DICTIONARY
OF
MODERN ITALIAN
HISTORY

DICTIONARY
OF
MODERN ITALIAN
HISTORY

Frank J. Coppa, Editor-in-Chief

Greenwood Press
Westport, Connecticut • London, England

Library of Congress Cataloging in Publication Data

Main entry under title:

Dictionary of modern Italian history.

   Includes bibliographic references and index.
   1. Italy—History—18th century—Dictionaries.
2. Italy—History—19th century—Dictionaries. 3. Italy
—History—20th century—Dictionaries. I. Coppa, Frank J.
DG545.D53 1985   945   84-6704
ISBN 0-313-22983-X (lib. bdg.)

Library of Congress Catalog Card Number: 84-6704
ISBN: 0-313-22983-X

First published in 1985

Greenwood Press
A division of Congressional Information Service, Inc.
88 Post Road West
Westport, Connecticut 06881

Printed in the United States of America

10 9 8 7 6 5 4 3 2 1

Contents

Editorial Advisory Board

Contributors

Angotti, Frank F. (FFA), Gannon University

Blatt, Joel (JB), University of Connecticut, Stamford

Brennan, John W. (JWB), Long Island University, Brooklyn

Brown, Benjamin F. (BFB), Institute for Research in History

Bucci, P. Vincent (PVB), St. John's University, New York

Bulman, Raymond (RB), St. John's University, New York

Cammett, John M. (JMC), John Jay College of Criminal Justice

Canepa, Andrew (ACan), San Francisco

Carrillo, Elisa (EC), Marymount College, Tarrytown

Cassels, Alan (ACas), McMaster University

Cohen, Jon S. (JSC), University of Toronto

Connelly, Owen (OC), University of South Carolina

Coppa, Frank J. (FJC), St. John's University, New York

Coppa, Rosina (RCo), New York

Cummings, Raymond (RCu), Villanova University

Cunsolo, Ronald S. (RSC), Nassau Community College

De Grand, Alexander J. (AJD), Roosevelt University

Delzell, Charles F. (CFD), Vanderbilt University

Devendittis, Paul J. (PJD), Nassau Community College

Di Gaetani, John L. (JLD), Hofstra University

DiScala, Spencer (SD), University of Massachusetts, Boston

Drake, Richard (RD), University of Montana, Missoula

Fink, Carole (CF), University of North Carolina

Gibson, Mary S. (MSG), John Jay College of Criminal Justice

Griffin, William D. (WDG), St. John's University, New York

Hess, Robert L. (RLH), Brooklyn College (CUNY)

Jensen, Richard (RJ), University of Minnesota

Kogan, Norman (NK), University of Connecticut, Storrs

LaVigna, Claire (CL), Erindale College, Toronto

Lavine, Marcia F. (MFL), Nashville

Leopold, John A. (JAL), Western Connecticut State College

Litchfield, R. Burr (RBL), Brown University

Lovett, Clara M. (CML), The George Washington University

Marchione, Margherita (MM), Fairleigh Dickinson University

Miller, Marion S. (MSM), University of Illinois, Chicago Circle

Noether, Emiliana P. (EPN), University of Connecticut, Storrs

Osofsky, Steve (SO), Nassau Community College

Paolucci, Anne (AP), St. John's University, New York

Paolucci, Henry (HP), St. John's University, New York

Pernicone, Nunzio (NP), Brooklyn, New York

Puzzo, Dante A. (DAP), City College of New York

Quinlan, B. Daniel (BDQ), St. John's University, New York

Rao, John C. (JCR), Notre Dame College, New York

Reece, Jack E. (JER), University of Pennsylvania

Reinerman, Alan J. (AJR), Boston College

Roberts, David D. (DDR), University of Rochester

Roberts, Elizabeth A. (EAR), Saddle Brook, New Jersey

Roberts, William (WR), Edward Williams College of Fairleigh Dickinson University

Rosengarten, Frank (FR), Queens College (CUNY)

Rossi, Ernest E. (EER), Western Michigan University

Saladino, Salvatore (SS), Queens College (CUNY)

Salomone, A. William (AWS), University of Rochester

Salvadori, Massimo (MS), Northampton, Massachusetts

Sarti, Roland (RS), University of Massachusetts, Amherst

Segre, Claudio G. (CGS), University of Texas, Austin

Slaughter, M. Jane (MJS), University of New Mexico

Wolff, Richard J. (RJW), St. John's University, New York

Zeender, John K. (JKZ), Catholic University of America

Preface

This volume surveys in alphabetical order the chief events, personalities, institutions, systems, and problems of Italy from the eighteenth century to the present. To date we have not had a reference-companion in English providing accurate, accessible, clear, and concise information on developments within modern Italy. Philip V. Cannistraro's *Historical Dictionary of Fascist Italy* (Greenwood Press, 1982) necessarily has a narrow focus. The present dictionary does not pretend to be all-inclusive. Nonetheless, an attempt has been made to deal with the major Italian political, economic, cultural, social, and religious issues from the eighteenth century to the 1980s. Within these pages there is special focus on the issues of industrialization, banking, regionalism, and political theory, with entries on newspapers, education, and the Enlightenment, among others.

In order to assure broad coverage in this one-volume dictionary, most of the entries are short, varying in length from 100 to 900 words. The longer ones include bibliographical references, and in many cases an effort has been made to accommodate the specialist as well as the general reader in providing additional references. An asterisk appearing after a term indicates the presence of an entry on that topic in this work.

In addition to the entries, there are five appendices providing a chronology of important events, and listings of ministries of Piedmont and Italy; presidents of the Italian Republic; kings of Piedmont and Italy; and popes.

The selection of topics for inclusion was made by the editor following consultation with the members of the Editorial Advisory Board. This is a collaborative work par excellence. The Editorial Advisory Board included Emiliana P. Noether for the eighteenth century, Clara M. Lovett for the *Risorgimento*, Salvatore Saladino for the Liberal Age, Charles F. Delzell for Fascist Italy, and Elisa Carrillo for post-World War II Italy. Their collective support was invaluable. In addition to providing topics for inclusion, they gave the editor suggestions concerning length of entries and prepared lists of likely contributors. They introduced the editor to a broad range of experts from different disciplines and a broad range of historiographical schools. The consultants also provided dates for the Chronology of Important Events (Appendix A) as well as short surveys of the period in which they are acknowledged experts. The latter have been included in the Introduction. Finally, they read all of the entries, proposing changes in both content and style. The task of executing those changes rested with the editor, who assumes ultimate responsibility for the work.

Frank J. Coppa

Acknowledgments

In editing the present volume I received the support of a good number of people. Without the efforts of the assistant editors and the contributors, this work would not have been possible. I am particularly indebted to Ronald Cunsolo, Charles Delzell, Salvatore Saladino, and Richard Wolff for agreeing to assume responsibility for additional entries when problems arose. Marion Duffy and Anna Marie Mannuzza, secretaries in the Department of History at St. John's University, typed and retyped, collated and filed entries, and played a part in the preparation of the manuscript from beginning to end. A number of graduate assistants in the department also helped in the preparation of the manuscript. Among those who assisted in the project were Angelo Araimo, Mark Blethroad, Joseph Bongiorno, Thomas Esposito, David Esposito, and Vincent Licata. Acknowledging the support and cooperation of these and others, as editor-in-chief I assume full responsibility for the shortcomings of this dictionary.

Abbreviations

AGIP	Azienda Generale Italiana Petroli (Italian General Petroleum Company)
AMG	Allied Military Government
CEU	Catholic Electoral Union
CGIL	Confederazione Generale Italiana del Lavoro (Italian General Confederation of Labor)
CGL	Confederazione Generale del Lavoro (General Confederation of Labor)
CI	Communist International
CLN	Comitato di Liberazione Nazionale (Committee of National Liberation)
CLNAI	Comitato di Liberazione Nationale per l'Alta Italia (Committee of National Liberation for Northern Italy)
CTV	Corpo Truppe Volontarie (Corps of Voluntary Troops)
CVL	Corpo Volontari della Libertà (Corps of Volunteers for Freedom)
ENI	Ente Nazionale Idrocarburi (National Fuel Trust)
FIAT	Fabbrica Italiana Automobili Torino (Italian Automobile Factory of Turin)
FUCI	Federazione Universitaria Cattolica Italiana (Italian Catholic University Federation)
GAP	Gruppi di Azione Patriottica (Groups of Patriotic Action)
GDD	Gruppi de Difese della Donna e per L'Assistenza ai Combattenti per la Libertà (Women Organized to Assist the Combatants for Liberty)
GIL	Gioventù Italiana del Littorio (Italian Youth of the Lictor)
IFI	Instituto Finanziario Industriale (Financial Institute)
IRI	Instituto per la Ricostruzione Industriale (Institute for Industrial Reconstruction)
IWW	International Workers of the World
MSI	Movimento Sociale Italiano (Italian Social Movement)
MSVN	Milizia Voluntaria per la Sicurezza Nazionale (Voluntary Militia for National Security)
ONB	Opera Nazionale Balilla (National Balilla Organization)
OVRA	An acronym, either meaningless or unknown, for Fascist Italy's secret police. Some believe it stood for Opera Volontaria Repressione Antifascista (Voluntary Organization for Anti-Fascist Repression)
PCI	Partito Comunista Italiano (Italian Communist Party)
PLI	Partito Liberale Italiano (Italian Liberal Party)

PNF	Partito Nazionale Fascista (National Fascist Party)
POI	Partito Operaio Italiano (Italian Worker Party)
PPI	Partito Popolare Italiano (Italian Popular Party)
PRI	Partito Repubblicano Italiano (Italian Republican Party)
PSDI	Partito Socialista Democratico Italiano (Italian Social Democratic Party)
PSI	Partito Socialista Italiano (Italian Socialist Party)
PSIUP	Partito Socialista Italiano di Unità Proletaria (Italian Socialist Party of Proletarian Unity)
UDI	Unione Donne Italiane (Union of Italian Women)

Introduction

The course of modern Italian history has been divided into a number of periods, which include Italy on the eve of the French Revolution, the *Risorgimento* and Italian Unification, Liberal Italy, and the Age of the Republic. While it is true that these are artificial divisions in the continuous flow of history, the changes in politics, economics, thought, and social relations during these years were of such magnitude as to warrant the conclusion that one age had finished and another commenced. This is apparent in the surveys of the periods which follow, written respectively by Emiliana P. Noether, Clara M. Lovett, Salvatore Saladino, Charles F. Delzell, and Elisa Carrillo.

I. EIGHTEENTH-CENTURY ITALY

For Italy the eighteenth century represented an age of sociopolitical change, economic revival, and intellectual ferment. At its end, the impact of the French Revolution, the Napoleonic imperium, and the Congress of Vienna settlement further changed and irreparably altered the peninsula's balance of power. Throughout the century most of the Italian states sought to introduce more efficient and modern governmental structures. A vast body of literature probed the causes of Italy's backward position vis-à-vis the rest of Europe and elaborated plans for reform. A few voices wondered whether part of the blame for Italy's decline did not originate in its division into small states, economically vulnerable and too weak to defend themselves against the encroachments of the larger powers. During the years of French hegemony over Italy this vaguely felt sense of national identity became a more clearly defined expression of nationalism which, after 1815, demanded independence and unity.

Three distinct phases mark the century: 1713 to 1748, 1748 to 1789, and 1789 to 1814. The first witnessed fundamental political realignments in the territorial map of Italy. The second saw the flowering of what may be called the Italian Enlightenment and the reform movement. The third brought Italy under French control and introduced a radically new political structure, as Italy was reorganized to suit Napoleon's imperial plans. These territorial shifts altered the way Italians thought of themselves and their country and sharpened their realization of the need for freedom and unity if Italy and its people were to cease to be the pawns of their neighbors.

During the first period (1713–48) major territorial and dynastic changes occurred. Under the terms of the peace settlement hammered out among the European powers at the end of the War of the Spanish Succession, Spain was forced to cede its Italian possessions, and Italy came under Austrian control. Actually, only Lombardy was ruled from Vienna, but Austria dwarfed the congeries of small and weak states into which Italy was divided. As a reward for its role in the War of the Spanish Succession, the Duchy of Savoy, traditional guardian of the northwest Alpine passes opening Italy to foreign invasion, attained the status of kingdom, and by 1735 was given control over the island of Sardinia in the Western Mediterranean. In that same year, Naples and Sicily were joined to form an independent kingdom under the Bourbon Charles, son of Philip V of Spain and his second wife, Elisabetta Farnese. With the dying out of the Medici and Farnese families, whose dynastic roots went back to the Renaissance, new rulers came to power in Tuscany and Parma-Piacenza in the 1730s. Francis II, duke of Lorraine and husband-to-be of Maria Theresa of Austria, succeeded the last Medici in Tuscany. Under him, and particularly under his son, Peter Leopold, Tuscany flourished and attained an internal equilibrium which made it a model for other states. As part of the general settlement following the War of the Austrian Succession, the claim to Parma-Piacenza by the second son of Elisabetta Farnese and Philip V was recognized. Thus, by 1748, when the succession wars (Spanish, Polish, and Austrian) were finally over, new dynasties and a new balance of power characterized Italy.

Change had not occurred everywhere, for among the remaining states the status quo continued until the Napoleonic invasion of Italy in 1796. The republics of Genoa and Venice maintained their oligarchies, while the political influence of the papacy declined as rulers throughout Europe sought to strengthen their position at the expense of the Church's political and economic privileges.

From 1748 to 1789, Italy, though still politically divided and in the shadow of Hapsburg power, enjoyed peace and stability. The kingdoms of Piedmont-Sardinia and of Naples gave it a voice among the rulers of Europe. The strong family ties that bound Tuscany and Parma-Piacenza to the Hapsburg and Bourbon dynasties, respectively, added a measure of prestige to these states' European status. Moreover, reforms introduced in both made them models of enlightened rule throughout the Continent. The changing balance of power in the Mediterranean itself also brought a measure of change. The decline of Turkish naval strength and the presence of Great Britain, with its base at Gibraltar, injected a new element into the diplomatic and commercial relations of the area.

In these years reform was talked about everywhere and practiced with varying degrees of success. Great economic advances occurred in Austrian Lombardy. Capital flowed into the countryside to increase production. In urban areas industry based on agricultural resources revived and an entrepreneurial middle class with links to both land and city developed.

The Kingdom of Piedmont-Sardinia remained rural and agricultural. Large quantities of raw silk were exported, mainly to France. The monarchs followed the military tradition of their dynasty and expended their resources in building a strong army. Reforms aimed at greater centralization of the state to enhance the King's power. A small middle class had little political or economic influence.

Venice, whose power had been declining since the sixteenth century, looked to its mainland territories to improve its economy. Textile industries were encouraged and plans for agrarian reforms designed, but few were enacted. The city of Venice itself remained immobile, transfixed by the memory of its past greatness, while its entrenched oligarchy refused to share power with the leaders of its mainland provinces.

Troubled by the continued rebellion in Corsica, Genoa sold the island to France in 1768. Genoa, in contrast to Venice, prospered as its banking activities brought wealth to the city. Its economy expanded with the establishment of a free port and the growth of its shipbuilding industry. Open to foreign ideas, Genoa, despite its minuscule size, continued to play a role as one of Italy's small but respected states. Severe internal social dissensions, however, created a precarious political stability.

Under the benign and enlightened rule of its new dukes, Tuscany flourished. One of the first states in Europe to introduce a modicum of free trade under Peter Leopold, the state's administrative, tax, and legal organization was restructured. In 1781 work was begun on a constitution, which, however, never became effective. Land reclamation projects brought new areas under cultivation, and the free port of Leghorn flourished as a center for English and Dutch shipping and trading activities in the Mediterranean.

With its reacquired independence as a kingdom after some two centuries of rule by a Spanish viceroy, the Kingdom of Naples and Sicily, despite a generally static economy based on traditional agriculture, tried to modernize. However, a parasitic class of noble landowners controlled most of the land and local power. Like Paris, the city of Naples concentrated the intellectual and fiscal resources of the state, including the only university on the mainland of southern Italy. The middle class sent its sons into the bureaucracy, and lawyers proliferated. In Sicily the pattern was little different.

After 1789 change accelerated. By 1815 the political structure of Italy had undergone radical alterations. Under Napoleon, three major political units emerged, bringing together areas of the peninsula which had a tradition of separateness. In the North, the French fostered the formation of the Cisalpine Republic, subsequently renamed the Italian Republic, and finally the Kingdom of Italy. In the South, the mainland Kingdom of Naples kept its independence. The rest of Italy eventually became part of France. Only Sicily and Sardinia remained outside the French orbit. Economically, while France placed a heavy burden on Italian resources, an industry geared to meet the war needs of Napoleon and a shift in land ownership created a new wealthy upper middle class.

The Congress of Vienna, ostensibly dedicated to restoring the status quo ante the revolution, disregarded its own guiding principle in the Italian settlement. The republics of Venice and Genoa, abolished by French fiat, were not revived. Venice became part of the Austrian possessions in Italy, while Genoa was joined to Piedmont-Sardinia.

An important feature of this century was its renewed intellectual activity. From Giambattista Vico in Naples at the beginning of the century to Cesare Beccaria in Milan toward its end, Italian thinkers made important contributions. After 1748 the Italian Enlightenment, whose roots went back to the beginning of the century, flourished and introduced new ideas and philosophies throughout the peninsula.

II. THE *RISORGIMENTO*

The term *Risorgimento* (''rebirth'') has traditionally been used to denote the formative period of the modern Italian state, approximately from the intervention of Napoleon's army in 1796 to the proclamation of the Kingdom of Italy in 1861. Contemporaries, however, used the term *rivoluzione italiana*, which described more accurately the conspiracies, uprisings, and wars that led to the dissolution of the Restoration governments and the emergence of a liberal, constitutional state.

The Italian Revolution was primarily a political revolution, but it included important cultural and social elements as well. The political struggle was initiated and led by liberal intellectuals and by enlightened members of the landed aristocracy and the bourgeoisie, who understood the relationship between economic progress and political change. Particularly in the period 1830–48, the principal goal of Italy's liberal leaders was to reform the existing governments along constitutional lines and to arrive at some form of federation similar to the German *Zollverein*. As early as 1831, however, Giuseppe Mazzini promoted the idea of territorial unification under one democratic and republican government. His solution to the ''Italian Question'' required considerable popular involvement in the making of a new state, while the solutions preferred by the liberals depended on diplomatic and military successes.

In the early 1840s, Italian leaders achieved a consensus on the need to end Austria's military domination of northern Italy (a consequence of the Congress of Vienna) and Austrian influence at several Italian courts. Mazzini advocated insurrections and guerrilla warfare to wear down Austrian resistance, while the moderate liberals attempted to win over the more enlightened Italian princes, including Pope Pius IX in 1846–47, and to secure the support of major European powers.

On the eve of the revolution of 1848, however, it became evident that no such consensus could be reached concerning the temporal power of the papacy, the second major obstacle to political reform or revolution in Italy. The Milanese insurrection of March 1848 and the subsequent intervention of King Charles Albert of Sardinia against Austria forced Pius IX to retreat from his previous position of support for political reform. His initial pronouncements on the Italian Question had lent credence to the thesis of the Piedmontese philosopher Vincenzo Gioberti that an Italian federation could be established under papal leadership.

The events of 1848–49 proved that the desire for Italian independence from foreign powers and, to a lesser degree, for unity had spread to all parts of Italy and to all social classes. Radical theorists like Giuseppe Ferrari and Carlo Pisacane then argued that a democratic political revolution was only a prelude to far-reaching social change and secularization.

Although unsuccessful, the revolution of 1848–49 marked a major turning point in the process of Italian unification. Not only did the revolution show that liberal and Mazzinian ideas had made headway everywhere in the country, it also brought together leaders from all regions to the major centers of conflict: Milan in the spring of 1848, Florence in the latter part of that year, Rome and Venice in 1849. After the revolution, those who had shared the experiences of war or barricade fighting also shared the experiences of exile, in Piedmont-Sardinia or abroad.

The inevitable reflections on what had gone wrong in 1848–49 brought into focus fundamental ideological and strategic differences between liberals and democrats (or radicals). In the 1850s, the liberals renewed their efforts to ally themselves with an Italian prince genuinely committed to constitutional government and willing to challenge Austria's military might. Eventually they found this prince, Victor Emmanuel II of Savoy, whose brilliant minister, Camillo Benso di Cavour, gained the support of France for war against Austria and the cooperation of the liberals' most important organization, the Italian National Society. Mazzini's followers and other democrats, on the other hand, remained committed to a strategy of popular insurrections. In 1857 Carlo Pisacane led the most ambitious of these—an attempt to incite the impoverished peasant masses of his native South to overthrow the Bourbon government. Pisacane's tragic failure won more supporters to Cavour's strategy, and by 1859 a new consensus emerged on the need to fight Austria again and to establish a united kingdom under Victor Emmanuel II. The annexation of Lombardy, the duchies of Tuscany, Parma, and Modena, and of a portion of the Papal States was the work of the Sardinian army and the moderate liberals. That the South also became part of the new kingdom in 1860 was due, however, to the military exploits of an old Mazzinian revolutionary, Giuseppe Garibaldi, the most colorful and popular Italian leader of the *Risorgimento* generation.

In March 1861, the Kingdom of Italy was proclaimed, although Venetia remained under Austrian rule until 1866 and Rome under papal rule until 1870. The *Risorgimento* came to a close with a victory of the liberals, who remained in control until the end of the nineteenth century. The creation of a new political and legal system was accompanied by partial secularization, in accordance with the liberal principle of separation between church and state. The *Risorgimento*, however, brought relatively minor changes in the social and economic condition of the Italian masses.

III. LIBERAL ITALY, 1861–1922

After decades of despairing hope and frustrated expectations, within the short span of a few years the dream of generations of Italian patriots was fulfilled: seven independent states were fused into one and a united Italy was born in 1861. But as a monarchy, however liberal, this was not the Italy of Mazzini's republican dreams, nor the democracy so dear to Garibaldi. Nor was it acceptable to the Church and to millions of its devout. Furthermore, even those who had fashioned this Italy according to their liberal monarchist preferences were aware of the enormous problems that political unification had not resolved, and of the many problems that the process of unification itself had created or aggravated.

To a papacy despoiled of its temporal domains, the liberal state made a gesture of conciliation with the offer of independence for its spiritual ministry and sovereign honors for its head in the Law of Papal Guarantees of 1871. The gesture was rejected in form, but the substance of the offer was gradually accepted in practice, regardless of the repeated papal protests against the loss of the Church's domains, protests that did not close the door to a reconciliation, proclaimed formally only by 1929. Equally slowly and laboriously, the country's political leaders addressed the problems of a predominantly agricultural South which, when combined with the problems of a developing industrial North, produced the Social Question, of which the emergence of a Socialist agitation was the symptomatic expression. These various social problems were faced spasmodically and with uncertainty, because of their intrinsic complexity and because of an ongoing political realignment of the right and left wings of Italian liberalism, a realignment conditioned by the practice of "transformism."

Further conditioning the transformation of Italian politics and its ability to address social problems were cares of foreign and colonial policy, all of which came to a head by the end of the century in a crisis that appeared to call the country's fundamental monarchical and parliamentary institutions into question. The crisis was surmounted; colonial expansion halted temporarily; foreign policy began its reorientation away from total dependency on the Triple Alliance; and with the advent of the Giolittian era social questions finally began to receive their due attention, facing Socialists with the dilemma of whether to work within the confines of the liberal state or to work for its destruction. For a time, the Giolittian compromise, which aimed at saving the liberal state by democratizing its political and social institutions, achieved some successes. But the decision to embark on colonial expansion with the Libyan War of 1911–12 put the compromise in jeopardy. The Socialist Party fell into the hands of its antiwar revolutionary wing; the elections of 1913, conducted under near-universal manhood suffrage and marking the full and open entry of Catholics into national politics, brought disarray into the varied Giolittian ranks; and the outbreak of World War I in 1914 found Giolitti out of power at a moment when the country was faced with a momentous decision. This decision, in favor of war, was made by Antonio Salandra of the Right in April-May 1915, in contrast to the preference of the Giolittian majority in parliament to remain neutral. There followed three and a half years of war, whose conduct and dubious fruits confirmed the worst fears of its opponents and the determination of its proponents to vindicate the course they had imposed on Italy in 1915. The politics of the immediate postwar period thus became a form of continuing referendum on the wartime experience, leading to the electoral successes of the neutralist Socialist and Catholic Popular parties in 1919, and to reactive responses on the part of interventionists of all shades, including the former Socialist, Benito Mussolini. Economic distress, fears of a Bolshevik-style revolution, territorial aspirations partially thwarted at the peace tables, and growing paralysis of a fragmented parliament all combined to produce a crisis situation aggravated and exploited by the Fascist movement. The culminating failure of the liberal parliamentary regime came in October 1922, when, in despair of other solutions, the government was entrusted to a man and a movement representing the negation of Italy's liberal past.

IV. THE FASCIST ERA, 1922–45

In the nineteenth century Italy was among the last major European countries to achieve national unification. Its liberal parliamentary system was approaching democratic maturity when World War I interrupted its evolution. In the twentieth century Italy was the first European country to discard such a system in favor of a Fascist government (October 1922).

Benito Mussolini became the new Fascist prime minister and soon was to make himself dictator. A maverick ex-Socialist and editor of the Milan newspaper *Il Popolo d'Italia*, he had supported Italy's intervention in the war. He organized his Fascist "Blackshirt" movement in Milan in March 1919. As leader (Duce), he attracted the support of ultranationalistic war veterans and youth, ex-syndicalists, Futurists, and lower-middle-class elements who feared that the country and their own social and economic status were being threatened by bolshevism.

Many of the workers and peasants had indeed been in a revolutionary mood at war's end because of the strains brought on by the prolonged conflict and by the heady news of Russia's Bolshevik Revolution. The introduction in 1919 of proportional representation, together with universal manhood suffrage and large electoral districts, had opened the way for an entirely new postwar political structure. The Catholics, led by Luigi Sturzo, had entered the political arena with a new Partito Popolare Italiano (PPI) that quickly won one hundred seats in the Chamber of Deputies. The Socialist Party's ranks swelled, making it the largest party in the country. The high point of Socialist and labor union agitation occurred in the late summer of 1920 when metalworkers occupied plants in the northern cities. After a few weeks, however, these strikers had to reach accom-

modation with the owners on the latter's terms. The revolutionary tide now
ebbed. Disillusioned left-wing extremists seceded from the main trunk of socialism to organize the Italian Communist Party (PCI) in January 1921, while
on the opposite side a revisionist Socialist Party (Partito Socialista Unitario,
PSU) under Filippo Turati and Giacomo Matteotti emerged.

At the same time, the Fascists were expanding from their original base in
Milan to win wide support from landowners in the lower Po Valley who were
determined to suppress the new Socialist and Catholic peasant organizations.
This "agrarian" Fascism, led by armed *squadristi* like Dino Grandi and Italo
Balbo, presented a challenge to Mussolini's leadership of the party, but he
managed to hang on to it. Virtual civil war characterized the period until 1922,
with the Fascists now clearly gaining the ascendancy. In a hurry to gain control
of the government, Mussolini shed his earlier republican rhetoric and openly
courted the King, the army, and the Church. The Nationalist Party threw its
support to the Fascists. So did the veterans of Gabriele D'Annunzio's postwar
adventure in Fiume. In Rome one weak liberal government after another collapsed.

At last, on October 28, 1922, when the Fascists were calling for a "march
on Rome," Victor Emmanuel III invited the Fascist Duce to form a coalition
government. At first the Fascist Party (PNF) held only a minority of the portfolios.
Premier Mussolini had to wait until after the parliamentary elections of April
1924 before he could hope to establish a completely Fascist government. When
the Socialist Matteotti publicly challenged the election outcome, Fascists assassinated him (June 10). This brought about a prolonged parliamentary crisis (the
Aventine Secession). Prodded by PNF consuls, Mussolini announced a coup
d'état on January 3, 1925. By November 1926 he completed the nailing down
of the "totalitarian state." All non-Fascist parties were dissolved, as were non-
Fascist labor syndicates. The PNF had its own armed force, the Militia (MVSN).
Censorship was imposed. A secret police and the special Tribunal for the Defense
of the State were established. Many of the opposition leaders were either arrested
or harried out of the land. Parliament was emasculated. A Fascist Grand Council
was formed as the party's top organ.

Though elitist in its hierarchical structure, the Fascist dictatorship differed
markedly from old-fashioned military and authoritarian regimes by its conscious
mobilization and indoctrination of the masses. A "radicalism of the Right,"
Fascism preserved private property and capitalism, but there was much governmental intervention in the economy. Strikes and lockouts were forbidden. Compulsory arbitration was enforced through labor courts. The Fascists repudiated
both liberalism and Marxist "class struggle," calling instead for "class conciliation" and national struggle. The Chamber of Deputies was replaced in due
course by the Chamber of Fasces and Corporations, which represented the single
party, and functional rather than either numerical or geographical constituencies.
Thus, the corporative state emerged piecemeal between 1923 and 1939. By then
only a few elements of the old system remained: the King (who still claimed
the allegiance of the regular army), the appointive and docile Senate, and the

Roman Catholic Church. Victor Emmanuel was quite willing to collaborate with Fascism in a "dyarchy" arrangement.

Pope Pius XI (1922–39) was happy to extend formal recognition to the Fascist State through the Lateran Pacts, signed on February 11, 1929. Consisting of a treaty, concordat, and financial agreement, these pacts settled half a century of hostility and proved to be the most enduring legacy of the dictatorship. They proclaimed Roman Catholicism to be the official religion of the state and called upon the latter to enforce canon law with respect to marriage. Though relations were generally good, a dispute between the authoritarian Church and the would-be totalitarian regime occurred in 1931 over the status of Catholic Action and related youth organizations. The Church was also displeased when Mussolini introduced anti-Semitic measures in 1938.

The Fascist economy went through a number of phases. Many traditional features of economic liberalism persisted until 1925. During the next two years there was much talk of creating the corporative state. From mid-1927 to 1935 Italy felt the effects of the Great Depression and high unemployment. Hoping to promote self-sufficiency, the Duce launched the "battle of grain" and other economic measures. These years also saw the rapid expansion of industrial monopolies and cartels. In January 1933 the regime created the Institute for Industrial Reconstruction (IRI) to help bail out financially troubled enterprises, thus starting a program of parastatal capitalism that was to be another important legacy of Fascism. The period 1935 to 1943 was characterized by a "war economy" and radical rhetoric against "plutocratic" capitalism.

Meanwhile, in the 1930s, Mussolini's attention was shifting from domestic to foreign policy, particularly after his announcement that Fascism was "for export." The bellicose dictator himself took control of the ministries of war, navy, and air in 1933. At the time of the Stresa Conference (April 1934) Italy was still aligned with France and Britain. But Mussolini broke away from this group when he declared war against Ethiopia (1935–36). He won this war despite sanctions imposed against Italy by the League of Nations. In 1936 Mussolini chose to align himself with Hitler in the Rome-Berlin Axis. The two Axis powers aided Franco's insurgents in the Spanish Civil War (1936–39). In 1937 Italy withdrew from the League and joined with Germany and Japan in the Anti-Comintern Pact. Meanwhile, Mussolini stopped supporting Austria's independence and acquiesced in Germany's annexation of that country in March 1938. He also approved Hitler's takeover of Czechoslovakia in 1938–39. In April 1939 Italy invaded Albania, and in May Italy and Germany signed the Pact of Steel, thereby becoming full-fledged allies.

When Hitler launched World War II by invading Poland in September 1939, Mussolini remained "nonbelligerent." But he hastily entered the conflict in June 1940 when he perceived the Nazi blitzkrieg overrunning France. Italy now became heavily engaged in fighting the British in the Mediterranean and North Africa. Mussolini decided to attack Greece in October 1940, but his forces suffered the humiliation of having to seek German help. Mussolini and Hitler divided up Yugoslavia in April 1941, and in June Italy joined Germany in the invasion of the Soviet Union. And in December, after the Japanese attack on Pearl Harbor, Italy and Germany declared war on the United States. Italy had now vastly overextended her capabilities.

The military tide turned against Fascist Italy in the autumn of 1942 when the Allies invaded French North Africa and defeated Axis forces in Egypt and Libya. Italy's cities and transportation system were constant targets of Allied bombings. The country's economy was in crisis. Strikes broke out in Turin and Milan in March 1943. The Allied invasion of Sicily on July 10 spelled the end of the dictatorship.

Meeting in Rome on July 24–25, 1943, the Fascist Grand Council, spearheaded by dissident Fascists (Galeazzo Ciano, Grandi, and Guiseppe Bottai), voted against Mussolini. The King thereupon named Marshal Pietro Badoglio to replace Mussolini, who was taken prisoner. The institutions of the Fascist regime collapsed while the Badoglio government secretly sought an armistice with the Allies. The armistice was announced on September 8, 1943, at the moment of the Allied invasion at Salerno. In the South, the Allies propped up the King and Badoglio.

In the confusion surrounding announcement of the armistice, German commandos rescued the sickly Mussolini. Hitler ordered him to establish a puppet regime, the Fascist Social Republic, in the German-occupied northern half of the peninsula. This shaky government tried in its rhetoric to appeal to the workers, but with scant success. It was confronted by the growing Armed Resistance, which received some military support from the Allies. When Allied forces finally overran the Po Valley in April 1945, Mussolini was captured by Italian partisans and executed near Lake Como on April 28. Fascism had come to a bloody and unlamented end in war-ravaged Italy. The German armies in Italy surrendered on May 2.

V. POST-WORLD WAR II ITALY

During the four decades that followed the end of World War II, Italy went through revolutionary changes. Twenty years of Fascist rule were quickly swept away; the House of Savoy was repudiated and a republic established; an alliance with the West was formed; and Italy achieved the greatest surface prosperity of her history, despite ministerial instability and increasing terrorism from the Left and Right after the late sixties.

Mussolini's downfall in 1943 was followed by King Victor Emmanuel III's appointment of Marshal Pietro Badoglio as premier. Under Badoglio's nonparty government, an armistice was signed with the Allies and war was waged against the Germans. Meanwhile, six anti-Fascist parties, the majority with roots in the pre-Fascist era, were organized: Communist, Christian Democratic, Socialist, Actionist, Labor Democratic, and Liberal. These parties formed the Central Committee of National Liberation. After the liberation of Rome by the Allies in June 1944, the anti-Fascist leaders refused to continue with Badoglio as premier. From June 1944 to November 1945, three governments, all composed of the representatives of the six parties, governed Italy: two were headed by Ivanoe Bonomi (June 1944–November 1944; December 1944–June 1945) and one by Ferruccio Parri (June 1945–November 1945). In December 1945 Alcide De Gasperi, the leader of the Christian Democrats, became the head of another government representing the Committee of National Liberation. He was to remain as premier until July 1953, but with a government predominantly Christian Democratic after 1946. In the June 1946 elections, in which the nation voted for a republic, the Christian Democrats emerged as the strongest party, a hegemony they were to retain for the succeeding three decades.

During the De Gasperi era, a peace treaty (the Treaty of Paris, 1947) was signed with the Allies. Despite Italy's cobelligerency after September 1943, the peace settlement was punitive. Italy ceded to Yugoslavia Istria and Fiume, to France several Alpine villages, and to Greece the Dodecanese Islands. Italy also surrendered her entire colonial empire in Africa, both the pre-Fascist and Fascist acquisitions.

The De Gasperi era also witnessed the adoption of a republican and democratic constitution that was largely inspired by the ideology of Christian Democracy. The implementation of the constitution was accompanied by economic recovery and identification with the West, as Italy accepted Marshall Plan funds, joined NATO, and became a member of the European Coal and Steel Community. The Communist Party under Palmiro Togliatti and the left-wing Socialists under Pietro Nenni constituted the government's major opposition on the Left, with the neo-Fascists (MSI, Italian Social Movement) on the Right.

The parliamentary elections of 1953 opened a period of uncertainty in Italy, and the Italian political situation became more fluid. The Christian Democratic Party became more independent of the Church, a development facilitated by the election of Pope John XXIII in 1958. As the process of industrialization and modernization accelerated in the 1960s, the Communist and Socialist parties as well as the more radical elements in the Christian Democratic Party demanded a larger role for the state in ensuring a more equitable society.

In the early 1960s a Center-Left coalition was forged which governed Italy with brief interruptions until the late 1970s. Under the Centro-Sinistra, economic planning became more institutionalized, regional governments with wide powers in administrative matters were established, the school system was expanded and democratized, and social security benefits were improved. In foreign affairs, relations were expanded with the Communist world at the same time that Italy retained its membership in NATO and the European Economic Community.

In the late 1960s and early 1970s, widespread unrest was triggered by inflation and recessionary conditions, aggravated by devastating floods and earthquakes. Ministries dissolved and reorganized, with names and policies more or less the same. In this atmosphere the ground became fertile for terrorism, and the Red Brigades were only the most famous of the terrorist groups that flourished. The most sensational act of terrorism was the kidnapping and murder of Premier Aldo Moro in the spring of 1978.

Meanwhile, the Communist Party, under the moderate leadership of Enrico Berlinguer, pursued a pragmatic approach to major policy issues. The party achieved extraordinary success in its efforts to enter social and economic groups beyond its traditional constituencies. Recognizing the nonrevolutionary character of the Communist Party, and seeking to establish a more stable government, the Christian Democrats hammered out an accord with the Communists in 1977–78. The accord proved to be of short duration because of the refusal of the Christian Democrats to give ministerial posts to the Communists.

As the decade of the 1980s opened, Italy was beset by many problems. Socioeconomic inequities persisted, despite surface appearances of general prosperity. Catholicism lost its hold on the majority of Italians (divorce and abortion were indicators of waning Catholic influence), but no religion or ideology rose to take the place of Catholicism. The democatic constitution proved its ability to survive major crises, but its cumbersome bureaucracy was a brake on progress and efficiency. Unemployment, especially among university graduates, remained high, and those who obtained positions depended heavily on the right connections. An impartial observer could well state that while much had been accomplished by post-Fascist Italy, a political, economic, and social structure more responsive to the changing conditions of Italian life was a prerequisite to further progress.

DICTIONARY
OF
MODERN ITALIAN
HISTORY

A

ABRUZZI, LUIGI AMADEO, DUKE DEGLI. This naval commander and explorer of the Arctic and Africa was born in Madrid on January 29, 1873, the third son of Amadeo, duke of Aosta and king of Spain, 1870–73. He was the first to ascend Mount Saint Elias in Alaska (July 31, 1897). In 1899–1900 he organized an arctic expedition, explored Franz Josef Land, and from his ship the *Stella Polare* sent out a sledding party which arrived at 86°34', the furthest north then recorded. He was also the first to ascend Mount Ruwenzori in Africa (1906). During the Italo-Turkish war (1911–12) he led a squadron, and during World War I,* from 1915 to 1917, served as commander in chief of the Italian navy. In 1920 he conducted an expedition into Ethiopia.* He died on March 18, 1933, in Italian Somalia.*

FJC

ABYSSINIA. See ETHIOPIA

ACCADEMIA DEI PUGNI. See BECCARIA, CESARE and CAFFÈ, IL

ACERBO ELECTORAL LAW. This was passed at the end of 1923 in preparation for the parliamentary elections of April 1924 and was a preliminary step in the establishment of the Fascist dictatorship. Drafted by Giacomo Acerbo (1888–1969), one of the Fascist undersecretaries, it stipulated that in subsequent elections the country would be treated as one constituency and that the party that polled the greatest number of votes, providing that it was over 25 percent of the total, would receive two-thirds of the seats in the Chamber of Deputies. It was supported by the Fascists as well as by the followers of Giovanni Giolitti,* Antonio Salandra,* and Vittorio Emanuele Orlando.* The opposition of some members of the Italian Popular Party* and the Reformist Socialists could not block its passage. Its approval assured the Fascists and their allies control of 356 seats out of 535 in the next Chamber.

FJC

ACQUARONE, PIETRO, DUCA D'. Born in Genoa on April 9, 1890, Acquarone commenced an army career, but left it in 1924 to enter the business world in Verona. In 1934 he was appointed to the Senate. Because of his administrative skills, Victor Emmanuel III* appointed him minister of the royal house in 1939, and in 1942 raised his status to duke. He became the King's most trusted counselor and planned the coup d'état of July 25, 1943, against Mussolini.* He accompanied Victor Emmanuel in the flight from Rome on September 9 and remained his close adviser until the abdication (May 1946). He died in retirement in San Remo on February 13, 1948.

CFD

ACTION PARTY. The Action Party, founded in July 1942, was heir to the pragmatic social progressivism of Gaetano Salvemini* and Piero Gobetti,* and to the liberal socialism of Carlo Rosselli.* It brought together former members of the Justice and Liberty movement,* the left wing of the Sardinian Action Party led by Emilio Lussu,* and small groups of liberal-socialist intellectuals inspired by the writings of the philosopher Guido Calogero.* In January 1943, the party began the clandestine distribution of its main organ, *L'Italia Libera*, whose first editor was the veteran anti-Fascist Leo Valiani.

The Action Party helped to form the Committees of National Liberation (CLN*) that became the political expression of the organized national Armed Resistance* movement from September 1943 to the end of World War II.* The party was intransigently opposed to the revival of traditional conservative and monarchical forces in Italy. It wanted the Resistance to begin a revolutionary transformation of Italian politics. But the Actionists were unable to overcome a schism between their radical and Socialist members. One of their leaders, Ferruccio Parri,* headed the first postwar Italian government in 1945. This was a brief moment of success, since the party's Rome Congress in February 1946 culminated in the withdrawal of the radical wing, which merged with the Italian Republican Party.* Most of the remaining members later entered either the Italian Communist Party (PCI)* or the Italian Socialist Party (PSI),* while others withdrew from politics altogether.

For further reference see: Emilio Lussu, *Sul Partito d'Azione e gli altri* (Milan: Mursia, 1968).

FR

ADELFI. The secret society of the Adelfi, organized around 1799, united various elements of the Left in common opposition to Bonapartist rule in Italy, seen as a betrayal of republican ideals. After the Restoration of 1814, the sect spread widely in northern Italy, especially Piedmont. Directed by Filippo Buonarroti* from Geneva, it sought to expel the Austrians and overthrow local Italian conservative regimes. It declined rapidly after the failure of the revolutions of 1820–21,* in which it had been involved.

AJR

ADMINISTRATIVE SYSTEM OF THE REPUBLIC. This system comprises the agencies and procedures by which national law and policy are carried out. It includes a complex network of ministries, policy-making and advisory bodies, special agencies, public and quasipublic corporations, and control agencies. The highest independent agencies that hold the public administration accountable are the Council of State and the Court of Accounts. The civil service is a classified merit system in which recruitment and promotion are based on competitive examinations. True merit, however, is often superseded by patronage and partisan influence. The bureaucracy is often criticized for being overcentralized, inefficient, and unproductive.

EER

ADOWA. A town in Tigre province, Ethiopia,* it was the site of a major battle on March 1, 1896. Beginning with the occupation of Massawa on the Red Sea coast in 1885, the Italians slowly advanced inland and occupied much of what is now Eritrea.* After the Treaty of Uccialli,* concluded between Ethiopia and Italy in 1889, there ensued a half decade of diplomatic controversy between the two states about the implications of the treaty for their relationship. When border skirmishes along the Eritrean-Ethiopian frontier broke out in January 1895, the Italians rapidly moved to occupy a large section of Tigre. Menelik II* then mobilized a large army, estimated at 100,000—of whom 10,000 had modern rifles—and met the 17,000 Italians and their 10,000 Eritrean colonial troops at Adowa on March 1, 1896. The Italians lost more than two-fifths of their fighting force in a military debacle that has been described as the most remarkable triumph of an African over a European army since the time of Hannibal. The Ethiopian victory at Adowa brought an end to Italian colonial expansion in the Horn of Africa for forty years. Subsequently it served as a bitter reminder to Mussolini* of Italy's military humiliation in Ethiopia, and revenge for Adowa became one of the rationales for the Italian invasion of Ethiopia in 1935.

RLH

ADUA. See **ADOWA**

AEGEAN ISLANDS. See **DODECANESE ISLANDS**

AFRICA ORIENTALE ITALIANA. See **ETHIOPIA**

AGIP. The Azienda Generale Italiana Petroli, a public corporation, was established by law on April 3, 1926, with a mandate to prospect for oil in Italy and abroad and to develop, refine, and market its discoveries. Its domestic prospecting before World War II* yielded little of immediate value, but its explorations in Iraq and Rumania, the former facilitated after 1931 by AGIP's controlling interest in the British Oil Development Company, gave it a basis of operations abroad. By 1939 AGIP produced over 1.4 million tons of oil products. Its contributions grew as a result of major natural gas discoveries in the Po Valley in 1946 and 1949. By 1953, when AGIP was absorbed by ENI,* it produced over 2 billion cubic meters of methane and supplied 9.4 percent of the nation's energy needs.

RS

AGNELLI, GIOVANNI. Industrialist and guiding genius of FIAT* (Fabbrica Italiana Automobili Torino), in the early years of this century Agnelli pioneered the introduction of serially produced standardized motor vehicles designed for a mass market. Born at Villar Perosa (Turin) on August 13, 1866, into a family of prosperous Piedmontese landowners, Agnelli attended a military academy and pursued a career in the cavalry until 1893. As chief administrator of FIAT (founded in July 1899), Agnelli soon gained control of that enterprise, which by 1918 had become the country's third largest business corporation. He adopted production techniques introduced by Henry Ford, whom he greatly admired, negotiated with organized labor, and cultivated political contacts. Although by preference a Giolittian liberal, Agnelli accepted Fascism* and worked closely with Mussolini,* who nominated him senator in March 1923. Charges of political collaboration with the regime were officially dropped shortly before Agnelli's death in Turin on December 16, 1945.

For further reference see: Valerio Castronuovo, *Giovanni Agnelli* (Turin: UTET, 1971).

RS

ALBANIA. Located across the strategic Strait of Otranto and a possible gateway to the Balkans, Albania was long a concern to Italian governments and a source of friction with Austria. During the decade before 1914, Italy nevertheless collaborated with Austria to obstruct Greek and Serbian ambitions in the area, promoting the creation of a neutralized independent Albania in 1912–13. With the outbreak of World War I,* Italy moved into southern Albania to check Greek expansionism, and in June 1917 proclaimed a protectorate over all Albania. Italian, Greek, and Yugoslav plans for Albania's partition were thwarted in 1919, when faced by resistance led by Ahmen Zogu. In 1920 Giovanni Giolitti* withdrew Italy's forces and recognized Albania's independence. The Greco-Italian rivalry helped lead to the Corfu Crisis* in 1923. The next year, Italo-Yugoslav differences over Albania were defused temporarily by a nonintervention agreement; but Mussolini's* policy of large-scale economic penetration and a military treaty with President Zogu (1927) again strained relations with Yugoslavia. From the early 1930s, Zogu (proclaimed King Zog I in 1928) attempted to reduce Italy's military presence in Albania, prompting Mussolini to invade the country in April 1939, making Victor Emmanuel III* its king. With the collapse of Italian forces in the Balkans in September 1943, Italy's direct influence in Albania came to an end.

SS

ALBERTARIO, DAVIDE. A prominent organizer of the Opera dei Congressi* and an associate of Don Luigi Sturzo,* Davide Albertario was born on February 16, 1846, in Filighera (Pavia). Ordained in 1868, Albertario joined the staff of the intransigent *Osservatore Cattolico* and became one of the founders of the Opera dei Congressi. A supporter of Catholic social action, the Catholic university, and the *non expedit*,* Albertario had a strong following among young Christian Democrats. His newspaper, with its motto "preparazione nell'astensione," lent its voice to the cause of Catholic Action* among the workers. In the turmoil of the Fatti di Maggio in 1898, Don Albertario was arrested and jailed for one year. After a lifetime of service to Catholic social action and eventual support for the Sturzo wing of the Opera, he died in Bergamo on September 21, 1902.

RJW

ALBERTINE CONSTITUTION. See STATUTO

ALBERTINI, LUIGI. Senator, historian, and director and co-owner of Milan's *Corriere della Sera*,* Albertini ranks as one of the notables of modern Italy. He was born in Ancona on October 19, 1871. He joined Salvatore Cognetti de Martiis' Laboratorio di Economia Politica in 1893 after having received his law degree from the University of Turin. Joining the *Corriere* in 1896, he rose to director and co-owner by 1900.

He made the *Corriere* into a formidable political organ that espoused his conservative liberal faith and tenacious adherence to the legacy of the Cavourian constitutional state of the *Risorgimento*.* Recognized as Italy's leading anti-Giolittian voice, Albertini fought what he saw as a betrayal of historical liberalism by "subversive" forces of socialism, clericalism, and, indeed, Giolittianism. The Libyan War (see Ouchy, Treaty of*) and the interventionist crisis of 1914–15 moved him toward a more conservative and patriotic stance. After the war, Albertini was a leading figure in the Congress of Oppressed Nationalities on the Yugoslav question, and he served as a delegate to the Washington Naval Disarmament Conference in 1922. World War I* and the "mutilated peace," however, led him to fear the death of liberal Italy under his nemesis, Giovanni Giolitti*; and he initially, although cautiously, welcomed Mussolini's* Fascist movement as an antidote to bolshevism and Giolittianism.

After 1923, however, he saw Mussolini as the direct heir of Giolitti's failures and mounted a courageous anti-Fascist campaign. Mussolini forced the Albertinis from ownership of the *Corriere*, which was "fascistized" in 1925. As senator, Albertini spoke forcefully against Fascist extremism, but constant threats and harassment compelled him to retire to an estate outside of Rome. From 1929 to 1941, in virtual isolation, he wrote his influential *Le origini della guerra del 1914* [Origins of the war of 1914], and his monumental five-volume memoirs, *Venti anni di vita politica* [Twenty years of political life]. He died in Rome on December 29, 1941.

PJD

ALERAMO, SIBILLA. This author's first and most famous book, *Una donna* [A woman] (1906), has been hailed as the book of Genesis in the Bible of feminism. Aleramo (pseudonym for Rina Faccio, 1876–1960) wrote other novels, as well as plays, short stories, and essays, but none matched the power and appeal of *Una donna*, which told the story of her liberation from an oppressive marriage. To free herself she had to surrender her child, and the pathos of the book derives from the tension between a woman's liberation and a mother's guilt. Thereafter, her numerous love affairs scandalized Italy, and she became known as the female D'Annunzio.*

From about 1910 until the early 1940s, Aleramo's writings reflected mainly belletristic concerns and recorded her relationships with the famous artists and writers who were her lovers. During the last ten years of the Fascist regime she received a pension from the government, which caused her acute mortification after the war. Under the tutelage of Palmiro Togliatti,* however, her social consciousness—expressed in the heroic work that she did for the peasants of the Agro Romano from 1904 to 1909—was revived. Aleramo's diaries from 1940 to 1960 describe this return to something akin to her earlier beliefs.

RD

ALFIERI, DINO. This fascist diplomat and minister was born in Bologna on June 8, 1886. Alfieri was trained in law. He was a "first-hour" nationalist and one of the founders of the Milan Nationalist Group, which he later headed. He volunteered to fight in World War I* and was decorated five times. Although a reluctant fusionist with Fascism,* Alfieri served the Fascists in many capacities. He was a member of the Fascist Grand Council, minister of popular culture in the mid-thirties, and ambassador to the Holy See (October 29, 1939). He was transferred to Berlin on May 13, 1940, where he remained until his dismissal on July 25, 1943. Convinced that the war was lost, at the Grand Council meeting of July 24–25 he voted for the Grandi resolution, which stripped the Duce of command. Alfieri died in Milan on January 2, 1966.

RSC

ALFIERI, VITTORIO. Born into a noble Piedmontese family in Asti on January 16, 1749, Alfieri was a poet and dramatist, many of whose writings called for a united and independent Italy. After finishing his studies, he entered the military and travelled widely in Italy and Europe. Becoming increasingly dissatisfied with his aimless life, he began to write. In 1775 his first play was produced in Turin. Its public acceptance gave Alfieri the goal he sought, and he determined to create a national theater for Italy. He resigned his military commission and began to study Italian, a language little known in Piedmont, where French and the local dialect prevailed.

In 1778, to escape government censorship, Alfieri decided to emigrate. He turned over his property to his sister in return for an assured life income and left Piedmont to live abroad. By the mid-1780s he had settled in Paris, where he remained until forced out in 1792 by the increasing revolutionary militancy. He ultimately settled in Florence and resided there until his death on October 8, 1803. He is buried in Santa Croce, memorialized by Antonio Canova's monument.

Until the outbreak of the French Revolution, Alfieri, like other eighteenth-century intellectuals, had believed that all evil in society resulted from absolutism. But the events after 1789 changed his outlook. Increasingly he came to hate the revolution and, by association, France, and to love Italy, for which he demanded unity and freedom.

His plays and poetry, written between 1775 and 1789, reflect the Enlightenment* philosophy and exalt moral and political ideals. After 1792 disillusionment permeated his writing, and it became bitter and satirical. One of his last major works was the *Misogallo* [Francophobe], an anti-French diatribe, written between 1790 and 1796.

Between 1776 and 1786 he wrote nineteen tragedies, all inspired by classical and historical themes. They dealt with human passions, excoriated tyranny, and praised freedom. His *Bruto primo* [The first Brutus] was dedicated to George Washington, whom he identified with the great defenders of liberty in the past. His last tragedy, the *Bruto minore* [The second Brutus], was dedicated to the "future people of Italy." His two important political treatises also contrasted tyranny and freedom. *Della tirannide* [Of tyranny] analyzed despotism, and *Del principe e delle lettere* [The prince and letters] examined the relationship between absolute monarchy and literature, concluding that princely patronage did not encourage great literature.

His autobiography, the *Vita*, was begun in 1790 and finished the year of his death. To subsequent generations he left a legacy of pride in Italy, which became an important source of nineteenth-century nationalism, distrust of French leadership, and faith in liberty and freedom, to which the Italian people, united into a nation, had a right.

For further reference see: Vittorio Alfieri, *The Prince and Letters*, trans. Beatrice Corrigan and Julius Molinaro (Toronto: University of Toronto Press, 1972); Vittorio Alfieri, *Of Tyranny*, trans. Molinaro and Corrigan (Toronto: University of Toronto Press, 1961); Gaudens Megaro, *Vittorio Alfieri: Forerunner of Italian Nationalism* (New York: Columbia University Press, 1930).

EPN

ALGECIRAS CONFERENCE. This diplomatic congress, held from January 16 to April 7, 1906, at Algeciras, Spain, dealt with Germany's protest over the

French threat to Morocco's independence. The German government actually hoped to break up the new Anglo-French Entente by confronting Great Britain and France with the possibility of a war between them and the Triple Alliance* of Germany, Austria-Hungary, and Italy. Italy, Great Britain, Russia, Spain, and the United States, however, all supported France at Algeciras. The conference decided to uphold Morocco's independence, but decreed that France and Spain should control its police system. Germany's confidence was shaken by Italy's defection at the congress. Italy was represented at the conference by the aged Emilio Visconti-Venosta.*

JKZ

ALLIED MILITARY GOVERNMENT (IN ITALY). This military government was established in Italy in 1943 by Great Britain and the United States. Its creation, which followed Allied occupation of the Italian peninsula, derived immediately from the Moscow Conference of November 1943. At this conference, the foreign secretaries of Great Britain, the United States, and the Soviet Union issued a joint "Declaration Regarding Italy," in which the Allied powers detailed the substance of Allied occupation policy in Italy. The resulting Allied Military Government, which later was followed by the Allied Control Commission, was a pivotal instrument for implementing this policy.

The Allied Military Government was under the jurisdiction of the commander of the Allied forces in Italy. The structure of the Allied Military Government for Italy consisted of divisions or sectors, each under the authority of an officer. These divisions or sectors reflected the different ramifications of Allied occupation policy in the Italian territory. The objectives of this policy were: (1) encouraging the institution of democratic government; (2) elimination of Fascist influence in local government and politics; and (3) restoration of normal conditions, with particular emphasis on public health, water supply, currency, foreign exchange, legal matters, and economic resources and supplies. These objectives were coordinated to aid the progress not only of the military government but also of the military operations still in progress. Toward the end of 1943, the functions of the Allied Military Government were assumed by the Allied Control Commission for Italy.

For further reference see: U.S. Congress, House of Representatives, "Declaration Regarding Italy," *House Miscellaneous Documents*, 78th Cong., 1st sess., 1943, Vol. 2 n.463.

PVB

ALMIRANTE, GIORGIO. See **MSI**

ALTO ADIGE. This is the Italian name for that northern section of the Trentino* referred to by the Austrians as the Suedtirol. Italian nationalists popularized the name at the turn of the century as part of their campaign to associate this predominantly Germanic region with Italy. The Alto Adige is characterized by the valleys surrounding the upper part of the river to which the province's name calls attention as well as by rugged Alpine terrain. Bolzano is the main city. Italian territory since 1918, it experiences certain ethnic tensions. The combined Trentino–Alto Adige presently forms one of five regions ruled by special statute.

JCR

AMENDOLA, GIORGIO. Giorgio Amendola was born in Rome in 1907 and died there in 1980. The anti-Fascist leader and Communist politician was the son of the liberal Giovanni Amendola.* He joined the Italian Communist Party (PCI)* in 1929 and was a leader of the party in exile during the 1930s. Active in the Resistance in France from 1940 to 1943, Amendola helped negotiate the "unity of action" agreement between the Italian Socialist Party (PSI)* and the Italian Communist Party (PCI)* and was an important organizer of the struggle to liberate Italy between 1943 and 1945. Amendola became an undersecretary in the first postwar governments (1945–46), served in every legislature after 1946, and became a leading exponent of a liberal "Italian road to socialism" within the Communist Party.

AJD

AMENDOLA, GIOVANNI. Born in Naples on April 15, 1882, Giovanni Amendola was a leader of the constitutional opposition to Fascism* from 1923 to 1926. In 1925 he founded the National Union of Liberal and Democratic Forces, which attracted a small but influential group of professional, largely middle-class intellectuals committed to the ideal of parliamentary democracy. His authority was based not only on the example he had set earlier, from 1921 to 1924, as a militant editor of the newspaper *Il Mondo*, but also on his successful effort to win a seat in the Chamber of Deputies in the elections of April 1924. In parliament he spoke out forcefully against various pieces of Fascist legislation, and founded the Unione Democratica Nazionale (1924).

Amendola's outspoken denunciations of the numerous acts of violence perpetrated by agents of the Fascist government earned him the enmity of the regime's henchmen, and he was savagely beaten on two occasions. The second beating, sustained on July 20, 1925, contributed to his premature death, which occurred in Cannes on April 7, 1926. Amendola's moral rigor and personal courage inspired a whole generation of Italian anti-Fascists, including his son Giorgio,* who combined his father's liberal convictions with his own allegiance to Marxism and to the Italian Communist Party (PCI).*

For further reference see: Simona Colarizi, *I Democratici all'opposizione— Giovanni Amendola e l'Unione Nazionale (1922–1926)* (Bologna: Il Mulino, 1973).

FR

AMG. See **ALLIED MILITARY GOVERNMENT (IN ITALY)**

AMICI PEDANTI. See **CARDUCCI, GIOSUÈ**

AMICIZIE CRISTIANE. These secret societies of Catholic clerics and laymen were organized to defend the faith against Jansenist, Enlightenment,* and Jacobin* attack in the period extending from the late 1770s until 1817. Founded by a Jesuit, Nikolaus von Diessbach (1732–98), after the suppression of the Society of Jesus, they spread from Turin to other Italian and foreign cities. The Amicizie have been looked upon as a prototype of later Catholic Action,* Diessbach encouraging adoption of modern methods to spread the Church's message. The aristocratic, legitimist, and ultramontane character of the societies caused them difficulties during the Napoleonic period. Pio Brunone Lanteri (1759–1830) altered and reinvigorated them in 1817 as the Amicizie Cattoliche.

JCR

ANARCHISM, ITALIAN. In his classic work *L'anarchia*, Errico Malatesta* defines anarchy as "the condition of a people who live without a constituted authority, without government." This antiauthoritarian, antigovernment (either of the Left or Right) tendency dominated Italian anarchism along with the call for direct action through propaganda by deed.

Although virtually born with the arrival of Mikhail Bakunin* in 1864, Italian anarchism has roots in the *Risorgimento** as a struggle for national liberation and in Proudhon's thought as interpreted by Carlo Pisacane.* Carbonari (see Carboneria,*), Garibaldinians, and Mazzinians helped establish anarchistic precedents through a tradition of conspiracy and insurrectionary deeds. The wars for unification and the expulsion of the Austrians brought more economic hardship to a country already suffering endemic agricultural distress. Whereas workers in the industrialized states of northern Europe looked to political parties or trade unions, the Italian workers, peasants, and artisans believed more in Bakunin.

Bakunin organized the Florentine Brotherhood and then the International Brotherhood before leaving Italy for Geneva in 1867. Even though the International Brotherhood was dissolved in 1869, Italian anarchists operated, loosely, under the umbrella of the Marxist International until expelled from world socialism by the Second International in 1896. A new generation of militants had risen in the 1870s, inspired by Bakunin's attacks on the aging Giuseppe Mazzini,* who had opposed socialism in all forms and had attacked the Paris Commune. The new anarchists were led by Malatesta and Carlo Cafiero,* and later by Andrea Costa.* The autonomy of Italian anarchism and the adherence to propaganda by the deed (not individualist terrorism, which was opposed) were determined at the Rimini Congress of 1872 and the Bologna Congress of 1873, although Malatesta and Cafiero did not promulgate the gospel of direct action until 1876. It was also during this year that the two leading anarchists moved away from Bakuninist collectivist anarchism to anarcho-communism and revolutionary insurrection.

In spite of the failures of the Bologna insurrection (1874) and the Benevento rising (1876), the movement still appeared viable in the face of mounting government repression. Then individual acts of violence, including an abortive attempt on the life of King Humbert I* and indiscriminate bombings, caused disenchantment among the masses and ever-increasing police persecution, arrests, and exile. Despite intense, dynamic activity by a few dedicated anarchists, the movement began to dwindle by the 1880s. Industrial development and parliamentary reformism began to cut the ranks of anarchists, who were excluded from the Italian Socialist Party (PSI),* formed in 1892. Costa defected to electoral politics, Cafiero succumbed to insanity, and Malatesta was constantly in prison or exile. Anarchist activities became sporadic, although as emigrés the Italians were prominent in the Levant, Latin America, and the United States. Unfortunately, the world better remembered Santo Caserio, Michele Angiolillo, Luigi Luccheni, and Gaetano Bresci,* political assassins rightly or wrongly linked with Italian anarchism.

Italian anarchism mingled with syndicalism* in the pre-World War I era, and some anarchists cooperated with Antonio Gramsci's* *Ordine Nuovo* manifesto in 1919 calling for the formation of factory councils (soviets). But these alliances were short-lived and fruitless. The Italian Anarchist Union Congress in November 1921 refused to even recognize the Soviet government. Neither the general strike and Red Week* of 1914 nor the occupation of the factories in 1920 could salvage anarchism, in spite of some momentary sparks of victory.

Fascist terrorism subdued Italian anarchism. The militants were killed or imprisoned, or they fled. But Italian anarchism by its very nature could not die. It remains one of the strongest of the scattered libertarian movements still in existence in the Western world.

For further reference see: Enzo Santarelli, *Il socialismo anarchico in Italia* (Milan: Feltrinelli, 1973); George Woodcock, *Anarchism* (New York: Meridian, 1971).

PJD

ANDREOTTI, GIULIO. Twice prime minister of postwar Italy, Giulio Andreotti was born to a poor Roman family on January 14, 1919. While pursuing a law degree at the University of Rome, Andreotti became a member and later president of the Federazione Universitaria Cattolica Italiana (FUCI),* the organization of Catholic university students, and forged friendships with Giovanni Battista Montini (later Paul VI*), Aldo Moro,* and other future Christian Democratic leaders.

A protégé of Alcide De Gasperi* and closely tied to the Roman Catholic establishment, Andreotti rose rapidly in the ranks of the Christian Democratic Party,* serving in various cabinet posts (finance, treasury, defense) before forming his own government in 1972, which lasted only one year. Again, in 1976, Andreotti became prime minister and struck the famous "Compromesso storico" with the Italian Communist Party (PCI).* In this informal agreement, the Communists agreed to refrain from voting against the government in matters that could result in its fall in return for concessions from the Christian Democrats. Andreotti presided over Italy in a period of political unrest, terrorism of the Left and Right, and the infamous kidnapping and assassination of Aldo Moro. His government fell in 1979, and with it the "Compromesso storico," as the Communists moved into opposition once again.

RJW

ANGLO-ITALIAN AGREEMENT OF 1938. This agreement, hastily concluded on April 16, 1938, represented a curious attempt by the British and Italian governments to achieve detente. Great Britain now recognized Italy's sovereignty in Ethiopia* and promised to take up the question of this Italian claim in the League of Nations Council. The Fascist government agreed to withdraw "Italian volunteers" from Spanish soil at the conclusion of the Spanish Civil War* and to end its anti-British propaganda in the Eastern Mediterranean. Both countries pledged to respect the Mediterranean and Red Sea status quo. While these issues warranted serious negotiations between the two governments, it is probable that they were both responding to the sudden conquest of Austria by Nazi forces in mid-March. British leaders hoped to divide Mussolini* and Hitler, and the Italian dictator desired to find a counterweight to his powerful German neighbor.

JKZ

ANNALI UNIVERSALI DI STATISTICA. An important *Risorgimento** journal (1824–71), it attempted to air themes and ideas designed to raise Italian public awareness and cohesiveness. It especially undertook the dissemination of economic and scientific information.

Founded by several prominent citizens of Milan in 1824, and placed under the general directorship of Francesco Lampato, its aim was, in five separate monthly reviews, to give a brief but salient analysis of the many works published throughout Europe on various subjects. After Melchiorre Gioia,* this review was edited by Gian Dominico Romagnosi,* and after Romagnosi, by his disciples Carlo Cattaneo,* Defendente Sacchi, Giuseppe Ferrari,* and Giuseppe Sacchi, who in 1848 succeeded Lampato as publisher. Abandoned by its collaborators and faced with officially promulgated statistics and public indifference, the *Annali* suspended publication in 1871.

FFA

ANSALDO. The Società Giovanni Ansaldo, initially a modest-sized privately owned company that produced goods used by engineering and shipbuilding firms, was transformed into a joint-stock company in 1903. From that date to World War I,* the company grew swiftly, expanding its productive capacity by integrating backward into the manufacture of iron products and forward into the production of finished goods. It was an integrated heavy industrial complex by 1913, and perhaps the major rival to the loosely knit group of heavy industrial firms controlled by the Banca Commerciale Italiana.*

During the war Ansaldo came into its own. Its rate of growth between 1915 and 1918 was spectacular. To give an idea of the firm's expansion, between 1915 and 1918 investment in plant and equipment was estimated at 588 million lire, while in 1914 this value had amounted to only 42 million lire. The number of workers employed by the company rose from roughly 6,000 in 1914 to 56,000 in 1918 (111,000 if employees of affiliates are included). In 1914 Ansaldo had been an important industrial enterprise, but one of many. By 1918 it was the largest and most powerful industrial complex in the country, a virtual industrial empire encompassing mining operations, iron and steel plants, electric power stations, engineering and shipbuilding facilities, and a merchant fleet. This growth, of course, was made possible by liberal support from the state and promoted by wartime demands of the military.

With the cessation of hostilities, government largesse and military demand also ceased. Ansaldo, along with other firms that had prospered because of the war, was saddled with substantial excess capacity and was strapped for funds. The directors of the company attempted, unsuccessfully as it turned out, to obtain control of the Banca Commerciale Italiana. A few years later the Ansaldo empire was restructured and scaled down. In 1933 control of Ansaldo was assumed by the Industrial Reconstruction Institute (IRI).*

JSC

ANSCHLUSS, ITALY'S RESPONSE TO. Italians opposed the German incorporation of Austria because they realized that this Austro-German union would bring German troops to the Brenner Pass and pose a threat to the hold Italy had gained on the Alto Adige* (South Tyrol) in 1919. Italian opposition to Anschluss was axiomatic and notably manifest in the crisis of 1934, occasioned by the murder of the Austrian chancellor Engelbert Dollfuss.* Yet, when Hitler effected incorporation in March 1938, Fascist Italy acquiesced. The change reflected Mussolini's* determination after the Ethiopian War, 1935–36, to side with his new Axis* partner. Nazi blandishments consisted of repeated recognition of the Brenner frontier and readiness to consider transfer of the German population from the Alto Adige. The actual Anschluss rendered an Italo-German military pact almost unavoidable, though the Pact of Steel* did not materialize until May 22, 1939.

ACas

ANTICLERICALISM. Anticlericalism in Italy derived not only from the secularism common to nearly all nineteenth-century liberals, but also from the hostility between church and state generated by the papacy's opposition to Italian unification and the despoilment of the Church's temporal power. The papacy's persistent refusal to recognize the existence of the Italian state before and after the Law of Papal Guarantees* (1871), the activity of Freemasonry,* regarded by the Church as a nefarious sect devoted to its destruction, and a number of laws and episodes all served to perpetuate anticlerical sentiment. The abolition of theology faculties in all universities (1873); an unratified "clerical abuses" bill (1877); compulsory lay elementary education (1877); another unratified bill, on compulsory civil marriage (1879); and disorders during the relocation of Pius IX's* mortal remains (1881) occasioned acrimonious debate, papal protests, and demands for the abolition of the Law of Guarantees of 1871. During the long political ascendancy of three Freemason prime ministers (Francesco Crispi,* 1887–91, 1893–96; Antonio Rudinì,* 1891–92, 1896–98; and Giuseppe Zanardelli,* 1901–3), anticlerical incidents and debates abounded. Crispi promoted the erection of monuments in Rome to Giordano Bruno (1889) and Giuseppe Garibaldi* (1895), both enemies of the Church. Pro-papal demonstrations by French pilgrims in Rome (October 1891) aroused much anticlerical clamor and demands for the repeal of the Law of 1871, both Rudinì and Crispi indicating that this law was not immutable. The major disturbances of May 1898 led Rudinì to dissolve numerous Catholic as well as Socialist organizations, eliciting papal protests and automatic anticlerical responses. The same occurred when Zanardelli introduced a divorce bill in 1902, prompting *L'Osservatore Romano** to refer to the King's ministers as instruments of Masonic sectarianism. With the advent of Giovanni Giolitti* (1903–5, 1906–9, 1911–14) and Pius X* (1903–14), there began a process of gradual accommodation between church and state, attenuating one of the primary causes of anticlericalism, which, though in decline, continued to manifest itself in several instances. In 1907 Ernesto Nathan,* a former grand master, was elected mayor of Rome where, two years later, Freemasons promoted a general strike in protest against the execution in Spain of a noted anticlerical. But the conclusion of an alliance between Liberal candidates and Catholic electoral organizations in the elections of 1913 (Gentiloni Pact*), although it led the most anticlerical party—the Radical Party*—to abandon Giolitti, was nevertheless an unmistakable sign of anticlericalism's political decline. Even the neutralist posture assumed by the Vatican and many Catholic organizations on the question of intervention in World War I* and the formation of a Catholic Popular Party (see Italian Popular Party*) in 1919 did not lead to a general anticlerical revival. During the Fascist era, anticlericalism (not altogether absent in Fascist ranks) remained subdued, because or in spite of the Lateran Accords* of 1929. In the post-Fascist period it has surfaced on such questions as the 1929 accords, divorce, and abortion, but it has not assumed the sustained intensity that characterized it during the nineteenth century.

For further reference see: Arturo Carlo Jemolo, *Chiesa e Stato in Italia negli ultimi cento anni* (Turin: Einaudi, 1949); J. Salwyn Schapiro, *Anticlericalism: Conflict between Church and State in France, Italy, and Spain* (Princeton, N.J.: Van Nostrand, 1967); José Mariano Sánchez, *Anticlericalism: A Brief History* (Notre Dame, Ind.: University of Notre Dame Press, 1972).

SS

ANTI-COMINTERN PACT. This agreement, signed on November 25, 1936, called for consultation and collaboration between Germany and Japan to counter the actions of the Third Communist International. The final agreement was drawn up by Major General Oshimà Hiroshi, the military attaché in Berlin; his counterpart in Tokyo, Colonel Eugen Ott; Joachim von Ribbentrop; and Shiratori Toshio. Italy joined on November 6, 1937, becoming the third party to the pact. Earlier, the Italian government, through its foreign minister, Count Galeazzo Ciano,* had signed the "October Protocols" of 1936. This too was, in part, an agreement to oppose the spread of communism.

Despite the fact that the Anti-Comintern Pact was not a military alliance, the Japanese army felt that this agreement would serve as a deterrent to the Soviet Union in Asia—which accounts for the primary role played by the army in its negotiation. After the pact was signed, Hitler recognized Japan's puppet government of Manchukuo, and Italy opened a consulate there. The Manchukuo government then joined the Anti-Comintern Pact. Rome, Berlin, and Tokyo never fully agreed on the meaning of the pact, with Germany refusing to consider Japan's war in China as one against communism. Germany interpreted the pact as applying only to the spread of communism within the boundaries of the nations that had signed the pact. Later the Allied nations used Mussolini's* term "Axis"* to describe not only the Rome-Berlin connection (as he had intended), but the agreement between Germany, Italy, Japan, and others, such as Spain, that signed the pact at later dates.

For further reference see: Leonid Kutakov, *The Diplomacy of Aggression: The Berlin-Rome-Tokyo Axis* (Woodstock, N.Y.: Beekman, 1975).

BDQ

ANTI-FASCISM. Anti-Fascism was the phenomenon of political opposition to the Fascist movement and to the regime of Mussolini* between 1919 and 1945. It embraced a wide ideological spectrum from anarchism* and communism to Catholicism and liberal conservatism. At first it was identified chiefly with the Socialist, Communist, and left-wing Popular parties, but after 1924 anti-Fascism widened its appeal. Following the murder of Socialist leader Giacomo Matteotti that same year (see Matteotti Crisis*), one hundred deputies withdrew from parliament to a symbolic Aventine, hoping to persuade the King to dismiss Premier Mussolini. The Aventine Secession* failed. Counterattacking, Mussolini imposed the totalitarian regime in 1925–26. Numerous Socialist leaders, including Filippo Turati,* Claudio Treves,* Pietro Nenni,* and others, escaped to France, where they organized the Anti-Fascist Concentration (see Concentrazione Antifascista*) (1927–34). In 1929 a liberal Socialist, Carlo Rosselli,* escaped to Paris and founded the rival Giustizia e Libertà (see Justice and Liberty movement*). Less activist-minded foes (e.g., Benedetto Croce* and Alcide De Gasperi*) stayed home.

The Communists remained apart until 1934, when they began a series of "unity of action" pacts with the Socialists. By the time of the Spanish Civil War* this Popular Front became the strongest anti-Fascist group. The shocking Nazi-Soviet Pact (1939–41) terminated it.

After the fall of France in 1940 numerous anti-Fascists (e.g., Carlo Sforza*) escaped to America and reorganized. Hitler's invasion of Russia (1941) caused Italian Communists to resume their links with the Socialists. By 1942–43 various anti-Fascist parties organized secretly in war-weary Italy. Anti-Fascism culminated in the Committees of National Liberation (CLNs*) that emerged in 1943 after the royal coup d'état of July 25 overthrew the dictatorship. The Armed Resistance* (1943–45) was the final phase of the struggle.

For further reference see: Charles F. Delzell, *Mussolini's Enemies: The Italian Anti-Fascist Resistance*, rev. ed. (New York: H. Fertig, 1974); Aldo Garosci, *Storia dei fuorusciti* (Bari: Laterza, 1953).

CFD

ANTI-FASCIST CONCENTRATION. See **CONCENTRAZIONE ANTIFASCISTA**

ANTONELLI, GIACOMO. This cardinal of the Catholic Church and papal secretary of state under Pius IX* was born in Sonnino near Terracina on April 2, 1806. He died in the Vatican on November 6, 1876. Giacomo attended the Roman Seminary and the University of the Sapienza, earned a doctorate in canon and civil law, and in 1830 entered the Prelatura—the higher civil and diplomatic service of the state. In 1835 he was appointed papal delegate to the province of Orvieto; the following year he was moved to Viterbo; and in 1839 he was transferred to Macerata.

Antonelli's loyalty to Rome and competence in economic matters won him the approval of Gregory XVI,* who in 1841 nominated him a canon of St. Peter's basilica. On this occasion he received holy orders up to the diaconate, resisting parental pressure to enter the priesthood. He never became a priest. In 1844 he was made deputy-treasurer under Cardinal Tosti, and with the latter's death in 1845 became treasurer-general. Mastai-Ferretti, who was elected pope in 1846, raised Antonelli to the dignity of a cardinal deacon in June 1847.

From 1846 to 1848 Antonelli seconded the moderate reformism of the Pope, serving as minister of finance while presiding over the newly established consultative assembly, or Consulta. He played a major role in drafting the constitution of the Papal States,* and in March 1848 was appointed secretary of state and given the responsibility of directing the constitutional ministry. Following the Allocution of April 29, 1848, in which Pius indicated that he could not wage war upon Catholic Austria, the entire ministry resigned, but Antonelli retained the Pope's confidence and served as prefect of papal palaces.

After the assassination of the Pope's minister, Pellegrino Rossi,* and the revolutionary upheaval in Rome of November 15–16, Antonelli arranged for Pius IX's flight to Gaeta,* acting as his secretary of state and chief adviser. It was Antonelli who issued the protests against the usurpations of the Holy Father's rights by the Roman revolutionists and appealed for the armed intervention of Austria, France, Spain, and Naples. Following the Pope's return to Rome in

April 1850, Antonelli served as the architect and prime minister of the papal government and was responsible for Vatican diplomacy.

After the emergence of the Kingdom of Italy* (1861) and the papacy's loss of Rome (1870), all sorts of personal and political accusations were launched against the cardinal, who excited the envy and anger of conservatives and liberals alike. Dubbed the "red pope" because of his habit, he allegedly gained ascendency over Pius and supposedly dragged him along a conservative course. This accusation was vigorously denied by contemporaries who had frequent access to both men, and the opening of the Vatican archives for this pontificate confirms that the policy of *non possumus* flowed from the principles of Pius rather than the intrigues of Antonelli.

Pius appreciated the loyalty and devotion of his secretary of state, who continued to serve him after the loss of the temporal power in 1870. It was Antonelli who advised the Pope not to leave Rome after the capital fell, correctly assessing that the situation had changed since 1848. It was also Antonelli who, during the course of the negotiations of September-October 1870, was able to obtain the restitution of some 5 million of Peter's Pence. This fund was carefully invested by the secretary of state, and it placed the Holy See on a sound financial basis, enabling the Pope to refuse the financial settlement proposed by the Italian government in the Law of Papal Guarantees.*

For further reference see: Roger Aubert, "Antonelli, Giacomo," *Dizionario Biografico degli Italiani*, 2: 484–93; Frank J. Coppa, "Cardinal Giacomo Antonelli: An Accommodating Personality in the Politics of Confrontation," *Biography* 2, no. 2 (Fall 1979): 283–302; idem, "Cardinal Antonelli, the Papal States and the Counter-Risorgimento," *Journal of Church and State* 16 (Autumn 1974): 453–71; Pietro Pirri, "Il Cardinale Antonelli tra il mito e la storia," *Rivista di Storia della Chiesa in Italia* 12 (1958): 81–120.

FJC

ARCARI, PAOLO. A leader of the democratic nationalists and a literary personality, Arcari was born in Fourneaux, Savoy, on October 25, 1879, to a family native to Bergamo. He took an interest in the emergent Christian Democratic movement (see Christian Democracy in Italy*), particularly its political and journalistic aspects. He then shifted allegiance to nationalism, serving as a member of the first central committee of the Italian Nationalist Association.* In December 1912, Arcari led the departure of democratic nationalists from the association. Professor of Italian literature at the Catholic University at Freiburg, and after 1931 dean of faculty, Arcari was instrumental in the continued diffusion of Italian culture in Switzerland. He died in Rome on February 4, 1955, leaving behind thirty volumes of diverse writings.

RSC

ARDEATINE CAVES, MASSACRE AT. See **GRUPPI DI AZIONE PATRIOTTICA**

ARDIGÒ, ROBERTO. The premier Italian positivist thinker, Roberto Ardigò was born in Casteldidone (Cremona) on January 28, 1828. Exposed to the ideological currents of the *Risorgimento*,* Ardigò left the priesthood in 1871. He held a number of teaching positions, including one at the University of Padua, 1881–1909. *La psicologia come scienza positiva* [Psychology as a positivist science] appeared in 1870; in it he maintained that knowledge was rooted in sensations and not in ideas, as the philosophic idealists maintained. In 1893 Ardigò wrote *La scienza dell'educazione* [The science of education], which argued that a sound educational system was based on self-knowledge and social utility, and not on abstract contemplation of the past and rote memorization. In the trilogy *Il vero* [The truth] (1891), *La ragione* [Reason] (1894), and *L'unità della coscienza* [The unity of conscience] (1898), Ardigò claimed that positivism, and the moral individualism that sustained it, were sufficient for man's hopes and needs. Ardigò died in Mantua, September 15, 1920.

RSC

ARDITI. The Arditi were specially trained shock troops deployed during World War I* to break the stalemate of trench warfare. Trained during the summer and fall of 1917, Arditi battalions participated in the battle of the Piave River, which halted the Austro-German advance after the battle of Caporetto* (October 1917), and in the battle of Vittorio Veneto,* which ended the war a year later. Approximately 10,000 Arditi joined the political Associazione fra gli Arditi d'Italia, founded in November 1918. The politicization of the Arditi and their frequent breaches of military discipline led to the disbandment of their formations in January 1919. In September 1919 former Arditi supported Gabriele D'Annunzio's* military takeover of Fiume,* and eventually many of them joined the Fascist squads. Their militarily organized attacks against political opponents gave Fascism* its permanent warlike character, while their presence in the movement strengthened its commitment to youth, action, and elitism.

RS

ARMED RESISTANCE. See **RESISTANCE, ARMED**

ARMISTICE WITH ITALY. In this protocol between Italy and the Allied powers, signed on September 3, 1943, the Italian government "accepted" the unconditional surrender terms requested by the Western powers. Although the armistice was signed on September 3, it did not become official until September 8, when Marshal Pietro Badoglio,* then head of the Italian government, announced the conclusion of the military hostilities in an emotional address to the Italian people over the state radio. The protocol signed on September 3 became known as the "Short Armistice," because it contained clauses dealing only with military affairs. These clauses provided for the immediate termination of military activities, the unconditional surrender of the Italian military forces, and the beginning of Anglo-American military government and jurisdiction over the entire Italian territory.

Another protocol, known as the "Long Armistice," was initialled on September 29, 1943. This armistice contained the political, economic, and financial conditions for the Allied occupation of Italy.

PVB

ARMONIA DELLA RELIGIONE COLLA CIVILTÀ, L'. This Catholic journal of intransigent character was published daily in Turin during the *Risorgimento** era. Founded in 1848, its guiding spirit and principal writer was Don Giacomo Margotti (1823–87). *L'Armonia*'s strong opposition to liberal and anticlerical trends in Piedmont, as well as to much of the nationalist program, made it a natural rallying point for Catholics in the Sardinian kingdom. It maintained close relations with the influential Jesuit periodical, *La Civiltà Cattolica.** Suppressed temporarily by Cavour* during the war of 1859,* it suffered irreversible decline with Margotti's departure in December 1863 to form the still more intransigent *L'Unità Cattolica. L'Armonia* ceased publication shortly after its transfer to Florence in 1866.

JCR

ARMY OF THE HOLY FAITH. See SANFEDISTI

ASCOLI, MAX. A political scientist, he was born on June 25, 1898, in Ferrara, Italy, scion of a distinguished Jewish family. A university teacher, militant anti-Fascist, and contributor to Piero Gobetti's* *Rivoluzione Liberale* and to Carlo Rosselli* and Pietro Nenni's* *Quarto Stato*, Ascoli was arrested briefly by the OVRA* in 1928 before leaving for the United States. Deeply committed as an American citizen to the worldwide defense of democracy and opposition to dictatorships of all hues, a close friend of influential New Dealers, and a founder, and president in 1941–43, of the Mazzini Society,* he campaigned successfully during World War II* for United States support of Italian democrats and for lenient peace terms. He was the founder and editor of *The Reporter*, acting as an authoritative voice among the American intelligentsia (1949–68). Among his works in English are *Intelligence in Politics, Political and Economic Democracy* (together with F. Lehmann), *Fascism for Whom?* (together with Arthur Feiler), and *The Power of Freedom.* Ascoli died in New York on January 1, 1978.

MS

ASINARI DI SAN MARZANO, ERMOLAO. A Piedmontese diplomat and signatory of the Albertine constitution, he was born in Costigliole of Asti on August 14, 1800. In 1825 he joined the Piedmontese legation in Vienna. He subsequently held posts as legation secretary in Madrid (1828) and Vienna (1830), chargé d'affaires in Bavaria (1835), and minister to Holland (1838) and the Kingdom of the Two Sicilies* (1841). San Marzano left Naples to become foreign secretary in October 1847. In that capacity he signed the *Statuto** issued by King Charles Albert of Savoy* on March 4, 1848. On March 10 he resigned, but soon after was nominated senator and appointed minister to Belgium. Recalled from Brussels in 1849, San Marzano retired. He died on October 15, 1864, in Turin.

                                                                        RJ

ASPROMONTE. Aspromonte was the site of a battle in southern Calabria where the supporters of Giuseppe Garibaldi* were prevented from marching toward Rome by Italian troops in 1862. Garibaldi organized the march on Rome in the belief that he had the tacit support of Urbano Rattazzi's* government. After gathering over 2,000 volunteers in Sicily, on August 24 his "Roman Legion" crossed the Straits to Calabria. Surrounded five days later on the heights of Aspromonte, Garibaldi was wounded in the encounter, surrendered, and was imprisoned. Amnestied in October 1862, Garibaldi became disenchanted with the Rattazzi government, whose performance during the episode occasioned its resignation in December 1862.

                                                                        SS

ASSAB. See **ETHIOPIA**

ASSOCIAZIONE ITALIANA DEI COTONIERI. See **CRESPI, SILVIO**

ASSOCIAZIONE NAZIONALE ITALIANA. See **ITALIAN NATIONAL-IST ASSOCIATION**

ATTOLICO, BERNARDO. An Italian diplomat and international technocrat between the world wars, Attolico was born in Canneto di Bari on January 17, 1880. He came to international affairs through service on Allied economic agencies during World War I.* This led to his becoming a stalwart in the League of Nations secretariat, 1920–27. Recalled to Italy's diplomatic service, which he had joined under Francesco Saverio Nitti's* patronage in 1919, he was successively ambassador to Rio de Janeiro, 1927–30, Moscow, 1930–35, and Berlin, 1935–40. It was in this last office that he earned most renown. He sought to prevent his country's total subservience to Nazi German diplomacy, and contributed significantly to Italy's decision for nonbelligerency in 1939. Overwork contributed to his death on February 9, 1942, in Rome while ambassador to the Vatican.

                                                                        ACas

AUDISIO, WALTER. Walter Audisio, a Communist Partisan commander known as "Colonel Valerio," was entrusted with the execution of Mussolini* and others at Dongo on Lake Como on April 28, 1945. His orders came from Luigi Longo,* commander of Garibaldini Partisans and vice-commander of the Volontari della

Libertà. The death sentence was decreed on April 25 by the CLNAI.* Born in Alessandria on June 28, 1909, Audisio had joined the clandestine Italian Communist Party (PCI)* in 1931. After the war he was elected to parliament.

For further reference see: Attilio Tamaro, *Due anni di storia, 1943–45* (Rome: Tosi, 1950).

MS

AUTARCHIA. Autarky, the pursuit of national economic self-sufficiency, officially became a goal of the Fascist regime with Mussolini's* speech of March 23, 1936, in the context of the Ethiopian War (see Ethiopia*) and the economic sanctions imposed against Italy by the League of Nations. According to Mussolini, autarky would enable the nation to pursue an independent foreign policy and face future military challenges. In reality, tentative autarkic measures had been taken as early as the mid-1920s, when tariffs were raised and agricultural production was expanded to improve the balance of payments and strengthen the currency. Italy's almost total dependence on imported fuel and raw materials made autarky an unattainable goal, but reliance on domestic substitutes benefited many national producers in textiles, chemicals, mining, and metallurgy.

RS

AVANGUARDIA SOCIALISTA. See **LABRIOLA, ARTURO**

AVANGUARDIE. See **BALILLA**

AVANTI! The history of *Avanti!*, organ of the Italian Socialist Party (PSI),* reflects the anguished history of Italian socialism itself in the first half of the twentieth century. Its first issue appeared on December 25, 1896, under the editorial direction of Leonida Bissolati,* who remained in that position until 1903. From 1903 to the beginning of World War I,* *Avanti!* underwent six major editorial changes. The prewar editors included Enrico Ferri,* Oddino Morgari, Bissolati again, Claudio Treves,* Giovanni Bacci, and Mussolini,* who was to be dismissed in October 1914 and ejected from the PSI. These changes mirrored basic tensions within the party between reformist and maximalist factions. Nonetheless, the paper succinctly stated the essential political ideals and policy recommendations of Italy's organized Left (see Sinistra, La*) opposition to the reactionary Pelloux laws, to imperialism, to arms increases and militarism, to the Libyan War (see Ouchy, Treaty of*) and World War I,* and support of universal (eventually including women's) suffrage. *Avanti!* was unequivocal in its denunciation of the extreme nationalist movement that arose in the opening years of the century and to Giovanni Giolitti's* method of governing.

During World War I the paper supported the party position, *né aderire, né sabotare* (''neither support, nor sabotage''). Its wartime editors included Costantino Lazzari,* who had invented that phrase. As the war drew to an end *Avanti!*'s pages bespoke the uncertain direction of the party, which remained badly divided in face of the postwar crisis, the challenge of the Russian Revolution, and the rise of the Fascist *squadristi*. When Fascist violence burned down the Milanese headquarters of the paper in 1919, followed by a similar attack on its Rome office in 1920, the paper began to falter. Though popular subscriptions helped restore an office (again destroyed in 1922), the split within the party and the debut of the Italian Communist Party (PCI)* in 1921 undermined any unified Socialist line that the paper might have adopted. Its editorial control passed into the hands of Giacinto Serrati and Pietro Nenni,* but Nenni refused to work with the Communists in an anti-Fascist front. As long as the formality of parliamentary government lasted (until 1926) *Avanti!* continued to attack Fascism* and was itself attacked until finally the paper was outlawed.

Between 1926 and 1940, *Avanti!* was irregularly issued in Paris, first under Ugo Coccia and later under Angelica Balabanoff,* who represented the maximalist position but remained equidistant from both the Second and Third internationals. During the 1930s, this line became increasingly irrelevant as the paper declined; it finally ceased publication in 1940.

In March 1930, Nenni began to publish a *Nuovo Avanti!** from Grenoble that was largely circulated in Switzerland. That year, too, the Italian Socialist Party of Proletarian Unity (PSIUP) was formed, a merger of Nenni's Socialists and the reformist faction (all in exile). *Nuovo Avanti!*, published in Zurich until 1933 and then in Paris from 1934 to 1940, struggled against communism and liberalized socialism. The Paris edition also filled the gap left by the death of Claudio Treves and his exile publication, *La Libertà*. Nenni was finally able to work out an alliance with the PCI in 1934, well in advance of the formal Popular Front of the Spanish Civil War* years. Before it ceased publication during the Nazi occupation of Paris in 1940, *Nuovo Avanti!* repeatedly warned against the danger of the coming war, and copies of it were smuggled into Italy, urging the proletariat to resist.

Avanti! reappeared in Italy in July 1943 in several clandestine issues, and began its two-year history as a journal of the Armed Resistance.* Its second issue (August 22, 1943) announced that it was the organ of the Partito Socialista Italiano di Unità Proletaria. Opposing Pietro Badoglio's* government, *Avanti!* espoused its immediate objective—total armed struggle until Italy was completely liberated—and its postwar vision of a socialist republic, unification of all workers' parties, nationalization of the means of production, and a massive agrarian reform.

Since 1945 *Avanti!* has been the official organ of the main body of Italian socialism, usually known as the Partito Socialista Italiano. Among its several postwar editors was Alessandro Pertini,* president of Italy since 1978.

For further reference see: Gaetano Arfè, *Storia del Avanti!* (Milan: Edizioni Avanti!*, 1956–58).

JMC

AVENTINE SECESSION. About 500 B.C. the Roman pleb withdrew to the Aventine hill as a sign of protest against the patriciate. The symbolic Aventine of 1924–26 was that part of the anti-Fascist opposition which abandoned its parliamentary seats on June 27, 1924, in protest against the Fascist assassination of Giacomo Matteotti (see Matteotti Crisis*), leader of the Unitary Socialist Party. About one hundred deputies withdrew—mostly Socialists, Popolari, Republicans, and Democratic Liberals. The Communists took part only briefly. Giovanni Amendola,* a Democratic Liberal, led the Aventine, which sought to raise a moral protest against Mussolini* and persuade Victor Emmanuel III* to dismiss him. The strategy failed. Paralyzed by dissension, the Aventine did not present its case effectively. The King refused to pay attention, and the Vatican was unsympathetic. Mussolini counterattacked on January 3, 1925, and during the next year or so deprived the Aventine protesters of their seats and outlawed the opposition parties.

                                                                        CFD

AXIS, THE ROME-BERLIN. This expression, coined by Mussolini,* refers to the relationship between Fascist Italy and Nazi Germany that was based on their agreement of October 25, 1936, announced in Milan by Count Galeazzo Ciano* and Joachim von Ribbentrop. They had earlier reached an understanding on Austria, and in the new convention Germany now recognized Italy's position in Ethiopia.* The two signatories agreed to pursue an economic treaty and to collaborate on common policies toward the League of Nations and communism. Mussolini's respect for Hitler and German power grew in the following year. He was shaken by Hitler's unilateral military solution of the Austrian question in March 1938 and his destruction of the rump Czechoslovak state a year later; nevertheless, he suddenly decided to conclude a military alliance (the Pact of Steel*) with Germany in May 1939. Mussolini apparently assumed that Hitler would soon achieve hegemony in Europe and that Italy could win new territories as Germany's major ally. In fact, he had already seized Albania* on April 7 while Europe was still reacting to Hitler's occupation of Prague.

   For further reference see: Elizabeth Wiskemann, *The Rome-Berlin Axis* (London: Collins, 1966).

                                                                        JKZ

AZEGLIO, EMANUELE D'. Minister to London and close collaborator of Cavour,* D'Azeglio was born in Turin on October 16, 1816, son of the Marquis Robert and the Marchioness Constance Alfieri. Educated at Turin, he began his diplomatic career in 1838. After serving at Monaco, Vienna, and Brussels, he became, in 1847, legation head at London, where, except for short sojourns in St. Petersburg and Paris, he remained, becoming minister plenipotentiary in 1850 and working effectively to strengthen political and economic ties with England. He died in Turin on March 4, 1880.

                                                                        FFA

AZEGLIO, LUIGI TAPARELLI D'. A Jesuit philosopher, political theorist, and journalist, he was born in Turin on November 24, 1793. He entered the nucleus of the restored Society of Jesus in 1814. After ordination in 1820, he served as rector of the Roman College (1824–29), provincial in Naples (1829–33), and professor at the Collegio Massimo in Palermo (1833–50). From 1850 until his death in Rome on September 21, 1862, he was one of the editors and principal writers of the influential intransigent Jesuit journal, *La Civiltà Cattolica.**

Instrumental in the Italian revival of Thomism, D'Azeglio wrote his main work on natural law, *Saggio teoretico di diritto naturale appoggiato sul fatto* [A theoretical study of natural law based on fact] (1841–43). His *Esame critico degli ordini rappresentativi nella società moderna* [Critical examination of representative orders in modern society] (1854) demonstrates both his debt to de Maistre and his political differences with his brother, Massimo D'Azeglio.*

For further reference see: Gabriele De Rosa, *Storia del movimento cattolico in Italia. Dalla restaurazione all'età giolittiana* (Bari: Laterza, 1966).

JCR

AZEGLIO, MASSIMO TAPARELLI D'. One of the foremost Piedmontese liberals of the *Risorgimento*,* D'Azeglio was born in Turin on October 24, 1798, to an aristocratic family. In his youth he rebelled against the conservative environment of his family and of the Piedmontese capital, and he moved to Milan to write and to study painting. In that city's literary circles he met Alessandro Manzoni,* whose daughter, Chiara, he married. In the 1830s he published his best-known historical novels, *Ettore Fieramosca o La disfida di Barletta* [Ettore Fieramosca or the tournament of Barletta] and *Niccolò de' Lapi ovvero i Palleschi e i Piagnoni* [Niccole de' Lapi or the Palleschi and Piagnoni]. *Fieramosca* became especially popular for its portrayal of Italian courage in the face of foreign occupation. A third novel, *La Lega lombarda* [The Lombard League], was published posthumously.

D'Azeglio's political career began in the 1840s under the guidance of his cousin, Count Cesare Balbo.* In 1845 D'Azeglio agreed to make a trip through the Papal Legations* under the auspices of the liberal clubs of Turin. His report, *Degli ultimi casi di Romagna* [On the recent events in the Romagna] (1846), was highly critical of Mazzinian revolutionaries who were attempting the violent overthrow of the papal regime; at the same time, it condemned that regime and urged major reforms. The advent of Pius IX* to the papal throne led D'Azeglio, like other liberals, to believe that those reforms were possible and imminent. He outlined his own political preferences in his *Proposta di un programma per l'opinione nazionale italiana* [Proposal for a program on Italian national opinion].

At the outbreak of war in northern Italy, D'Azeglio supported Charles Albert of Savoy's* decision to intervene in Lombardy* and joined his army. He engaged in bitter polemics with supporters of Giuseppe Mazzini* and with separatists in Lombardy and Venetia. Having passed a major political test of liberal principles and monarchical stability, D'Azeglio was offered the premiership of the new constitutional Kingdom of Sardinia, but he accepted it only after the second defeat of the Sardinian army by the Austrians in 1849.

During his premiership D'Azeglio succeeded in protecting the constitutional government against the attacks of Austrian diplomacy and of Piedmontese conservatives. He was also instrumental in the passage of the Siccardi Laws* (1850), which altered radically the relationship between church and state. The rapprochement (*connubio**) between Cavourian liberals and the parliamentary faction led by Urbano Rattazzi* spelled the end of D'Azeglio's ministry in October 1852, but he remained active on the political scene and was assigned to several diplomatic missions. In 1853–54 he supported Cavour's* policy of intervention in the Crimean War* and, later, the anti-Austrian policy that led to the War of 1859.* In the late 1850s, however, D'Azeglio's main contribution was made through the press. In 1859 he published a series of anti-Austrian articles in the British *Morning Chronicle*, and in 1860 the pamphlet *De la politique et du droit chrétien au point de vue de la question italienne* [On politics and Christian law from the point of view of the Italian question]. At the moment of unification, however, he broke with Cavour and the Italian National Society (see Società Nazionale Italiano*). He opposed the unification of North and South, which he regarded as premature, and in 1861, in the pamphlet *Questioni urgenti** [Urgent issues], he opposed the designation of Rome as the capital of united Italy. He withdrew from political life in the 1860s and wrote his memoirs, *I miei ricordi* [My memoirs] (1867), which were published after his death. D'Azeglio died in Turin on January 15, 1866.

CML

AZIENDA GENERALE ITALIANA PETROLI. See **AGIP**

AZIONE CATTOLICA ITALIANA. See **CATHOLIC ACTION**

B

BACCARINI, ALFREDO. See **PENTARCHY**

BADOGLIO, PIETRO. A leading participant in the ouster of Mussolini,* Badoglio still remains a figure of controversy. He was born on September 28, 1871, in Grazzano Monferrato (Asti), where he died on November 1, 1956. A career soldier, Badoglio achieved distinction in August 1916 when, as a colonel, he led a successful assault on the Austrian stronghold of Monte Sabotino, near Gorizia. At the time of the Italian defeat of Caporetto* (October-November 1917), he was commanding general of the Twenty-seventh Army Corps, for whose rout some have held Badoglio himself responsible. The new supreme commander, General Armando Diaz,* nevertheless chose him as his deputy chief of staff. The two coordinated the resistance to the Austro-German offensives on the Piave (November-December 1917) and Monte Grappa (June 1918), and prepared the Italian victory at the battle of Vittorio Veneto* (October-November 1918). After the war, Badoglio served as army chief of staff (1919–21) and on several diplomatic missions. During the crisis of October 1922, he is reported to have assured the government of the army's loyalty against a Fascist coup. Eventually reconciled to Fascism,* in June 1925 he was appointed to the newly created post of Chief of the General Staff of the Armed Forces. The next year he was named marshal of Italy, and in 1929 he became marquis of Sabotino and governor of Libya.* Replacing General Emilio De Bono* in November 1935, Badoglio completed the conquest of Ethiopia* by May 1936, after which he was named duke of Addis Ababa. He disapproved of Italy's involvement in the Spanish Civil War,* on the grounds of unpreparedness, and of its entry into World War II* in June 1940, which he characterized as suicidal. He nevertheless did not resign his post until December 1940, after the calamitous invasion of Greece. On July 25, 1943, Badoglio replaced Mussolini as head of the government. He negotiated an armistice with the Allies in September, succeeded in persuading the anti-Fascist parties to enter his government only by April 1944, and was forced to resign in June.

For further reference see: Pietro Badoglio, *Italy in the Second World War* (New York: Oxford University Press, 1948); Amedeo Tosti, *Pietro Badoglio* (Milan: Mondadori, 1956).

SS

BAKUNIN, MIKHAIL. Revolutionary conspirator and leading nineteenth-century anarchist, Bakunin was born at Tver, Russia, on May 30, 1814, of an aristocratic family. He was educated at a military school in St. Petersburg. Leaving the army in 1835, he enrolled at Moscow University and thereafter went to Berlin in 1840 to study German philosophy. He travelled throughout Europe from 1843 to 1848, meeting with and learning from leading radicals, including Marx and Proudhon.

He took part in the 1848 upheavals at Paris and Prague. Arrested at Dresden, he was imprisoned, condemned to death, and then extradited to Russia in 1851. After imprisonment in Moscow and Siberian exile, he escaped to London in 1861. Turning his attention to Italy, he travelled the length and breadth of the peninsula between 1864 and 1867, establishing the International Brotherhood (Naples, 1865) and the International Alliance of Social Democracy (Bologna, 1867).

The program of these revolutionary organizations combined a destructive mixture of anarchism* and nihilism. Bakunin had once written, "The urge to destroy is also a creative force." He rejected organized religion, championed communal autonomy, and urged the masses to rebel against the state and private property, which were "a hindrance to true liberty." His success was scant, but through his disciples Carlo Cafiero* and Giuseppe Fanelli he helped shape the beginnings of modern working-class consciousness in Italy.

Influenced by Hegel, Comte, Marx, and especially Proudhon, he was not an original thinker. Yet he was idefatigable in his conspiratorial zeal. His concept of a bloody mass uprising, led by a few ruthless men, ranks him as a forerunner of the totalitarian movements of the twentieth century.

Bakunin took part in uprisings at Lyons (1870) and Bologna (1874) before his death in Berne, Switzerland, on July 1, 1876.

FFA

BALABANOFF, ANGELICA. A major figure in the international Socialist movement, the Italian Socialist Party (PSI),* and, after 1947, the Italian Social Democratic Party, Balabanoff was born near Kiev in 1869. She left Russia in 1898, breaking ties with her wealthy Jewish landowning family by her decision to pursue university studies and a life of political activism. Completely dedicated to Socialist politics for over a half century, Balabanoff faced the innumerable struggles and contradictions that characterized the movement.

In Italy as a party organizer, editor, and, in 1912, member of the Socialist Party executive committee, she sided with the maximalist group against the reformist faction. A staunch opponent of the war in 1914, Balabanoff denounced nationalist politics and continued to support the efficacy of the Second International. Joining the Bolshevik Party in 1917 and serving as secretary of the Comintern in 1919, she reaffirmed her belief in working-class revolution, yet ultimately could not accept party tactics and Bolshevik political maneuverings. In exile from both Russia and Italy (1921–45), she was an outspoken critic of Mussolini* and a leader of Italian anti-Fascism.* At the same time, she vehemently opposed Stalinist politics and any association with international communism. These sentiments led her to support the founding of the Social Democratic Party in 1947. Until her death in Rome in 1965 she served as a party officer, responsible for organizing women, and as a member of the International Council of Social Democratic Women. As a woman Socialist, Balabanoff denied affiliation with feminism, which she considered bourgeois, yet spent a great deal of her energy organizing women and defending women's rights. She died in Rome on November 25, 1965.

For further reference see: Angelica Balabanoff, *My Life as a Rebel* (1938; reprint Westport, Conn.: Greenwood Press, 1968); Nancy Eshelman, "Forging a Socialist Women's Movement: Angelica Balabanoff in Switzerland," in *The Italian Immigrant Woman in North America*, ed. Betty Boyd Caroli, Robert Harney, and Lydio Tomasi (Toronto: The Multicultural History Society of Ontario, 1978), pp. 44–75; Jane Slaughter, "Humanism versus Feminism in the Socialist Movement: The Life of Angelica Balabanoff," in *European Women on the Left*, ed. Jane Slaughter and Robert Kern (Westport, Conn.: Greenwood Press, 1981), pp. 179–94.

MJS

BALBO, COUNT CESARE. This Piedmontese historian and political figure was born in Turin on November 21, 1789. He died there on June 3, 1853. Balbo was educated by his father, Prospero Balbo, in exile in Barcelona and Bologna, and later at the University of Turin after Prospero became rector there in 1802. In 1808 Cesare served Napoleonic Italy in Tuscany and Rome, and later in Paris as auditor of the Council of State. Only in 1814, after entering the Piedmontese army, did he work against Napoleon for an Italian cause. While in Spain (1818–19), Balbo began his career as a historian with an account of the Spanish wars of independence (1808–14). Admiring the British constitution, Balbo sought to counsel Charles Albert of Savoy* on the Piedmontese events of 1821, an attempt which the new king, Charles Felix,* did not accept. Returning from exile in 1824, Balbo dedicated himself to historical writing with his *Storia d'Italia* [History of Italy] (1830), *Vita di Dante* [Life of Dante] (1839), and *Meditazione storiche* [Historical meditations] (1842). For him historical writing served to formulate national opinion toward ultimate independence.

Balbo's concern for a realistic means of ridding northern Italy of Austria diplomatically while maintaining an important balance of power led to *Delle speranze d'Italia*￼* [On the hopes of Italy] (1844). Serving as editor of *Il Risorgimento* beginning in December 1847, Balbo also helped to prepare the electoral laws in 1848 and served as Piedmont's first prime minister. His liberal conservatism led him to combat the democratic factions, while his religious commitments prevented him from supporting the anticlerical Siccardi Laws of 1850 and the institution of civil marriage in 1852. Balbo's historical writings often revealed his dislike of the French Revolution, of the emerging concepts of popular sovereignty, and of the break that revolution had caused with gradual reform movements.

For further reference see: Nino Valeri, "Cesare Balbo," in Cesare Balbo, *Pagine scelte* (Milan: Instituto editoriale cisalpino, 1960); Eugenio di Carlo, ed., *Lettere inedite di Cesare Balbo e Luigi Taparelli d'Azeglio* (Turin, n.p., 1923).

MSM

BALBO, ITALO. Fascist politician, pioneering aviator, and military leader, Balbo was born in Quartesana (Ferrara), June 6, 1896, the son of schoolteachers. Following a youthful career as a republican, interventionist, and war veteran, Balbo first gained prominence in the Fascist hierarchy for his military leadership of the Ferrara Blackshirts. Quadrumvir of the March on Rome,* then head of the Fascist militia (MVSN) (see Voluntary Militia for National Security*), his career nearly foundered in 1924 when he was indirectly implicated in the murder of the anti-Fascist priest Don Giovanni Minzoni. After a brief term as undersecretary to the minister of national economy, Balbo was appointed undersecretary (1926–29) and then minister (1929–33) of the air force. He achieved an international reputation as a pioneering aviator for personally leading a series of mass training flights (*crociere*) between 1928 and 1933. For leading the "Crociera del Decennale" (July 1933) from Orbetello to Chicago and back, he was named air marshal.

Appointed governor of Libya* in January 1934, he modernized the colony and initiated mass colonization programs (1938–39) aimed at transforming Libya into an extension of the mother country ("fourth shore"). A vociferous critic of Mussolini's* pro-German policies, anti-Semitic legislation, and intervention in World War II,* Balbo nevertheless remained loyal to the regime, and was appointed commander of Italian armed forces in North Africa. His airplane was accidentally hit by Italian batteries over Tobruk, June 28, 1940, and he died in the crash.

For further reference see: Claudio G. Segre, "Italo Balbo," in *Uomini e volti del fascismo*, ed. F. Cordova (Roma: Bulzoni, 1980); A. Berselli, "Balbo," *Dizionario Biografico degli Italiani* (Roma: Istituto della Enciclopedia Italiana, 1963).

CGS

BALDISSERA, ANTONIO. Italian general, colonial administrator, and exponent of the moderate school of colonial policy of the nineteenth century, he was born in Padua on May 27, 1838, and died at Florence on January 8, 1917.

He was chief commander in the Eritrean campaign of 1888–89 and opposed the policies that led to the disaster at Adowa* (1896). After the battle he served as colonial governor and concluded the peace treaty with Menelik II.* After returning to Italy he became military commander at Ancona and, in 1904, was named senator.

WR

BALILLA. Formally organized as the official Fascist youth movement on April 3, 1926, the Opera Nazionale Balilla (ONB), headed by Renato Ricci, consisted of three main branches: the Balilla (eight- to fifteen-year-olds), the Avanguardie (fifteen–eighteen), and the Piccole Italiane (the girls' group). Many teachers staffed the ranks of the ONB as leaders and organizers, and by 1928 all youth groups outside of the ONB were declared illegal and dissolved. At its height the ONB controlled all physical education and organized sports. In 1937 the ONB was replaced by the GIL (Gioventù Italiana del Littorio).

The purpose of the youth groups of the ONB was to encourage the development of Fascist ideals and loyalty to the Duce among the youth. The controversial nature of the Opera was revealed in its clashes with the Church, the bureaucracy of the Ministry of National Education, and even with elements of the Fascist Party itself. On a day-to-day basis, these youth groups served as methods of checking the political orthodoxy of teachers and school administrators and as effective instruments of propaganda.

RJW

BANCA COMMERCIALE ITALIANA. The Banca Commerciale Italiana (Comit) was established on October 10, 1894, with 20 million lire worth of equity capital, the bulk of which was held by Germans. The strong presence of German financial interests in Italy represented a change from the preceding twenty years, during which the principal sources of foreign financial capital were French. In any case, Italian capitalists were quick to see the potential of the bank, so that by 1913 a majority of shares were owned by Italians.

The bank expanded very rapidly; by 1903 it had a capital of 80 million lire, and by 1911, 130 million lire. Savings and demand deposits held went up five times between 1903 and 1911. By 1913 the Comit was the largest corporation in Italy as measured by the value of its assets, and held approximately 40 percent of the total assets of the ordinary credit banks.

The first twenty years of the bank's existence coincided with a rapid growth of Italy's industrial capacity. Whether or not the Comit and other credit banks played a causal role in this expansion (it is a controversial issue among economic historians), it is certainly beyond dispute that these banks, especially the Comit, were actively involved in financing a great many industrial enterprises. The funds were provided in various ways—through loans, advances, overdrafts, underwriting services, direct participation in equity capital—and in most cases involved a long-term relationship between the bank and the enterprise. Although the

Comit's interests covered most of the major industrial sectors, the bank was particularly involved in electric power and electrochemicals, chemical fertilizers, iron and steel, shipbuilding, and the merchant marine.

It is worth pointing out that any time a financial institution commits a substantial share of its assets to one type of risky investment (in this case, investments in industry) the institution is running a risk. Thus it was with the Comit and the other ordinary credit banks. Prior to and during World War I,* industrial production continued on the whole to expand, and the stock market remained buoyant. The same was true, after a brief, sharp recession, in the postwar period up to 1925. The Comit allocated a growing share of its portfolio to industrial investments during these years, especially during the speculative boom between 1921 and 1925. After 1925, however, the economic climate worsened and the Comit found itself in serious trouble. Industrial growth stagnated and stock prices fell. In effect, the value of the Comit's liabilities remained more or less constant while the value of its assets dropped. By 1930, with the capitalist world, including Italy, in a deep depression, the situation of the Comit became desperate. At this point, the government stepped in, took over the illiquid assets of the Comit, created the Industrial Reconstruction Institute (IRI),* and transformed the Comit into a public institution. The Comit was no longer permitted to invest long term in industrial assets; it became instead a strictly commercial bank. Thus, the current Banca Commerciale Italiana is, in its banking policies, only a distant relation of the original bank.

For further reference see: A. Confalonieri, *Banca e Industria in Italia, 1894– 1906*. vol. 2: Il sistema bancario tra due crisi (Milan: Banca Commerciale Italiana, 1975).

JSC

BANCA DI GENOVA. See **CREDITO ITALIANO**

BANCA D'ITALIA. The Bank of Italy was created through the banking law of August 10, 1893. The country at the time was in the midst of the most severe financial crisis in its short history, one that threatened to topple not only the entire banking system but also a substantial part of Italy's modern industrial sector. The reorganization of the banks of issue (those banks authorized by law to issue bank notes), through which the Bank of Italy came into existence, was absolutely imperative if the country's banking system were to survive the crisis and if similar crises were to be avoided in the future.

Prior to the law of 1893, there were six banks of issue in Italy: the Banca Nazionale nel Regno (by far the largest), the Banca Toscana di Credito, the Banca Nazionale Toscana, the Banca Romana, the Banco di Napoli, and the Banco di Sicilia. The Bank of Italy was essentially an amalgam of the first three banks. It also assumed the responsibility of liquidating the assets of the Banca Romana, which was compelled to declare bankruptcy (see Banca Romana, Scandal of the*). The Bank of Naples and the Bank of Sicily, for various reasons, retained the right of note issue along with the Bank of Italy until the bank legislation of 1926 gave to the Bank of Italy the exclusive right to issue paper money.

The bank contributed to the Italian economy in many ways. First, because its activities were regulated by law and its books inspected at regular intervals, the Bank of Italy (along with the two southern banks of issue) provided the country with a money supply whose acceptability was never questioned. Second, although this was not appreciated until much later, the Bank of Italy provided the government with an institution through which it could regulate the supply of money and credit and thus influence economic activity in the country. Finally, it can be argued that, at least until the major reform of the financial system in 1936, the most important contribution of the Bank of Italy to the stability of the Italian economy and to the growth of industry was in its capacity as a lender of last resort. On numerous occasions it saved leading credit institutions from bankruptcy and averted serious financial crises. Although at times the bank may have been too liberal with its assistance, it seems reasonable to argue that the long-run performance of the economy was enhanced by the lender-of-last-resort facilities provided by the bank.

For further reference see: A. Confalonieri, *Banca e Industria in Italia,* Vol. 2: *Il sistema bancario tra due crisi* (Milan: Banca Commerciale Italiano, 1975); R. De Mattia, ed., *I bilanci degli istituti di emissione italiani dal 1845 al 1936*, 2 vols. (Rome: Banca d'Italia, 1967); R. De Mattia, ed., *Storia del capitale della Banca d'Italia e degli istituti predecessori*, 2 vols. (Rome: Banca d'Italia, 1977).

JSC

BANCA GENERALE. The Banca Generale was established in 1871 by a group composed mainly of Italian financiers, with some capital provided by foreign bankers. The bank was committed from its inception, as was the Credito Mobiliare Italiano,* to financing every sort of industrial undertaking, from railroads to mining ventures to iron and steel plants, irrigation projects, and so on. In fact, its assets were concentrated primarily in three areas: government bonds and municipal loans; securities of joint-stock companies held primarily for speculative purposes; and various types of credits (including holding of securities) provided to companies in which the bank played an entrepreneurial role.

The size of the bank, when compared with the major savings banks, cooperative banks, or banks of emission, was relatively modest. This was partly intentional, but it was also a result of the bank's limited access to funds either through the capital market or through demand and savings deposits. In spite of its size, however, the bank was an important source of credit for many major enterprises in the economy, including Terni,* Ferriere Italiane, the Societa SS. FF. Mediterraneo, Risanamento Napoli, F. Casaroni, and others.

The bank went into liquidation in 1894. Its collapse was due partly to exogenous factors, partly to poor management, and partly to the underdeveloped nature of the Italian economy, which prevented an industrial credit bank such as the Banca Generale from spreading its risks adequately across different types of assets.

JSC

BANCA ITALIANA DI SCONTO. See **SOCIETÀ BANCARIA ITALIANA**

BANCA ROMANA, SCANDAL OF THE. In December 1892, the republican Socialist deputy Napoleone Colajanni* read in the Chamber portions of an 1889 inquiry, kept secret for fear of severe financial repercussions, alleging excessive and fraudulent circulation of currency by the Banca Romana, one of Italy's six banks of issue. Prime Minister Giovanni Giolitti* appointed a select committee whose report in March 1893 of fraud and other irregularities was even more alarming than Colajanni's revelations. Giolitti thereupon proposed a reform of all banks of issue, adopted in August. The scandal grew in November 1893, when the report by another committee censured all governments from 1880 to 1892 for improper supervision of the banks of issue; named newspapers and parliamentarians involved in questionable relations with the Banca Romana; and, although partially absolving Giolitti of allegations of using money borrowed from the bank for partisan electoral purposes, censured him for nominating the bank's governor, Bernardo Tanlongo, to a senatorship in November 1892. The shaken Giolitti thereupon resigned. The scandal was revived in 1894 with charges of improper relations between the bank and Francesco Crispi,* Giolitti's successor and opponent. Crispi carried the charges to his grave; during Giolitti's subsequent long career, virulent opponents rarely failed to raise the accusatory cry of "Banca Romana!"

SS

BANCO DI ROMA. The Banco di Roma was founded on March 9, 1880, and opened for business two months later. For the first twenty years or so of its life, the bank remained a relatively modest local institution, engaged mostly in making short-term loans to farmers, local merchants, and small local banks. Bank policies, however, began to change after 1898, when its assets, which until then had remained stable, expanded swiftly. It established branches throughout the country and abroad, and by the turn of the century, began to provide long-term capital to industry, much along the lines followed by the other banks of ordinary credit. The Banco di Roma appears to have had a particular penchant for investments outside of Italy, notably in Turkey, the Balkans, Egypt, and Libya*—areas in which Italy's political interests were expanding. During World War I* and the interwar period, the Banco di Roma pursued policies similar to those followed by the other large ordinary credit banks and encountered the same difficulties in the late 1920s and early 1930s. It became a public institution during the Great Depression, and was transformed into a purely commercial bank in 1936.

JSC

BANDINI, SALLUSTIO ANTONIO. A priest and economist of the early Enlightenment,* Bandini was born in 1677 into a wealthy patrician Sienese family that was linked to the Piccolomini and traced its origins back to the fourteenth century. He received a degree in civil and canon law at the University of Siena in 1699, entered holy orders in 1705, and from 1708 until his death in 1760 served, among other benefices, as a canon of the Cathedral of Siena. Bandini is known chiefly for his writings on economic matters. Through the Sienese academies of his day he became acquainted with and developed themes of French economists of the late seventeenth century, particularly Vauban and Boisguilbert. His writings dealt with the economic decadence of the State of Siena under the Medici dukes of Tuscany, and with the problems of the sparsely populated and unproductive region of the Maremma, between Siena and the Mediterranean coast, where his family and others of the Sienese aristocracy owned large estates. In 1715 he wrote *Memoria sul magistrato dell'abbondanza* [Recollection on the magistracy for the distribution of grain], which examined the strict controls on marketing of grain exercised through the provisioning legislation of the Grand Duchy to keep grain prices artificially low. In a 1718 manuscript entitled *Sul corso delle monete* [On the course of money] he examined the lack of specie in this region. His major work, the *Discorso sopra la Maremma di Siena* [Discourse on the Maremma of Sienna], was written in 1737 and published posthumously in 1775. Here, Bandini referred to the ancient privilege of the Maremma to export grain freely, and argued that the best means for restoring its agricultural productivity was to permit a more liberal commerce in grain, thus allowing proprietors to respond to the stimulus of a natural market. The publication of the *Discorso* in the midst of the discussion of Physiocratic theories (see Physiocracy*) in the 1770s has led some to label Bandini a direct precursor of that school of thought. Bandini's aim, however, was to obtain a kind of mercantilistic agricultural protection for the Maremma. Nonetheless, elements of his thought, and particularly his critique of a solely monetary theory of value, were precursors of later theoretical developments.

For further reference see: George R. F. Baker, *Sallustio Bandini* (Florence: Olschki, 1978).

RBL

BANK OF ITALY. See **BANCA D'ITALIA**

BARATIERI, ORESTE. The principal military figure held responsible for Italy's defeat at Adowa,* Ethiopia,* on March 1, 1896, ending Francesco Crispi's* policy of colonial expansion, Baratieri was born on November 13, 1841, in Condino (Trent), and died on August 7, 1901, in Vitipeno (Bolzano). A volunteer among Giuseppe Garibaldi's* "Thousand" in 1860, author of numerous military works, and member of parliament from 1876 to 1896, in 1892 Baratieri was appointed governor of Eritrea.* In 1894–95 he achieved a number of victories in Tigré province; but the entry of Emperor Menelik II* into the conflict led to the disastrous encounter at Adowa, which left about 6,000 Italians dead. The defeat ended Baratieri's military and political career and led to Crispi's fall from office.

SS

BARD OF DEMOCRACY. See **CAVALLOTTI, FELICE**

BARRÈRE, CAMILLE. French ambassador to Italy from 1897 to 1924, Barrère (1851–1940) was a patriot who valued Italian support against Germany. From 1897 to 1914 he patiently worked to separate Italy from the Triple Alliance.* During World War I* he cooperated closely with Sidney Sonnino* as a means to ease Franco-Italian friction. During the Paris Peace Conference* Barrère favored a compromise with Italy on Fiume* and bitterly opposed Premier Georges Clemenceau's* pro-American position. From 1919 to 1924 he renewed his quest for closer Franco-Italian relations against Germany. His hostility to socialism, communism, and the liberal internationalist Francesco Nitti* contributed to his sympathy for the rise of Italian Fascism.* From 1922 to 1924 Barrère conciliated Mussolini,* but without suggesting major French territorial concessions.

For further reference see: E. Serra, *Camille Barrère e l'intesa italo-francese* (Milan: A. Giuffrè, 1950).

JB

BARZILAI, SALVATORE. A noted republican, Barzilai was above all an irredentist, irreconcilably opposed to the Triple Alliance* as an insuperable obstacle to the unification of the "unredeemed" lands with Italy (see Irredentism*). He was born on July 5, 1860, in Trieste,* and died on May 1, 1939, in Rome. Imprisoned at eighteen by the Austrian authorities for irredentist activity, he emigrated to Italy, pursued a career in law and journalism, authored several works on penology and foreign affairs, and served as foreign affairs editor of the *Tribuna* of Rome (1883–90). Elected to parliament from Rome (1890–1919), he sat at the Extreme Left (see Sinistra, La*) with the Republican Party,* which he abandoned in 1912 because of its opposition to the Libyan War (see Ouchy, Treaty of*) and increased military expenditures. From the outset of World War I,* he favored Italy's intervention against Austria. He supported the policies of Antonio Salandra,* whose government he entered in June 1915 as minister without portfolio for the liberated territories. He fell from office with Salandra in June 1916. Giovanni Giolitti* appointed him senator in 1920.

SS

BASSO, LELIO. An important postwar Socialist leader, Basso was born in Varazze (Savona), on December 25, 1903. He became active in the Socialist movement while very young, writing for *Critica Sociale** and other Socialist reviews, and founding his own journal. In 1928 he was arrested by the Fascists, but after his release in 1931 he helped organize Italian Socialist Party (PSI)* sections clandestinely. In 1943 he became a member of the Socialist directorate and became secretary-general from 1947 to 1948. He was elected to the Constituent Assembly of 1946* and later to parliament. With the split of the Socialist Party after the Center-Left coalition of 1963, Basso joined the resulting splinter party, the PSIUP, and later became its president.

SD

BASTIANINI, GIUSEPPE. Giuseppe Bastianini, a Fascist hierarch and diplomat, was born in Perugia on March 8, 1899, and died in Milan on December 17, 1961. A rightist war veteran, he founded the *fasci* in Umbria in the fall of 1920 and was named a vice secretary-general of the Fascist Party in 1921. He helped plan the March on Rome* from Perugia (October 1922). Bastianini was appointed to the Fascist Grand Council (1922–26) and became secretary of the *fasci all'estero* ("abroad") (1923–26). He was elected to parliament in 1924 from Perugia. In 1927 Bastianini began a diplomatic career, serving first in Tangier. He was minister to Portugal (1928–29) and Greece (1929–32), and ambassador to Poland (1932–36) and Britain (1939–40). From June 1941 till February 1943 he was governor of Dalmatia.* Thereafter, he became undersecretary of foreign affairs, a post he had also held from 1936 to 1939. He backed Dino Grandi* against Mussolini* in the Grand Council session of July 24–25, 1943. He retired in August 1943 and went into hiding. The Fascist Special Tribunal in Verona sentenced him to death *in absentia* in January 1944. In 1947 Bastianini was cleared by a Rome purge court.

For further reference see his memoirs: *Uomini, cose, fatti* (Milan: Vitigliano, 1959).

CFD

BATTAGLIA DEL GRANO. The Battle for Wheat, launched with great fanfare in the summer of 1925, envisaged an all-out effort by government, industry, and landowners to expand the domestic production of wheat. A concrete manifestation of the Fascist regime's commitment to rural society, its immediate causes were large deficits in the balance of payments, due in large measure to grain imports and a consequent erosion of the lira on international money markets. Wheat production increased through protective tariffs, greater use of chemical fertilizers, mechanization, and improved agricultural techniques. The area devoted to wheat underwent a modest increase from 4.7 million hectares in 1926 to 5.1 million in 1940. By that time, the Battle for Wheat had virtually achieved its goal of national self-sufficiency. The economic and social costs, in the form of higher prices, reduced per capita consumption, and losses in the production of potentially more profitable crops, had been high.

RS

BATTISTI, CESARE (GIUSEPPE). Italian irredentist hero born in Trent, February 5, 1875, Battisti studied at the Istituto dei Studi Superiori in Florence. He promoted a series of irredentist causes in Italy and sought to prepare Austria's Italian subjects for autonomy. In 1911 he succeeded A. Avancini as the Socialist deputy from Trent in the Austrian parliament. On August 12, 1914, Battisti secretly crossed the frontier and campaigned ardently for Italian intervention on the Allied side. Based on his intimate knowledge and extensive study, Battisti provided the Italian high command with valuable strategic information on the war zones. Seeking front-line service, Battisti was made lieutenant of a company of Alpinists. He was captured by the Austrians on July 10, 1916, near Mt. Corno, along with the Istrian Fabio Filzi. Both were found guilty of high treason and sentenced to death. Battisti and Filzi were hanged on July 12, 1916, in Trent.

RSC

"BATTLE FOR GRAIN." See **BATTAGLIA DEL GRANO**

BAUER, RICCARDO. A political theorist and activist, Bauer was born in Milan on January 6, 1896. He was a volunteer in World War I* and a militant anti-Fascist from 1919 on. Together with Ernesto Rossi* and others, he was instrumental in organizing the Justice and Liberty movement* in Italy after it had been founded by Carlo Rosselli* and other exiles in the fall of 1929. Arrested in October 1930 and sentenced to twenty years' imprisonment, he regained his freedom after the overthrow of the Fascist dictatorship in July 1943. He was a member of the Military Committee of the Central Committee of National Liberation (see CLN*) during the Armed Resistance* of 1943–45 and edited *Il Caffè* in the mid-twenties and *Realtà Politica* in the late forties. Author of numerous books, including *Alla ricerca della libertà* and *A B C della democrazia*, and president of L'Umanitaria, the Italian League of the Rights of Man, and of Peace and Justice, in the post-World War II period Bauer was one of the most authoritative and respected spokesmen for democracy. He died in 1982.

For further reference see: Charles F. Delzell, *Mussolini's Enemies* (Princeton: Princeton University Press, 1961).

MS

BECCARIA, CESARE. A reformer best known for his work on criminal reform, *Dei delitti e delle pene* [On crimes and punishments] (published anonymously in 1764), Beccaria was born in Milan on March 15, 1738, and died there on November 28, 1794.

A member of the Accademia dei Pugni, a society of enlightened young Milanese organized in 1761 by the nobleman and reformer Pietro Verri* to air new ideas, Beccaria participated actively in its discussions. The administration of law and justice, with its reliance on torture to extract confessions from prisoners, figured prominently in the group's considerations. Beccaria was encouraged to analyze what might more appropriately be called injustice.

In his book, written in clear, unadorned language, Beccaria effectively demonstrated that injustice was being perpetrated in the name of justice. Punishments were harsh and not proportionate to the gravity of the crime, and hardly deterred further ill-doing. Torture favored the physically strong, so that while innocence or guilt played no part in eliciting a confession, physical stamina did. Inspired by a utilitarian and contractual view of society, rather than by humanitarian feelings, Beccaria wrote that punishment for crimes should be such as to maintain the maximum happiness for the greatest number. Excessive use of punishment became self-defeating, and the death penalty was neither "useful" nor "necessary."

His book met with instant success and aroused much controversy. By 1765 it had gone through three Italian editions, and in 1766 it appeared in a French translation, receiving high praise from D'Alembert, d'Holbach, Diderot, Helvetius, and Voltaire. Widely read in its French version, Beccaria's work had far-reaching effects. It started the movement for penal reform which finally succeeded in introducing more just and humane legal codes and practices in most Western countries during the nineteenth century. More immediately, it inspired Catherine of Russia to appoint a commission to review the legal code of her country.

Unaffected by the success of his book, Beccaria, except for a brief visit to Paris, spent the rest of his life in Milan teaching and serving the government in various offices, both as an economist and as a legal reformer.

For further reference see: Marcello T. Maestro, *Voltaire and Beccaria as Reformers of Criminal Law* (New York: Columbia University Press, 1942); Franco Venturi, *Settecentro riformatore*, Vol. 1: *Da Muratori a Beccaria* (Turin: Einaudi, 1969).

EPN

BEI, ADELE. This Communist leader and longtime anti-Fascist was born in Cantrano (Pesaro) on May 4, 1904, and died there in 1975. She joined the Italian Communist Party (PCI)* in 1925, worked clandestinely in it, and was arrested in 1933 and imprisoned until July 1943, when she joined the Armed Resistance.* After the war she was elected to the Constituent Assembly of 1946*; she then served as senator. She also served on the PCI Central Committee and the Council of the Confederazione Generale Italiana del Lavoro (CGIL).

MJS

BELGIOJOSO, CRISTINA TRIVULZIO DI. A political activist and writer, Cristina Trivulzio was born June 28, 1808, in Milan, where she died on July 5, 1871. At age sixteen she married Prince Emilio Barbiano di Belgiojoso-Este. After separating from him in the early 1830s, she travelled to Switzerland, Genoa, and Marseilles, where she became involved with Mazzinian organizations. In 1833 she helped finance Giuseppe Mazzini's* abortive insurrection in Savoy. In the 1840s she settled in Paris, where she became mistress of a famous literary salon.

At the outbreak of the revolutions of 1848* she headed for Naples, where she recruited volunteers for the war against Austria. She became a strong advocate of the union of Lombardy* with Piedmont-Sardinia—a point of view reflected in her newspapers, *Il Crociato* and *Lo Scudo di Savoia*. Upon the return of Austrian troops she fled to Switzerland and then to Rome, where she organized a military hospital for the defenders of the Roman Republic.

Unable to return to Italy, from 1849 to 1853 she travelled extensively in the Middle East and wrote an account of her travels, *Asie mineure* [Asia Minor] (1858). During this trip, it seems, she became addicted to opium—a habit that wrecked her already frail health. In 1853 she returned to the glitter of the French capital but spent most of her time at home, seeing only a few close friends. In 1856 she was granted permission to return to Lombardy on the condition that she live at her country estate in Locate. There she wrote the *Histoire de la maison de Savoie* [History of the House of Savoy] and, in 1860, launched the liberal newspaper *L'Italie*. Her personal behavior, however, became more and more eccentric, especially after the mysterious death of her young farm manager, with whom she had a stormy liaison. The last years of her life were spent in almost complete seclusion. But she remained intellectually active, writing on women's rights and education and on social problems. In 1869 she published a notable essay on the Lombard peasantry, *Gli affittaiuoli della Bassa Lombardia* [The tenant farmers of Lower Lombardy].

CML

BENADIR PORTS. See **ITALIAN EAST AFRICA COMPANY**

BENEDICT XV. Elected pope on September 3, 1914, Benedict devoted much of his pontificate to ending the war and mitigating its effects. Born Giacomo Della Chiesa on November 21, 1854, in Genoa, he died on January 22, 1922, in Rome. Ordained in 1878, he became secretary (1882–87) to the apostolic nuncio to Spain, Mariano Rampolla Del Tindaro.* Della Chiesa continued as Rampolla's secretary when the latter became secretary of state in 1887, and in 1901 became undersecretary of state. In 1907 he was named archbishop of

Bologna and, surprisingly, was elected pope only two months after being made cardinal. He repeatedly urged all belligerents to put an end to "the suicide of Europe"; his Note of August 1, 1917, the substance of which anticipated most of the Wilsonian Fourteen Points, was received coldly by both sides. In Italy, the note's reference to the war as "useless carnage" aroused the ire of interventionist elements as an instigation to defeatism. After the war he sought an accommodation with the Italian government and did not obstruct the formation of the Italian Popular Party,* definitively repealing the *non expedit.**

SS

BERGAMINI, ALBERTO. This journalist, born June 1, 1871, at San Giovanni in Persiceto (Bologna), is best known for his service from 1901 to 1923 as editor of Sidney Sonnino's* Rome newspaper, *Il Giornale d'Italia.** In March 1901, Bergamini was approached by Sonnino to head the new daily he and other liberal conservatives proposed to found in Rome. As editor Bergamini made the paper one of the nation's most influential dailies and set new standards of style and reporting as well as promoting various innovations, notably the beginning of the *terza pagina** feature. Bergamini remained a spokesman of the Sonnino political conservatism throughout his editorship.

Despite a brief period of admiration for Mussolini* and editorials supporting him, Bergamini's attacks on the Fascists in 1923 caused him to be driven from public life, particularly after a beating by *squadristi*. He withdrew into retirement in Umbria until July 1943, when, at Mussolini's deposition, he returned to head *Il Giornale d'Italia* for a few weeks. Arrested by the invading Germans in the fall of 1943, Bergamini was soon able to escape and go into exile in the Vatican.

Bergamini was elected to the Consulta in 1945 and to the Constituent Assembly of 1946.* By virtue of his having been named a senator in 1920, he sat by right in the Senate* of the First Legislature of the Republic. In 1953 Bergamini campaigned unsuccessfully for election to the Senate as a monarchist. He remained active in public life, notably as president of the National Press Association, and died in Rome on December 22, 1962.

BFB

BERLIN, CONGRESS OF, AND ITALY. This European congress, which met between June 13 and July 13, 1878, dealt with the problems created by earlier national uprisings in the Balkans against the Ottoman Empire and Russia's treaty demands on the same state after their war of 1877–78. The final settlement provided for the independence of Montenegro, Rumania, and Serbia, autonomy for a small Bulgarian principality, and concessions to Austria-Hungary, Great Britain, and Russia. Italian public opinion held the highly optimistic view that the Italian foreign secretary, Count Corti, could win the Trentino* and Trieste* as Italy's share in return for the conference's concessions to Austria-Hungary, the holder of those territories, Corti did not share their illusions, and he was proven correct.

JKZ

BERLINGUER, ENRICO. See **ITALIAN COMMUNIST PARTY (PCI)**

BERNERI, CAMILLO. Berneri was an anarchist, born in Lodi on May 20, 1897. A disciple of Errico Malatesta,* his anarchism was a synthesis of Proudhonism and revisionist socialism. During World War I* he collaborated with Antonio Gramsci* in the neutralists' campaign against the Allies. A close friend of Spanish anarchists, he was one of nearly 4,000 Italian exiles who joined the Republicans fighting against Franco. Together with his friend Francesco Barbieri, he was assassinated in Barcelona by Stalinists on May 5, 1937.

MS

BERNETTI, TOMMASO. Born at Fermo on December 29, 1779, Bernetti rose rapidly in the papal administration, although he always remained a deacon and never took holy orders. Pope Leo XII* named him a cardinal in 1827 and secretary of state in 1828–29. He was again named to that post by Gregory XVI* in 1831. During the next five years, he suppressed the revolutionary outbreaks of 1831–32 (see Revolutions of 1831*) with Austrian aid, carried out limited reforms in the papal regime, and sought to maintain a policy of independence and neutrality in international affairs. He lost the trust of Gregory XVI in 1836 and left office, but remained influential in the Curia until his death at Fermo on March 21, 1852.

AJR

BERTANI, AGOSTINO. Distinguished surgeon, republican, and social reformer, Bertani was for nearly two decades a leader of the Extreme Left (see Sinistra, La*), serving in parliament from 1860 to 1880 and from 1882 to 1886. He was born on October 19, 1812, in Milan, and died on April 30, 1886, in Rome. He contributed his medical skills during the Milanese rising against Austria in March 1848, which he helped organize; served in a similar capacity in defense of Giuseppe Mazzini's* Roman Republic in 1849; and was a chief medical officer among Giuseppe Garibaldi's* volunteers in the war of 1859* against Austria. The next year Bertani helped form a medical service among Garibaldi's Thousand in Sicily, and did the same during Garibaldi's abortive attempt to take Rome by force in 1867. In parliament he opposed the transformism* practiced by Agostino Depretis.* In 1872 Bertani proposed and helped prepare the famous inquiry on the conditions of Italian agriculture completed in 1885.

SS

BERTOLINI, PIETRO. Politician and author of several volumes on public administration and local government, he was born on July 24, 1859, in Venice. Elected deputy from Treviso in 1891, he served as finance undersecretary (July 1894–March 1896), interior undersecretary (May 1899–June 1900), and public works minister (November 1907–December 1909). Bertolini helped negotiate the peace treaty of Ouchy* with Turkey (October 18, 1912). As minister of colonies (November 1912–March 1913), he organized the colony of Libya.* Bertolini was nominated in 1919 to be the Italian representative to the inter-Allied reparations commission at Paris. He died on November 28, 1920, in Turin.

RJ

BIANCHI, MICHELE. This Fascist leader, born in Belmonte Calbro (Cosena) on July 22, 1883, began his career as a Socialist and labor organizer. He joined Mussolini* in calling for Italian intervention in World War I,* becoming a founder of the Fascist movement (see Fascism*) in March 1919 and one of Mussolini's closest collaborators. Bianchi was one of the four commanders of the March on Rome* and served briefly as general secretary of the Fascist Party in late 1922. He became undersecretary at the Ministry of Public Works in 1925, undersecretary at the Interior Ministry in 1928, and minister of public works from 1929 until his death in Rome on February 3, 1930.

AJD

BISMARCK, OTTO VON. The Prussian statesman who created the second German Empire between 1866 and 1870 and then led it as chancellor till 1890, Bismarck was born into an old Junker family at Schönhausen, Brandenburg, on April 1, 1815, and died at Friedrichsruh near Hamburg on July 30, 1898. After becoming Prussian minister-president in 1862, he put his state at the head of the national unification movement. After Prussia's three wars—with Denmark (1864), Austria (1866), and France (1870)—Bismarck set up a national government dominated by the Prussian monarchy.

As German chancellor Bismarck won respect throughout Europe by his efforts to maintain peace. In domestic affairs, however, he was often arbitrary in his treatment of the Reichstag and the political parties. His legacy to the German people was a powerful national state and excessive emphasis upon authority and bureaucratic government.

For further reference see: Gordon A. Craig, *Germany 1866–1945* (New York: Oxford University Press, 1980); Otto Pflanze, *Bismarck and the Development of Germany: The Period of Unification, 1915–1871* (Princeton: Princeton University Press, 1963).

JKZ

BISSOLATI, LEONIDA. Bissolati was a founder of the Italian Socialist Party (PSI)* in 1892. He was born in Cremona on February 20, 1857. As a young man he went to the University of Bologna with Filippo Turati* and began his political activity as a labor organizer on the land. In 1896 he became the first editor of *Avanti!*,* a post he held until 1903, when he was replaced by the left-wing leader Enrico Ferri.* He again became editor in 1908 with the return of the reformists to power within the party, but resigned when his faction, the "reformists of the Right," clashed with Turati, the party leader.

Bissolati's current faction advocated the eventual replacement of the Socialist Party by a "labor party" on the English model and based upon the General Confederation of Labor (see CGL*). He had the support of that organization's chief, Rinaldo Rigola, but was outmaneuvered by Turati. Bissolati advocated Socialist support and entrance into "bourgeois" cabinets as a means of securing democratic reforms. He also became convinced of the inevitability of a European war and caused further consternation in the party by refusing to follow its policy of opposing requests for arms appropriations in the Chamber and the country. In 1911 Turati dissuaded him from accepting an offer to join Giovanni Giolitti's* cabinet, but Bissolati touched off a crisis by publicly consulting with the King. He opposed the Socialist condemnation of the Libyan War (see Ouchy, Treaty of*) and supported the government's position, for which the party expelled him and his friends in 1912. After his expulsion Bissolati founded the Partito Socialista Riformista Italiano, which remained a splinter party despite some initial electoral success.

With the outbreak of World War I* Bissolati became the prime exponent of "democratic interventionism," that is, Italian intervention on the Allied side to defend democracy. He later took part in wartime cabinets, but resigned in December 1918 because his Wilsonian ideas clashed with Sidney Sonnino's* nationalistic aspirations. He died on May 6, 1920, in Rome.

For further reference see: Leonida Bissolati, *La Politica Estera dell'Italia dal 1897 al 1920* (Milan: Treves, 1923); Raffaele Colapietra, *Leonida Bissolati* (Milan: Feltrinelli, 1958).

SD

BIXIO, NINO (GEROLAMO). This sailor, follower of Giuseppe Garibaldi,* and general was born in Genoa on October 2, 1821. At an early age he left for the Americas; upon his return he enrolled in the Sardinian navy. Finding this monotonous, he left the service and sought new adventure on board an American ship bound for Sumatra. This, too, did not please his free spirit, and he returned to Genoa via New York. When Piedmont entered the war against Austria he was among the first to join, fighting at Vicenza and Treviso. Toward the end of

1848 he entered Garibaldi's Italian legion, and his impetuosity and valor won him the admiration of the general, whom Bixio served in the defense of the Roman Republic.

Following the Restoration, Bixio returned to Piedmont and served in the Sardinian merchant marine. In 1859 he joined Garibaldi's Cacciatori delle Alpi, and after the armistice of Villafranca* was one of the most enthusiastic supporters of the expedition of the Thousand. In the expedition to Sicily, he commanded the ship *Il Lombardo* to Marsala, fought at Calatafimi, and was wounded while entering Palermo. Promoted to lieutenant general in the Italian army, afterward he was made general. He sought to bring Garibaldi and Cavour* together after the proclamation of the Kingdom of Italy.* He fought in the second battle of Custozza (1866)* and in 1870 was nominated to the Senate. Soon after he took part in the Italian seizure of Rome. He died of cholera in Sumatra in 1873.

FJC

BOCCHINI, ARTURO. See **OVRA**

BOLSHEVIK OF THE ANNUNZIATA. See **GIOLITTI, GIOVANNI**

BOMBA. See **FERDINAND II OF THE KINGDOM OF THE TWO SICILIES**

BONCOMPAGNI, CARLO. Piedmontese politician, lawyer, and writer, Boncompagni was born in Turin on July 25, 1804. He served in various capacities in the Aostan government before becoming, in 1848, Piedmont's minister of public instruction. In 1849 he was one of the negotiators for peace with Austria. In 1852 he was minister of agriculture and commerce (January–November) and then of charity and justice (November–May). He was president of the Chamber of Deputies from 1853 to 1856, commissioner to Florence up to the armistice of Villafranca,* and then governor of Emilia and Tuscany.

He wrote, with Cavour,* the proclamation of March 27, 1861, which announced that Rome would be the capital of Italy. Appointed senator of the realm in 1874, his last years were devoted to politics and to teaching law in Rome and Florence. Among his many works on a variety of subjects, his *Introduzione alla scienza del diritto* [Introduction to the science of law] (1848) stands out. He died in Turin on December 14, 1880.

FFA

BONGHI, RUGGIERO. Classical scholar, historian, and philosopher, Bonghi, born on March 21, 1826, in Naples, was one of the leading spirits of the "historical Right" (see Destra, La*) during his nearly thirty years in parliament from 1860 to the 1890s. In 1871 he was rapporteur for the Law of Papal Guarantees,* which he defended with eloquence and success. As minister of education (1874–76) in the last government of the Right until the 1890s, he reformed the university system. Loyal to the traditions of the Cavourian Right, Bonghi resisted the practice of transformism.* In 1893 he published an article, "The Office of the Prince in a Free State," in which he called for the restoration of the King's autonomy from transient parliamentary majorities. He died on October 22, 1895, in Torre del Greco.

                                                                                        SS

BONIFICA INTEGRALE. Land reclamation (bonifica integrale) had been practiced in Italy since the eighteenth century, but the Fascist regime made it a national crusade with strong ideological overtones. By labeling it integral, the regime denoted its commitment to transforming waste and marginal lands through comprehensive works of drainage, irrigation, soil improvement, reforestation, and the construction of roads and buildings. Though financing was to be both public and private, private investment proved minor while the government spent 9.2 billion lire by 1939 to carry out complete or partial improvements on approximately 350,000 hectares of land. Means and goals were indicated in the so-called Mussolini Act of December 24, 1928, which noted that the ultimate objective was "to reclaim the land, and with the land the men, and with the men the race."

                                                                                        RS

BONOMI, IVANOE. Born in Mantua on October 18, 1873, Bonomi belongs to the second generation of the historical leaders of the Italian Socialist Party (PSI).* He began his political activity on the land and was influential in turning the peasant movement in his native region toward socialism. In the course of his activities he met Leonida Bissolati,* his closest associate, and the other major Socialist leaders—Filippo Turati,* Anna Kuliscioff,* and Camillo Prampolini. It was in Turati's *Critica Sociale** that Bonomi published his first theoretical writings, joining Turati's faction within the party. In 1898 Enrico Ferri,* who had been entrusted with the editorship of *Avanti!** after Bissolati's arrest, called Bonomi to Rome, where he became *de facto* editor for several months. After 1899 Bonomi supported Turati's policy of strengthening Italian democracy both in the party and in the Chamber of Deputies by collaborating with democratic "bourgeois" political groups.

   In 1907 Bonomi made the most serious attempt to make revisionism a viable theoretical force in Italy with his famous book, *Le vie nuove del socialismo* [The new paths of socialism]. This attempt had as little success as his and Bissolati's efforts to found a "labor party" in Italy. With Bissolati, Bonomi became a leader of the "reformists of the Right," advocating Socialist support of or entrance into government coalitions as the best method of securing reforms such as universal suffrage. Bonomi objected to the Socialist Party's opposition to the Libyan conflict of 1911–12, thus provoking his own and his faction's expulsion at the Congress of Reggio Emilia in 1912. After his expulsion Bonomi participated in the founding of the Partito Socialista Riformista Italiano.

With the outbreak of World War I* Bonomi shared Bissolati's "democratic interventionist" position and volunteered for active service when Italy entered the war. In June 1916 Bonomi became minister of public works, subsequently serving in several cabinets, and moved steadily toward nationalist positions as the war ended, a development that produced a cooling of relations with Bissolati. In July 1921 Bonomi became premier, but his cabinet lasted only a short time.

With the triumph of Fascism,* which he opposed, Bonomi retired to private life to write. He resumed his political activity in 1942 through his contacts with anti-Fascist conspirators. In June 1943 plans for a Badoglio*-Bonomi cabinet which would overthrow Fascism and end the German alliance were drawn up, but the King opted for a military government instead. After the armistice of September 8, 1943, Bonomi became president of the Committee of National Liberation (CLN*), which included all the anti-Fascist parties.

When the Allied troops entered Rome in June 1944, the CLN pressed for and obtained an anti-Fascist cabinet headed by Bonomi, who skillfully defused the revolutionary pressures that had built up in the country. The new moderate policy of the Italian Communists, the "Svolta di Salerno," contributed to this result. Bonomi resigned in June 1945, and although his name was proposed on several occasions he never returned to power. He died in Rome on April 20, 1951.

For further reference see: Ivanoe Bonomi, *La politica italiana da Porta Pia a Vittorio Veneto* (Turin: Einaudi, 1966).

SD

BORDIGA, AMADEO. An early leader of Italian communism, Bordiga was born in Resina (Naples) on June 13, 1899, and died in Formia on July 24, 1970. By the age of twenty-three he had received a degree in civil engineering. Following in his father's footsteps, he taught for a while in the Scuola Superiore di Agricoltura in Portici and then worked for a year as a railroad engineer.

His political activity was precocious and his rise in the Italian Left (see Sinistra, La*) was meteoric. In 1910 he joined the Socialist Youth Federation and initiated his enduring attack on the "morbid degeneration" of Neapolitan and Italian socialism. His campaign against the reformists and against opportunism in general brought him a national reputation as early as 1912. His unremitting opposition to any form of support for World War I* enhanced his reputation, as did his early (May 1917) demand for the expulsion of the reformists from the Italian Socialist Party (PSI).* By the war's end, he was the acknowledged leader of the Extreme Left of Italian socialism and was so recognized at the Congress of Bologna of 1919. Although attacked by Lenin for his rigid "absentionism" (absolute rejection of parliamentarianism), Bordiga's great administrative gifts ensured him the leadership of the new Italian Communist Party (PCI)* founded at Livorno in January 1921.

Bordiga was a very effective speaker and a persuasive leader with great physical presence. At first his ideological "purity" seemed wholly appropriate to lead the new party in the revolutionary phase of the postwar crisis. However, his shortcomings soon became apparent. Bordiga's thoroughly deterministic conception of the historical process, for example, led him to believe that a party of resolute militants possessed of a body of revolutionary principles would be sufficient to ensure success when the correct "moment" was at hand. He therefore underestimated the importance of active intervention of the party and the masses in the revolutionary process, and regarded trade-union work and concrete historical assessments of Italy and his time as unimportant.

For these reasons he soon quarreled with the leadership of the Communist International and rejected its prescriptions for a united front and for a renewed merger with the main (nonreformist) body of the PSI. Shortly after Bordiga's arrest in 1923 Antonio Gramsci* and his Turinese collaborators began to take over the leadership of the party. The long and often harsh struggle was completed with Gramsci's victory at the Third Congress of the PCI in Lyons in 1926. Bordiga was once again arrested at the end of 1926. He was released after three years and thereafter retired from political activity. In March 1930 he was expelled from the PCI.

For further reference see: Earlene Craver, "The Rediscovery of Amadeo Bordiga," *Survey* 20 (Spring/Summer 1974): 160–75; Franco Livorsi, *Amadeo Bordiga, il pensiero e l'azione politica, 1912–1970* (Rome: Editori Riuniti, 1976).

JMC

BORELLINI, GINA. A Communist activist renowned for her partisan activities, Borellini was born in Modena on October 24, 1919. She joined the Armed Resistance* in September 1943 to aid her husband and brother. When her husband was captured she took his place. She also helped organize the GDD (see Gruppi di Difese della Donna. . . *) in Modena. After the war she was elected provisional councillor in Modena, president of the Modena Unione Donne Italiane (UDI)*, and deputy in the first three chambers.

MJS

BORGESE, GIUSEPPE ANTONIO. This literary critic and writer was born in Polizzi Generosa (Palermo) on November 12, 1882. He founded the reviews *Hermes* and *Medusa* (1903), worked successively on the *Mattino* of Naples, on *La Stampa** of Turin as Berlin correspondent, and on the *Corriere della Sera** of Milan. In 1910 he was named professor of German literature at the University of Rome, and later taught in Milan. In 1931 he refused the oath to the Fascist regime, which was required of university professors, and went into exile in the United States, where he became professor of Romance languages at the University of Chicago. His *Goliath, the March of Fascism* (1937) was one of the first and strongest indictments of Fascism.* He died in Florence on December 4, 1952.

AJD

BORGHESE, SCIPIONE. Scipione Borghese (1871–1927), traveller and essayist, was best known for competing successfully with Luigi Barzini of the

*Corriere della Sera** in an auto race from Paris to Peking in 1907. In 1913 he lost a bid to enter parliament to the leader of the Italian Nationalist Association,* Luigi Federzoni.* He is also remembered for his travel books on Asia.

AJD

BORGHI, ARMANDO. An anarchist, he was born on April 6, 1882, in Castel Bolognese (Ravenna). In his youth Borghi was close to Amilcare Cipriani and to Errico Malatesta.* A militant labor organizer, he was secretary-general (1912–20) of the anarcho-syndicalist Unione Sindacale Italiana and a founder of the Alleanza del Lavoro. Repeatedly arrested after 1902, in 1923 he chose exile, first in France and then (1926–45) in the United States. After his return to Italy he became editor of *L'Umanità Nuova* and was deeply involved in disputes among anarchists. He died in Rome on April 21, 1968.

MS

BOSELLI, PAOLO. At age seventy-eight, Boselli crowned forty-six years of parliamentary activity when chosen in June 1916 to head a wartime national union government. He was born on June 8, 1838, in Savona, and died on March 10, 1932, in Rome. He had a varied career, as a lawyer and practiced administrator; liberal conservative deputy in 1870; professor of financial sciences at the University of Rome (1871); author of a major work on maritime law (1885); and negotiator of navigation agreements with France (1886). Boselli held five ministerial posts: education (1888–91), agriculture (1893–94), finance (1894–96), treasury (1899–1900), and education (1906), serving in governments of both the Left (see Sinistra, La*) and Right (see Destra, La*). He supported Antonio Salandra's* decision to enter the war (May 1915). Boselli succeeded him in 1916, but proved unable to invigorate Italy's war effort owing to irreconcilable differences within the government. Voted out of office during the early days of the Caporetto* military disaster (October 25, 1917), he was appointed senator in 1921. In 1924 he accepted honorary membership in the Fascist Party.

SS

BOTTAI, GIUSEPPE. Giuseppe Bottai, a Fascist politician, was born in Rome on September 3, 1895, and died there on January 9, 1959. He was elected to parliament in 1921 on the Fascist Party list and commanded a column of Blackshirts during the March on Rome.* From 1926 to 1943 Bottai was successively undersecretary at the Ministry of Corporations (1926–29), minister of corporations (1929–32), governor of Rome (1935–36), and minister of national education (1936–43). He was also a member of the Fascist Grand Council (1926–43) and joined with Dino Grandi* in the plot to oust Mussolini* on July 24–25, 1943. In 1944 he escaped to North Africa, where he joined the French Foreign Legion, and served in France, Germany, and North Africa from 1944 to 1948. On his return to Italy he resumed a career as a journalist. From 1953 to 1959 he edited the political review *abc*.

As minister of corporations Bottai attempted to create a state-directed, planned capitalist economy but was blocked by Mussolini and major industrialists. He was responsible for the School Charter of 1939, a general reform of the schools to make them conform to the rural and populist features of Fascism.* Bottai played an important role in rallying the younger generation to the regime through his editorial and cultural activities. The reviews *Critica Fascista, Archivio di Studi Corporativi*, and *Primato*, and the School of Corporative Studies at the University of Pisa were the most important.

For further reference see: G. B. Guerri, *Giuseppe Bottai: Un fascista critico* (Milan: Feltrinelli, 1976); A. De Grand, *Bottai e la cultura fascista* (Bari: Laterza, 1978).

AJD

BOVIO, GIOVANNI. Neo-Hegelian philosopher, prolific author, and lecturer on the philosophy of law (Naples, 1875), Bovio was elected to parliament for eight successive legislatures (1876–1903), where he sat at the Extreme Left (see Sinistra, La*) as an independent among democratic republicans. He was born on February 6, 1837, in Trani (Apulia), and died in Naples on April 15, 1903. Bovio consistently supported the separation of church and state, championed the extension of suffrage, supported irredentism,* and opposed the transformism* practiced by Agostino Depretis* of the Left, in reaction to which he helped found the Fascio della Democrazia (1883), in association with the Socialist Andrea Costa* and the radical democratic leader Felice Cavallotti.* In 1890 Bovio rallied to the Pact of Rome,* calling for radical political and socioeconomic reforms, nevertheless remaining, as always, opposed to violent solutions.

SS

BRASCHI, GIOVANNI ANGELO. See PIUS VI

BREDA, ERNESTO. Breda was an industrialist, born on October 6, 1852, into a family of prosperous rural notables from the town of San Martino (Padua). After obtaining a degree in civil engineering, he went to work for a cousin, Vincenzo Stefano Breda, who manufactured railroad equipment. Travels in northern Europe in 1882 made him aware of the backward state of Italian manufacturing; after unsuccessful attempts at joining foreign firms, he decided to establish his own company in 1886. In December 1899 it became the joint-stock Società Italiano Ernesto Breda per Costruzioni Meccaniche. The enterprise initially produced pig iron and machinery but soon branched out into the production of artillery, munitions, locomotives, and, during World War I,* ships and aircraft, always relying heavily upon government contracts. Breda died on November 6, 1918, while listening to the announcement of victory in the war.

RS

BRESCI, GAETANO. Assassin of King Humbert I,* Bresci belonged to that part of Italian anarchism* espousing revolutionary acts of violence. He was born on November 10, 1869, in Coiano (Prato), and became a skilled textile worker. In December 1897 he immigrated to the United States, joining the Italian anarchist colony in Paterson, New Jersey. There, feelings against King Humbert were intense because of his approval of the repression of the disturbances of 1898. Bresci returned to Italy in mid-1900, and on July 29 shot and mortally wounded the King at Monza. Sentenced to life imprisonment, Bresci committed suicide on May 22, 1901, in the penitentiary of Porto Santo Stefano. All political groups in Italy, including some anarchists, condemned Bresci's act.

SS

BRIGANDAGE. Brigandage was the term that government sources used to describe frequent outbreaks of armed rebellion occurring from 1861 to 1865 in many mainland provinces of the former Kingdom of the Two Sicilies.* By describing these acts of insurgency as brigandage, the government of the recently unified Kingdom of Italy* obscured the social and political grievances underlying the phenomenon and disguised its civil war character. Unemployment, peasant frustation over the absence of land reform, rapid demobilization of the defeated Neapolitan army, hostility toward Piedmontese military conscription, cultural acceptance of the outlaw as a hero, and political intrigue by clericals and Bourbon royalists contributed in varing measures to the rebellions. By 1862 the insurgents, organized in bands of several hundred members, may have totaled 80,000. In isolated instances they seized entire villages and towns, but in spite of widespread peasant support they failed to form a unified movement. The insurgents shared no common ideology and lacked a clearly defined political goal; they were mostly young, male, unmarried, and socially marginal; they found no support among the urban middle classes and the intelligentsia. Stern repressive measures by the army came with the imposition of martial law on most of the South in August 1863 and continued until the end of 1865, when the region was pacified. At the height of the repression the army deployed 120,000 troops, and from 1861 to 1865 it killed in combat or otherwise executed 5,212 rebels and arrested an additional 5,044. Brigandage as a sociopolitical phenomenon was eliminated, but its underlying causes were not.

For further reference see: Franco Molfese, *Storia del brigantaggio dopo l'unità* (Milan: Feltrinelli, 1964).

RS

BRIN, BENEDETTO. As minister of the navy, he was primarily responsible for the development of the modern Italian navy. Born in Turin on May 17, 1833, Brin died in Rome on May 24, 1898. He gained an international reputation for innovative designing of cruisers, antisubmarine devices, bigger guns, and more resourceful strategy.

RSC

BRUNETTI, ANGELO. One of the leading figures in the revolutionary events of 1848 in Rome, he was known as Ciceruacchio. All sorts of explanations have been provided for his nickname, among them that it derived from Cicero and was given to him because of his pompous speech. He was born in the Campo Marzio district of Rome on September 27, 1800, and worked as a wine carter. It is believed that he was initiated into politics by Pietro Sterbini* and Felice Scifoni. In 1827 he was inscribed in the Carbonari (see Carboneria*) and in 1833 in Mazzini's Giovine Italia.* During the cholera epidemic of 1837, he won broad support in the capital because of his generosity in aiding the unfortunate, as well as for his ability to lead and organize the common people. With the accession of Pius IX* in 1846, Brunetti emerged as a personality of major political importance.

During the first two years of Pius IX's pontificate, Brunetti was at the head of the giant demonstrations in honor of the Pope; many of them were in fact organized and orchestrated by him. Thus, when Pius issued the decree on the Consulta, it was Brunetti who coordinated the massive demonstration at the Quirinale, the papal residence. More than anything else, Brunetti's impressive figure and oratory preserved order in the capital and prevented the early demonstrations from degenerating into violence and revolution. Small wonder that he was received by the Pope in audience on several occasions, and his fame transcended the Papal States.*

This intermediary between the masses and the government was courted by the Popular Club and two of its most influential members, the Prince of Canino and Pietro Sterbini. Since Brunetti's attachment to the Pope was personal rather than ideological, and since his ideas lacked both clarity and precision, the club members were able to sway him. As the Pope showed himself unwilling to commit himself to the national cause, the Prince of Canino and Sterbini pushed Brunetti along a more radical course. Dissatisfied with the selection of Pellegrino Rossi* as Pio Nono's chief minister, it is believed that Brunetti and Sterbini apparently planned Rossi's assassination (November 15, 1848) together with Ciceruacchio's son Luigi.

Following the flight of the Pope from Rome to Gaeta* and the establishment of the Roman Republic, Brunetti was no longer the idol of the populace. However, he did reemerge as a leader of importance when the Roman Republic was attacked by the armies of the Catholic powers—Austria, France, Spain, and Naples—and he acted energetically to defend the capital. During this period, Giuseppe Garibaldi* appeared to have had the greatest influence upon Brunetti and his sons Luigi and Lorenzo. With the fall of Rome to the French early in July 1849, Ciceruacchio and his sons joined a group that followed Garibaldi in his attempt to reach Venice, which was still resisting the Austrians. As the group tried to cross the border into the Veneto they were betrayed to the Austrians, and Brunetti and his sons were shot at Ca' Tiepolo on August 10, 1849.

For further reference see: F. Venosta, *Ciceruacchio, il popolano di Roma* (Milan, 1863); "Brunetti, Angelo," *Dizionario Biografico degli Italiani*, 14: 569–71.

FJC

BUONARROTI, FILIPPO. Buonarroti, a Tuscan revolutionary, was born in Pisa on November 11, 1761. After a musical and legal education in Florence, he became a bookseller and journalist. In 1789, inflamed with revolutionary zeal, he moved to Corsica, where he later denounced Pasquale Paoli* to the National Convention. A friend of Robespierre in Paris, he was appointed by the Committee of Public Safety as administrator and commissioner of occupied territories at Oneglia on the Ligurian coast, a Jacobin center for organizing Italian revolutionaries into a larger French network. He shared leadership with Gracchus Babeuf in the Conspiracy of Equals of May 10, 1796, and, escaping the death penalty, was imprisoned until 1806 in Sospello. Following his release, he supported himself as a teacher of music while in exile in Geneva and then Brussels until 1830. He also wrote an account of the 1796 conspiracy, and organized a series of secret societies—Adelfi,* Filadelfi, Apofasimeni, Société des amis du Peuple, Veri Italiani—each in a tight hierarchy imitative of Freemasonry,* with apprentices, masters, and grand masters. Buonarroti saw the Italian Revolution in an international context, opposed federalism and localized revolts, and believed that in Italy only a centralized egalitarian republic resting on popular sovereignty could destroy the regional power bases of vested landowning interests. In 1830, nearly blind, he returned to Paris, where he was frequently at odds with the more moderate Italian exiles. His cooperation with Giuseppe Mazzini* in 1833 was short-lived because of ideological and methodological differences. The growing social concerns of an industrializing French society led him to new organizations such as the Société des Familles. The revolutionary scene was changing at the end of his life, as exemplified by the Lyons strikes and government repression in 1834. Buonarroti died in Paris on September 14, 1837.

For further reference see: Elizabeth Eisenstein, *The First Professional Revolutionist: Filippo Michele Buonarroti (1761–1837)* (Cambridge, Mass.: Harvard University Press, 1959); A. Galante Garrone, *Filippo Buonarroti e i rivoluzionari dell'ottocento (1828–1837)* (Turin: Einaudi, 1972).

MSM

BUOZZI, BRUNO. Born near Ferrara on January 31, 1881, he was secretary-general of the Italian General Confederation of Labor (see CGL*) until November 1926, when he immigrated to Paris. There he edited the anti-Fascist labor newspaper *L'Operaio Italiano*, in which he opposed both the Fascist corporative system and the Communist doctrine of proletarian dictatorship. He waged an effective ideological campaign against the Fascist labor syndicates.

In the late 1930s, Buozzi joined the Italian Socialist Party (PSI).* In 1943 and 1944, after Mussolini's* ouster, he worked in Rome to rebuild an independent Italian labor movement. He was assassinated by Germans on June 3, 1944, during the course of the German army's retreat from the Italian capital.

FR

C

CABRINI, ANGIOLO. One of the major influences on the Italian labor movement, Cabrini was born on March 9, 1869, in Codogno (Milan) and died in Rome on May 7, 1937. He became a member of the Partito Operaio Italiano and was a founder of the Italian Socialist Party (PSI)* in 1892, although he objected to its Marxist program and remained aloof for a number of years. In 1895 he fled to Switzerland to avoid the repression under Francesco Crispi* and organized Socialist organizations in the Canton Ticino.

Cabrini's sojourn in Switzerland gave him an enduring feeling for the emigrant problem. Indeed, Cabrini was perhaps the major Italian expert on social legislation during the late nineteenth and early twentieth centuries. In 1902 he became secretary of the Resistance and in 1906 of the General Confederation of Labor (see CGL*), which he was instrumental in founding. Cabrini stayed in Italy during the Fascist period to study and write about labor problems and, like other early labor leaders who elected to stay in Italy, he has been accused of conferring respectability on the Fascist regime.

In political life, Cabrini was "the most reformist of the Italian reformists," a follower of Filippo Turati* first and then of Leonida Bissolati.* Cabrini was expelled from the Socialist Party in 1912 and joined the Reformist Socialist Party. He was a deputy from 1900 to 1919.

SD

CABRINI, FRANCESCA SAVERIA. The founder of the Roman Catholic order of the Missionary Sisters of the Sacred Heart of Jesus was born on June 15, 1850, in Sant'Angelo, Italy. Mother Cabrini founded her order in Italy and in 1889 began a long series of visits to North and South America to establish schools, hospitals, orphanages, and camps to aid Italian immigrants. She became a U.S. citizen in 1909, and died on December 22, 1917, in Chicago, Illinois. Within twenty-five years of her death, Mother Cabrini was credited with four miraculous healings, and on July 7, 1946, she became the first United States citizen to be canonized by the Roman Catholic Church. Her order still assists immigrants of all nationalities worldwide.

WR

CADORNA, LUIGI. Commander in chief during the disaster of Caporetto* (October-November 1917), Cadorna remains the most controversial figure in Italy's efforts during World War I.* He was born on September 4, 1850, in Pallanza, son of General Raffaele Cadorna*; he died on December 21, 1928, in Bordighera. Commissioned in 1868, he served as a general staff officer and held several field commands from 1892 to July 1914, when he became army chief of staff. An excellent organizer and a rigid disciplinarian, he was insensitive to criticism. He failed to exploit the advantage Italy had on the Austrian front in May 1915. Instead, until 1917 he pursued a strategy of attrition costing hundreds of thousands of lives, with meager results. The rout of Caporetto cost Cadorna his command in November 1917, when he was replaced by Armando Diaz.* The report of a commission of inquiry (1919) held Cadorna responsible for faulty deployment of forces, disregard of intelligence of an impending enemy offensive, failure to curb the actions of subordinate commanders, brutal discipline, indifference to the morale of the troops, and an independent attitude toward civilian authority. To his credit are his preparation of the army for war between July 1914 and May 1915, frequently with inadequate resources; his containment of a major Austrian offensive in the Trentino* (May-July 1916); the taking of the bastion of Gorizia (August 1916); his partial and costly successes in August 1917; and his masterly preparation of a defensive line on the Piave River during the retreat from Caporetto, which held despite repeated Austro-German assaults. In 1924 the Fascist government promoted him to the rank of Marshal of Italy.

For further reference, see: Luigi Cadorna, *La guerra alla fronte italiana*, 2 vols. (Milan: Treves, 1923); also the critical appraisal by Enrico Caviglia, *La dodicesima battaglia* (Milan: Mondadori, 1933).

SS

CADORNA, RAFFAELE. Career officer, Partisan commander, and scion of an aristocratic Piedmontese family, Cadorna was born in Pallanza (Novara) on September 12, 1889. He was the son of Luigi Cadorna, who was army chief of staff during World War I.* His grandfather, also named Raffaele, had commanded the Italian troops that occupied Rome in 1870. Under the Fascist dictatorship he had friends among militant anti-Fascists. After the armistice was signed on September 3, 1943, troops under his command fought valiantly against the Germans at Monterosi and Bracciano. At the request of the CLNAI* and of the Allied Fifteenth Army Group he went into enemy-occupied territory. In November the CLNAI appointed him supreme commander of the Partisans reorganized as Volontari della Libertà (Freedom Volunteers), with Ferruccio Parri* of the Action Party* and Luigi Longo* of the Italian Communist Party (PCI)* as vice-commanders. His book, *La riscossa dal 25 luglio alla liberazione*, is a valuable and reliable document. Appointed chief of staff of the Italian armed forces after the German surrender, and later elected to the Senate* (1948–63), he died in 1973.

MS

CAETANI, GELASIO. This aristocratic supporter of early Fascism* was born in Rome on March 7, 1877, of an American mother. He pursued a successful career in mining engineering in the United States until 1914. His American background induced Mussolini* to make Caetani his first ambassador in Washington where, from 1922 to 1925, the most pressing issues concerned war debts and the attitude of Italo-Americans to the new Fascist regime. Returning to Italy, he served as consultant to the Pontine Marshes drainage project but spent most of his last years systematizing his family's extensive archive. He died in Rome on October 23, 1934.

ACas

CAFFÈ, IL. This periodical was published at Milan every ten days from June 1764 to May 1766. Called the *"Encyclopédie* of the Italian Enlightenment,"* *Il Caffè* was the voice of the Milanese Accademia dei Pugni (Academy of the Fisticuffs), which brought together an active, eclectic group of Milan's young intellectuals under the leadership of Pietro* and Alessandro Verri.* Interested in the ideas of English and French reformers and *philosophes*, they launched *Il Caffè* to stimulate and promote discussion among a wide audience. In its pages appeared articles on a varied range of topics—from agriculture to language, from social customs to national rivalries and false pride. It sought to air new ideas, demolish accepted concepts, attack conformity, and support reform. Like its writers, it was often brash and abrasive, always stimulating, and never dull. Its very success led to its demise, for the intensity of its effort could not be sustained. *Il Caffè* accomplished much in its two years of existence, for in questioning everything it provoked public discussion. Many of its writers went on to become government officials and tried to effect the reforms they had called for in its pages.

EPN

CAFIERO, CARLO. A leading Italian social revolutionary, anarchist, and political thinker of the nineteenth century, he was born in 1846 at Barletta of a wealthy landed family, and died in 1892 at Nocera Inferiore. Early on Cafiero abandoned a diplomatic career for anarchism.* He knew both Marx and Engels personally in London, and therefore participated in the establishment of the First International in Italy. He became the chief exponent and principal financial backer of Mikhail Bakunin,* collaborated on Socialist journals such as *La Compagna,** and participated in the attempted insurrections in Bologna (1874) and Matese

(1877). He was arrested many times in both Italy and Switzerland. Cafiero published a summary of Marx's *Capital* that had a wide circulation.

WR

CAIROLI, BENEDETTO. Thrice prime minister, Cairoli was more successful as a patriot than as a political leader. He was born on January 28, 1825, in Pavia. With his four brothers, Cairoli participated in all the wars for independence (see Revolutions of 1848*; War of 1859*; War of 1866*), helped plan the Mazzinian rising in Milan in 1853, organized and followed Giuseppe Garibaldi's* Thousand, and was wounded in the capture of Palermo (1860). A member of parliament from 1860 to his death, Cairoli first sat among the republicans, agitated for the redemption of Rome and Venetia, and opposed the 1871 Papal Law of Guarantees* as too generous to the papacy. Originally a supporter of Agostino Depretis,* he became his opponent because of the slowness of the latter's reform program and succeeded him as prime minister in March 1878. Cairoli was held accountable for the failure at the Congress of Berlin* (June-July 1878), from which Italy's "honest" diplomacy emerged with "hands clean" but empty. He regained a measure of esteem when wounded in defense of King Humbert I* against an assassin's dagger (November 1878), but some nevertheless held Cairoli indirectly responsible for the attempt because of his and Giuseppe Zanardelli's* permissive policy on civil liberties. He fell from office in December 1878 on this issue; returned as prime minister in July 1879; and was joined by his predecessor, Depretis, as minister of the interior, when Cairoli formed his third and longest ministry (November 1879–May 1881). Acting as his own foreign minister, he was faced by worsened relations with Austria owing to irredentist agitation (see Irrendentism*) and by France's ambition for supremacy in Tunisia, culminating in France's protectorate (May 1881), after which Cairoli resigned in an atmosphere of general reproach for failing to protect Italy's interests in North Africa. Declining health reduced his political activity thereafter, forever characterized as honest but inept. He died on August 8, 1889, in Naples.

For further reference see: Michele Rosi, *I Cairoli*, new ed., 2 vols. (Bologna: L. Cappelli, 1929); Erminia Ghiglione Giulietti, ed., *Adelaide Cairoli e i suoi figli* (Pavia: Cortina, 1960).

SS

CALAMANDREI, PIERO. Piero Calamandrei was born in Florence on April 21, 1889, and died there on September 27, 1956. He was an eminent professor of civil and constitutional law. After the fall of Fascism,* he became rector of the University of Florence and was elected (Action Party*) to the Constituent Assembly of 1946* and parliament. In 1945 he founded the political review *Il Ponte*.

CFD

CALOGERO, GUIDO. This professor of the history of philosophy, born in Rome on December 4, 1904, was jailed in 1942 for founding the anti-Fascist

"Liberalsocialismo" movement. It is described in his book, *Difesa del liber-alsocialismo* (Rome, 1945). In 1946 Calogero represented the Action Party* in the National Consultative Assembly.

CFD

CAMORRA. Complete with elaborate rituals, oaths, and tests of loyalty, the Camorra was a secret society that originated under the Neapolitan Bourbons in the first half of the nineteenth century. Often compared with the Sicilian Mafia* because it was composed of notorious criminal elements organized into gangs who practiced extortion, smuggling, robbery, and murder, the Camorra effectively dominated the ill-governed city of Naples during the last years of Bourbon rule. In 1860 its leaders transferred their allegiance to Giuseppe Garibaldi,* and the Camorra played a part in overturning the Bourbon monarchy and winning the former Neapolitan state to the Italian national cause. But since the new Italian government was in the hands of Garibaldi's political adversaries, it owed nothing to the Camorra. This attitude it made clear by its repeated and largely successful efforts during the last decades of the nineteenth century to suppress the society.

The last notable incident involving the secret society occurred in 1906, when Camorra thugs murdered a couple named Cuocolo who were thought to be police informers. After a five-year investigation thirty accused perpetrators of this crime were tried, convicted, and imprisoned. The Camorra never recovered from this setback and all but disappeared after World War I* as a consequence of the vigorous campaign of repression directed against it by Fascist authorities. Despite frequent allegations to the contrary, the gangsterism and corruption found in contemporary Naples therefore has nothing to do with that long-extinct society.

JER

CAMPIERI. Campieri were armed, mounted field-guards hired by Sicilian land-owners to protect their livestock and crops from the assaults of poverty-stricken and potentially insurgent peasants. Living outside the law and unhampered by the presence of an effective local police force, these men routinely practiced the worst forms of violence and crime against the island's agricultural population. Easily identified by the distinctive slouch hats and bandoliers they wore and by the laconic delivery of their speech, many campieri accumulated much capital and acquired an increasingly large share of the land of their employers. These "men of respect," as they were usually called, eventually became known as mafiosi (see Mafia*) as they successfully contested Sicily's traditional landed class for control of the island during the middle decades of the nineteenth century. Less ambitious campieri served as the paid retainers of ex-field-guards who had become powerful mafiosi, acting as the violent enforcers of their will in those areas of the island that had fallen under their dominion.

JER

CAMPO FORMIO, TREATY OF. This treaty ended a phase of the French Revolutionary Wars. Signed October 17, 1797, by Napoleon I* and Austrian representatives, it set the seal on his victories in northern Italy. The specifically Italian provisions included (1) Austria's acquisition of Venetia as far as the Adige, with the city of Venice, Istria,* and Dalmatia*; (2) Austria'a recognition of the Cisalpine Republic,* comprising Milan, Modena, Ferrara, Bologna, and Romagna*; and (3) Austria's indemnification of the Duke of Modena with the Breisgau.

WDG

CAMPAGNONI, GIUSEPPE. See **JACOBINS**

CANEVARO, FELICE NAPOLEONE. A naval commander and diplomat, Canevaro was born of Genoese parents on July 7, 1838, in Lima, Peru. He fought in the naval campaigns of 1859–61 and 1866 (see War of 1866*). In February 1897 Admiral Canevaro assumed command of the European fleets sent to mediate Crete's revolt against Turkey. Elected deputy in 1882 and nominated senator in 1896, in June 1898 he became navy minister. Foreign minister in Luigi Pelloux's* first cabinet (June 29, 1898–May 14, 1899), he presided over an international antianarchist conference in Rome from November 24 to December 21, 1898. His failure in March 1899 to secure Italian control over China's San-Mun Bay precipitated the government's resignation. Canevaro died in Venice on December 30, 1926.

RJ

CANOSA, ANTONIO CAPECE MINUTOLO, PRINCE OF. A Neapolitan political figure and polemicist, he was born in Naples on March 5, 1768, and died in exile at Pesaro on March 4, 1838. A militant supporter of Old Regime traditions, papal authority, and monarchy bolstered by a privileged nobility and clergy, he fought the French occupation of the Neapolitan kingdom (1799, 1806–15), was ambassador to Spain (1814–15), and twice briefly served Ferdinand I* as minister of police (1816, 1821). On both occasions his extraordinarily repressive police tactics caused his dismissal. Exiled in 1822, he moved about Italy working and writing on behalf of reaction.

RCu

CANTALUPO, ROBERTO. A political journalist and writer who served Mussolini,* Cantalupo was born in Naples on January 17, 1891. His nationalist views led to an association with Fascism.* Elected a deputy in 1924 and 1929, he was undersecretary for colonies from 1924 to 1926. He moved into diplomacy as minister to Egypt, 1930–32, and served as ambassador to Brazil, 1933–37. From February to April 1937 he was special emissary to General Franco, but his advice that Italy disengage from the Spanish Civil War* was rejected. After World War II* he sat in the Italian and European parliaments.

ACas

CANTÙ, CESARE. Popular historian and prolific writer, Cantù was born in Brivio on December 5, 1804. Early on he achieved recognition with the romantic poem *"Algiso"* (1828) and the regional study *Storia della città e della diocesi di Como* [*The history of the city and diocese of Como*] (2 volumes, 1829). His popular historical novel, *Margheria Pisterla*, appeared in 1838. In 1836 he began, and six years later completed, the monumental thirty-five volume *Storia universale* [Universal history]. Its publication made Cantù the wealthiest and best known Italian writer of the time. After a brief exile in Turin and Switzerland in 1848, he returned to Milan and continued his formidable literary output. While often magisterial and vivid in style, Cantù's works are marred by poor judgment and religious and political prejudice.

For a short time (1860–61) he sat in the Chamber of Deputies, but, failing to be reelected, he retired to revise earlier works and to serve as the director of the Lombard Archives. He died in Milan on March 11, 1895.

FFA

CAPORETTO. This battle was fought during World War I* between the Italians under General Luigi Cadorna* and the Germans and Austrians under General Otto von Below. In a coordinated effort to knock Italy out of the war, seven German and eight Austrian divisions attacked the Italian Isonzo front (see Isonzo, Battles of the*) near Caporetto on October 24, 1917, quickly forcing an Italian retreat to the Piave line. After advancing seventy miles into Italy, von Below was finally halted in a four-day battle (December 11--15, 1917) in the Brenta Valley. The Italians lost 45,000 dead and wounded and 275,000 prisoners.

WDG

CAPPELLARI, BARTOLOMEO. See **GREGORY XVI**

CAPPONI, CARLA. A Communist activist, she was awarded a gold medal for valor in the Armed Resistance.* Born in Rome on December 7, 1921, Capponi was a law student who joined the Resistance in September 1943 as part of the Gruppi di Azione Patriottica* unit, of which she became vice-commander. She was involved in numerous acts of sabotage and combat situations. After the war (1953) she was elected to the Chamber of Deputies* from the Italian Socialist Party (PCI)* lists.

MJS

CAPPONI, GINO. This statesman and historian contributed much to the promulgation of the ideas and spirit of the *Risorgimento.* Born in Florence on September 13, 1792, and educated at Vienna and Florence, the wealthy Capponi began a long period of travel in 1814. Upon returning to Italy in 1820, he founded, with G. P. Vieusseux, the journal *Antologia*. Modeled on the *Edinburgh Review*, it promoted the economic and educational welfare of Tuscany. He also helped found and contributed to the journals *Archivio Storico, Giornale Agrario Toscano*, and *Guida dell'Educatore*.

In 1844, he lost his sight; nevertheless, he maintained constant contact with the liberals of Italy. Thus, when Tuscany was granted a constitution in 1848, he was named prime minister. After the reaction, he returned to writing his great *Storia della Repubblica di Firenze* [History of the Florentine republic] (1875), which, though partially obsolete, remains a standard work. He died in Florence on February 3, 1876.

FFA

CARBONERIA. This secret society of the first half of the nineteenth century began in southern Italy during the reign of King Joachim Murat,* probably due to a schism within Masonic lodges (see Freemasonry*). Around 1813–14 it spread to northern Italian regions through the Papal States* and the Romagna,* and there it came in contact with the democratic organization of Filippo Buonarroti* and others. In the early 1820s the society also spread to France and Spain. The Carboneria's most important moment was the Neapolitan Revolution of 1820–21 (see Revolutions of 1820–21*). The failure of that revolutionary movement and of other initiatives by Lombard and Piedmontese Carbonari precipitated a crisis. Later, the society was reconstituted by Buonarroti as the Carboneria Riformata and the Carboneria Democratica Universale. Members of the society, who called one another "cousin," were dedicated to the overthrow of despotic regimes and the attainment of constitutions. Carbonari played a major role in the revolutions of 1831* in central Italy as well as in the 1834 revolt in Lyons. But the French political trials of 1835, the death of Buonarroti in 1837, and the success of Giuseppe Mazzini's* rival organization, Giovine Italia* (Young Italy), marked the demise of the movement.

CML

CARDUCCI, GIOSUÈ. Italy's leading poet in the post-*Risorgimento** period, Carducci was born in Valdicastello on July 28, 1835. He was raised in the wilds of Maremma, south of Livorno, by a violent misanthropic father. Schooled in Florence and Pisa, Carducci took a degree in philosophy and philology in 1856. During the next four years he taught school, wrote poety, edited Italian literary classics, and founded a short-lived journal, *Il Poliziano*. His critical writings attracted favorable attention, and in 1860 he was offered a professorship at the University of Bologna. This became Carducci's base for the rest of his career.

Carducci's central poetic vision, filled with the images of antiquity, began to take shape in his earliest work, *Juvenila* [Youthful writings] (1850–60). With his school friends in Pisa, he formed the Amici Pedanti, a classical literary society opposed to romanticism, which they dismissed as a foreign importation.

Influenced by Giuseppe Mazzini's* "Third Rome" rhetoric, the Pedantic Friends proposed a literary program for Italy that was based on native classical traditions. Carducci's own poetry was intensely patriotic, and some of his best known poems celebrated the *Risorgimento** as the modern epic of the Italian people.

The poems published in Carducci's next two collections, *Levia gravia* [Light and Serious Poems] (1861–71) and *Giambi ed epodi* [Iambics and Epodes] (1867–79), however, revealed his disappointment with the new Italy. Frequently using the pseudonym "Enotrio Romano," he expressed the anticlerical state of mind to be found on the Garibaldian and republican Left (see Sinistra, La*) during the 1860s. His image as an incurable rebel became complete when the republicans disavowed his notorious "Inno a Satana" [Hymn to Satan] (1863), which he intended as a defense of reason against the oppressive theology of Christianity, but which they interpreted as an antidemocratic attack on Mazzini's principle of "God and People."

This poem pointed toward the elitist aesthetic theories that Carducci espoused in the 1880s. His greatest literary success, *Odi barbare* [The barbarian odes] (1877), won the approval of the young aesthetes who helped to launch Angelo Sommaruga's* *Cronaca Bizantina** in 1881—Giulio Salvadori,* Gabriele D'Annunzio,* Edoardo Scarfoglio,* and Cesario Testa. During the next four years Carducci was the central figure of this group. Disillusioned by what they perceived to be a disjunction between the promised Third Rome and Umbertian Italy, the *bizantini* held up Carducci as their poetic ideal.

A stroke in 1885 broke Carducci's health, but his hold on the affection of the cultural elite as the nation's reigning man of letters remained firm. He continued to write poetry and criticism and to speak out as a Crispian nationalist on political questions. By the 1890s he clearly had distinguished himself as a cultural pillar of the monarchical establishment and was named a senator by royal decree. A few months before his death on February 16, 1907, Carducci became the first Italian to win the Nobel Prize for literature.

For further reference see: Paolo Alatri, *Carducci giacobino: L'evoluzione dell'ethos politico* (Palermo: Libreria Prima, 1953); Mario Biagini, *Il poeta della terza Italia* (Milan: Mursia, 1961).

RD

CARLI, GIAN RINALDO, COUNT. Italian economist, public servant, and historian during the Enlightenment,* he was born at Capodistria on April 11, 1720, and died on February 22, 1795. After some years as professor of astronomy and navigation at the University of Padua, he moved to Milan and entered the service of Austrian Lombardy.* Charged with the economic administation of the province, he wrote extensively on fiscal matters. Among his works are *Delle monete e della instituzione delle zecche d'Italia* [On money and the mints of Italy] and *Ragionamento sopra i bilanci economici delle nazione* [Discourse on the economic accounts of nations]. In the tradition of Lodovico Muratori* he also published the very valuable *Antichità italiche* [Antiquities of Italy], which discussed all aspects of Italian life from Roman times until the fourteenth century. In *L'Uomo libero* [The free man] he confuted Rousseau's *Social Contract*, and in the *Lettere americane* [American letters] he tried to present a comparative study of human societies.

WR

CARTA DEL CARNARO. The Charter of Carnaro was a corporativist constitution devised in 1920, ostensibly for the "Regency" that Gabriele D'Annunzio* established in the disputed city of Fiume* in 1919. D'Annunzio gave the document its rhetorical form, but the substance was provided by the syndicalist Alceste De Ambris,* head of the Fiume cabinet during 1920. The constitution sought to provide the structure for a new, more communitarian kind of state based on common productive roles (see Corporativism*). The legislature was to be based on the ten occupational groupings, or corporations, into which all the producers in the society would be organized. The economy would be politicized, with private property deemed a social instrument, and a labor magistracy would be established to adjudicate labor conflicts.

In this short-lived regime there was no chance to test the constitution in practice, but D'Annunzio and De Ambris were chiefly interested in the document's wider propaganda value. D'Annunzio hoped to pressure the Italian government, while De Ambris was seeking the basis for a non-Socialist revolutionary coalition. Each was disappointed, but the Carta del Carnaro proved a major vehicle of neosyndicalist influence on young Fascists seeking an alternative to both liberalism and socialism.

DDR

CARTA DELLA SCUOLA. Written by the left-wing Fascist minister of national education, Giuseppe Bottai,* and promulgated by Mussolini* on February 15, 1939, the Carta della Scuola was a reform of the educational system designed to infuse Fascist principles into the schools.

Bottai regarded the 1923 Gentile Reform* as incomplete and "bourgeois." Only the elementary schools were sufficiently Fascist, argued the minister, while the upper levels retained a measure of independence and thus fostered class elitism. The Carta della Scuola was instituted for the purpose of bringing the education of the individual into harmony with the goals of the party and the corporative state. To this end, official Fascist youth organizations (GIL) were recognized as integral to the educational system. The Carta even required all university students to enroll in the Gioventù Universitaria Fascista (GUF).* The 1939 reform also provided for mandatory manual labor from the fourth grade on. This was to aid the Italian economy and to instill in the child respect for all forms of labor. The Carta reorganized the grade levels, establishing a uniform scuola media to combat the system's "elitist tendencies."

Despite the fanfare surrounding its promulgation, the Carta della Scuola, due to the continued influence of the Church and the outbreak of World War II,* had little success in fulfilling Bottai's promises.

For further reference see: Giorgio Gabrielli, *Principi, fini e metodi della scuola fascista secondo la Carta della Scuola* (Florence: La Nuova Italia, 1940); Richard J. Wolff, "Catholicism, Fascism and Italian Education from the Riforma Gentile to the Carta della Scuola, 1922–1939," *History of Education Quarterly* 20, no. 1 (Spring 1980): 3–26.

RJW

CARTA DEL LAVORO. This basic document of Fascist corporativism* was issued by the Grand Council on April 21, 1927. It consisted of thirty articles that embodied general guidelines affecting labor relations, public and private initiative, employment, and social welfare programs. The Labor Charter was framed after an extensive process of consultation with leaders of labor unions, employer organizations, and the party. Its provisions reflected the sometimes discordant ideas of these groups and of such Fascist personalities as Giuseppe Bottai,* Alfredo Rocco,* and Edmondo Rossoni. Starting from the premise that "the Italian nation is an organic entity whose goals, needs, and means take precedence over those of private individuals and interest groups," the charter asserted that only officially recognized associations of workers and employers could conclude legally binding labor contracts, that the state could intervene in labor disputes through special labor courts, and that corporations of workers and employers would play a role in organizing and managing production. The vagueness of the charter's language was calculated to reconcile differences of opinion among the leadership. Thus, while the charter guaranteed the sanctity of private property and described private initiative as the most effective means of production, it also declared that the state had ultimate responsibility for protecting the public interest in production and labor relations. The provisions of the charter lacked the force of law, but in 1928 the government was authorized to issue implementing measures, and in 1941 the charter was incorporated into the new civil code. The charter was officially abrogated in 1944, when the institutions of the corporate state were dismantled.

For further reference see: *La Carta del Lavoro illustrata da Giuseppe Bottai* (Rome: Edizioni del Diritto del Lavoro, 1928).

RS

CASATI LAW. Promulgated on November 13, 1859, by Victor Emmanuel II* during the Second War of Independence (see War of 1859*), the Casati Educational Law established an organized system of public instruction for Piedmont and Lombardy.* Following unification, the jurisdiction of the Legge Casati was extended to the entire peninsula.

Named for the King's minister, Gabrio Casati, this first comprehensive educational act provided for a highly centralized Ministry of Public Instruction, which regulated most public instruction and supervised all private education. In the public sector, only military, nautical, and vocational schools and kinder-gartens were exempted from direct rule by the minister. The ministry itself was composed of four general departments, a Central Office of Inspection responsible for site visits to elementary and secondary schools, and an advisory council to the minister, the Superior Council of Public Instruction.

The law also established local school boards on the provincial level which were under the control of the prefect. These provincial bodies were to oversee the activities of municipal school councils, which were popularly elected and charged with the establishment of public elementary schools.

The Legge Casati, although subject to subsequent minor modification, re-mained the only major comprehensive educational law until the passage of the Gentile Reform* in 1923.

For further reference see: Giuseppe Talamo, *La Scuola dalla Legge Casati alla inchiesta del 1864* (Milan: A. Giuffrè, 1960).

RJW

CASTAGNOLA, STEFANO. See **MASSARI-CASTAGNOLA REPORTS**

CASTELFIDARDO. See **LAMORICIÈRE, LOUIS CHRISTOPHE LÉON**

CASTEL GONDOLFO. A small town in Lazio situated eighteen miles southeast of Rome on the shore of Lake Albano, Castel Gondolfo is most famous as the summer residence of the Roman Catholic pontiff. The papal villa itself was given to the popes in 1596 by the Savelli family as payment for a debt and has been a seasonal home for the pontiffs since the seventeenth century.

RJW

CASTELLI, MICHELANGELO. *Risorgimento** statesman and journalist, Castelli was born in Racconigi (Cuneo) on December 4, 1808. His original Mazzinian sentiments were later tempered along the more moderate lines drawn by such men as Massimo D'Azeglio,* Cesare Balbo,* and Terenzio Mamiani della Rovere.* His position was elaborated in works like the *Saggi sull'opinione politica moderata in Italia* [Essays on moderate political opinion in Italy] (1847), which encouraged work within the peninsula's political framework. Soon after, he became a member of Cavour's* circle and director of the journal *Risorgimento*.

Castelli developed some skill as an unofficial mediator in delicate political matters. He helped to negotiate the *connubio** of Cavour and Urbano Rattazzi,* served as liaison between provincial leaders and Turin, was useful in several diplomatic maneuvers, and facilitated relations between the government and the King. His career took him to the Camera, the Senate, and the directorship of the State Archives in the years between 1848 and the 1860s. Castelli died in Turin on August 20, 1875.

JCR

CASTIGLIONE, VIRGINIA VERASIS, COUNTESS DI. This noblewoman, born Virginia Oldoini in Florence on March 22, 1835, played an important role in Italian and European diplomacy in the mid-nineteenth century. A beautiful child, she developed into a voluptuous woman who attracted attention first at the court in Turin and later at the imperial court in France. Married in 1854 to Count Francesco Verasis di Castiglione, the "divine countess" did not love her husband and was not faithful to him. Count Cavour* appreciated her appeal and sent her to Paris to enlist the Emperor Napoleon III* in the cause of Italian unification. The countess succeeded in becoming Napoleon's mistress for a number of years, but her impact on the formation of the Franco-Sardinian alliance against Austria, and the subsequent war for the liberation of northern Italy, remains obsure. In 1860 she fell from the Emperor's favor. Vain and self-centered, this captivating woman did not age gracefully and spent her last years as a recluse in her apartment in the Vendôme. She died in Paris on November 28, 1899.

FJC

CASTIGLIONI, FRANCESCO SAVERIO. See **PIUS VIII**

CATHOLIC ACTION. Originally founded as the Opera dei Congressi* in 1874, the term *Catholic Action* was first employed by Pope Pius X* to apply to the work of the Catholic laity, but it was Pope Pius XI* (1922–38) who elevated the organization to national prominence.

With the dissolution of the Opera dei Congressi in 1903 because of its independent political tones and the "infection" of Modernism,* Pius X placed his own mark upon the Catholic lay movement. In his encyclical *Il fermo proposito* (1905), the Pope relaxed the *non expedit** and established the Unione Popolare, the Unione Economico-Sociale, and the Unione Elettorale as the main organizations of the Catholic Action. The Unione Popolare was to be the directing force of the movement, but it was not invested with overall authority, which was left to each bishop. It was not until the 1915 reforms of Benedict XV* that Catholic Action, under Giuseppe Dalla Torre, regained the tight, centralized leadership of the pre-1903 years.

Active in many social areas, Catholic Action was eclipsed in the political arena with the founding in 1919 of the Catholic Partito Popolare (see Italian Popular Party*) headed by Don Luigi Sturzo,* but regained importance with the election of Achille Ratti as Pius XI in 1922. During the Fascist period, Catholic Action, strongly protected by the Pope, managed to organize Catholic youth associations and became an effective competitor in some areas with official Fascist groups. Although the leadership was rather conservative, the organization harbored many anti-Fascists and served as the nucleus for the reemergence of the Christian Democrats in 1944.

For further reference see: G. De Rosa, *Storia politica dell'Azione Cattolica in Italia*, 2 vols. (Bari: Laterza, 1953–54).

RJW

CATTANEO, CARLO. Cattaneo was born in Milan on June 15, 1801, and died at Castagnola di Lugano, Switzerland, on February 5, 1869. A disciple of Gian Dominico Romagnosi,* he graduated from the University of Pavia in 1824 and pursued a career as a teacher and publicist. From 1833 to 1838 he was a major contributor to Romagnosi's *Annali Universali di Statistica*,* writing on commerce, finance, and agriculture as well as philosophy. In 1839 he founded his own journal, *Il Politecnico*, which became a milestone of Lombard progressive culture. The journal and the *Notizie naturali e civili sulla Lombardia* [Natural and civil information on Lombardy], published in 1844, established his reputation as a scholar whose advice the Hapsburg authorities often sought before 1848.

Although he did not take part in conspiracies, Cattaneo lost confidence in the possibility of major reforms under the Hapsburgs, and during the Five Days of Milan (March 18–22, 1848) he headed the revolutionary war council. His republican and democratic ideas brought him into conflict with the Lombard patricians who had asked for the intervention of Charles Albert of Savoy.* Cattaneo lost to them, but he remained firm in his conviction that Lombardy* should not be annexed to Sardinia and that a revolutionary war (*guerra di popolo*) was needed to prevent the return of the Austrian armies.

On August 6, 1848, when Milan was again occupied by Austrian troops, Cattaneo and his Irish-born wife, Anna Pyne Woodcock, fled to Switzerland. They settled in the small village of Castagnola, near Lugano. Cattaneo taught at the local liceo and formed a partnership with the publisher Alessandro Repetti, owner of the Tipografia Elvetica. With the cooperation of many political exiles, they published the series *I documenti della guerra santa* [The documents of the Holy War] and the *Archivio triennale delle cose d'Italia* [Triennial archive of events in Italy], which remain important sources for the history of the revolutions of 1848.*

While remaining active in the movement for Italian independence, Cattaneo in the 1850s resumed his scholarly pursuits and wrote historical and philosophical essays in which he argued for a federation of democratic republics in Italy. In 1860 he was elected to the first Italian Parliament but chose not to take his seat or return to Italy. Even so, his political ideas remained very influential among progressive intellectuals of the post-*Risorgimento* and among the critics of monarchy and of liberal hegemony in the twentieth century.

CML

CAVALIERI, ENEA. See *RASSEGNA SETTIMANALE, LA*

CAVALLOTTI, FELICE. Playwright, poet, journalist, and consummate orator, known as the "Bard of democracy," Cavallotti was the chief protagonist of non-Socialist radicalism for nearly two decades. He was born on October 6, 1842, in Milan, and died on March 6, 1898, in Rome, as the result of the last of more than thirty duels. When not yet eighteen, he followed Giuseppe Garibaldi* in the liberation of Sicily and Naples (1860), joining him again in the war of 1866.* Cavallotti continued his literary activity, begun as a youth, after his election to parliament in 1873, where he sat at the Extreme Left (see Sinistra, La*). Dissatisfied with the Left's moderate reforms after its rise to power in 1876, he supported Garibaldi in 1879 in the demand for universal suffrage and led the democrats' campaign to this end in 1881. Because the electoral reforms of 1882 stopped far short of this goal, in 1883 he joined the republican Giovanni Bovio* and the Socialist Andrea Costa* in forming the Fascio della Democrazia. In 1890 Cavallotti rallied the whole Extreme Left around a program of advanced socioeconomic reforms (Pact of Rome*). Intolerant of compromise, he was vitriolic in his attacks on Agostino Depretis'* transformism.* Toward Francesco Crispi* he was a veritable nemesis, especially for the former's repressive domestic and adventurous foreign policies.

For further reference see: Raffaele Colapietra, *Felice Cavallotti e la democrazia radicale in Italia* (Brescia: Morcelliana, 1966); Allessandro Galante Garrone, *Felice Cavallotti* (Turin: UTET, 1976).

SS

CAVOUR, CAMILLO BENSO, COUNT DI. This second son of a Piedmontese aristocratic family served as the architect of Italian unification. His diplomacy converted what Metternich* described as a "geographical expression" into the Kingdom of Italy,* while his liberalism assured that the new state would be constitutional and parliamentary.

Born in Turin on August 10, 1810, when the city was under French control, the young Cavour was sponsored in baptism by the Emperor's sister, Pauline Bonaparte, and her husband, Prince Camillo Borghese, after whom he was named. Following his education at home, he entered the Military Academy of Turin and in July 1824 was named a page to Charles Albert,* prince of Carignano and later king of Sardinia (1831–49). Commissioned a second lieutenant in the Corps of Engineers in 1826, he resigned from the army at the end of 1831. The count tended his father's estates, pursued a number of business interests, and served as mayor of Grinzane from 1832 to 1848. He travelled widely in Europe, particularly in France, Switzerland, and Britain, and was impressed with English institutions, the advantages of free trade, and the need for railways in the peninsula. Cavour did not travel much in Italy and never ventured south of Florence. His interests were European rather than Italian, and while he was fluent in French, he always spoke Italian as a language learned later in life.

In 1847 Cavour was one of the leaders urging Charles Albert to grant his people a constitution. Cavour was first elected to the Sardinian parliament in

June 1848. In 1850 he entered the cabinet as minister of agriculture, becoming prime minister in 1852 following his *connubio*,* or political alliance, with Urbano Rattazzi.* During the Crimean War* he allied Sardinia with Britain and France and in 1856 presented the Italian case at the Congress of Paris.* At Plombières (1858) he obtained Napoleon III's* support for a war against Austria (see Plombières Agreement*) and in 1859 provoked that country into declaring war. With the assistance of the French, the National Society (see Società Nazionale Italiana*), and Giuseppe Garibaldi,* the Kingdom of Italy was proclaimad in 1861, and Cavour became its first prime minister. He died shortly afterward, on June 6, 1861, calling for Rome, which was still in papal hands, to become capital of the new Italy and offering to settle the conflict with the Catholic Church on the basis of "a free Church in a free State."

For further reference see: Frank J. Coppa, *Camillo di Cavour* (New York: Twayne Publishers, Inc., 1973); Denis Mack Smith, *Victor Emmanuel, Cavour and the Risorgimento* (London: Oxford University Press, 1971); Rosario Romeo, *Cavour e il suo tempo* (Bari: Laterza, 1969–77); Luigi Chiala, ed., *Lettere edite ed inedite di Camillo di Cavour* (Turin: Roux e Favale, 1882–87).

                                                                                          FJC

CAVOUR, GUSTAVO BENSO, MARQUIS DI. Born in Turin on June 27, 1806, Gustavo Benso was from adolescence inclined to reflective and philosophical studies, in marked contrast to his younger brother Camillo's* propensity for action. He abandoned his career in the foreign service to devote full time to his scholarship. A follower of the classical school of economics, he was acquainted with the works of Smith, Ricardo, and Malthus. In politics he favored a moderate liberalism and championed constitutionalism. Initially his religious sentiments were aconfessional and tended toward deism.

The turning point in his intellectual life occurred as a result of his friendship with the philosopher and priest Antonio Rosmini-Serbati,* whose work seemed to reconcile religion and reason. Under his influence Gustavo came to believe that it was possible for Christianity and progress to march together and concluded that the diffusion of moderate liberal ideas could parallel a Christian renewal in Europe. His optimism was reflected in his *Essai sur la destination de l'homme* [Essay on the destiny of man] (1837–38) and *Des idées communistes et des moyens d'en combattre le développement* [On Communist ideas and the means of combating their development] (1846). Gustavo hoped that Rosmini-Serbati could effect a conversion in his younger brother and draw him back to orthodox Catholicism. This proved impossible, and Gustavo's passage from "liberal philosopher" to "philosophical theologian" made any reconciliation between the brothers impossible.

In 1848 Gustavo was one of the founders and directors of the Turin journal *L'Armonia della Religione colla Civiltà**; he truly believed that religion and civil society could be brought into harmony. As *L'Armonia* became increasingly reactionary under the direction of Father Giacomo Margotti, Gustavo realized that the journal could not effect such a reconciliation and withdrew from it in 1851.

Following the death of his first son in the battle of Goito, Gustavo became increasingly isolated and prone to solitary meditation. He viewed his brother's political program with a mixture of admiration and criticism that earned him the suspicion of clericals and liberals alike. Elected to the Piedmontese Chamber of Deputies in 1849, he served in it until his death in Turin on February 26, 1864.

For further reference see: P. E. Schazmann, "Un carteggio inedito di Gustavo di Cavour," *Archivio Storico della Svizzera Italiana* 16 (1941): 203–23; Bianca Montale, "Gustavo di Cavour e *L'Armonia*," *Rassegna Storica del Risorgimento*, 41 (1954): 456–66.

FJC

CENTRO-SINISTRA. See **CHRISTIAN DEMOCRATIC PARTY**

CERATI, GASPARE. Born in 1690 into a patrician family of Parma, where he received his early education, Cerati entered holy orders. He was appointed rector of the University of Pisa by Gian Gastone De Medici in 1733, a position he held until his death. He occupied an important place among Italian men of letters in the middle years of the eighteenth century and was important in the transformation of the University of Pisa. Among his friends and correspondents were Passionei, Montesquieu, Voltaire, and Ferdinando Galiani.* At Pisa, Cerati was the protector of professors—such as Gualberto De Soria, in philosophy, and Giuseppe Marie Lampredi, in law—who introduced Enlightenment* ideas into the university. Cerati died in 1769.

RBL

CERRUTI, VITTORIO. Cerruti was a professional diplomat specializing in central European affairs before and after World War I.* He was born in Novara on May 25, 1881, and joined Italy's foreign service in 1904. A decade as secretary in the Vienna embassy ended unhappily with war in 1915. Later, Cerruti headed Italian missions in Budapest, 1919–20, Peking, 1921–26, Moscow, 1927–30, Rio de Janeiro, 1930–32, and Berlin, 1932–35. After crossing swords with Major Mario Renzetti, Mussolini's* personal liaison with the Nazis, he was transferred to the Paris embassy from 1935 to 1937. Differences with Galeazzo Ciano* led to his premature retirement in 1938. He died on April 25, 1961, in Novara.

ACas

CGII. See **CONFINDUSTRIA**

CGL. The Confederazione Generale del Lavoro was a national labor union founded in Milan on October 1, 1906, and associated with the Italian Socialist Party (PSI).* Its initial membership of 190,000 grew to 384,000 by 1911 and reached a high point of over 2.2 million in 1920, when it represented about one-half of all organized workers. Its principal constituents were northern industrial workers belonging to trade unions, but it also included less skilled workers, organized locally in chambers of labor, and landless agricultural workers from the Po Valley. In 1920 landless workers made up about one-third of the CGL's membership. The preponderance of skilled trade-union workers gave the CGL a generally moderate reformist orientation that was best exemplified by Rinaldo Rigola, who held the post of secretary-general from 1906 to 1918, and by his successor, Ludovico D'Aragona.* Its relationship with the Socialist Party did not impair its autonomy as a labor organization. Reformist Socialists like Filippo Turati* found their position within the party strengthened by the influence of the CGL, particularly in the years from 1908 to 1912, when the party was most committed to working through parliament. Before World War I* the CGL's centralized structure contributed to orderly collective bargaining and reduced violent confrontations between labor and management. The widespread social turbulence and rising worker expectations of the immediate postwar years posed the greatest challenge for the CGL's reformist leaders, who found themselves increasingly out of step with the rank and file. During the worker occupation of the factories in September 1920, when talk of revolution was in the air, the CGL adopted a cautious policy that helped defuse the threat of violence and put the entire labor movement on the defensive. In 1921 its membership dropped to 1,130,000 under the double blows of economic recession and escalating antilabor violence by Fascist squads. The Fascist seizure of power beginning with the March on Rome* in October 1922 ushered in even harder times for the CGL. Worker discouragement, government repression, and aggressive recruitment by Fascist labor unions further thinned out its ranks. The syndical reforms of 1925–26 deprived non-Fascist labor organizations of the right to conclude legally binding labor contracts, this eliminating the CGL's reason for being. On January 4, 1927, the CGL dissolved itself, and many of its leaders went into exile. An attempt to resurrect the CGL in the region of Campania in 1943–44 failed amid party rivalries.

For further reference see: *La confederazione Italiana del Lavoro negli atti, nei documenti, nei congressi (1906–1926)* (Milan: Edizione Avanti, 1962).

RS

CHABOD, FEDERICO. A historian, from 1955 until his death in Rome on July 14, 1960, he was president of the International Committee of Historical Sciences. Chabod was born in Aosta on February 23, 1901. A prolific scholar who served the historical profession in many capacities, Chabod studied the problem of the state in *Del "Principe" del Niccolò Machiavelli* [On the "Prince" of Niccolò Machiavelli] (1926). His *Per la storia religiosa dello stato di Milano durante il dominio di Carlo V* [The religious history of Milan during the reign of Charles V] (1938) examined ethical-political forces, while *La politica estera italiana dal 1871 al 1896* [Italian foreign policy from 1871 to 1896], Volume 1, *Le premesse* [The antecedents] (1951), underlined the role of men, values, and ideas. An Alpinist, Chabod commanded partisan bands during the Armed Resistance.* In the immediate postwar period he tenaciously defended his Valle d'Aosta against French annexationist designs.

RSC

CHAMBER OF DEPUTIES OF THE REPUBLIC. The Chamber of Deputies is the lower or popular house of the Italian Parliament. Since 1963 the Chamber of Deputies has had 630 members, who are elected for a five-year term by direct universal suffrage. The list system of proportional representation is used for elections, and, since 1975, citizens who have reached eighteen years of age may vote. The Chamber of Deputies exercises full legislative powers, holds the government responsible, supervises the executive branch, enacts constitutional amendments, and acts as an electoral college for various offices. Although it shares its powers equally with the Senate of the Republic,* the Chamber of Deputies is the more influential body.

EER

CHARLES ALBERT OF SAVOY. King of Sardinia from 1831 to 1849, Charles Albert was born in Turin on October 29, 1798. His parents, Charles Albert of Carignano and Maria Cristina of Saxony-Courland, were known at the Savoy court for their liberal political convictions. The young Charles Albert was educated in Paris and Geneva, and he received a commission in the Napoleonic army. In May 1814, he returned to Turin as heir presumptive to the throne of Sardinia. In 1817 he married Maria Teresa, daughter of the grand duke of Tuscany.

Although ambitious and filled with dynastic pride, Charles Albert grew very impatient with the stifling, bigoted atmosphere of the Sardinian court in the last year of Victor Emmanuel I's* reign. Thus, he became close to young aristocrats of liberal persuasion such as Santorre di Santarosa.* Through these friends he was certainly informed of the liberal conspiracy leading to the Piedmontese uprising of March 1821, but the extent of his involvement in the conspiracy itself remains much less clear. When Victor Emmanuel abdicated, however, Charles Albert, as regent, gave in to liberal demands for a constitution modeled after the Spanish one of 1812. His actions were disowned by the new king. Charles Felix,* who banished him to a garrison at Novara. From there Charles Albert moved to his father-in-law's court in Florence. In the summer of 1823 he fought at Trocadero against the Spanish liberals. This action found great favor in the eyes of the conservative Charles Felix, but it outraged Sardinian liberals, who had already felt betrayed by Charles Albert's equivocal behavior in 1821.

Upon his accession to the Sardinian throne on April 22, 1831, Charles Albert surrounded himself with conservative advisers and championed legitimist causes. During the early years of his reign the Sardinian government entered a military alliance with Austria and engaged in relentless persecution of liberals, Carbonari (see Carboneria*), and Mazzinians. Although conservative and paternalistic,

Charles Albert's government was considerably more enlightened than those of his predecessors. Feudal privileges that had survived the French Revolution were abolished, as were many internal barriers to trade and economic development. A major reform in 1837 created uniform legal codes for the heterogeneous parts of the Kingdom of Sardinia.

The unfolding of the Eastern crisis of 1840 caused Charles Albert to change his foreign policy. Perceiving the possibility of expansion in northern Italy, he turned against Austria. In 1848 he reaped the fruits of his anti-Austrian policy. After he had granted a constitution (*Statuto**) to his own subjects and thereby atoned for his conservative rule in the 1830s, Charles Albert was invited to send his army into Lombardy.* The liberal patricians who had led the anti-Austrian insurrection known as the Five Days of Milan regarded him as a logical choice for a new constitutional state in northern Italy. But Charles Albert failed twice to win a decisive military victory over Austria. On March 23, 1849, after his second defeat at the battle of Novara,* he abdicated in favor of his son, Victor Emmanuel II,* and took refuge in Oporto, Portugal, where he died on July 28, 1849.

CML

CHARLES FELIX, KING OF PIEDMONT-SARDINIA. Born in Turin on April 6, 1765, he became king of Piedmont-Sardinia upon the abdication of his brother, Victor Emmanuel I,* in 1821. He had earlier been viceroy of Sardinia. Rigid and reactionary, and hating the changes that had taken place under the French occupation, upon returning to the mainland in 1814 he resided at the court of his nephew in Modena. After Victor Emmanuel's abdication, Charles Albert of Savoy,* the heir presumptive, assumed the regency and conceded a constitution. Charles Felix renounced this concession, had the Austrian army put down the uprising, and exiled the regent to Florence. Returning to Turin in October, Charles Felix prosecuted the rebels, expanded police power, and exacted loyalty oaths. Cracking down on the university, he said, "All the bad are literate, all the good are ignorant." His short reign, however, had positive aspects: he improved the civil administration, favored economic development, supported the Academy of Science, and founded the Egyptian Museum. He died without heirs in Turin on April 27, 1831.

FFA

CHIARAMONTI, BARNABA. See **PIUS VII**

CHRISTIAN DEMOCRACY IN ITALY. Christian Democracy refers to the movement and ideology that inspired the formation of the Italian Popular Party* (Partito Popolare Italiano) in 1919 and the Christian Democratic Party* (Democrazia Cristiana) in 1943. The ideology of Christian Democracy stresses personalism, pluralism, social justice, and structural changes through democratic, legal means. Pope Leo XIII,* Giuseppe Toniolo,* Romolo Murri,* Luigi Sturzo,* and Alcide De Gasperi* figure prominently among its founders.

This movement has its historical roots in the era of Italian unification, when the Kingdom of Italy* was formed at the expense of the Papal States.* In 1875 Italian Catholics formed a national organization, the Opera dei Congressi,* to protect the Church against further aggresssion. These papal defenders saw the Italian bourgeoisie, the founders of the unified Italian state, both as the enemy of Catholicism and the enemy of the working classes. Italian Catholics established a network of labor unions, rural cooperatives, and credit unions using Leo XIII's *Rerum novarum* as a guideline.

The more militant Catholics (the so-called Christian Democrats) were led by Don Romolo Murri, a priest from the Marches, and envisaged a mass party of Catholics. Their program, announced in 1899, included the organization of professions and occupations as "corporations"; the democratization of political life through the referendum, the initiative, and proportional representation; and the protection of small landowners and agricultural workers. Other Italian Catholics, led by the Milanese lawyer Filippo Meda,* viewed the Christian Democrats as extremists; they themselves had no compunction about cooperating with the bourgeois Italian state. Factionalism within the congress movement became so rife that Pope Pius X* dissolved the Opera in 1905. At the same time he modified the long-standing ban on Catholic participation in national politics, granting to Catholics permission to vote whenever anticlerical candidates might be elected in the absence of Catholic votes.

At the end of World War I* Benedict XV* completely rescinded the electoral ban, thereby making possible the organization of an interclass party of Christian Democratic inspiration, called the Italian Popular Party. Led by the Sicilian priest Don Luigi Sturzo, the party called for governmental decentralization, proportional representation, women's suffrage, an elective senate, agrarian reform, social legislation, and disarmament. The Roman Question,* that is, the quarrel between church and state, was not mentioned because Sturzo was opposed to the party's involvement in ecclesiastical matters. He also resisted any confessional designation for the party, even though its ideology was Christian and the bulk of the members were Catholics.

In the elections of 1919 the Popularists won one-fifth of the seats in the Chamber of Deputies, an extraordinary feat for a new party. The party was not united, however, having developed both right and left wings. The right wing placed great emphasis on administrative and financial reforms, while the left wing favored drastic social and economic reforms in the name of "Christian proletarianism." Ideological differences and lack of political sophistication prevented the Popularists from cooperating with other anti-Fascist parties to halt the tide of Fascism.*

Although the Popular Party entered the first Mussolini* ministry (1922), hoping that Mussolini would be won over to constitutionalism once confronted with the reality of government, it soon joined the opposition. The party remained disunited, with many of its right-wing members sympathetic to Fascism. Pope Pius XI,* suspicious of the Popular's Party's socioeconomic program, was also fearful that the party might obstruct the settlement of the Roman Question. Vatican pressure forced Don Sturzo to resign the party secretaryship and go into exile. With Alcide De Gasperi as party secretary, Popularists participated in the Aventine Secession,* a protest movement following the murder of the Socialist deputy Matteotti by Fascist thugs (see Matteotti Crisis*). The Aventine Secession failed to topple Mussolini, and in 1926 parliament declared that the electoral mandate of the Aventine deputies had lapsed. The prefect of Rome decreed the dissolution of the Popular Party.

Despite the conclusion of the Lateran Accords* in 1929, Catholicism and Fascism proved incompatible, as Pius XI indicated in his encyclical *Non abbiamo bisogno.** After Italy entered World War II,* and especially after the newswires carried home monotonous stories of Italian defeats on the field of battle, Catholics came together to revive Christian Democracy and to form a new party that would guide the nation through the postwar trauma. In July 1943 the members of Italian Catholic Action,* the Guelf movement of Lombardy,* and the Federazione Universitaria Cattolica Italiana (FUCI)* (Catholic university students and graduates) joined with former members of the Popular Party to form the Christian Democratic Party. Alcide De Gasperi was elected president of the party's Central Committee. The platform of the new party drew its inspiration from popularism but also strongly mirrored the new political, social, and economic realities. In the elections of 1946 it emerged as the strongest party and retained its political hegemony for the next three decades.

For further reference see: Elisa Carrillo, "Christian Democracy," in Edward Tannenbaum and Emiliana Noether, eds., *Modern Italy* (New York: University Press, 1973); Richard A. Webster, *The Cross and the Fasces* (Stanford: Stanford University Press, 1960).

EC

CHRISTIAN DEMOCRATIC PARTY. This Italian political party (Democrazia Cristiana) of Christian Democratic ideology was founded in July 1943 through a fusion of various pre-World War II groups: the former Popularists, Giorgio La Pira's* circle of Catholic Action* in Florence, the Guelf movement in Lombardy,* and the Federazione Universitaria Cattolica Italiana (FUCI)* (university students and graduates). The first party platform called for regionalism; a bicameral legislature; workers' participation in the management, capitalization, and profits of their companies; agrarian reform; tax reform; protection for unions; the formation of an international organization to maintain peace; and progressive disarmament. The Christian Democratic Party rapidly became a heterogeneous mass party, composed of trade unionists, landless peasants, large and small landowners, industrialists, small shopkeepers, devout Catholics, agnostics, and others.

Alcide De Gasperi,* last head of the Italian Popular Party,* emerged as the leader of the Christian Democratic Party, becoming premier in December 1945 and remaining in this post until August 1953. In April 1948, in the first parliamentary elections to be held under the new republican constitution, the Christian Democrats captured 48 percent of the vote (52 percent including that of their allies), and throughout the postwar period they retained control of the government, though with diminishing strength. In the June 1979 elections the Christian Democrats emerged with 38 percent of the votes. The Italian Communist Party (PCI)* remained their principal rival throughout the postwar period.

The De Gasperi governments were coalitions, with the bulk of the posts held by Christian Democrats and the others going to the Social Democrats (right-wing Socialists), Liberals, and Republicans. The Christian Democrats were divided into factions from the outset, with a center (the strongest) represented by De Gasperi, a right wing with close ties to the Church and especially to Catholic Action, and a fragmented left wing with Giuseppe Dossetti* representing the most influential faction. Under De Gasperi, party positions were generally those of the center "current."

With the passing of De Gasperi, the Christian Democratic Party entered a new era, signaled by the election of Amintore Fanfani* as party secretary at the Fifth National Congress, held in Naples in June 1954. Clerical influence on the party diminished, a development facilitated by the election of Pope John XXIII* in 1958. With the loosening of ties between the Socialists led by Pietro Nenni* and the Communists, a Center-Left coalition became possible. At the Christian Democratic Party congress held in January 1962 in Naples an overwhelming majority voted for an "Opening to the Left"—Centro-Sinistra. The program adopted by the Center-Left coalition called for increased participation by the masses in the exercise of political power, the nationalization of the electrical industry, the democratization of the educational system, the expansion of regional governments, and improvements in agriculture. In foreign affairs, the program reaffirmed Italy's alignment with the West, but pledged to work for an easing of East-West tensions. The two Christian Democrats credited with the birth of Centro-Sinistra were Amintore Fanfani and Aldo Moro.* The latter was assassinated by the Red Brigades* in 1978. He had served as premier from 1963 to 1968 and from 1974 to 1976.

Despite internal stresses and strains and some brief interruptions, Center-Left governments continued to govern Italy through the sixties and seventies. The economy deteriorated, however, and political kidnappings and terrorism increased after the mid-1970s. In 1975 Benigno Zaccagnini, a political ally of Aldo Moro, became party secretary. Zaccagnini was not averse to reaching a programmatic accord with the Communist Party in return for Communist support of the Christian Democratic coalition in parliament. In March 1978 the Communists and three other parties agreed to support the Christian Democratic government of Giulio Andreotti.* Less than six months later, however, the Communists withdrew their support, alleging that the conservative wing of the Christian Democratic Party had come to exercise increasing influence with the government. Among other things, the government's decision to bring Italy into the European Monetary System was opposed by the Communists. In June 1979 parliamentary elections saw the Communists lose ground for the first time since the end of World War II.* The Christian Democrats also lost votes, but only .4 percent since the elections of 1976, as opposed to 4 percent for the Communists.

Between August 1979 and June 1981 coalition governments dominated by Christian Democrats ruled Italy. The revelation that party officials belonged to a secret Masonic lodge—Lodge P-2 (see Freemasonry*)—caused a scandal that brought down the Christian Democratic government of Arnaldo Forlani in May 1981. In June Giovanni Spadolini, a senator and secretary of the small Republican Party,* became head of a five-party coalition government (Christian Democrats, Republicans, Socialists, Social Democrats, Liberals). Although fifteen of the twenty-seven ministerial posts went to the Christian Democrats, Spadolini was the first premier since World War II not of their ranks.

For further reference see: Elisa Carrillo, "Christian Democracy," in *Modern Italy*, ed. Edward Tannenbaum and Emiliana P. Noether (New York: New York University Press, 1974); Giuseppe Mammarella, *Italy after Fascism* (Notre Dame: University of Notre Dame Press, 1965).

EC

CIALDINO, ENRICO, DUKE DI GAETA. This general, political figure, and diplomat was born in the Duchy of Modena on August 10, 1811. He fought in the revolutions of 1831,* then in Spain and Portugal. In 1848 he reentered Italy and took part in the war against Austria, fighting in the battle of Novara.* In 1855 he commanded a brigade in the Crimean War.* During the Italian War of Liberation (see War of 1859*) he raised the Alpine brigade, and in 1860 he commanded the troops besieging Gaeta.* Following unification he directed the suppression of brigandage* in the South. He fought in the war of 1866* against Austria, and with Alphonso La Marmora* compromised on the strategy that led to the Italian defeats. The following year (1867) he stopped Giuseppe Garibaldi* at Aspromonte* and prevented his March on Rome.* Subsequently Cialdini served as Italian ambassador to Paris (1876–82). He died on September 8, 1892.

FJC

CIANO, COSTANZO. This naval hero of World War I* and Fascist hierarch was born in Livorno on August 30, 1876, and died in Ponte a Moriano on June 27, 1939. Ciano gained fame through a series of daring sea raids and took part in Gabriele D'Annunzio's* Fiume* adventure. A conservative monarchist, he was elected as a Fascist deputy in 1921, participated in the March on Rome,* was appointed undersecretary of the merchant marine in Mussolini's* first cabinet, and later became minister of posts and communications (1924–34) and president of the Chamber of Fasces and Corporations (1934–39).

MFL

CIANO, GALEAZZO. Foreign minister and hierarch in the Fascist government, Galeazzo Ciano was regarded as the heir apparent to Mussolini,* his father-in-law. He was the author of a diary that has become an important source on the period 1935 to 1943. Born on March 18, 1903, in Livorno, the son of naval hero Costanzo Ciano,* Galeazzo spent his early years in Livorno and other seaports, completing his university education in law in Rome in 1925. During his university years, Ciano dabbled in journalism, playwriting, and criticism. He was only minimally involved in the Fascist movement.

In 1925 Ciano entered the diplomatic service, working first in the cipher section of the ministry and in low-level posts in South America and the Orient before returning to Rome in a post at the Holy See in 1930. There, on April 24, 1930, he married Edda, Mussolini's eldest child. Ciano was subsequently restationed and distinguished himself in higher-level posts in Shanghai and Peking.

Mussolini recalled Ciano in 1933 to become head of his newly formed press office, which Ciano's ambition and interest in journalism upgraded to an undersecretariat (1934) and later to the Ministry of Press and Propaganda (1935), always with himself as head. Ciano left the ministry only to enter the Ethiopian War as a bomber pilot, a means to better his Fascist credentials. On July 9, 1936, Ciano was named foreign minister, an appointment criticized because of his egomania, indiscretion, dearth of experience, and too-rapid rise. The first years of his tenure were marked by emulation of Mussolini and his policies, concentration of power in the minister and his "gabinetto," removal of career diplomats from influence, and a diplomacy based upon Ciano's personality and friendships.

Among those policies in which Ciano played a significant role were the Italian intervention in the Spanish Civil War,* the takeover of Albania,* and continuing efforts to dismember Yugoslavia. Ciano's independent influence reached its zenith in the summer of 1939 when he successfully promoted Italian nonbelligerency in World War II.* German strength and Ciano's personal weaknesses ended nonintervention and limited Ciano's influence, which was ultimately destroyed by the debacle of the Italian invasion of Greece ("Ciano's War") in 1940–41.

Ciano remained figurehead foreign minister until February 5, 1943, when he was demoted to ambassador to the Holy See. There he came into contact with many conspirators seeking the overthrow of Mussolini, and at the Grand Council meeting of July 25, 1943, he voted for Dino Grandi's* resolution censuring Mussolini. For that action, Ciano was tried and executed as a traitor to the regime on January 11, 1944, in Verona, at German insistence and Mussolini's behest.

For further reference see: Galeazzo Ciano, *Diario 1939–1943* (Milan: Rizzoli, 1946); Giordano Bruno Guerri, *Galeazzo Ciano: Una vita 1903/1944* (Milan: Casa Editrice Valentino Bompiani e C., 1979).

MFL

CICERUACCHIO. See **BRUNETTI, ANGELO**

CIRCOLO COSTITUZIONALE. See **JACOBINS**

CISALPINE REPUBLIC. This was a satellite state created by Napoleon I* in northern Italy. Founded in June 1797, the Cisalpine Republic included Lombardy,* Modena, the Legations,* and the Valtelline. Its constitution, modeled on the French one of 1795, provided for a plural executive, the Directory, and an elected assembly, the Grand Council. Milan was the capital. Never more than a facade for French domination and exploitation, it had no true independence and enjoyed little public support. In 1802 Napoleon merged it with the Italian Republic which he had created.

AJR

CIVILTÀ CATTOLICA, LA. A semi-official journal of the Vatican under the direction of the Society of Jesus, *La Civiltà Cattolica* was founded by Carlo M. Curci* in April 1850. Its original spirit was legitimist and anti-*Risorgimento*, and it was no accident that it was first established in Naples, the capital city of the Bourbon Kingdom of the Two Sicilies.* Continuing uninterrupted publication from 1850 to 1870, the Jesuit Fathers suspended *La Civiltà*, then headquartered in Rome, in 1870 to protest the seizure of Rome by Italian troops. Later that year the editors moved its offices to Florence, refusing to remain in a nonpapal Rome. Only in 1888 did *La Civiltà* return to the Eternal City, taking offices in the Via di Ripetta, where it remains to this day. Many of the most famous Italian Jesuits have written for and edited *La Civiltà*, including Luigi Taparelli D'Azeglio,* Antonio Bresciani, and Enrico Rossi. *La Civiltà* has always exhibited intense loyalty to the Vatican, thus earning the right to be considered a mouthpiece for the popes.

RJW

CLARENDON, GEORGE WILLIAM FREDERICK VILLIERS, EARL OF. Born in London on January 12, 1800, Clarendon entered the British diplomatic service in 1820 as attaché at St. Petersburg and later served with distinction as envoy to Madrid during the Carlist War. In 1838 he succeeded his uncle as fourth earl of Clarendon. Enlightened in his political views, he held posts in two Whig cabinets before accepting the Foreign Office in Aberdeen's coalition government in 1853. For all his vaunted knowledge of European politics, however, Clarendon lacked the comprehensive vision of a Castlereagh or the personal dynamism of a Palmerston, and his accomplishments as foreign secretary were meager. His vacillation in the face of Russia's occupation of the Danubian Principalities in 1853–54 helped bring Britain into the Crimean War.* Despite his memorable speech at the Congress of Paris* denouncing Austria's presence in Italy, he remained dubious of British efforts in favor of Italian independence, especially during the years 1859–60. He served twice more as foreign secretary, in 1865–66 and 1868–70, and died in office on June 27, 1870, shortly before the Franco-Prussian War ushered in a new Europe he would have found unrecognizable.

JWB

CLEMENCEAU, GEORGES. French premier from 1906 to 1909 and from 1917 to 1920, Georges Clemenceau (1841–1929) was an Italophobe, but his perception of French interests determined his policy toward Italy at the Paris Peace Conference.* In 1914 he hoped for immediate Italian entry into World War I*; in 1918 he condemned Italian delay in launching a major offensive. In April 1919 Clemenceau acquiesced in Woodrow Wilson's obduracy against any compromise with Italian leaders over Fiume.* When hard-pressed by the American president, Clemenceau chose the United States over Italy.

For further reference see: J.B. Duroselle, "Clemenceau et l'Italie," in *La France et l'Italie pendant la première guerre mondiale* (Grenoble: Presses Universitaires de Grenoble, 1976), pp. 492–511.

JB

CLN. Modeled on the French Conseil de la Résistance and the Yugoslav National Liberation Front, the Italian Committees of National Liberation (CLN) led the Armed Resistance* movement from 1943 to 1945. The committees were based on the principles of cooperation and unity of purpose common to the five anti-Fascist parties that created them: the Italian Communist Party (PCI),* the Italian Socialist Party (PSI),* the Action Party,* the Christian Democratic Party,* and the Liberal Party.* The first committee was formed in Rome in September 1943 and included outstanding veterans of the anti-Fascist movement.

Despite profound differences in their political orientations, the five parties were able to agree that united action on all fronts was the only way anti-Fascist Italians could contribute decisively to the final defeat of Fascism* and Nazism. But many divisive issues presented themselves during the course of the Resistance. The character and function of the partisan movement, relations with the Allied governments, and the institutional structure of postwar Italy were among the questions that strained the unity of the CLN. Yet this unity survived until the end of the war, due in large part to the moderating role played by two of Italy's most skillful political tacticians, the Communist Palmiro Togliatti* and the Christian Democrat and future prime minister, Alcide De Gasperi.*

For further reference see: Guido Quazza, Leo Valiani, and Edoardo Volterra,

Il governo dei C.L.N.—Atti del Convegno dei Comitati di Liberazione Nazionale a Torino 9–10 ottobre 1965 (Turin: G. Giappichelli, 1966).

FR

CLNAI. Beginning in November 1943, the work of the Committees of National Liberation in the regions of Liguria, Piedmont, Lombardy,* Venetia, and Emilia was coordinated by a central committee in Milan that on January 31, 1944, assumed the name Comitato di Liberazione Nazionale per l'Alta Italia (Committee of National Liberation for Northern Italy). The CLNAI directed the political and military activities of the Italian Armed Resistance* movement. Among its leading members were the Communist Luigi Longo,* the Liberal Filippo Jacini, the Socialist Alessandro Pertini,* the Actionist Feruccio Parri,* the Christian Democrat Achille Marazza, and the Liberal Alfredo Pizzoni.

FR

COCCHI, ANTONIO. Cocchi was a Florentine doctor (1695–1758) whose career was indicative of the early Enlightenment* in Tuscany. He travelled as a young man to France, Holland, and England, maintained a correspondence with English and Dutch scientists, and was associated during the 1730s with the group involved with the first Masonic lodge in Florence. He taught medicine at Pisa and Florence, became director of the Ospedale di Santa Maria Nuova, wrote treatises on medicine, natural history, and English and French literature, and was one of the founders of the Società Botanica Fiorentina. His diary, which remains unpublished, contains much of interest on his times.

RBL

CODIGNOLA, ERNESTO. Ernesto Codignola was born in Genoa on June 23, 1885. Founder of the Fascio di Educazione Nazionale (1919), a teachers' organization characterized by its nationalist and idealist sentiments, Codignola led the post–World War I opposition to the "democratic" schools of the liberal period. He strongly believed in a meritocratic educational system which would weed out the lower classes, who were, in his view, unfit for advanced schooling. A supporter of Giovanni Gentile* and Fascism,* Codignola eventually voiced reservations concerning the activities of the Opera Nazionale Balilla,* which he ridiculed as a distraction to serious-minded students and useless as a tool of political education. He preferred to rely on the school curricula to train loyal citizens of Fascist Italy. A scholar of some repute, he founded a number of journals, such as *Levana* (1922–28), *La Nuova Scuola Italiana* (1923–38), and *Scuola e Città* (1950–). He died in Florence in 1965.

RJW

COLAJANNI, NAPOLEONE. This follower of Giuseppe Garibaldi* and Giuseppe Mazzini,* instrumental in provoking the scandal of the Banca Romana,* was born in Castrogiovanni (today Enna) on April 27, 1847. In 1860, when only thirteen, he attempted to join the Red Shirts. A friend of the family brought him back home. He did manage to fight with Garibaldi at Aspromonte* and during the war of 1866* fought under him in the Trentino.* Afterward he studied medicine at the University of Naples where, along with Edoardo Pantano and Giorgio Imbriani, he got into difficulty because of his republican agitation. In 1871, after receiving his degree in medicine, he left for South America, where he practiced his profession for a number of years.

Intensely interested in politics, he was elected to the Chamber from Caltanisetta in 1890. A convinced federalist and a champion of honesty in government, in 1892 he exposed the irregularities in the Banca Romana and the political cover-up which led to the collapse of the first government of Giovanni Giolitti* (1893). He reflected on these events in his volume *Banche e parlamento* [Banks and parliament]. Subsequently he was named professor of statistics at the University of Naples. Although he favored an expansionist democracy, he condemned military conquests and adventures. He therefore opposed the Libyan War (see Ouchy, Treaty of*) but favored intervention in World War I.* He died in Castrogiovanni on September 2, 1921.

FJC

COLONNA DI CESARÒ, GIOVANNI ANTONIO. Giovanni Antonio Colonna di Cesarò, who was born in Rome in 1878 and died there in 1940, was a political leader who prominently supported the war against Austria in 1914–15. He was a member of the wartime Fascio Parlamentare and a founder of the Social Democracy Party in the post-1918 period. He was minister of posts in the 1922 government of Luigi Facta* and a member of Mussolini's* first cabinet (1922–24). He broke with Fascism* during the Matteotti Crisis* of June 1924 and joined the Aventine Secession.* His political career ended in 1926 with the suppression of the opposition to the Fascist regime.

AJD

COMIT. See **BANCA COMMERCIALE ITALIANA**

COMITATO DI LIBERAZIONE NAZIONALE. See **CLN**

COMITATO DI LIBERAZIONE NAZIONALE PER L'ALTA ITALIA. See **CLNAI**

COMMON MAN'S MOVEMENT. L'Uomo Qualunque or Common Man's movement was an Italian political movement founded by Guglielmo Giannini in 1945. Inspired by a newspaper of the same name, it made its appeal to the "good sense" of the middle classes, criticized political professionalism, and honored the past regime, while defaming the Armed Resistance.* It came into existence as a protest against the inaction of the Christian Democratic government and was quickly infiltrated by neo-Fascists. It disintegrated after the 1948 elections. The MSI* subsequently absorbed much of its membership.

WR

COMMUNIST PARTY. See **ITALIAN COMMUNIST PARTY (PCI)**

COMPAGNA. This title applied to a variety of women's publications after 1922. It first appeared in March 1922 as an Italian Communist Party (PCI)* publication. Beginning in July and August of 1944 women's groups of the Italian Socialist Party (PSI)* in Piedmont, Lombardy,* and Emilia-Romagna published newssheets titled variously *Compagna* or *La Compagna* for the purpose of mobilizing women in Armed Resistance* activities. The title continued to be used for a Socialist women's publication after 1945.

MJS

COMPROMESSO STORICO. See **ANDREOTTI, GIULIO** and **MORO, ALDO**

CONCENTRAZIONE ANTIFASCISTA. The Concentrazione Antifascista was an interparty alliance founded in Nérac, France, in March 1927, on the initiative of Luigi Campolonghi and Alceste De Ambris.* It was essentially a coalition of left-wing republicans, labor unions, and Socialists belonging to the Italian Socialist Party (PSI),* the Socialist Party of Italian Workers, the Italian Republican Party,* the General Confederation of Labor (CGL*), and the Italian League of the Rights of Man. In 1931 the Justice and Liberty movement* also joined the alliance. The Socialist Claudio Treves* was managing editor of the Concentrazione's principal organ, *La Libertà*, until his death in 1933.

Through its weekly newspaper and by means of rallies and its organizational network, the Concentrazione documented Fascist crimes, raised money to help the victims of Fascist persecution, and tried to create links in Italy with potential or already existing centers of anti-Fascist activity. Among the Concentrazione's most consistent campaigns was its espousal of European unity based on the principles of liberalism, federalism, and democracy. *La Libertà* also waged an effective campaign against the Lateran Accords* of February 11, 1929, between the Italian state and the Holy See. Disputes over tactical and ideological questions led to the demise of *La Libertà* and to the dissolution of the Concentrazione in May 1934.

For further reference see: Santi Fedele, *Storia della Concentrazione Antifascista 1927/1934* (Milan: Feltrinelli, 1976).

FR

CONCILIATORE, IL. This weekly newspaper was published in Milan between September 3, 1818, and October 17, 1819. The title signifies its intention of accommodating any school of thought that would contribute to the progress of

Italian culture. In literary matters, however, it was a strong defender of romanticism. Its founders were the counts Luigi Porro Lambertenghi and Federico
Confalonieri.* Silvio Pellico,* a revolutionary romantic, was its editor. As part
of his circle, Vincenzo Monti, Giovanni Berchet, and Ugo Foscolo,* among
others, contributed to *Il Conciliatore*. At first devoted almost exclusively to
foreign literature, the newspaper increasingly involved itself with Italian themes
and during its short existence became the vehicle around which were gathered
the enemies of Austrian hegemony.

Because of Austrian censorship, it was necessary to avoid overtly political
themes. Nevertheless, in the late summer of 1819 censorship increased, and in
early October Pellico was warned about the too explicitly political tone of *Il
Conciliatore*. Finding it impossible to continue, Pellico suspended publication
on October 17, 1819. The demise of *Il Conciliatore* left a vacuum that handi-
capped the work of reform up to 1848. The moderate liberals, faced with obstacles
to public intellectual activity, then turned to conspiracy.

FFA

CONCORDAT UNDER THE REPUBLIC. This agreement was one of three
documents constituting the Lateran Accords* signed on February 11, 1929, which
brought to an end the historic Roman Question.* With the signing of the accords
reconciliation was achieved between the Italian government and the Vatican,
and the Concordat regularized relations between church and state. The Concordat
consists of forty-five articles which establish a *modus vivendi* of unique significance in church-state relations. It provides for the teaching of Catholic doctrine
in public schools and the protection of the Catholic clergy, conferring upon the
Roman Catholic Church the authority to dissolve the matrimonial bond. Together
its stipulations grant the Roman Catholic Church a privileged position in Italy.

To everyone's surprise, in March 1947 the Constituent Assembly,* responding
to political stimuli, included the accords, and hence the Concordat, in the new
constitution. Thus, Article 7 affirms that "the State and the Catholic Church
are...independent and sovereign. Their relations are regulated by the Lateran
Pacts." Under the constitution of the Republic of Italy, the Concordat enjoys
the force of a regulatory norm since the provisions of the constitution form the
basic law of the state.

From the first, some were dissatisfied with this decision. The *aggiornamento*
("bringing up to date") in the Church and the "Opening to the Left" in politics
prompted the call for a revision of the accords, especially of the controversial
Concordat. After much delay, in 1968 Italy and the Holy See opened negotiations.
To date no revision has been agreed upon. The impasse involves two crucial
issues: the sacramental character of matrimony, and religious instruction in the
public schools. In the interim, the state has unilaterally approved a limited divorce
law despite the opposition of the Vatican.

For further reference see: Italy. Assemblea Constituente, *Atti 1946–1948*, vol. 3 (March 4, 1947–April 15, 1947); Senato della Repubblica, *Elementi di documentazione sulla revisione del concordato* (May 1980).

PVB

CONFALONIERI, FEDERICO. Confalonieri, a Lombard patrician and patriot, was born in 1785. His liberal views were shaped under the Napoleonic Kingdom of Italy, but his first political action came in April 1814, when he and other Lombard nobles opposed Prince Eugene de Beauharnais, Napoleon's viceroy in the Kingdom of Italy who considered French above Italian interests. This was followed by his condemnation of the Vienna settlement, which attached Lombardy* to Austria. Travel within Italy (1815–16) led to a widening of his liberal friendships, especially with the Tuscan Gino Capponi.* Trips in France and England resulted in his advocacy of an eclectic group of social and economic reforms: gas illumination, mechanization of the textile industry, steamship navigation of the Po, the institution of the Lancastrian school system, and the establishment of a Milanese Athenaeum. Many of these ideas were presented in the pages of *Il Conciliatore*,* with which he was associated. His identification with romanticism was political, since classicism was supported by the Austrian government. His Carbonari contacts (see Carboneria*) and his involvement with Charles Albert of Savoy* and the 1821 Piedmontese revolution (see Revolutions of 1820–21*), with aspirations for a provisional government in Lombardy, led to his arrest on December 13, 1821. In his *Memorie politiche* [Political memoirs] he tells of his trial, the commutation of the death sentence to life imprisonment, and the persistence of his wife, Teresa Casati, in securing his release in 1835. Police surveillance during his brief stays in Milan enforced a life of political restraints, while ill health plagued his peregrinations in western Europe and the Near East until his death in Switzerland in 1846.

For further reference see: Federico Confalonieri, *Memorie e lettere*, ed. G. Casati (Milan: Ulrico Hoepli, 1889); Federico Confalonieri, *Carteggio*, ed. G. Gallavresi (Milan: Tipo-litografia Ripalta, 1910–13).   MSM

CONFEDERAZIONE AGRARIA. This is the common designation for the Confederazione Generale dell'Agricoltura, the national association of large landowners founded in Bologna in November 1909. In the anticipation of its founders, the Confederazione was to be the nucleus of a conservative agrarian party, but that goal was never achieved. Instead, the Confederazione became an influential lobby composed of local agrarian associations (*agrarie*) located primarily in the Romagna,* Piedmont, and Apulia. Giolittian in orientation, the Confederazione took up the fight against Socialist and Catholic leagues of peasant workers. It remained aloof from the Fascist movement after 1918, thereby alienating pro-Fascist landowners, who established the rival Federazione Italiana Sindacati Agricoltori Fascisti, which in February 1924 took over and absorbed the Confederazione Agraria. An independent Confederazione Generale dell'Agricoltura Italiana was reconstituted after World War II.*

RS

CONFEDERAZIONE GENERALE DEL LAVORO. See **CGL**

CONFEDERAZIONE GENERALE DELL'INDUSTRIA ITALIANA. See **CONFINDUSTRIA**

CONFINDUSTRIA. This national industrial organization was established in 1910 but was relaunched on a broader organizational basis on April 8, 1919. It then assumed the task of forming a united business front in the face of mounting social turmoil and the economic crisis resulting from the conversion to peacetime production. Although Confindustria claimed to represent all industrial interests, its protectionist views and its stand in favor of currency revaluation alienated the textile industry and other light industries oriented toward exports. Its membership consists of trade and regional associations of industrialists rather than individuals or firms. Confindustria's administration is divided into a syndical section, which formulates general policies for dealing with organized labor, and an economic section, which seeks to influence government policy in matters of trade, taxation, spending, credit, and money supply. The activities of the two sections are coordinated by a general assembly representing all member associations, a much smaller executive committee, and a presidency. The presidents of Confindustria have generally been industrialists of national prominence, including Ettore Conti, Antonio Stefano Benni, Alberto Pirelli,* Giuseppe Volpi,* Angelo Costa, and Gianni Agnelli. Gino Olivetti (not related to the manufacturers of office machines), who held the post of secretary-general for Confindustria's inception until 1934, was primarily responsible for Confindustria's organizational success.

With the emergence of the Fascist regime, Confindustria attained a representational monopoly over industrial firms which made it the most influential pressure group in the country. The syndical and corporative reforms enacted between 1925 and 1934 made it an integral part of the machinery of government, but Fascist officials seldom interfered in its internal affairs. Confindustria officials, in turn, seldom took a position on purely political questions, particularly in the area of foreign affairs. But they did try, often successfully, to limit the scope and cost of social programs and to uphold the principle of managerial autonomy. The abolition of corporative agencies in 1944 reduced Confindustria to the status of a still powerful but wholly private pressure group.

For further reference see: Roland Sarti, *Fascism and the Industrial Leadership in Italy, 1919–1940* (Berkeley: University of California Press, 1971).

RS

CONGRESS OF BERLIN. See **BERLIN, CONGRESS OF, ITALY AT**

CONGRESS OF PARIS. See PARIS, CONGRESS OF

CONGRESS OF VIENNA. See VIENNA, CONGRESS OF

CONNUBIO. This term was given to the marriage fashioned in January–February 1852 between the liberal Cavour* and the democratic Left-Center guided by Urbano Rattazzi.* Often traced to fears of potentially reactionary consequences developing in Italy in the wake of Louis Napoleon's *coup d'état* (December 1851), the *connubio* stimulated creation of a new "centrist" party. It also aided Cavour's rise to power. The arrangement became public during the debate concerning the new and more restrictive press law supported by the government of Massimo D'Azeglio,* of which Cavour was a part. Count Ottavio di Revel (see Thaon di Revel, Ottavio*) baptized the alliance with the name by which it has subsequently been known.

JCR

CONSALVI, ERCOLE. Papal secretary of state from 1800 to 1823, Consalvi was born in Rome on June 8, 1757. He never took holy orders, remaining a deacon; nonetheless, he rose rapidly in the Roman Curia. As secretary of the conclave of 1800, he played a leading role in promoting the election of Pope Pius VII,* who made him a cardinal and secretary of state. An open-minded realist, he saw that the French Revolution had drastically transformed European society and that the papacy must adapt if it hoped to survive. He dedicated the rest of his life to this process. He negotiated a series of concordats, beginning with that of 1801 with Napoleon I,* which placed church-state relations on a more modern basis and marked a notable advance for papal authority. After 1804 he was preoccupied by the demands of Napoleon for papal acceptance of his claims to authority over the Church and papal support in his conflict with England. Angered by Consalvi's resistance, Napoleon first forced his resignation, in 1806, and then imprisoned him in 1809. Released at Napoleon's fall in 1814, his first task was to represent Rome at the Congress of Vienna,* where he secured the restoration of virtually all the Papal States.* On his return to Rome, he turned to reforming the Papal States, where popular discontent was growing rapidly: years of Napoleonic rule had accustomed the people to efficient secular government, and they resented the revival of the inefficient ecclesiastical regime. In 1816 he drew up a reform plan which would have modernized the administration and admitted laymen to it in large numbers; unfortunately, the reactionary faction at Rome, the *Zelanti*,* were able to prevent most of his reforms from going into effect. In international affairs, he saw cooperation with Austria as the best hope of protection for the Papal States against revolution or invasion. However, after 1820 Metternich* sought to increase Austrian control over Italy and Consalvi took the lead in defeating his plans. The death of Pius VII in 1823 and the election of the *Zelante* Pope Leo XII* marked the end of Consalvi's influence. He died at Anzio on January 25, 1824.

For further reference see: Ercole Consalvi, *Memorie*, ed. Mario Naselli Rocca di Corneliano (Rome: Signorelli, 1950); Alan J. Reinerman, *Austria and the Papacy in the Age of Metternich. Volume 1: 1809–1830* (Washington, D.C.: Catholic University of America Press, 1979).

AJR

CONSTITUENT ASSEMBLY OF 1946. This representative body drafted and adopted the constitution of the Italian Republic. The Constituent Assembly was composed of 556 deputies who were elected on June 2, 1946, in the country's first postwar national election. Although the Christian Democratic,* Italian Socialist,* and Italian Communist* parties controlled 75 percent of the seats, smaller parties were also influential. The assembly completed its work on December 22, 1947, when by a vote of 453 to 62 it adopted the constitution, which went into effect on January 1, 1948. The assembly also elected Senator Enrico De Nicola* as the provisional president of the Republic on June 28, 1946, and it ratified the Italian Peace Treaty on July 31, 1947.

EER

CONSTITUTION OF 1948. The fundamental law of the Italian Republic, the constitution was adopted by the Constituent Assembly of 1946* on December 22, 1947, and went into effect on January 1, 1948. Constructed by a multiparty assembly, the constitution reflects liberal, socialist, and Catholic influences and the consequent marks of compromise and self-contradiction. The constitution incorporates the principles of popular sovereignty, cabinet responsibilty to parliament, bicameralism, separation of powers, judicial review of legislation, and decentralization of authority. Italy is proclaimed to be a "democratic Republic founded on work." Citizens are guaranteed a large number of political and civil liberties together with an equal number of social and economic rights. Both private property and public ownership of productive property are recognized. The Lateran Accords* of 1929 that protected the Catholic Church's interests were fully incorporated into the system. Innovations from the pre-Fascist Albertine *Statuto** include: republicanism, a popularly elected Senate,* a Constitutional Court* exercising the power of judicial review of legislation, regional governments, a Superior Council of the Judiciary to protect the independence of judges, and popular initiative and referendum. There were extensive delays by the parliament in implementing some of the most important organs established by the constitution.

For further reference see: Mauro Cappelletti, John Henry Newman, and Joseph M. Perillo, *The Italian Legal System* (Stanford, Calif.: Stanford University Press, 1967); John Clarke Adams and Paolo Barile, *The Government of Republican Italy*, 3rd ed. (Boston: Houghton Mifflin, 1972).

EER

CONSTITUTIONAL COURT. This judicial body determines the constitutionality of national and regional laws and decrees in the Italian Republic. The court also resolves jurisdictional disputes between major state organs, between the state and the regions, and between regions. It determines the admissibility of referendum proposals and hears impeachment cases against the president of the Republic* and cabinet ministers. The court is composed of fifteen judges, one-third selected by the president of the Republic, one-third by parliament in joint session, and one-third by the highest ordinary and administrative courts. Judges serve for nine years (originally twelve) and are not immediately eligible for reappointment. Since its establishment in 1956, the court has been active in protecting civil liberties and the rights of regions.

EER

CONTARINI, SALVATORE. Contarini was an archetypal and influential Italian career diplomat during Fascism's* rise to power. Born in Palermo on August 6, 1867, he joined the Foreign Ministry in 1891, rising through posts almost exclusively in Rome to become its secretary-general in 1920. By dint of this office and his own forceful personality he was instrumental in persuading most of Italy's diplomatic corps to serve Mussolini* after 1922. Contarini shared the Nationalists' ambition of raising Italy's international stature and hoped to employ Fascism to this end. He resigned, however, in 1926, more over personal than political differences with the Duce. Although a member of the Senate and the Council of State, he played no further public role. He died in Rome on September 17, 1945.

ACas

CONTRI, VALENTINO. See **JACOBINS**

COPPINO, MICHELE. See **COPPINO LAW**

COPPINO LAW. This educational law of 1877 established free and compulsory schooling for children in Italy between the ages of six and nine. It also abolished compulsory religious teaching in elementary schools, and was part of the reform movement of the government of Agostino Depretis.* Neglect of enforcement, however, made the law only partially effective. It was named for Michele Coppino, minister of education.

WR

COPPOLA, FRANCESCO. A Fascist official and political writer of nationalist orientation, Coppola was born in Naples on September 27, 1878. Elected to the first central committee of the Italian Nationalist Association* in 1910, he was an incorrigible reactionary and was accused of anti-Semitism. Coppola volunteered to fight in World War I.* His *La pace coatta* [The forced peace] (1929) interpreted that conflict in Darwinian terms. Coppola served on the Fascist state's Commission of Eighteen for the revamping of the liberal regime. In 1923 and 1925 he headed the Italian delegation to the Geneva disarmament conference.

He was an original member of the Fascist-sponsored Italian Academy. From 1929 to 1939 Coppola was professor of diplomatic history at the University of Perugia. He died in Anacapri in 1957.

RSC

CORFU CRISIS. This incident was an early instance of Fascist international belligerence. Ostensibly as a guarantee of reparation for the murder of an Italian general who was delimiting the Greek-Albanian frontier near Janina, an Italian naval squadron seized the Greek island of Corfu on August 31, 1923. Its strategic location off the Albanian coast and at the mouth of the Adriatic served Italian nationalist interests. Heaviest causalties during the operation were sustained by Armenian refugees sheltered on Corfu by the League of Nations. Greece's appeal for League action was countered by Mussolini's* threat to withdraw Italy from the Geneva organization. Instead, the dispute was mediated by the Allied Conference of Ambassadors; Athens was constrained to pay a 50 million lire indemnity for the Janina crime—in effect, a price for the return of Corfu. Nevertheless, a veiled threat to use the British navy to enforce evacuation was also needed before Italian forces left the island on September 29. In pitting Fascist Italy against the League and Britain, the Corfu incident anticipated the Ethiopian crisis (see Ethiopia*).

ACas

CORPORATIVISM. This form of sociopolitical organization based public life on occupational groupings and was intended to avoid the alleged excesses of liberal individualism and class-based socialism. Corporativism has been important in Catholic social thought, but it was especially significant in Italian Fascism,* apparently offering the institutional alternative to parliamentary liberalism that many Fascists sought.

Fascist corporativism grew out of syndicalism* and nationalism, but since these two movements were opposed in important respects there was ambiguity about the purpose of Fascist corporativism—and about how it was to work. Some, like Sergio Panunzio* from the syndicalist Left, viewed corporativism as the basis for more constant popular involvement in public life; others, like Alfredo Rocco* from the nationalist Right, saw corporativism as a way of extending the sovereignty of the state over private associations, especially trade unions, left unchecked under liberalism. However, all Fascist corporativists were seeking to enhance production, to maximize technical competence in public life, and to minimize the purely political sphere of elections and politicians.

Fascism began to commit itself to a corporativist direction in August 1924, when Mussolini* was searching for a new *raison d'être* during the Matteotti Crisis.* With convinced corporativists continuing to push, a series of innovations followed on a piecemeal basis, from the trade union law of 1926 to the Chamber of Fasces and Corporations of 1939. Fascist corporativists never considered the system finished, and they were often critical of the bureaucratic and party interference that undermined the corporative institutions in practice. Partly because Mussolini lacked confidence in the system, the corporations established in 1934 were never given broad powers. Nevertheless, corporativism served the regime as a myth in the 1930s, affording the illusion that Fascism offered a depression-ridden world a revolutionary alternative to outmoded liberalism and misguided communism.

For further reference see: David D. Roberts, *The Syndicalist Tradition and Italian Fascism* (Chapel Hill: University of North Carolina Press, 1979); Bruno Uva, *La nascità dello stato corporativo e sindacale fascista* (Assisi and Rome: Beniamino Carucci, n.d.).

DDR

CORPO VOLONTARI DELLA LIBERTÀ. See **CVL**

CORRADINI, ENRICO. Enrico Corradini, leader of the Italian nationalist movement, was born at Sarminiatello, near Florence, on July 20, 1865. He was a leader of the Italian Nationalist Association* from its birth on December 4, 1910, until its fusion with Fascism* on March 1923. Corradini taught Italian literature in high school, wrote many plays, novels, and short stories, and co-founded and directed several Florentine periodicals of art and literature that attained only limited recognition. He became committed to nationalism after the defeat Italy suffered at Adowa,* Ethiopia,* on March 1, 1896. With his weekly political review, *Il Regno** (1903–6), Corradini began to alert the Italian people to issues of national importance. He submitted internal solutions of a populist-conservative nature, which called for unity at home to enhance Italy's stature abroad. His final formulation was the ideal of a producers' society, composed of a citizenry of proletarians, all dedicated to the fatherland and structured in a corporative commonwealth. With the demise of the *Regno*, Corradini had to wait for the outrage that arose in Italy due to Austria's outright seizure of Bosnia on October 6, 1908, for the opportune moment to begin in earnest the campaign for a formal nationalist movement.

Corradini employed his talents as a journalist most effectively. Among his works were *Julius Caesar*, a political treatise of 1902; *La patria lontana* [The distant homeland], a patriotic doctrinal novel of 1910; and *La marcia dei pro-duttori* [The march of the producers] (1916), a collection of significant speeches on the internal objectives of World War I.* He was in the forefront of the propaganda drive for Libya* and for the intervention on the Allied side during World War I. The war would add Italia Irredenta to Italy (see Irrendentism*) and lead to territorial expansion overseas. Corradini pushed for a merger of the elitist Italian Nationalist Association with the mass-oriented Fascist Party. Following fusion he became a member of the Fascist Grand Council and of the Commission of Eighteen, and, later, senator. Before his death in Florence on December 11, 1931, Corradini, perhaps not unexpectedly, had become disillusioned because of the cult of the Duce (see Mussolini, Benito*) that had arisen at the expense of the real hero—Italy. He was buried in the church at Santacroce, in Florence.

For further reference see: Ronald S. Cunsolo, ''Enrico Corradini e la teoria del nazionalismo proletario,'' *Rassegna Storia del Risorgimento* 65, fasc. 3 (July-September 1978): 341–55.

RSC

CORRIDONI, FILIPPO. This leading revolutionary syndicalist labor organizer was born in Pausula (Marche) on October 23, 1888. Corridoni gravitated to Milan in 1905 and quickly emerged as a forceful, charismatic leader in the left wing of the Milanese labor movement. He was arrested thirty times—as, for example, in 1913, when he spearheaded a series of militant strikes as head of the Unione Sindacale Milanese. But the failures of syndicalism* by 1914 led Corridoni to conclude that radical political change, not led by the proletariat, was necessary before the syndicalist blueprint would be applicable to Italy. A leading interventionist, Corridoni was killed at the Carso front on October 23, 1915. He subsequently became a cult figure, first for the interventionist Left, then for Fascism.*

DDR

CORRIERE DELLA SERA. The *Corriere della Sera* was founded by Eugenio Torelli Viollier in Milan in 1876. From 1885 to 1895, with the backing of Lombard industrialists, the *Corriere* became a prominent voice of bourgeois public opinion and established a tradition of support for the liberal state of the *Risorgimento.* *

Luigi Albertini* joined the staff in 1896 and built the *Corriere* into a political organ of great impact widely respected in Italy and Europe. He introduced technical and administrative improvements that made his daily the largest in Italy and a powerful podium for conservative liberal principles.

In the Giolittian era the *Corriere* became the universally recognized public organ of opposition to Giolittian democratic liberalism, an independent political force in its own right. It editorialized against Giovanni Giolitti's* democratic reforms as well as the intrusions of clericalism and socialism in the liberal state. In support of the Libyan War (see Ouchy, Treaty of*) and as the strongest interventionist vehicle during the 1914–15 crisis, authoritarian and patriotic rhetoric became a pronounced tendency of the *Corriere*. After World War I* the journal continued this nationalistic thrust. Although critical of Mussolini's* Blackshirts for excesses, it initially saw Fascism* as the extreme wing of national, patriotic politics.

Cautious support for Fascism continued until 1923, when the *Corriere* found its conscience and became a leading opposition forum. In 1925 Mussolini forced the Albertini brothers from ownership, and it became Fascist. Luigi Albertini persuaded most of his staff to remain, however, and the newspaper weathered the Fascist storm, so that when democracy returned the *Corriere* regained its moderate liberal credentials and its standing as one of Italy's largest and finest newspapers.

PJD

CORRIERE DI SICILIA, IL. See **NEWSPAPERS**

CORSO FORZOSO. The *corso forzoso* was introduced by the Italian government in 1866. It meant that notes of the banks of emission (initially the notes of the Banca Nazionale del Regno and later those of the other note-issuing banks) were no longer convertible into gold or silver coin. Foreign transactions were still settled in metallic currency, and lira remained pegged internationally to gold (and silver), but domestically Italians could not exchange paper money for metallic currency.

The *corso forzoso* was considered a risky but unavoidable policy move. The dangers were high and included inflation and the collapse of the government's already poor international credit rating. As it was, however, the government's need for funds was substantial and growing, its revenue base was restricted and stagnant, and its ability to borrow abroad was limited. To avert a serious financial crisis (it had obligations to meet but did not have the money to meet them), the government had only one recourse—to borrow from the Banca Nazionale del Regno. The bank set as a condition for the loan the inconvertibility of its bank notes. As it turned out, the negative effects of the *corso forzoso* were less serious than many had anticipated, and its positive impact was much greater than many had thought it would be. There was no runaway inflation, and the government's credit rating did not plummet. On the other hand, because the gold premium on the lira rose, Italian exports became relatively cheaper for foreign customers, while the price of imported goods for Italians went up. Thus, export industries received a boost from the *corso forzoso*, and the country's current accounts position in the balance of payments improved.

The *corso forzoso* was envisioned as a temporary measure but, for various reasons, it was not abandoned until April 1883. To facilitate the return to convertibility, the government borrowed 644 million lire abroad to be paid in gold. The funds were used to redeem bank notes and to provide metallic reserves to the banks to meet conversion demands. The return to convertibility went smoothly, perhaps too smoothly. There was no rush on the part of the public to convert its paper money into metal, the money supply rose moderately, and there was a sharp increase in the overall liquidity of the economy. Some analysts contend that the injection of so much high-powered money into the economy by the government made possible the speculative excesses of the late 1880s.

JSC

CORTE COSTITUZIONALE. See **CONSTITUTIONAL COURT**

CORTI, LUIGI. See **BERLIN, CONGRESS OF, AND ITALY**

COSIMO III DE MEDICI, GRAND DUKE OF TUSCANY. The sixth and longest reigning duke of the Medici line, Cosimo (1639–1723) was the eldest son of Ferdinando II, whom he succeeded in 1670. During his reign Tuscan society reached the nadir of its post-Renaissance involution, with economic stasis, social immobility, and Church dominance of cultural life. From an early age Cosimo exhibited unusual piety. He was unhappily married in 1661 to Margherita Luisa of Orleans, a protégée of Louis XIV of France. She bore Cosimo three children, but proved to be antipathetical to the duke and was exiled to France in 1675. In internal policy Cosimo continued the mercantile protectionism of his predecessors in a period when markets for Florentine textiles were not expanding. Besides a strict regulation of the distribution of grain, little was done to encourage Tuscan agriculture. The power of the Church brought about the decline of scientific speculation in the Florentine academies, which had been encouraged by the duke's uncle, Cardinal Leopoldo De Medici (d. 1675). Foreign policy became dominated by the problem of the Medici succession. Neither Cosimo's brother, Cardinal Francesco Maria (who left the Church to be married in old age and died in 1711), nor any of his three children—Ferdinando (d. 1713), Anna Maria Luisa (d. 1743), and Gian Gastone (d. 1737)—had any heirs. In negotiations that accompanied the Peace of Utrecht, Cosimo attempted unsuccessfully to secure acceptance of a hopeless scheme to restore the Florentine Republic after his death and thus escape plans to determine the fate of Tuscany by the Bourbon or Hapsburg dynasties. On his death, the succession of his youngest son, Gian Gastone, marked, in effect, the end of the Medici dynasty.

For further reference see: Gaetano Pieraccini, *La stirpe De Medici di Caffaggiolo*, vol. 2 (Florence: Vallecchi, 1924).

RBL

COSSA, EMILIO. See **COSSA, LUIGI**

COSSA, LUIGI. This economist, born in Milan on May 22, 1831, served as professor of political economy at the University of Pavia from 1858 to his death on May 10, 1896. Cossa was among those who organized the Association for the Progress of Economic Studies, which had its first congress in Milan in 1875 and had as its organ the *Giornale degli Economisti*, which appeared that same year in Padua. One of his students, Vito Cusumano, brought the German "socialism of the chair" to Italy, making known the thought of that part of the scholarly community that advocated government intervention to correct glaring abuses in the economic and social system. Cossa wrote a series of articles and books, which have been translated into many languages. His *Introduzione allo studio dell'economia politica* [Introduction to the study of political economy] is among the classic works in economics. Cossa's son Emilio (1863–1908) also dedicated himself to economic studies and taught first at the technical institute in Bologna, and from 1904 to 1908 at the University of Messina. Emilio died in the earthquake that devastated Messina in 1908.

FJC

COSTA, ANDREA. This political figure, born in Imola on November 30, 1851, was one of the founders of the Socialist movement in Italy and the first Socialist to be elected to the Italian Chamber of Deputies. He studied at the University of Bologna and had Giosuè Carducci* as one of his teachers and Giovanni Pascoli* and Severino Ferrari as friends. He was attracted to the ideas of Mikhail Bakunin* and joined the International. In 1871 he initiated the publication of the *Fascio Operaio* in Bologna and in 1874 began the *Martello*. Soon thereafter he was condemned for his revolutionary action in the Romagna,* and after his release from prison left for Paris in 1876.

In Paris he met Anna Kuliscioff* and abandoned his violent tactics in favor of legitimate means of altering the system, moving from Bakuninism to Marxism. He returned to Italy and in 1880 founded the *Rivista Internazionale del Socialismo* in Milan and in 1881 the weekly *Avanti!* in Imola. In 1882 he was elected deputy from the college of Ravenna. Ten years later he was responsible for the Congress of Genoa,* in which the Italian Socialist Party (PSI)* was formed under the name of the Partito dei Lavoratori Italiani.

Arrested in Milan in 1898 during the state of siege, he was soon released and called for the cooperation of all Socialist forces. Esteemed even by his adversaries for his honesty and for the sincerity of his convictions, in 1909 he was elected vice-president of the Chamber. He died in Imola on January 19, 1910.

FJC

COUNCIL OF MINISTERS OF THE REPUBLIC. The executive power of the Italian government is headed by the president of the Council of Ministers (prime minister) and includes other cabinet ministers. The prime minister and cabinet are appointed by the president of the Republic,* but the government must receive a separate vote of confidence by both houses of parliament. The Council of Ministers exercises the executive powers of government and provides policy-making leadership to parliament. Since no single party has been able to command a majority in parliament, the cabinet has usually been composed of a coalition of political parties or a minority Christian Democratic government. These coalitions have been unstable, resulting in more than forty-three cabinets since the Republic was established in 1946.

EER

CRAXI, BETTINO. This Socialist politician and first Socialist prime minister of Italy (August 1983) was born Benedetto Craxi in Milan on February 24, 1934. The son of a Socialist father who migrated from his native Sicily to find work, Bettino joined the Italian Socialist Party (PSI)* at the age of eighteen, the same year he enrolled at Milan University to study law. He found politics more interesting than the law and immersed himself in party activities, leaving school without receiving his degree. His career in the party, however, was spectacular. In 1957, prior to his twenty-third birthday, he was elected to the party's central committee; he became provincial party secretary in 1965. Befriended by Pietro Nenni,* the venerated leader of the Socialists, he was first elected to the Chamber of Deputies* in 1968 and has sat there since; in 1969 he became deputy party secretary. In 1976 he was elected party secretary. Craxi's persistence and hard work, as well as his support for the North Atlantic Treaty Organization* and his suspicion of the Soviet Union, contributed to his presiding over Italy's forty-fourth cabinet in the post-World War II period.

FJC

CREDITO ITALIANO. The Credito Italiano was founded on February 6, 1895, with a paid-in capital of 14 million lire. It was created out of the Banca di Genova, a local credit institution, but quickly became a major national bank. Initial shares were subscribed in part by shareholders of the Banca di Genova and in part by German and Swiss banking houses. In this latter respect, the Credito Italiano was similar to the Banca Commerciale Italiana* (Comit), which also originally relied on German capital. It is worth noting that by 1907 the French had for the most part displaced the Germans as the main foreign participants in these banks—a return, as it were, to the traditional source of foreign capital in Italy.

The Credito Italiano was, in terms of the value of its assets, the second largest ordinary credit, or "mixed," bank in Italy during the period between its foundation in 1895 and its transformation in the mid-1930s. It grew quickly during the first twenty years of its existence. The equity capital of the bank reached 75 million lire by 1913, and its savings and demand deposits grew at an annual average rate of almost 20 percent between 1900 and 1913.

Although burdened initially by poor investments inherited from the Banca di Genova, the Credito Italiano became, along with the Comit, an important source of external funds for Italian industry during the relatively prosperous years 1896–1913. As with the Comit, the Credito Italiano was involved with major firms in most sectors of the economy, including iron and steel, electric power, sugar refining, urban transportation, chemicals, and so on. The Credito Italiano supplied loans and underwriting services and often held some shares of companies in its portfolio. It even provided technical expertise on occasion.

In the post-World War I boom (1922–25), the Credito Italiano, along with the other mixed banks, increased substantially the share of its assets invested in industrial securities. The decline in share prices after 1925 and the slowdown in economic expansion created serious difficulties for the Credito Italiano, as it did for the other mixed banks. By 1932 most of these banks were threatened with insolvency. The Credito Italiano was saved by the intervention of the government and the Banca D'Italia,* but was, in the process, fundamentally transformed. It became a publicly owned institution, and it was no longer permitted to invest long term in industrial assets. Since 1936, the Credito Italiano, along with the Comit and the Banco di Roma,* has been essentially a commercial bank.

JSC

CREDITO MOBILIARE ITALIANO. The Credito Mobiliare was founded in 1863 by a group of Italian and French banking interests, including, in particular, both the French and Spanish Crédit Mobilier. The bank was modeled explicitly on the French Crédit Mobilier, the industrial credit bank established by the Périer brothers a decade or so earlier in Paris. This meant, in effect, that the Credito Mobiliare was committed to financing all types of productive economic activities in the country. And, indeed, as Maffeo Pantaleoni* observed in an article written in 1895, the Credito Mobiliare, along with the Banca Generale,* was involved in the financing of almost all manufacturing enterprises in Italy.

The Credito Mobiliare provided funds to industry primarily through the purchase of securities (stocks and bonds) of favored companies. The bank would, in principle, hold these securities in its portfolio when stock markets were weak and liquidate them in bull markets. The consolidated balance sheet of the Credito Mobiliare for the thirty-one years of its existence indicates that, in fact, corporate securities were in most years the single most important item in the bank's portfolio, often amounting to one-third of the value of total assets.

Although the Credito Mobiliare was larger than its main rival, the Banca Generale, it was smaller than the largest savings, cooperative, and emission banks. And its growth was relatively modest over its lifetime. As with the Banca Generale, this slow growth and modest size may have been the result of conscious policy decisions by the bank's directors, but it was also the consequence of limited access to funds. The bank ceased operations at the end of 1893. The directors, beginning in 1891, tried to increase the liquidity of the bank's portfolio, but they began too late. As with the Banca Generale, poor investments and exogenous factors contributed to the ultimate failure of the bank.

JSC

CRESPI, MARIO. Mario Crespi, an industrialist and newspaper magnate, was born into a family of prominent Lombard manufacturers on September 3, 1879, at Nembro (Bergamo). His paternal uncle, Cristoforo Benigno Crespi (1833–1920), pioneered the production of cotton textiles; his father, Benigno Crespi (1848–1910), branched out into production of hydroelectric power and, in 1882, acquired an interest in the Milanese newspaper *Corriere della Sera.* Co-ownership of the *Corriere* enabled Mario Crespi and his brothers Aldo and Vittorio to oust the Albertini brothers from the directorship of the newspaper in November 1925, at a time when the Albertinis' liberal opposition to the Fascist regime was unwelcome to Mussolini* and Fascist extremists like Roberto Farinacci.* Mario Crespi's Fascist sympathies, his sponsorship of the coveted Mussolini Prizes awarded to prominent scholars and artists, and his image as an energetic captain of industry brought him much public recognition under Fascism,* including his appointment to the Senate in January 1934. He died in Milan in 1962.

RS

CRESPI, SILVIO. An industrialist, business organizer, and public figure, Crespi was born on September 24, 1868. From his father, Cristoforo Benigno Crespi, he inherited the bulk of the family interests in cotton manufacturing. In 1893 he founded the Associazione Italiana dei Cotonieri, a major business pressure group that also served as a cartel for cotton manufacturers. Elected to serve in parliament at the age of thirty, he retained his seat in the Chamber until 1919. During and immediately after World War I* he held important government posts, including the ministry for supplies and consumption, and sat on many interallied councils. These experiences he recounted in his book *Alla difesa d'Italia in guerra e a Versailles* [In defense of Italy in the war and at Versailles] (1937). In his private capacity as a businessman he extended the family influence in banking, holding the presidency of the Banca Commerciale Italiana* from 1919 to 1930. In October 1920 he was nominated senator by Giovanni Giolitti.* Although not a Fascist, he nevertheless favored Mussolini's* appointment as prime minister in October 1922, and was awarded membership in the Fascist Party (see Fascism*) in October 1925. He died in 1944.

RS

CRIMEAN WAR. Engaging Britain, France, and later Sardinia against Russia on a small peninsula in the Black Sea, the war (September 1854–February 1856) was fought ostensibly to settle the conflicting claims of Christian sects to the Holy Places in Jerusalem, but actually to secure the territorial integrity of the Ottoman Empire against Russian expansion into the Balkans. Despite serious failings in leadership and preparedness, especially in medical services, the allies succeeded in taking the main Russian base at Sebastopol; its loss, coupled with an Austrian ultimatum, forced the Russians to agree to peace. For Sardinia, the dispatch of 10,000 of her troops to the Crimea resulted in a seat at the Congress of Paris,* where Cavour* was able to plead the Italian case before the Great Powers and proceed with his search for a potential ally against Austria. For Europe as a whole, the war marked the final collapse of the conservative alliance of Austria, Russia, and Prussia, which since the end of the Napoleonic wars had impeded the progress of liberalism and nationalism on the Continent.

JWB

CRISPI, FRANCESCO. One of the most prominent political figures of nineteenth-century Italy and the first southerner to become prime minister, Crispi was born at Ribera (Agrigento), Sicily, on October 4, 1819. Although he earned a law degree from the University of Palermo in 1837, he achieved his initial fame in journalism there. Feeling frustrated by the poor conditions of the island, he moved to Naples in 1845 to accept a judgeship he had won in public competition. He soon became prominent in Neapolitan republican circles and worked to win a constitution from Ferdinand II* and also to keep in touch with democratic circles in Sicily.

When Palermo rose in rebellion in January 1848, Crispi returned and offered his services to the revolutionary government and also founded the newspaper *L'Apostolato* to propagate his political views. He became a member of the Sicilian parliament. There he took a seat on the Extreme Left, argued for total war against the Bourbons in Naples, and sponsored the motion that abolished their rule in Sicily. At this time he also favored a constituent assembly for delegates from all of Italy. These activities were ended by the return of Bourbon rule, which forced Crispi into exile in Piedmont.

In Turin he again became active in journalistic circles, promoting democratic government, but when the Piedmontese government rounded up exiles suspected of involvement in the February 1853 riots in neighboring Milan, he was among those expelled. Having kept in close touch with Sicilian democrats, he now went to Malta, where he was more advantageously situated to continue this work and where his relationship with Giuseppe Mazzini* became well known. In December 1853 he was given two weeks to leave Malta, and in that period he married Rosalia Montmasson, with whom he had lived for some years.

Crispi next moved to London, where he became personally acquainted with Mazzini. Unable to find work there, he went to Paris, where he remained until, in 1858, in the aftermath of Felice Orsini's* attempted assassination of Napoleon III,* the repressive atmosphere caused him to move on to Portugal and again to England.

As conditions in Italy moved closer to revolution, Crispi returned to Sicily in July 1859 to promote an uprising there. At the end of the year he played a decisive role in convincing Giuseppe Garibaldi* to organize The Thousand. Crispi returned to Sicily as Garibaldi's political secretary and was named dictator of the island when it fell to the invasion. He went on to be a minister in Naples when it was conquered later in the year. Despite his republican past, he advocated the fusion of the South into a monarchy governed by Victor Emmaneul II.*

In the elections of 1861, Crispi was elected to the Chamber of Deputies from Sicily and remained a member of parliament for the rest of his life, occasionally being elected in five or more constituencies. As a deputy, he opposed Cavour* and the Old Right (see Destra, La*), often vehemently, but he also began drifting away from Mazzini. He broke definitively with Mazzini in 1865, commenting that "the monarchy unites us; the republic would divide us."

Because of his prominence, Crispi was offered ministerial positions, but he remained an adamant critic of the Right, although he did not break with the Left (see Sinistra, La*). In the 1870s he became a harsh critic of Quintino Sella* and Marco Minghetti* for their financial policies and for the latter's proposal of exceptional laws to combat Sicilian brigandage.*

With the advent of the *Sinistra storica* in 1876, Crispi was passed over for a ministerial position because of his extreme stands, but he was elected president of the Chamber. Agostino Depretis,* recognizing his stature, sent him on a mission to meet Otto von Bismarck* in 1877, an encounter that molded Crispi's views on foreign policy for the remainder of his career. When Giovanni Nicotera* resigned as minister of the interior, Depretis named Crispi to replace him in December 1877. Despite his success in maintaining order through the critical moments of the deaths of Victor Emmanuel II and Pius IX* in early 1878, a newspaper campaign accusing him of bigamy forced his resignation and that of the entire cabinet in March. Crispi's original marriage to Rosalia Montmasson, which had not been legally contracted, had ended earlier, and in 1877 he married Lina Barbagallo, the mother of his daughter. Although he was absolved of any legal guilt, Crispi's reputation was temporarily soiled, and he held no other cabinet position for a decade.

In the intervening years, Crispi continued to be the advocate of the "pure Left" in the Chamber and joined the Pentarchy* in 1883 in protest against the *trasformismo* (transformism*) of Depretis. Regardless of his opposition to Depretis, Crispi was of sufficient stature that when the government was reformed in 1887, he was made minister of the interior. At Depretis' death in late July of that year, Crispi succeeded to the Prime Ministry and also assumed the Ministry of Foreign Affairs.

The decade that followed, during which Crispi was prime minister for all but two years, began a new era in national politics. In his first governments, to 1891, he sought to strengthen the executive powers of the prime minister and also sponsored an impressive number of reform measures. The suffrage was extended in reform of local governments so that all literate males paying five lire in taxes were eligible to vote. Larger towns were accorded the privilege of electing their own mayors. Prison and police reforms were instituted, public health legislation was begun, and charitable organizations were reorganized and placed under public lay control. The penal code was totally revamped in the law that bore Giuseppe Zanardelli's* name but which was promoted by Crispi himself. For the first time, legal measures were enacted for the protection of emigrants.

In foreign affairs, Crispi adopted an assertive stance, strengthening the Triple Alliance* by adding an Italo-German military convention in 1888 and starting a trade war with France. Although he had initially opposed colonial expansion, Crispi reversed his position by promoting enlargement of the territories held along the Red Sea, a policy that led to the signing of the Treaty of Uccialli* in May 1889 with Menelik II.*

The trade war and worsening internal economic problems forced Crispi's resignation in February 1891. The succeeding governments of Antonio Di Rudinì* and Giovanni Giolitti* were unable to alter the course of affairs. Following the scandal of the Banca Romana,* which toppled the latter's government in 1893, Crispi returned as the savior of the nation.

Domestic difficulties plagued the new government from its start, particularly with the Fasci Siciliani* rebellion and its counterpart in the Lunigiana region of

Tuscany, both of which Crispi suppressed by the use of martial law. Financial matters were, however, improved by a severe austerity program instituted by the minister of finance, Sidney Sonnino,* who ultimately succeeded in balancing the budget. Meanwhile, however, conditions in the colony of Eritrea* worsened, leading to war with Menelik, which culminated in the disastrous defeat of the Italian forces at Adowa* on March 1, 1896. Crispi was forced from office and threatened with official investigations to ascertain the cause of the military disgrace, and his reputation did not recover until after his death. Despite his condemnation of *trasformismo*, his career is still considered a prime example of that form of political conduct. Crispi died in Naples on August 12, 1901.

For further reference see: Massimo Grillandi, *Crispi* (Turin: UTET, 1969); Crispi, *Discorsi parlamentari*, 3 vols. (Rome: Tipografia della Camera dei Deputati, 1915); idem, *The Memoirs of Francesco Crispi*, 3 vols. (London: Hodder & Stoughton, 1912–14).

BFB

CRITICA, LA. See **CROCE, BENEDETTO**

CRITICA SOCIALE. This theoretical journal, published by Filippo Turati* and Anna Kuliscioff,* disseminated Marxism in Italy. In 1891 Turati took over *Cuore e Critica*, founded by his friend Archangelo Ghisleri, changed its name to reflect his more "scientific" brand of socialism, and moved it to Milan, where the review became a major cultural and political force. It helped create the conditions that brought about the successful foundation of the Italian Socialist Party (PSI)* in 1892 and thereafter remained one of the most important influences in Italian cultural and political life.

Contributors were not restricted to Socialists, and the most important Italian writers of the late nineteenth and twentieth centuries lent their names to the journal.

Publication of the *Critica* was suspended in 1898 during the government crackdown against Socialists but resumed in 1899. The review ceased publication in 1926, when the Fascists ended liberty of the press, but reappeared after World War II,* when it again took its place as an important forum for the discussion of the issues affecting Italian life. Postwar editors have included Ugo Guido Mondolfo, Giuseppe Faravelli, and Ugoberto Alfassio Grimaldi.

SD

CROCE, BENEDETTO. Croce, who was born in Pescasseroli d'Aquila, Abruzzi, on February 25, 1866, and died in Naples on November 20, 1952, is the best known and most influential Italian philosopher of the twentieth century. Equally celebrated as a thinker, moralist, theoretician of historiography, and master of literary criticism, Croce is one of the great stylists in the history of Italian literary expression. In April 1915 Croce published a short work entitled *Contributo alla critica di me stesso*, which his friend, the English philosopher

R. G. Collingwood, translated as *Autobiography*, in which he looked back at himself and his work critically. The *Contributo* is a sort of prism crystallizing and reflecting the entire *cursus* of Croce's material life and development.

Born of a well-to-do South Italian (Abruzzese and Neapolitan) landowning family of Bourbon *galantuomini*, Croce did not initially feel the patriotic fervor stirring in the peninsula. He was sent to a Catholic boarding school from which, in his words, he emerged a "nonbeliever." On July 28, 1883, while vacationing on the island of Ischia, the family was caught in the earthquake that destroyed Casamicciola. It killed his mother, father, and sister and left him buried in the ruins for hours. This experience haunted Croce the rest of his life and contributed to the sense of anguish that led him to think of suicide. For three years (1883–86) Benedetto and a younger brother who had also survived the tragedy were received as wards by Silvio Spaventa,* their cousin. There they were surrounded by a sophisticated circle of politicians, intellectuals, writers, and critics.

Benedetto matriculated at the University of Rome to pursue courses in law but was soon bored by the subject and his professors. He sought relief by attending the classes in moral philosophy given at the university by Antonio Labriola,* who was to have a lasting impact upon Croce's life and thought. A follower of the philosophy of Johann Friedrich Herbart (1776–1841), Labriola emphasized, among other things, the strict relationship between education and morality in the formation of the personality. Later Labriola was to have a second and more dramatic impact on the substance and direction of Croce's thought as the most outstanding Italian interpreter of Marxism.

In 1893 Croce published his first truly theoretical essay, entitled *History Subsumed under the General Concept of Art*. In these pages he tore asunder the false connection that the nineteenth century had made between the realm of history and art and that of science. As a result of this essay, in which Croce "saved" history from the spurious embrace of "science" and reduced it to an "art," he became famous. In 1895 Labriola sent Croce a copy of a manuscript on Marx's *Communist Manifesto*, which stimulated the latter to undertake a historical analysis of the development of revolutionary doctrines in general and those of the modern Socialist movement in particular. This led him to write a series of essays between 1896 and 1900, published in a volume entitled *Materialismo storico ed economia marxistica* (1900). In its later editions it included a devastating postscript on the "birth and death of theoretical Marxism in Italy."

The first years of the twentieth century mark a turning point in Croce's intellectual life. Before then Croce had written much in various guises—as historian, critic, theorist, passive antiquarian, and committed ideologue—but there was not evident a single unitary feature nor a single mode of expression. After 1900, to the eve of Italy's entry in World War I,* Croce, as director and editor of the review *La Critica*, was a respected publicist and controversial commentator on Italian and European cultural affairs. He was, above all, an Italian philosopher of European, indeed world, stature. It was during this decade and a half that Croce may be said to have had a strategy of creative labor. Though he gave it the name of *Filosofia dello spirito* [Philosophy of the spirit] only after it was complete, he reared a philosophic structure of four major parts or forms. Croce launched upon his true career as a philosopher with the treatise *Estetica come scienze dell'espressione e linguistica generale* [Aesthetic as science of expression and general linguistic] (1902), which remains the best introduction to a theory of aesthetics that offers an autonomous interpretation of the relation between intuition and image.

In 1909 Croce published his *Logica come scienza del concette puro* [Logic as the science of pure concept], which seeks to deny the validity of all systems of metaphysics that transcend the humanism of the historical world. In it Croce emphasized the centrality of human will and action in shaping the character of the "interior man" and the destiny of the human world. It ultimately proved to be the basis of the subsequent Crocean identification of philosophy and history. Yet it was the third "pillar" of the *Filosofia dello spirito*, which he also published in 1909, under the title *Filosofia dello pratica, economia ed etica* [Philosophy of the practical], that eventually came to be regarded as more original and, in a sense, more enduring, than the *Estetica* and the *Logica*. In the *Pratica* Croce analyzed the nature of the economy and practical action in the world of men as well as the interrelationship between the will and moral activity.

The fourth pillar of the *Filosofia dello spirito* was on a subject apparently unrelated to those treated in its three predecessors: it was the *Teoria e storia della storiografia* [History: its theory and practice], first published in its separate parts in academic journals and reviews, and in book form in Italian in 1917. The *Teoria e storia* was in fact a culmination of Crocean thought directly or indirectly related to the problems raised in the previous three works. History was an art of recreation achieved not merely by intuition and fantasy but also by thought, and as such, therefore, as a function of philosophy. Croce was to return to the concepts formulated in his *Teoria e storia* in 1938 with the publication of his *La storia come pensiero e come azione*, translated as *History as the Story of Liberty* (1941).

Croce accepted Giovanni Giolitti's* invitation to serve as minister of public instruction in the great statesman's last cabinet (1920–21). Afterward he observed Fascist activity with a kind of benign tolerance, not dissimilar to that of Giolitti. It was only after the Matteotti Crisis,* when Mussolini,* in January 1925, openly proclaimed his intention of establishing a dictatorship, that Croce decided to assume an anti-Fascist stance. When his old friend Giovanni Gentile* issued the *Manifesto of the Fascist Intellectuals,** Croce countered with a *Manifesto of Anti-Fascist Intellectuals*. Through almost twenty years Croce maintained his position with dignity.

After 1925 Croce plunged into a historical tetralogy which, when completed, was almost symmetrical to the earlier philosophical tetralogy. The four parts of the new historiographical structure succeeded one another: *Storia del Regno di Napoli* [History of the kingdom of Naples] (1925); *Storia d'Italia dal 1871 al 1915* [History of Italy from 1871 to 1915] (1928); *Storia dell'eta' barocca in Italia* [History of the age of the baroque in Italy] (1929); and, finally, *Storia d'Europa nel secolo XIX* [History of Europe in the nineteenth century] (1932). The four volumes of this historical tetralogy are characterized by conceptual vigor and stylistic elegance. All are histories of cultures and ideas, but all can also be subsumed under the general framework of ethical political history. The most attractive, and in due time the most controversial, of Croce's historical tetralogy were the *History of Italy* and the *History of Europe*. In the former Croce indicated that after a decade of scandal and difficulty, the coming of the era of Giolitti (1901–14) brought Italy one of the most productive periods in her long history. Croce, who had thrived during these years, penned a sort of apologia of the Giolittian era. His *History of Europe*, in turn, was greeted as Croce's apologia for the "religion of liberty" that had characterized European history during the nineteenth century.

For Croce the historicist relativism of the philosophic tetralogy had ultimately given way to the humanism of freedom and the absolute historicism of the historical tetralogy. For him now history was indeed "the story of liberty" predicated upon the inherently dialectical process operating within the Vichian "world of human society." But Croce's dialectic is not merely one of opposites, idealistic, as in Hegel, or materialistic, as in Marx. It is rather a dialectic of "distincts," of distinctions between varieties of elements whose sole eternally stirring common denominator is the striving for freedom. But now, for the old philosopher, this striving for freedom is neither a late restatement of the theological doctrine of grace or providential salvation, nor is it a new version of Hegel's "spirit of the world." Theoretically it does operate within the sphere of Vico's "storia ideale eterna" (ideal eternal history). But in fact freedom, for Croce, is a special "prime mover" immanent in all human life: it is, therefore, a form of that life and a sign of its capacity for endless self-redemption.

The works of Benedetto Croce amount to over seventy volumes, excluding his writings through forty years on his review, *La Critica* (1903–46). His closest friend and biographer, Fausto Nicolini, estimates that Croce wrote, "between large and small pieces," more than three hundred, perhaps four hundred. There is no opportunity here to list all or even the most important works of Croce besides those referred to above.

To those who desire a view of practically the whole vast biobibliographic range of Croce's intellectual production, the following three books are strongly recommended: Giovanni Castellano, *Introduzione allo studio delle opere di Benedetto Croce* (Naples: Ricciardi, 1919); Fausto Nicolini, *Benedetto Croce* (Turin: UTET, 1962), containing, on pp. 508–19, a bibliographical analysis of the Crocean opus; and Benedetto Croce, *Filosofia-Poesia-Storia: Pagine tratte da tutte le opere a cura dell'Autore* (Milan: Ricciardi, 1951), Croce's own final work containing excerpts and extracts from his works and, on pp. 1182–87, a bibliographical summary.

AWS

CRONACA BIZANTINA. The Roman *Cronaca Bizantina*, founded June 15, 1881, and terminated March 16, 1885, was published by Angelo Sommaruga* and began as an aesthetic literary showcase for the poetry of Giosuè Carducci* and his followers. At the peak of its fame the journal boasted 12,000 subscribers, but in October 1884 the so-called *bizantini maggiori*—Gabriele D'Annunzio,* Edoardo Scarfoglio,* Giulio Salvadori*—and other staff members bolted because of Sommaruga's financial support of Pietro Sbarbro's yellow *Forche Caudine*. When that publication was shut down by the government of Agostino Depretis* on February 15, 1885, Sommaruga's entire publishing house was threatened and eventually destroyed. Prince Maffeo Sciarra took over the defunct journal and brought it back to life on May 3, 1885, under the name *Domenica Letteraria-Cronaca Bizantina*; twenty-eight numbers were published, until November 7. On November 15, the so-called *Cronaca Bizantina Dannunziana* was born when Sciarra made D'Annunzio editor; its final issue appeared on March 28, 1886.

RD

CUOCO, VINCENZO. This writer and political figure, born in Civitacampomarano in Molise on October 1, 1770, wrote the *Saggio storico sulla rivoluzione napoletana* [Historical study of the Neapolitan revolution] (1801), the best analysis by a contemporary of the Neapolitan revolution. Although Cuoco had ventured to Naples in 1787 to study and practice public law, he soon revealed his talent in philosophical and historical studies.

Cuoco played a minor role in the republic established after the French entered Naples in January 1799. Nonetheless, following the Restoration of the Bourbons, his house was ransacked, his patrimony was confiscated, and he was condemned to twenty years of exile. He ventured to Marseilles, Paris, and Savoy, and returned to Italy after the battle of Marengo* (1801). It was at this time that he published his three-volume *Saggio*, which was less a history than a series of reflections on the revolution and the Parthenopean Republic.* He concluded that the revolution in Naples had failed because it had been "passive" and had not met the concrete needs of the people.

In Milan, Cuoco founded and assumed direction of the journal *Il Giornale Italiano* and in 1804 published *Platone in Italia*, a history of Italy before the Romans in the form of a novel. He returned to Naples in 1806 but in 1815 was stricken by a mental illness that troubled his remaining years. He died in Naples on December 14, 1823.

FJC

CUORE. See **DE AMICIS, EDMONDO**

CURCI, CARLO MARIA. This Jesuit writer, born in Naples on September 4, 1810, entered the Society in 1826. He dedicated himself to preaching and teaching Hebrew and sacred scripture. Initially well disposed to Vincenzo Gioberti* and his *Del Primato morale e civile degli Italiani* [On the moral and civil primacy of the Italians], he resented his criticism of the Jesuits in the *Prolegomeni*, and this prompted him to write *Fatti ed argomenti in risposta alle molte* *parole di Vincenzo Gioberti* [Facts and arguments in response to the many words of Vincenzo Gioberti]. In it he not only defended his order, but also attacked the notions that churchmen should make themselves the apostles of civilization or use religion on behalf of revolution. In 1850, with the encouragement of Pius IX,* he founded the *Civiltà Cattolica** in Naples and served as its first director.

After the fall of Rome to the Italians, the ardent defender of the temporal power concluded that the Vatican should accommodate itself to the political reality because Christianity suffered as a result of the church-state conflict. He defended his views in *Lezioni esegetiche e morali sopra i quattro Evangeli* [Exegetical and moral lessons on the four gospels] (1874), which provoked controversy in conservative Catholic quarters. Constrained to leave his order in 1877, he wrote three additional books defending his liberal ideas; all three were placed on the *Index librorum prohibitorum*, the list of books forbidden to its members by the Roman Catholic Church. In 1891, months before his death, he accepted the condemnation of his works and was readmitted to the Society. He died in Careggi near Florence, on June 9, 1891. A depressing autobiography of sorts, entitled *Memorie utili di una vita disutile* [Useful memories of a useless life], was published posthumously in 1892.

FJC

CURCIO, RENATO. See **RED BRIGADES**

CURIEL, EUGENIO. Born of Jewish parents in Trieste (December 11, 1912), Eugenio Curiel became a militant anti-Fascist. He edited the student newspaper at the University of Padua, *Il Bò*, from 1937 to 1938. In prison from 1939 to 1943, he thereafter headed the Communist Fronte della Gioventù in Milan and edited *L'Unità* and *La Nostra Lotta* until a Fascist squad shot him on February 24, 1945.

For further reference see: Eugenio Curiel, *Scritti 1939–1945*, ed. F. Frassati (Rome: Riuniti, 1973).

CFD

CUSTOZZA, BATTLE OF (1848). This battle was fought during the Wars of Independence between the Piedmontese under King Charles Albert of Savoy* and the Austrians under Field Marshal Joseph Radetzky.* Charles Albert, preparing to besiege Mantua, had strung out his 70,000 men on a long front, permitting Radetzky to concentrate his 100,000 troops and break through on July 23. The Piedmontese regrouped and counterattacked at Custozza on July 24. Despite an initial success, they were routed by Radetzky on July 25. A vigorous Austrian pursuit led to the reoccupation of Milan and Charles Albert's retreat into his own territory.

WDG

CUSTOZZA, BATTLE OF (1866). This battle was fought in the Wars of Independence between the Italians under Marchese Alfonso Ferrero de La Marmora* and the Austrians under Archduke Albert. Having crossed the Mincio, La Marmora, with 80,000 men, advanced upon the archduke's 74,000 troops covering Verona. La Marmora's columns were slowed by hilly terrain, and, as they debouched successively upon the plains of Custozza, were defeated in detail by the Austrians. La Marmora retreated across the Mincio, but despite the victory political circumstances forced Austria to cede Venetia to Italy.

WDG

CVL. The Corpo Volontari della Libertà was the military arm of the Italian Armed Resistance* movement in central and northern Italy, 1944–45. Its headquarters were in Milan. The CVL was entrusted with the task of coordinating the operations of partisan units, and had among its main functions the maintenance of contact with Allied military, diplomatic, and intelligence authorities in Italy, Switzerland, and France. The name—Corps of Volunteers for Freedom—expressed the desire of anti-Fascist Italians to contribute in a decisive manner to their own liberation. In addition to its military functions, the CVL had a counterespionage division, a counterfeit document center, and a press office.

FR

CYRENAICA. See **LIBYA**

D

DABORMIDA, GIUSEPPE. This Piedmontese general, deputy, and senator was born in Verrua (Turin) on November 21, 1799. A cadet in the artillery in 1815, he became captain in 1824 and instructor in the military academy in 1828. In 1838 he was called to court to instruct the royal princes. He remained at court until 1841. During the campaign of 1848 against Austria, he substituted as minister of war while General Franzini followed King Charles Albert of Savoy* into the field. Promoted to major general, he served as minister of war in Cesare Alfieri's government after the Salasco armistice. A deputy since 1848, in 1852 he was made senator at the same time that he assumed the post of minister of foreign affairs in the ministry of Massimo D'Azeglio.* He retained this post under Cavour* but resigned in 1855 because he did not approve the conditions under which Piedmont proposed to enter the Crimean War.* After Villafranca* he held the Ministry of Foreign Affairs for a short time in the Rattazzi*-La Marmora* government (July 1859–January 1860). In the Senate he joined those who opposed the cession of Nice and Savoy to France. In 1863 he was made a count. He died in Buriasco di Pinerolo on August 10, 1869.

FJC

DALLA TORRE, GIUSEPPE. See **CATHOLIC ACTION**

DALMATIA. In part possessions of the Venetian Republic until 1797, the coastline and islands of the Dalmatian region across the Adriatic passed to Austrian control in the nineteenth century. Austria favored the numerically superior Slavic element against the Italian-speaking population. Promised to Italy in the Pact of London* that led Italy to intervene in World War I,* all of Dalmatia except Zara and several islands was nevertheless assigned to the new Yugoslav kingdom after the war in the treaties of Saint-Germain (1919) and Rapallo* (1920). Dalmatia was a frequent source of friction between Yugoslavia and Italy during the Fascist period. Occupied by Italy and Germany in April 1941, Dalmatia was returned to Yugoslavia after the end of World War II.*

SS

DANEO-CREDARO LAW. This educational law, passed in 1911, radically modified the scholastic structure of Italy by giving control of education to the provinces instead of to the small communes, which could not fully afford the state programs. It also created large grants-in-aid by the government, enlarged the role of inspectors and vice-inspectors, created a number of new grades, and raised compulsory elementary education to six years. This law worked to create a better educated electorate for the newly extended suffrage.

WR

D'ANNUNZIO, GABRIELE. Of provincial middle-class origin, born in Pescara on March 12, 1863, D'Annunzio was a brilliant but erratic student at Prato's Collegio Cicognini. In his mid-teens he wrote a critically acclaimed book of verse, *Primo vere* [In early spring] (1879), Carduccian in inspiration. D'Annunzio moved to Rome in 1881 and soon afterward became a principal collaborator on the *Cronaca Bizantina.** He wrote for other Roman publications as well, notably *La Tribuna*.

There was a palpable tension in D'Annunzio's creative writing during the 1880s as he wavered between an esoteric aestheticism in his poetry (*Canto novo* [New song], 1882; *Intermezzo di rime* [Interlude of poems], 1883; and *Isaotta Guttadauro ed altre poesie* [Isaotta Guttadauro and other poems], 1886), and a verism in his short stories (*Terra vergine*, 1882; and *San Pantaleone*, 1886). The tension was eased in the successful *fin de siècle* novels that he wrote, beginning with *Il piacere* [The child of pleasure] (1889). Here and in the other Romanzi della Rosa novels, *L'innocente* [The intruder] (1892) and *Il trionfo della morte* [The triumph of death] (1894), D'Annunzio combined his warring gifts in a unique style marked by vivid imagery, brazen sensuality, telling detail, and unsurpassed technical mastery.

D'Annunzio's interest in politics was foreshadowed in numerous works that he wrote during the 1880s and 1890s, but especially in the Nietzschean *Vergini delle rocce* [The maidens of the rocks] (1895). Two years later he ran successfully for parliament, taking a seat on the Extreme Right (see Destra, La*). The "Deputy of Beauty," however, was deeply impressed by the Socialist struggle against the ministry of Luigi Pelloux* after the May Days of Milan in 1898. He therefore took a seat on the Extreme Left (see Sinistra, La*), saying, "As a man of intellect, I go toward life."

D'Annunzio's parliamentary career ended in 1900, but he entered the most productive period of his literary career, the so-called Capponcina years. His marriage to the Duchess Maria Hardouin di Gallese had virtually ended, and in 1898 he took up residence in the luxurious Tuscan villa, La Capponcina, with Eleonora Duse. This became one of the most well-publicized love affairs of the *belle epoque*, with D'Annunzio himself doing much of the publicizing in his autobiographical novel, *Il fuoco* [The flame of life] (1900). While at La Capponcina he wrote the first three books of *Le laudi* [Praises] (1903–4), including what many critics regard as his poetic masterpiece, *Alcyone*, but it was Duse who inspired him to write for the theater. His decision to cast her rival, Sarah Bernhardt, in the premiere of *La città morta* [The dead city] (1898) wounded Duse; nevertheless, their tempestuous collaboration continued for several years, and his major plays of this period were *La gioconda* [Gioconda] (1899), *La gloria* [Glory] (1899), *Francesca da Rimini* (1902), and *La figlia di Iorio* [The daughter of Jorio] (1904).

In 1910 mounting debts drove D'Annunzio into French exile. World War I* completely transformed his image from a decadent aesthete to a martial hero with a distinguished record in all three military services. Disgusted by the failure of the Italian negotiators at Versailles to secure Fiume,* he led an assault on that city in September 1919. To the mortification of Francesco Nitti's* government, D'Annunzio held Fiume for more than a year and did not surrender until compelled to by Giovanni Giolitti's* massive show of force.

In 1921 he retired to a sumptuous villa near Gardone on Lake Garda. His political ambitions were forestalled by fatigue, war wounds, a mysterious fall in 1922, and the presence of Mussolini,* to whose success and style the Fiume episode had made an important contribution. The Fascist seizure of power in October 1922 left him with little to do but transform the villa—now officially called the Vittoriale degli Italiani—into a memorial for his own career, write books of reminiscences, and prepare the Vittoriale edition of his life's work. In 1924 D'Annunzio became, by royal decree, the prince of Montenevoso, and he presided as a decorative figure in the Fascist cultural establishment, ending his days as the president of the Accademia d'Italia. He died in Gardone Riviera on March 1, 1938.

For further reference see: Guglielmo Gatti, *La vita de Gabriele D'Annunzio* (Florence: Sansoni, 1956); Francesco Flora, *D'Annunzio* (Naples: Ricciardi, 1926).

RD

D'ARAGONA, LUDOVICO. One of the major Socialist leaders of the General Confederation of Labor (CGL*), D'Aragona was born on May 23, 1876, in Cernusco sul Naviglio (Milan), and died in Rome on June 17, 1961. He was a moderate, generally following the reformist line in his labor activities. He occupied several important positions in the labor movement and in 1918 became secretary-general of the CGL.

D'Aragona was elected to parliament in 1919 and supported Emanuele Modigliani's call for a constituent assembly. D'Aragona's main concern was for the CGL's welfare, and he was unwilling to take risks that might endanger the workers' organizations. Thus, he moved to prevent the Italian Socialist Party

(PSI)* from using the factory occupation of 1920 for revolutionary purposes, focusing instead on the issue of worker control of the factories.

In an attempt to protect the CGL from Fascist reprisals, D'Aragona softened the union's stand against Mussolini* and even met with him, but this policy failed. He resigned as secretary-general in 1925, two years before the CGL's dissolution. Until 1929 D'Aragona participated with other former Socialists who were allowed some freedom by the regime to study the problems of labor, but he withdrew from public life after that year.

In June 1946 he was elected to the Constituent Assembly.* He joined the Socialist Party of the Italian Workers and subsequently served in several cabinets.

SD

DC. See **CHRISTIAN DEMOCRATIC PARTY**

DE AMBRIS, ALCESTE. This labor organizer, Socialist theorist, and leading partisan of revolutionary syndicalism* before World War I* was born in Licciana Nardi (Lunigiana) on September 15, 1874, and died at Brive (Guyene), France, on December 19, 1934. As head of the Parma Chamber of Labor, De Ambris led one of the classic syndicalist strikes in 1908. Persistently critical of the reformist Confederazione Generale del Lavoro (see CGL*), he helped organize the rival Unione Sindacale Italiana in 1912. In August 1914 De Ambris was one of the first Italian Socialists to propose Italian intervention in the war, which he portrayed in relatively orthodox terms as an international crusade against German militarism and imperialism. However, interventionism contributed to the doctrinal revision that made him a national corporativist after the war. De Ambris remained active in the labor movement, as a leader in the anti-Bolshevik Unione Italiana del Lavoro, but he sought especially to forge a non-Socialist coalition to make a corporativist political revolution. To this end, he maintained close ties with Fascism* in 1919–20 and collaborated throughout 1920 with Gabriele D'Annunzio's* Fiume* regency, providing the substance of its corporativist constitution, the Carta del Carnaro.* But De Ambris soon grew disillusioned with Mussolini* and diverged from his many syndicalist colleagues, who saw Fascism as the vehicle for corporativist revolution. He went into exile in France in 1923 and never returned to Italy.

DDR

DE AMICIS, EDMONDO. This popular post-*Risorgimento* writer was born in Oneglia on October 31, 1846. De Amicis graduated from the military school in Modena and served in the army at the battle of Custozza (1866).* After the war with Austria he collaborated on the review *Italia Militare*, contributing sketches, which were eventually collected in *La vita militare* [The military life] (1868). The success of this book and of the other short story collections that immediately followed, *Novelle* (1872) and *Ricordi del 1870–71* [Memoirs of 1870–71] (1872), induced him to give up the army and devote all of his time to writing, as a journalist, as a collaborator on literary reviews, and—less felicitously—as a poet.

De Amicis became a master of the travel memoir, and he wrote six of these during the 1870s: *Spagna* [Spain] (1873), *Ricordi di Londra* [Memoirs of London] (1873), *Olanda* [Holland] (1874), *Marocco* (1876), *Costantinopoli* (1878–79), and *Ricordi di Parigi* [Memoirs of Paris] (1879). In the following decade he concerned himself with the problem of education in Italy; many of his books stressed this theme, but one surpassed all the others in popular appeal. This was *Cuore* [An Italian schoolboy's journal] (1886), published in dozens of Italian editions and in twenty-five foreign languages, the second most popular book in Italy after Collodi's *Pinocchio*.

The moralistic and sentimental ideas in *Cuore* characterized his thinking about the problem of Italian emigration* found in his *Sull' oceano* [On the ocean] (1889). He embraced socialism in 1891 and described his new political outlook in the novel *Il primo maggio* [The first of May]. De Amicis continued to produce novels, short stories, memoirs, and scholarly works on language, adding to his reputation as one of post-*Risorgimento* Italy's most patriotic and civic-minded writers. Many of his books remain landmarks of Italian taste during the Umbertian period. He died in Bardighera on March 11, 1908.

RD

DE BONO, EMILIO. General and Fascist leader, born in Cassaro d'Adda (Milan) on March 19, 1866, he commanded the Ninth Army Corps during World War I,* adhered to the Fascist Party (see Fascism*) in 1922, and helped organize the March on Rome.* De Bono was put in charge of public security and the Fascist Voluntary Militia for National Security* from 1922 to 1924 but was forced to resign during the Matteotti Crisis* of June 1924. Tried and acquitted of complicity in Matteotti's murder, De Bono became governor of Tripolitania (1925–28) and minister of colonies in 1929. He was a key figure in the preparations for the Ethiopian war of 1935 and briefly commanded Italian forces until replaced by Marshal Pietro Badoglio.* At the meeting of the Fascist Grand Council of July 24–25, 1943, De Bono joined the majority in voting against Mussolini.* He was seized by the Fascist Social Republic (see Salò, Republic of*), then tried and executed at Verona on January 11, 1944.

AJD

DE BOSIS, ADOLFO. The young De Bosis, born in Ancona on January 3, 1863, left the provinces to begin a literary career in Rome. Strongly influenced by the Pre-Raphaelites, he also looked to Gabriele D'Annunzio's* work as a model for his poetry. *Amori ac silentio sacrum* [For love and silence of sacred things] (1900) and *Rime sparse* [Collected poems] (1914) are examples of these influences. His translations of Shelley drew universal praise from contemporaries. However, his most memorable enterprise, begun in collaboration with D'Annunzio, was the *Convito* [The banquet], a twelve-volume anthology of essays, stories, novels, poems, and art sketches on the many variations on one theme, pure beauty. This work was intended as a protest against the shabbiness of modern life. The editors planned to bring out all twelve volumes in 1895, but midway through the project D'Annunzio's interest waned, and De Bosis carried on alone. The last volume appeared in 1907, and the entire set constitutes the best primary source for *fin de siècle* aesthetic politics in Italy. He died in Ancona on August 28, 1924.

RD

DEDALO. See **OJETTI, UGO**

DE FELICE-GIUFFRIDA, GIUSEPPE. This journalist and Socialist leader was born in Catania on September 17, 1859. In 1891 he founded a workers' *fascio* in Catania and through it sought to provide guidance for the poorly focused unrest that spread through Sicily in 1893–94 and became known as the movement of the Fasci Siciliani.* Following the military repression of the movement De Felice-Giuffrida was court-martialed and sentenced to eighteen years in prison but was amnestied in March 1896. Elected to parliament in 1892, he emerged as a spokesman for the South, frequently castigating the corrupt electoral practices which enabled liberal leaders, particularly Giovanni Giolitti,* to secure majorities in Sicily. While remaining a Socialist, De Felice-Giuffrida differed from most party leaders in his view that colonial expansion was a means for solving the problem of the South. From his parliamentary seat he spoke out in favor of war against Turkey to capture Libya* in 1911–12 and in favor of Italian intervention in World War I* in 1914–15. He volunteered for military service after Italy declared war on Austria-Hungary on May 24, 1915. He died in Catania in 1920.

RS

DE GASPERI, ALCIDE. Premier of Italy from 1945 to 1953 and principal founder of the Italian Christian Democratic Party,* De Gasperi was born in Pieve Tesino (Trentino), Austria-Hungary, on April 3, 1881, and died on August 19, 1954, in Sella Valsugana, Italy. Of middle-class background, De Gasperi received his secondary education in Trent and his higher education at the University of Vienna, from which he graduated in 1905. During his youth he was active both in the Italian Catholic social movement of the Trentino* and in the Trentine Popular Party. The party stood for the administrative autonomy of the predominantly Italian-speaking Trentino and for the application of the principles of Christian Democracy* to the socioeconomic problems of the day. In 1911 he was elected to the Austrian parliament, in which he represented the Trentino until the end of World War I.* During the war he devoted himself to the alleviation of the sufferings of Italians who were refugees or who had been placed in Austrian internment camps.

With Italy's annexation of the Trentino under the terms of the Treaty of Saint-Germain, De Gasperi became a subject of the Kingdom of Italy. He immediately became active in the Italian Popular Party* founded by Don Luigi Sturzo,* and he was elected to the Chamber of Deputies of 1921. Both on the floor of the Chamber and through his newspaper, *Il Nuovo Trentino*, De Gasperi denounced Fascism* as an ideology inherently opposed to that of popularism. He was willing to collaborate with right-wing Socialists in an effort to stem the tide of Fascism, but such collaboration was effectively vetoed by Pope Pius XI* in 1924. De Gasperi took part in the Aventine Secession,* which the anti-Fascist deputies organized after the murder of Giacomo Matteotti by Fascist hoodlums (see Matteotti, Crisis*). The Aventine Secession failed to topple Mussolini,* and thus in 1926 De Gasperi was among the deputies deprived of their parliamentary seats. In 1927 Mussolini's police arrested him, alleging attempted clandestine expatriation. In 1929, after his release from prison, De Gasperi entered the employ of Pope Pius XI as a cataloguer in the Vatican Library, rising by 1939 to the position of secretary of the Vatican Library. Mussolini unsuccessfully tried to have the Pope dismiss him.

In December 1945 De Gasperi became the first Christian Democratic premier. He remained at the head of the Italian government for eight and a half years, presiding over eight consecutive ministries. His first ministries included members of the Italian Communist Party (PCI)* and the Italian Socialist Party (PSI),* but in May 1947 De Gasperi expelled the Communists and their left-wing Socialist allies (Nenni Socialists). Subsequently De Gasperi's ministries were made up of Christian Democrats, Liberals, Social Democrats (right-wing or Saragat Socialists), and Republicans. The parliamentary elections of 1948 gave the Christian Democrats a hegemony that they were to retain for the next several decades.

After a brief period of neutrality in foreign affairs, De Gasperi aligned Italy with the West. Italy accepted Marshall Plan* funds, joined the North Atlantic Treaty Organization* (NATO), and became a member of the European Steel and Coal Community. On the domestic front he supported conservative monetary policies, a mixed economy of private and state enterprises, and the development of southern Italy. The agrarian reform was the most controversial economic measure enacted by De Gasperi, and this cost him the support of the Liberal Party.*

Within his party De Gasperi hewed to a center line, endeavoring to maintain a balance between its right and left wings. De Gasperi was willing to accept the aid of the Catholic Church in electoral contests, but resisted any efforts to form a "Catholic Party" or to join neo-Fascists to prevent Communist electoral victories.

In the summer of 1953, after the Christian Democrats and their allies among the smaller parties had failed to obtain a clear majority in the parliamentary elections, De Gasperi was willing to consider a Centro-Sinistra government (see Christian Democratic Party*) with the Nenni Socialists. The continuation of the Pact of Unity between the Socialists and the Communists rendered abortive this first attempt at Centro-Sinistra. De Gasperi resigned as premier in July 1953, but as secretary of the party, a post to which he was elected in October 1953, he sought to continue to guide the party. At the time of his death in August

1954 he was championing the cause of European unity. De Gasperi is buried in Rome in the Church of San Lorenzo Fuori le Mure. He was married to Francesca Romani, by whom he had three daughters.

For further reference see: Elisa Carrillo, *De Gasperi, the Long Apprenticeship* (Notre Dame: University of Notre Dame Press, 1965); Maria Romana Catti de Gasperi, *De Gasperi, uomo solo* (Milan: Mondadori, 1964); Pietro Scoppola, *La proposta politica di De Gasperi* (Bologna: Il Mulino, 1977).

EC

DELCASSÉ, THÉOPHILE. Delcassé, French foreign minister (1898–1905, 1914–15) and minister of the Navy (1911–13), was born in Pamiers on March 1, 1858. Italy played an important role in his diplomatic strategy from 1898 to 1905. He worked closely with his ambassador and friend in Rome, Camille Barrère.* In 1898 Delcassé reached a commercial accord with Luigi Luzzatti.* Delcassé improved Franco-Italian relations in order to further French colonial ambitions in the Mediterranean and as a function of French rivalry with England. In 1900 France and Italy exchanged recognition of their respective penetrations of Morocco and Libya.* Two years later Delcassé and Barrère achieved their major goal of separating Italy from Germany. The previous colonial accord was strengthened, and Italian leaders agreed to declare neutrality if Germany initiated a war against France. In 1904, as foreign minister in the anticlerical government of Emile Combes, Delcassé participated in breaking relations with the Vatican. In 1912 Navy Minister Delcassé achieved passage of a naval law that assumed concentration of the French fleet in the Mediterranean. Foreign minister again after the outbreak of World War I,* he worked to attract Italy to the side of the Triple Entente.* He died on February 27, 1923.

For further reference see: Christopher Andrew, *Théophile Delcassé and the Making of the Entente Cordiale: A Reappraisal of French Foreign Policy 1898–1905* (New York: St. Martin's Press, 1968).

JB

DELLA CHIESA, GIACOMO. See **BENEDICT XV**

DELLA GENGA, ANNIBALE SERMATTEI. See **LEO XII**

DELLA VALLE, CLAUDIO. See **JACOBINS**

DELLE SPERANZE D'ITALIA. See *SPERANZE D'ITALIA, DELLE*

DE MEIS, ANGELO CAMILLO. This scientist and philosopher was born in Bucchianico (Chieti) on July 14, 1817. He studied at the University of Naples and sought to apply Hegelian principles to physiology and biology. In 1848 he was elected deputy to the Neapolitan parliament, but following the death of his father in April 1848 he left the Kingdom of the Two Sicilies* and eventually settled in Turin. Subsequently he was nominated director of the Medical College at Naples and later held the chair of the history of medicine at the University of Bologna. Regarding Italy's political condition, he considered it the historic mission of the monarchy to serve as mediator between the higher and lower elements in the population. He died in Bologna on March 6, 1891.

FJC

DEMOCRATIC INTERVENTIONISM. See **BISSOLATI, LEONIDA** and **BONOMI, IVANOE**

DEMOCRAZIA CRISTIANA. See **CHRISTIAN DEMOCRATIC PARTY**

DE NICOLA, ENRICO. This statesman, respected for his honesty and intelligence, unfortunately was also a prototype of the many pre-Fascist Liberals who strongly resented Fascism* but did not oppose it. Born in Naples on November 9, 1877, he acquired a reputation as a prominent jurist. Elected to parliament in 1909 as a follower of Giovanni Giolitti,* he joined the government in 1913. As speaker of the Chamber of Deputies from 1920 to 1923, he failed to protest when Mussolini, the newly appointed prime minister, expressed his contempt for parliamentary institutions. At the general elections of 1924 he was included in the Fascist-led *listone* which received two-thirds of the popular vote, and in 1929 he accepted appointment as senator. After the armistice signed on September 3, 1943, he helped his close friend Benedetto Croce* in peacefully effecting the difficult transition, first from dictatorial to constitutional rule, and then, in 1946, from a monarchical to a republican regime. The Constitutional Assembly of 1946* elected him provisional head of state. He was president of the Republic* during the interval between the enactment of the constitution and the election of the first regular parliament, speaker of the Senate* from 1948 to 1953, and president of the Constitutional Court* (Italy's Supreme Court) from 1956 to 1957. He died in Torre del Greco on October 1, 1959.

MS

DEPRETIS, AGOSTINO. Three times prime minister between 1876 and 1887, and virtual parliamentary "dictator" during this period, Depretis acquired the reputation of manipulator of men and elections, the very embodiment of transformism.* He was born on January 31, 1813, in Mezzana Corti (Pavia), and died on July 29, 1887, in Stradella. A lawyer and a Mazzinian in his early years, Depretis entered politics in 1848 as a democrat and was elected uninterruptedly for sixteen legislatures of the Piedmontese, and later, Italian, parliament. Although Depretis opposed Cavour's* financial policies and involvement in the Crimean War,* Cavour nevertheless chose him as governor of liberated Brescia in 1859. In 1860 Giuseppe Garibaldi* accepted him as his pro-dictator in Sicily, where Depretis clashed with Francesco Crispi.* Five times vice-president of the Chamber of Deputies between 1849 and 1866, he joined Urbano Rattazzi's* Left government in 1862 as minister of public works, and Bettino Ricasoli's* coalition cabinet, first as navy minister (1866) and later at finance (1867). After Rattazzi's death in 1873, Depretis succeeded him as leader of the Left (see Sinistra, La*), propounding in 1875 a monarchy democratized by such reforms as extended suffrage, compulsory education, administrative decentralization, and a more equitable tax structure. With the fall of Marco Minghetti* in March 1876, ending nearly fifteen years of rule by men of the Right (see Destra, La*), Depretis formed his first ministry, which won an overwhelming victory in the elections held the following November, reducing the Right to a fragment and introducing into the Chamber a host of new, untried, and disunited deputies, nominally of the Left but lacking in party discipline. It was this varied composition of his nominal parliamentary majority that convinced Depretis of the need to move slowly with the promised reforms and seek support from the Right whenever his own party would not follow him in his moderation. For eleven years his dominance was interrupted only by three administrations led by Benedetto Cairoli,* in the last and longest of which (November 1879–May 1881) he served as minister of the interior. During Depretis' long ministry (May 1881–July 1887), four times recomposed, he achieved a number of significant though partial reforms: extension of the suffrage; repeal of the hated grist tax (see Macinato*); the beginning of an accident insurance program; and the reorganization and expansion of the railroads. He brought Italy into the Triple Alliance,* without abandoning the hope of better relations with France; and entered with reluctance the race for colonies in Africa. But these achievements did not disarm his critics, who viewed him as a corruptor of politics, although personally honest. His defenders characterized him as the great pacifier of the volatile parliamentary scene. Dissension among the various factions constituting the Left obliged Depretis to make into a system—transformism—the art of compromise with nominal opponents of the Right. Former and future colleagues on the Left, including Cairoli, Crispi, and Giuseppe Zanardelli,* rebelled; and opponents from the Right, such as Minghetti, accepted and gave collaboration. He made a virtue of the necessity of compromise, hoping thereby to avoid political polarization into the intractable antagonism of a two-party system that would give the country not a clear choice but rather an irreparable division. He lived for his office and power, and died poor.

For further reference see: Giampiero Carocci, *Agostino Depretis e la politica interna italiana dal 1876 al 1887* (Turin: Einaudi, 1956); Giuseppe Talamo, *La formazione di Agostino Depretis* (Milan: A. Giuffrè, 1970).

SS

DE RICCI, SCIPIONE. This son of a Florentine patrician family (1741–1820), educated for the clergy at Rome and the University of Pisa, was first employed in the nunciature of Florence. In 1780 he was nominated bishop of Pistoia and Prato by the Grand Duke Peter Leopold of Hapsburg-Lorraine.* Ricci was a proponent of the type of Fabbronian Jansenism that gained support in Tuscany and Lombardy* in the 1780s. His innovations at Pistoia and Prato included establishment of new seminaries, removal of images, and introduction of a vernacular liturgy. These were at first supported by the duke, who aimed at ecclesiastical reforms in redistricting of parishes and suppression of superfluous convents and monasteries. Ricci went further, and encountered opposition within his diocese, from the Tuscan clergy, and from Pius VI.* He was obliged to renounce his bishopric in 1791. He fell under suspicion during the conservative reaction of 1799, and died in obscurity.

RBL

DE RUGGIERO, GUIDO. A liberal political thinker and historian of philosophy, he was born in Naples on March 23, 1888, and died in Rome on December 29, 1948. Initially a disciple of Benedetto Croce* and especially Giovanni Gentile,* De Ruggiero remained within Croce's orbit, but he developed his own brand of liberalism. He was influential in political journalism from 1912 until 1926, then again in the 1940s, when he contributed regularly to Luigi Salvatorelli's* *La Nuova Europa.*

Disillusioned with the failure of liberalism after World War I,* De Ruggiero sought to reexamine the liberal patrimony in *The History of European Liberalism* (1925), a major document in European political thought. He called for a more socially responsive, reformist variety of liberalism, but he also insisted on the radical incompatibility of liberalism and orthodox socialism. Seeking to counter the influence of Marxist categories, De Ruggiero called for renewed confidence on the part of the liberal middle class—confidence in its legitimacy as a ruling class, as well as in the validity of the liberal conception of politics. However, his conception was not rigidly elitist: in principle, everyone has the capacity for freedom and political vision, and those with power must ensure that all have the opportunity to develop it.

De Ruggiero was among the founders of the Action Party* in 1942–43, and he served as minister of education in 1944. However, he quickly grew disillusioned with postwar Italian politics—especially with the ongoing appeal of Marxist categories. When the Action Party split in February 1946, he moved to the Republican Party,* but he had begun to conclude that in a mass age, the liberal intellectual must eschew active politics and attend to the cultural foundations.

DDR

DE SANCTIS, FRANCESCO. The leading literary critic of the post-*Risorgimento* years, De Sanctis was born at Morra Irpina on March 28, 1817. After studying rhetoric and literary criticism in Naples with Basilio Puoti, a major figure in the *movimento purista*, De Sanctis began his career as a grammar school teacher and curator of critical editions of early modern texts. But the revolutions of 1848,* which he supported, interrupted his work and led to his imprisonment from 1850 to 1853. Allowed to leave the Kingdom of the Two Sicilies,* he fled to Turin, where he gave a series of public lectures on the *Divine Comedy* and resumed his study of literature and philosophy. In 1855 he was appointed to a chair of Italian literature at the Polytechnic of Zurich, where he developed a chronological framework for a general course and also taught a monographic course on Petrarch. Letters written from exile to family and friends reveal that De Sanctis experienced a deep crisis of alienation and loneliness that probably heightened his understanding of Petrarch and led him to study and interpret early romantic writers. Close to Cavour* and the moderate liberals in the late 1850s, De Sanctis was rewarded with the post of minister of education in 1861. During the 1860s, however, he moved toward more democratic positions, and in 1878 he once again became minister of education, but in a government of the *Sinistra storica* (see Sinistra, La*). While serving in Parliament he taught and published his milestone works, *Saggi critici* [Critical essays] (1866), *Storia della letteratura italiana* [History of Italian literature] (1870–71), and *Letteratura italiana nel secolo XIX* [Italian literature in the nineteenth century], edited by Benedetto Croce* and published posthumously in 1897. De Sanctis died in Naples on December 29, 1883.

                                                                                        CML

DE STEFANI, ALBERTO. This economist and political figure was born in Verona on October 6, 1879. He studied at the Ca' Foscari in Venice and the University of Padua before being appointed to the faculty of the University of Naples in 1922. An early supporter of Fascism,* he was named minister of finance in the first Mussolini* cabinet, and in 1923 was also entrusted with the Ministry of the Treasury. A liberal economist by training, he sought to free private enterprise from rigid state control. He thus abolished the commissions that fixed prices, withdrew government subsidies from cooperatives, destroyed the life insurance monopoly created by Giovanni Giolitti,* and returned the telephone companies to private control. He also turned his attention to balancing the budget, and in 1925 an excess of receipts over expenditures was recorded for the first time in the postwar period. Dismissed from his position on July 10, 1925, he was appointed full professor at the University of Rome, where he presided over the new faculty of political science. He also served on the Fascist Grand Council and voted against Mussolini during the stormy session of July 24–25, 1943. Condemned to death in 1944 in Verona, he managed to elude Fascist revenge. After the war he was brought before the high court in Rome but acquitted. Thereafter, he wrote articles for *Il Tempo* and in 1963 had his memoirs published. He died in Rome on January 15, 1969.

For further reference see: Alberto De Stefani, *Fuga del tempo* (Perugia: Donnini, 1948).

                                                                                        FJC

DESTRA, LA. By this term (the Right) is meant the political formation, shaped during the unification period, devoted to constitutional government, moderate social conservatism, and, in economics, laissez-faire. Believing that unification could be achieved and preserved only under the initiative and authority of a liberal monarchy, the Right included conservatives side by side with former republicans and federalists disenchanted by the failures of 1848. It was fashioned into an instrument of government by Cavour*; his political heirs of the Right completed unification by 1870, implemented a tolerable *modus vivendi* with the Church in the Law of Papal Guarantees* (1871), centralized the administration, and established a sound, if burdensome, fiscal structure. Undemocratic in its opposition to universal manhood suffrage and insistent on the authority of the laic state, the Right nevertheless remained liberal in its respect for individual liberties. After its fall from power in 1876, some of its leaders (Marco Minghetti* and Antonio Di Rudinì*) transacted with the Left (see Sinistra, La*); but others, especially Sidney Sonnino,* attempted toward the end of the century to revive the "Historical Right" of the unification period and resisted the transformism* characteristic of the Giolittian era. Its last major leader was Antonio Salandra.* The Destra is not to be confused with the illiberal and antiparliamentarian Nationalist Right of the early twentieth century.

SS

DE VECCHI, CESARE MARIA. Cesare Maria De Vecchi, Count of Valcismon, who was born in Monferrato on November 14, 1884, and died in Rome on June 23, 1959, was the Fascist leader (ras) of Turin before the Fascists seized power. He was elected to parliament in 1921 and served as a leader (quadrumvir) of the March on Rome* of October 28–30, 1922. De Vecchi was named undersecretary at the Ministry of Pensions and then at the Ministry of Finance in late 1922 and early 1923 before being appointed governor of Somalia,* a post which he held from 1923 to 1928. He was a representative of the conservative and Catholic wing of Fascism* and served as ambassador to the Vatican after the signing of the Lateran Accords* in 1929. Subsequently, he served as minister of national education in 1935 and 1936 and then as governor of the Dodecanese Islands* after 1937. On July 24–25, 1943, De Vecchi, a senior member of the Fascist Grand Council, voted against Mussolini* but without taking a leading role in either the plotting or the debates.

AJD

DE VITI DE MARCO, ANTONIO. As an economist, academic, polemicist, and member of parliament, De Viti De Marco spoke forcefully on behalf of the South. Born in Lecce (Puglie) in 1858, he belonged to the first generation of *meridionalisti*, who in the last twenty years of the nineteenth century exploded the myth of a naturally rich South held back by centuries of corrupt administration. From 1900 to 1921 he sat in parliament as a member of the Radical Party,* but it was as a spokesman for economic liberalism that he made his strongest mark in public life. His appointment to teach economics and finance at the University of Rome in 1887 was followed by years of intense activity as a writer for such influential periodicals as the *Giornale degli Economisti* and Gaetano

Salvemini's* *L'Unità*.* Through these and other journals he argued in favor of trade as a means of developing the agriculture of the South, charged that economic protectionism widened the economic gap between North and South, and criticized the government's fiscal and spending policies for diverting capital from productive investments. In 1931 he lost his academic appointment for refusing to take the loyalty oath to the Fascist regime. He died in Rome in 1943.

RS

DIAZ, ARMANDO. Army chief of staff during the last year of World War I,* Diaz reorganized the Italian forces after the defeat of Caporetto* (October-November 1917). He was born in Naples on December 5, 1861, and died in Rome on February 29, 1928. At the beginning of the Caporetto disaster, Diaz led the Twenty-third Army Corps in orderly retreat to the Piave River. As the new commander in chief, replacing General Luigi Cadorna,* he held fast on the Piave for nearly eight months, after which he prepared the triumphal battle of Vittorio Veneto* (October-November 1918), for which he was named Duca della Vittoria in 1921. He joined Mussolini's* first government as minister of war (October 1922); after his retirement in 1924 he was appointed marshal of Italy. There is some controversy concerning just what advice Diaz gave the King regarding the army's possible role in halting the Fascist March on Rome* in October 1922.

SS

DI RUDINÌ, ANTONIO. See RUDINÌ, ANTONIO STARABBA, MARQUIS DI

DIVINI ILLIUS MAGISTRI. Issued by Pope Pius XI* in December 1929, this encyclical on the education of youth reflected not only the traditional position of the Church, but also the struggle between Catholicism and Fascism* over the training of young Italians.

In *Divini illius magistri* the Pope articulated the Church's view of the relative rights and duties of religion, parents, and the state in the education of Christian youth. The encyclical contended that the family has "priority rights" in education, that the Church has "preeminent rights," and that the state, with its resources, has the duty to complement but not to supplant the other two institutions. Pius asserted the Church's prerogatives in both "educazione" and "istruzione" and insisted that the Church possessed "the independent right to judge whether any other system or method of education is helpful or harmful to Christian education." The pontiff vigorously opposed a state monopoly in education and compulsory attendance in state-controlled schools. The encyclical was generally greeted warmly in the Catholic world outside of Mussolini's* Italy.

RJW

DIVORCE. Divorce as a civil institution was rendered possible in Italy by the enactment of a legislative proposal—*disegno legge* No. 898—on December 1,

1970. The journey of divorce legislation in Italy encompasses a period of ninety-two years—from 1878 to 1970. Within the contemporary period, efforts to institute divorce in Italy began in the fall of 1954, when Renato Sansone, a member of the Italian Socialist Party (PSI),* introduced legislation that would have permitted divorce in five cases. But those who opposed divorce—principally the Christian Democrats, under pressure from the Holy See—sought to prevent the legislation from reaching the floor of parliament, or to await adjournment of the legislative session, thus killing the proposal. This tactic became known as *insabbiamento*.

In the fall of 1965, Louis Fortuna, another Socialist, introduced a second proposal. As before, the end of the legislative session disposed of it. He tried again in the spring of 1968. In the fall of that year, another proposal was introduced by Antonio Baslini, a member of the Liberal Party.* The two deputies agreed on a unified version, the Fortuna-Baslini *disegno di legge 898*, which was formally introduced in the Chamber of Deputies* in April 1969. After the Commission on Justice of the Chamber approved the proposed legislation, it was referred to the floor for discussion and vote. On November 28, 1969, the Chamber of Deputies approved the divorce bill 325 to 283. All parties voted for the proposal with the exception of the Christian Democrats, the Monarchists, and the Italian Social Movement (see MSI*).

Victory was not complete. Another year elapsed before the Senate* acted on the proposal. On October 9, 1970, the upper house approved the legislation by a vote of 164 to 150. The law instituting civil divorce in Italy for the first time was promulgated on December 1, 1970. It became operative December 3, 1970.

The opponents of divorce—*gli antidivorzisti*—resolved to undo what had been accomplished. Their strategy was, first, to challenge the constitutionality of the law because it violated Article 7 of the Constitution of 1948*; and second, to follow the procedure established under Article 75 of the constitution by requesting a referendum on the law, hoping that Catholic Italy would abrogate it. Both options entailed risks. If the Italian Constitutional Court* were to assert the constitutionality of the law, then the Lateran Accords* could not be considered necessarily constitutional norms, despite being an integral part of the constitution (Article 7). Should the Christian Democrats resort to the referendum and lose, this would cause a further erosion of their influence.

In fact, both options failed. On December 11, 1973, in two historic decisions, the Constitutional Court ruled that the divorce law did not contravene Article 7 of the constitution. Less than a year later, the referendum of May 12–13, 1974, approved, by a comfortable margin, the law in question.

Under the law, divorce is permitted when one of the partners is sentenced to at least fifteen years in prison; has been sentenced for the physical or sexual abuse of members of the family; has been judged incurably insane and has been confined to an insane asylum for a period of not less than five years; or when the partners have been separated for a period of at least five years.

For further reference see: Italy, *Gazzetta Ufficiale della Repubblica Italiana*, Parte Prima, no. 306 (December 3, 1970) (Rome: Tipografia della Camera, 1970); Gabrio Lombardi, *Divorzio, referendum, concordato* (Bologna: Il Mulino, 1970).

PVB

DODECANESE ISLANDS. This group of twelve islands, located between Turkey and Greece, is also known as the Aegean Islands. The Dodecanese have been under several flags. Turkey ruled them for four centuries. Italy acquired possession in 1912, with the conclusion of the Italo-Turkish war. Following World War II* and the peace treaty concluded between Italy and the Western powers, the islands were ceded to Greece, which has administered them ever since.

PVB

DOGALI. Dogali was the site of an early colonial battle in Eritrea* (now Ethiopia*) where Italian troops were defeated on January 26, 1887. With 500 men, Lieutenant Colonel Tommaso De Cristoforis suffered a surprise attack while bringing provisions and reinforcements from Moncullo to a besieged garrison at Saàti. Ambushed at Dogali by 7,000 Abyssinian soldiers under the command of the ras Alula, he lost over four-fifths of his men. Following the defeat, Prime Minister Agostino Depretis* introduced successful legislation to finance the sending of reinforcements to Africa. Several years elapsed, however, before significant further expansion was undertaken by Francesco Crispi's* government.

MSG

DOLLFUSS, ENGELBERT. This Austrian chancellor, born in Texing in 1892, was killed during the attempted Nazi coup of July 25, 1934. A Christian Socialist, Dollfuss had become chancellor in May 1932. Mussolini* befriended him, as he wanted to preserve the Austrian state as a buffer against Nazi irredentism. In imitation of Italian Fascism,* Dollfuss suppressed the "party state," created the Fatherland Front, and promulgated an authoritarian constitution. Anxious to annex his homeland, Hitler sought to undermine the government of Dollfuss. When a native Austrian Nazi group assassinated Dollfuss, Mussolini sent troops to the Brenner Pass as a demonstration of support for an independent Austria.

JAL

DONATI, GIUSEPPE. Giuseppe Donati, born near Bologna in 1890, was among the most eloquent Catholic opponents of the Fascist regime. From 1923 to 1925 he was managing editor of *Il Popolo*. Many of his editorials were intransigent repudiations of Fascist statism, nationalism, and corporativism.* He also played a leading role in defending a free press against the restrictions imposed by various Fascist decrees in the years 1923 to 1925. In 1925 he emigrated to

Paris, where he continued his anti-Fascist activities as editor of *Il Corriere degli Italiani*. In several articles he espoused the kind of united anti-Fascist action that was later to assume concrete form in the Armed Resistance.* Donati died in Paris on August 16, 1931.

FR

DOPOLAVORO. The largest mass institution of Fascist Italy, the Opera Nazionale Dopolovaro was established in 1926 to promote broad support for Fascism through national organization of leisure time and coordination of recreational facilities, sports, and cultural activities. It covered urban and rural areas and incorporated all socioeconomic groups and classes. Hierarchical and traditional values were stressed. By 1936 there were over 20,000 local centers, having 2,755,000 members. It originally had considerable popular appeal; after 1936, however, as the regime became noticeably oppressive, the Dopolavoro gradually came to be seen as an instrument of fascistization and ideological conformity. It did not survive Fascism.*

For further reference see: Victoria de Grazia, *The Culture of Consent: Mass Organization of Leisure in Fascist Italy* (New York: Cambridge University Press, 1981).

RSC

DOSSETTI, GIUSEPPE. Born in Genoa on February 13, 1913, Dossetti came from a devout middle-class Catholic family. After a classical secondary education, he entered the University of Bologna in 1930 and received a degree in law in 1934. In 1935 Dossetti began to teach canon law at the Catholic University of the Sacred Heart at Milan. Here he came into contact with diverse cultural influences, and by 1938 he was questioning the Fascist regime. Beginning in 1940 he and others at the university began to meet regularly to consider alternative solutions to Italy's problems. During World War II* he assisted the partisans and became the head of the Committee of National Liberation (see CLN*) in Reggio Emilia. In July 1945 he became vice-secretary of the Christian Democratic Party* there. As a member of the Directory of the national party, he was regarded as a representative of the new and younger generation that had joined with the ex-Popularists in forming the successor to the Italian Popular Party.* Dossetti was elected to the Constituent Assembly of 1946* and in 1948 became a member of the Chamber of Deputies* of the new parliament.

From the outset of his political career, Dossetti took a stance that was independent of Alcide De Gasperi* and the party's center. The Dossetti wing became the most important of the leftist currents. The journal *Cronache Sociali* served as the mouthpiece for him and his followers. The group espoused integralism, that is, a close relationship between Catholic moral positions and political action. In Dossetti's opinion, Italy's problems stemmed from three sources: the existence of two great world imperialisms, the Russian and the American, with Italy caught in the middle; the inability of the Christian Democratic Party, because of its strong right wing, to come to terms with the Italian Communist Party (PCI),* which understood the socioeconomic realities of Italy; and a Church weighed down both by past errors and a theologically illiterate laity. In foreign affairs Dossetti favored neutrality for Italy in the East-West struggle, and he opposed Italy's entry into the North Atlantic Treaty Organization.* These views collided with those of De Gasperi, who considered Dossetti dogmatic and impractical. In 1951 Dossetti suddenly retired from politics to become a priest. He founded a monastic community in Bologna, and although he returned to political life, he never regained his former influence. In 1967 he was appointed pro-vicar general for the diocese of Bologna.

For further reference see: Salvatore Fangareggi, *Il Partigiano Dossetti* (Florence: Vallecchi, 1978); Paolo Pombeni, *Il Gruppo Dossettiano e la fondazione della democrazia italiana* (Bologna: Il Mulino, 1979).

EC

DOUHET, GIULIO. This Italian military officer and early advocate of strategic airpower, sometimes referred to as "the Mahan of airpower," was born at Caserta on May 30, 1869. He entered the army's artillery corps and from 1912 to 1915 headed Italy's first aviation batallion. As a result of his blistering criticism of his country's conduct of the war, he was court-martialed and imprisoned. The debacle of Caporetto* (1917) proved that his criticism had been warranted and led to his rehabilitation. Removed from the retired list, he was put in charge of the Italian aviation service. After the war he attained the rank of major general (1921) and wrote a number of works putting forward his ideas. He conceived of a *guerra fulminante*, or blitzkrieg, in which airpower would be employed as a stategic force to destroy the enemy's potential to wage effective war. In *Il dominio dell'aria* (Command of the Air) (1921), he revealed how the massive use of airpower could paralyze and help defeat an opponent. Douhet also sought the creation of an independent air unit having the autonomy of the army and navy and called for the coordination of the various fighting forces. He died in Rome on February 15, 1930, too early to see the great impact his theories would have on the course of the fighting in World War II.*

For further reference see: Giulio Douhet, *Scritti inediti* (Florence: Scuola di Guerra Aerea, 1951).

FJC

DRONERO, DISCORSO DI. See **GIOLITTI, GIOVANNI**

DUCE. See **MUSSOLINI, BENITO**

DURANDO, GIACOMO. This general, writer, and political figure was born in Mondovì on February 4, 1807, and exiled from Piedmont in 1831 for having participated in the revolutionary events of that year (see Revolutions of 1831*). After a brief stay in Switzerland, he fought for liberty in Belgium, Portugal, and Spain. In France he published his *Della nazionalità italiana*, which sought a moderate and constitutional solution to the Italian problem. In 1847 he returned to Piedmont, founded the journal *L'Opinione*, and was one of the journalists who persuaded Charles Albert of Savoy* to grant a constitution. In 1848–49 he commanded a corps of volunteers in the war against Austria and fought at the battle of Novara.* After the defeat, he seconded the policies of Cavour* and supported Piedmontese participation in the Crimean War.* In 1856 he was appointed ambassador to Constantinople; in 1862 he served as foreign minister and sought a settlement of the Roman Question.* During the war of 1866* he fought and was wounded in the second battle of Custozza (1866).* Subsequently, he was appointed prefect of Naples (1867), later entering the Senate, over which he presided from 1884 to 1887. He died in Rome on August 21, 1894.

FJC

DURANDO, GIOVANNI. This general, brother of Giacomo Durando,* was born at Mondovì on June 23, 1804. An officer in the Piedmontese army who did not appreciate its conservative climate, he resigned his commission and fought in Spain and Portugal on behalf of liberal principles. He returned to Italy in 1842 and during the war of 1848 led the papal army of Pius IX.* Following Pius IX's allocution against participation in the war and the defeat of those who had disobeyed the papal directive, he returned to service in the Piedmontese army and fought at the battle of Novara.* Subsequently, he fought in the Crimean War* as well as in the Franco-Piedmontese war of 1859* against Austria. The following year he was named senator and promoted to general. He died in Florence on May 27, 1869.

FJC

E

ECONOMIC MIRACLE. After World War II* Italy took part in the economic resurgence of Western Europe known as the "economic miracle." Through wise government policies, efficient management, and the ingenuity of producers such as FIAT,* the gross national product of the 1950s and early 1960s increased at an annual rate of 6 percent, while industrial production averaged a yearly increase of about 8.5 percent. Italy at this time had the world's third highest gold reserves. There was an overall improvement in the standard of living, with gains occurring in the consumption of all goods, in travel, and in the construction of schools and housing. Unemployment was reduced by approximately 6 percent during this period, as the economy expanded in all sectors.

WR

EDUCATION, 1859–1980. This history of education in unified Italy may be divided into three major phases: the parliamentary period (1859–1922), the Fascist period (1923–43), and the postwar period (1943 to the present). In each phase, educational philosophy and practice have been characterized by unique problems and distinct approaches to solutions.

The first distinguishable phase of Italian education was regulated by the Casati Law,* promulgated in Piedmont in 1859 and gradually extended to the unified Italian state. The most pressing problems confronting a new Italian educational system were the absence of a national school organization, the need to impart a notion of the *Italianità* to the various provinces, and the extremely high illiteracy rate, which in the South hovered around 80 percent until the turn of the century. The Legge Casati provided for a centralized national Ministry of Public Instruction which regulated and inspected education for the entire kingdom. This centralized system was designed to assist in standardizing educational practice and to form citizens loyal to the new Italy, rather than to local and regional interests. During this period elected municipal school councils were responsible for the establishment of local elementary schools, but in many areas of the country these councils simply refused to allocate sufficient monies.

In 1911 the parliament, recognizing the failure of the councils to care for elementary education, revoked this right from those municipalities judged negligent. Thus, in the overwhelming number of cases, the administration of local elementary schools passed to the province, and the financial concerns came directly under the ministry in Rome. The problem of illiteracy remained a constant one, and in the end the greatest successes in this struggle were made not by the schools themselves, but by the army, which instructed draftees in basic skills during their terms of service.

The final years of the parliamentary regime saw a growing dissatisfaction with the educational system, as increasingly vocal nationalist critics, such as Ernest Colignola,* proclaimed, "La scuola ha fatto Caporetto!"(The Italian school system was responsible for the defeat of Caporetto). Blaming the quality of education for Italy's ills, the nationalists called for a complete reform, and in 1918 a royal commission urged that serious changes be implemented on the national level. Certain of these recommendations, such as one encouraging the "establishment of compulsory schools in every municipality" and one which would have instituted "compulsory schools for illiterate adults up to the age of 45," pointed to the failures of the previous decades.

The coming to power of Mussolini* in 1922 brought major redirections in Italian education. The appointment of Giovanni Gentile* as minister of public instruction resulted in the idealistic reshaping of the educational system and the issuing of the Gentile Reform* in 1923, which the Duce heralded as the "most Fascist of all reforms." The reform reflected Mussolini's desire to placate the Church and to weaken its support for the opposition Catholic political party, the Italian Popular Party,* in that religion classes were initiated in the lower grades, Catholic graduates were permitted to sit for state examinations, and crucifixes were returned to the classroom. Gentile attempted to broaden elementary education, while restricting access to the secondary schools and the universities. His idealism envisioned schools that formed the character, will, and spirit of the students. The business of making young Fascists was left to the elementary schools and to the array of Fascist youth groups from the Balilla* to the Gioventù Universitaria Fascista* (GUF).

Certain elements of the party objected to the meritocratic structure of the Gentile system, which in 1939 was educating only 2.5 percent of the university-aged population. Terming education in Italy "bourgeois," Giuseppe Bottai* instituted the Carta della Scuola* in 1939 in order to infuse Fascist ideals into the schools. The youth organizations, which were hitherto only supplementary to the school system, were integrated into the educational hierarchy. The Carta even required that all university students enroll in the GUF. The outbreak of World War II* in 1939 and the fall of the regime in 1943, however, minimized the effect of the Carta on Italian schools.

Until 1968 the post-World War II years saw few major structural reforms in the educational system with the exception of the eradication of Fascist influence. Enrollments in schools increased dramatically between 1950, when only 9.2

percent of the fourteen-to-eighteen-year age group were in postcompulsory attendance, and 1970, when 37.9 percent were similarly enrolled. The 1968 unrest at the universities resulted in the broadening of access to univeristy facilities, which previously had been restricted almost exclusively to graduates of the classical liceo. By 1980 approximately 23 percent of the university-aged population were in attendance at the universities; the academic and physical plant, however, remained virtually unchanged from 1939 to 1980. The pressures of overcrowding, growing unemployment among the *laureati* or graduates, and the apparent political inertia of the nation resulted in the increasing popularity of extremists groups, such as the Red Brigades,* among the students.

For further reference see: D. Bertone Jovine, *Storia dell' educazione popolare in Italia* (Rome: Laterza, 1966); Barbara Burns, *The Emerging System of Higher Education in Italy* (New York, 1973); Richard J. Wolff, ''The University under Mussolini,'' *The History of Higher Education Annual* 1 (1981): 132–53.

RJW

EIGHTEENTH-CENTURY ITALY, ADMINISTRATIVE REFORMS IN.

Before unification the regional states of Italy had complex administrative systems which had emerged in the late Middle Ages. By the eighteenth century even the republics of Venice, Genoa, and Lucca* had developed a hierarchy of permanent bureaucratic functionaries who responded to the will of the ruler. This type of princely absolutism had mitigated the effects of the refeudalization of Italy during the seventeenth-century economic downturn and had continued to absorb small independent jurisdictions into the major states. During the eighteenth century the impetus to reform was greater in some states than in others. Most progressive were the Duchy of Milan and the Grand Duchy of Tuscany under the Austrian Hapsburgs and the Kingdom of Naples and the Duchy of Parma under the Bourbons, both new dynasties established in Italy early in the century. There were also important changes in Piedmont (the Kingdom of Sardinia under the Savoy) and in the Duchy of Modena under the Este. Venice, Genoa, Lucca, and the Papal States* changed little during the century. Important in carrying out reforms were functionaries in the existing native bureaucracies, many of whom were lawyers and practical professional administrators. Among these was Bernardo Tanucci,* who was trained in law at Pisa and later became the principal minister of Carlo Borbone at Naples. Pompeo Neri,* also trained at Pisa, began his administrative career under the Medici at Florence, was transferred to Milan to become president of the commission for a new *Catasto* (tax survey) for Lombardy* in 1748, and later returned to Tuscany, where he became one of the chief ministers of the Grand Duke Peter Leopold.* Reform efforts varied from place to place, but the reforms in general aimed to make state administrations more efficient. Reform of law codes, such as the one partly enacted under Victor Amadeus II in Piedmont with the *Costituzioni Piemontesi*, developed early in the century. The War of the Austrian Succession and the Seven Years War spurred tax reform, especially in the Hapsburg dominions. High grain prices and scarcity during the 1760s inspired efforts to free the grain trade and stimulate economic progress. Eighteenth-century reformers attempted to reduce the size of debts and to restore direct taxation on land, an aim similar to the single tax proposals of the French Physiocrats. In Hapsburg Lombardy the effort to increase tax revenue, which began with the new Austrian administration in 1714, involved an entirely new geometric land survey of the entire duchy, which was completed in the 1750s, and the creation of new local councils in every community to administer the tax. Overcentralization of the Lombard administration from Vienna provoked opposition at Milan during the 1780s. In Tuscany tax reform was carried out in the 1770s and 1780s on the basis of the existing assessments, and resistance to the regime was less intense. Still, throughout Italy centralization imposed by eighteenth-century administrative reform aroused widespread opposition.

For further reference see: F. Valsecchi, *L'assolutismo illuminato in Austria ed in Lombardia* (Bologna: Zanichelli, 1931); D. M. Klang, *Tax Reform in Eighteenth Century Lombardy* (New York: Columbia University Press, 1977); L. Dal Pane, *La finanza Toscana dagli iniziii del secolo XVIII alla caduta del Granducato* (Milan: Banca Commerciale Italiana, 1965).

RBL

EIGHTEENTH-CENTURY ITALY, INDUSTRY IN. With the general economic upturn of the eighteenth century, manufacturing in the Italian states experienced a revival and also the beginnings of the reorganization of production which led ultimately to industrialization. The seventeenth century had witnessed a shift in the center of European economic activity from the Mediterrean to ports on the Atlantic and, with state protection, the emergence of national markets in England and France. Traditional centers of Italian textile production in northern Italy did not expand in this period. Wool production declined, although through guild protection export of quality silk cloth continued in eighteenth-century Piedmont, Lombardy,* Venice, and Tuscany, as did production of cloth of all kinds for local consumption throughout the peninsula. There were also centers for production of other specialized products such as paper, ceramics, glass, leather goods, and firearms. Guild regulation, which extended from the dominant cities over the subordinate countryside, had particular importance in Italy, where it tended to separate higher-quality products of the cities, on which export depended, from products of common consumption, which might be produced in the countryside. During the eighteenth century the traditional textile industries of the major cities in the North continued to suffer from French and English competition, which, especially with the mechanization of cotton texile production, was aiming at mass production of cheaper textiles for common use. Gradually Italian producers sought to adopt similar strategies. The guilds made it difficult to introduce new methods of production, but they were gradually suppressed in Tuscany and Lombardy through the Hapsburg reforms of the 1770s and 1780s, and elsewhere during the Napoleonic period or shortly thereafter. In the silk industry reorientation of production using foreign techniques caused the decline of some traditional centers, such as Florence and Lucca,* which did not survive the end of guild protection; but the silk industry expanded in Piedmont and Lombardy, where French methods of production were successfully adopted. The technology for industrialization in the early nineteenth century was mostly imported from abroad. Its successful adoption depended on the native skills of Italian artisans. This was a period of difficult transition for the artisans of Italian cities. The disappearance of guild regulation was combined with little improvement in wages, a rising cost of living in the late eighteenth century, increasing competition for employment, and a deterioration of traditional skills.

For further reference see: Bruno Caizzi, *Storia dell'industria italiana dal XVIII secolo ai giorni nostri* (Turin: Unione tipografico-editrice torinese, 1965); Luigi Dal Pane, *Storia del lavoro in Italia dagli inizii del secolo XVIII al 1815* (Milan: Giuffrè, 1958).

RBL

EIGHTEENTH-CENTURY ITALY, LAW CODES IN. In *Dei delitti e delle pene* Cesare Beccaria* lamented the outdated legal practices of his day, but in the eighteenth century Italian legal studies and legislation kept pace with advances in other parts of Europe. Legal procedure was based on Roman law, canon law, and the maze of legislation of the different Italian states. Italian universities, such as those of Pisa, Bologna, and Rome, taught exclusively Roman and canon law. Inspired by the rational ideas of the Enlightenment,* the eighteenth century witnessed a revival in legal studies that included a new interest in practical legislation and in codification of the law. The works of the French jurist Montesquieu and the Italian theorists, like Lodovico Antonio Muratori* at Modena, Cesare Beccaria* at Milan, Gaetano Filangieri at Naples, and Lampredi at Pisa, stimulated a concern with the more theoretical aspects of law and shifted the focus from simple codification to rational concepts of natural law and utility, although, in practice, eighteenth-century efforts at codification resulted mostly in the compilation of collections of existing statutes. Such was the *Costituzioni Piemontesi* compiled for Victor Amadeus II of Sardinia-Piedmont and published in 1723. The effort to compile a law code for the Grand Duchy of Tuscany, first attempted under Pompeo Neri* in the 1740s, encountered difficulties in the inability to determine an appropriate model for a general code. Modena was more successful with the *Codice Estense* of 1771. In Tuscany, an extensive reform of criminal procedure in 1786, which abolished capital punishment, is sometimes called the *Codice Leopoldino*, but Tuscany did not acquire a true criminal code until 1853, and a civil code had still not been completed before Italian unification. Milan benefited from the work of Austrian jurists, as the Austrian civil and criminal codes were extended to Lombardy* in 1815. In general, the French law codes of the Revolution and Napoleon I* had an important impact in Italy, both through their temporary adoption and through the impetus they gave to the elaboration of new native codes after the Restoration: in the

Papal States* in 1817, in the Kingdom of the Two Sicilies* in 1819, in Piedmont in 1837, and in Modena in 1851.

For further reference see: V. P. Mortari, *Tentativi di codificazione nel Granducato di Toscana nel Secolo XVIII* (Naples: Liguori, 1971).

RBL

EIGHTEENTH-CENTURY ITALY, POPULATION GROWTH IN. During the early decades of the seventeenth century, Italy's population remained practically stable or even decreased. However, there was a recovery in the last decades of the seventeenth century, and in the eighteenth century, the population began the long-term increase that has continued, with acceleration, to the present:

Year	Population (in thousands)	Fifty-Year Increase (per 100)	Annual Increase (per 1,000)
1600	13,272		
1650	11,543	− .13	− 2.6
1700	13,373	+ .16	+ 3.1
1750	15,484	+ .16	+ 3.1
1800	18,091	+ .17	+ 3.3
1851	24,162	+ .34	+ 6.7
1901	33,370	+ .38	+ 7.6
1951	47,159	+ .41	+ 8.2

Italy thus participated in the general population upswing of eighteenth-century Europe that preceded industrialization. While the population of the largest cities slightly decreased in the seventeenth century, it began to grow again in urban centers during the eighteenth century. Regionally, the rural population grew slightly more rapidly in the South (including Sicily) in the eighteenth century than in the Center and in much of the North, a difference that continued through the nineteenth century. This led to transoceanic migration from the South and ultimately to the influx into the northern industrial cities.

For further reference see: K. J. Beloch, *Bevolkerungsgeschichte Italiens* (Berlin, 1961), vol. 3; M. Livi-Bacci, *A History of Italian Fertility during the Last Two Centuries* (Princeton: Princeton University Press, 1977).

RBL

EIGHTEENTH-CENTURY ITALY, RURAL CONDITIONS IN. The eighteenth century saw an improvement in the Italian countryside in a period when the vast majority of the population continued to live directly from agriculture. The extent of the upturn depended on the trend of demand, the nature of landholding, and the agricultural technology. In the eighteenth century the population of Italy, which had remained static in the seventeenth century, began to increase.

Prices of agricultural products rose steadily from the 1750s onward, parallel to the trend of prices in Europe generally. In response, Italian agricultural production increased, chiefly through extensive improvements in cultivation. More units of land, previously uncultivated wooded and marshy areas, were brought under cultivation, a development that affected the entire peninsula and accounted for an increase of agricultural production in the South as well as in the North. Intensive improvement, based on utilization of new techniques of farming and higher-yield crops, was mainly restricted to the North and Center, where rural capitalism was more developed. In the Po Valley there were experiments with artificial pastures, dairy farming, and cultivation of higher-yield cereals, such as maize. There was also domestic production of linen and hemp, an expansion in the cultivation of silk, and some carding and spinning of rough wool. Intensive development occurred less easily in central and southern Italy. In the Center, and particularly in Tuscany, progress was hindered by the prevalence of share-cropping (see *mezzadria**), which made it difficult to enlarge estates and change the traditional pattern of promiscuous cultivation (grain, vines, and olives in the same fields). Sharecroppers were unable to take initiative independently, and despite much discussion of agricultural techniques landlords were slow to promote innovations. In the Kingdom of the Two Sicilies,* in the South, feudal tenure of the large estates continued until the Napoleonic legislation of 1805–1806. Although Sicily remained a center of grain production of some importance, feudal landlords in the South paid little attention to the rural economy. Medium-sized owners were relatively few, the material condition of peasant laborers was very poor, and intensive improvement was hardly begun. These were contributing causes of the growing economic disparity between North and South.

RBL

EIGHTEENTH-CENTURY ITALY, URBAN GRAIN SUPPLY IN. During the late Middle Ages and the Renaissance the Italian states evolved an elaborate system for supplying grain to the major cities, a reason for the relatively large urban population of the North. The system was abandoned in the late eighteenth century with the introduction of free trade in grain. The provisioning legislation of Tuscany and the *Abbondanze* of Florence and Siena—the urban magistracies that provided for distribution of grain—show how the system worked. Export of grain from Tuscany was prohibited, and its internal marketing was tightly controlled. The *Abbondanza* bought grain from local producers at low prices after the harvest or imported grain through the port of Livorno in years of dearth, and maintained storehouses. In good years, or until prices rose in the spring, consumers bought grain on the open market. In periods of high prices or of shortage the *Abbondanza* supplied grain to bakers and regulated production of bread. Disadvantages of the system were its excessive regulation and inefficient bureaucratic functioning, which removed market incentives to increase local production, and the huge cost of importing grain, sometimes from as far away as the Baltic. Urban consumers thought the system favored their interests, and this produced a brief reaction in Tuscany after provisioning was abandoned in 1768. Although higher prices assured sufficient supply of grain by private merchants, grain prices rose alarmingly and caused controls to be temporarily reintroduced in 1793.

RBL

EINÀUDI, LUIGI. President of the Republic* from 1948 to 1955, prominent postwar politician, and well-known economist, Luigi Einàudi was born in Carrù (Cuneo) on March 24, 1874. After graduating from the University of Turin, Einàudi embarked on a teaching career in both Turin and Milan, authoring many well-received works in economic theory and finance. In 1908 he assumed the editorship of the journal *Riforma Sociale* and shortly thereafter began to write for *La Stampa** and the prestigious Milanese daily *Corriere della Sera.** In 1960 he published the first of his monumental eight-volume series on the Italian economy, *Cronache economiche e politiche di un trentennio* [Economic and political chronicles of three decades] (1960–65).

In 1935 Einàudi's liberal economic theory, which attacked both communism and the Fascist corporative system, began to generate suspicion among the authorities. It was not, however, until 1943, shortly after being elected president of the Ateneo Torinese, that he was forced to flee to Switzerland. With the final defeat of Mussolini,* Einàudi returned to Italy and in 1944 was named president of the Banca d'Italia.* A member of the Constituent Assembly of 1946* as a Liberal, he also served as deputy premier, charged with stabilizing the lire, in Alcide De Gasperi's* first government, before being elected the first president of the Republic on May 11, 1948. At the end of his term, Einàudi returned to his academic life, defending liberal economic theory in his many books and articles. He died in Rome on October 30, 1961.

For further reference see: A. Bernardino, *La vita di Luigi Einàudi* (Padova: CEDAM, 1954).

RJW

EL ALAMEIN. A major battle (October 23–November 4, 1942) in World War II* between the Germans and Italians under Field Marshal Erwin Rommel and the British under General Bernard Montgomery. The British 8th Army had stopped an Axis* advance on Cairo in July 1942 along a line stretching inland from the Egyptian coastal village of El Alamein. In October the British thrust westward from that line with 200,000 men and 1,000 tanks against Rommel's 53,000 Germans and 43,000 Italians (with 200 and 300 tanks respectively). After 10 days of fierce fighting, the remnants of Rommel's shattered army retreated across Libya* into Tunisia. Libya was occupied by the British.

WDG

ELECTORAL SYSTEMS UNDER THE REPUBLIC. The procedures by which Italian voters have selected government officials since 1946. A wide variety of forms are used at the national, regional, provincial, and communal levels. Only legislators are directly elected by the people; executives and judicial officials are either appointed or elected by other bodies. Various types of proportional representation systems predominate in direct elections, but these systems are often mixed with preferential voting, single-member district majority systems, limited voting, and split-ticket voting. Suffrage is direct, universal, and free; women voted for the first time in 1946. In 1975, the minimum age for voting was lowered from twenty-one to eighteen, except for Senate* elections where it remained at twenty-five.

EER

ELENA OF MONTENEGRO. Queen of Italy, 1900–1946, wife of Victor Emmanuel III* and mother of Humbert II.* She was born January 8, 1873, at Cettigne, and died November 28, 1953, at Montpellier. Her early years spent with relatives at the autocratic court in St. Petersburg influenced her later support of the Fascist regime and her fear of Italian Liberalism. She shared Victor Emmanuel's anticlericalism, and after his abdication in May 1946, resided with him in exile in Alexandria, Egypt, until his death.

WR

ELLENA, VITTORIO. Economist, career bureaucrat, and member of parliament, Ellena made his major contributions as a gatherer and compiler of statistics. Born on May 11, 1844, he received his first appointment to a minor post in the Ministry of Agriculture in 1862. From there he transferred to the Ministry of Finance in 1877, where he held the important post of chief customs collector. His many publications brought him recognition as an expert in matters of finance, trade, production, and emigration.* His survey of industrial production and working conditions, *La statistica di alcune industrie italiane* (1880), made a case for industrial protectionism. He was elected to parliament in 1886 and appointed Minister of Finance by Giovanni Giolitti* in May 1892. He resigned for health reasons on July 7 and died on July 19, 1892.

RS

EMIGRATION. Characterized as Italy's "safety-valve," emigration has played a major role in its social and economic history. Between 1871 and 1900, the population present in Italy grew by 5.646 million (from 26.801 million to 32.447 million). During the same period, approximately 5.9 million Italians emigrated; and although before 1902 there are no reliable statistics on repatriation (which at times exceeded 50 percent), the permanent exodus was nevertheless immense. Between 1901 and 1920, the population present increased by 3.461 million; total emigration for the period exceeded 9.854 million, with a peak of 872,600 in 1913. Although about 2.75 million were repatriated from transoceanic areas (no figures are available for repatriation from European and adjacent countries), the permanent exodus surpassed by far the country's net population growth. Between

1921 and 1940, the population grew by 6.652 million (from 38.023 to 44.675 million), with a total emigration of 3.281 million. Repatriation from all areas is estimated at 1.968 million, with a total permanent emigration of 1.313 million, marking a sharp decline in the ratio between permanent expatriation and population growth, reflecting emigration-immigration policies as well as changes in economic conditions in both Italy and countries of destination. From 1941 to 1955, Italy's population grew by 3.199 million (to 48.185 million), with a permanent emigration of 1.523 million, once again increasing the emigration ratio to population growth, and showing a return to the pattern of emigration characteristic of the period 1870 to 1886, when emigration to European areas far exceeded that overseas, with France, Austria, Germany, and Switzerland the countries of preference. From 1887, and especially after 1900, the trend was markedly altered in favor of North and South America. Between 1901 and 1913, 58.2 percent of all emigrants went overseas, and the rest to European and adjacent areas. By 1902, emigration to the United States far exceeded that to Brazil and Argentina combined, and in 1913 reached the peak figure of about 377,000. After 1921, owing in part to restrictive U.S. legislation, the trend was reversed in favor of European areas and has remained generally so ever since.

In 1876, over 86 percent of all emigrants came from northern Italy; in 1890 the figure dropped to 49.9 percent, whereas that of the South rose from 6.6 percent to 40.1 percent, rising further to 46 percent during the period 1901 to 1913. Significantly, during the latter period about 75 percent of northern emigrants went to European countries, whereas more than 90 percent of southern emigrants went overseas. And although for the period 1876 to 1955 nonagricultural emigrants consistently exceeded agriculturists in total numbers (except for 1885–1889, 1891, and 1895–1896), southern emigrants were prevalently agriculturists or unskilled workers, whereas northern emigrants were generally more skilled. Given the more than doubling of Italy's population from 1871 to the present (26.8 million to about 57 million in 1981) and the paucity of the country's economic resources, emigration, emigrant remittances, and well-to-do repatriates all contributed to making emigration a veritable safety-valve for what otherwise might have been uncontainable socioeconomic pressures. Others have nevertheless viewed emigration as the squandering of precious human resources to the benefit of foreign countries and have used this argument as justification for colonial expansion.

For further reference see: Robert F. Foerster, *The Italian Emigration of Our Times* (Cambridge, Mass.: Harvard Univeristy Press, 1924); Angelo Filipuzzi, *Il diabattito sull'emigrazione, 1861–1914* (Florence: F. Le Monnier, 1976); Zeffiro Ciuffoletti, *L'emigrazione nella storia d'Italia, 1868–1975* (Florence: Vallecchi, 1978).

SS

ENCICLOPEDIA ITALIANA. See **GENTILE, GIOVANNI**

ENI. The Ente Nazionale Idrocarburi, a state holding corporation, was established by law on February 10, 1953. Its initial charge was to explore and develop oil deposits in the Po Valley, but when no commercially significant oil deposits were found it turned to oil exploration abroad. Under the energetic and controversial leadership of its first director, Enrico Mattei,* ENI contracted to buy oil from the Soviet Union and obtained concessions from Iran, Egypt, Libya,* and other oil producers on the basis of a 75-25 profit-sharing formula that broke the standard 50-50 agreements practiced by major oil companies. ENI also developed oil fields off the coast of Sicily. In 1963 it processed about 4 million tons of oil, or 18 percent of the national need. In its operations, which cover the gamut from prospecting to distribution, ENI exemplifies a model of industrial production which combines public and private investments in state-owned enterprises.

RS

ENLIGHTENMENT. This period was the Italian counterpart of the French Enlightenment. Most of the writers associated with it were active in the 1750s and 1760s, but echoes of it persisted until the 1780s. Its origins go back to the end of the seventeenth century, when the ideas of René Descartes, John Locke, and Isaac Newton began to reach Italy. Already, Italian intellectuals had begun to rebel against the conformity imposed by the Counter-Reformation, and the foreign philosophies further expanded their views on man and society. By 1750 the new ideas were dominant. At this time, moreover, the changed political situation in Italy enabled Italians to have greater contacts outside their country. Many travelled widely. At the same time, foreigners came to Italy and a lively intellectual exchange ensued.

In Italy the Enlightenment focused on all sorts of reform. A vast literature examined the problems endemic to Italian life and suggested concrete remedies. The role of the Church and the clergy, the power of the nobility, the restraints on trade and commerce, inequitable laws and taxation, censorship, and over-emphasis on the past were all examined. In Naples, Antonio Genovesi* used his university post to advocate far-reaching changes in the social and economic structure of Neapolitan society and to train a generation of practical reformers who tried to put his ideas into practice. In Milan, *Il Caffè* * attacked the status quo. After its demise, its writers continued their reforming drive both as private individuals and as public officials.

While most Italian Enlightenment writers concentrated on specifically Italian issues, addressing an Italian audience, there were a few exceptions whose work transcended national interests. Cesare Beccaria's* indictment of contemporary criminal justice, for instance, gained a wide consensus and became the basis for the penal reform movement that slowly developed throughout Europe. Ferdinando Galiani's* treatise on money also broke new ground and found a European audience, while Gaetano Filangieri's study of legislation complemented and crowned earlier French and English writings.

Naples, Milan, and Florence were the epicenters of the Italian Enlightenment, for in these states administrators tried to put into effect, at various times and with varying degrees of success, reforms advocated by enlightened thinkers. The influence of new ideas, however, spread throughout the peninsula, and plans for practical reforms, penned by the Italian counterparts of the French *philosophes*, proliferated. Wherever there was an educated Italian, the works of the Enlightenment were read and discussed. Exposed to its critical spirit, Italians became increasingly aware of how far behind Italy had fallen since the Renaissance. They probed the reasons for this decline and elaborated plans for Italy's revival. Thus, for Italy the Enlightenment was a period of intense desire for renewal, progress, and fundamental change in the political, religious, economic, and social structures of the country.

For further reference see: Franco Venturi, *Italy and the Enlightenment. Studies in a Cosmopolitan Century* (New York: New York University, 1972); idem, *Settecento riformatore*, 2 vols. (Turin: Einaudi, 1969, 1976).

EPN

ENOTRIO ROMANO. See **CARDUCCI, GIOSUÈ**

ENTE NAZIONALE IDROCARBURI. See **ENI**

ERITREA. Now a province of Ethiopia,* it was known until 1890 as the *Bahr Nagash*, "coastal territory." Beginning in 1869 with the purchase of the Red Sea port of Assab by the Rubattino Shipping Company, the Italian presence in northeast Africa was asserted definitively by the occupation of Massawa in 1865. In the following four years, much of the coastal lowlands was occupied by the Italans, despite fierce resistance from the local population. After the death of Emperor Yohannes IV, his successor, Menelik II,* sought Italian support as a means to consolidate his power and concluded in May 1889 the Treaty of Uccialli (see Uccialli, Treaty of*), which formally recognized the Italian possession of the coast. In 1890 the Colony of Eritrea formally came into being, evoking the classical Greek nomenclature of the Red, or Erythraean ("Eritrean") Sea. Some 100,000 Italian farmers were eventually settled in the highlands of Eritrea, a railroad was constructed between Massawa and the colonial capital at Asmara, and Eritrea became a staging area for the second invasion of Ethiopia in Italy in 1935. During World War II* a British force conquered the Italian colony. Italy surrendered all claims to the territory in the peace treaty of 1947. The British occupation ended in September 1952, when Eritrea entered into a federation with Ethiopia. Ten years later the Eritrean Assembly, closely controlled by the Ethiopian government, voted for complete union with Ethiopia. Most of the Italians remaining in the country subsequently departed. A large portion of the Eritrean population refused to accept annexation by Ethiopia, and a series of liberation movements has struggled for nearly twenty years to create an independent Eritrea, free of all contacts with Ethiopia.

RLH

ETHIOPIA. Although Italian artists and traders were present in Ethiopia as early as the fifteenth century, the involvement of Italy in Ethiopian affairs began in 1869 with the purchase of the port of Assab by the Rubattino Shipping Company. In 1882 Assab formally became an Italian colony, and three years later the port of Massawa was occupied by an Italian force. Resistance by local chieftains and Emperor Yohannes IV limited the Italian occupation for the most part to the insalubrious coastal lowlands of Eritrea.* When Menelik II* became emperor after the death of Yohannes IV, he quickly concluded a Treaty of Perpetual Peace and Friendship with Italy at Uccialli (see Uccialli, Treaty of*) on May 2, 1889.

The Italian government then formally established the Colony of Eritrea and proclaimed to the European powers that it had a formal protectorate, "Italian Abyssinia," over the Ethiopian Empire. Although most European powers recognized the protectorate as legal and binding, Menelik II denounced the Treaty of Uccialli in February 1893. Following months of desultory warfare and border skirmishes, an Italian army invaded northern Ethiopia and advanced as far as Adowa,* the capital of Tigre province. There the Italians suffered a catastrophic defeat in 1896. Prime Minister Francesco Crispi's* government fell, and his dream of empire collapsed.

Although Italy attempted to use its entry into World War I* as a means to reassert its claims to Ethiopia (see London, Treaty of*), events in Europe undermined these plans. During the 1920s and early 1930s the Italians greatly strengthened their military position in Eritrea and Somalia,* which eventually became staging grounds for a full-scale second invasion of Ethiopia in 1935. First under the regency (1917–30) and then under the monarchy (1930–73) of Haile Selassie I,* Ethiopia actively courted the European powers, who responded by providing the African state with large numbers of modern rifles.

Italy's second Ethiopian war began with the bombardment of Adowa on October 3, 1935, and the invasion by an army of more than 100,000 men. Although Haile Selassie appealed to the League of Nations, which eventually adopted economic sanctions against Italy, it was all in vain. Italian military supremacy, including the use of poison gas, overwhelmed the Ethiopian armies. On May 9, 1936, Mussolini* formally annexed Ethiopia, and much of the country was occupied by the Italians for the ensuing five years. Fascist plans called for the rapid construction of a highway network in Ethiopia, to the virtual exclusion of all other economic development, and for the large-scale settlement of Italians in the fertile highlands of Ethiopia. By 1939 approximately 130,000 Italians resided in Ethiopia and Eritrea. Ethiopian resistance was dealt with ruthlessly, but Italians never gained full control over the countryside. The Italian occupation of Ethiopia, or Africa Orientale Italiana, as it was briefly designated, came to an end in 1941, when British armies and Ethiopian guerrilla units rapidly defeated the Italian army. On May 5, 1941, Haile Selassie returned to Addis Ababa, marking the final chapter in the brief history of Italian imperialism. In September 1974 he was ousted in a coup. Haile Selassie died in detention in 1975.

RLH

EUROPEAN RECOVERY PLAN. See **MARSHALL PLAN, ITALY AND THE**

EXEQUATUR. Exequatur is the approval given by secular rulers to papal bulls, briefs, or other documents, required for them to have binding force in their territories. Devised as a means of increasing the control of secular rulers over the Church within their territories, at the expense of the papacy, the exequatur first appeared in the late Middle Ages. In Italy, it was first introduced by Martin I of Sicily and Alfonse I of Naples in the early fifteenth century. After the unification of Italy, a decree of March 5, 1863, asserted the necessity of the exequator for all papal acts within the kingdom. The Law of Papal Guarantees* of 1871 eliminated the need for the exequatur for most acts, except those granting major benefices or ecclesiastical properties. The exequatur was finally abolished by the Concordat of 1929 (see Lateran Accords*).

AJR

F

FABBRICA ITALIANA AUTOMOBILI TORINO. See FIAT

FABBRONI, GIOVANNI VALENTINO MATTIA. Fabbroni was a Florentine natural scientist and political economist of the late Enlightenment* (1752–1822). As a youth he served as assistant to the mathematician Felice Fontana, who was charged with organizing the Florentine Museum of Natural History by Duke Peter Leopold of Hapsburg-Lorraine* in 1766. In 1775 he accompanied Fontana to Paris and London, where he became a Freemason, and established contacts with Jefferson, Franklin, Priestley, and others, with whom he continued to correspond. He was a convinced proponent of Physiocracy, the theories of which he developed in *Reflexions sur l'etat actuel de l'agriculture* [Reflections on the actual state of agriculture] (1780) and *Dei provvedimenti annonari* [On provisioning] (1804), and was well known among scientists of the revolutionary period. After the Napoleonic occupation of Tuscany he participated in the imperial administration of Italy and became professor at the University of Pisa and director of the Florentine museum, positions that he continued to hold after the Restoration until his death.

RBL

FACCIO, RINA. See ALERAMO, SIBILLA

FACTA, LUIGI. Last president of the council of ministers of Liberal Italy, Facta was born in Pinerolo, Turin, on November 16, 1861. A member of parliament from 1892, he filled several ministerial posts, particularly under Giovanni Giolitti.* Facta then formed his own government, in February 1922. Following its collapse on July 19, 1922, Facta reconstituted his ministry on August 1. Doubts persist over Facta's objectives and behavior during the parliamentary crisis of October 1922. He tried to negotiate secretly with Mussolini* and possibly with Gabriele D'Annunzio.* While the March on Rome* was in progress, Facta personally delivered to Victor Emmanuel III* the martial law decree deliberated by the government. The King dissented. Following Mussolini's takeover Facta retired from public life, although appointed a senator in 1924. He died in Pinerolo on November 5, 1930.

RSC

FALCO, GIAN. See PAPINI, GIOVANNI

FANFANI, AMINTORE. Prime minister, president of the Senate,* and economic historian, Amintore Fanfani was born in Arezzo in 1908. Author of a number of important works on economics, Fanfani accepted a chair at the Catholic University of Milan in 1936. He was active in Catholic youth groups during the Fascist period, especially the Federazione Universitaria Cattolica Italiana (FUCI)* and the Laureati, and emerged in 1946 as one of the younger leaders of the Christian Democrats.

Elected to the Constituent Assembly of 1946* on the Christian Democratic list, he joined Alcide De Gasperi's* cabinet a year later. In 1953 he was appointed minister of the interior under Giuseppe Pella* and subsequently became secretary-general of the Christian Democrats (1954–59). From 1954 to the mid-1960s, Fanfani's influence both in the party and in national politics was at its height. Under his direction, the Christian Democratic Party* embarked upon a campaign of social activism, and in 1958 he was called upon to form a government of his own. But Fanfani's coalition of Republicans, Social Democrats, and Christian Democrats lasted only a few months. In the early sixties, he became the architect of the Center-Left coalition. He served as premier from 1960 to 1963 and again in the early eighties. In 1968 he became president of the Italian Senate.

For further reference see: Piero Ottone, *Fanfani* (Milan: Longanesi, 1966).

RJW

FANTI, MANFREDO. This Italian general was active in the events surrounding the annexation of central and southern Italy in 1860. Born in Capri on February 28, 1808, Fanti was exiled in 1831 for involvement in revolutionary activities. He returned to Piedmont in 1848 and entered its service in the war against Austria. In 1859–60 Fanti organized the army of the Central Italian League, took part in the invasion of the Papal States,* and became minister of war. Clashes with Giuseppe Garibaldi* and his volunteers over their role in the unification movement and in the Italian army weakened his position. Fanti later commanded an army corps in Florence, where he died on April 5, 1865.

JCR

FARINACCI, ROBERTO. Roberto Farinacci, a Fascist politician, was born in Isernia on October 16, 1892, and died at Vimercate on April 28, 1945. He entered politics as a reformist Socialist and labor organizer. He supported Italy's entry into World War I* and became a collaborator on Mussolini's* newspaper, *Il Popolo d'Italia.* In 1919 he joined the new Fascist movement and headed its squads in Cremona, where he became infamous for the brutality of his attacks on the Socialist and Catholic worker organizations.

Farinacci entered parliament in 1921 and participated in the March on Rome.* From the beginning he represented the most aggressive wing within the regime, which sought total party control over the state. Mussolini, whose tactics carried him toward a compromise with the established order, rarely allowed Farinacci much leeway. Farinacci's moment seemed to arrive, however, when, as a result of the crisis provoked by the murder of Giacomo Matteotti (see Matteotti Crisis*) in 1924, he was appointed secretary of the Fascist part (see Fascism*) in February 1925. His term in office lasted little more than a year, during which time he centralized power in the hands of the party secretariat. Mussolini, who disliked Farinacci intensely, forced him out in March 1926 and never again offered him such an important government post. From his base in Cremona Farinacci became an exponent of the alliance with Nazi Germany after 1936, of harsh measures against Italian Jews in 1938, and of cultural primitivism when he launched the artistic competition for the Cremona Prize during the late 1930s.

Farinacci favored war on the side of Germany in 1940 and served briefly in Albania.* On July 25 he voted against Dino Grandi's* motion to strip Mussolini of his power over war policy. Farinacci was a power behind the scenes during the brief history of the Italian Social Republic (see Salò, Republic of*) (1943–45). In April 1945 he was seized and executed by the Armed Resistance* forces at Vimercate.

For further reference see: Harry Fornari, *Mussolini's Gadfly: Roberto Farinacci* (Nashville, Tenn.: Vanderbilt University Press, 1971).

AJD

FARINI, LUIGI CARLO. *Risorgimento** statesman and historian, he was born on October 22, 1812. Farini's medical career did not preclude his involvement in revolutionary activities. He was exiled from the Papal States* under Gregory XVI,* but returned with Pius IX's* amnesty and held several political positions in Rome.

Farini's public life after 1848 was associated with the Kingdom of Sardinia, which he served in a variety of capacities, particularly during the period of expansion in 1859–60. Cavour,* at this time, sent him to central Italy to arrange its annexation to Piedmont, and to Naples as viceroy to facilitate its union with the Sardinian kingdom. Quarrels with the Garibaldians and a lack of understanding of the South made this latter mission an arduous one. A brief tenure as prime minister in 1862–63 was troubled by illness. Farini authored *Storia dello stato romano dal 1815 al 1850* (1850–53). He died in Quarto on August 1, 1866.

JCR

FASCI DI COMBATTIMENTO. See MUSSOLINI, BENITO

FASCIO DELLA DEMOCRAZIA. See CAVALLOTTI, FELICE

FASCIO DI EDUCAZIONE NAZIONALE. See **CODIGNOLA, ERNESTO**

FASCIO RIVOLUZIONARIO D'AZIONE INTERNAZIONALISTA. See **OLIVETTI, ANGELO OLIVIERO**

FASCI SICILIANI. This network of industrial and agrarian workers' clubs (*fasci*) gave its name to the wave of popular unrest that spread throughout Sicily in 1893–94. The first *fasci* were urban, with the Catania *fascio*, founded in 1891 by Giuseppe De Felice-Giuffrida,* and the Palermo *fascio*, established in 1892 by Rosario Garibaldi Bosco, being the principal centers of activity. In May 1893 representatives of the local organizations meeting in Palermo adopted a Socialist program, joined the Socialist Workers' Party, and decided to carry their political campaign to the countryside. The peasant response was surprisingly favorable. Economic conditions in the countryside had been deteriorating for several years due to economic depression and a tariff war with France, which hurt production of wine and fruit. In the western part of the island the sulphur industry was in crisis due to competition from U.S. producers. The demands of those workers and peasants who joined the *fasci* included the renegotiation of labor contracts, tax reductions, admininstrative reforms in local government, and distribution of former common land appropriated by large landowners in the 1860s. By September 1893 the leaders of the movement claimed a membership of 300,000, but that figure was probably highly inflated. Nevertheless, political candidates sponsored by the *fasci* scored impressive victories in local elections, indicating broad popular support.

In the autumn of 1893 the movement turned to direct action characterized by spontaneous occupations of the land by peasants, loud demonstrations, and confrontations with the police. The reactions of landowners and prefects to these developments revealed a deep-seated fear of popular initiatives. Their fears were shared by Francesco Crispi,* who in December 1893 took over as head of the national government, replacing the more flexible Giovanni Giolitti.* Apparently convinced that a separatist plot fomented by subversives and foreign agents was behind the disturbances, Crispi reacted by placing the island under martial law and sending 40,000 troops to restore order. His fears of a separatist plot to detach the island from the national state had little basis in fact, as no single goal or political creed united the members. Some demonstrators marched behind religious banners, while others rallied in the name of the King, Giuseppe Garibaldi,* or Giuseppe Mazzini.* From the point of view of the local notables, the most dangerous aspect of the movement was its popularity, particularly among peasants, for they saw that as a threat to their control of local politics.

For further reference see: S. F. Romano, *Storia dei Fasci Siciliani* (Bari: Laterza, 1959).

RS

FASCISM. Fascism was an Italian political movement of the Radical Right founded by its Duce, Benito Mussolini,* in Milan on March 23, 1919, and remaining in power from October 28, 1922, to July 25, 1943. As a generic term, fascism (small *f*) refers to analogous movements in a number of European and other states. Only in Mussolini's Italy and in Hitler's Germany did fascist movements become regimes.

Italian Fascism went through various phases. The first one was from 1919 to 1922. The Fasci di Combattimento (Fighting Leagues), founded by the ex-Socialist Mussolini, were nationalistic, antiliberal, and anti-Bolshevik. They expressed the confused dreams for national grandeur and social reform felt by many war veterans and young people from the lower and middle strata of the bourgeoisie. A foretaste of Fascism could be found in Italy's Nationalist Party, Georges Sorel's revolutionary syndicalism,* Catholic corporativism,* Futurist irrationalism, D'Annunzian ritualism, and Nietzschean voluntarism. But without the social disruptions brought on by World War I* and the Russian revolutions (plus the frustration felt by Italy at the Paris Peace Conference*), it is unlikely that Fascism would have become a significant movement in 1919. Initially, it was republican, anticlerical, and somewhat radical in its economic program. After the electoral setback of November 1919, however, Mussolini, a pragmatist, shifted to the Radical Right to court the monarchy, the army, and the Church. In 1920–21 landowners and *squadristi* in the lower Po Valley added a reactionary, violent new dimension to Fascism. After the collapse of the Socialist strikes in the metal industries in September 1920, the movement pushed ahead rapidly and soon adopted the name Partito Nazionale Fascista (PNF). A threatened Fascist March on Rome* caused Victor Emmanuel III* to invite Mussolini to form a coalition government (October 28, 1922).

A new chapter began between January 3, 1925, and November 1926, when the Duce imposed the totalitarian state, outlawed opposition parties, and arrested many of their leaders. This was triggered by the Fascist murder in 1924 of Giacomo Matteotti (see Matteotti Crisis*), leader of the Unitary Socialist Party, and the ensuing Aventine Secession*. The Duce's corporative state emasculated parliament and abolished free trade unions and the right to strike, but preserved capitalism. The regime promoted public works and autarky (see Autarchia*) but did nothing to modernize the agricultural sector. In 1933 it created the Industrial Reconstruction Institute (IRI)* to subsidize faltering banks and industries. Much of the resulting parastatal capitalism has survived. The most enduring action of the regime, however, was the signing of the Lateran Accords* (concordat, treaty, and financial accord) with the Vatican on February 11, 1929, thereby reconciling church and state. In 1932 Mussolini belatedly wrote his "Doctrine on Fascism," but action always outstripped theory in his amorphous ism.

Soon Fascism embarked upon a new phase—military aggression. In 1935–36 Italy conquered Ethiopia* in defiance of the League of Nations. From 1936 to 1939 Mussolini sent "volunteers" to help General Franco in the Spanish Civil War.* In April 1939 Italy invaded Albania.* Meanwhile, the Duce approved the Rome-Berlin Axis* (1936), expanding it into an alliance in May 1939. He introduced anti-Semitic decrees in Italy in 1938–39.

Mussolini did not join Hitler in the war against France and Britain until June 1940. During the next two years he also declared war on Greece, Yugoslavia, Soviet Russia, and the United States. A series of military debacles and a vote of nonconfidence in the Duce by the Fascist Grand Council set the stage for Victor Emmanuel III to carry out a coup d'état against the sickly dictator on July 25, 1943. The new regime of the King and Marshal Pietro Badoglio* began to dismantle Fascist institutions and signed an armistice with the Allies.

In September 1943 German forces overran northern Italy, rescuing Mussolini and propping him up in a puppet Italian Social Republic (see Salò, Republic of*). He tried to give it a pseudo-leftist orientation in the vain hope of outbidding the Armed Resistance* for support from the workers. Mussolini was caught and executed by Italian partisans on April 28, 1945, when Allied troops were driven into the Po Valley.

For further reference see: Renzo De Felice's multivolume *Mussolini* (Turin: Einaudi, 1965–   ), the major archival study of Fascism; also idem, *Interpretations of Fascism* (Cambridge, Mass.: Harvard University Press, 1977), and Stanley G. Payne, *Fascism: Comparison and Definition* (Madison: University of Wisconsin Press, 1980), for the historiography.

CFD

FASCIST PARTY. See FASCISM

FASCIST SOCIAL REPUBLIC. See SALÒ, REPUBLIC OF

FATTI DI MAGGIO. See KULISCIOFF, ANNA

FEDERALISM. Federalism is an ideology, and sometimes a political movement, which emphasizes the need for democratic and decentralized government. A strong federalist current existed among Italian intellectuals in the eighteenth century. This became obvious in 1796 when several federalist entries were submitted for a competition on the theme, "Which form of free government is best suited to the welfare of Italy." In contrast to Giuseppe Mazzini,* who advocated a unitary republic, Vincenzo Gioberti* favored a federation of Italian states under the aegis of the Pope, while his fellow Piedmontese, Count Cesare Balbo,* preferred accommodation with Austrian interests. The failure of Gioberti's neo-Guelf federalism (see Neo-Guelf movement*) in the late 1840s gave way to a new, democratic formula of which Carlo Cattaneo* and Giuseppe Ferrari* were the leading advocates. The former believed that the creation of small republics on the Swiss model would make it easier for Italy's democratic leaders to raise the level of political sophistication of the masses and to teach them self-government. Both were convinced that Italy's traditions, especially the continued vitality of ancient, once autonomous cities, were not conducive to the growth of a centralized nation-state on the French or Spanish model. When just such a state was established in 1860, democratic federalists shifted their strategy to a defense of local autonomies vis-à-vis the central government. Cattaneo's disciples Gabriele Rosa and Archangelo Ghisleri became the chief spokesmen for this new version of federalism, which found support among the postunification Republican,* Radical,* and Italian Socialist* parties. Federalism, however, remained largely an intellectual movement until after World War II,* when Ernesto Rossi,* Altiero Spinelli, and others founded the Movimento Federalista Europeo. In the tradition of Cattaneo's writings on "A United States of Europe" and of Ferrari's *La federazione repubblicana*, they advocated a democratic Italian republic with strong regional autonomy within the context of a federation of Western European democracies.

CML

FEDERATI. One of the numerous secret societies of the Restoration, the Federati were formed, apparently in 1818, from the union of various liberal and nationalist organizations of Piedmont and Lombardy.* Their aims were Italian independence, to be gained by expelling the Austrians, and the creation of a constitutional regime. They played an active role in the revolutions of 1820–21* but disappeared soon after their failure.

AJR

FEDERAZIONE UNIVERSITARIA CATTOLICA ITALIANA (FUCI). The Federazione Universitaria Cattolica Italiana was founded in 1896 as a branch of Catholic Action* dedicated to work among Italy's university students. Strongly linked to the nascent Christian Democratic movement (see Christian Democracy in Italy*) of Don Luigi Struzo* and Don Romolo Murri,* the Federazione enjoyed considerable autonomy from the lay leadership of Catholic Action and generally cultivated direct relations with the Vatican. The organization consisted of two branches, male and female (its members known as *fucini* and *fucine*) with a lay president and an *assistente ecclesiastico* appointed by the Vatican.

Generally viewed as in the camp of liberal Catholicism, in 1898 the Federazione was accused by Antonio di Rudinì's* government of complicity in the disturbances of the *Fatti di Maggio* (see Kuliscioff, Anna*) in Milan and was often at odds with the conservative leadership of Catholic Action. In 1906 Pius X,* mindful of the university students' attachment to the papacy, granted the Federazione permission to hold national congresses separate from those of Catholic Action.

With the advent of Fascism* the Catholic university students, identified as they were with the Partito Popolare (see Italian Popular Party*), were the object of considerable political harassment. This culminated in the 1931 dissolution of the group by Mussolini* and its subsequent reorganization. Under the guidance of Igino Righetti* and Giovanni Battista Montini (later Pope Paul VI*), the Federazione struck a decidedly anti-Fascist pose until 1933. After a brief period of harmony with the government, FUCI leaders Aldo Moro* and Giulio Andreotti* again led the Catholic students away from the regime.

Individual *fucini* assisted immeasurably in the formation of the postwar republic, and most of the important Christian Democratic politicians at one time or another passed through the ranks of the Federazione.

For further reference see: Renato Moro, *La formazione della dirigente cattolica, 1929–1937* (Bologna, 1979); Richard J. Wolff, "The Makings of Christian Democracy: The Federazione Universitaria Cattolica Italiana, 1925–1943" (Ph.D. diss., Columbia University, 1979).

RJW

FEDERZONI, LUIGI. A distinguished Fascist minister of Nationalist origins, Federzoni was born on September 27, 1878, in Bologna, where he studied under Giosuè Carducci,* majoring in letters. As a novelist, art critic, and political writer, he used the acronymous pseudonym "Giulio de Frenzi." He was on the organizing committee of the Italian Nationalist Association.* In 1913 he wrested Rome's first electoral college from Socialist Antonio Camponozzi. He volunteered for military service in 1915. Federzoni served the Fascist regime and supported the merger between Nationalism and Fascism.* Federzoni was minister of colonies from October 28, 1922, to June 5, 1924, when, following the assassination of Giacomo Matteotti (see Matteotti Crisis*), he became minister of the interior. On November 6, 1926, he returned to the colonial post and remained in it until December 18, 1928. Federzoni was president of the Senate from April 20, 1929, until March 15, 1939, and was made president of the Italian Academy in March 1938. At the Interior Ministry, Federzoni brought the Fascist Party apparatus under state control. His instructions to the prefects for muzzling the press were notorious.

Doubts surrounding Federzoni's conduct during the March on Rome,* his momentary hesitation over fusion between the Fascists and Nationalists, his efforts at disciplining party chieftains, and his strong monarchical sympathies aroused suspicions among some Fascists. At the Fascist Grand Council meeting of July 24–25, 1943, Federzoni backed Grandi's* majority resolution. The Fascist tribunal in Verona condemned him to death *in absentia*. Tried and sentenced to imprisonment by the Italian Supreme Court, Federzoni was pardoned in December 1947. He died in Rome on January 24, 1967.

For further reference see: Alexander De Grand, *The Italian Nationalist Association and the Rise of Fascism in Italy* (Lincoln: University of Nebraska Press, 1978).

RSC

FERDINAND I OF THE KINGDOM OF THE TWO SICILIES. Ruler of the unified Kingdom of the Two Sicilies* from 1816 to 1825, he had previously reigned as Ferdinand IV of Naples and Ferdinand III of Sicily. He was born in Naples on January 12, 1751, and succeeded to the thrones of the two kingdoms as a minor in 1759, when his father became king of Spain as Charles III. Until the French Revolution shook Europe, Ferdinand's ministers, most notably Bernardo Tanucci,* were able to pursue a reforming program. This reformism diminished after Ferdinand's masterful wife, Maria Carolina, engineered Tanucci's fall in 1776. Ferdinand joined the Second and Third Coalitions against the French and sought refuge in Sicily from invading French armies in 1799 and again from 1806 to 1815. Ferdinand granted Sicily a constitution under English pressure in 1812 and, after his restoration in 1815, created a centralized administration for Naples and Sicily, which preserved reforms introduced by the French but repudiated constitutionalism and alienated liberals. Forced by revolution in 1820 (see Revolutions of 1820–21*) to concede a constitution, he quashed it with the help of Austrian armies after having attended the Congress of Laibach in 1821. Ferdinand embraced reaction until his death at Naples on January 4, 1825.

For further reference see: Harold Acton, *The Bourbons of Naples* (London: Methuen and Co., 1956); Michelangelo Schipa, *Nel regno di Ferdinando IV Borbone* (Florence: Vallecchi Editore, 1938).

RCu

FERDINAND II OF THE KINGDOM OF THE TWO SICILIES. He succeeded his father, Francis I, as King of the Two Sicilies (1830–59) on November 8, 1830. Born in Palermo on January 12, 1810, upon becoming king he granted an amnesty to political prisoners, lowered taxes, and promoted the nation's economy, but he resisted agitation for constitutional government or for the Italian national cause. Cherishing independence, he followed a policy of nonalignment in foreign affairs.

Revolt in Palermo in January 1848 led Ferdinand to grant a constitution, while popular pressure pushed him to war against Austria in April. He managed to initiate counterrevolutionary measures in May, and by late spring 1849 had shelved the constitution and subdued Sicily. Labeled "King Bomba" by his critics for the bombardment of Messina, Ferdinand henceforth pursued a stubborn policy of reaction, centralization, neutrality, and opposition to the national movement. He died at Caserta on May 22, 1859.

RCu

FERDINAND III OF HAPSBURG-LORRAINE, GRAND DUKE OF TUSCANY. Second son of the Grand Duke Peter Leopold,* Ferdinand (1769–1824) was educated at Florence through the period of reforms effected by his father. He succeeded as duke when his father became emperor in 1790, and was married to Maria Luisa, daughter of Ferdinand IV of Naples. Ferdinand III proved to be a conscientious but not active ruler. He followed internal policies set forth by his father's administrative reforms. The outbreak of the French Revolution evoked few immediate repercussions in Tuscany, although in response to high grain prices free trade in grain was restricted in 1793. The death penalty was restored for crimes of *Lesa Maesta'* (high treason) in 1795. The duchy withdrew from the First Coalition in 1795 and was not occupied by the French until 1799, when

Ferdinand escaped into exile in Austria. After the battle of Marengo,* the Treaty of Lunéville in 1801 replaced him with Ludovico Borbone and the Regno di Etruria, which lasted until the duchy was annexed to the French Empire in 1807. In recompense Ferdinand was made grand duke of Wurtzburg in Austria. He returned to Tuscany in 1814, restored the progressive prerevolutionary administration of the duchy, and retained the Napoleonic commercial code. Under the Restoration Ferdinand governed through capable councillors Neri Corsini and Vittorio Fossombroni, and continued reforms initiated in the eighteenth century. The ducal government started new drainage and hydraulic projects, built roads, and began a new cadastral tax survey that was completed in the 1830s. It also restricted the powers enjoyed earlier by local communal government through more strict central control. Foreign policy under the Restoration was directed by Austria. Ferdinand was succeeded in 1824 by his son, Leopold II.

For further reference see: A. Zobi, *Storia civile della Toscana* (Florence: L. Molini, 1850–52), vols. 4–5.

RBL

FERRARA, FRANCESCO. A prominent economist of the liberal era, Ferrara was born in Palermo on December 7, 1810. Arrested by the Bourbon government for his liberal ideas, he was elected to the Sicilian parliament in 1848 and headed a delegation that offered the crown of Sicily to a son of the King of Sardinia. In exile in Piedmont after the revolution, he served on the editorial board of Cavour's* *Il Risorgimento* and taught political economy at the University of Turin. He also participated in the Sicilian Provisional Government of 1860. Thereafter he held several administrative posts and served in the national parliament, becoming minister of finance in 1867 and senator in 1881. He was the leading Italian proponent of classical economic theory. His ideas can be traced in several prefaces that he wrote for the series *Biblioteca dell'economista* (1850–70). These prefaces were reprinted in 1889–90 in the two-volume work *Esame storico critico di economisti e dottrine economiche* [Critical historical examination of economists and economic doctrines]. His university lectures, *Lezioni di economia politica* [Lessons of political economy], circulated widely in Italy, as did his essays on the currency and on the grist tax (see Macinato*). He died in Palermo on January 22, 1900.

CML

FERRARI, GIUSEPPE. A major proponent of democratic federalism and socialism in the *Risorgimento*,* Ferrari was born to a middle-class family in Milan on March 7, 1811. After earning a law degree at the University of Pavia and studying philosophy with Gian Dominico Romagnosi,* in 1838 Ferrari immigrated to France in search of greater political freedom and intellectual stimulation than were possible in Hapsburg Lombardy.* He moved in Saint-Simonian and Socialist circles there and became acquainted with Pierre Leroux, Georges Sand, and François Buloz, editor of the *Revue des Deux Mondes.* Ferrari wrote for the

Revue and for Leroux' *Revue Indépendante*, but at the same time took courses at the Collège de France, where he met Jules Michelet and Edgar Quinet. Following in their footsteps, he published philosophical treatises, with an eye to an academic appointment, which he obtained at the University of Strasbourg in 1841. His lectures on early modern Europe became a cause célèbre when Louis Veuillot, editor of the ultramontane newspaper *L'univers*, attacked the rector of the university for allowing an atheist as well as liberal Catholics and Protestants to teach there. Ferrari was forced to resign, and he accepted a post at the lycée of Rochefort-sur-mer, where he became involved in left-wing conspiracies. Ultimately, he fled Rochefort to escape arrest. The Bonapartist coup of December 2, 1851, put an end to his academic aspirations, and he joined Proudhon and other intellectuals in intransigent opposition to the Second Empire. In the 1850s he wrote his most important political works (*Filosofia della rivoluzione* [Philosophy of the revolution], *La federazione repubblicana* [The republican federation], and the *Histoire des révolutions d'Italie* [History of the Italian revolutions]) and collaborated with Carlo Cattaneo* in the publication and dissemination of works on the revolutions of 1848.* Although he had become a French citizen in 1842, Ferrari returned to Italy and ran for parliament in 1861. Until his death in Rome on July 1, 1876, he represented the rural district of Gavirate-Luino in northern Lombardy. In parliament he became one of the best known and most outspoken critics of the economic and ecclesiastical policies of the *Destra storica* (see Destra, La*) and also of Garibaldian adventurism. He urged his colleagues on the Left (see Sinistra, La*) to play the role of "loyal opposition" to the moderate liberals and to press for fiscal and social reform as well as for the radical secularization of Italian society. In the last decade of his life he resumed the philosophical studies of his youth and developed a generational explanation of historical change, discussed in his *Teoria dei periodi politici* [Theory of political periods] (1874). Ferrari expounded his radical ideas not only in parliament, but also in his lectures at the universities of Turin and Florence and in meetings of the Consiglio Superiore per la Pubblica Istruzione, on which he served in the mid-1860s.

For further reference see: Silvia Rota Ghibaudi, *Giuseppe Ferrari. L'evoluzione del suo pensiero, 1838–1860* (Florence: Olschki, 1969); Clara M. Lovett, *Giuseppe Ferrari and the Italian Revolution* (Chapel Hill: University of North Carolina Press, 1979).

CML

FERRERO, GUGLIELMO. Guglielmo Ferrero, a historian and novelist once internationally famous for his *Grandezza e decadenza di Roma* [The greatness and decline of Rome] (1902–7), was born in Naples on July 21, 1871. He studied literature in Bologna (1891) and law in Turin (1893) where, in collaboration with the eminent Jewish-Italian criminologist Cesare Lombroso, he coauthored *La donna criminale* [The female criminal] (1893). After marrying Lombroso's daughter in 1901, Ferrero produced his five-volume Roman history, which was popularly hailed as a startling reinterpretation of his subject. The Fascist regime forced him into exile in 1929. Residing and teaching in Geneva, Switzerland, he thereafter wrote mostly in French, publishing books on Napoleon I,* Talleyrand, and political power, as well as several novels, before he died on August 3, 1942.

HP

FERRI, ENRICO. This Socialist was born on February 25, 1856, in San Benedetto Po (Mantua) into a middle-class family. His father was a businessman, while his mother came from peasant origins. Ferri completed high school in Mantua and obtained his *laurea* in jurisprudence at Bologna (1877). His thesis won Cesare Lombroso's admiration and launched Ferri as one of the founders of the noted Italian school of positivist criminology. Both Ferri and Lombroso eventually developed international reputations in the field. Ferri's academic career in jurisprudence began with his appointment as professor of penal law in Bologna, and later in Siena, Pisa, and finally Rome (1884–1925). In addition, Ferri gained popular recognition for his defense of 200 arrested peasants at the well-publicized trial known as "la boje" in 1884–85. Well known among a variety of groups in the Cremona-Mantua area, Ferri launched a parallel career in politics and was first elected deputy from the moderate Left (see Sinistra, La*) in 1886. He continued to hold a parliamentary seat through 1919 and was again reelected in 1921. After 1893, however, he sat as a Socialist member of the newly formed Partito Socialista Italiano (see Italian Socialist Party, PSI*).

In his early years as a Socialist, Ferri defended a moderate position that partly reflected his intellectual commitments. He sought a mode to accommodate Marxism and the precepts of scientific positivism, which he accepted from his early years as a student. The effort to reconcile the ideas of the class struggle with the environmentalist, evolutionary thought of Darwinism was published in his *Socialismo e scienza positiva. Darwin, Spencer, Marx* [Socialism and positive science: Darwin, Spencer, Marx] (1894). Here, the absolute positivist belief in progressive change and adaptation was merged with the broad Socialist vision of the unfolding of history. Ferri's intellectual views logically argued for a moderate, even reformist, stance within the party.

Such, however, was not the case. Between 1896 and 1908, especially during 1903–8, when he edited *Avanti!*,* Ferri frequently adopted the most intransigent positions on strategy, defending all but the most extreme exponents of noncollaboration. To further complicate matters, despite this position he often compromised considerably with supporters of more accommodating postures. The end result was that he became more obsessed with the world of party tactics than with the real problems in Italy. By 1908 he lost his following, resigned from *Avanti!*, and left Italy for a one-year lecture tour in Latin America. He never regained any major role in the PSI.

Ferri also wavered on his antimilitarism. Opposed to imperialism during the 1890s, he voted for the annexation of Libya* in 1912. In 1914–15, however, he remained neutralist. At the end of the war, he was invited to preside over the government commission to reform the penal code, and in 1921 the fruits of its labors were embodied in a new code. This change was short-lived, for the Fascist government essentially adopted a repressive, authoritarian penal procedure which ignored Ferri's long-developed understanding of criminal behavior. Notwithstanding, Ferri moved close to Fascism* with the success of Mussolini.* In 1926 he denounced socialism as a "gaseous degeneracy" and even argued that Matteotti had been murdered by enemies of Mussolini (see Matteotti Crisis*). In turn, Ferri was to be installed as a senator, but died in Rome on April 12, 1929, shortly before the ceremony.

For further reference see: Franco Andreucci, "E.F.," in *Il movimento operaio italiano. Dizionario biografico* (Rome: Ed. Riuniti, 1976) 2: 342–48.

JMC

FIAT. Fabbrica Italiana Automobili Torino is not only Italy's largest manufacturer of automobiles but also its biggest privately owned corporation, with a labor force of 238,000 in 1980. It was founded on July 1, 1899, by thirty Turinese investors, several of whom were titled noblemen. Among the original founders was Giovanni Agnelli,* who assumed primary responsibility for running the enterprise. The economic crisis of 1907 brought about a reorganization that enabled Agnelli to launch production of the first serially produced vehicles at lower prices. A policy of negotiating generous contracts produced a reliable labor force before the outbreak of World War I.* During the war FIAT experienced rapid expansion; the company branched out into production of armaments, and its labor force grew from 4,000 to 40,000. The problems of rapid growth were exacerbated in 1919–20 by political instability in the country. During those years FIAT experienced bitter labor confrontations that subsided with the economic crisis of 1921. During the Fascist period FIAT consolidated its position as the country's leading automobile manufacturer. A major step in that direction was the establishment on July 27, 1927, of the holding company IFI (Instituto Finanziario Industriale), which also consolidated the Agnellis' hold on FIAT.

RS

FIBBI, LINA (GIULIETTA). Fibbi was born in Florence on August 4, 1920. Her anti-Fascist family was in exile in France after 1923. She joined the French Young Communist League and was in and out of prison (1939–43). During the Armed Resistance* Fibbi was attached to the General Command of the Garibaldi Brigades and helped organize women in Milan. After the war she was part of the Italian Communist Party (PCI)* directorate, served as national secretary of the Italian Federation of Textile Workers, and was elected to the Chamber of Deputies* in 1963 and 1968.

MJS

FILONARDI, VINCENZO. He was the first Italian consul in Zanzibar (1885) and the founder of V. Filonardi e Compagnia, the largest Italian commercial enterprise in East Africa. Politically ambitious for Italy, Filonardi strove to gain Zanzibari recognition of Italy as a major power in East African affairs alongside Britain and Germany. Meeting with only modest success, Filonardi subsequently arranged, through the intermediary of the Imperial British East Africa Company, for the rental of Zanzibar's coast ports in Somalia* to the Filonardi Company (1893–96); but the trading potential of the area did not live up to his expectations, and he sought to sell his company to other interests. The Ethiopian victory at Adowa,* however, reduced the Italians' interest in colonial enterprises, and the Somali region drifted until finally, in 1905, the Filonardi holdings became the colony of Italian Somalia.

RLH

FINANZA ALLA MAGLIANI. See **MAGLIANI, AGOSTINO**

FINOCCHIARO-APRILE, CAMILLO. Political figure and jurist born in Palermo on January 28, 1851, he commenced his career as a devoted disciple of Giuseppe Mazzini.* A close friend of Francesco Crispi,* he held a number of administrative posts in Palermo before his election to the Chamber of Deputies in 1882. For thirty-four years Sicily returned him to the Chamber. Vice-president of that body from 1907 to 1911, he served as minister of posts and telegraph communications in the first cabinet of Giovanni Giolitti* (1892–93) and subsequently presided over the Ministry of Justice under Luigi Pelloux* and Alessandro Fortis,* and during the fourth Giolitti ministry from 1911 to 1914. Interested in educational and juridical matters, he was instrumental in introducing a number of reforms. He died in Rome on January 26, 1916.

FJC

FINZI, ALDO. Aldo Finzi, born in 1891, was a veteran of Gabriele D'Annunzio's* expedition to Fiume* in 1919 and 1920. He subsequently joined the Fascist movement and was active in the squads of the Po Valley. After his election to parliament in 1921, Finzi became one of Mussolini's* most trusted political agents. In October 1922 he was appointed undersecretary of the Ministry of the Interior, where he carried out Mussolini's policy of curbing the power of local Fascist leaders and dividing the anti-Fascist opposition. In June 1924 he was forced from the government because of his involvement in the murder of the Socialist deputy Giacomo Matteotti (see Matteotti Crisis*). Not politically active after 1924, Finzi was arrested in 1943 for anti-Fascist activities and was executed by the Nazis in the Ardeatine Cave massacre of March 24–25, 1944 (see Gruppi di Azioni Patriottica*).

AJD

FIORDELLI, PIETRO. The spiritual leader of the diocese of Prato achieved notoriety for being the first bishop of the Catholic Church to be tried by the civil authorities since the inception of the Kingdom of Italy* in 1861. This event was of unique juridical significance because, under Article 7 of the Italian constitution, "the State and the Catholic Church are, each in its own sphere, independent and sovereign."

Fiordelli was born in 1916 in a town near Perugia. He pursued a brilliant career within the Church and served as editor of the weekly *La Voce*. His trial before the First Penal Section of the Tribunal of Florence stemmed from a letter that he wrote and ordered read to the faithful on August 12, 1956. In it, he condemned Mauro Bellandi and Loriani Nunziati for having entered into marriage only civilly, thus violating Article 34 of the Concordat (see Lateran Accords*). He therefore branded them "public sinners," whereupon the couple brought suit against him for criminal defamation of character. The bishop was found guilty of this charge, but the tribunal decreed that the sentence be suspended for five years and that no judicial record be made thereof. In an appeal the decision was reversed.

For further reference see: Giorgio Moseon, "Il vescovo, lo stato, e il cittadino," *Il Ponte*, no. 1 (January 1958); P. Vincent Bucci, *Chieso e Stato: Church-State Relations in Italy within the Contemporary Constitutional Framework* (The Hague: Martinus Nijhoff, 1969).

PVB

FIRMIAN, CARLO. This functionary in the Hapsburg administration of Lombardy* was born in Trent in 1718 into a noble family already employed in imperial service. Made a councillor of state by Francis I in 1752, he served first as ambassador to Naples and to Rome before becoming governor of Lombardy in 1759, where he remained until his death in 1782. There he became not only the protector of Milanese intellectuals and reformers, but also the agent of increasingly unpopular measures introduced by Joseph II from Vienna.

RBL

FIRST VATICAN COUNCIL. See **VATICAN COUNCIL I**

FIRST WAR FOR NATIONAL LIBERATION. See **REVOLUTIONS OF 1848**

FIRST WORLD WAR. See **WORLD WAR I, ITALY IN**

FISIOCRAZIA. See **PHYSIOCRACY**

FIUME (RIJEKA). Not as significant as Trent and Trieste* in the anti-Austrian slogans of Italian irredentist agitation, the Adriatic city of Fiume became the focus of a clamorous confrontation at the Paris Peace Conference* of 1919 between the Italian delegation and President Woodrow Wilson, who supported Yugoslav claims to the area. Fiume was erected into a free state by the compromise Rapallo Treaty of 1920,* but in December 1920 Giovanni Giolitti's* government forcibly ended Gabriele D'Annunzio's* occupation of the city, which he had seized in September 1919. It was acquired by Italy in an agreement with Yugoslavia in January 1924. Occupied by Yugoslav forces in May 1945, Fiume was assigned to Yugoslavia by the Paris Peace Treaty of February 1947.

SS

FIVE DAYS OF MILAN. See **CHARLES ALBERT OF SAVOY**

FOGAZZARO, ANTONIO. This author was born in Vicenza in 1842 and died there in 1911. Trained as a lawyer at the University of Padua, Fogazzaro underwent a profound religious experience in 1873 after reading Auguste-Alphonse Gratry's *Philosophie du credo* (1861). Gratry's book suddenly recalled him to the Catholic values that he had received as a young man from his eminent teacher, Giacomo Zanella.

His earliest poetry, *Miranda* (1873) and *Valsolda* (1876), was poorly received. He found his true métier as a novelist, beginning with *Malombra* (1881), the spiritual values of which inspired Matilde Serao to dub him "the knight of the Holy Spirit." Fogazzaro's first great success was *Daniele Cortis* (1885), where he expressed in mature form the religious and moral preoccupations that would characterize all of his later books. The most famous of these was *Piccolo mondo antico* [The little world of the past] (1895), which established his reputation as a writer who belonged in the company of Giovanni Verga and Gabriele D'Annunzio.* The more rarefied *Piccolo mondo moderno* [The sinner] (1900) and *Il santo* [The saint] (1905) enjoyed less success, precisely because they lacked the details of caricature and dialect so richly present in the first book of his trilogy.

At the peak of his literary success Fogazzaro found himself embroiled in the controversy over Modernism,* with friends and foes alike regarding him as a supporter of the movement to reform Church dogma. His *Santo* was placed on the *Index* in 1906, and in the following year Pius X* condemned Modernism. A devout son of the Church, Fogazzaro accepted this chastisement, but even his last novel, *Leila* (1910), ran afoul of Catholic censors. Benedetto Croce* was largely responsible for the negative critical reaction that destroyed Fogazzaro's image as a great novelist. However, his reputation as a local colorist without equal in depicting nineteenth-century bourgeois provincial life has endured.

RD

FORGES DAVANZATI, ROBERTO. Roberto Forges Davanzati was born in Naples on February 23, 1880, and died there in 1936. This Fascist publicist and politician had an early career as a Socialist and syndicalist before helping found the Italian Nationalist Association* in 1910. From 1907 to 1914 he was Rome correspondent of the *Corriere della Sera*ted* of Milan and after 1911 was an editor of *L'Idea Nazionale*.* After 1919 he played a leading role in the alliance between the Italian Nationalist Association and the Fascist Party (see Fascism*). After the merger of the two parties in March 1923, Forges became, for a brief period, a secretary of the Fascist Party. From 1933 to 1936 his radio program, "Cronache del Regime," made him one of the most effective propagandists of Fascist Italy.

AJD

FORLANI, ARNALDO. See **CHRISTIAN DEMOCRATIC PARTY** and **PROPAGANDA DUE**

FORTIS, ALESSANDRO. Prime minister from 1905 to 1906, Fortis' evolution from radical republicanism to reconciliation with monarchy and eventually to governmental responsibility marked the transformation experienced by many of Giuseppe Mazzini's* one-time followers. He was born on September 16, 1841, in Florì, and died on December 4, 1909, in Rome. A follower of Giuseppe Garibaldi* in the war of 1866* and in the abortive attempt to take Rome by force (1867), he was among a group of republicans subjected to preventive arrest in 1874. Convinced of the futility of conspiratorial action, Fortis adopted the legalitarian course, was elected deputy in 1880, and served as Francesco Crispi's* undersecretary of state for the interior (1887–90). Minister of agriculture under Luigi Pelloux* (June 1898–May 1899), he broke with the government because of its increasingly repressive policy and became a lieutenant to Giovanni Giolitti,* whom he succeeded as prime minister from March 1905 to February 1906. Fortis was firm in dealing with a strike by railwaymen, carried through the nationalization of the railroads, and dared conclude an unpopular commercial treaty with Spain, all Giolittian-sponsored measures.

SS

FORTUNATO, GIUSTINO. This writer, political figure, and champion of the cause of the Italian South, or Mezzogiorno, was born on September 1, 1848, in Rionero in the Basilicata. Educated at the Jesuit college in Naples, from 1878 to 1880, he served as the Neapolitan correspondent of *La Rassegna Settimanale*,* founded by Leopoldo Franchetti* and Sidney Sonnino.* Elected to the Chamber of Deputies from the college of Melfi in 1880, he sat on the Right (see Destra, La*) with the followers of Sonnino. He remained in the Chamber until April 1909, when he was nominated to the Senate. A political educator more than a politician proper, on more than one occasion he refused to participate in the government. Intensely interested in social questions, and above all in conditions in the South, he was instrumental in overturning the "Mito del Mezzogiorno," which saw the region as a garden that was either exploited by the government or ruined by those who lived there. Fortunato revealed that the South's problems were geographic and economic as much as political and suggested a series of remedies. In his most important work, *Il Mezzogiorno e lo stato italiano* [The

South and the Italian state] (1911), he not only examined the problems of the South, but proposed a comprehensive program to bring about its regeneration. He died in Naples on July 23, 1932.

FJC

FOSCOLO, UGO. A poet, dramatist, and novelist born in 1778 on the Venetian-controlled Ionian island of Zante and strongly influenced by Greek culture, Foscolo moved to Venice in 1792, where he later observed Napoleonic politics. His play *Tieste* (1797) was followed by the novel *Le ultime lettere di Jacopo Ortis* [Last letters of Jacopo Ortis] (1802), a Wertherian work with Italianate overtones credited with inspiring nationalism of various political hues. Vacillation in Foscolo's support for Napoleon I* appears in the poems *Dei sepolcri* [On sepulcres] (1807), and later in his 1811 satire of the Emperor in the play *Ajace* [Ajax]. In 1806 he ended two years in the Napoleonic army to pursue a brief academic career as professor of Italian rhetoric at Pavia. Opposed to an Austrian-controlled Lombardy,* he spent his final years in England, where he died in 1827.

In England he worked on his poem *Le Grazie* [The graces], translated the *Iliad*, and pursued a new career as literary critic and historical interpreter of Italy for the *Edinburgh Review*, the *Westminster Review*, and other English journals. Foscolo aspired to a balance between romanticism and classicism. Aristocratic and cosmopolitan, he declined to cater to bourgeois taste, yet professed admiration for simple poetry evolved from primitive and popular cultures.

For further reference see: Glauco Cambon, *Ugo Foscolo* (Princeton: Princeton University Press, 1980); Mario Fubini, *Ugo Foscolo: Saggio critico* (Florence: La Nuova Italia, 1962).

MSM

FOUR-POWER PACT. This covenant, initiated on June 6, 1933, by representatives of the Italian, German, British, and French governments, was based on an earlier, more ambitious proposal of Benito Mussolini.* The Italian dictator had wished to shift the discussion and resolution of major diplomatic issues like disarmament and revision of boundaries from the League of Nations (in which France and her eastern European allies had dominant influence) to a smaller grouping in which Italy and Germany would carry greater weight. Mussolini's original draft had called for a parity of armaments for Germany and revision of its boundaries with Poland. France's allies protested, and the British and French governments then insisted that Mussolini's specific recommendations be omitted from the proposal. The pact, which referred to the League of Nations and treaties of international peace and arbitration, was soon ignored.

JKZ

FRANCHETTI, LEOPOLDO. Franchetti was a wealthy Florentine landowner, born on May 31, 1847. In the course of his political career he advocated colonial expansion as a means of solving the land problem. An early *meridionalista* (together with Sidney Sonnino* he carried out studies of southern agriculture in the 1870s), he argued that settlement colonies would help solve the Southern Question.* His ideal was a conservative rural democracy based on an economically secure peasantry. He joined the influential *Rassegna Settimanale*,* through which he publicized his ideas. Elected to the Chamber in 1882, he served there until 1909, when he was appointed to the Senate. Although his land settlement venture in Eritrea* collapsed after 1896, he continued to advocate similar ventures for Libya* and Asia Minor. Disheartened by the news of Caporetto,* Franchetti committed suicide in Rome on November 4, 1917.

RS

FRANCIS I OF THE KINGDOM OF THE TWO SICILIES. Francis succeeded his father, Ferdinand I* of the Neapolitan Bourbon line, as king in 1825 and reigned until 1830. Born in Naples on August 14, 1777, he displayed liberal inclinations as a young man. This made it convenient for Ferdinand to designate Francis temporarily as his vicar when he was pressed by England's Lord Bentinck to grant a constitution to Sicily in 1812 and when he was forced by Neapolitan revolutionaries to grant a constitution in 1820. As vicar in 1820–21 Francis evidenced a readiness to abide by the constitution and defend it against invading Austrian armies. As reaction triumphed, however, his sentiments shifted strongly against liberalism.

Weak in will and body, Francis proved to be an inept monarch whose reign was characterized by inefficiency and corruption. In 1826 he substituted Swiss mercenaries for peasant troops and in 1828 savagely repressed an uprising in Cilento. He died in Naples on November 8, 1830.

RCu

FRANCIS II. Last king of the Two Sicilies, Francis II was born in Naples on January 16, 1836. He ascended the throne on May 22, 1859, upon the death of his father, Ferdinand II.* Lacking confidence and experience, he clung to his father's policy of absolutism and opposition to Italian nationalism. Guiseppe Garibaldi's* invasion of Sicily in May 1860 led him *in extremis* to grant a constitution, which failed to rally support. Forced from Naples, he held out at Gaeta* until February 13, 1861, when he fled to Rome. From Rome he plotted to regain his throne. He died at Arco, in the Trentino,* on December 27, 1894.

RCu

FRANCIS IV OF MODENA. See MENOTTI, CIRO; MISLEY, ENRICO; and REVOLUTIONS OF 1831

FRANCIS JOSEPH. Born on August 18, 1830, at Schoenbrunn, he became emperor of Austria in the midst of the revolutions of 1848.* With the support of Russia he was able to repress the revolutions in 1849. During the 1850s he lost Russian support by his equivocal conduct during the Crimean War* and was left alone to face France and Piedmont in the war of 1859*; the result was the loss of Lombardy* and the end of Austrian predominance in Italy. He was equally unsuccessful in meeting the threat from German nationalism, now guided by Otto von Bismarck* of Prussia: in the war of 1866* he was forced not only to renounce Austria's old predominance in Germany, but to cede Venetia to Italy, Prussia's ally. These defeats led to a revival of liberal and nationalist pressures in the empire, to which he had to yield in the end: during 1860–68 he slowly liberalized the government of the empire, while in the Compromise of 1867 he gave Hungary equal status with Austria in a dual monarchy of Austria-Hungary. Other national groups remained dissatisfied, however, particularly those that could look to national states outside the empire: Italians, Yugoslavs, and Rumanians. In foreign affairs, he now sought to follow a policy of peace and conservation of his remaining territories, based upon the Triple Alliance* of 1882 with Germany and Italy. Nonetheless, the last years of his life saw a series of crises with Serbia, which, backed by Russia, encouraged Yugoslav agitation within the monarchy. In 1914 the assassination of his heir, Francis Ferdinand, by Yugoslav terrorists led to the outbreak of World War I.* He died on November 21, 1916, before he could see the disintegration of his empire under the strain of defeat.

AJR

FRANCIS STEPHEN OF HAPSBURG-LORRAINE, HOLY ROMAN EMPEROR AND GRAND DUKE OF TUSCANY.

Second son of Duke Leopold of Lorraine, of the Lotharingian dynasty, and nephew of Duke Charles V of Lorraine, who had been *condottiere* in the service of the Hapsburgs and liberator of Vienna from the Turks in 1683, Francis Stephen (1708–65) succeeded as duke of Lorraine in his own right in 1729. In imperial service he was made governor of Hungary in 1732. Chosen to be consort of Maria Theresa, daughter of Emperor Charles VI, he was married to her in 1736, and in 1745 was elected Holy Roman Emperor. Ten years earlier (1735), as a result of complicated diplomatic maneuvers that followed the War of the Polish Succession, he had been forced to exchange the Duchy of Lorraine for the Grand Duchy of Tuscany. Then, France recognized the Hapsburg candidate for the throne of Poland; in return, the unsuccessful French candidate, Stanislaus Lesczynsky, was awarded the Duchy of Lorraine. In Italy the Hapsburgs ceded the Kingdom to Naples to the Bourbon Don Carlos. In compensation, Francis Stephen was designated the heir to the Duchy of Tuscany at the death of the last Medici duke. After his accession in 1737, Francis Stephen spent less than a year in Florence, preferring to govern Tuscany through a council of regents from Vienna. The Grand Duchy, although benefiting from some administrative reforms, was financially exploited by an impoverished imperial treasury during the War of the Austrian Succession and the Seven Years War. On his death Francis Stephen was succeeded as emperor by his first son, Joseph II, and as grand duke of Tuscany by his second son, Peter Leopold.*

For further reference see: A. Wandruska, *The House of Hapsburg* (Garden City, N.Y.: Doubleday, 1964).

RBL

FRANSONI, GIACOMO FILIPPO. This cardinal and long-term prefect of the Congregation for the Propagation of the Faith was born in Genoa on December 10, 1775. Fransoni early entered the service of the papacy. He was among those exiled from Rome as a result of Pius VII's* quarrel with Napoleon I.* Appointed apostolic nuncio to Portugal in 1823, he was named cardinal by Pope Leo XII* three years later. Fransoni was entrusted with a variety of positions between 1827 and 1834, but is remembered most for his more than twenty-two years with the Propagation. He died in Rome on April 24, 1856.

JCR

FRANSONI, LUIGI. The imprisonment and exile of this archbishop of Turin in 1850 helped to sharpen the battle between the Kingdom of Sardinia and the Church. Born in Genoa on March 29, 1789, Fransoni took possession of the See of Turin in 1832. He gained a reputation for opposing all liberal innovations in Piedmont. The archbishop's imprisonment in May-June 1850 followed his criticism and personal violation of the Siccardi Laws.* A refusal to allow absolution to be granted to a dying member of the government, the Count of Santa Rosa, helped to ensure his exile in September. Fransoni, looked upon by some Catholics as a hero, by others as an unbending reactionary, lived thereafter in Lyons, where he died on March 26, 1862.

JCR

FREEMASONRY. This secret society claims that its esoteric ritual can be traced to ancient and medieval times. Its modern version appeared among intellectuals in Britain around 1710. Its cosmopolitan outlook, humanitarian emphasis, deistic temperament, and faith in both reason and unlimited progress drew inspiration from the underlying assumptions of the Enlightenment.* Freemasonry reached the Italian states between 1720 and 1750. It became radically anticlerical and laic, particularly under Adriano Lemmi, Ernesto Nathan,* and Ettore Ferrari, who were grand masters between 1885 and 1919. Various popes launched over 400 denunciations, beginning with Clement XII's excommunication decree of April 28, 1738. The Italian Nationalist Association* declared Freemasonry incompatible with nationalism in 1912, as did the Italian Socialist Party (PSI)* in 1914. The Fascist government suppressed Freemasonry in 1925.

Italian Freemasonry was reconstituted after World War II* and reverted to the wider movement's international stance, scaling down much of its anti-Church hostility and abandoning most of its secrecy. In 1975 there were 876 lodges in Italy, with 20,000 members.

For further reference see: Rosario F. Esposito, *La massoneria e l'Italia dal 1800 ai nostri giorni*, 5th ed. (Rome: Paolini, 1979).

RSC

FRENZI, GIULIO DE. See **FEDERZONI, LUIGI**

FRISI, PAOLO. Milanese priest, mathematician, and scientist of the Enlightenment,* Frisi (1728–84) taught in the Barnabite College at Pavia, and then at the University of Pisa from 1754 to 1764, when he returned to Milan to be employed in the Scuole Palatine and to become involved with the group of *Il Caffè.** For this journal he wrote the article "Saggio su Galilei" [Essay on Galileo] in 1765, which took issue with d'Alembert's preliminary discourse of the *Encyclopédie* in calling attention to Italian science. He was a strong supporter of the Hapsburg reform movement in Lombardy.* His later writings included his *Saggio sopra l'architettura gotica* [Essay on gothic architecture] (1767), one of the first works of the Gothic revival; *Ragionamento sopra la podestà temporale de' principi e l'autorità spirituale della chiesa* [Arguments on the temporal power of princes and the spiritual authority of the Church] (1768), on church-state relationships, and *Della meccanica* [On mechanics] (1783), a work on civil engineering.

RBL

FUCI. See **FEDERAZIONE UNIVERSITARIA CATTOLICA ITALIANA**

FUORUSCITI. The *fuorusciti* were the anti-Fascist exiles who had to flee abroad during the dictatorship. The term, of medieval origin, was employed in a derogatory sense by the Fascists, but the exiles gave it a positive meaning. Among them many political and intellectual *fuorusciti* were Francesco S. Nitti,* Carlo Sforza,* Luigi Sturzo,* Gaetano Salvemini,* Filippo Turati,* Pietro Nenni,* Alessandro Pertini,* Giuseppe Saragat,* Ignazio Silone,* Palmiro Togliatti,* Carlo Rosselli,* and others. Most sought to regroup in France, but after 1940 the United States and Latin America became their major centers.

For further reference see: Aldo Garosci, *Storia dei fuorusciti* (Bari: Laterza, 1953).

CFD

FUSION, PACT OF. See **MARAVIGLIA, MAURIZIO**

FUTURISM. Futurism was an influential Italian movement in the arts, launched by Filippo T. Marinetti* with a clamorous manifesto in Paris in 1909. To counter a cultural tradition that seemed especially stifling in their country, the Italian Futurists sought a new aesthetic based on the rhythms of the modern machine age. Though its pronouncements were extreme and sometimes ridiculous, Futurism constituted Italy's first major contribution to the European artistic vanguard in over a century. The painters Umberto Boccioni, Carlo Carrà, Giacomo Balla, Gino Severini, and Luigi Russolo transformed cubist techniques in order to convey motion, energy, and the dynamic interaction of the object with its environment. In music, Luigi Russolo devised an "art of noises," to be produced with novel noise-making machines, and Ballila Pratella wrote orchestral compositions conveying the sounds of the modern industrial city. Publicized by a series of provocative manifestoes and "entertainments," Futurism exerted considerable influence on artistic movements in France, England, and Russia by 1914. And ultimately the Futurist style—the combination of shock and humor, the sustained assault on bourgeois values—affected Dada and much of modern art.

The Futurists enjoyed considerable prestige in Italy by 1913, thanks partly to the support of Giovanni Papini,* Ardegno Soffici,* and their review *Lacerba*, but "classical" Futurism proved short-lived. With their belief in the "hygienic" properties of war, the Futurists were in the forefront of the interventionist movement, but several would not survive the war, and the wartime cultural challenge led others in new directions. Marinetti collaborated with Mussolini* in 1919, and Futurism remained loosely associated with Fascism* throughout the years of the regime. It failed to extend its earlier ideas during this period, but aspects of Futurism—the cult of youth and dynamism, the antibourgeois invective, the antitraditional nationalism—contributed significantly to the Fascist style and self-image.

DDR

G

GAETA. A town located fifty-nine miles northwest of Naples on the Tyrrhenian Sea, in the nineteenth century it possessed a powerful citadel which made it one of the most formidable defensive positions in the Kingdom of the Two Sicilies.* In 1806, for example, it took French invaders under General Massena over five months to subdue this fortress for Joseph Bonaparte. Forced by disorders to flee Rome in November 1848, Pius IX* sought refuge in Gaeta, where he was hosted by Ferdinand II* and joined in February 1849 by the Grand Duke of Tuscany, a fellow refugee. It was from Gaeta in 1849 that the Pope solicited advice from the bishops of the world concerning the definition of the dogma of the Immaculate Conception.

After Naples fell to Giuseppe Garibaldi* on September 7, 1860, Gaeta became the final stronghold of the last king of Naples, Francis II.* His dogged defense from October 1860 to February 13, 1861, against the besieging Piedmontese enabled him to cover his fall from power with a certain aura of heroism. Aiding his resistance was the presence before Gaeta of a French fleet commanded by Admiral de Tinan, which prevented a blockade of the fortress until January 19.

RCu

GALDI, MATTEO. See **JACOBINS**

GALIANI, FERDINANDO. Economist and writer, and a disciple of the French Enlightenment, Galiani was born in Chieti in 1728. In *Della moneta* [On money] (1751) he outlined a very advanced economic theory of value based on utility and the scarcity of goods, demonstrating an equilibrium theory based on supply and demand. A great work when written, its suppositions are still valid today. From 1759 to 1769 he served as secretary to the Neapolitan ambassador to France and joined the brilliant circle of Parisian Enlightenment figures, maintaining a lifelong correspondence with many of them. He seemed to turn against his earlier economic liberalism with the publication in 1770 of *Dialoghi sul commercio dei grani* [Dialogues on the grain trade], which held that economic conditions are strictly tied to a specific time and place. After returning to Naples in 1769, he held a number of high economic positions. He wrote the libretto to Giovanni

Paisello's *Socrate immaginario* (1775), *Dialetto napoletano* [The Neapolitan dialect] (1779), and *Doveri dei principi neutrali* [Duties of neutral princes] (1789). He died in Naples in 1787.

FFA

GARIBALDI, GIUSEPPE. The foremost guerrilla leader of the *Risorgimento*,* Garibaldi was born in Nice, then a part of the Kingdom of Sardinia, on July 4, 1807. The son of a merchant marine captain, Garibaldi spent much of his youth working on ships that travelled back and forth between Liguria and the Eastern Mediterranean and the Black Sea. During one such trip in 1833, he was introduced to Giuseppe Mazzini's* Giovine Italia* by another Ligurian sailor, Giovanni Battista Cuneo. In 1833 he took part in an abortive insurrection in Savoy and was sentenced to death *in absentia*. He fled to Marseilles and found work as captain of a small ship bound for Brazil, where he remained from January 1836 until the outbreak of the revolutions of 1848* in Italy. With other exiles he fought on the side of the separatists in the state of Rio Grande do Sul. During these campaigns he met the Brazilian Anna Maria (Anita) Ribeiro da Silva, whom he married in 1842 and who accompanied him upon his return to Italy.

Garibaldi played a major role in the revolution of 1848, especially in the defense of the Roman Republic. Upon the collapse of the revolution, he resumed the seafaring life of his youth, travelling as far away as China and Peru. In the early 1850s he remained active in Mazzinian circles. However, around 1856 he began to subordinate his republican ideas to the belief that only the army of the King of Sardinia could drive the Austrians out of northern Italy. From the founding of the Società Nazionale Italiana* to the unification, Garibaldi supported Cavour's* foreign policy and accepted the leadership of Victor Emmanuel II* of Savoy. In the North Italian campaign of 1859 Garibaldi coordinated the activities of volunteer troops that assisted the Franco-Sardinian forces. He was profoundly disappointed when Napoleon III* and Victor Emmanuel II decided to sign the Villafranca armistice* in July 1859, leaving Venetia to the Austrians. Shortly thereafter, however, he began to plan for the military expedition (*Spedizione dei Mille*) that overthrew Bourbon rule in Sicily and Naples in 1860. The expedition had the tacit support of Cavour and of the British government. When Garibaldi decided to use his strong southern base to move against the papal government, Cavour withdrew his support and indeed persuaded the King to send troops into central Italy. Not wishing a confrontation with royal troops, Garibaldi gave up his attempt to conquer Rome, only to try again in 1862 and 1867.

As Italy's most popular revolutionary figure, in the decade after unification Garibaldi became the focal point of attempts to complete the territorial unification through the liberation of Rome and Venetia. Although a member of parliament, on several occasions he led his enthusiastic followers in *coups de main* against the wishes of the kingdom's constitutional governments.

In 1866 he again led volunteer troops in a campaign against Austrian forces near Verona, and in 1870–71 he went to the aid of republican France against the Prussians.

Once Italy's unification was completed, Garibaldi returned to the radical ideology of his youth, moving beyond the Mazzinian notion of social progress through interclass cooperation to a form of socialism. He became active in the Società Operaie* and later joined the First International. His anticlericalism was even stronger than his proclivity for socialism. Throughout his life Garibaldi was a rabid opponent of organized religion, especially in its Roman Catholic form. His views on the role of the Church in Italian life were publicized in the novel *Clelia, o il governo del monaco* [Clelia, or the government of the clergy]. He also wrote two novels concerning the 1860 expedition (*Cantoni il volontario* [Cantoni the volunteer] and *I mille* [The thousand]) and the *Memorie autobiografiche*, begun in Tangier around 1850. Garibaldi died on the island of Caprera, where he owned a small farm, on June 2, 1882.

For further reference see: Jasper G. Ridley, *Garibaldi* (London: Constable, 1974); Denis Mack Smith, *Garibaldi: A Life in Brief* (New York: Knopf, 1957); idem, *Cavour and Garibaldi, 1860: A Study in Political Conflict* (New York: Cambridge University Press, 1954).

CML

GAROSCI, ALDO. An authoritative spokesman for socialism as the fulfillment of liberal principles, values, and institutions, Garosci was born at Meana di Susa (Piedmont) on August 13, 1907. In the mid-twenties he was an active organizer in Turin of student anti-Fascist demonstrations. When repression made overt opposition impossible, he turned to covert activities, joining the Justice and Liberty movement* and editing the clandestine *Voci d'Officina* [Factory voices]. Having escaped arrest, he went into exile in France, where he cooperated closely with Carlo Rosselli.* He was wounded while fighting for the Republicans in the Spanish Civil War.* After the fall of France he reached the United States, where he joined the Mazzini Society.* He was parachuted near Rome in January 1944, joining the Action Party* partisans. After World War II* Garosci was professor of history at the universities of Turin and Rome. He contributed regularly to *Il Mondo* and other publications while writing valuable works such as *Vita di Carlo Rosselli* [Life of Carlo Rosselli], *Storia dei fuorusciti* [History of exiles from Fascism], and *Storia della Francia moderna* [History of modern France].

MS

GASPARRI, PIETRO. This cardinal served as secretary of state for both Benedict XV* and Pius XI,* holding this key office from 1914 to 1930. Born in Macerata on May 5, 1852, he soon revealed his scholarly inclinations and his deep religious spirit and was ordained in March 1877. An expert in canon law, he was the central figure in the codification of the *Codex iuris canonici*, to which he devoted the years from 1904 to 1917. He was also preoccupied by the Roman Question* and played a key role in the conciliation achieved by the signing of the Lateran Accords* on February 11, 1929. At heart an anti-Fascist, Gasparri sought in these agreements with Mussolini* to protect the interests of the Church in Italy and to secure the international and financial position of the papacy. During the Vatican's polemic with Fascist Italy over the interpretation of the Lateran Pacts, personality and policy differences between the cardinal and Pius XI led to his replacement by Eugenio Pacelli (later Pius XII*), who became secretary of state in February 1930. Gasparri retired to his studies and died in Rome on November 18, 1934.

FJC

GAYDA, VIRGINIO. This journalist was born in Rome on August 12, 1885. He covered the Balkans and Central Europe for *La Stampa** of Turin prior to World War I,* and subsequently became war correspondent on the Russian front. When peace returned, Gayda entered the diplomatic service. Between 1926 and 1943 he was editor of *Il Giornale d'Italia.** Because this Roman daily reflected the views of the Ministry of Foreign Affairs and because the outlook of his books on international relations was pro-Fascist, Gayda acquired a reputation as a semiofficial spokesman of the Fascist regime in foreign policy. He died in Rome on March 14, 1944, from injuries suffered in an aerial bombardment.

RSC

GAZZETTA DI VENEZIA. See **NEWSPAPERS**

GAZZETTA PIEMONTESE. See **NEWSPAPERS** and *STAMPA, LA*

GDD. See **GRUPPI DI DIFESA DELLA DONNA E PER L'ASSISTENZA AI COMBATTENTI PER LA LIBERTÀ**

GENERAL CONFEDERATION OF AGRICULTURE. See **CONFEDERAZIONE AGRARIA**

GENERAL CONFEDERATION OF INDUSTRY. See **CONFINDUSTRIA**

GENERAL CONFEDERATION OF LABOR. See **CGL**

GENOA, CONFERENCE OF. This thirty-four nation summit conference was hosted by Italy from April 10 through May 19, 1922. Inspired by British Prime Minister David Lloyd George, the conference was called by the Allied Supreme Council to promote European reconstruction and the resumption of ties between Soviet Russia and the West. After the first week, on Easter Sunday, Germany and Russia signed a separate treaty at Rapallo that undermined the conference. During the next five weeks, Italian Premier Luigi Facta,* Foreign Minister Carlo Schanzer, and the economic expert Francesco Giannini worked diligently to obtain agreement at Genoa on the Soviets' repayment of debts, the restitution of foreign property, the terms under which new capital would enter Russia, and also on general principles of European financial, economic, and transport cooperation.

There was no agreement at Genoa, and a subsequent meeting at The Hague in June–July 1922 also proved fruitless. For Italy, the Genoa conference represented a major investment of effort by a shaky coalition government in what proved to be a futile bid for British support in Central Europe, the Near and Middle East, and Africa. Italy also failed to expand its ties with Moscow and further worsened its relations with France and its allies. Genoa thus represented a failure for Italian diplomacy. Mussolini* was one of its most severe critics.

CF

GENOVESI, ANTONIO. Economist, reformer, and leading figure of the Neapolitan Enlightenment,* Genovesi was born in Castiglioni, Salerno, on November 1, 1713, and died in Naples on September 23, 1769. Trained for the priesthood, he took holy orders in 1737 and went to Naples the next year. Here he became aware of and began to study the new French and English philosophies. This earned him the disfavor of traditional circles, and he failed to get appointed to the chair of theology at the University of Naples. After this failure Genovesi turned to economic and social issues and from 1754 to 1769 made notable contributions to the reform movement in the southern kingdom. He began to write in Italian, and his works, especially the *Lezioni di commercio* (1766–67), were widely read. Through Bartolomeo Intieri, an influential Florentine banker active in Naples, he was appointed the first professor of "commerce and mechanics" at the University of Naples on November 5, 1754. His lectures, delivered in Italian and open to the public, attracted a wide audience. Besides writing and lecturing on the many aspects of Neapolitan social and economic life that needed reforming, Genovesi was instrumental in having important English and French works on these problems translated into Italian. His reform program encompassed fundamental changes in society. He advocated the curtailment of Church ownership of land; the encouragement and stimulation of agriculture, industry, and commerce; and education for all, which he believed should provide practical training in the skills needed to make people productive. He supported a moderate protectionism in foreign trade and the greatest possible freedom in the internal passage of goods, especially after the famine of the 1760s. He believed that the greatest wealth Naples possessed was its people and that they should be nurtured and protected. Frequently consulted by the government on foreign and domestic matters, in 1767, when the Jesuits were expelled from Naples, he was asked to draw up a plan for a general reform of education in the realm.

Most of the reforms he advocated were never activated, but he trained a generation of Neapolitan reformers and thinkers who spread his ideas throughout southern Italy.

174

For further reference see: Emiliana P. Noether, *Seeds of Italian Nationalism, 1700–1815* (New York: Columbia University Press, 1951); Franco Venturi, *Settecento reformatore*. Vol. 1: *Da Muratori a Beccaria* (Turin: Einaudi, 1969).

EPN

GENTILE, GIOVANNI. This idealist philosopher, creator of the new system of Actualism, educator, and general editor of the *Enciclopedia Italiana* was born in Caltanisetta, Sicily, on May 27, 1875, and died in Florence on April 15, 1944. After his early education in Sicily, Gentile attended the Scuola Normale Superiore di Pisa, where he studied with some of the masters of modern Italian philosophy, history, and literature. In 1897 he received his degree with a thesis on *Rosmini and Gioberti* (see Rosmini-Serbati, Antonio*; Gioberti, Vincenzo*). He had in the interim made contact with Benedetto Croce,* who was impressed with Gentile's literary criticism. They thus began a correspondence and a personal and professional friendship that was cemented during the next decade and a half. In 1903 Gentile was asked to teach philosophy at the University of Naples and while there accepted Croce's invitation to collaborate as the only other contributor to Croce's recently founded review, *La Critica.*

In 1907 Gentile published an important work on Giordano Bruno in which he established, among other things, the basis for an antipositivist approach to the anti-Aristotelian strands of the Italian Renaissance and early modern philosophy. During the seven years before World War I,* Gentile wrote a series of studies on critical philosophy dealing with Kant, Hegel, and sixteenth- and seventeenth-century Italian philosophers. He closed this period with a first article launching his novel interpretation of idealism as Actualism under the title "L'atto del pensiero come atto puro" (1911; 1913). In 1914 Gentile moved to the Scuola Normale Superiore di Pisa to occupy the chair of theoretical philosophy. At the outbreak of World War I* Gentile joined the interventionists. He remained in Pisa until 1918 and then transferred to the University of Rome, where he produced a series of influential works on the historical-cultural life of the special regions of Italy.

With the advent of Fascism* and the formation of the Mussolini* ministry in November 1922, Gentile was asked to join the cabinet as minister of public instruction. He did so on condition that constitutional, public liberties be restored throughout Italy and that the state establish a standard examination for graduation from Italian secondary schools. In office he sought to reform the entire public education system. The Riforma Gentile (see Gentile Reform*) introduced religious instruction first on the elementary levels and later (1930) in the secondary schools for all those pupils whose parents did not request an exemption. Special state examinations were provided for both teachers and students, while the upper range of the "middle schools" was divided between technical-professional and liberal-humanistic sectors. A small but brilliant group of disciples sought to maintain the momentum of the Gentile Reform, but they were opposed by other Fascist ideologues who disagreed with the philosophy of the program.

Following the assassination of Matteotti (see Matteotti Crisis*), Gentile resigned his post as minister of public instruction, but in 1925 he was named president of a commission to establish the Giovanni Treccani Institute, charged with the publication of the *Enciclopedia Italiana*, of which Gentile was to be general editor. Gentile obtained the collaboration of a brilliant group of young scholars, and with the assistance of members of the older Italian intelligentsia brought forth a monumental, collective work of scholarship. Volume fourteen contained an important article on "Fascismo," which was intended to give Italians and the world an official formulation of the theory, practice, and history of Fascism. Although the section of the article that presented the fundamental ideas of Fascism was signed by Mussolini, it was actually written by Gentile.

In 1925, as Gentile was preparing to launch his work on the *Enciclopedia*, he was called upon to pen and issue above the signature of prominent personages of Italian culture a *Manifesto of the Fascist Intellectuals*.* This Manifesto came out on April 21, 1925. Within a few days, on May 1, at the suggestion of the Liberal anti-Fascist Giovanni Amendola,* Benedetto Croce countered with the publication of a *Manifesto of Anti-Fascist Intellectuals*, which contained a list of eminent protesters against the Fascist dictatorship and its Gentilian ideological justification. The break between the two philosophers and old friends was now beyond redress. As the totalitarian state relentlessly proceeded to its culmination and downfall, the twin Italian philosophers of neo-idealism placed their apparently irreconcilable versions of it into absolute historicism (Croce) and absolute Actualism (Gentile).

Although Gentile showed no enthusiasm for the Fascist racial decrees, his faith in Mussolini's dedication and judgment did not falter. On February 9, 1943, he delivered a speech on "Our Religion" in which he reaffirmed his sense of the immanent spiritual meaning of the raging storm of war. One month before the fall of Mussolini (June 24, 1943), Gentile delivered another speech in which he reasserted his loyalty to the Duce of Fascism. Following the creation of the Social Republic of Salò* under Nazi protection in northern Italy, Gentile, who moved to Florence, proclaimed his support. There the philosopher continued to praise Mussolini. It was for this, among other reasons, that the anti-Fascist groups operating in the Florence areas known as the GAP (Gruppi Di Azione Patriottica*) decided to assassinate Gentile. They carried out the execution in the courtyard of his villa on April 14, 1944.

The complete works of Giovanni Gentile are as numerous as those of Benedetto Croce: fifty-five volumes, plus nine volumes of correspondence. The publishing house of G. C. Sansoni, which the Gentile family owned during the Fascist period and in large part still directs in Florence, has assumed the task of the publication of his *Opera omnia*, and to date has published over forty volumes. These are divided as follows: *Systematic Works* (volumes 1–9); *Historical Works* (volumes 10–35); *Miscellaneous Works* (volumes 36–46); *Essays, Special Studies, Fragments of Philosophy* (volumes 47–55); and nine independent volumes of his *Correspondence*.

For further reference see: Gabriele Turi, *Il Fascismo e il consenso degli intellettuali* (Bologna: Il Mulino, 1980); idem, *Il pensiero di Giovanni Gentile. Atti del convengo tenuto a Roma dal 26 al 31 maggio 1975.* 2 vols. (Rome: Istituto della Enciclopedia Italiana, 1977). The bibliography of works on Gentile in volume 2 (pp. 915–1000) contains no less than 2,265 entries and is unsurpassed in range, reliability, and scholarly utility.

AWS

GENTILE REFORM. Promulgated on July 16, 1923, the Gentile Reform was the first major reform issued by the Fascist government and the first reorganization of the Italian school system since 1859. Named for the philosopher who was Mussolini's* first minister of public instruction, Giovanni Gentile,* the reform attempted to infuse the idealistic philosophy into the schools, replacing the positivism of Johann Friedrich Herbart, which had dominated Italian pedagogical theory and practice. For Gentile, the aim of education was to produce men, to form their minds and their hearts, and to develop the pupil's spirit, character, and will. He was extremely critical of education that focused exclusively on intellectualism.

The reform itself provided for a reduction in the number of secondary schools; a revision of the curriculum including the discouraging of early specialization; the introduction of religious education on the elementary level; and a limitation on the number of students eligible for free secondary education. Advancement was tied to a strict examination system, thus accentuating the meritocratic nature of the reform and reflecting Gentile's maxim, "poche ma buone" ("few but good"), in reference to the schools. To be sure, the provisions concerning religious education, the display of the crucifix in the classroom, and the right of graduates of Church schools to sit for state examinations were greeted warmly by the Vatican.

For further reference see: L. Minio-Paluello, *Education in Fascist Italy* (New York: Oxford University Press, 1946.)

RJW

GENTILONI PACT. The Gentiloni Pact was an agreement allegedly made in 1913 between the president of the Council of Ministers, Giovanni Giolitti,* and the president of the Catholic Electoral Union (CEU), Count Ottorino Gentiloni. This pact supposedly allowed the Giolitti government to cope with the quasi-universal manhood suffrage introduced in the elections of that year by permitting Catholics to vote for those liberal candidates who accepted Catholic guidelines. The charge that a pact had been made followed an interview Gentiloni granted to the anti-Giolittian *Giornale d'Italia,** which sought to explain the role played by the Catholic Electoral Union in the recent election and the disclosure of *L'Osservatore Romano** that Catholic support had been given to 228 of the elected deputies. In the aftermath, all sorts of accusations were made.

What is known is that the prohibition of the *non expedit** was lifted in 330 constituencies, and those candidates who desired the support of the Catholic Electoral Union were asked to sign a statement indicating that they supported its position on liberty of conscience and association, divorce, religious corporations, education, fiscal reform with social justice, and morality in society. The seven points of the CEU were labeled the "seven commandments." Although Gentiloni made it clear that individual candidates, acting on their own initiative, accepted or rejected the conditions of the CEU and that there had been no pact with the government, the charge persisted. Thus, the Congress of the Radical Party,* scandalized by the alleged pact, called upon the Radical deputies to withdraw their support from the government, and in March 1914 they did so. Two days later, on March 10, Giolitti's fourth ministry collapsed.

For further reference see: Frank J. Coppa, "Giolitti and the Gentiloni Pact between Myth and Reality," *Catholic Historical Review* 53, no. 2 (July 1967): 217–28.

FJC

GEORGOFILI, ACCADEMIA DEI. One of the first agrarian academies of eighteenth-century Europe, the Georgofili was founded by Ubaldo Montelatici and his associates among the aristocracy of Florence in 1753. Montelatici was a parish priest of the upper Arno Valley who published in 1752 a work entitled *Ragionamento sopra i mezzi più necessari per far rifiorire l'agricoltura* [Discourse on the best means for the reflowering of agriculture] that was inspired by the works of French agronomists, and by the need to educate landlords and peasants about new agricultural techniques. His associates in the Accademia dei Georgofili included other Florentine economists and some of the major landowners. The academy attracted foreign members of note and through its memoirs and publications remained an important institution for progressive Tuscan landowners through the nineteenth century. The *Atti* of the Georgofili were published continuously from 1791.

For further reference see: Marco Tabarrini, *Degli studi e delle vicende della R. Accademia dei Georgofili* (Florence: M. Cellini, 1856).

RBL

GERMINAL. A Florentine literary review, *Germinal* (December 20, 1891– January 15, 1893) was founded and directed by Enrico Corradini,* Luigi Rasa, and Carlo Cordara. Corradini became the most important figure of the three, as the chief ideologue and organizer of early twentieth-century Italian nationalism. In the mid- and late-1890s, before finding his true voice as a radical right-wing literary intellectual, he imitated Gabriel D'Annunzio's* style in plays and novels. *Germinal* remains historically significant because it expressed Corradini's very first literary point of view, which was strongly anti-D'Annunzian. In this earliest phase Corradini's literary hero was Henrik Ibsen, and *Germinal* proclaimed itself to be a manifesto of art serving humanity. The journal was never popular, and it failed because of unspecified editorial conflicts between Corradini and his colleagues.

RD

GIAN GASTONE DE MEDICI, GRAND DUKE OF TUSCANY. This seventh and last of the Medici dukes (1671–1737) was the second son of Cosimo III. From his youth he exhibited a listless and melancholy spirit. He was married in 1697 to Anna Maria Francesca, princess of Saxony, but produced no heirs. On his accession as duke in 1723 it was clear that he would be the last of his line, and he lived out his reign enclosed in the Palazzo Pitti surrounded by dissolute companions. His accession marked little change of internal policy, besides the dismissal of the clerical advisers of Cosimo III. Through the treaties of London and Vienna of 1718 and 1725 the Medici succession was fixed by the Great Powers, at first on Carlo Borbone, the son of Philip V of Spain and Elisabetta Farnese, heiress of Parma and Piacenza. Carlo was proclaimed heir of Gian Gastone at Florence in 1731. But this arrangement was reversed by the invasion of Naples by Carlo in 1734, where he became king. At the same time, Duke Francis Stephen, who was consort of Maria Theresa in Vienna, was compensated in Tuscany for the loss of Lorraine and for the Hapsburg loss of Naples. Consequently, on the death of Gian Gastone in 1737, regents from Lorraine in the service of Francis Stephen arrived in Florence to take possession of the Grand Duchy, and Tuscany entered the sphere of Hapsburg influence in Italy.

For further reference see: Gaetano Pieraccini, *La stirpe De Medici di Caffaggiolo*, Vol. II (Florence: Vallecchi, 1924).

RBL

GIANNI, FRANCESCO MARIA. This Tuscan political economist and functionary under the Hapsburg regency and Peter Leopold* was one of the most interesting figures of the Tuscan reform movement of the late eighteenth century. Born into a patrician family of Florence in 1728, he received his higher education in the Florentine bureaucracy, where he was employed after 1750 in the central administration of finances. Gianni held a number of offices, beginning with the directorship of the Dogana of Pisa in 1754. He was made a senator of Florence in 1761, and under Peter Leopold became a councillor of state in 1789. In the 1760s and 1770s his practical knowledge of local administration led him to oppose the more doctrinaire application of physiocratic theories by other advisers to the duke, such as Angelo Tavanti and Pompeo Neri.* Although a stronger supporter of the adoption of free trade in grain in 1767, on gaining more influence at the end of the 1770s Gianni opposed implementation of a single tax on agriculture and favored a degree of tariff protection for traditional urban manufactures. Popular opinion, however, associated him with the freeing of the grain trade, and after the serious shortages and grain riots of 1790 he lost favor. He left the Council of State on the accession of Ferdinand III.* During the French occupation of 1799, he had some association with pro-French Florentine patriots and left Tuscany during the reaction that followed the victory of the Second Coalition. He died in Genoa in 1821. Several of his administrative and economic treatises, which reveal his pragmatic views, were published in the *Raccolta degli economisti toscani* of 1848.

For further reference see: Furio Diaz, *Francesco Maria Gianni: Dalla burocrazia alla politica sotto Pietro Leopoldo di Toscana* (Milan: Ricciardi, 1966).

RBL

GIANNINI, GUGLIELMO. See **COMMON MAN'S MOVEMENT**

GIANNONE, PIETRO. Historian and jurisconsult, Giannone (1676–1748) served as a bridge between Socinianism of the seventeenth century and the deistic world of the eighteenth. He studied jurisprudence at the University of Naples and was influenced by the Neapolitan Accademia degli Investiganti. The publication in 1723, after twenty years of work, of his *Istoria civile del Regno di Napoli* (Civil history of the Kingdom of Naples) led to exile and excommunication. Influenced by the works of Livy, Machiavelli, and Sarpi, Giannone traced the history of the Kingdom of Naples from Roman times to 1700 and identified the conflict between church and state as the cause of its economic and social problems. Defending civil authority, Giannone advocated placing the Church under state jurisdiction. The work was translated into English between 1729 and 1731. While in exile in Vienna, Giannone began *Triregno*, another historical anticlerical piece that analyzed the pre-Christian earthly kingdom, early Christianity's heavenly kingdom, and the final reign of the papal one, which he saw as dogmatic, superstitious, and divorced from the humanity of early Christianity. Forced to flee Vienna in 1734, Giannone settled in Geneva, where he was attracted to but resisted conversion to Calvinism. At the time of his arrest in 1736 by Savoyard agents, the *Triregno* manuscript was left with a Calvinist pastor, Jacob Venet, but ultimately reached the Roman Inquisition. Though a version was published in Venice in 1768, only in 1783 was the full version printed in Naples. From 1736 until his death in 1748 Giannone languished in Piedmontese prisons. His autobiography, written between 1736 and 1741, reveals his identification with the rational, scientific world of the emerging Enlightenment* and his concern for social and economic reform.

For further reference see: Lino Marini, *Pietro Giannone e il giannonismo a Napoli nel settecento* (Bari: Laterza, 1950); Brunello Vigezzi, *Pietro Giannone riformatore e storico* (Milan: Feltrinelli, 1961).

MSM

GIARDINO, GAETANO ETTORE. Giardino was an Italian soldier born in Montemagno (Alessandria) on January 24, 1864. He entered the army in 1882 and at the outbreak of World War I* served as chief of staff of the Fourth Corps. Fighting at Gorizia, he was promoted to brigadier general. He became corps commander in June 1917, and soon after was appointed minister of war. In February 1918 he was appointed to the Supreme Inter-Allied Council at Versailles, where he remained until April. He then returned to the front, defeating the Austrians at the battle of Vittorio Veneto* during October-November 1918. He served as governor of Fiume,* 1923–24, and then as minister of state. In 1926 he was made marshal; he died in 1935. He is buried on Mount Grappa, which he helped liberate.

For further reference see: Georgio Rochat, *L'esercito italiano da Vittorio Veneto a Mussolini* (Bari: Laterza, 1967).

FJC

GINZBURG, LEONE. Born in Odessa in 1909, Leone Ginzburg was one of a group of Turinese intellectuals who joined the Justice and Liberty movement* in the mid-1930s. In 1936 he served a short prison sentence and lost his professorship at the University of Turin because of his refusal to sign an oath of loyalty to the Fascist government. He was active in the Armed Resistance* and in 1943 joined the editorial staff of the Action Party's* clandestine organ, *L'Italia Libera*. Suffering from a heart ailment and unable to endure the beatings inflicted on him by his interrogators, he died in a Roman prison on February 5, 1944. His widow, Natalia, is a distinguished novelist.

FR

GIOANETTI, GIUSEPPE. See **JACOBINS**

GIOBERTI, VINCENZO. This *Risorgimento** priest, philosopher, and statesman was born in Turin on April 5, 1801. He was ordained in 1825 and became professor of theology at the University of Turin and a court chaplain in 1831. Gioberti was charged with involvement in revolutionary activities and imprisoned in 1833; he left for exile in Paris and Brussels shortly thereafter.

Gioberti achieved recognition in three different realms: the philosophical, as he developed his distinct version of "ontologism"; the polemical, due to a critique of the Society of Jesus; and the political, as he formulated a moderate, nonviolent approach to the question of Italian unification, encouraging establishment of an Italian federation under the presidency of the Pope. His most influential political work is *Del primato morale e civile degli Italiani* [On the moral and civil primacy of the Italians] (1843). The stir created by this book helped to propel him, upon return from exile to Turin in 1847, to the presidency of the Camera and to the post of prime minister (1848–49). Gioberti lived in France after this date, his vision rendered impossible by Pius IX's* opposition to unification and the placing of his works on the *Index*. He died in Paris on November 26, 1852.

For further reference see: A. Anzilotti, *Gioberti* (Florence: Vallecchi, 1931); A. Omodeo, *Vincenzo Gioberti e la sua evoluzione politica* (Turin: Einaudi,

1941); Giovanni Giammona, *La problematica filosofica e pedagogica di Vincenzo Gioberti* (Catania: Edigrof, 1973).

JCR

GIOIA, MELCHIORRE. A political thinker and economist (1767–1829), Gioia's associations with Jansenism and Jacobinism (see Jacobins*) helped formulate his moderate republicanism. While jailed in 1797 for Jacobin involvement, he wrote an essay, "Quale dei governi liberi meglio convegna alla felicità d'Italia," advocating popular sovereignty and condemning monarchical and oligarchical governments. It won a prize in a competition sponsored by the Cisalpine government. Gioia hoped to instill patriotism by emphasizing the need of the individual to devote himself to the state. With Ugo Foscolo* he favored unity and opposed the policy of the Directory in the creation of independent republics, fearing the French would use Italy as a pawn. His journalistic endeavors, *Monitore Italiano*, *Il Censore*, *Gazzetta Nazionale della Cisalpina*, and *Giornale Filosofico Politico*, were often short-lived. Convinced of the need for a greater Italian unity, Gioia's economic philosophy of free trade and his role as statistician for the Kingdom of Italy served to advocate the promotion of economic modernization in Lombard commerce. After the Vienna settlement of 1815, Gioia joined the *Il Conciliatore** group and maintained an anti-Austrian position, which led to his imprisonment in 1820–21.

MSM

GIOLITTI, GIOVANNI. This liberal-democratic statesman who dominated Italian political life from 1901 to 1914 was born in Mondovi, province of Cuneo, on October 27, 1842. Five times prime minister, Giolitti sought to extend to all Italians the benefits of liberal democracy. Upon graduation from the University of Turin, where he received a degree in law (1860), Giolitti served in the administration of the Historical Right (see Destra, La*), working with Marco Minghetti, Quintino Sella,* and Giovanni Lanza* as they coordinated the structure of the new state. After the "parliamentary revolution" of March 18, 1876, which brought the Sinistra* to power, Giolitti moved to serve the Historical Left and was named secretary-general of the Corte dei Conti. Giolitti held office in this administrative, fiscal, and legislative high court and general accounting office until 1882, when Agostino Depretis* named him councillor of state. That same year he was elected to the Chamber of Deputies; he retained his seat during the next forty-six years.

From 1889 to 1890 Giolitti served as minister of the treasury in Francesco Crispi's* cabinet, a collaboration that led to conflict between the pragmatic Piedmontese minister and the fiery Sicilian. From May 1892 to November 1893, Giolitti exercised his first ministry, calling elections in October 1892 and prevailing through a combination of normal and "innovative" electoral methods of dubious legality. This ministry was brought down by the scandal of the Banca

Romana* of 1893, and it was only in his electoral speech in Caraglio (1897) that Giolitti publicly spoke of the "persecution" he had endured as a consequence.

Since Giolitti's ministries and their "prologue" and "epilogue" constitute a unity, the following summary of his governmental activity is provided. Giolitti served as minister of the interior of Giuseppe Zanardelli's* government from February 1901 to October 1903. This was followed by Giolitti's second ministry (November 1903 to March 1905), his third or "long" ministry from May 1906 to December 1909, the fourth or "great" ministry from March 1911 to March 1914, and finally the fifth ministry from June 1920 to July 1921. It was during the "prelude," while Giolitti was minister of the interior, that he emerged as the champion of a new liberalism which combined features of the classical liberalism of the nineteenth century and the radical and democratic liberalism of the twentieth. He made it clear that the government would no longer seek to protect the privileges and rights of the proprietary classes vis-à-vis the popular classes and called for a solution to the social question.*

With the expertise gained through a long apprenticeship at the highest level of administration, Giolitti operated the mechanism of the state almost to perfection. By means of the prefects, whom he controlled with an iron grip, the Piedmontese minister virtually controlled the elections in 1904, 1909, and 1913. Reform was not lacking, however, and in 1913, by the passage of the great Electoral Reform Bill, sponsored by Giolitti himself, the male suffrage was extended from 3 million to 8.5 million. In the interim he had also insured the right of workers to organize, peaceably protest, agitate, and strike. From 1901 to 1914 Giolitti also contributed to the restoration of the parliamentary and constitutional structure of the kingdom that had been momentarily threatened by the authoritarian measures of the Crispi and Luigi Pelloux* regimes. There were important economic innovations as well. Northern Italy became increasingly prosperous, particularly the fortunate industrial, commercial, financial, and "cultural" triangle formed by Milan, Turin, and Genoa. The Giolitti government seconded and contributed to the industrial spurt forward from 1896 to 1906 that rapidly brought Italy to near equality with the advanced Western European countries. The South, despite Giolitti's law for the Basilicata and program for the industrialization of Naples, remained backward and a land of emigration.* This was cause for complaint.

Likewise, Giolitti's appeal to the Socialists on the Left and Catholics on the Right provoked criticism from Gaetano Salvemini* and Luigi Sturzo,* among others. Following the outcry raised by the Gentiloni Pact* (1913), the Radical Party* defected from the government coalition, leading to the collapse of the fourth ministry. Giolitti suggested Antonio Salandra,* a rigid southern conservative, as his successor, perhaps expecting that he would play the role of temporary lieutenant as Tommaso Tittoni,* Alessandro Fortis,* Sidney Sonnino,* and Luigi Luzzatti* had done earlier. He was to be disappointed as he watched from his native Piedmont the tragic consequences of World War I,* and the Italian intervention, which he opposed.

Giolitti reappeared on the Italian political scene with an unexpectedly critical and defiant electoral speech, delivered to his constituents at Dronero on October 12, 1919. This discourse not only launched accusations; it was also a vast program for an organic national reconstruction that called for a renovation of the nation's political structure and the fulfillment of the needs of the masses. Never again, Giolitti insisted, should there be any "possibility that a bold minority or a government without intelligence and without conscience might succeed in dragging a people to war against its will." Thus, the prosaic old man of Italian politics was suggesting a radical change in the relations and exercise of power between the crown, the parliament, and the electorate as consecrated in the Italian constitution. For his suggestions the conservative ruling classes branded Giolitti "the Bolshevik of the Annunziata."

Following the fall of Francesco Nitti's* government on June 15, 1920, Giolitti formed his fifth and final ministry. A number of notables joined his cabinet, including Count Carlo Sforza* in the Foreign Office, the Catholic Filippo Meda* in the Treasury, the former Socialist and independent syndicalist Arturo Labriola,* and, perhaps most extraordinarily, the philosopher, historian, and literary critic Benedetto Croce* as minister of public instruction. During the course of this ministry Giolitti and his close collaborators confronted and overcame some of the most serious problems threatening postwar Italy, including the workers' occupation of the factories in August-September 1920, and Gabriele D'Annunzio's* occupation of Fiume.* Concomitantly, Giolitti resolved such problems as the so-called political price of bread, the question of registration of stocks, and the Crocean attempt at the reform of public education. Socialist agitation and Fascist violence, however, continued.

Giolitti sought to maintain a neutral stance in the violence that erupted between Fascists and Socialists, mistakenly interpreting Fascist violence within the framework of the older disorders he had witnessed in the peninsula. He saw it as mere youthful exuberance in search of an outlet and believed that, like Marxism, it would be "relegated to the attic." Confronted with Socialist, Communist, and Catholic opposition or noncooperation, in May 1921 Giolitti called for new general elections, which he hoped would create a bloc in favor of the liberal state and enable him to govern effectively. The results proved disastrous for the Giolittian Center, and the thirty-four Fascists who entered the Chamber as part of the Center bloc proved to be disruptive and nonsupportive. On June 21, 1921, Giolitti submitted his cabinet's resignation.

Initially tolerant, if not supportive, of the Fascist government, he chaired the parliamentary commission that approved the Acerbo Electoral Law,* which all but assured Fascist control of the Chamber of Deputies. Following the Matteotti Crisis* and the establishment of the dictatorship, however, Giolitti withdrew his support from the government and in his last political act, months before his death, spoke out against the Fascist electoral law of 1928. He died in his mother's house in the town of Cavour on July 17, 1928.

For further reference see: A. William Salomone, *Italian Democracy in the*

Making: Italy in the Giolittian Era, 1900–1914 (Philadelphia: University of Pennsylvania Press, 1960); Giovanni Giolitti, *Memorie della mia vita* (Milan: Fratelli Treves, 1922); Frank J. Coppa, *Economics and Politics in the Giolittian Era: Planning, Protectionism and Politics in Liberal Italy* (Washington, D.C.: Catholic University of America Press, 1971); Emilio Gentile, *L'eta' giolittiana, 1899–1914* (Naples: Edizioni Scientifiche Italiane, 1977).

AWS

GIORNALE DI SICILIA. See **NEWSPAPERS**

GIORNALE D'ITALIA, IL. This influential Rome newspaper was founded by Sidney Sonnino* with generous backing by wealthy business, financial, and agrarian leaders primarily from northern and central Italy. The daily was launched to promote the liberal conservative ideas of the Sonninian Center in parliament. Sonnino undertook this journalistic endeavor following the purchase in 1900 of *La Tribuna* by backers of Giovanni Giolitti* and also as a response to the advent in February 1901 of Giuseppe Zanardelli* to the Prime Ministry, with Giolitti as interior minister. *Il Giornale d'Italia* thus began as an organ of opposition to the leftist liberalism in Italy in the first decade of the century.

Il Giornale d'Italia, under the editorship of Alberto Bergamini,* began publication on November 16, 1901. From its first weeks, the paper drew wide attention for its crisp style, acute analyses, and authoritative firsthand news stories, together with its emphasis on news from the Italian South. Bergamini soon added new types of coverage, which ultimately evolved into the uniquely Italian journalistic feature, the *terza pagina*.*

This journal regularly opposed Giolitti's social and economic policies, which it considered unfaithful to the traditions of liberal constitutional monarchical principles. Nevertheless, the paper's independence was demonstrated by its backing of the Modernists (see Modernism in Italy*) against Pius X,* its campaign for universal male suffrage, and for the first announcement of the Gentiloni Pact.*

In foreign affairs, *Il Giornale d'Italia* faithfully reflected the views of Sonnino and his closest political ally, Antonio Salandra,* by favoring unswerving loyalty to the Triple Alliance,* Italian colonial expansion in Africa, and Italian interests in the Balkans.

Only the largesse of its founders kept the newspaper alive until it achieved self-sufficiency in 1911. In January 1912 publication of *Il Piccolo Giornale d'Italia* began; this was an extra edition in tabloid format which lasted until 1944. The weekly supplement *Il Giornale d'Italia Agricolo*, launched in 1918, expanded the paper's service to its agrarian constituents.

Bergamini and *Il Giornale d'Italia*, initially sympathetic to Mussolini,* were among the first supporters of Fascism* to turn away from the movement and suffer its repressive wrath. The death of Sonnino in 1922 weakened the paper's organization, and a *squadrista* beating of Bergamini in late 1923 caused him to relinquish the editorship to Vittorio Vettori in December of that year.

Il Giornale d'Italia continued publication until 1976, but its historic mark in Italian journalism was made in its first two decades. The paper's character changed markedly early in 1924, and it never recovered the respected position it enjoyed under Sonnino and Bergamini.

BFB

GIORNALE DI VENEZIA. See **NEWSPAPERS**

GIOVENTÙ ITALIANA DEL LITTORIO. See **BALILLA**

GIOVENTÙ UNIVERSITARIA FASCISTA (GUF). The Fascist youth organization of university students, the Gioventù Universitaria Fascista, organized students enrolled during the Mussolini* years in the faculties of the universities and the "Istituti superiori." The GUF was autonomous from the structure of the universities but was firmly positioned within the hierarchy of Fascist youth groups, its members being expected to have passed through the Balilla* and the Avanguardista. The organization, headed by the secretaries of the Fascist Party (see Fascism*), involved students in a series of activities, ranging from propaganda lectures and patriotic rallies to sporting and cultural events. Both the "Coppa di Duce," an annual athletic award, and the "Littoriali," a national competition of written, oral, and artistic presentations, were major GUF activities. The organization also published a weekly newspaper entitled *Libro e Moschetto*.

RJW

GIOVINE ITALIA. This society was founded by Giuseppe Mazzini* in Marseilles in July 1831. Although it operated underground and its members were sworn to secrecy, Giovine Italia advertised its program openly in the newspaper of the same name (1931–34) and later in *L'Italia del Popolo* and other democratic publications. In contrast to other secret societies with which Mazzini was affiliated in his youth, Giovine Italia did not aim to create a revolutionary elite but rather to spread the ideology of democratic nationalism among the Italian people generally. Thanks to its national and democratic ideology and to the dedication of Mazzini's followers, in the 1830s and early 1840s the society was more successful than any of its forerunners, spreading to every part of the peninsula. Members were admitted without regard to sex, religion, or social position, and they were put through an elaborate initiation ritual borrowed in part from the Carboneria.*

Despite the dedication of Mazzini's followers, Giovine Italia suffered a severe setback early in its development, when it attempted in 1833 to lead a popular insurrection in Savoy. The attempt ended with numerous arrests and with a death sentence *in absentia* against Mazzini himself. This debacle did not hinder the growth of the society outside Piedmont, but it led Mazzini to the conclusion that an international network of revolutionary societies was needed, hence the founding of Young Europe. He also recognized the need to avoid premature *coups de main* and to concentrate instead on the political education of the Italian people. Giovine Italia followed this strategy until the revolutions of 1848,* when Mazzini founded the Associazione Nazionale Italiana (see Italian Nationalist Association*).

CML

GIULIANO IL SOFISTA. See **PREZZOLINI, GIUSEPPE**

GIUSTIZIA E LIBERTÀ. See **JUSTICE AND LIBERTY MOVEMENT**

GIZZI, PASQUALE. See **PIUS IX**

GOBETTI, ADA MARCHESINI PROSPERO. This journalist, literary figure, and liberal political activist was born in Turin on July 23, 1902, and died there on March 15, 1968. In Turin in the 1920s she worked on the anti-Fascist journal *La Rivoluzione Liberale* with her husband Piero,* and in the 1930s her home was a center for Giustizia e Libertà conspirators (see Justice and Liberty movement*). She helped found the Action Party* in 1942; was an active partisan after September 1943, and served as inspector for the Piedmontese regional command with the rank of major in the Fourth G & L Division. After the war she was elected vice-mayor of Turin, was one of the founders of the Federazione Democratica Internazionale Femminile, and was a member of the Unione Donne Italiane* (UDI).

MJS

GOBETTI, PIERO. Piero Gobetti, a neoliberal thinker and organizer of Italian political culture, was born in Turin on June 19, 1901, and died in Paris on February 15, 1926. Remarkably precocious, Gobetti began publishing his first review, *Energie Nove*, in Turin in 1918. He was initially a partisan of Gaetano Salvemini's* enlightened reformism, but by 1920 he had grown disillusioned with the standard forms of democratic politics and the standard abstractions about the rights of man. Gobetti decided that liberalism, when crystallized in established governmental institutions, meant stasis, but he was impressed with the societal autonomy and initiative that he saw in the Russian Revolution and in the factory council movement in Turin, spearheaded by the Communists around Antonio Gramsci.* The task for frustrated liberals was to encompass within the liberal tradition the striving for freedom underlying such movements.

Borrowing from Vilfredo Pareto,* Gaetano Mosca,* Georges Sorel, and Benedetto Croce,* Gobetti developed a novel synthesis, with liberalism defined as the ongoing process through which new social groups struggle for freedom and autonomy, in opposition to the inertia embodied in governmental institutions. For the present, Gobetti decided, the working class could best play this liberal role, reinvigorating the political process; liberal intellectuals should offer support, though recognizing that since the struggle for freedom is endless, the workers' Socialist ideals were only myths.

Especially through his Turin review, *La Rivoluzione Liberale* (February 12, 1922–November 8, 1925), Gobetti became the focus for an impressive group of anti-Fascist intellectuals, including Aldo Garosci,* Carlo Levi, Lelio Basso, and Tommaso Fiore. Though Gobetti himself died in exile in 1926, his ideas provided a major stimulus to the political rethinking of the Resistance period, especially the attempt to renew Italian liberalism in light of Fascism.* However, Gobetti's revolutionary liberalism proved an unstable mixture; much as Gramsci had anticipated in 1926, Gobetti proved but a stepping-stone for many frustrated intellectuals on their way to a more complete commitment to the working class than Gobetti himself had envisioned.

For further reference see: Anna Maria Lumbelli, *Piero Gobetti "Storico del presente"* (Turin: Deputazione Subalpina di Storia Patria, 1967); Claudio Pogliano, *Piero Gobetti e l'ideologia dell'assenza* (Bari: De Donato, 1976).

DDR

GONELLA, GUIDO. A prominent member of the right wing of the postwar Christian Democratic Party,* he was born in Verona on September 18, 1905. While pursuing degrees in both philosophy and law, Gonella was an active leader of the Federazione Universitaria Cattolica Italiana (FUCI).* An inveterate anti-Fascist, he was elected to the Chamber of Deputies* in 1948, and subsequently served in various cabinet posts under Alcide De Gasperi,* Antonio Segni,* Andone Zoli,* Fernando Tambroni, and Giovanni Leone.* Gonella was also political secretary of the Christian Democrats from 1950 to 1953 and a deputy to the European Parliament. A professor of the philosophy of law at the Papal Lateran University, he championed the cause of penal code reform and served as president of the national organization of journalists.

RJW

GORANI, GIUSEPPE. Born into a noble family of Milan in 1740, he undertook the career of a professional soldier during the Seven Years War and later lived as a writer and adventurer. He was successively a supporter of Pasquale Paoli* in Corsica, an intimate of Cesare Beccaria* and his circle at Milan, a political theorist and admirer of enlightened despotism in his *Il vero despotismo* [The true despotism] (1770), and in later life a protagonist of the Gironde at Paris during the French Revolution. He died in 1819. His *Memoires secrets et critiques des cours, des gouvernements et des moeurs des principaux etats d'Italie* [Secret and critical memoirs of the courts and customs of the principal states of Italy] (1793) provides a lively retrospective account of his adventures and changing opinions.

RBL

GRAMSCI, ANTONIO. Antonio Gramsci was born in Ales (Cagliari) on January 22, 1891. The Gramscis, of Albanian origin, were a petty bourgeois family.

Antonio's father, Francesco, became involved on the wrong side of a political vendetta and was imprisoned from 1898 to 1904. His Sardinian mother, Giuseppina Marcias, struggled to bring up her seven children. For Antonio things began badly. At the age of four he had a bad fall and developed a physical deformity. In 1902 he graduated from elementary school but had to interrupt his education to go to work. From 1908 to 1911 he attended a classical liceo in Cagliari. There he stayed with his older brother Gennaro, who probably introduced him to socialism. Initially, Antonio seems to have been attracted to regional patriotism (*sardismo*) and to cultural movements such as those led by Benedetto Croce* and Gaetano Salvemini.*

In 1911 Gramsci's life changed when he won a scholarship and began attending the University of Turin, a leading center of Italian culture. There he met Angelo Tasca,* Umberto Terracini,* Palmiro Togliatti,* and others later well known in the history of Italian communism. In 1913 he joined the Italian Socialist Party (PSI)* and began writing for its local newspaper, *Il Grido del Popolo*. His career in the party nearly ended when he briefly and partially supported Benito Mussolini's* call for intervention in World War I.* By late 1915, however, he was back at *Il Grido* and also began writing a special column on Turin for *Avanti!*,* the national party newspaper. In February 1917 he published a special number entitled *La Città Futura* for the Piedmontese Socialist Youth Federation. It is here that the ideas of the young Gramsci are most fully expressed: insistence on the will as a creative factor in history; the importance of the cultural struggle; and total rejection of positivism, determinism, and reformism.

In 1917 Gramsci also became the secretary of the Turin section of the PSI, following the riots of August and the subsequent arrest of most of the leadership. In November he published his now famous article, "The Revolution against *Kapital*," where he asserted that in Russia *Kapital* had become "the book of the bourgeoisie." It was used to demonstrate the fatal necessity that capitalism and bourgeois civilization must develop in Russia before a proletarian revolution could occur. But, said Gramsci, the crisis of the war had made it possible for willful action to become the "shaper of objective reality."

The end of the war brought the revolutionary crisis to the West and so began Italy's "Red Years" of 1919–20. Gramsci's new journal, *L'Ordine Nuovo* (May 1, 1919), represented an attempt to bring the crisis to fruition. He envisioned the fulcrum of the Italian revolution in the "factory councils," representative organs of all the workers in each factory. In his journal, Gramsci provided the theory of their nature and scope and helped to organize them. In a few months the councils became the major expression of "worker democracy" in Turin. The isolation of Turin and the incapacity of the party leadership (torn as it was between timid reformists and bombastic "maximalists") were main causes of the collapse of the councils after the occupation of the factories in September 1920.

Meanwhile, the various left-wing factions of the PSI had agreed on a program to expel the reformist leadership and to establish the Italian Communist Party

(PCI)* at the next congress. Indeed, the newly formed Communist International (CI) had insisted on those steps in its "Twenty-One Points" for admission. Thus, the PCI was established at Livorno on January 21, 1921. For Gramsci this event was no cause for rejoicing. The foundation came after the crest of the revolutionary wave, and instead of uniting the great majority of the proletariat behind it, the new party was much smaller than what remained of the old PSI. Moreover, Gramsci and his group were a distinct minority within the PCI. The party was led by Amadeo Bordiga,* a brilliant orator and organizer but a rigid determinist who eschewed the development of a flexible strategy to confront the incipient reaction.

For the next two to three years, Gramsci seems to have entered a period of political inertia. Beyond writing a series of articles on the nature of the Fascist movement and giving some support (despite Bordiga's opposition) to a broad-based armed resistance against the Blackshirts, he did very little. Then, in May 1922, Gramsci was sent to Moscow as the party representative to the Executive Committee of the Communist International. There he met Julia Schucht, who later became his wife, attended the Fourth Congress of the Communist International, and received his first direct exposure to Leninism.

Because of the increasing threat of reaction in Europe, the CI had urged a united front of all proletarian parties in each country and, in the case of Italy, a fusion of the PCI and the PSI (from which the reformists had finally been ejected). Gramsci accepted the first in principle and proved willing to merge with at least the so-called Third-Internationalist faction of the PSI. He recognized that his party needed the moral and material support of the CI and had to play a more active role in the fight against Fascism.*

Thus began Gramsci's struggle against Bordiga for the leadership of the PCI. After moving to Vienna in November 1923, Gramsci was elected to the Chamber of Deputies the following April. His parliamentary immunity permitted him to return to Italy in May 1924. After a struggle Gramsci and his forces were able to consolidate their control of the party. At the Congress of Lyons, held in January 1926, 90.8 percent of the delegates approved his leadership. The PCI grew from fewer than 9,000 members in 1923 to about 25,000 in 1925. A police report in the fall of 1926 concluded that in nearly every region the PCI had become the only organized anti-Fascist force, and the only one presenting any real danger to the regime.

Nevertheless, the struggle against Fascism was a failure. Following the assassination of Matteotti (see Matteotti Crisis*), the PCI joined the Aventine Secession.* Once the Aventine leadership rejected use of the general strike or any mass action to overthrow the regime, Gramsci concluded that the Communist program would be better served by a return to parliament. In November 1926, Mussolini was able to proclaim the "exceptional laws" and put an end to all legal opposition. Gramsci's career as leader of the PCI was ended with his arrest on November 8.

After confinement on the island of Ustica and in a Milanese prison, Gramsci was transferred to Rome, where on June 4, 1928, he was sentenced to more than twenty years of imprisonment. He was confined in the prison at Turi di Bari until the end of 1933, when his delicate health completely collapsed and he was transferred to medical clinics, first in Formia and then in Rome. There he was struck by a cerebral hemorrhage and died on April 27, 1937.

Gramsci's fame rests on his *Prison Notebooks*, the 2,848 pages of essays and observations that he compiled between 1929 and 1935. Togliatti had them published between 1948 and 1951 (the critical edition appeared in 1975). Despite incompleteness and restrictions imposed by censorship, the *Notebooks* were immediately recognized for their originality. Gramsci's overriding purpose was to explain the defeat of the postwar Italian revolution, but this led him to much broader concerns. Among the most important results were an intriguing Marxist interpretation of the history of Italy; considerations on the role of intellectuals in history and society; and novel reflections on the nature of revolution in the West.

For further reference see: Antonio Gramsci, *Selections from the Prison Notebooks*, ed. and trans. Q. Hoare and G. Nowell Smith (New York: International Publishers, 1971).

JMC

GRANDE ITALIA, LA. This political newspaper is one of a number whose origins are traceable to the revival of Italian patriotism triggered by Austria's uncontested incorporation of Bosnia in October 1908. *La Grande Italia* was a four-page weekly established in Milan on April 17, 1909, with Ambrogio Codara as editor. Following the Florence inaugural congress (December 1910) of the Italian Nationalist Association,* the newspaper merged with the *Carroccio* of Rome. The *Grande Italia e Carroccio* folded due to the secession of the democratic nationalists at the association's Rome congress in December 1912.

RSC

GRANDI, DINO. Dino Grandi, the Fascist hierarch who plotted Mussolini's* overthrow in July 1943, was born in Mordana (Bologna) on June 4, 1895. In his youth he was active in a Catholic labor current and later in the Italian Socialist Pary (PSI),* but broke with them in 1915 when he volunteered for military service.

In 1919 Grandi earned a law degree and joined Mussolini's Fascist movement. He organized *squadristi* in Bologna province and promoted Fascist national syndicates. He was secretary-general of the Confederazione Nazionale del Lavoro Intellettuale. In 1921 Grandi sharply opposed Mussolini's ''pacification pact'' with the Socialists, but the two men reconciled their differences at the Congress of Rome (November 1921). In 1921 he was elected to parliament but was denied a seat because of his age.

Grandi served as chief of staff of the *quadrumvirs* in the March on Rome* (1922). He was elected to parliament in 1924 and served in the twenty-sixth, twenty-seventh, twenty-eighth, and twenty-ninth legislatures. Secretary of the Fascist parliamentary group, he was later vice-president of the Chamber of Deputies. He was also a member of the Fascist Grand Council and lieutenant general of the MVSN (see Voluntary Militia for National Security*).

During the Matteotti Crisis* (1924) he served briefly as undersecretary of the interior. In 1924–25 he was named undersecretary of the Foreign Ministry. From September 1929 to July 20, 1932, Mussolini entrusted him with the post of foreign minister. He was ambassador to Britain from 1932 to 1939. During the 1930s Grandi's views moderated considerably. He sought to improve Fascist Italy's image abroad in spite of Mussolini's aggressive foreign policy. On July 12, 1939, he was named minister of justice and worked on the new civil codes. On November 30, 1939, he also became president of the new Chamber of Fasces and Corporations.

Despite earlier reservations, Grandi supported Mussolini's declaration of war in June 1940. But after the debacle in Greece he hinted to the King (May 1941) the need for a new government. At the Fascist Grand Council meeting on July 24–25, 1943, Grandi, with support from Galeazzo Ciano* and Giuseppe Bottai,* presented the resolution that brought about Mussolini's downfall. Grandi failed, however, to be named to the new government and in August left for Lisbon. In November 1943 the Fascist Tribunal in Verona sentenced him *in absentia* to death. In Rome an anti-Fascist tribunal also condemned him, but soon he was granted amnesty. In 1948 Grandi moved from Lisbon to Brazil; he returned to Italy in the 1960s. He has turned over his personal archives to Renzo De Felice, who used them in writing the fifth volume of his biography of Mussolini.

CFD

GRAZIANI, RODOLFO. Rodolfo Graziani, chief of staff and combat general during World War II,* was born at Follettino (Frosinone) on August 11, 1882. He fought in World War I,* helped pacify Libya* in the 1930s, became marshal of Italy and viceroy of Ethiopia* in 1936, and commanded Italian forces in East Africa in 1941. He also served in Mussolini's* Republic of Salò* (1943–45) as a military commander. Surrendering to the Allies on May 1, 1945, he was tried and found guilty of collaboration by the supreme Italian military tribunal, and condemned to nineteen years of solitary confinement. After being granted amnesty on May 3, 1950, Graziani wrote his apologia, *Ho difeso la patria* [I defended the fatherland]. He died in Rome on January 11, 1955.

RSC

GREGORY XVI. Born Bartolemeo Cappellari at Belluno on September 18, 1765, the future pontiff became a Camaldolese monk in 1783. During the Napoleonic era, he won a reputation through his works defending papal authority. Named a cardinal in 1825, he was elected pope in the conclave of 1831. Shortly afterward, revolt broke out in the Papal States,* and soon all but Rome was lost. Only Austrian intervention restored papal authority. The Powers (England,

France, Russia, Prussia, and Austria); foreseeing new revolts if popular discontent was not appeased, urged him to grant reforms, but Gregory XVI, essentially conservative, did little in that direction. Public opinion turned steadily against the papal regime, as the conviction spread that only its overthrow could bring reform. Uprisings in 1843 and 1845 were crushed, but discontent continued to grow. In response, Gregory became increasingly hostile to all manifestations of modern civilization. This hostility dominated his attitude toward more progressive trends within the Catholic Church, as demonstrated by his condemnation of Felicité Robert de Lamennais, the founder of liberal Catholicism, in 1832. In international affairs, he aligned the papacy with the conservative powers. In general, the effect of his pontificate was to make the papacy seem increasingly to be the foe of modern civilization and to render the Church increasingly out of touch with the progressive currents of the age, while stimulating in the Papal States the growth of popular hostility that was undermining the foundations of the temporal power. He died in Rome on June 1, 1846.

For further reference see: A. Bartoli et al., *Gregorio XVI. Miscellanea commemorativa*, 2 vols. (Rome: Pontifica Università Gregoriana, 1948).

AJR

GRIST TAX. See MACINATO

GRONCHI, GIOVANNI. A prominent Catholic politician and president of the Republic* from 1955 to 1962, Gronchi was born in Pontedera (Pisa) on September 10, 1887. Active in Catholic youth movements, he became one of the founders of the Partito Popolare Italiano (see Italian Popular Party*), winning election as a deputy after World War I* and becoming the secretary-general of the party's "White Unions" in 1922. For a brief period he was one of the Popolari who participated in Mussolini's* first government, but when the Fascists continued to persecute Catholic organizations and journals, he moved into the ranks of the anti-Fascists.

In the post-World War II period, Gronchi, who was trained as a teacher, served as a cabinet minister in the governments of Alcide De Gasperi,* Ivanoe Bonomi,* and Ferruccio Parri.* He was the first president of the Chamber of Deputies* and was elected president of the Republic in 1955. Considered by the Christian Democrats' former general secretary Benigno Zaccagnini as "one of the most eminent figures of the Italian Republic," Gronchi died on October 17, 1978, at the age of ninety-one.

RJW

GRUPPI DI AZIONE PATRIOTTICA. The Gruppi di Azione Patriottica (GAP) were assault groups of audacious youths organized by the Communist Garibaldi Brigades and, to a lesser extent, by the Action Party* after September 1943 to carry on the Armed Resistance* inside the cities. They attacked German and Fascist officials, military commands, depots, units in transit, and rail and power stations. These groups were difficult to organize because of the high risks involved and the reluctance of many to engage in cold-blooded terrorism. The most famous GAP action was the ambush of 33 German soldiers on Rome's Via Rasella on March 23, 1944. This led to the German massacre of 335 people in reprisal at the Ardeatine Caves.

CFD

GRUPPI DI DIFESA DELLA DONNA E PER L'ASSISTENZA AI COMBATTENTI PER LA LIBERTÀ. This mass organization was founded in Milan in November 1943 to mobilize women for Armed Resistance* activities. The GDD enlisted women as couriers, provisioners, and nurses for partisan units and organized strikes and demonstrations as well as all-female fighting detachments. The GDD also emphasized recognition of women's social, economic, and political rights. Membership centered in the north and crossed party lines, though groups were identified predominantly with the Left. Recognized formally as a mass organization by the CLNAI* in October 1944, most of the estimated 70,000 members of the GDD were absorbed into the Unione Donne Italiane* (UDI) by the end of 1945.

MJS

GUERRA FULMINANTE. See **DOUHET, GIULIO**

GUERRAZZI, FRANCESCO DOMENICO. See **REVOLUTIONS OF 1848**

GUF. See **GIOVENTÙ UNIVERSITARIA FASCISTA**

GUCCIARDINI, FRANCESCO. See *RASSEGNA SETTIMANALE, LA*

H

HAILE SELASSIE I. Haile Selassie I, Emperor of Ethiopia,* was born Tafari Makonnen in Harar in 1892. The second cousin of Menelik II,* he became regent of Ethiopia in 1916, while Menelik's daughter Zawditu became empress. As regent, he continued the modernization process begun by Menelik, all the while consolidating his power. Upon the death of Zawditu, Tafari Makonnen became emperor, assuming the throne name Haile Selassie I (literally, ''Power of the Trinity''). He was forced into exile (1935–41) following the Italian invasion of Ethiopia. Despite his appeals to the League of Nations, Haile Selassie was unable to attract effective support against the Italians, although obtaining considerable world sympathy for his eloquent statesmanship. He returned to Ethiopia in 1941 under the protection of the British army. Following World War II,* Haile Selassie continued an internal policy of modernization and an external policy of rapprochement with Italy while assuming a role of leadership on the African continent. Addis Ababa became the site of the UN Economic Commission for Africa and the secretariat of the Organization for African Unity. The forces of modernization eventually turned against Haile Selassie, who was deposed in the course of the Ethiopian Revolution of 1973–75 and died in detention in 1975.

RLH

HAPSBURG-LORRAINE DYNASTY. The modern history of Hapsburg power in Italy began with a double crisis: the extinction of the Spanish branch of the dynasty with the death of Charles II in 1700, and the death of Charles VI of the Austrian branch without male heirs in 1740. The Spanish crisis was resolved through the War of the Spanish Succession, the accession to the throne of Spain by the Bourbon dynasty in the person of Philip V, and the transfer of Spain's Italian possessions (the Duchy of Milan and the Kingdom of Naples and Sicily) to the Austrian Hapsburgs. In 1735 the southern Italian kingdom was lost by Austria to Charles Bourbon, son of Philip V of Spain, who became king of an independent state of Naples and Sicily. The Austrian crisis was resolved by a series of related events, beginning with the Pragmatic Sanction of 1713, which permitted Charles VI's daughter Maria Theresa to succeed him; the marriage of Maria Theresa to Francis Stephen,* duke of Lorraine, which united the Hapsburg and Lorraine dynasties; the War of the Austrian Succession, which vindicated the Pragmatic Sanction; and the numerous progeny (sixteen children) of Maria Theresa and Francis Stephen. As a result of a dispute in 1735 over the succession to the throne of Poland, Francis Stephen of Lorraine had been forced to exchange Lorraine for the Grand Duchy of Tuscany. In 1737, at the death of the last Medici grand duke of Tuscany, Francis Stephen had come into possession of Tuscany. Unlike the Duchy of Milan, which was ruled as a province of Austria by a governor appointed by Vienna, Tuscany was not incorporated into the Hapsburg family possessions but instead was governed separately as a *secondogenitura*. Thus, after the death of Stephen Francis in 1765, Tuscany passed to his second surviving son, Peter Leopold,* while his first son, Joseph, ruled the Austrian possessions jointly with his mother, Maria Theresa, and became Holy Roman Emperor. At the death of Maria Theresa in 1780, Joseph became sole ruler, and when he died without children in 1790 his brother, Peter Leopold, grand duke of Tuscany, inherited the possessions and royal title. Leopold's first son, Francis, was designated to succeed him as emperor in Austria (which occurred in 1792), while his second son, Ferdinand, became grand duke of Tuscany. As Francis II, Leopold's first son ruled as emperor until his death in 1835, when he was succeeded by his son, Ferdinand I, who was forced to abdicate in 1848 and was succeeded in turn by his nephew, Francis Joseph,* who died in 1916.

Hapsburg influence in Italy was further extended through marriage. A daughter of Maria Theresa, Maria Carolina, was married to Ferdinand IV of Naples (see Ferdinand I of the Kingdom of the Two Sicilies*), and a son, Ferdinand, was married to Maria Beatrice d'Este, the heiress of Modena, which brought this state under Hapsburg rule. Then, at the Congress of Vienna,* Maria Luisa, who had been married to Napoleon Bonaparte (see Napoleon I*) in 1808, was awarded the Duchy of Parma and Piacenza.

After the Congress of Vienna the Hapsburgs thus ruled five Italian states: Tuscany, Parma-Piacenza, Modena, and Lombardy-Venetia, which included the Duchy of Milan and the territory of the Republic of Venice definitely annexed in 1814.

For further reference see: Adam Wandruska, *The House of Hapsburg* (Garden City, N.Y.: Doubleday, 1964).

                                                                                              RBL

HERMES. A Florentine periodical of art and literature, it was founded by Giuseppe A. Borgese* on January 1, 1904. Self-proclaimed pagans in religion, aristocrats in culture, idealists in philosophy, and individualists in life, the youthful contributors were outspoken followers of Gabriele D'Annunzio* and admirers of Enrico Corradini.* Beauty was to be elevated as the sole criterion of art and as the reliable mirror of the soul. *Hermes* sought to harmonize the D'Annunzian approach to beauty with Benedetto Croce's* aesthetic theories. Having fulfilled its promise of twenty-four issues, *Hermes* discontinued publication on December 15, 1906.

RSC

HOARE-LAVAL AGREEMENT. This was an agreement initiated by French Foreign Minister Pierre Laval and signed, on December 9, 1935, by British Foreign Minister Sir Samuel Hoare. It attempted to appease Mussolini* by recognizing Italian rule in more than half of the then conquered Abyssinia (see Ethiopia*). Public protest in England caused the agreement to be abandoned. In retaliation, Mussolini denounced the earlier Rome accords and Stresa agreements (see Stresa Front*), thereby preventing a possible reconciliation between Italy and the Western powers.

WR

HUDSON, JAMES, SIR. Born in Yorkshire in 1810, Hudson entered the diplomatic service in 1838 after an early career at court and served in junior posts before being named envoy at Turin in 1851. Popular with Italians and occasionally at odds with his superiors, he served there for twelve years. Though accused by Tories of sympathizing with extreme nationalists, Hudson was in fact a staunch Cavourian, and through his association with Giuseppe Massari* frequently reflected Cavour's* outlook in his dispatches. In 1855 he was instrumental in arranging Sardinia's entry into the Crimean War*; in the summer of 1859, when Cavour was out of office and British policy was officially noninterventionist, Hudson gave considerable unofficial support to the Italian cause. He retired in 1863 but continued to live in Italy until his death in 1885. He was buried at Florence.

JWB

HUMBERT I. Long known as "the Good," Humbert I lost much of his benevolent reputation during the crises at the end of the nineteenth century. Born on March 14, 1844, in Turin, son of Victor Emmanuel II,* then duke of Savoy, and Maria Adelaide, archduchess of Austria, he died by an assassin's hand on July 29, 1900, at Monza. Given a military education in accordance with Savoyard tradition, he commanded a division at the battle of Custozza (1866),* bravely covering the retreat, for which he received the gold medal for valor. In April 1868 he married his first cousin, Margherita of Savoy,* who bore him an only son, Victor Emmanuel III,* on November 11, 1869. Military commander of the Naples area (1868) and of an army corps in Rome (1870), Humbert ascended the throne on his father's death (January 9, 1878). On November 17, 1878, he was the target of Giovanni Passanante's assassination attempt in Naples, arousing much sympathy for the new King, especially after he commuted Passanante's death sentence. His popularity increased with his gestures of concern when he visited flooded areas of the Veneto (1882), earthquake-stricken Casamicciola

(1883), and cholera-infested Naples (1884). But some of Humbert's policies eventually diminished his popularity. His championing of the Triple Alliance* alienated irredentists (see Irredentism*) and Francophiles; his support of Crispi's* policies of colonial expansion and a large army lost him the favor of the Extreme Left (see Sinistra, La*) and some fiscal conservatives; Crispi's massive repression of the Fasci Siciliani* (1893–94) and Antonio Di Rudinì's* repression of the May 1898 disturbances alienated even some liberals of the Left, especially when Humbert decorated the general who had used artillery against Milanese rioters. After the May 1898 crisis, Humbert contemplated ruling by decree; and it was the royal decree power exercised by Prime Minister General Luigi Pelloux* in June 1899 that precipitated the crisis of parliamentary obstructionism in the first half of 1900. In a climate of growing hostility toward the monarchy, the anarchist Gaetano Bresci* shot and killed the King in July 1900. Even admirers of Humbert I agree that, although well-intentioned, he was weak.

For further reference see: Ugoberto Alfassio Grimaldi, *Il re "buono"* (Milan: Feltrinelli, 1970); Eugenio Pedrotti, *Vita e regno di Umberto I* (Naples: Jovene, 1900).

SS

HUMBERT II. The last king of Italy, son of Victor Emmanuel III* and Queen Elena (see Elena of Montenegro*), was born in Racconigi on September 15, 1904. He received his military commission in 1923, and in 1930 married Princess Marie Jose of Belgium. His support of the Fascist regime was minimal. Humbert exercised much of his father's authority after June 1944, when he became lieutenant general of the kingdom. His twenty-six-day reign was from May 9, 1946, until June 2 of the same year, when a referendum ended the monarchy. Although he never abdicated, he was forced to reside in exile and died in Geneva of bone cancer on March 18, 1983.

WR

I

IDEA NAZIONALE, L'. This Nationalist political weekly was founded by Enrico Corradini,* Francesco Coppola,* Roberto Forges Davanzati,* Luigi Federzoni,* and Maurizio Maraviglia* on March 1, 1911, the fifteenth anniversary of Adowa.* Its founders' prominence, the newspaper's location in Rome, and the energetic promotional activities of its editors gave the weekly an official tone and earned for it an advanced place in Italian journalism. A daily from October 1, 1914, on *L'Idea Nazionale* was partly subsidized by munitions and industrial trusts. From birth, the Nationalist newspaper campaigned for Libya* and favored intervention on the Allied side in 1914–15, expecting maximum imperialist returns. It also unfolded a conservative domestic program and adopted a guarded attitude toward Fascism.* It was absorbed into the *Tribuna* on January 1, 1926, with Forges Davanzati as editor.

RSC

ILLUMINISMO. See ENLIGHTENMENT

ILVA. The Società Ilva was established in February 1905 by a group of metallurgical firms that included the Siderurgica di Savona, Metallurgica Ligure, and Terni,* and was expanded after a brief interval to include the Società Elba and Ferriere Italiane. Ilva was set up to take advantage of legislation introduced by the government in 1904 that reserved a portion of the iron ore mined on the island of Elba for firms producing in the South, especially in the Naples area. Thus, Ilva was to construct and operate a modern iron and steel complex at Bagnoli.

The economic crisis of 1907 and the subsequent slowdown in the rate of economic growth placed many of Italy's major iron and steel firms, which had expanded capacity very quickly prior to the crisis, in serious financial difficulties. In an attempt to regulate output five major firms in the sector—the Società Elba, Piombino, Ferriere Italiane, Siderurgica di Savona, and Metallurgica Ligure (most of which were involved in creating Ilva)—formed an association in 1911 and gave Ilva a mandate to manage their plants for the next twelve years. The plants controlled by Ilva in 1913 produced almost all of Italy's pig iron and 58 percent of its smelted steel.

In 1918 Piombino absorbed all the other metallurgical firms in the association with the exception of Elba and became the Società Ilva Alti Forni e Acciaierie d'Italia. Ilva by the war's end was a virtual conglomerate; aside from its metallurgical activities it had interests in mining, electric power production, shipbuilding, shipping lines, and engineering firms. Iron and steel production in Italy is now controlled by the Industrial Reconstruction Institute (IRI).*

JSC

IMBRIANI, MATTEO RENATO. A protagonist of irredentism,* he was born on November 28, 1843, in Naples, and died on September 12, 1901, in San Martino Valle Caudina. A volunteer in the war of 1859,* Imbriani followed Giuseppe Garibaldi* in 1860, participated in the war of 1866,* and conspired in the Mentana expedition of 1867 (see Mentana, Battle of*), after which he turned republican and in 1870 abandoned his military career. With his founding of the Italia Irredenta Association in 1877, he expanded his long apostolate for the redemption of Trent and Trieste* from Austrian rule. He was a prolific publicist and orator, and his election as deputy in 1889 brought his irredentism into the parliamentary forum, where he opposed the Triple Alliance* and colonial expansion as contrary to Italy's primary goal of acquiring its unredeemed provinces.

SS

INCHIESTA IN SICILIA. See **SONNINO AND FRANCHETTI, *IN-CHIESTA IN SICILIA***

INDUSTRIAL RECONSTRUCTION INSTITUTE (IRI). IRI was created by the Royal Law Decree on November 23, 1933, in order to strengthen Italy's financial system during the Great Depression.

The portfolios of the banks of ordinary credit (or of the holding companies that they owned) were swollen with industrial assets, which they could liquidate only by sustaining catastrophic losses. Furthermore, the Banca d'Italia,* acting in its capacity as lender of last resort, had made substantial advances (over 50 percent of its outstanding circulation) to the banks of ordinary credit, which these banks could not repay because they were saddled with their practically worthless industrial assets. Finally, there was the problem of industrial credit itself. If the banks of ordinary credit were to cease providing long-term credit to industry (and everyone involved agreed that this step was desirable), then industry would be without such credit at a time of great need.

IRI provided a solution, in effect, to all three problems. It took over the holdings of the banks and thus gave them a new lease on life. The amount, it should be noted, came close to 10 percent of the gross national product. At the same time, IRI assumed the debt these banks owed to the Banca d'Italia, thus freeing the central bank's assets. IRI and, later, companies of which it was the major shareholder became a source of long-term financing for industry. IRI financed all its operations through bond issues to the public and through funds provided by the state.

Although IRI was initially conceived as an emergency institute that would disappear when its job was completed, in 1937 it became a permanent body and continued to operate in the post-Fascist era. The companies in which it owns shares are private and behave accordingly; IRI is, at least in principle, just another shareholder. In this respect, it would be incorrect to view companies in which IRI is a major shareholder as nationalized. However, in these same companies, because of its majority position, IRI is able to influence corporate decisions and in so doing may take into consideration social as well as private benefits and costs.

JSC

INSTITUTIONAL QUESTION IN 1946. The question of whether Italy should retain the institution of the monarchy or adopt a republican form of government was resolved by a popular referendum on June 2, 1946, when 12,717,923 votes were cast for the Republic and 10,719,284 votes were cast for the monarchy. Monarchist sentiment was strong in the South and the islands, but was overcome by the larger republican showing in the more populous North and Center. The abdication of King Victor Emmanuel III* in favor of the crown prince, later Humbert II,* and support for the monarchy by the Church were insufficient to save the institution.

EER

IRI. See **INDUSTRIAL RECONSTRUCTION INSTITUTE**

IRREDENTISM. This term is used primarily to refer to the movement for the redemption of Italian-speaking territories that remained under Austrian control after the war of 1866.* Irredentism was a major cause of continued strains in Austro-Italian relations and of domestic agitation. The territories in question stretched from the Trentino* to Istria* and Dalmatia,* although for the sake of brevity the movement's rallying cry was simply "Trent and Trieste."* The phrase "unredeemed lands" was coined by Matteo Imbriani,* founder of the Italia Irredenta Association in 1877 and lifelong apostle of the movement; but the desire to acquire Italy's "natural" frontiers was a concern to all Italian governments after 1866. The movement grew rapidly after 1878, following Italy's failure to extract any concessions from Austria in the Trentino at the Congress of Berlin,* prompting Giuseppe Garibaldi* to consider plans for forays to liberate the unredeemed lands. Following Italy's entrance into the Triple Alliance* in 1882, irredentism also became a rallying point for those opposed to the alliance with autocratic Austria and Germany. During the 1890s colonial ventures, domestic disturbances, and the rise of an antiexpansionist socialism worked against the irredentist movement, which experienced a revival early in the 1900s, centered around demands for the creation of Italian universities in Trieste and Trent, but rejected by Austria. To the old democratic-irredentist movement, there was now added an openly imperialistic element of Corradinian and D'Annunzian nationalism, which preached expansion to the whole of the Adriatic-Mediterranean basin. Violent encounters between Italian and Austrian students at Innsbruck (1903, 1904), Vienna (1908), and Graz (1913), and anti-Italian measures in Trieste (1913) kept the movement alive. It reached its culmination in May 1915, when Italy declared war against Austria for the acquisition of the strategically located unredeemed lands.

For further reference see: Nicola Lapegna, *L'Italia degli Italiani: Contributo alla storia dell'irredentismo* (Milan: Società Editrice Dante Alighieri, 1932–35); Augusto Sandonà, *L'irredentismo nelle lotte politiche e nelle contese diplomatiche italo-austriache*, 3 vols. (Bologna: Zanichelli, 1932–38); Angelo Vivante, *L'irredentismo adriatico* (Florence: Libreria della "Voce," 1912).

SS

ISONZO, BATTLES OF THE. A mountainous area in northeastern Italy adjacent to the Isonzo River, the Isonzo was the scene of twelve battles between Italian and Austrian troops during World War I,* the last of which was the catastrophic defeat of Caporetto.* Chosen by the Italian supreme commander, General Luigi Cadorna,* as the gateway to the Austrian heartland, from May–June 1915 to August–September 1917 eleven Italian offensives were launched on the Isonzo front, with indecisive results and Italian casualties exceeding 725,000 in dead, wounded, and prisoners. The twelfth battle of the Isonzo (Caporetto), initiated by an Austro-German offensive on October 24, 1917, forced the Italian armies to retreat seventy miles to the Piave River by November 9, with about 340,000 casualties, leading to Cadorna's dismissal.

For further reference see: Pietro Maravigna, *Le undici offensive sull'Isonzo* (Rome: Libreria del Littorio, 1928); Enrico Caviglia, *La dodicesima battaglia: Caporetto* (Milan-Verona: Mondadori, 1933).

SS

ISTRIA. A triangular peninsula in the upper Adriatic with three important ports (Trieste,* Fiume,* and Pola), Istria—and especially Trieste—formed the center of Italian Adriatic irredentism* after the war of 1866,* straining relations first with Austria and later with Yugoslavia. Acquired by Italy after World War I,* the whole peninsula except for Trieste was assigned to Yugoslavia in 1947. Erected into a Free Territory, the Trieste area became the source of acute international disputes, which were resolved in 1954, the city and a coastal strip (Zone A) going to Italy, the rest (Zone B) to Yugoslavia.

SS

ITALIA IRRENDENTA. See **IRREDENTISM**

ITALIA IRREDENTA ASSOCIATION. See **IRREDENTISM**

ITALIA LIBERA. Italia Libera was the name of the first non-Communist underground anti-Fascist movement that succeeded in making a real impact on the Italian political scene. The movement had members in virtually all of the major Italian cities and represented a cross-section of the population, from postal clerks to professors, from railroad workers to lawyers. It was composed mainly of war veterans like Raffaele Cristofani, Ernesto Rossi,* Nello Traquandi, and Raffaele Rossetti, who were disgusted by the pro-Fascist collaborationism of the National War Veterans Association. The members of Italia Libera wanted to perpetuate the democratic values for which they believed Italy had entered World War I.*

From 1923 to 1925 Italia Libera published clandestine manifestoes denouncing the Fascist regime, staged street demonstrations, covered the walls and billboards of Italian cities with anti-Fascist slogans, and rallied support for the parliamentary opposition after the murder of the Socialist deputy Giacomo Matteotti on June 10, 1924 (see Matteotti Crisis*). The Florentine contingent of the movement published an important clandestine newspaper, *Non Mollare!* ("Don't Give In!"), which summoned the Italian people "to resist those who constantly attempt to intimidate us with threats of violence, who buy off witnesses and judges to condemn us, who burn our meeting places, who confiscate our newspapers."

For further reference see: Luciano Zani, *Italia Libera—Il primo movimento antifascista clandestino 1923/25* (Bari: Laterza, 1975).

FR

ITALIAN COMMUNIST PARTY (PCI). The PCI was founded on January 21, 1921, at Livorno. Its foundation was inspired by the call of the Communist International at its Second Congress (the "Twenty-one Points") and by the failure of the Second International to prevent the outbreak of World War I.* However, the reformism and the ineptitude of the Italian Socialist Party (PSI)* during the "Red Years" (1919–20) also inspired the new party. Three groups shared leadership in the action at Livorno: (1) Amadeo Bordiga,* the first party leader, and his abstentionist faction based at Naples; (2) Antonio Gramsci* and his "Ordine nuovo" group based at Turin; and (3) a heterogeneous group of older "maximalist" leaders.

The PCI proved to be a distinct minority of the Italian Left. By October 1922, the March on Rome* forced the new party into semilegality. Though the Comintern was now urging an accommodation with the Socialists, Bordiga and the whole party leadership refused any such cooperation. Gramsci, who had been sent to Moscow as the party representative to the Comintern, proved more willing than the rigid Bordiga to accept joint action with at least some of the Socialists. By 1924 he returned to Italy as a parliamentary deputy and the new party leader. Following the Matteotti Crisis,* Gramsci had some success in increasing the unity and strength of the party. By the end of 1925, the PCI had almost 25,000 members, as compared to the 9,000 of 1923. The Communists withstood the attacks of the Fascist regime somewhat better than the Socialists and by 1926 provided the only real opposition to the regime. Gramsci's "Lyons Theses," written for the Third Congress of the PCI (Lyons, January 1926), represented a first attempt to create a strategy for revolution based on a serious analysis of Italian history and society. Though Gramsci accepted Bolshevik leadership in the Communist movement, his famous letter of October 1926 to the Communist Party of the USSR (CPUSSR) showed that he would not refrain from criticizing Moscow.

By November 1926 Gramsci and much of the party leadership were imprisoned. Palmiro Togliatti* assumed leadership, and the PCI went underground and did not emerge until July 1943. During that period the party remained little more than a small band of professional revolutionaries. Unlike the French and even the Spanish Communist parties, it had practically no mass political experience before World War II.* In 1939 even its Central Committee had been dissolved by order of the Comintern.

This small band of dedicated revolutionaries prepared for a different future, learning from their defeats. Togliatti's Moscow lectures of 1935 on the idea of Fascism* as a "mass reactionary regime" maintained that a mass democratic revolution would be required to overthrow Mussolini.* Togliatti, who had helped to formulate the new line of the "popular front," was the leading representative of the Comintern in Spain during the Spanish Civil War.* There he developed his theme of a "mass democracy of a new type," and there too the cadres of the PCI received invaluable experience in armed struggle against Fascism.

Thus, by 1943 the PCI was prepared to lead the *Resistenza* (see Resistance, Armed*) for the redemption of Italy from Fascism and the Nazi occupation. No other party could match its cadres, tempered by imprisonment, exile, and battle. On March 27, 1944, Togliatti arrived at Naples, where he called for the construction of a new kind of Communist Party, a "positive, constructive" force which would use the anti-Fascist experience to build a democracy capable of far-reaching structural reforms. The new party, he said, would cooperate with all others so long as they remained anti-Fascist. With the completion of the *Resistenza* and the adoption of the anti-Fascist and socially oriented constitution, the PCI did indeed become a mass party. By the end of 1945, it had more than 1.7 million members, a figure that it has by and large maintained until the present.

With the Fifth Congress of December 19, 1945–January 19, 1946, the ranks of the party were opened to all who accepted its program. Until the end of 1947 the effective line of the party was the search for an "Italian road to socialism," though the phrase itself was not then employed. During this period the great mass organizations of Italian communism were developed (representing trade unions, cooperatives, peasants, women, and youth) as the PCI became an indispensable part of the fabric of Italian social life. In foreign policy, however, it retained a wholly uncritical attitude toward the USSR.

With Alcide De Gasperi's* expulsion of the Communists from the government in May 1947, the Cold War began in Italy. For the next nine years the PCI moved closer to the USSR; the healthy state of the world economy and the anti-Communist crusade considerably reduced the party's influence over intellectuals and even some workers. Only the publication of Gramsci's *Prison Notebooks* impelled the party's leaders and cadres to study seriously the nature of Italian history, modern capitalist society and culture, and the revolutionary process in advanced countries.

The year 1956 began a new period in the history of the PCI, one which is arguably still being enacted. The Twentieth Congress of the CPUSSR, with Khrushchev's denunciation of Stalin, and the intervention of the Soviet army in Hungary forced sweeping changes in the PCI. By the Eighth Congress (Rome, January 1957), the strategy of an "Italian road to socialism" was made explicit, as was the rejection of a "leading" Communist state or party. The Yalta Memorandum, Togliatti's last political act, ensured the continuation of the independence of the PCI. Meanwhile, the party had more than recouped the losses it sustained during the Cold War. Its new policy of cultural openness and freedom of expression achieved considerable success among the intellectuals.

Luigi Longo,* who was Piedmontese and a hero of the Spanish Civil War and the *Resistenza*, succeeded Togliatti as general secretary. A strong supporter of Alexander Dubček and the "Prague Spring" of 1968, Longo's rejection of the Soviet intervention was particularly strong and was supported by the majority of the rank and file. Longo also furthered the idea of political "pluralism"— that the Italian state (even a Socialist one) should include elements from the Italian democratic and liberal traditions.

At the conclusion of the Thirteenth Congress in March 1972, Enrico Berlinguer (1922–1984) succeeded Longo as general secretary. He was the first leader to have spent his entire career in the "New Party" established after 1944. As such, Berlinguer mirrored the great changes that had occurred in both the party and in the country since the end of World War II. He was perhaps best known as the leading proponent of Eurocommunism and for his strategy of the "historical compromise," or the attempt to establish a political understanding with the Christian Democratic Party.* This phase ended in 1979 and has since been replaced by a program to create a Left "alternative" with the PCI and other groups.

Perhaps the most important development of the Berlinguer years was the great success of the PCI in establishing itself as a permanent part of Italian political life, even on the highest national and parliamentary levels. Though it has experienced defeats as well as victories, the PCI has maintained its mass character and organization and its solid role in a powerful trade-union movement. The following table gives the number and percentage of PCI votes in Italian political elections from 1946 to 1979:

Year	PCI Votes	Percentage
1946	4,356,686	19.0
1948 (with PSI)	8,137,047	31.0
1953	6,121,922	22.6
1958	6,704,706	22.7
1963	7,763,854	25.3
1968	8,551,347	26.9
1972	9,068,774	27.1
1976	12,620,509	34.4
1979	11,107,883	30.4

For further reference see: Paolo Spriano, *Stroia del PCI*, 5 vols. (Turin: Einaudi, 1967–75); Franco Andreucci and Malcom Sylers, "The Italian Communists Write Their History," *Science and Society* 40 (Spring 1976): 28–56.

                                                                                                JMC

ITALIAN EAST AFRICA COMPANY. The Italian East African Company was the predecessor of the Filonardi Company (see Filonardi, Vincenzo*), proposed by the British in 1888 as the vehicle by which Zanzibari territories on the Somali coast could be conveyed to Italy. The plan called for the Sultan of Zanzibar to give the Imperial British East Africa Company (IBEAC) a fifty-year concession of the Benadir ports (Mogadishu, Brawa, Kismayu, Merka, and Warsheik), with full administrative powers and rights similar to those granted for the coast of Kenya. The IBEAC would then transfer these ports to an Italian East Africa Company sponsored by the Italian government on identical terms. In other words, Italian imperialism would be the junior partner of British imperialism on the East African coast. Five years of intensive diplomatic activity were required before the plan was put into effect in 1893, when Vincenzo Filonardi took possession of the Benadir ports, ending a period of cooperative imperialism and beginning a period of colonial government by chartered company.

                                                                                                RLH

ITALIAN LIBERAL PARTY. Spurred mainly by French *philosophes* but also by British thinkers, liberalism appeared in Italy (particularly among the Milanese, Neapolitan, and Florentine intelligentsia) during the second half of the eighteenth century. Some of its main tenets were the priority of reason over the irrational; constitutionalism founded on individual rights, the rule of law, and parliament; freedom of the press; religious tolerance; and a market economy. Between 1796 and 1814 Liberals cooperated with regimes set up in Italian states by the French. A small minority in the nation, Liberals were nonetheless more numerous than other *Risorgimento** patriots such as Republicans, monarchical Federalists, and neo-Guelphs (see Neo-Guelph movement*). Liberals were involved in the two unsuccessful attempts of 1814–15 to organize constitutional states; in the revolutions of 1820–21* and 1831*; in the agitation that led to the granting of constitutions in 1848 (see Revolutions of 1848*); and in the *Risorgimento* wars. They successfully governed Piedmont (the Kingdom of Sardinia) from 1848 to 1860. With the help of the French Empire and of Republicans, they established the Kingdom of Italy* in 1861 and governed it until 1922.

Liberals were not formally organized in political parties, but from the 1850s to the 1880s they were clearly and sharply divided between moderates (La Destra*) and progressives (La Sinistra*). Just before World War I,* when traditionalists (*clericali*) underwent a deep transformation and entered the political arena together with new forces (Socialists, Nationalists, Syndicalists), Liberals were divided between a national-liberal Right, a democratic Center, and a progressive Left, whose major leaders in 1914 were Antonio Salandra,* Giovanni Giolitti,* and Francesco Nitti,* respectively. Under the pressure of growing anti-Liberal forces (to which Communists and Fascists were added between 1919 and 1921), in 1922 Center Liberals formed the Liberal Party,* led by Giolitti and organized by Alberto Giovannini. Progressive Liberals found their Voice in Piero Gobetti's* *Rivoluzione Liberale*. In 1924 the Liberal Left, led by Giovanni Amendola,* in conjunction with the Catholic Italian Popular Party,* the Socialist parties, and smaller groups, organized a constitutional opposition to Mussolini's* government (see Aventine Secession*); in 1925 it created the Unione Democratica Nazionale. Party and union were outlawed in 1926, the year in which Amendola and Gobetti died of wounds inflicted by Fascists. After the overthrow of the Fascist dictatorship, the Liberal Party was reorganized under the leadership of Benedetto Croce.* It took an active part in the events of 1943–46, both in Allied-occupied and German-occupied areas. When, at the instigation of the Allies, a Badoglio*-CLN* government was formed (April 1944), Croce had the distinction of being its most prominent member.

At the general election of June 2, 1946, the Liberal Party, allied to kindred groups, received 8 percent of the votes. The successful attempt of extreme monarchists to control the party weakened it considerably, although the first two presidents of the Republic* (Enrico De Nicola* and Luigi Einàudi*) were Liberals, and the party continued to be a member of the *quadripartito*—the pro-NATO Center alliance of Christian Democrats, Social Democrats, Republicans, and Liberals that governed Italy during most of the 1950s. The election of Giovanni Malagodi,* who aimed at competing with the Christian Democrats in appealing to the conservative vote, as secretary-general of the party led progresive Liberals (Carandini, Cattani, Villabruna, and others) to secede and, in 1956–57, to form the Radical Party.* This party, however, failed to elect a single deputy or senator and was dissolved after a few years. The Radical Party of the late seventies had only a tenuous connection with its predecessor. With the replacement of Malagodi by V. Zanone as secretary-general, and with the adoption of progressive policies while continuing support for NATO (see North Atlantic Treaty Organization*) and the EEC, the Liberal Party moved toward the creation of a lay democratic front with Republicans, Social Democrats, and Socialists; but this move came too late to regain the ground lost in the electorate.

For further reference see: Arnaldo Ciani, *Il Partito Liberale Italiano* (Naples: ESI, 1968); Manlio di Lalla, *Storia del liberalismo italiano* (Bologna: ISMLI, 1976).

MS

ITALIAN NATIONALIST ASSOCIATION. It was formed in December 1910 in Florence by Enrico Corradini* and Luigi Federzoni.* Its subsequent growth into one of the most important right-wing movements in Italian history was aided by the outburst of patriotism produced by the Libyan war of 1911–12 (see Ouchy, Treaty of*) and the crisis of the traditional political system caused by the introduction of universal manhood suffrage for the parliamentary elections of 1913.

By 1914 the Nationalists had elaborated an alternative political strategy for Italy, based on state-sponsored cartels for production and marketing, high levels of tariff production, colonial expansion, state control of worker unions, elimination of the political function of the Italian Socialist Party (PSI),* and a stronger executive authority. The Italian Nationalists rejected racism and mysticism in favor of a pragmatic appeal to industrial and agricultural interests, which they saw as threatened by socialism.

The Italian Nationalist Association and its newspaper, *L'Idea Nazionale,** helped lead the campaign for Italian intervention in World War I,* and during the war the Nationalists worked successfully to impose an outlook that identified victory with the total realization of Italy's territorial demands in Dalmatia,* Albania,* and Africa.

The Nationalists allied after 1921 with the growing Fascist movement in order to steer it along monarchist and conservative paths. In March 1923 the two movements merged. Thereafter, the Nationalists exerted an enormous intellectual and political influence on Fascism,* especially with the appointments of its leaders: Luigi Federzoni as interior minister in June 1924 and Alfredo Rocco* as justice minister in January 1925. Federzoni and Rocco ensured that the establishment of a full-scale dictatorship in 1925 and 1926 would operate within the limits of the state rather than the party bureaucracy.

For further reference see: Franco Gaeta, *Il nazionalismo italiano* (Naples: Edizioni Scientifiche Italiane, 1965); A. De Grand, *The Italian Nationalist Association and the Rise of Fascism in Italy* (Lincoln: University of Nebraska Press, 1978).

AJD

ITALIAN NATIONAL SOCIETY. See **SOCIETÀ NAZIONALE ITALIANA**

ITALIAN POPULAR PARTY. The political expression of the Christian Democratic movement in Italy (see Christian Democracy in Italy*), this party became possible only when Pope Benedict XV* completely rescinded the ban on Italian Catholic participation in national elections (1918). The principal founder of the Popular Party was the Sicilian priest Don Luigi Sturzo.* He favored an interclass party, nonconfessional in character but of Christian inspiration, open to all who would accept its platform. The chief tenets of the party were an elective senate, proportional representation, corporatism, agrarian reform, women's suffrage, political decentralization, independence for the Church, and social legislation. From the outset the party had a right and a left wing. The right wing was sympathetic toward Mussolini,* while the left wing was Marxist-oriented. The party's strongest support came from the trade unions and the lower clergy. The first national congress of the party took place in Bologna in June 1919. By this time, it had 56,000 card-carrying members, distributed among 850 precincts.

In the elections of 1919 the Popularists won 100 seats out of 508. After his election to parliament in 1921, Alcide De Gasperi* became the president of the Popularist parliamentary group, although the real leader of the group was its secretary, the Lombard conservative Stefano Cavazzoni. During 1922 Fascists repeatedly attacked the headquarters and presses of the Popular Party. Popularism proved incapable of opposing the march of Fascism for several reasons: lack of political expertise, disunity within its ranks, and ideological inability to join forces with the Italian Socialist Party (PSI).*

Popularists joined the first ministry formed by Mussolini in October 1922, hoping that the realities of government would tame Mussolini and place him on the path of constitutionalism. Fascist violence, however, did not abate, and when the party, acting under the direction of De Gasperi, asserted its autonomy, Mussolini expelled it from his government. The party also suffered from the Pope's antagonism. Pius XI* feared that a party composed of Catholics would alienate Mussolini and thereby prevent a solution to the Roman Question.* Vatican pressure was also responsible for the resignation of Don Sturzo from the party secretaryship and for his exile from Italy. In May 1924 the National Council of the party elected De Gasperi political secretary, thus uniting in one mandate the presidency of the parliamentary group and the party secretaryship. By this time, however, the right wing of the party (the "Clerico-Moderates") had defected to Mussolini.

The last act of organized defiance of Mussolini on the part of the Popularists was participation in the Aventine Secession,* wherein the anti-Fascist opposition voted to boycott parliament until the reign of violence ceased. The Aventine Secession was a political failure, for Mussolini weathered the storm created by the murder of the Socialist Giacomo Matteotti by Fascist hoodlums (see Matteotti Crisis*). On June 28–30, 1925, the Popular Party held its fifth and last national congress. De Gasperi dominated the proceedings, and while he admitted that the battle had been lost, he sketched plans for renewal of the party in the future. In 1926 all the members of the Aventine Secession were deprived of their parliamentary seats, and in province after province the Popular Party was forced to close down. The party was reborn after 1943 in the form of the Christian Democratic Party.*

For further reference see: Gabriele de Rosa, *Storia del Partito Popolare* (Bari: Laterza, 1958); Richard A. Webster, *The Cross and the Fasces* (Stanford: Stanford University Press, 1960).

EC

ITALIAN REPUBLICAN PARTY. Three factors explain the political weight in Italy of a small left-of-center party, the PRI or Partito Repubblicano Italiano, which in recent general elections has received only 3 percent or so of the popular vote. These include the role Republicans played in the *Risorgimento** and in opposition to Fascism*; the high proportion of Republicans in the political class as distinct from the population at large; and the sincere commitment and high intellectual and moral caliber of twentieth-century leaders such as Eugenio Chiesa, G. Conti, Cipriano Facchinetti, Ugo La Malfa,* and B. Visentini.

In its contemporary form, republicanism appeared in Italy primarily under the impact of French Jacobinism (see Jacobins*). In spite of their small numbers, Republicans played a role in the six ephemeral republics established by French revolutionary armies in Italy between 1796 and 1799. Many *Carbonari* (see *Carboneria**) and members of other secret societies of the first half of the nineteenth century were Republicans as well. After 1830 republicanism was shaped mainly by Giuseppe Mazzini,* whose organic and monistic concept of society and state was the antithesis of the Liberals' individualism and pluralism. The Mazzinian vision included a factionless government by the people or nation (the population minus the privileged classes), deontological ethics linked to belief in God (not necessarily the Christian God), monopoly of media and education, a cooperative economy, and—at the international level—a federation of self-governing nation-states. A minority strain was represented by Carlo Cattaneo,* an enthusiastic admirer of Swiss liberal democracy. In the wake of Liberal failures in 1848, Republicans pursued the struggle against despotism in Venice, Rome, and Florence until defeated militarily by Austria and France. In the 1850s those for whom unification was the paramount goal—including Giuseppe Garibaldi,* among many others—seceded from Mazzinian republicanism. A small, cohesive, and dynamic Republican Party survived and from 1920 on was militantly anti-Fascist. Many Republicans went into exile and later fought in the Spanish Civil War.* Others were active in the anti-Fascist underground, on their own or cooperating with Liberal Socialists in the Justice and Liberty movement.* During the Armed Resistance* of 1943–45, most Republicans joined the Action Party* and its partisan formations. When World War II* ended, the most authoritative representative of the Mazzinian tradition in the PRI was Randolfo Pacciardi,* who had been an exile in Switzerland, France, and the United States, and who had distinguished himself fighting in Spain against Franco's Nationalists. His major opponent was Ugo La Malfa, undoubtedly the most influential spokesman for progressive liberalism in the postwar period, who had joined the PRI after the collapse of the Action Party. When a majority of party members, including many staunch Mazzinians, elected La Malfa as party secretary-general, Pacciardi left the PRI, rejoining it in 1981. As a member of the *quadripartito*—the pro-NATO alliance of Christian Democrats, Social Democrats, Republicans, and Liberals—the PRI participated in most governments of the 1950s, a period of cultural dynamism, economic expansion, and radical social transformation. The PRI was instrumental in bringing together Christian Democrats and Socialists, thus replacing the Center coalition of the fifties with the Center-Left coalition of the sixties, when dynamism, expansion, and transformation continued with renewed impetus. In view of the worsening situation in the seventies (economic difficulties, financial scandals, terrorism, growth of fringe movements bent on destroying the democratic republic), La Malfa, twice vice-prime minister, advocated the formation of a government of national unity, excluding only neo-Fascists, New Left anarcho-communists, and kindred groups. The plan did not materialize, but it created conditions favorable to the support the Italian Communist Party (PCI)* gave in parliament to the ruling coalition in the late seventies, and to the choice of Giovanni Spadolini, La Malfa's successor as leader of the PRI, as prime minister in 1981.

MS

ITALIAN SOCIAL DEMOCRATIC PARTY. See ITALIAN SOCIALIST PARTY (PSI) and SARAGAT, GIUSEPPE

ITALIAN SOCIALIST PARTY (PSI). The first modern Italian political party, the Italian Socialist Party (Partito Socialista Italiano, PSI) was established in 1892 and took this title at its third congress. The PSI suffered from numerous divisions from the beginning, an important factor explaining its inability to take full advantage of the widespread support it has had in the country during different periods.

In 1901 Filippo Turati's* policy of alliances with "bourgeois" political groups under nonemergency conditions prevailed, and the Socialist deputies voted for a cabinet for the first time. In 1903 and 1904, however, the left wing put through a rule forbidding votes in favor of governments, which led to an exacerbation of the struggle between the party apparatus and the Socialist deputies. By 1908 the reformists, who controlled the labor movement, achieved complete dominance once again and kept it until 1912. In that year the left wing, led by Giovanni Lerda* and Benito Mussolini,* took control at the Congress of Reggio Emilia. Mussolini became editor of *Avanti!** and preached violence revolution from that forum. His articles helped provoke a short-lived revolt in the Romagna* in June 1914—Red Week.* The PSI championed neutrality during the debate preceding Italy's entrance into World War I* and urged the Italians to neither support nor sabotage the war effort when the country intervened in the conflict.

The divisions within the PSI worsened after the war, with the "maximalist" majority calling for a violent revolution on the Soviet model and the still influential reformists advocating nonviolence and gradualism. The PSI became the largest party in the Chamber of Deputies, but its leaders blocked the deputies from taking constructive political action while at the same time failing to organize a revolution. In 1921 the left wing broke off, convinced that the PSI could not organize a revolution, and formed the Italian Communist Party (PCI).* In 1922 Turati sought a political solution to the Fascist onslaught and was expelled. Under his leadership the reformists founded the Unitary Socialist Party. Thus divided, the Left proved incapable of opposing the March on Rome* in 1922, and, after the murder of Matteotti in 1924 (see Matteotti Crisis*), of preventing the establishment of Mussolini's dictatorship.

The major Socialist leaders went into exile in Paris, where they reunified the two parties in 1930. After the Communists adopted the "popular front" tactic, the Socialists agreed to join them in a "unity pact" in 1934. The Socialists fought the Fascists during the Spanish Civil War* and during World War II.*

After the overthrow of Fascism* in 1943 the exiles linked up with Socialist groups in Italy, took the name Italian Socialist Party of Proletarian Unity (PSIUP), and participated in postwar governments through the Committees of National Liberation (CLN*). In January 1947 Giuseppe Saragat* split from the party, objecting that it had come under excessive Communist influence. He formed a new party, which (in 1951) took the name Italian Social Democratic Party (Partito Socialista Democratico Italiano, PSDI) and participated in the postwar cabinets. In the 1950s the PSIUP's ties with the Communists loosened, spurred on by the desire for autonomy and especially by the revelation of Stalin's crimes and the Hungarian revolution.

By 1959 relations between the PSI (which had changed its name again) and the PCI had cooled to such a degree as to allow serious discussion of a Center-Left reforming coalition which would include Socialists and Christian Democrats. The negotiations proved difficult and lengthy, but with the encouragement of the Kennedy and Johnson administrations they came to fruition in December 1963, when Socialists joined Aldo Moro's* cabinet. The PSI and the PSDI reunited in 1966 but split again in 1971. During the 1970s the Center-Left fell apart, but by the end of the decade the PSI was pursuing an aggressive policy designed to bring it to power under its new secretary, Bettino Craxi.*

For further reference see: Spender DiScala, *Dilemmas of Italian Socialism: The Politics of Filippo Turati* (Amherst, Mass.: University of Massachusetts Press, 1980); Gaetano Arfé, *Storia del socialismo italiano* (Turin: Einaudi, 1965).

SD

ITALIAN SOCIALIST PARTY OF PROLETARIAN UNITY (PSIUP). See **ITALIAN SOCIALIST PARTY (PSI)**

ITALIAN SOCIAL MOVEMENT. See **MSI**

ITALIAN SOCIAL REPUBLIC. See **SALÒ, REPUBLIC OF**

ITALIAN-TURKISH WAR. See **MILLO DI CASALGIATE, ENRICO**

ITALIAN WAR OF LIBERATION. See **WAR OF 1859**

ITALO-GERMAN CONVENTION. This agreement, signed on October 25, 1936, marked the formal commencement of the Rome-Berlin Axis.* The other powers and the League of Nations had condemned Italy's attack on Ethiopia* and Germany's remilitarization of the Rhineland during the previous winter, but Italo-German relations had been strained by Hitler's interference in Austrian affairs and his initial reserve on the question of Italy's claim to Ethiopia. In the spring of 1936, however, Hitler showed sympathy toward Italy on that issue, and in July he agreed to respect Austria's independence. The German government formally recognized Italy's sovereignty in Ethiopia in the convention of October 25, and the two signatories promised to conclude an economic agreement and to develop common policies toward communism and the League of Nations.

JKZ

ITALO-YUGOSLAV NONAGGRESSION PACT. This treaty, signed on March 25, 1937, by foreign ministers Galeazzo Ciano* and Milan Stoyadinovic, reduced the long-standing enmity between Italy and Yugoslavia, which had its roots in Yugoslavia's membership in the French alliance system and in Mussolini's* support of separatist movements in Yugoslavia. The Yugoslav government's desire to improve relations with Italy reflected its awareness of Germany's growing power in central Europe and the developing ties between the Nazi and Fascist regimes. The Italo-Yugoslav treaty provided for a joint guarantee of their boundary, Yugoslavia's recognition of Italy's sovereignty in Ethiopia,* favorable trade concessions by Italy to Yugoslavia, and improved cultural conditions for the Yugoslav minority in the Italian state.

JKZ

ITALY, KINGDOM OF, PROCLAIMED IN 1861. In January 1861, following the liberation of Lombardy* and Giuseppe Garibaldi's* acquisition of the Kingdom of the Two Sicilies,* national elections were held. The parliament that met in February 1861, representing the whole peninsula save the Veneto and the area around Rome, opened as the eighth session of the Sardinian parliament and closed as the first of the Italian Kingdom. On March 17 it passed a bill unanimously proclaiming Victor Emmanuel II* King of Italy. The preservation of the King's old title and the retention of the Sardinian *Statuto* * of 1848 tied the new state to the old monarchy of Savoy, which it succeeded. On March 27, following Cavour's* speech calling for a "free Church in a free State," the Chamber proclaimed Rome capital of the Kingdom of Italy. Unfortunately,

Cavour, who had been most responsible for the appearance of the new kingdom, died in June 1861, barely three months after its proclamation.

FJC

ITALY, NAPOLEONIC KINGDOM OF. This was a French satellite state in northeastern Italy. The Italian Republic, which had evolved out of the Cisalpine Republic* of 1797, was in its turn transformed into the Kingdom of Italy in 1805, following Bonaparte's creation of a monarchy in France. Formed out of the old duchies of Milan, Modena, and Mantua, as well as parts of papal, Venetian, and Swiss territory, it gained subsequent additions at the expense of the Pope (1808) and Austria (Venetia and the southern Tyrol, 1809). At its greatest extent, it covered 35,000 square miles, with a population of almost 7 million. Eugene de Beauharnais ruled as viceroy at Milan on behalf of Napoleon I.* His administration was notable for its efficiency in financial and educational matters, and for its military contribution to the Napoleonic cause, in which Italian troops sustained particularly heavy casualties. Although the Kingdom was swept away in April 1814, its influence as a catalyst for Italian nationalism and liberalism would persist throughout the Restoration era.

WDG

J

JACINI, STEFANO. This conservative leader was born into a family of prosperous landowners from Cremona (Lombardy*) on June 20, 1826. Known primarily for his sponsorship of the parliamentary investigation of national agriculture carried out from 1877 to 1885 (*Inchiesta agraria*), Jacini actually conducted a lifelong crusade on behalf of progressive agrarian capitalism. His reputation as an agricultural expert was established by his pioneering study of land ownership in Lombardy, published in 1857. Cavour* chose him as minister of public works in 1860, a post which he also held under General Alfonso La Marmora* from 1864 to 1866. He was nominated to the Senate in February 1870. The *Inchiesta agraria*, proposed by the radical deputy Agostino Bertani* as an investigation of living conditions among the rural populations, was transformed by Jacini into a survey of agriculture. The tone and conclusions of the *Inchiesta* were generally pessimistic, pointing to high taxes and government indifference to the needs of capital-intensive agriculture. In the 1880s Jacini argued for the need to form a national conservative party based on enlarged suffrage and reconciliation with the Church. His sudden death on March 25, 1891, cut short his work as president of the recently formed National Conservative Association.

RS

JACOBINS. Rooted in late eighteenth-century Freemasonry,* Italian Jacobins were organized in clubs throughout the peninsula and were active throughout the decade of revolution, 1789–99, especially during the "triennio" of 1796–99, when the French presence in Italy contained Jacobin activities.

The Italian Jacobins were theoretically egalitarian, democratic, republican, anticlerical, cosmopolitan, and unitarian. Actually, their views had originated in the conditions and intellectual atmosphere of prerevolutionary Italy, and there were significant differences between them and their French counterparts, both in ideology and in action. Frequently the Italian Jacobins' anticlericalism was combined with an idea of spiritual regeneration, or expressed in a type of Christian Democracy which they did not find incompatible with their radicalism.

Generally they were exiles, wandering from region to region, republic to republic, and from Italy to France. Finally, in action they proved unable to build ties with the masses (in particular the peasantry), and so were unable to sustain the political institution of the *giornate* (the French *journées*), that is, the stirring of a popular rising to force through their program, the technique so effectively used by the French.

Regional differences modified ideas and actions among Italian Jacobins. Melchiorre Gioia* favored the unitary state and advocated legal equality, but not equality of wealth. However, the Roman Jacobin Claudio della Valle, in his "Dalla 'Grammatica Repubblica,'" attacked the unequal distribution of land and the tyranny of the rich few over the masses. The Modenese Jacobin Canon Valentino Contri stressed vast educational programs to instruct illiterate workers and peasants and to neutralize the antipatriotic propaganda of the aristocracy and the clergy. Bologna's *Circolo Costituzionale*, where peasant and noble often ate side by side in the name of brotherhood, was a center of Jacobin activities. The city's most articulate Jacobin, Giuseppe Gioanetti, advocated egalitarianism.

Numerous regional and local journals described Jacobin views on constitutional issues, public instruction, commerce, and redistribution of wealth and land. Jacobins like Matteo Galdi, Antonio Ranza, and Giuseppe Campagnoni were active political propagandists for such Milanese journals as *Il Giornale de' Patrioti d'Italia*, *Tribuno del Popolo*, *Termometro Politico della Lombardia*, the *Genio Democratico* of Bologna, and the *Monitore Napolitano*.

On the political reforms in the various republics set up in the 1790s the Jacobins were frequently outnumbered and outvoted by moderates. Thus, the legislation that was passed during the *triennio* seemed a continuation of eighteenth-century reform in the hands of moderate landowners and bourgeois reformers. For example, in the Cisalpine Republic* moderates succeeded in inserting in the constitution that equality of all men could not exist. Cisalpine Jacobins did succeed, however, in terminating primogeniture, permitting civil marriage, and establishing the equality of women to men in intestate inheritances. In the Roman Republic of 1798–99,* local Jacobins, along with fellow exiles from other states, kept French authorities on the alert to prevent networks from going beyond the republic's borders. The Parthenopean Republic* at Naples did not last many months before the 1799 revolution, but Jacobins pushed to abolish feudalism. Southern Jacobins failed to recruit the peasantry as allies because a moderate, wealthy landowning class, the *galantuomini*, whose aim was to secure more land for themselves from continuing sales of ecclesiastical property, did not permit Jacobins to promote distribution of land to the peasantry.

Many factors limited Jacobin reform programs. Along with the curtailment of their activities by Italian moderates and the French, Jacobins faced attacks by the Church. In areas where Jacobinism was strongest, such as in the Romagna,* Piedmont, and southern Italy, the Church marshalled anti-Jacobin forces through Sanfedist crusades (see Sanfedesti*). The one led by Cardinal Fabrizio Ruffo* in southern Italy in 1799 was both anti-French and anti-Jacobin. By 1799 many Jacobins joined with moderates in protesting French pillaging, requisitions, or solicitations of contributions in money and kind. Others, however, were torn between an emerging Italian patriotism and a dedication to a cosmopolitan and international ideal. Piedmontese Jacobins, for example, faced the dilemma of supporting or opposing French annexation of their state. Some Jacobins, for example, Giovanni Ranza, voted for annexation in order to avoid further sacking and requisitions, while others organized a new secret group, the Società dei Raggi, whose goals were a Piedmont independent of France, and a united Italy.

In the post-1799 period, Italian Jacobins became part of a wider revolutionary tradition, both Italian and European, leading to the revolutions of 1820–21,* 1831,* and 1848.* Whether within Carbonari societies (see Carboneria*), "parties of action," or Young Italy (see Giovine Italia*), elements of Italian Jacobinism survived.

For further reference see: Delio Cantimori, *Utopisti e riformatori italiani 1794–1847* (Florence: Sansoni, 1943); Renzo De Felice, *Italia Giacobina* (Naples: Edizioni Scientifiche Italiane, 1965).

MSM

JEWS IN ITALY. Italian Jewry is the oldest continuous settlement of the Diaspora. Though Italian Jewry predates the Christian era, the ethnic-cultural composition and geographic distribution of the community crystallized only in the 1600s, when amalgamation of Ashkenazic and Sephardic immigrant groups with native Italian elements was nearly complete and 95 percent of the Jewish population was concentrated in central and northern Italy. The regime of civil, political, and economic interdictions was intensified in the eighteenth century; in spite of the Enlightenment,* no major Italian *illuminista* sponsored Jewish equality. On the eve of the French Revolution the Italian Jewish community, which numbered about 30,000, was among the poorest and most disfranchised in Western Europe. At the same time, it was culturally the most integrated with the surrounding Christian population, and anti-Jewish violence was relatively unknown on the peninsula.

1796–1815. Jewish emancipation, first introduced in Italy by the French invasion of 1796, was artificial and precarious, as evidenced by sporadic anti-Semitism among Italian Jacobins* themselves and by the reaction of 1799, during which the populace engaged in the only pogroms in modern Italian history (Siena, Sinigaglia). Italian Jewry by and large warmly supported the new regime, but only a few benefited from the political and economic opportunites offered by equality. Individual fortunes were made in military provisions and confiscated Church lands, and the economic activities of the Jewish bourgeoisie, especially in Piedmont and the lower Po Valley, expanded beyond credit and commerce to agriculture and the textile industry. However, just as the secularizing *prominenti* who attended the Paris Assembly of Notables (1806) and Sanhedrin (1807) did not represent the great mass of Italian Jews, so too the good fortune of a few was offset by the progressive impoverishment of the community as a whole, severely hit by Napoleon I's* Continental System of economic warfare against England.

1815–70. The Restoration witnessed a general return to pre-Napoleonic legislation and a return of the interdictions in Piedmont and the Papal States.* Conditions for Jews were best in Tuscany,* Parma, and Lombardy-Venetia. The economic progress of the Jewish elite was not arrested, and this, along with the growth of liberalism, gave rise to a campaign in favor of emancipation beginning around 1830. Italian Jewry prepared for improved conditions both through reform of its educational and charitable institutions and through active involvement in the conspiracies and battles of the *Risorgimento.* Jewish participation was greatest where long-established rights had bred civic consciousness (Tuscany, Lombardy-Venetia) and was practically nonexistent in the Roman community, whose Jewish population was the most oppressed and abject in Italy. Characteristic of the contributions of Jews to the *Risorgimento* was their role as financiers and messengers and their concentration in the moderate liberal camp.

Full emancipation was granted in various localities in 1848 but was maintained only in the Kingdom of Sardinia, whose decrees were then extended to the rest of Italy with the process of unification. In 1870 Rome's 4,800 Jews (the largest community) were finally enfranchised. The juridical form of emancipation (a single legal act rather than a series of installments), the brevity of the debate on the issue, and the undivided stand of the liberals determined that after the *Risorgimento* Jewish equality was more solid and less questioned in Italy than in other European states.

1870–1922. The following fifty years revealed the unique success of emancipation on the peninsula, in both its positive and negative aspects: security and acceptance, and erosion of Jewish identity. Jews were fully integrated into society and politics and had access to careers in diplomacy and the military, generally closed to them elsewhere. The first Jewish minister of war and the first Jewish premier in Europe were Italians: Giuseppe Ottolenghi (1902–3) and Luigi Luzzatti* (1910–11). Anti-Semitism was a marginal phenomenon, and the clerical campaign (1883–1903) served only to further isolate Catholics from Italian politics. On the other hand, the post-*Risorgimento* period was marked by progressive assimilation, indicated by increased secularization and irreligion, growth of mixed marriages, and a sharp drop in the Jewish birthrate. Economically, there was a continuing *embourgeoisement* of Italian Jews, but as late as 1912 one-third of the community was still supported by charity.

Countercurrents of Jewish revival surfaced in the first two decades of the century, especially in Rome, Tuscany, and Emilia, with the emergence of Zionism, the formation of a school of historical studies at the rabbinical college of Florence, the Pro Cultura circles, the proliferation of Jewish periodicals, and the founding of a Jewish youth movement.

1922–45. The situation of Italian Jewry did not change with the advent of Fascism.* Jewish rights were safeguarded, and on the whole the Jewish community, because of its largely middle-class makeup, accepted the regime, so that by 1933 some 7,300 Jews had enrolled in the Fascist Party. In 1930–31 royal decrees established the Union of Italian Jewish Communities, giving a uniform legal status to Italian Jewry and providing a stable base for Jewish religious, cultural, and charitable activities. Assimilation continued largely unabated, and in 1938 43.7 percent of married Jews had non-Jewish spouses.

A radical turnabout in the Fascist attitude began in 1936 with the pro-German reorientation of Italian diplomacy, and culminated in the discriminatory "racial laws" of 1938, which were occasioned by Mussolini's* policy of ideological alignment with Nazi Germany. Jewish political rights were lost, intermarriage was forbidden, and Jews were barred from government employment and the public schools. During the German occupation (1943–45), 7,749 Italian Jews perished in Nazi death camps.

Postwar Italy. In 1945 the Jewish population in Italy was reduced to 28,000 and by 1975 had reached only 35,000, with 70 percent concentrated in Rome and Milan. Rome, the largest, least assimilated, and poorest community, is also the only one with a self-sustained demographic growth, while Milan's Jewish population has increased mostly through immigration from Eastern Europe, North Africa, and the Middle East. Jewish equality is secure, though since the 1960s there have been anti-Semitic polemics in neo-Fascist circles and in the anti-Zionist Left.

ACan

JOHN XXIII. The 259th Roman pontiff, who changed the course of Catholicism with his 1962 convening of Vatican II,* Angelo Giuseppie Roncalli was born on November 25, 1881, at Sotto il Monte (Bergamo) in northern Italy. His parents, Giovanni Battista and Marianna, were both of peasant families that had lived for generations in this small Lombard town.

In 1892 young Angelo entered the minor seminary at Bergamo, studying there and at the diocesan seminary until 1901, when he left for the Appolinaire, Rome's major seminary, to continue his training. Roncalli distinguished himself at the Appolinaire, taking the prize for Hebrew, but his studies were interrupted when he was compelled to undertake his one-year military obligation. This he did from November 30, 1901, to November 30, 1902, being promoted to the rank of sergeant in the process. In 1904 he received his doctorate in sacred theology, and in the same year he was ordained a priest at Santa Maria in Monte Santo (Rome).

For sixteen years Father Roncalli worked in various capacities in his home diocese of Bergamo; he was secretary to Bishop Giacomo Radini, professor of Church history at the seminary, and an active member of Azione Cattolica (see Catholic Action*). After three years of service in Rome at the Propaganda Fide and the Lateran University, Roncalli was appointed apostolic visitor to Bulgaria in 1925 and was raised simultaneously to the rank of archbishop. In 1935 he was sent to Turkey as the apostolic administrator, and in 1944 he became nuncio to Paris.

Monsignor Roncalli resumed his pastoral career in 1953 after twenty-eight years in the diplomatic corps, when he was given the red hat of a cardinal and appointed patriarch of Venice by Pius XII.* Upon the death of Papa Pacelli in 1958, Roncalli, taking the name of John, was elevated to the papal throne after a conclave of three days. An engaging and popular pope who mixed easily with people, exhibiting genuine warmth and sense of humor, Pope John spoke eloquently of the Christian's responsibilities toward the poor and oppressed (in the encyclical *Mater et magistrum*) and toward peace (*Pacem in terris*).

With Vatican II John exposed the Church to the modern world, updating the liturgy and Church ceremony, launching a serious ecumenical movement, and promoting the cause of social justice. On June 3, 1963, the peasant pope died, leaving the work of the council in the hands of his successor, Paul VI.*

For further reference see: Ernesto Balducci, *John the Transitional Pope* (New York: McGraw-Hill, 1965); Carlo Falconi, *The Popes of the Twentieth Century* (Boston: Little, Brown, 1968).

RJW

JUDICIAL SYSTEM OF THE REPUBLIC. This comprises the organization, procedures, and functions of Italian courts since 1948. The Constitutional Court* stands apart from the ordinary court system and is the only court authorized to declare laws unconstitutional. The ordinary court system is a unified national network of lower and appellate civil and criminal courts. At the apex of the network stands the Supreme Court of Cassation, which hears appeals on points of law from lower civil and criminal appellate courts. Separate administrative courts include the Council of State and the Court of Accounts. Most judges are in a career service which is supervised by the Superior Council of the Judiciary.

EER

JUSTICE AND LIBERTY MOVEMENT. From its founding in 1929 until 1942, the Justice and Liberty movement played an important role in the history of Italian anti-Fascism.* But by 1938 the movement had lost some of its momentum as a consequence of the assassination in June 1937 of its principal founder and theorist, Carlo Rosselli,* and because of the inability of its leading intellectuals to overcome their differences concerning the movement's nature and aims.

From 1929 to 1933, under the leadership of such figures as Rosselli, Alberto Tarchiani, Emilio Lussu,* and Fausto Nitti, who directed the movement's activities in Paris, and of Ernesto Rossi,* Riccardo Bauer,* and others, who worked clandestinely in Italy, the movement aimed primarily to mobilize the non-Communist opposition to Fascism* through the dissemination of propaganda, the elaboration of a political program embracing republicanism and democratic socialism, and sporadic attempts to organize armed resistance against Mussolini's* regime.

From 1932 to the early 1940s, Justice and Liberty was preeminently an activist movement, but it contributed also to the ideological struggle against Fascism in its newspaper and in its theoretical organ, *Quaderni di Giustizia e Libertà*. Basically, the movement strove for a creative reinterpretation of socialism, whose tenets it sought to reconcile with those of classical liberalism.

For further reference see: various authors, *Giustizia e Libertà nella lotta antifascista e nella storia d'Italia—Attualità dei fratelli Rosselli a quaranta anni dal loro sacrificio* (Florence: La Nuova Italia, 1978).

FR

K

KULISCIOFF, ANNA. This Socialist and cofounder of the *Critica Sociale** was born on January 9, 1854, in Moskaya (Kherson), Russia, and died on December 29, 1925, in Milan, Italy. She studied engineering at the University of Zurich, Switzerland, 1871–72, and studied medicine at the University of Berne, Switzerland, 1882–84, receiving a degree in medicine from the University of Naples in 1886. Kuliscioff practiced medicine in Milan from 1887 to 1891 and was cofounder and administrator of *Critica Sociale* from 1891 to 1910 and editor of *La Difesa delle Lavoratrici*, 1911–12.

The Italian Socialist Party (PSI),* from its founding in 1892 until its dissolution by the Fascists in 1926, bore Kuliscioff's imprint. Her lifelong commitment to socialism began soon after she was introduced into Russian populist circles at the University of Zurich. Abandoning her studies, she returned to Russia, first to take part in the ill-fated "go to the people" movement in the summer of 1874 and later to work with clandestine anarchist groups. Threatened by arrest in 1877, she fled Russia to join other Bakuninist anarchists in Lugano, Switzerland. There she became acquainted with Italian Socialists, particularly the young anarchist leader Andrea Costa.*

Late in the 1870s, doubting the efficacy of anarchist methods but holding firm to her populist belief in working directly with the people, Kuliscioff converted to Marxism. She is believed to have influenced a similar conversion in Costa.

Following the dissolution of her liaison with Costa, Kuliscioff met Filippo Turati.* Soon after, he too became a Marxist. During the thirty-five years of the Turati-Kuliscioff partnership, they founded the *Critica Sociale* in 1891; contributed decisively to the founding of the PSI in 1892; and guided that party for over thirty years, particularly in parliament, where Turati, a Socialist deputy, was influenced by daily letters of advice from Kuliscioff.

In the 1890s Italian governments practiced a policy of repressing the young PSI. Thus, following the tumults in Milan in May 1898, the *Fatti di Maggio*, Kuliscioff was arrested, charged with having contributed to these violent uprisings through her efforts to organize women into labor unions, and sentenced to two years in prison.

In the Giolittian era (1901–14), unresolved tensions between the political views of the two partners—Turati emphasizing parliamentary action, Kuliscioff favoring more work on the grass-roots level within the PSI—were in large measure responsible for the political hesitancy so often attributed to Turati.

The massive funeral that marked Kuliscioff's death in 1925 was a last political manifestion of the PSI before the Fascist government silenced all opposition.

For further reference see: Anna Kuliscioff and Filippo Turati, *Carteggio 1898–1925*, 6 vols. (Turin: Einaudi, 1977); Franco Damiani and Fabio Rodriguez, eds., *Anna Kuliscioff: Immagini, scritti, testimonianze* (Milan: Feltrinelli economica, 1978); Alessandro Schiavi, *Anna Kuliscioff* (Rome: Opere Nuove, 1955).

CL

L

LABRIOLA, ANTONIO. Labriola was born on July 2, 1843, and died on February 2, 1904, in Rome. His significance in modern Italian and European history was insured by any one of several major contributions. As a brilliant philosopher, his writings were original and noteworthy and reflected his shift from Hegelianism to Marxism. As an intellectual who hated the potential sterility of pure theory, he struggled for a merger between thought and realistic political action. As a teacher he convinced a generation of future leaders of the constant need to work through the theoretical and practical tension of thought and action. As a man of letters who saw that neither democracy nor socialism could develop in a nation of illiterates, he labored arduously to develop Italian educational institutions that would serve to lift the cultural level of the masses. His last fifteen years were devoted to the introduction and critical analysis of the Marxian corpus in Italy.

Labriola inspired numerous students, including Benedetto Croce,* as well as numbers of Socialist and labor leaders. He also translated and transported Marxian socialism into the Italian intellectual consciousness, an effort that coincided with the early years of the history of the Partito Socialista Italiano (see Italian Socialist Party, PSI*). Labriola attempted to work with PSI members during the 1890s, but he was frequently uncomfortable, impatient, bitterly polemical, and even contemptuous of many who called themselves Socialists and yet appeared blind to the needs of the masses. His tolerance was very limited for those who considered themselves Socialists but ignored the vast work required in creating class consciousness in the broader context of historical consciousness.

Labriola did not arrive at his Socialist convictions until 1887–88. As a child he had been sent by his father, a schoolteacher, to the abbey school at Montecassino, from which Labriola entered the Faculty of Letters and Philosophy at Naples, where Hegelianism reigned supreme. Much influenced by that world view, especially in the lectures of Bertrando Spaventa,* Labriola went on to develop an intellectual interest in various Germanic schools concerned with the psychology of peoples and linguistics. To earn a living, he first worked in the secretariat of the Neapolitan police section (the *Questura*) and from 1866 to 1871 taught in a *ginnasio*, a job which he disliked. He prepared a thesis at Naples and entered several essays in competitions, which eventually led to the university appointment he desired. In 1874 he was named to a chair of philosophy and education in Rome. By then he had also developed a reputation as a journalist and had attracted the attention of Ruggiero Bonghi.* In Rome, Bonghi opened a "museo"—actually an institute to study and improve Italian education as well as help prepare teachers—which Labriola headed from 1877 to 1891. Labriola's interest in education led him to produce lengthy studies of comparative public educational practices in six countries.

Labriola's interests turned in a decidedly political direction in the seventies and eighties. He sought to determine how to minimize clerical influence in the national formation of a people; how to transform a nation into a modern community; how to train a corps of teachers in a philosophical approach that could be applied in popular classrooms; and what immediate and practical steps the state ought to take in order to alleviate the sufferings of millions of unemployed and to support the disabled. By the end of the eighties, Labriola found sufficient answers in dialectical materialism combined with a study of history.

His lectures examined the world of Europe since the French Revolution to clarify the limitations of the bourgeois revolutions and societies. He likewise began to deliver lectures to audiences of unemployed construction and steel workers; worked closely with Andrea Costa,* Filippo Turati,* and the PSI leadership for a brief period; corresponded regularly with Engels (who died in 1895); and even attended one meeting of the Second International (Zurich, 1893), where he met Engels. He nearly exhausted himself in his crusade for popular education and popular universities. His activism lasted until 1895.

In the mid- and late 1890s he began publishing his famous essays in Georges Sorel's *Devenir Social*, later published as the *Saggi*, which synthesized his understanding of Marxism and history and which laid forth a philosophy of *praxis* that has motivated a stream of twentieth-century activists. His last writings included bitter attacks on revisionists as well as the curious arguments in defense of Italian imperialism in Tripoli, which Labriola insisted was required by modern economic and political forces. He died at sixty-one, following an operation.

For further reference see: Luigi Dal Pane, *Antonio Labriola nella politica e nella cultura italiano* (Turin: Einaudi, 1975); Antonio Labriola, *Essays on the Materialist Conception of History*, trans. Charles H. Kerr (Chicago: Charles H. Kerr and Co., 1908).

JMC

LABRIOLA, ARTURO. Arturo Labriola, an early leader of the revolutionary syndicalist current in Italian socialism, was born in Naples on January 22, 1873, and died there on June 23, 1959. Labriola's Neapolitan background shaped his conception of Italian problems, as he looked for solutions to industrialization and the emerging industrial proletariat. In 1902 he moved from Naples to Milan, where he founded the journal *Avanguardia Socialista* as a weapon against reformist socialism. He felt that the reformists, with their emphasis on parliamentary politics and their complicity in the Giolittian system, would undermine the capacity of the proletariat to develop new values and institutions. Thus, he began to emphasize the role of an autonomous labor movement in creating socialism.

Although he favored the Libyan War (see Ouchy, Treaty of*) in World War I,* Labriola did not share in the revision that led many syndicalists to corporativism.* The failure of syndicalism* in practice prompted him to work for reforms to undermine the monarchical and protectionist forces that had so far impeded normal syndicalist development. He won election to parliament as an independent Socialist in 1913.

After the war, Labriola served as minister of labor under Giovanni Giolitti,* then joined the reformist Partito Socialista Unitario (Unitary Socialist Party). Hostile to Fascism* as a backward form of the general postwar reaction, he participated in the Aventine Secession,* then went into exile in France in 1927.

Labriola returned to Italy in 1935, during the Ethiopian war. Long concerned about Italy's position in the Mediterranean, he approved of Mussolini's* turn to a more aggressive foreign policy, but he remained apart from Fascist politics. After World War II* he served as a deputy in the Constituent Assembly of 1946,* then as a senator in the Republic.

For further reference see: Dora Marucco, *Arturo Labriola e il sindacalismo rivoluzionario in Italia* (Turin: Fondazione Luigi Einaudi, 1970).

DDR

LACERBA. See **FUTURISM**

LA FARINA, GIUSEPPE. This revolutionary, journalist, and leader of the Italian National Society (see Società Nazionale Italiana*) was born in Messina on July 20, 1815. La Farina won his law degree in 1835 and quickly became involved in revolutionary activities in the Kingdom of the Two Sicilies.* He lived in Florence during the 1840s, but returned to Sicily in 1848 and held several positions in the revolutionary government. Exiled in 1849, he remained in France until 1853.

La Farina's career after 1856 was connected with Turin, Cavour,* the Italian National Society, which promoted the prime minister's policies, and *Il Piccolo Corriere d'Italia*, which served as its official organ. He aided the expedition of Giuseppe Garibaldi,* with whom he nevertheless clashed. Representing southern Italy in the parliament of the new kingdom after 1860, La Farina died in Turin on September 5, 1863. His books include *Istoria documentata della Rivoluzione*

Siciliana del 1848–1849 [Documented history of the Sicilian revolution of 1848–1849] (1850), and *Storia d'Italia dal 1815 al 1850* [History of Italy from 1815 to 1850] (1851–52).

JCR

LA MALFA, UGO. This postwar secretary of the Partito Repubblicano Italiano (PRI) (see Italian Republican Party*) and prominent lay politician was born on May 16, 1903, in Palermo. He received his degree in foreign affairs from the University of Palermo and was an active anti-Fascist during the Mussolini* years. Arrested once, he remained in the Armed Resistance,* founded the Action Party* in 1941, and was compelled to flee Italy in 1943. In 1946 he became a member of the PRI and was elected to the Chamber of Deputies* from the Bologna area in 1948. La Malfa held ministerial posts under a number of prime ministers, including Ferruccio Parri,* Alcide De Gasperi,* and Amintore Fanfani.* Known for his austere economic views, La Malfa was chosen secretary of the PRI in 1965, a post he held until his death in 1979.

RJW

LA MARMORA, ALFONSO FERRERO DE. Soldier, administrator, and statesman of the *Risorgimento** era, La Marmora was born in Turin on November 18, 1804. He gained a reputation for skilled and heroic action during the 1848 war against Austria. He was minister of war almost without interruption from 1849 until 1860, and commander of the Sardinian forces in the Crimean War* in 1855. Twice prime minister, in 1859–60 and again in 1864–66, his latter term of office witnessed the conclusion of the Prussian alliance. La Marmora's subsequent career was somewhat clouded because he was held responsible for the defeat at the battle of Custozza (1866).* He died in Florence on January 5, 1878.

JCR

LA MASA, GIUSEPPE. This Sicilian revolutionary associated with Giuseppe Garibaldi's* expedition in 1860 was born in Trabia on November 30, 1819. La Masa's early involvement with revolutionary causes led to his emigration from the island. He returned to Sicily to help lead the revolutions of 1848,* during which he headed a band of volunteers against the Austrians. A second exile carried him to France and to Turin. La Masa led 200 volunteers from the Italian National Society (see Società Nazionale Italiana*) in Garibaldi's Sicilian expedition. He developed a reputation for somewhat theatrical behavior but later attained the rank of major general in the Italian army. La Masa also served as a deputy associated with the Left (see Sinistra, La*). He died in Rome on March 29, 1881.

JCR

LAMBROSO, CESARE. See *RASSEGNA SETTIMANALE, LA*

LAMBRUSCHINI, LUIGI. This cardinal served as papal secretary of state under Gregory XVI* from 1836 to 1846. Born at Sestri Levante on May 16, 1776, Lambruschini became a noted theologian, first at Macerata, then at Rome. In 1819 he became archbishop of Genoa. In 1827 he was sent to Paris as nuncio; however, his hostility to the July Revolution led the new king, Louis Philippe, to demand his recall in 1831. In 1836 he became papal secretary of state; in that post he adopted a strong antiliberal stance and aligned Rome firmly with the conservative powers. He was the favored conservative candidate in the conclave of 1846, in which Pius IX* was elected. Disapproving of the new pope's liberal policies, he left Rome in the fall of 1848, only returning with the counterrevolution in 1849. He died in Rome on May 12, 1854.

AJR

LAMI, GIOVANNI. This Florentine priest (1697–1770) of the Enlightenment* became editor, in 1740, of the *Novelle Letterarie*, one of the first Italian journals of national and foreign literature. He received a degree in law at Pisa in 1720; was active in the Florentine literary academies; travelled to France, Holland, and Switzerland; served as librarian to the Riccardi family in Florence; and taught Church history at the Studio Fiorentino. He also published works of theology, literary biography, and Florentine history. His eighteen-volume *Deliciae eruditorum* [Delights of the scholar] (1736–69) and his *Lezioni di antichità toscane* [Lessons from Tuscan antiquity] (1766) were large and important collections of medieval and Renaissance chronicles and treatises.

RBL

LAMORICIÈRE, LOUIS CHRISTOPHE LÈON. A French general and commander of the papal army, he was born in Nantes on February 15, 1806. Lamoricière achieved prominence as a military leader and governor-general in Algeria. A supporter of the Second Republic, his opposition to Louis Napoleon (see Napoleon III*) caused his arrest and exile after Napoleon's coup in December 1851. On April 9, 1860, he took command of Pius IX's* volunteer army of approximately 18,000 men. Sardinia's invasion of the Papal States* led to his defeat by vastly superior numbers at Castelfidardo (September 18, 1860) and to his surrender at Ancona ten days later. He died in Prouzel, near Amiens, on September 11, 1865.

RCu

LAMPATO, FRANCESCO. See *ANNALI UNIVERSALI DI STATISTICA*

LAMPEDUSA, GIUSEPPE TOMASSI, PRINCE DI. This Sicilian aristocrat wrote *The Leopard* (1958), one of the greatest novels of the twentieth century. He was born in 1896 in Palermo and died soon after completing his great work in 1957. A man of deep culture and wide learning, he published nothing until the age of sixty, when he set out to write a book which would combine historical exposition and psychological confession. The *Risorgimento** events in the background of *The Leopard*'s beginning symbolize the passing of the old and the advent of the new as seen through the intelligent eyes of Prince Salina, an enlightened figure who combines "feline suppleness with dangerous strength and regal majesty." During the rest of the fifty years that the book encompasses, the traditional world disappears; the Prince is forgotten, his fortune scattered, his palaces ruined. In *The Leopard* Lampedusa portrays the eternal themes of inner struggle, frustrated humanity, and psychosocial ambivalence.

Other works, published posthumously, are: *Racconti* (1961), *Lezioni su Stendhal* (1971), and *Cinquecento* (1979).

FFA

LAMPERTICO, FEDELE. This economist and political figure was born in Vicenza on June 13, 1833. A professor at the University of Padua, he entered the Chamber of Deputies in 1866 and in 1873 was named to the Senate. An acute observer of the political and cultural life of the times, he was especially critical of the inadequacies of laissez-faire economics and sought an alternative. In 1875 he called the Congress of Italian Economists in Milan, which favored state intervention in economic affairs. Nonetheless, ten years later, in 1885, he was among those in the Senate who opposed an increase in the duties on grain. His major work, the five-volume *Economia dei popoli e degli stati* [The economy of peoples and states] (1874–84), saw economic science as evolving within the framework of a people's intellectual, physical, and moral development. Lampertico died in Vicenza on April 6, 1906.

FJC

LANCIANI, RODOLFO AMADEO. An archeologist, he was born in Montecelio (Rome) on January 1, 1847. Although he received his degree in engineering, he studied the classics and was intensely interested in the topography and antiquities of the Eternal City. Appointed secretary of the communal archeological commission in 1872, he was involved in the various excavations in the capital, Tivoli, and Ostia, and published his findings. In 1893 he published the *Forma Urbis Romae* [Plan of the City of Rome], which documented and illustrated the history of the monuments of ancient, medieval, and modern Rome. He also published a number of works in English, among them *Ancient Rome in the Light of Modern Discoveries* (1888), *Pagan and Christian Rome* (1892), *The Ruins and Excavations of Ancient Rome* (1897), and *Wanderings in the Roman Campagna* (1909). He died on May 21, 1929, in the city he loved and studied throughout his life.

FJC

LAND RECLAMATION UNDER FASCISM. See **BONIFICA INTEGRALE**

LANZA, FERDINANDO. Lanza, a general of the Kingdom of the Two Sicilies,* was born in Palermo in 1788. He led an army against the Roman Republic in 1849 when Ferdinand II* marched into the Papal States* on behalf of Pius IX.* Giuseppe Garibaldi* checked Lanza's forces near Palestrina (May 4) and inflicted further casualties upon the retreating Neapolitans in a skirmish at Velletri (May 19). In 1860 Francis II* appointed Lanza as his *alter ego* in Sicily. The general's incompetence enabled Garibaldi to seize Palermo in three days of fighting (May 27–29). An armistice concluded on May 30 terminated with Lanza's surrender (June 6). He died in 1865.

RCu

LANZA, GIOVANNI. Prime minister from 1869 to 1873 and the last of Cavour's* political heirs in the progressive Piedmontese Right (see Destra, La*), Lanza helped consolidate the financial and foreign policies of the young Italian state. He was born on February 15, 1810, in Casale Monferrato (Alessandria), and died on March 9, 1882, in Rome. A physician who volunteered in the war of 1848 against Austria, Lanza was elected to parliament the same year and was reelected uninterruptedly until his death. At first he sat at the Left (see Sinistra, La*), but moved gradually toward the Cavourian Right. He was prominent in the Chamber as its vice-president (1853–55) and president (1860–61, 1867–68, 1869). Minister of education (1855–58) and of finance (1858–59) under Cavour, he rose to the Ministry of the Interior under General Alfonso La Marmora* (1864–65), supporting the September Convention* with France as a step toward making Rome capital of Italy. However, he broke with La Marmora and Finance Minister Quintino Sella* over the grist tax (see Macinato*), which Lanza opposed. His appointment as prime minister in December 1869 marked a victory of parliamentary—as opposed to royal—direction of government. He came to accept Sella's stringent fiscal policies as necessary for the solvency of the state. Sentimentally a Francophile, he nevertheless successfully opposed Victor Emmanuel II's* inclination to support France in the war of 1870, daring to take Rome by force in September of the same year, after which he promoted the passage of the conciliatory Law of Papal Guarantees* in 1871. With Foreign Minister Emilio Visconti-Venosta,* Lanza charted a course of noninvolvement in the Franco-German rivalry after 1871 and remained constant in support of Sella's fiscal policies, the unpopularity of which led to the ministry's resignation in June 1873, ending more than a decade of Piedmontese hegemony in united Italy. Personally modest and frequently in the shadow of more forceful figures, Lanza remains among the less appreciated makers of the Italian state.

For further reference see: Enrico Tavallini, *La vita e i tempi di Giovanni Lanza*, 2 vols. (Turin: Roux, 1887).

SS

LANZILLO, AGOSTINO. Agostino Lanzillo, a Fascist publicist in the revolutionary syndicalist tradition, was born in Reggio Calabria on August 31,

1886, and died in Milan on March 13, 1952. He was influential especially during the formative period of Fascism* from 1918 to 1922, analyzing the impact of the war, the limits of orthodox socialism, and the requirements for new political forms. Although he was a member of various Fascist bodies, including the Commission of Eighteen, Lanzillo maintained a relatively independent posture within the regime, criticizing, for example, the syndical law of 1926 and the move toward autarky (see Autarchia*) in the 1930s. Though sometimes in trouble with Fascist Party authorities, he pursued an academic career in economics and continued to publicize his relatively open and pluralistic corporativist conception.

DDR

LA PIRA, GIORGIO. Christian Democratic mayor of Florence and an international figure in the cause of peace and justice, La Pira was born on January 9, 1904. He received his law degree from the University of Florence and became active in postwar Christian Democratic politics. In 1951 he was elected mayor of Florence, but devoted much of his later life to the goal of world peace. La Pira travelled widely for this purpose, addressing the Soviet parliament on peace and disarmament in 1959, marching in the United States for civil rights, and attempting to negotiate peace between the United States and North Vietnam. A devoted Roman Catholic, he once wrote, ''My life is guided by one, unique norm: to be always, at whatever price, in the Church and with the Church, my Mother.'' He died on November 5, 1977.

RJW

LATERAN ACCORDS. These agreements were reached between Fascist Italy and the Holy See in 1929 and incorporated into the Constitution of 1948.* By the second decade of the twentieth century the climate of opinion in Italian ecclesiastical and governmental circles had become conducive to a settlement of the Roman Question.* The advent and speedy consolidation of Fascism undoubtedly hastened a solution. Mussolini* saw in a reconciliation with the Church not only a way to enhance the prestige of Fascism but also a means of ensuring the permanent dissolution of the Italian Popular Party.* The negotiations that terminated in the Lateran Accords began in August 1926 with private exchanges of views between Francesco Pacelli, legal consultant to the Holy See and brother of Monsignor Eugenio Pacelli (later Pius XII*), and Domenico Barone, councillor of state in the Italian government. The negotiations were frequently interrupted by renewed Fascist violence against Catholic organizations and by Fascist attempts to bring all youth organizations under the direction of the Fascist Opera Nazionale Balilla (see Balilla*). Pope Pius XI* protested against the efforts of the Fascist government to dissolve Catholic youth organizations, but the secret negotiations continued and were concluded on February 11, 1929, when three accords were signed by the representatives of the Holy See and the Kingdom of Italy.

Under the terms of the Conciliation Treaty Italy recognized Roman Catholicism as the sole religion of the state. It also recognized the right of the Holy See to communicate freely with the bishops, clergy, and laity of the entire Catholic world without interference from the Italian government. The sovereignty and independence of a new state, Vatican City, were acknowledged, together with the right of the Vatican to send and receive diplomatic representatives. The Holy See declared Vatican City to be "neutral and inviolable territory." It also declared the Roman Question settled and recognized the Kingdom of Italy under the House of Savoy with Rome as its capital.

Under the Concordat Italy guaranteed to the Catholic Church free exercise of spiritual power, free and public exercise of worship, and jurisdiction in ecclesiastical matters. No ecclesiastic could be employed or remain in the employment of the Italian state without the express permission of the diocesan bishop. Before the appointment of a bishop, the Holy See was to communicate the name of the person to the Italian government to ensure that the latter had no objection of a political nature. All bishops, moreover, were required to take an oath of loyalty to the head of the state. The civil effects of a canonical marriage were to be recognized by the state. Religious instruction was to be provided in public elementary and secondary schools, and teachers of such instruction had to have the approval of the ecclesiastical authorities. The Italian state recognized the auxiliary organizations of Italian Catholic Action.* All religious were forbidden to enroll or to take part in any political party.

The Financial Convention was intended to provide partial compensation for papal territories annexed by Italy during the era of unification. The Pope was promised 750 million lire in cash and 1 billion lire in government bonds. The Lateran Accords brought enormous prestige to the Fascist government of Mussolini.

For further reference see: Francesco Margiotto Broglio, *Italia e Santa Sede dalla grande guerra alla conciliazione* (Bari: Laterza, 1966); Daniel Binchy, *Church and State in Fascist Italy* (New York: Oxford University Press, 1941).

EC

LATERZA, GIOVANNI. Giovanni Laterza was born in 1873 in Putigliano, Puglia. He was the son of Vito Laterza, who in 1855 had founded a small publishing house that moved to Bari in 1889. Giovanni took it over in 1901. To promote his business he went to Naples, where he met Benedetto Croce* and Francesco Nitti,* whose books he proceeded to publish, to their profit and his own. From 1903 on he printed Croce's *La Critica*. During the twenty-year Fascist dictatorship Laterza managed to maintain sufficient autonomy to publish works recommended by Croce, including those of such anti-Fascist intellectuals as Guido De Ruggiero,* Francesco Flora, Arturo Labriola,* Giorgio Morandi, Adolfo Omodeo, Luigi Russo, and Mario Vinciguerra.* He died in Bari in 1943.

MS

LAVORO, IL. See **NEWSPAPERS**

LAW OF PAPAL GUARANTEES. See **PAPAL GUARANTEES, LAW OF**

LAZZARI, COSTANTINO. This founder of the Partito Operaio Italiano and one of the founders of the Lega Fascista Milanese and the Partito Socialista Italiano (see Italian Socialist Party, PSI*) was born in Cremona on January 1, 1857, and died in Rome on December 29, 1927. He received a technical school certificate at age fifteen and then worked in a warehouse to support himself. He returned to school and eventually obtained a teacher's diploma, although he had difficulty in finding a suitable teaching position.

His political life began and ended in poverty and prisons. He was repeatedly arrested in the 1880s—for political organizing among workers; for speaking out on behalf of Socialist principles; for agitation (1898) in the wake of the Adowa* defeat in the Fatti di Milano; for so-called defeatist propaganda in 1918; and finally, in 1927, by the Fascists. Throughout Lazzari remained unshaken in his views about the Socialist road to power. Despite a brief flirtation in 1899 with the politics of collaboration, Lazzari remained attached to a politics of intransigence, opposing any collaboration on the parliamentary level with bourgeois parties and equally opposing any reformist drift within his own party. His pamphlet, "La necessità della politica socialista in Italia" (1902), summed up his philosophy of action. It argued that socialism required a permanent battle with bourgeois forces, that it would be achieved only through conscious revolution and not coups, and that evolutionary reformism was the wrong approach. He believed that bourgeois political systems would inevitably crumble and be replaced by triumphant socialism.

His famous phrase, delivered in a speech during a May 1915 party congress— "né aderire, né sabotare" [neither support, nor sabotage]—encapsulated PSI policy during World War I.* It was also consistent with his long antimilitarist record, beginning at an 1891 party congress where he attacked Italian imperialism in Africa, and reiterated in 1896–98, 1911–12 (against the Libyan War [see Ouchy, Treaty of*]), and at the start of World War I. When the editor of *Avanti!*,* Mussolini,* published his famous statement in October 1914 regarding Italian participation in the war, Lazzari moved quickly to expel him from the party and then took over *Avanti!* himself.

With the founding of the Third International, Lazzari led that section of the PSI which refused to join the new Italian Communist Party (PCI)* but wanted to join the new International, a position which the PSI did not accept. He was successful, however, in leading the expulsion of reformists from the PSI in 1923.

Attacked physically by Fascists in the parliament in 1926, he spent several months in prison in the following year, only to be released to a grinding poverty that contributed to his death in his seventy-first year.

For further reference see: Armando Parlato, "Costantino Lazzari," in *Enci-*

clopedia dell' antifascismo e della Resistenza (Milan: La Pietra, 1976) 3: 294–95; Luigi Crotesi, *Il socialismo italiano tra reforme e rivoluzione, 1892–1921* (Bari: Laterza, 1969).

JMC

LAZZARONI. A name of Spanish derivative, originally meaning "lepers," it was applied to the common people of Naples. In the seventeenth century it referred to the plebes of the Mercato district of the city who revolted against the Spanish in 1647. Sporadically applied to the rebellious plebes in other southern cities, the term persisted only in Naples, where the *lazzaroni* became famous for their fierce devotion to the Bourbon dynasty. They aroused admiration for their bravery in fighting the French in 1799. After 1815 the Bourbon regime used the ragged and excitable *lazzaroni* against its liberal enemies, who despised them as a vile and reactionary rabble.

RCu

LEFT. See **SINISTRA, LA**

LEGATIONS. The four northern provinces of the Papal States*—Bologna, Ferrara, Forli, and Ravenna—were called Legations, from the legates or papal governors who ruled them. In 1797 they were forcibly detached from the Papal States by Napoleon I,* who added them first to the Cisalpine Republic,* and later to the Italian Republic. In 1815 they were returned to papal rule by the Congress of Vienna.* However, two decades of modern and secular French rule had left the people of the Legations with little enthusiasm for a return to the inefficient ecclesiastical rule of the papacy. Discontent grew rapidly, and a revolution in February 1831 was put down only by Austrian intervention. Thereafter, the Legations became a stronghold of the *Risorgimento*,* playing a leading role in the revolutions of 1848* and 1859. In 1860 they were finally added to the Italian state.

AJR

LEGGE CASATI. See **CASATI LAW**

LEO XII. Born Annibale Sermattei della Genga on August 22, 1760, at Genga near Spoleto, the future pope (1823–29) took holy orders in 1783 and rose rapidly in the papal diplomatic service: he served as nuncio in Cologne from 1794 to 1799 and as nuncio in Munich from 1802 to 1808. In 1814, after the fall of Napoleon I,* he was sent by Pius VII* to Paris to negotiate the return of the Papal States* with the victorious Allies, but travelled so slowly that he arrived after the Peace of Paris had been signed. He became a leading figure among the *Zelanti** after 1815, and his election as Pope Leo XII in 1823 marked a reactionary turn in papal policy. He abolished Ercole Consalvi's* reforms and restored the outdated papal administration to its prerevolutionary state; this provoked growing discontent, and the revolutionary secret societies flourished. It was during his reign, in fact, that the decline of the temporal power first became obvious. In foreign policy, he aligned the papacy closely with the conservative powers. He died in Rome on February 10, 1829.

AJR

LEO XIII. Roman pontiff from 1878 to 1903 and most famous for his encyclical on the condition of the working man, Leo XIII was born Gioacchino Pecci on March 2, 1810, in Carpineo (Frosinone). Educated by the Jesuits, Pecci was ordained in 1837 after studies at the Accademia dei Nobili Ecclesiastici and the University of Sapienza. The young cleric was taken into the administration of the Papal States* by Pope Gregory XVI,* who sent him as apostolic delegate first to Benevento, and then to Perugia. After a brief career as nuncio to Belgium (1843–46), Pecci returned to Italy to become the archbishop of Perugia. While Giacomo Antonelli* reigned in Rome as cardinal secretary of state, Archbishop Pecci was distrusted and considered imprudently liberal. Given a red hat in 1853, he was almost sixty-eight when elected to the chair of Peter on February 20, 1878.

Taking the name Leo, Pecci remained in the Vatican for twenty-five years, slowly but deliberately bringing the Church into the modern world. Patient and nonjudgmental, Leo's encyclical writings encouraged biblical scholarship (*Providentissimus Deus*, 1893), accepted democracy (*Libertas*, 1888, and *Sapientiae christianae*, 1890), and embraced the workers' movement and rights of labor (*Rerum novarum*,* 1891). At the outset of his papacy, Leo hoped to solve the Roman Question* through direct negotiation with the Italian Kingdom, but soon despaired of success. He then attempted, especially under secretary of state Mariano Rampolla del Tindaro,* to negotiate the issue on the international plane. This, too, ended in failure, and the territorial question remained unsolved at his death on August 30, 1903.

For further reference see: E. Soderini, *Il pontificato di Leone XIII*, 3 vols. (Milan: Mondadori, 1932–33).

RJW

LEONARDO. A Florentine periodical of philosophy founded and directed by Giovanni Papini* (Gian Falco) and Giuseppe Prezzolini* (Giuliano il Sofista), it appeared on December 1, 1902, and was issued thrice monthy. It represented a reaction against positivist trends, increasing specialization, advancing materialism, and the conformity of the age. The name *Leonardo* symbolized the youthful collaborators' search for liberation, universality, and spontaneity. *Leonardo* also sought to complete the *Risorgimento** by giving the Italian people an overriding sense of mission. Failing to evoke a national response, Papini and Prezzolini ceased publishing the periodical in August 1907.

RSC

LEONE, GIOVANNI. Elected president of the Italian Republic* on December 24, 1971, Giovanni Leone was forced to resign in June 1978 because of alleged financial improprieties connected with the Lockheed scandals. A prominent lawyer and postwar politician, Leone was born in Naples on November 3, 1908. He received a law degree in 1929 from the University of Naples and began a career as a professor that culminated in his appointment to the chair of criminal trial law at the University of Rome in 1956.

Leone's political career was launched in 1946 when he was elected on the Christian Democratic list to the Constituent Assembly.* After serving in the Chamber of Deputies* for fifteen years, eight of which were spent as chairman of the Chamber, he became prime minister in 1963 and again in 1968, both governments lasting only a few months.

Leone's successful career reached its apex in 1971 with his election to the presidency. His reputation, however, was badly tarnished when his name surfaced as an alleged beneficiary of Lockheed Corporation bribes for government contracts.

RJW

LEONINE CITY. The name is applied to that part of Rome, including the Vatican, Castel Sant'Angelo, and the Borgo, that Pope Leo IV surrounded with a defensive wall after the Saracen raid of 846. In 860 Pope Nicholas I transferred the papal residence from the Lateran Palace to the Vatican; thereafter, the Leonine City became the center of the papal administration and of Roman religious life. After the Italian occupation of Rome in 1870, the government offered to allow the papacy to retain the Leonine City, but Pope Pius IX* rejected the offer. Only the Vatican remains under papal authority today by virtue of the Lateran Accords* of 1929.

AJR

LEOPARDI, GIACOMO. Leopardi was a poet (1798–1837) whose patriotic verses, "All'Italia" and "Sopra il monumento di Dante" (1818), inspired many in the *Risorgimento*.* The self-taught son of an orthodox Catholic, Count Monaldo Leopardi of Recanati, Giacomo found solace in friendships with Pietro Giordani, with members of the Florentine Gabinetto Vieusseux, and especially in later years with the Neapolitan Antonio Ranieri. Leopardi's Florentine associates often helped support him and his publications and brought him membership in the Accademia della Crusca. The poet was plagued by ill-health and a sense of despair, and his *Operette morali* (1824–27) reflected boredom and unhappiness. Earlier *Canzoni* (1818–22) defended the world of illusions and dreams against reason, but later works such as the allegorical "Paralipomeni della Batracomiomachia'' (begun in 1831) reflected the conflict between liberals and reactionaries in the Romagna* in 1831. During that conflict Leopardi was elected deputy on March 19, 1831, but refrained from accepting.

For further reference see: *Appunti e ricordi* (1819), *Le Ricordanze* (1829), and *Zibaldone* (1821), all largely autobiographical.

MSM

LERDA, GIOVANNI. Giovanni Lerda was a prominent leader of the left wing of the Italian Socialist Party (PSI)* during the late nineteenth and early twentieth centuries. The author of several books, he advocated intransigence for the party, arguing against alliances with ''bourgeois'' political groups and opposing the tendency of the Socialist deputies to vote for cabinets.

During 1911 and 1912 he successfully organized the left wing in order to challenge reformist control of the party. With his wife Oda and several friends he established the newspaper *La Soffitta*, which served both as a forum for the discussion of leftist ideas and as a powerful organizing force. Lerda, however, was unable to provide the revolutionaries with a viable theoretical position; indeed, he raised a number of issues that embarrassed his colleagues.

After 1912 Lerda reluctantly agreed to fold *La Soffitta* in order not to compete with *Avanti!*,* which had come under left-wing control. At the Congress of Reggio Emilia (1912) Lerda resigned from the party after the delegates approved a motion stating that membership in the party was incompatible with Freemasonry.* Lerda withdrew his resignation at the delegates' request, saying that he would remain in the party as an ordinary ''soldier.''

SD

LIBERAL PARTY. Divided into two loose coalitions (*La Destra*,* the Right; *La Sinistra*,* the Left) made increasingly indistinct by transformism,* Italy's Liberal Party dominated political life from the time of unification to the advent of Fascism.* The Right, in power until 1876 and inspired by Cavour's* legacy, was devoted to constitutional monarchy, social conservatism, limited suffrage, administrative centralization, and balanced budgets. The Left, also monarchical, nevertheless included a greater number of former republicans; it generally promoted enlarged suffrage, experimented with deficit financing for social reform purposes, and held power with few interruptions from 1876 until World War I.* Individual differences aside, both coalitions favored a laic state and a foreign policy designed to safeguard Italy's interests within a European balance of power.

SS

LIBERALSOCIALISMO MOVEMENT. See **CALOGERO, GUIDO**

LIBERTÀ, LA. See **CONCENTRAZIONE ANTIFASCISTA**

LIBYA. Consisting of the two impoverished Ottoman provinces of Tripolitania and Cyrenaica, Libya became an Italian colony as a result of the Italo-Turkish War of 1911–12. Italian imperialist writers had long promised that the vast, thinly populated desert territories could be transformed into a major settlement colony, a "fourth shore" (to add to Italy's Tyrrhenian, Adriatic, and Sicilian shores) similar to French Algeria.

Liberal governments, preoccupied with World War I* and postwar domestic crises, made little headway in developing the colony. The military conquest of Libya and its subsequent colonization were almost entirely Fascist enterprises. The conquest began in 1922, and by 1924 Tripolitania was subdued. The Sanusi-led rebellion in Cyrenaica, however, lasted until 1931 and was repressed with particular ferocity. Colonization, under a succession of governors—Count Giuseppe Volpi* (July 1921–July 1925), General Emilio De Bono* (July 1925–December 1928), and Marshal Pietro Badoglio* (January 1929–December 1933)—proceeded slowly. Programs of government grants and subsidies to colonists and investors yielded unsatisfactory results. Instead of the anticipated small farms worked by Italian emigrants, large plantations (devoted primarily to almonds, olives, and vineyards) dependent on Libyan labor developed.

The colony developed most rapidly from 1934 to 1940, thanks to peaceful internal conditions, heavy government investment, and the dynamic leadership of Governor Italo Balbo.* Communications improved, and the administration was united. Colonization companies, financed by the government and by social welfare organizations, directed intensive land settlement by Italian emigrants. The coastal region, where the bulk of the 110,000 Italians (1940) was concentrated, became an extension of the mother country. This transformation was given legal recognition in 1939 when the four coastal provinces were incorporated into the Kingdom of Italy.

In the long run, however, the transformation failed economically and politically. Libya's economy remained heavily dependent on Italian subsidies. Politically, the Italians' "separate but equal" policy never won the loyalty of the 800,000 Libyans, many of whom rallied to the Sanusi banner (in alliance with the British) during World War II.* The Libyans rejected Italian claims for even a limited period of trusteeship over Tripolitania after World War II, and Libya became independent in 1951. The last remnants of the Italian colonists, numbering some 14,000, were finally expelled after the 1970 Libyan revolution.

For further reference see: Claudio G. Segrè, *Fourth Shore: The Italian Colonization of Libya* (Chicago: University of Chicago Press, 1974); E. E. Evans Pritchard, *The Sanusi of Cyrenaica* (London: Oxford University Press, 1949); F. Malgeri, *La guerra libica* (Rome: Edizioni di Storia e Letteratura, 1970).

CGS

LIBYAN WAR. See **OUCHY, TREATY OF**

LIGURIAN REPUBLIC. This was one of the French-inspired sister republics established after Napoleon Bonaparte's (see Napoleon I*) first Italian campaign and conquest of the Po Valley in 1796–97. Through the clandestine activity of the French resident Tilly, Genoa became a center of Jacobin activity in Italy after the outbreak of the War of the First Coalition (see Wars of the First and Second Coalitions*) with France in 1792. On the French invasion of Italy, Genoa was revolutionized through the actions of local patriots and occupation by the French, and a republic inspired by France replaced the old, oligarchic republican state. The constitution was based on the French constitution of 1795. In the War of the Second Coalition, the French army was blockaded in Genoa in the winter of 1798. Although the Ligurian Republic was revived in 1800, with the creation of the Kingdom of Italy in 1805 Genoa was annexed to France.

RBL

LISSA. This battle was fought in the Third War for National Liberation between the Italians under Admiral Count Carlo di Persano and the Austrians under Admiral Wilhelm von Tegethoff. The Italians, with ten ironclads, were besieging the Adriatic island of Lissa (modern Vis, Yugoslavia) when, on July 20, 1866, they were attacked by an Austrian squadron of seven ironclads and a few obsolete wooden ships. Tegethoff formed a wedge, with his flagship at the apex, and broke the Italian line as it steamed across his bows. The Austrians rammed and sank Persano's flagship, and the besiegers were driven off with a loss of two ironclads. Despite this blow to the embryonic Italian navy, Austria's problems elsewhere prevented her from following up the advantage.

WDG

LOCAL GOVERNMENT UNDER THE REPUBLIC. These institutions make and administer subnational policy. Units of local government comprise 20 regions, 94 provinces, 8,000 rural and urban communes, and numerous special purpose bodies. Each level of government includes a popularly elected council, an executive group, and a chief executive. Local governments make policy appropriate to their levels and also administer national policy. With the creation of regional governments in the Republic, the functions of provinces have declined and in some regions the province serves only as a unit of national administration. Local government is supervised by national administrative officers and agencies, including the provincial prefect, the regional commissioner, and the *questore*, the provincial chief of the national police.

EER

LOCARNO PACT. This covenant, consisting of several treaties signed at Locarno on December 1, 1925, essentially dealt with the controversial boundaries that the Allies had imposed on Germany in 1919. In a treaty of mutual guarantee Germany and France and also Germany and Belgium agreed to maintain the status quo of their boundaries with each other, while Great Britain and Italy signed the pact as its guarantors. Germany also entered into treaties of arbitration with France, Belgium, Poland, and Czechoslovakia, but refused to guarantee her existing boundaries with her two eastern neighbors. France, their patron, concluded pacts of mutual assistance with Poland and Czechoslovakia. In the wake of Locarno, Germany was to be admitted to the League of Nations as a permanent member.

JKZ

LOMBARDO-RADICE, GIUSEPPE. A prominent educator and collaborator of Giovanni Gentile,* Lombardo-Radice was born in Catania in 1879. A professor of education at the University of Catania, he became a spokesman for the new nationalist and idealist education of Gentile, and in 1923 joined the Ministry of Public Instruction as the director-general of elementary schools. After playing an important role in the formation of the Gentile Reform,* he returned to teaching and research, establishing a number of journals, the most famous of which was *Educazione Nazionale*, and writing many monographs and scholarly articles. He died in Cortina d'Ampezzo in 1938.

RJW

LOMBARDO-VENETIAN KINGDOM. This was a province of the Austrian Empire, 1814–1859/66. The Congress of Vienna* having awarded Lombardy* and Venetia to Austria, the provinces were joined together to form a single administrative entity. Metternich* had intended to give the Kingdom genuine local autonomy under a Hapsburg archduke, as a means of countering Italian nationalism; however, his plan was rejected by Emperor Francis I, who was intent on centralizing his monarchy. The Kingdom remained under tight control from Vienna, which aroused growing resentment and stimulated a rapid rise in Italian national consciousness. These provinces played a leading role in the revolutions of 1848,* during which they were briefly independent but soon reconquered by Austria. In consequence of the war of 1859,* Lombardy was merged with the unified Italian state, while Venetia was added after the war of 1866.*

AJR

LOMBARDY. An important region in north-central Italy, in 1713 it passed from Spanish to Austrian rule, and new forces began to change Lombardy from within. In the process of reforming its own governmental structure, Austria gave impetus to administrative and fiscal reforms in its Italian province. Despite the continuing economic dominance of the landed aristocracy and the Church, an entrepreneurial middle class began to emerge, often enriching itself at the expense of the very nobles it served.

While keeping control of ultimate political decision-making power, Austria entrusted the educated nobility of Lombardy, and more particularly of Milan, with administrative responsibility for Lombardy's internal affairs, and they defended their rights against imperial encroachments. After 1748, however, under Maria Theresa and then Joseph II, a process of consolidation and reorganization of the Hapsburg state gained momentum, and Lombardy felt the impact of imperial pressure. In the long run it benefited from this greater integration because it lost its provincial isolation, and its people and goods became part of a cosmopolitan empire.

In 1796 Napoleon I* led his army into Italy. His victory over the Austrians opened the way to Milan, which he entered in triumph on May 16, 1796. By 1800, after a brief period of renewed Austrian rule, Lombardy passed under French control following Napoleon's second Italian campaign. It became the nucleus for the Cisalpine Republic,* later to become the Italian Republic, and then the Kingdom of Italy under the empire. The administrative center of northern Italy under the French, Lombardy achieved a leading position, and Milan emerged as one of the major centers of the peninsula. Of all the Italian states in the eighteenth century, Lombardy displayed the most dynamic growth in political sophistication, economic development, and intellectual effervescence, particularly from 1748 to 1814.

For further reference see: Bruno Caizzi, *Industria, commercio e banca in Lombardia nel XVIII secolo* (Milan: Banca Commerciale Italiana, 1968); Roberto Pracchi, *Lombardia*, 2nd ed. (Turin: UTET, 1971).

EPN

LONDON, PACT OF. This secret treaty of alliance, concluded April 26, 1915, between Italy and the Triple Entente,* stipulated the terms of Italy's entry into World War I* against Germany and Austria and their allies. Although a member of the Triple Alliance* (*Triplice*) since 1882, Italy declared her neutrality on August 3, 1914, on the grounds that the *casus foederis* (an attack on one of the high contracting parties) had not occurred. At the same time, Italy asserted that Article 7 of the *Triplice* provided for compensation to her because the status quo of the Balkans had been altered by Austria's actions against Serbia, an issue that had rankled in Rome since Austria's annexation of Bosnia-Herzegovina in 1908.

In the fast-moving diplomatic events of August 1914, Italy began negotiations with Vienna and Berlin on her claims under the *Triplice* agreement and also with the Entente powers because of advances they made seeking to lure Italy to their side. Despite German pressure. Austria's inflexibility on Italian demands during the winter of 1914–15 made the Entente's demarches more attractive and ultimately led to serious negotiations in London. The lengthy and complex discussions were conducted in secrecy, primarily in the British capital, by Ambassador Guglielmo Imperiali on instructions from Foreign Minister Sidney Sonnino.*

The pact that resulted provided for military and naval conventions between the four nations and for Italy's commitment of her forces against all enemies of the Entente. In return, Italy was to receive at the end of the conflict the regions of the South Tyrol and Trentino* ruled by Austria, thus taking her border to the Brenner Pass. In addition, Italy was to acquire Trieste,* Gorizia, the Istrian peninsula, and a large portion of Dalmatia* and the neighboring islands, excluding the city of Fiume.* Other clauses provided for an Italian protectorate

over Albania and recognition of Italian sovereignty over the Dodecanese Islands,*
occupied since 1912 in the Tripolitan War. Also, in the event of a partitioning
of the Ottoman Empire, Italy was to be given the Anatolian region of Adalia.
Furthermore, should Great Britain and France divide Germany's African colonies
at the war's end, Italian holdings in Libya,* Somalia,* and Eritrea* were to be
enlarged. Two final declarations provided that none of the signatory powers
would conclude a separate peace, and that, on Italy's insistence, the Holy See
would be excluded from peace negotiations at the end of the war.

The treaty committed Italy to declare war within one month, which she did
against Austria-Hungary on May 23, despite significant noninterventionist sentiment in parliament. Declarations of war against Austria-Hungary's allies continued throughout 1915 and culminated on August 28, 1916, in the declaration
against Germany.

Italy's failure to achieve the goals she expected from this treaty at the Paris
Peace Conference* of 1919 exacerbated critical domestic problems created by
the war. Not the least of Italy's laments was the sentiment that she had been
denied compensation for her sacrifices when her claims under the treaty were
challenged by Woodrow Wilson's policies on self-determination. The text of the
treaty was leaked by the Soviets in 1917 and first published by a Swedish
newspaper.

Various aspects of the treaty's history are treated in the extensive literature
on World War I. Its text can be found in F. Seymour Cocks, *The Secret Treaties
and Understandings* (London: Union of Democratic Control, 1918), pp. 27–42.
Although somewhat dated, the standard monographs are Mario Toscano, *Il patto
di Londra*, 2nd ed. (Bologna: Zanichelli, 1934), and Rene Albrecht-Carrie, *Italy
at the Paris Peace Conference* (New York: Columbia University Press, 1938).
From more recent memoir material, see the relevant volumes in Sidney Sonnino,
Opera omnia, 8 vols. (Bari: Laterza, 1972–81).

BFB

LONGO, ABBATE MARCHESE ALFONSO. Milanese aristocrat and cleric,
scientist and economist of the Enlightenment,* Longo (1738–1804) passed from
his education at Rome to participate, along with Pietro Verri,* Cesare Beccaria,*
and Paolo Frisi,* in the group of *Il Caffè** and to a chair in law at the University
of Milan in 1769. He was one of the important links between the Milanese reform
group of the 1760s and 1770s and the pro-French patriots of the Cisalpine
Republic* of the *Triennio*. Before the French Revolution he maintained an
important correspondence with the elder Marquis de Mirabeau in France on
matters of political economy. On the French occupation of Lombardy* he was
one of the signers of the Constitution of the Cisalpine Republic in 1797 and
became active in drafting legislation on ecclesiastical and economic reform.

RBL

LONGO, LUIGI. A founder and later secretary-general of the Italian Communist Party (PCI),* Luigi Longo was born to a peasant family on March 15,

1900, in Fubine Monferrato (Alessandria). Finishing three years of study as an engineer, he was drafted into the army and in 1920 joined the Italian Socialist Party (PSI).* He participated in the labor unrest of the post-World War I period and eventually abandoned the Socialists, helping to establish the PCI. Arrested twice by the Fascist police, Longo fled Italy for Switzerland in 1927. He continued his anti-Fascist activities abroad, serving with the Republican forces in both the Spanish Civil War* and in the Italian Armed Resistance.*

Longo began his parliamentary career in 1946 as a Communist delegate to the Constituent Assembly.* By 1948 he was vice-secretary of the PCI and was elected to the Chamber of Deputies.* Reelected with increasing pluralities in the Milan region, his career in the party culminated when he was chosen secretary-general upon the death of Palmiro Togliatti* in 1964. He held this post until 1972, when he was succeeded by Enrico Berlinguer. In 1979 he was made president of the PCI.

RJW

LORIA, ACHILLE. An economist, he was born in Mantua in 1857. Although he was a Socialist, his historical materialism was permeated by a current of idealistic philosophy. Loria proposed a reform of society, eliminating private property and land rental, and dividing the rewards of labor and capital more equally between the entrepreneur and the workers. He died at Luserna San Giovanni (Turin) in 1943.

RSC

LUCCA. This Tuscan city was the capital of an independent state until 1847. In 1744 the city had 20,770 inhabitants, while the entire territory of the Republic of Lucca, which extended to the Mediterranean at Viareggio, contained some 106,600. Although its ecclesiastical institutions were very ancient, the city did not become seat of an archbishop until 1726. In the Middle Ages and the Renaissance Lucca escaped dominance by Florence, and in the mid-sixteenth century its institutions became more closed, with the result that the Republic of Lucca survived into the eighteenth century under the government of a small oligarchy, and with the diplomatic tolerance of Spain, Tuscany,* and Modena. The later fortunes of the city derived from its silk industry, which expanded in the sixteenth century and then declined at the end of the eighteenth. The modern history of Lucca began with the War of the Second Coalition (see Wars of the First and Second Coalitions*), when the Republic was occupied by the French in February 1799. Converted into a principate for Felice Baciocchi, the husband of Napoleon I's* sister Elisa, Lucca became a pawn of Bourbon and Hapsburg diplomacy at the Congress of Vienna.* The new duchy was settled on Maria Luisa of Bourbon, from the house that had earlier ruled Parma, with the proviso that on the death of Marie Louise of Hapsburg (the consort of Napoleon who had been awarded the Duchy of Parma) the Bourbon line would be restored at Parma, and Lucca would be absorbed into the Grand Duchy of Tuscany. The reign of Maria Luisa (and of her son Carlo Ludovico, who succeeded his mother in 1824) was moderate and progressive: roads and aqueducts were built, and Viareggio was developed as a small port. In 1847, in anticipation of the Vienna agreement, Carlo Ludovico ceded Lucca to Leopoldo II of Tuscany, and the Duchy was incorporated into the administration of the Grand Duchy as an independent province.

RBL

LUCETTI, GINO. See **OVRA**

LUSSU, EMILIO. Emilio Lussu, who was born in Armungia (Cagliari) in 1890 and died in Rome in 1975, was a Socialist and anti-Fascist. He began his career as a representative of the Sardinian Action Party in the Italian Parliament (1921–26). Lussu was arrested by the Fascists in 1926 but escaped to France with Carlo Rosselli* in 1929. While in France he helped found the Justice and Liberty movement* and wrote anti-Fascist tracts. After the fall of Mussolini* in 1943, Lussu became an organizer of the Action Party.* He served as minister in Ferruccio Parri's* government and in the first governments of Alcide De Gasperi* (1945–46); as senator for the Italian Socialist Party (PSI)* (1948–64); and as leader of the Italian Socialist Party of Proletarian Unity* (1964–75).

AJD

LUZZATTI, LUIGI. Prime minister (March 1910–March 1911) and five times treasury minister, his major achievements were in the fields of public finance and commercial treaties. He was born on March 1, 1841, in Venice, and died on March 29, 1927, in Rome. Luzzatti was a student of law, economics, and social questions. His championing of cooperatives and mutual aid societies forced him to leave Austrian-ruled Venice in 1863. A prolific writer, he was professor of economics at Milan's Technical Institute (1863), and of constitutional law (Padua, 1866). Although loyal to the leaders of the postunification Right (see Destra, La*), during fifty years of parliamentary life (1871–1921) his expertise made him a welcome collaborator to the Left (see Sinistra, La*) as well. Assistant to Marco Minghetti* as secretary-general for agriculture (1869) and at the Treasury (1873–76), after the fall of the Right in 1876 Luzzatti joined Minghetti in collaborating with governments of the moderate Left and for more than three decades helped fashion most of Italy's commercial treaties. Twice treasury minister under Antonio Di Rudinì* (1891–92, 1896–98), Luzzatti worked toward a balanced budget, although he opposed reduction of military expenditures. As treasury minister to Giovanni Giolitti* (1903–5) and Sidney Sonnino* (1906), he prepared the grand conversion of the national debt from 5 to 3.75 percent. He served as minister of agriculture under Sonnino (December 1909–March 1910) and succeeded the latter as Italy's second prime minister of Jewish extraction (Sonnino was the first). He effected a major reform of elementary education, and proposed an extension of suffrage, achieved on a wider scale by his successor, Giolitti, in 1912. On relations with the Church, his motto was "Free religions in the sovereign state." In foreign policy, he favored rapprochement with France, negotiating in 1898 the end of the tariff war. He also supported the Libyan War (see Ouchy, Treaty of*) and Italy's participation in World War I.* Briefly treasury minister under Francesco Nitti* (March–May 1920), he was named senator by Giolitti in 1921 and was eulogized by Mussolini* in 1927 as one of "the wise and good men...keepers of eternal truths."

For further reference see: Luigi Luzzatti, *Memorie autobiografiche e carteggi*, 3 vols. (Bologna: N. Zanichelli, 1931–66).

SS

M

MACCHI, MAURO. A leading social activist of the *Risorgimento*,* Macchi was born in Milan in 1818. In his youth he was deeply influenced by Carlo Cattaneo,* whose leadership he followed at the outbreak of the Milanese revolution of 1848 (see Revolutions of 1848*). Macchi distinguished himself during the revolution by leading to the barricades men and women from the poor neighborhoods where he had grown up. After the failure of the revolution, he took refuge first in the Lugano area and then in Turin. In the early 1850s he worked closely with Cattaneo on publishing materials about the revolution. Later, in Piedmont, he became a successful journalist, known for his polemics against moderate liberals and Mazzinian republicans. He also became interested in the civic and political education of workers, in the regulation of child labor, and in women's rights. He championed these causes in the democratic press and in the national parliament until his death in Rome in 1880.

CML

MACINATO. A grist tax on all grains was authorized by parliament on July 7, 1868. Of all the taxes introduced after national unification, the *macinato* was the most unpopular. Shortly after it went into effect on January 1, 1869, angry demonstrators in the countryside of Emilia, Romagna,* and Tuscany sacked mills where the tax was levied, attacked municipal offices, and destroyed tax records. In confrontations with troops sent in to restore order some 250 people died. Minister of Finance Quintino Sella* and most leaders of the Historical Right (see Destra, La*) supported the tax as a means of balancing the budget. The Liberal Left (see Sinistra, La*), led by Agostino Depretis,* opposed it and promised to abolish it once in power. However, it was only in July 1880, four years after Depretis came to power, that parliament agreed to phase it out gradually over a period of four years. From 1871 to 1880 the *macinato* yielded some 69 million lire per year, or slightly more than 5 percent of all government revenues.

RS

MAFIA. Although the words *Mafia* and *mafioso* did not come into common usage until the 1860s in Sicily, the social phenomena they describe have been enduring features of the island's historical landscape for centuries. The historical outcome of local Sicilian efforts to cope with more than a millennium of repeated invasions, foreign rule, poverty, and mainland neglect, the *Mafia* has been described by anthropologist Anton Blok as a phenomenon involving the private use of unlicensed violence, within a framework of connivance with constituted authority joined to extortion and other forms of coerced and/or purchased protection. Confined to the western half of the island and endowed with no regular leadership or formal organizational structure, the *Mafia* is best understood as an informal network of powerful local bosses who by means of violence, favors, and political influence dominate completely the communities in which they live. In practice, however, these *mafiosi* function as intermediaries between the local population in Sicily and central governmental authorities on the mainland—delivering justice to the former even as they exploit them economically, while serving as agents for the latter to maintain the political control of the island for Rome and for the distribution of patronage.

Mafia influence in Sicily grew enormously during the heyday of liberal Italy from 1860 to 1922. Little of importance transpired on the island during these years without the knowledge and assent of powerful local *mafiosi*. This amounted to a policy of abandonment of Sicily to its historic fate, as successive mainland governments showed themselves unwilling to challenge powerful *mafiosi* for authority on the island. Nor indeed could they, for virtually every ruling coalition in the national capital between 1860 and 1922 had as its core (and depended for its majority on) a compact body of deputies from Sicilian constituencies tightly controlled by so-called *mafioso* grand electors who demanded in return that the central government not interfere in the affairs of the island.

This mutually advantageous system came to an end after 1922, when the Fascist regime suspended free parliamentary elections and thus destroyed the political nexus between *Mafia* bosses in Sicily and the mainland political class in Rome. In 1925, moreover, Fascist authorities launched a highly publicized campaign against the *Mafia* in Sicily and at the end of the decade announced its successful conclusion. In fact, however, only small-fry mafiosi landed in prison, while the most powerful *Mafia* bosses were simply integrated into the hierarchical system of Mussolini's* political machine.

With the Allied invasion of Sicily and the subsequent collapse of Mussolini's government in July 1943, leading *mafiosi* on the island initially supported the Sicilian independence movement. But when Anglo-American authorities made clear that they favored the retention of Italian sovereignty over the island and promoted the ascendancy of the Christian Democrats in Rome, these *mafiosi* ended their support of Sicilian independence. Following the mainland's concession of a regime of local autonomy for Sicily, the political and electoral nexus between Rome and the *Mafia* that had been so profitable for both parties between 1860 and 1922 was reestablished. So it has happened that *Mafia* political bosses—secure in their control of the regional government in Palermo—today enjoy far greater sway in Sicily than at any other time in the long and unhappy past of that island.

For further reference see: Michele Pantaleone, *The Mafia and Politics* (London: Chatto & Windus, 1966); Gaetano Falzone, *Storia della mafia* (Milan: Pan Editrice, 1975).

JER

MAGENTA, BATTLE OF. This important French-Sardinian victory took place in the Second War of Italian Independence (see War of 1859*). Piedmontese troops took no active part in the encounter, which pitted the French, under Napoleon III,* against a slightly larger Austrian force commanded by Franz Gyulai on June 4, 1859. French victory was assured by the appearance of General MacMahon with reinforcements late in the battle. The results of the rather bloody encounter were manifest. The Austrians were forced to abandon Lombardy,* Napoleon III and Victor Emmanuel II* demonstrating this fact by making a triumphal entry into Milan on June 8. Uprisings against Austrian client states throughout Italy were then facilitated.

JCR

MAGLIANI, AGOSTINO. A late nineteenth-century liberal economist and minister of finance, he was born in Laurino (Salerno) on July 23, 1824. Magliani studied and lived in Naples until 1860. Moving to Turin, Florence, and Rome in his career with the Corte dei Conti, he was made a senator in 1871 and became known as an expert on monetary theory. Magliani was minister of finance almost without interruption from 1878 until 1888. His efforts to conceal expenses under the guise of capital investment gave rise to the accusation that he was an illusionist with figures and led to the expression *finanza alla Magliana*. He died in Rome on February 20, 1891.

JCR

MAJORANA CALATABIANA, ANGELO. Born in Catania on December 4, 1865, Majorana studied law there and became a professor of law at the University of Catania. Elected to the Chamber of Deputies in 1897, he was returned to that position until his death in Catania on February 9, 1910. Majorana wrote extensively on constitutional law and public finance.

Throughout his career, Majorana was a loyal follower of Giovanni Giolitti,* whom he served as minister of the treasury and as minister of finance between

1904 and 1907. In this capacity, he achieved particular fame for his June 1906 conversion of the Italian debt in such a manner as to restore international confidence in the nation's finances.

                                                                                                    BFB

MALAGODI, GIOVANNI. This leader of the post-World War II Partito Liberale Italiano (PLI) (see Italian Liberal Party*) was born in London on October 10, 1904. He received a law degree from the University of Rome and in 1933 became the director-general of the Banca Commerciale Italiana.* Malagodi became active in politics after the fall of Mussolini* and was elected to the Chamber of Deputies* as a PLI candidate from Milan in 1953. In the following year he was chosen secretary-general of the Liberal Party, a post which he held for eighteen years. He also served as minister of the treasury in the first government of Giulio Andreotti* (1972–73) and was elected to the Italian Senate* in 1979.

                                                                                                    RJW

MALAGODI, OLINDO. A journalist, novelist, and poet during the period of Giovanni Giolitti's* ascendancy, he was born in Cento di Ferrara on January 28, 1870. Malagodi spent much of his professional life with the Roman, liberal, "Giolittian" daily, *La Tribuna*. He served as its London correspondent from 1895 until 1910 and as its director from 1910 until 1921. In 1921 Malagodi was named a senator. His writings include *Imperialismo: La civiltà industriale e le sue conquiste* [Imperialism: industrial civilization and its conquests] (1901), *Il focolare e la strada* [The hearth and the road] (1904), and several novels and books of poetry, as well as sketches illuminating World War I* and the Italian statesmen active in it. He died in Paris on January 30, 1934.

                                                                                                    JCR

MALAPARTE, CURZIO. Curzio Malaparte was the pseudonym of Kurt Erich Suckert, who was born in Prato in 1898 and died in Rome in 1957. Author and journalist, he volunteered in World War I* and joined the Fascist Party (see Fascism*) in 1921. After a brief career in diplomacy, he directed the Fascist paper *La Conquista dello Stato* and then *Il Mattino* of Naples and *La Stampa* of Turin between 1924 and 1929. Malaparte was arrested in 1933 after conflicts with Italo Balbo* and the publication in France of his *Technique of the Coup d'État* (1931). He resumed his activity as a journalist in 1937, writing of World War II* from behind the German lines in *Kaputt* and of the American occupation of Italy in *La pelle* [The skin].

                                                                                                    AJD

MALATESTA, ERRICO. Errico Malatesta, anarchist journalist, activist, propagandist, and revolutionary, was born in 1853 in Santa Maria Capua, near Naples. A medical student at the University of Naples who belonged to the Garibaldian Republican movement, he was expelled from the university for taking part in a demonstration. Soon thereafter he became a follower of Mikhail Bakunin,* who had promoted the Italian anarchist movement while residing in Italy from 1864 to 1867.

Malatesta was one of the major members of a triumvirate of the younger generation of anarchist militants of the 1870s that included Carmelo Palladino and Carlo Cafiero,* all of whom were educated and came from Italian landowning families. In 1876 Cafiero and Malatesta became missionaries of "propaganda by the deed," a belief in insurrection as the most effective form of propaganda. At the 1876 Florence anarchist congress they dominated the proceedings and succeeded in modifying the official organizational program toward anarchist communism instead of Bakuninist collectivism, a shift that linked Malatesta with the doctrine of Peter Kropotkin, Bakunin's successor as the major theoretician of anarchism.*

Malatesta helped instigate peasant insurrection at Benevento in 1877; in the aftermath of its suppression, he wandered through the Middle East, Greece, Rumania, and France. He spent more years in exile in London than anywhere else, although he also lived in Argentina (1884–85) and in the United States, where he was wounded in Paterson, New Jersey. Returning to Italy in 1913, he lived in Ancona and participated in the highly successful general strike of June 1914 (Red Week*). Exiled again, he moved to London, but was smuggled back into Italy at the end of 1919 and welcomed as a popular hero. He opposed his ideological mentor Kropotkin's support of the Allied cause during World War I,* an issue that split the world anarchist movement.

Malatesta adhered to Kropotkin's view that the human instinct of mutual aid or cooperation was the key to the highest development of the species and that government was the major repressive agent holding back the instinctive socialism of the people. In reply to critics demanding the details of his new anarchist order before they took the revolutionary leap in the dark, he proclaimed in his most famous work, L'Anarchia (1891), that anarchism was merely a method, not a set of blueprints. The method was to allow the free initiative of all and the reign of free agreements following the abolition of private property by revolutionary action, with the consequent creation of equality for all to dispose of social wealth. He argued that the collective abilities and good will of the people, once they were liberated, would provide for the needs of all in a continuously spontaneous and hence unpredictable pattern. He had none of the Socialists' scruples about choice of allies for promoting the revolution.

He reestablished the Italian anarchist daily newspaper of Milan, Umanità Nova, in 1920 and expressed some sympathy for Gabriele D'Annunzio's* "revolution" in Fiume.* In October 1920 he was arrested again and was held ten months without trial before being acquitted in 1922. His death in Rome in 1932 at the age of eighty-two, while under Fascist house arrest rather than in prison, testified to a limited measure of respect that was accorded him by the Fascist regime.

For further reference see: "Malatesta, Errico," *Enciclopedia dell'Antifascismo e della Resistenza*, vol. 3 (Milan: Edizioni La Pietra, 1976).

SO

MAMIANI DELLA ROVERE, TERENZIO. This *Risorgimento** philosopher, poet, and statesman was born in Pesaro on September 27, 1799. Early literary interests led him to friendship with such men as Giacomo Leopardi* and Niccolò Tommaseo. Mamiani's involvement in revolutionary activities in 1831 included participation, as minister of the interior, in the central government established in Bologna. Captured and imprisoned by the Austrians, he ultimately went into exile in France until 1847. There he developed his philosophical views, his *Del rinnovamento della filosofia antica italiana* [On the renewal of the ancient Italian philosophy] (1836) beginning with a controversy with Antonio Rosmini-Serbati.* It was also in France that the moderate political position expressed in *Nostro parere intorno alle cose italiane* [Our opinion on Italian matters] (1839) was defined.

Returning to Italy in 1847, Mamiani held several positions, including that of minister of the interior, in the Papal States.* He encouraged close cooperation with other Italian states against the Austrians. The victory of the Roman radicals ended his power, and Mamiani eventually left the city for Genoa and Turin. His later activity involved the foundation of the Accademia di Filosofia Italica (1850), chairs in the philosophy of history in Turin (1857) and Rome (1871), several governmental and diplomatic responsibilities, and senatorial dignity (1864). He died in Rome on May 21, 1885.

For further reference see: D. Gaspari, *Vita di Terenzio Mamiani* (Ancona: A. G. Morelli, 1888); F. Partini, *Terenzio Mamiani e i suoi tempi* (Rome, 1911).

JCR

MANCINI, PASQUALE STANISLAO. A leader of the *Risorgimento** and later famous as a political figure of united Italy, Mancini was born on March 17, 1817, at Castel Baronia (Avellino). At age twenty he went to Naples, where he earned a law degree and joined liberal political groups. In the 1840s he became influential in the more progressive circles that were gaining the confidence of King Ferdinand II.* Mancini first distinguished himself as a member of the Neapolitan Assembly of 1848 with his proposal to abolish the death penalty as well as through his authorship of a protest against the May 15, 1848, Naples massacre of demonstrators demanding progressive reforms. He rapidly fell out of favor with the monarchy and was forced into exile. He moved to Turin, where the university created for him its first chair of international law.

In 1851, in Turin, Mancini published *La nazionalità come fonte del diritto delle genti* [Nationality as the fount of the law of nations], which brought him fame in circles seeking Italian unification and which also provided a legal doctrine justifying the goals of the *Risorgimento*. This work aroused the ire of both the

Austrian and Neapolitan governments because of the influence it achieved in areas of Italy still under their rule.

In April 1860 Mancini was elected to the Chamber of Deputies, a seat he held until his death. That same year he was sent by the government in Turin to serve with the council presiding in Naples over southern regions conquered by Giuseppe Garibaldi.* In that capacity he succeeded in suppressing religious orders in the old Kingdom of the Two Sicilies* and in renouncing the Concordat between the papacy and Naples. He also proclaimed the rights of the state over religious properties.

On his return to Turin, Mancini was briefly minister of public instruction in March 1862 in Urbano Rattazzi's* government. As a member of the *Sinistra storica* (see Sinistra, La*), he held no other government offices until that group came to power in 1876. In the intervening years he distinguished himself in the parliamentary campaign to limit the application of the death penalty and also as the most eloquent advocate of state control over the Church. He also devoted time to the study of international law, which served him well in the 1880s.

With the advent of the Left to power, Agostino Depretis* named Mancini minister of justice. In that office, he extended freedom of the press, abolished imprisonment for debt, and guaranteed freedom of action for the conclave that elected Leo XIII* in 1878.

When Depretis returned to the Prime Ministry in 1881, Mancini became minister for foreign affairs, the position on which his greatest fame is based. In October of that year he accompanied King Humbert I* to Vienna on a state visit that led to the May 20, 1882, signing of the first treaty of the Triple Alliance.* Mancini was particularly successful in winning international support for Italian colonial aspirations. In 1882 he initiated Italy's first colonial activity when he purchased the Rubattino Company's station at Assab on the Red Sea. However, that same year he refused England's invitation to join in the international intervention in Egypt. Still, in close relations with Great Britain, whose approval he had, he enlarged Italy's Red Sea holdings by sending an expedition to claim Massawa. It was his intention to enlarge this undertaking to include Zeila, but parliamentary opposition to his colonial policy forced his resignation in June 1885.

Mancini is remembered as the architect of Italy's entry into the Triple Alliance and as the founder of its colonial empire. He was widowed in 1869 when his wife, the poet Laura Beatrice Oliva, died. Mancini himself died in Rome on December 26, 1888.

For further reference see: P. S. Mancini, *Discorsi parlamentari*, 8 vols. (Rome: Tipografia della Camera dei Deputati, 1893–97); idem, *Diritto internazionale* (Rome: Unione Tipografica Manuzio, 1905).

BFB

MANIFESTO OF ANTI-FASCIST INTELLECTUALS. See **GENTILE, GIOVANNI**

MANIFESTO OF THE FASCIST INTELLECTUALS. After the Fascist and Nationalist parties merged in 1923, the latter group sought to give the Fascist ideology a more conservative, "statist" tone. Thus, the *Manifesto of the Fascist Intellectuals* was issued on April 2, 1925, by Giovanni Gentile,* a neo-Hegelian philosopher who had served until 1924 as Mussolini's* first minister of education. His rhetorical declaration was signed by numerous cultural leaders. Gentile's manifesto angered the liberal Benedetto Croce,* who responded on May 1, 1925, with a scathing *Countermanifesto*, signed by dozens of anti-Fascist intellectuals.

For further reference see: Emilo R. Papa, *Storia di due manifesti* (Milan: Feltrinelli, 1958).

CFD

MANIN, DANIELE. The leader of the Venetian Revolution of 1848 (see Revolutions of 1848*) and a prominent supporter of Cavour's* diplomacy a decade later, Manin was born in Venice on May 13, 1804. He was the son of a lawyer whose Jewish ancestors had converted to Christianity and changed the family name from Medina to Manin in the eighteenth century. A precocious youngster, Manin graduated with a law degree from the University of Padua in 1821 and returned to Venice to practice law. In the 1840s he became active in the anti-Hapsburg opposition movement. Just before the outbreak of revolution in 1848 he was arrested along with his fellow conspirator, the Dalmatian Niccolò Tommaseo. Manin was freed by the Venetian populace during demonstrations that followed news of the revolution in Vienna. He did not agree with the liberal patricians who were willing to settle for a constitutional government under the Hapsburgs. Instead, he organized a popular movement that ousted the Venetian Provisional Government and proclaimed the Republic of St. Mark on March 22, 1848. Manin was elected president of the new republic and was given the mandate to establish ties with other revolutionary governments in Italy. To the chagrin of radicals like the actor Gustavo Modena of Treviso, Manin supported the annexation of Lombardy* to Piedmont-Sardinia and the attempt by King Charles Albert's* army to occupy Venetia. After Charles Albert's second defeat in 1849, however, Manin and his government were left solely responsible for defending the Venetian Republic against the returning Austrians. They resisted, amidst famine and disease, until August 22, 1849. Manin then fled with his family to Paris, where he remained until his death on September 22, 1857. Active in political exile circles, Manin was often called upon to mediate conflicts between democratic and liberal elements in the Italian independence movement. Having witnessed the failure of Mazzinian conspiracies and attempted insurrections, he concluded in the mid-1850s that a compromise with the Sardinian monarchy was necessary if Austria's military predominance in northern Italy were ever to be destroyed. Thus, in 1856 he joined the Lombard patrician Giorgio Pallavicino Trivulzio* in establishing the Società Nazionale Italiana* with a program that accepted King Victor Emmanuel II* of Savoy as leader of the national revolution.

The society attracted prominent liberals from all parts of Italy and was instrumental in the success of Cavour's anti-Austrian strategy of 1857–59.

For further reference see: George M. Trevelyan, *Manin e la rivoluzione veneziana* (Bologna: Zanichelli, 1926); Paul Ginsborg, *Daniele Manin e la rivoluzione veneziana del 1848–1849* (Milan: Feltrinelli, 1978); idem, *Daniele Manin e Giorgio Pallavicino. Epistolario politico (1855–1857)*, ed. B. E. Maineri (Milan: Bortolotti, 1878).

CML

MANZONI, ALESSANDRO. One of Italy's greatest novelists, he was the author of *I promessi sposi* [The betrothed] (1827), a literary masterpiece to be ranked with the major works of Dante, Petrarch, Boccaccio, Ariosto, and Machiavelli. Born in Milan on March 7, 1785, Manzoni was the grandson (on his mother's side) of Cesare Beccaria,* author of *Dei delitti e delle pene* [On crimes and their punishments]. He was raised as a Voltairian rationalist; but his major writings date from his "return" to Roman Catholicism, after the conversion of his wife, a Swiss Calvinist. His poems place him, along with Petrarch and Giacomo Leopardi,* in the first rank of Italian lyricists; among them are *Inni Sacri* [Sacred hymns] (1812–22) and "Cinque Maggio" [The fifth of May] (1821), on the death of Napoleon I.* He also penned two romantic plays on the vexing question of the long-delayed unification of Italy and wrote major treatises on the history of torture, persecution, and Catholic morals. But his singular masterpiece remains *I promessi sposi*, a model of modern Italian prose. Through the novel's plot, involving the trials of seemingly ill-starred lovers in seventeenth-century Milan, Manzoni creates an entire world and presents a sweeping spectacle of a Christian providential, and in large measure Jansenist, view of the human condition. Honored in his last years for his exemplary patriotism as well as for his Christian faith, Manzoni died in Milan on May 22, 1873.

For further reference see: Jean-Pierre Barricelli, *Alessandro Manzoni* (Boston: Twayne, 1976).

AP

MARAVIGLIA, MAURIZIO. This Fascist official was born in Paola (Calabria) on January 15, 1878. From revolutionary socialism he turned to nationalism, and was chosen for the first central committee of the Italian Nationalist Association* and later for its executive board. With Enrico Corradini* and Luigi Federzoni,* Maraviglia signed the Pact of Fusion between the Nationalist Association and the National Fascist Party (see Fascism*) on February 27, 1923. He was codirector of *L'Idea Nazionale** and assistant director of *La Tribuna* of Rome when it absorbed the former on January 1, 1926. After fusion, Maraviglia entered the Fascist Grand Council; became a member of the national directorate of the Fascist Party; and served as deputy from Calabria and Basilicata, and as senator from 1939 until his death in Rome in 1955.

RSC

MARCHIANI, IRMA. Born in Florence on February 6, 1911, Marchiani symbolizes the role of 35,000 women partisans of the Italian Armed Resistance.* She served early partisan bands as a *staffetta*, and by spring 1944 she had become vice-commander of a partisan brigade in the Modena area. Involved in active combat, after her second arrest by the Germans she was shot at Pavullo (Modena) prison on November 26, 1944. She was awarded the gold medal posthumously.

MJS

MARCH ON ROME. The March on Rome of October 27–29, 1922, was a political and military operation by which Benito Mussolini* was appointed premier on October 28. It began as a mobilization of the Fascist squads on October 27. The aim was to seize provincial rail and communication centers as a prelude to a general assault on the capital. The march was led by four Fascist quadrumvirs—Michele Bianchi,* Italo Balbo,* Emilio De Bono,* and Cesare Maria De Vecchi.* It was, however, only partially a military exercise because the poorly armed squads were no match for the regular army. The strategy was to use the threat of civil war to force King Victor Emmanuel III* and the conservative politicians to accelerate their plans to bring the Fascists into the government.

Premier Luigi Facta* attempted to secure emergency martial law powers in order to block the Fascists, but the King rejected the government's request on the morning of October 28. Instead, the monarch turned to Antonio Salandra,* a former premier and leader of the parliamentary Right, to form a government with Fascist participation. Mussolini, who directed overall strategy from his headquarters in Milan, rejected Salandra's offers and claimed the premiership for himself. Acting on the advice of industrial leaders and conservative politicians, including Salandra himself, the King offered the post of premier to Mussolini on October 28. Only then, on October 29, did the Fascist Blackshirts complete their march on the capital. Thus, the March on Rome was a semiconstitutional seizure of power. The key to its success was the benevolent neutrality of the army and the clearly expressed desire of the conservative leaders to use the Fascists to break the political power of the Italian Socialist Party (PSI)* and its unions.

For further reference see: A. Repaci, *La Marcia su Roma*, 2 vols. (Rome: Canesi, 1963).

AJD

MARCONI, GUGLIELMO. This inventor of wireless telegraphy was born in Bologna on April 25, 1874. Marconi improved the inventions of Heinrich R.

Hertz and Edouard Branly in electromagnetic waves and introduced a practical antenna. In 1885 he sent longwave signals more than one mile. Unable to interest the Italian government, Marconi, at the urging of his mother, patented his experiment in Britain in 1896. On October 21, 1901, in St. John's, Newfoundland, he received the first Atlantic impulses transmitted from his station at Poldhu, Cornwall. In 1916 Marconi turned his attention to shortwaves and from 1930 concentrated on microwaves. Marconi shared the 1909 Nobel Peace Prize and served as president of the Italian Academy from 1933 until his death in Rome on July 20, 1937.

RSC

MARCORA, GIUSEPPE. Born in Milan on October 14, 1841, Marcora studied law and in his youth joined Giuseppe Mazzini's* Action Party.* He fought with Giuseppe Garibaldi's* forces in the war of 1859* and the war of 1866.* Once Italian unification was achieved, he accepted the monarchy as an expression of national will but continued to work in various democratic organizations on the Left (see Sinistra, La*).

In 1876 Marcora was elected to the Chamber of Deputies on the Radical Party* ticket and was returned to parliament in each election until 1921, except for the term between 1890 and 1892. As a deputy, he distinguished himself in the campaign for achieving a national control over primary schools and as a principal contributor to the Zanardellian Criminal Code of 1890, which abolished capital punishment and unified all penal legislation. He spoke frequently in favor of Italian *irredenta* territories (see Irredentism*) but opposed Italian colonial expansion.

Because of his favorable inclinations toward Giuseppe Zanardelli* and Giovanni Giolitti* in 1901, Marcora broke with the Radical Party. In 1904, as the Giolittian candidate, he was elected president of the Chamber of Deputies, a post he held until 1906 and again from 1907 to 1919. He also wrote various juridical and political works and served on the Milan City Council.

Marcora was named senator in May 1921 and died in Milan on November 4, 1927.

BFB

MARENGO, BATTLE OF. A battle in the French Revolutionary Wars between the French under General Napoleon Bonaparte (see Napoleon I*) and the Austrians under General Baron Michael von Melas, it was fought on the plain of that name southeast of Alexandria in Piedmont. Bonaparte, advancing to frustrate a threatened Austrian invasion of France, was caught with his forces scattered and had only 18,000 men at hand when the Austrians attacked with 31,000 on the morning of June 14, 1800. Melas' victory seemed assured until French reinforcements drove the Austrians back into Marengo. Cavalry charges turned the Austrian retreat into a rout in which half their army was lost. Bonaparte was left master of northern Italy.

WDG

MARGHERITA OF SAVOY. Queen of Italy from January 9, 1878, to July 29, 1900, she was the wife of Humbert I* of Savoy and the mother of Victor Emmanuel III.* Margherita was born on November 20, 1851, in Turin, and died on January 4, 1926, in Bordighera. She sought to reconcile parties of the Right (see Destra, La*) and Left (see Sinistra, La*) as well as Roman society to the monarchy. She was an influential force in Italian fashion; the poet Giosuè Carducci* was devoted to her and frequented her salon. A fervent nationalist who was known for wanting to make Italy a feared and respected world power, in her later years she supported Benito Mussolini.*

EAR

MARGOTTI, DON GIACOMO. See *ARMONIA DELLA RELIGIONE COLLA CIVILTÀ, L'*

MARINETTI, FILIPPO TOMMASO. Filippo Tommaso Marinetti, poet and leader of the Futurist movement in the arts launched in 1909 (see Futurism*), was born in Alexandria, Egypt, on December 22, 1876, and died in Bellagio (Como) on December 2, 1944. The wealthy and dynamic Marinetti began his literary career in Paris during the first decade of the twentieth century, associating with Alfred Jarry and others in the avant-garde; he published the controversial review *Poesia* in Milan from 1905 to 1909. Though he remained an active poet, Marinetti was most influential as a propagandist, devising the provocative manifestoes and "entertainments" that made Futurism famous in European cultural capitals by 1914.

Convinced of the curative properties of war, Marinetti promoted Italian intervention in 1914–15 and served as a volunteer officer at the front, winning a decoration. The struggle for intervention brought him into contact with Mussolini,* and he was elected to the central committee of Fascism* at the movement's founding meeting in March 1919. Marinetti was also a leader in the violent anti-Socialist demonstration of April 1919. However, Fascism's tendency to compromise with established institutions provoked Marinetti's disillusionment in 1920. He supported the regime from 1923 on, but he concentrated on his poetry—lauding air flight and war—and was not significant politically. A member of the Italian Academy of 1929, Marinetti served as an ornament, affording Fascism a tenuous association with artistic modernism.

DDR

MARIO, JESSE MERITON WHITE. Patriot and writer, wife of Alberto Mario, she was born in Portsmouth, England, on May 9, 1832. She was enlisted into the Italian national cause when she met Giuseppe Garibaldi* in Nice in

1855. Upon returning to London, she befriended Giuseppe Mazzini* and organized a series of public lectures in England and Scotland to gain sympathy for the Italian patriots (1856–57). In June 1857, involved in an abortive revolution in Genoa, she was arrested and expelled with the young intellectual and revolutionary, Alberto Mario, whom she wed several months later. She continued to raise funds abroad and performed charitable work in various parts of Italy. She was involved as a nurse in several campaigns with Garibaldi, and at times negotiated for wounded prisoners. In disagreement with Alberto, she accompanied Garibaldi on the latter's French campaign of 1870. She wrote *I Garibaldini in Francia* (1871), *La miseria di Napoli* (1877), and *The Birth of Modern Italy* (1909). She died in Florence on March 5, 1906.

FFA

MARSHALL PLAN, ITALY AND THE. This crucial economic program for European recovery was proposed by U.S. Secretary of State George C. Marshall in a commencement address delivered at Harvard University on June 5, 1947. The plan, officially known as the European Recovery Program, offered aid to all European countries, irrespective of political posture, provided they guaranteed maximum effectiveness of the American assistance. Italy accepted the offer, but the decision was not approved by all. The Marshall Plan was *l'ordre du jour* during the electoral campaign in the "critical" 1948 elections. The victory of the Christian Democrats in that year paved the way for Italian participation in the European Recovery Program.

Participation in the Marshall Plan proved beneficial for Italy. Under the program, which commenced in 1948 and terminated in 1952, Italy received $1.515 billion in economic assistance. This quadrennium was characterized by marked advances, both economically and politically. In the economic sector, the impact of the Marshall Plan, in addition to saving Italy from economic stagnation, revitalized the industrial apparatus of the country.

The Marshall Plan had a critical impact on Italy. There was a political corollary to the plan: the achievement of governmental stability as a result of the 1948 elections, relative social peace, and the effective anti-inflationary measures of the minister of finance, Luigi Einàudi,* who in 1948 became president of the Republic.* Finally, the results of the Marshall Plan contributed to the economic miracle* that Italy experienced in the 1960s.

For further reference see: "Elezioni politiche in Italia dal 1946 ad oggi," *Testimonianze documenti* (Sulmonai: Italia Editoriale, 1972); Amintore Fanfani, *Anni difficili ma non sterili* (Bologna: Cappelli, 1958).

PVB

MARTINI, FERDINANDO. This noted writer, political figure, and journalist was born in Florence on June 30, 1841. He taught at Vercelli and Pisa, wrote a number of plays and essays, and founded and directed many literary reviews. In the 1870s he was drawn into politics and entered the Chamber of Deputies, and in 1884 was named undersecretary in the Ministry of Public Instruction. During Giovanni Giolitti's* first ministry, 1892–93, Martini served as minister of public instruction and introduced a number of reforms, particularly in university studies. From 1897 to 1907 he served as governor of Eritrea* and from 1914 to 1916 was minister of colonies. In 1923 the Mussolini* government appointed him to the Senate, where he sat till his death in Monsummano on April 24, 1928.

FJC

MARTINO, GAETANO. A prominent postwar politician of the Liberal Party,* Martino was born into a well-known family of Messina on November 25, 1900. He took a degree in medicine in 1923 from the University of Rome, pursuing a distinguished academic and medical career until the fall of Fascism.* In 1948 he was elected to the Chamber of Deputies* and in 1954 became minister of education. Subsequently he served as minister of foreign affairs. A strong proponent of the North Atlantic Treaty Organization* and decidedly pro-American, Martino negotiated the 1954 border agreement between Italy and Yugoslavia and played a major role in the negotiation of the Treaty of Rome (1957), which created the Common Market. He continued his career in foreign affairs, serving as president of the European Parliament from 1962 to 1964, and heading various Italian disarmament delegations to Geneva, until his death in July 1967.

RJW

MARZOCCO. This Florentine periodical of art, sculpture, and literature was established by Adolfo and Angelo Orvieto on February 2, 1896, with Enrico Corradini* as editor. *Marzocco* endured until 1932. Its main contributors— Gabriele D'Annunzio,* Mario Morasso, the Orvieto brothers, Giovanni Pascoli,* Luigi Pirandello,* and Corradini—debated many ideas. An aesthete, Corradini unsuccessfully attempted to lead the review to a concept of beauty equated with aristocratic standards, against vulgar and commercialized tastes identified with democracy. Corradini left the review on February 18, 1900.

RSC

MASCAGNI, PIETRO. The composer of one of the most popular Italian operas, *Cavalleria rusticana*, Mascagni was born in Livorno on December 7, 1863, to a nonmusical family. He was a student at the Milan Conservatory but left after two years. The music publishing firm of Sonzogno held a contest for new one-act operas, and *Cavalleria* won in 1888. When the opera was staged in Rome in 1890, it became an instant success. The success was repeated all over Europe and in North and South America and established a new operatic style for the next twenty years, *verismo*. Mascagni's other works never were as popular as *Cavalleria* but are still performed occasionally. Of his seventeen operas, the major ones (with year of first performance) are: *L'amico Fritz* (1891), *Iris* (1898), *Le maschere* (1901), *Lodoletta* (1917), and *Il piccolo Marat* (1921). The reputation of his last years was clouded by his enthusiastic endorsement of Mussolini* and the Fascist movement. He died in Rome on August 2, 1945.

JLD

MASSARI, GIUSEPPE. A political activist and writer, he was born in Taranto on August 11, 1821. After studies in literature and medicine, he went to Paris in 1839, becoming friendly with leading Italian political exiles. He returned to Italy in 1843 but was soon expelled from Milan for revolutionary activity. He returned to Paris and collaborated on the *Gazzetta Italiana*.

In 1847 he returned to Milan, where he took part in the May 15 uprising. Fleeing to Naples, he was elected to the new parliament. When it was dissolved in March 1849, he fled to Turin, and helped Vincenzo Gioberti* compile *Il saggiatore*. Massari became director of the *Gazzette Officiale* in 1856. He also wrote articles for various journals and undertook diverse diplomatic missions for Cavour.* He remained active as a politician and writer until his death in Rome on March 13, 1884.

FFA

MASSARI-CASTAGNOLA REPORTS. These reports were presented by deputies Stefano Castagnola (1825–91), a former Mazzinian, and Giuseppe Massari* (1821–84), an old-time opponent of the Bourbon regime in Naples, as members of a parliamentary commission appointed to study the Southern Question.* The reports were presented to the Chamber of Deputies in secret session on May 3 and 4, 1863, and focused on the problem of armed popular unrest in the southern provinces, which many political leaders sought to dismiss as mere brigandage.* The reports drew attention to the long-term causes of rural misery and the popular desire to protest against traditional injustices. Among the immediate causes the authors listed Bourbon and papal intrigues to restore the deposed dynasty, errors committed by government officials after national unification, and corruption in local administrations. This first classic exposition of the social problems of the South was kept secret by parliament, which chose to deal with brigandage by military means.

RS

MASSAWA. See **ERITREA**

MASTAI FERRETTI, GIOVANNI. See **PIUS IX**

MATTEI, ENRICO. This industrialist, more than any other, is identified with the creation of the Ente Nazionale Idrocarburi (ENI*), or the National Fuel Trust. A member of the left wing of the Christian Democratic Party,* he sat in the Chamber of Deputies* from 1948 to 1953. In 1953 he proceeded to dismantle the Italian Petroleum Agency, which was a residue of Fascism.* Under his leadership Italy's consumption of energy increased fivefold.

He was also instrumental in the exploration for natural gas all over Italy. Abroad he obtained important concessions in the Middle East and entered into trade agreements with the Soviet Union.

Mattei, who was born in 1906, died in 1956 in an airplane crash.

PVB

MATTEOTTI CRISIS. On June 10, 1924, Giacomo Matteotti, secretary of the Partito Socialista Unitario (Unitary Socialist Party) and ''spiritual son'' of Filippo Turati,* was kidnapped and killed by Fascist thugs. In the Chamber of Deputies Matteotti had strongly denounced Fascist atrocities, especially those committed during the April election. He had also written a book destroying Fascist claims to have ended the postwar crisis.

When Matteotti's body was discovered and Mussolini's role in the affair surfaced, revulsion ensued throughout the country, invading even Fascist ranks, and touched off a crisis which, it appeared, would help topple the regime.

Mussolini's opponents, however, failed to take full advantage of the situation. They withdrew from parliament in the Aventine Secession,* designed to focus the nation's moral indignation on the Duce, but did little to translate their condemnation into concrete political action. Furthermore, the King, Victor Emmanuel III,* decided to retain Mussolini out of fear that a Socialist government would result from the crisis.

As it became clear that Fascism's* opponents had not mobilized the country against him, and as the wave of revulsion subsided, Mussolini recovered. He took advantage of his opponents' absence from the Chamber of Deputies to introduce repressive legislation. It was these laws, passed in 1925 and 1926, that definitely ended Italian liberty and transformed Mussolini's government into a dictatorship destined to last until 1943.

For further reference see: Philip C. Cannistraro, ed., *Historical Dictionary of Fascist Italy* (Westport, Conn.: Greenwood Press, 1982).

SD

MATTINO, IL. See **NEWSPAPERS**

MAZZEI, PHILIP. Mazzei was born in Poggio a Caiano, Florence, on December 25, 1730, and died in Pisa on March 19, 1816. He travelled on three continents, lived in ten countries, and participated in the American and French revolutions and in the short-lived Polish constitutional reform of 1791. He was a surgeon in Florence, Leghorn, Constantinople, and Smyrna; a merchant and language teacher in London; an agriculturalist and zealous Whig in Virginia; a writer and diplomat in Paris; and a royal chamberlain and privy councillor in Warsaw.

Arriving in Virginia in 1773, he befriended and collaborated with the Virginia leaders in their struggle for independence. He promoted American ideals and defended the American cause in Europe and America. An excerpt from "Instructions of the Freeholders of Albemarle County to their Delegates in Convention," written in 1776, was used by Jefferson in his attempt to produce a new state constitution.

Sent to Europe as Virginia's agent in 1779, Mazzei returned to Virginia in 1783 and founded the Constitutional Society. This organization sought to preserve the republican form of government from its adversaries. He joined Jefferson in Paris in 1785 and was never to return to America. In 1788 he published a four-volume history of the American colonies and entered the diplomatic service of the king of Poland. The second partition of Poland ended his diplomatic career, and he retired to Pisa in 1792 where, at the age of eighty, he completed his memoirs—*My Life and Wanderings*—a rich source-book for the life and mores of the eighteenth century.

On learning of Mazzei's death, Jefferson wrote, "He was of solid worth: honest, able, zealous in sound principles, moral and political, constant in friendship and punctual in all his undertakings. He was greatly esteemed in this country...."

A transmitter of European ideas to the Americans and a bearer of American ideas across the Atlantic, Mazzei was in contact with the most prominent figures of the day on both continents.

For further reference see: Margherita Marchione, *Philip Mazzei: Jefferson's "Zealous Whig"* (New York: American Institute of Italian Studies, 1975); *Philip Mazzei: My Life and Wanderings*, trans. S. E. Scalia, ed. Margherita Marchione (New York: American Institute of Italian Studies, 1980); *Philip Mazzei: The Comprehensive Microform Edition of His Papers, 1730–1816*, ed. Margherita Marchione (Millwood, N.Y.: Kraus Microform, 1981).

MM

MAZZINI, GIUSEPPE. The most influential and significant leader of the Italian national revolution, Mazzini was born in Genoa on June 22, 1805. His father, Giacomo, was a physician and an active participant in the Ligurian Jacobin movement. His mother, Maria Drago, practiced a rigorous form of Christian morality, perhaps due to the influence of Jansenist ideas. This influence was also evident in her choice of her son's first teachers, both of whom were Jansenist clergymen. At age sixteen Mazzini was already enrolled at the University of Genoa. Along with other students he took part in the liberal movement of 1821. But his full-time commitment to political activity began only later in the decade, under the oppressive regime of King Charles Felix.* A sign of his growing involvement in politics was his editorship of *L'Indicatore Genovese* (1828) and his contributions to Francesco Domenico Guerrazzi's *L'Indicatore Livornese*. From 1827 to 1830 Mazzini was also active in the Carboneria* and was briefly imprisoned in connection with a conspiracy. After his release from the Savona fortress, Mazzini was given a choice between internment in a small village and exile abroad, and he chose the latter. He broke with the Carboneria, which he had come to regard as an elitist, arcane movement not sufficiently rooted in the popular consciousness. From Marseilles in October 1831 Mazzini announced the founding of a new national movement with a democratic and republican ideology and based upon the principle of cooperation among all social classes. This movement, Giovine Italia,* spread quickly in the 1830s and 1840s from Piedmont and Lombardy* to regions as far away as Sicily and Apulia. In part, its success was due to Mazzini's ability to recruit members of older secret societies. But it was also due to its appeal to a new generation of Italians too young to remember the Jacobin movement or the liberal movements of 1820–21.

Too confident of his success, as early as 1833 Mazzini urged his followers to attempt an insurrection in Savoy. A costly failure, this fiasco drove him again into exile and threw him into a deep depression. He came out of this crisis determined to continue building the Giovine Italia network and also to launch Young Europe, an international organization that would bind together all European movements for national liberation. Through Young Europe, Mazzini became a revolutionary leader of international importance; he was hunted by police everywhere he went and remained constantly on the move. His entire life was devoted to the cause of the Italian Revolution, which precluded a stable occupation and a normal family life. Only the devotion of his followers and the unstinting support of his mother saved him again and again from imprisonment, starvation, and illness.

In January 1837, accompanied by his friends and devout followers, the brothers Ruffini of Genoa and Angelo Usiglio of Modena, Mazzini moved to England. Until 1848, when he returned to Italy to join the revolution, he contributed articles to several English newspapers, winning the sympathy and help of intellectuals and politicians for the Italian cause. In this period he wrote his most important essays on nationalism and democracy. His appeal was directed not only to the educated middle classes in the host country and in Italy, but also to urban artisans and workers. Evidence of Mazzini's commitment to them and concern for their needs is the fact that he helped establish a school for the children of working-class Italians in London.

From England Mazzini travelled to Milan in April 1848 at grave personal risk. He was disappointed to find that the revolution there had been channeled in a monarchist direction by the moderate liberals, and he clashed with Carlo Cattaneo* and Giuseppe Ferrari,* who envisioned a Lombard republic within a democratic Italian federation. Mazzini held firm to his conviction that the revolution must lead to a unified Italian republic with its capital in Rome.

The opportunity to establish such a republic presented itself early in 1849, when Pope Pius IX* broke with the liberals in his constitutional government and sought the protection of the King of the Two Sicilies in Gaeta.* With many other democratic leaders, Mazzini went to Rome to participate in a new phase of the Roman Revolution, which led to the proclamation of a republic. Although short-lived, the republican experiment in Rome represented an attempt to change not only the form of government but the relationship between church and state, the distribution of wealth, the suffrage, and so forth. The republican constitution reflected the enormous influence of Mazzini's thought on the Italian revolutionary movement.

In June 1849 the Roman Republic fell under the blows of French military power. Mazzini then fled to the Lugano area, where other leaders of the revolution gathered in the 1850s to reflect on their errors and achievements and to prepare for a resumption of the struggle. While fellow revolutionaries of a more introspective disposition, especially Cattaneo, wrote lengthy accounts of the revolution and engaged in bitter polemics, Mazzini felt increasingly frustrated by lack of action against the restored conservative governments. Thus, in the early 1850s he did not try to dissuade younger or more militant followers from attempting insurrections in Lombardy, Liguria, and the Lunigiana. The failure of those attempts, however, brought criticism even from people, both in Italy and abroad, who sympathized with Mazzini's ultimate goal. Even the tragic Sapri expedition led by Carlo Pisacane* was blamed, albeit erroneously, on Mazzini.

On the eve of unification Mazzini found himself in a very paradoxical position. His ideas and his organizational genius had prepared intellectually and trained for action the cadres of successful national revolution. Yet his personal prestige was at a low ebb, and the leadership of the revolution had passed to the Società Nazionale Italiana,* many of whose members had once been ardent Mazzinians.

Although the Kingdom of Italy proclaimed in 1861* was a far cry from the democratic republic of his dreams, Mazzini drifted back to his native country and settled in Pisa, a guest of Janet Nathan Rosselli. He could neither travel freely nor engage in overt political activity due to a death sentence issued against him *in absentia* for his role in the abortive Savoy insurrection of 1833. Despite protests by democratic members of parliament, Mazzini was never pardoned. From the Rosselli home, however, he kept in touch with followers who were active in the democratic press and in the Società Operaie.* He died in Pisa on March 10, 1872.

For further reference see: Franco Della Peruta, *Mazzini e i rivoluzionari italiani* (Milan: Feltrinelli, 1974); Alessandro Levi, *Mazzini* (Florence: Barbèra, 1955); and the essay on Mazzini by Giuseppe Berti in *I democratici e l'iniziativa meridionale nel Risorgimento* (Milan: Feltrinelli, 1962), pp. 15–61.

CML

MAZZINI SOCIETY. Inspired by Gaetano Salvemini,* late in 1940 a group of Italian exiles and Italian-American anti-Fascists created this association in the United States. It was dedicated to counteracting Fascist influence among Italian-Americans, and, clandestinely active in Italy, it sought to commit the U.S. government and the Allies to a policy aimed at replacing the Fascist dictatorship in Italy with a democratic republic. Some of the society's prominent members were Max Ascoli,* the first president, Carlo Sforza,* Alberto Tarchiani, and

Lionello Venturi. Its headquarters were in New York. Though its membership never exceed 2,000, the Mazzini Society had the support of the Italian-American Labor Council, organized immediately after Pearl Harbor by Luigi Antonini, August Bellanca, and other labor leaders, through which nearly 200,000 Italian-Americans were mobilized. The Mazzini Society published *Mazzini News*, replaced in 1942 by *Nazioni Unite*, and several pamphlets. Contacts with the White House, the State Department, and prominent New Dealers were established. In 1943 numerous exiles returned to Europe to participate in the Armed Resistance.* Having fulfilled its mission, the Mazzini Society was dissolved shortly after World War II.*

MS

MEDA, FILIPPO. Publicist and political figure, Meda led the first Catholic deputation in the Italian Parliament (1909) and worked for reconciliation between church and state. He was born on January 1, 1869, in Milan, and died there on December 31, 1939. Meda, a teacher and lawyer, was editor (1898) and later publisher (1902) of the Milanese *Osservatore Cattolico*. An active participant in lay Catholic organizations, he avoided the Modernist controversy (see Modernism in Italy*) and the more extreme forms of Christian Democracy,* remaining loyal to papal supremacy. He advocated Catholic involvement in local politics as an avenue toward penetration into and reconciliation with the liberal state. His formula, "preparation in abstention," was vindicated by the papacy with the partial relaxation of the *non expedit** in the general elections of 1904, and again in 1909, when Meda and about twenty others entered parliament not as "Catholic deputies" but as deputies who were Catholic. Although a neutralist at the outbreak of World War I,* he supported the war effort after 1915, joining the cabinets of Paolo Boselli* and Vittorio Orlando* (June 1916–June 1919) as finance minister. In 1919 he was one of the founders of the Italian Popular Party,* as leader of which he served as treasury minister (June 1920–April 1921) in Giovanni Giolitti's* last ministry. Twice, in February and July 1922, he refused the mandate to form a government. When Mussolini* received the appointment in October 1922, Meda counselled, in vain, against Popular participation; but in 1923 he supported the Acerbo Electoral Law,* against his party's majority. Consequently Meda was not presented as a candidate of his party in the 1924 elections, after which Mussolini offered him a senatorship. Meda refused it and retired from politics to professional and scholarly pursuits.

For further reference see: Gabriele De Rosa, *Filippo Meda e l'età liberale* (Florence: Le Monnier, 1959).

SS

MEDICI, LUIGI. A prominent minister of Ferdinand I of the Kingdom of the Two Sicilies* (1759–1825) and of his successor, Francis I* (1825–30), he was born in Naples on April 22, 1759. Medici proved to be especially adept at directing state finances. An ambitious technician, he avoided party politics and stressed economic development while trying to steer a middle course between reaction and revolutionary liberalism. He represented Naples at the Congress of Vienna,* engineered the fusion of Naples and Sicily into a single kingdom (1816), signed a concordat with the papacy (1818), and dominated governmental policy under Francis I. He died in Madrid on January 25, 1830.

RCu

MEDICI SUCCESSION. See **COSIMO III DE MEDICI, GRAND DUKE OF TUSCANY**

MEDITERRANEAN AGREEMENTS. The first of these pacts was based on a series of notes exchanged by Great Britain, Italy, Austria-Hungary, Germany, and Spain between February 12 and May 21, 1887. It committed the signatory states to the maintenance of the status quo in the Mediterranean, inclusive of the Adriatic, Aegean, and Black seas, where they feared both Russian and French ambitions. If the status quo broke down, they were to agree on changes. Great Britain promised in that case to support Italy's aims in North Africa in return for Italy's approval of her policy in Egypt. Only Great Britain, Austria-Hungary, and Italy joined in the second covenant, which was signed on December 12, 1887. It affirmed their commitment to the status quo in the Eastern Mediterranean and their affirmation of the Ottoman Empire's rights in Bulgaria, the Straits, and Asia Minor. Germany welcomed the second pact because it posed a barrier to Russian expansion in the Near East, but did not participate in it because Otto von Bismarck* had signed a nonaggression treaty with Russia on June 18, 1887.

JKZ

MELZI D'ERIL, FRANCESCO. This statesman was born in Milan on October 6, 1753, and died in Bellagio on January 17, 1816. He played an important role in Italian affairs under Napoleon I* as vice-president of the Italian Republic. Melzi d'Eril belonged to the wealthy landed nobility of Lombardy.* After finishing his studies, he travelled, living abroad for several years. From this experience he acquired a moderate political outlook, later strengthened by his contacts with older Milanese reformers such as Pietro Verri* and Cesare Beccaria.*

He initially followed the events in France after 1789 with sympathy, but as the revolutionary excesses increased he became disenchanted. After Napoleon's victory over the Austrians at Lodi in 1796, he was persuaded to head a Milanese delegation to the French. He impressed Napoleon, who subsequently used him on various missions and finally appointed him vice-president of the Italian Republic, of which Napoleon was president.

As vice-president of the new state, Melzi had wide discretionary powers in domestic matters. He restored northern Italy's finances and credit, built roads, encouraged agriculture, commerce and industry, broadened the educational system, and curtailed abuses. In this sense, he may be said to have continued the programs initiated by earlier Lombard reformers under Austrian rule.

Melzi d'Eril soon realized that an Italian state could never achieve any real viability as a French satellite. He envisaged an independent position for the Italian Republic in which it would enjoy real control over its own affairs and serve as a buffer state between Austria and France. Austria proved receptive to his proposal, but Napoleon refused to discuss it. He had other plans for Italy in a French-dominated Europe.

When Napoleon established the Empire, republics became anachronistic; thus, the Italian Republic was transformed into the northern Kingdom of Italy (see Italy, Napoleonic Kingdom of*) under Eugène de Beauharnais. In the new political organization there was no place for Melzi d'Eril, who was promoted to an honorary court position and named duke of Lodi by Napoleon in 1807.

With the end of the Napoleonic hegemony, Melzi d'Eril tried unsuccessfully to resurrect his plan for a truly independent state in northern Italy, but with Napoleon defeated, the Austrians saw no need for such a political entity. Credit must be given to Melzi d'Eril for being one of the first Italians to have had a realistic political vision of the role Italy could play among the larger powers and for having tried to secure autonomy at least for northern Italy.

For further reference see: *I carteggi di Francesco Melzi d'Eril, duca di Lodi*, 8 vols. (Milan: Museo del Risorgimento, 1958–65).

EPN

MEMORANDUM OF 1831. The Memorandum of 1831 was a reform plan for the Papal States.* After the revolutions of 1831* had revealed the danger for the papal regime and the peace of Europe posed by discontent in the Papal States, the representatives of the great powers (Austria, France, England, Prussia, and Russia) met at Rome to discuss reforms that would avert future revolutions. On May 21, 1831, they presented to Pope Gregory XVI* a memorandum, listing the reforms they considered most urgent: admission of laymen to most posts in the civil government; reform of the judicial system; municipal self-government by elected city councils; provincial councils to express provincial wishes to the Pope; and a Junta or council in Rome to supervise state finances, staffed by laymen. Though the memorandum would not have satisfied dedicated liberals, it would have done much to pacify public opinion in the provinces. Unfortunately, Rome failed to implement the memorandum; it thus missed the opportunity to win over moderate opinion and made inevitable the growth of revolutionary discontent that would ultimately overthrow the temporal power.

AJR

MENABREA, LUIGI FEDERICO. Prime Minister Menabrea's tenure (October 1867–November 1869) marked a period of political conservatism and royal ascendancy. He was born on September 4, 1809, in Chambéry, Savoy, and died on May 25, 1896, in Saint-Cassin. Officer of Engineers, and instructor in mathematics and engineering at the Turin military academy (1839–48), Menabrea performed diplomatic-military missions in 1848–49, and in the campaigns of

1859–60 rose to the command of the Corps of Engineers, receiving the gold medal for valor. He entered parliament in 1848 as a liberal of the Left (see Sinistra, La*); gradually moved toward the clerical Right (see Destra, La*); and in 1860 became a senator after the cession of Savoy to France. Navy minister under Bettino Ricasoli* (June 1861–March 1862) and minister of public works in the Farini*-Minghetti* government (December 1862–September 1864), Menabrea was a plenipotentiary in the negotiations ending the war of 1866* with Austria. At the end of October 1867, during the crisis with France and the papacy provoked by Giuseppe Garibaldi's* attempt to take Rome by force (the battle of Mentana*), Victor Emmanuel II* appointed Menabrea prime minister with a government composed predominantly of senators. Menabrea obstructed Garibaldi's foray and ordered his arrest. He faced a storm of protest from the Chamber for failing to prevent the return of French troops to Rome, and lost a vote of confidence in December 1867. The King nevertheless reconfirmed Menabrea in office; he was faced with a severe fiscal crisis, which he sought to meet with higher taxes, including the hated grist tax (see Macinato*) and a project for private participation in the state tobacco monopoly. Menabrea lost support from the Right after the severe repression of disturbances in North-Central Italy early in 1869. Shaken further by a scandal involving the tobacco monopoly and attacked for its "reactionary" public order policies, Menabrea's twice-reconstituted government resigned in November 1869, although the King did his best to retain his loyal minister. For the next quarter of a century, Menabrea served in various diplomatic posts.

For further reference see: Gaspare Finali, *La vita politica dei contemporanei illustri* (Turin: Roux, Frassati e C., 1895); Giuseppe Massari, *La vita e il regno di Vittorio Emanuele II*, 2 vols. (Milan: Treves, 1896).

SS

MENELIK II. Emperor of Ethiopia* from 1889 to 1913, Menelik (1845–1913) was one of the country's strongest monarchs. He greatly extended the boundaries of Ethiopia at the time when European imperialism in Northeast Africa was greatest. In 1889 Menelik concluded the controversial Treaty of Uccialli* with Italy, culminating in a brief war with Italy (1896) and a major setback to Italian colonialism in Northeast Africa. From 1889 to 1896 the European powers mistakenly assumed that Ethiopia had become an Italian protectorate. After defeating a large Italian army at Adowa,* Menelik then turned his attention to the task of beginning the modernization of Ethiopia by calling upon Britain, France, Russia, Germany, and Austria, as well as Italy, for technical assistance.

RLH

MENOTTI, CIRO. This entrepreneur and liberal conspirator was born in 1789 into a *nouveau riche* family. Menotti tried unsuccessfully to introduce steam-driven looms into silk manufacturing. His democratic philosophy came from the Jacobin Antonio Lugli. Meetings in 1830 of Menotti and Enrico Misley* with

Duke Francis IV of Modena have caused historians to overrate the duke's role in the 1831 conspiracy (see Revolutions of 1831*). As Menotti's agent among Italian exiles in France, Misley prepared the Modenese rising as part of a larger regional effort with a Parisian-based central committee to coordinate local *raggi* established in 1830 in the Romagna,* in Bologna, Florence, Parma, and Mantua. Their goals included a constitutional monarchy, an elected assembly, and Rome as capital; Menotti's contacts may have extended to the Bonapartist Roman conspiracy of December 1830. He ignored Filippo Buonarroti's* advice to await a national uprising. On February 3, 1831, the eve of the Modenese rising, ducal police arrested his group of forty; after the ducal restoration, he was hanged on May 26, 1831. Menotti's group cut across class lines from peasants and artisans to nobility. His attempts at a revolutionary network with France were seen as a continuation of post-1796 Jacobin connections (see Jacobins*). His organizations in central Italian cities provided a bridge between the declining Carbonari groups (see Carboneria*) and the emerging Giovine Italia.*

For further reference see: Giuseppe Silingardi, *Ciro Menotti e la rivoluzione dell'anno 1831 in Modena* (Florence: Tipografia editrice della Gazzetta d'Italia, 1880); Guido Ruffini, *Le cospirazioni del 1831 nelle memorie di Enrico Misley* (Bologna: Nicola Zanichelli, 1931).

MSM

MENTANA, BATTLE OF. Trusting in the covert support of the government (led by Urbano Rattazzi,* as at the time of the Aspromonte* episode in 1862) and in a popular insurrection in Rome itself, which never materialized, Giuseppe Garibaldi* made preparations once again to take Rome by force in October 1867. Protests by France over Italy's failure to halt these preparations led to Rattazzi's resignation (October 19), with the new government, headed by Luigi Menabrea,* cutting off reinforcements and supplies to Garibaldi. French troops, returned to Rome (Octobr 29) after their withdrawal in 1866, sealed the enterprise's fate at Mentana, at the outskirts of Rome, on November 3, 1867. After his final failure, Garibaldi became even more estranged from king and government; and France's forceful intervention aroused much anti-French sentiment in Italy.

SS

MERLIN, ANGELINA. A Turinese Socialist leader active in women's rights, Angelina Merlin was born at Pozzonuovo (Padova) on October 15, 1889, and died in 1979. As managing editor for several Socialist newspapers, she was arrested five times after 1926 and eventually spent five years in *confino*. Merlin joined the Armed Resistance* in 1943 and was one of the founders of the first Gruppi di Difese delle Donna* in Milan. She was also a founder of the Unione

Donne Italiane.* After 1945 she was elected not only to the Constituent Assembly* but also to the Senate* and Chamber of Deputies,* where she sponsored various laws dealing with women's issues.

MJS

MERLINO, FRANCESCO SAVERIO. Francesco Saverio Merlino, an independent Socialist thinker important in the European revisionist debates of the 1890s, was born in Naples on September 15, 1856, and died in Rome on June 30, 1930. A middle-class Neapolitan lawyer, Merlino began his political career as an anarchist and spent the years from 1884 to 1894 in exile. His ideas began to have European resonance with the publication of a series of articles in the Belgian review *La Société Nouvelle* from 1889 to 1893. Some of them, criticizing German social democracy, proved especially challenging to Eduard Bernstein. However, Merlino's independent inquiry caused him to break with anarchism* by 1897, when he published *Pro e contro il socialismo* [For and against socialism], which introduced his mature conception.

Merlino criticized anarchism for its extreme individualism and Marxism for its authoritarian tendencies and overemphasis on economics. Socialism, he insisted, rested on the human aspiration for justice and social solidarity and should not be linked to socioeconomic class struggle. To avoid the utopian excesses of both anarchism and collectivism, Socialists should examine actual social movements for new juridical relationships and new forms of social harmony. Ultimately, socialism could only emerge gradually, as the result of a variety of social tendencies; it could not be created through political conquest.

Merlino had a major impact on the early syndicalist thinking (see Syndicalism*) of Georges Sorel, who corresponded with Merlino during 1897–99, and who contributed to Merlino's *Rivista Critica del Socialismo* [Critical review of socialism], published during 1899.

Although he had been persistently attacked by orthodox Socialists, Merlino joined the Italian Socialist Party (PSI)* around the end of 1899. He remained relatively isolated, however, and gradually withdrew from political life.

For further reference see: Francesco Saverio Merlino, *Il socialismo senza Marx: Studi e polemiche per una revisione della dottrina socialista (1897–1930)*, ed. with a biographical profile by Aldo Venturini (Bologna: Massimiliano Boni, 1974).

DDR

MERODE, FREDERIC DE LA. Merode was a Belgian prelate who acted as minister of war and almoner of Pius IX.* Born in Brussels on March 20, 1820, he attended its military academy and fought with the French army in Algeria, but abruptly left for Rome in 1847 to enter the priesthood. Ordained in 1849, he was given charge of the Roman prison system in 1850. In 1860 Merode persuaded Pius IX, over Cardinal Giacomo Antonelli's* objections, to give General Louis Lamoricière* of France command of the papal army. Merode served as war minister from 1860 until 1865, after which, as papal almoner, he devoted himself mainly to charity. He died in Rome on July 10, 1874.

RCu

MERRY DEL VAL, RAFAEL. Papal secretary of state (1903–14) under Pius X,* Merry Del Val, the son of a Spanish diplomat based in London, was born on October 10, 1865. After entering the priesthood, he was graduated from the Accademia dei Nobili Ecclesiastici and the Gregorianum, and went directly into the Vatican diplomatic corps. Given the red hat of a cardinal and made secretary of state by Pius X, he was an archenemy of Modernism.* Under Pius XI he became secretary of the Holy Office and was a convinced supporter of the *Conciliazione*. He died in Rome on February 26, 1930.

RJW

MESSAGGERO, IL. See **NEWSPAPERS**

MESSEDAGLIA, ANGELO. This economist and statistician, born in Villa-franca (Verona) on November 2, 1820, was remarkably versatile and produced juridical tracts, literary works, and studies of navigation, among other things. After receiving his degree in law at the University of Pavia, he taught there before assuming the chair of political economy and statistics at the University of Padua. Subsequently he moved to the capital where in 1888 he was entrusted with the chair of political economy at the University of Rome. Among his economic studies are his works on population, including the noted *Malthus e dell' equilibrio della popolazione colla sussistenza* [Malthus and the equilibrium of population and subsistence], in which he disproved Malthus' contention that population tended to increase geometrically while the food supply increased arithmetically. Inclined more to detailed analysis than bold synthesis, his solidly based monographs presented pragmatic and empirical solutions to economic questions. Messedaglia sat in the Chamber of Deputies from 1866 to 1883, and in 1884 was appointed to the Senate. He died in Rome on April 1, 1901.

FJC

METTERNICH-WINNEBURG, CLEMENT VON. This Austrian chancellor (1809–48) was born in Coblentz on May 15, 1773, of an aristocratic family of the Rhineland. Driven from his home by the French revolutionary armies, he entered the Austrian diplomatic service in 1794 and rose rapidly. In 1809 he was appointed foreign minister, after Austria had suffered a disastrous defeat by France. For the next few years he concentrated upon ensuring Austria's survival by cultivating Napoleon I's* good will. After Napoleon's defeat in Russia in 1812, Metternich reasserted Austria's independence and played a leading role in the coalition that defeated France. At the Congress of Vienna* his brilliant diplomacy secured the restoration of Austria's possessions, as well as her hegemony over Italy and Germany. For the next three decades he managed to keep the Italian states under control by adroit diplomacy, utilizing Hapsburg family connections, military alliances, and offers of protection against revolution. His success was endangered by the 1820 revolution at Naples (see Revolutions of 1820–21*); after securing the approval of the other powers at the Congress of Troppau, which formally proclaimed the right of the powers to intervene against revolution, he was able to suppress the Neapolitan revolt in March 1821. When a revolt broke out in Piedmont a few weeks later, he was able to suppress it without difficulty. This brilliant success led to his appointment as chancellor, the highest post in the Austrian Empire. For the next two decades he had little difficulty in maintaining Austrian hegemony over Italy: the revolutions of 1831* were suppressed, the plots of Giuseppe Mazzini* held in check, and the Italian princes kept firmly in the Austrian orbit. The 1840s, however, saw the decline of his system. The election of Pope Pius IX* was a great blow, marking the end of the Union of Throne and Altar against revolution, stirring up great popular enthusiasm for the *Risorgimento*,* and convincing Charles Albert* of Piedmont that the time had come to challenge Austria. Hampered by domestic opposition and in poor health, Metternich was unable to formulate a constructive response to the Italian crisis. In March 1848 revolution broke out (see Revolutions of 1848*), not only in Italy but throughout the empire, and the old chancellor was forced into exile. He later returned to Vienna, but was unable to prevent Francis Joseph* from sending the ultimatum to Piedmont that provoked the war of 1859.* He died in Vienna on June 11, 1859.

For further reference see: Heinrich Ritter von Srbik, *Metternich*, 3 vols. (Munich: Bruckmann, 1925); Alan J. Reinerman, *Austria and the Papacy in the Age of Metternich* (Washington, D.C.: Catholic University of America Press, 1979).

AJR

MEZZADRIA. *Mezzadria* is a type of land contract and tenure whereby owner (*padrone*) and tenant family (*famiglia colonica*) share the costs of cultivation and divide the produce and profits from the land. Although present in every part of the country, the central regions of Tuscany, the Marches, and Umbria are the regions where *mezzadria* contracts have appeared in their most clear-cut form. The details of the *mezzadria*, however, vary from place to place and are often determined by custom. In general, agreements are made on a yearly basis, with the owner providing land, fixed assets, and most operating capital. The tenant families, for their part, provide labor, tools, upkeep, and part of the cost of machinery. Although the concept of *mezzadria* implies an even division of produce and profits, in practice tenants tended to receive no more than one-third. Until the early years of this century *mezzadria* was valued for its social benefits, including considerable security of tenure for tenants. Market-oriented landowners denounced its economic disadvantages, arguing that it discouraged major improvements and crop specialization. A crisis of *mezzadria* developed in the early

1950s due to the flight of workers from the land and government legislation designed to transform tenants into small independent owners.

RS

MEZZOGIORNO, CASSA PER IL. This special government agency was established by parliament on August 10, 1950, to stimulate the economic development of the South. Before the Cassa was established, government efforts were limited to providing incentives for private investments. By 1950 the economy had recovered sufficiently from the war to deal with questions of long-term development. The Cassa was the first and most massive program of the postwar years to deal with the problem of regional economic imbalances. Criticized in the beginning by the parties of the Left as inadequate to the task, it indicated a strong commitment by the governing Center coalition to the elimination of the economic dualism between North and South. Geographically, the Cassa covered not only the southern regions on the mainland, but also the islands of Sardinia and Sicily, other minor islands, including Elba, and certain depressed provinces in the regions of Latium, the Marches, and Tuscany. The Cassa was charged with funding and managing special development projects in agriculture, transport and communications, waterworks, and tourism. It was endowed with broad operational autonomy to minimize bureaucratic and political interference.

Initially, the law authorized annual expenditures of 100 billion lire guaranteed for ten years, but this level of funding proved inadequate to the task. By 1960 the Cassa had authorized expenditures of 1,403 billion lire, 77 percent of which was allocated to agriculture, 11.5 percent to waterworks, 9 percent to roads and communications, and 2.5 percent to tourism. The concentration on agricultural projects at a time when the exodus from the countryside was already well under way was immediately criticized as economically unwise. By the late 1950s the Cassa began to pay greater attention to encouraging industrialization in certain designated areas by providing credit, fiscal, and social security incentives to private investors. Most major industrial projects in the South, however, have occurred by means of direct public investments through the state-owned Institute for Industrial Reconstruction (IRI).* It is therefore difficult to assess the impact of Cassa projects on the economic development of the South. Incomes and investments have risen substantially, but not as spectacularly as they have risen in the industrial North. As a result, the economic gap between North and South has actually increased since 1950, and the population exodus from the rural South continues at a rapid pace.

For further reference see: Joseph A. Martellaro, *Economic Development in Southern Italy* (Washington, D.C.: Catholic University of America Press, 1965).

RS

MICHELS, ROBERT. A sociologist, he was born in Cologne on January 9, 1876, and became a naturalized Italian citizen. Michels taught at the universities of Basel, Turin, Perugia, and Rome. Influenced by the theories of Vilfredo

Pareto* and Gaetano Mosca,* Michels was interested in tracing the development of mass parties in the modern age. His primary discovery was the unavoidable domination exercised by the party organization over the membership, and by the oligarchical leadership over the bureaucracy, thus severely restricting democratic practices and thwarting the initiative and will of the masses. He strove to go beyond the purely psychological and personal in motivational explanation, unfolding ideas that were substantially sociological. His *Zur Soziologie des Parteiwesens in der modernen Demokratie* [On the sociology of political actions in modern democracy] (1911) is still seriously reviewed. Becoming increasingly pessimistic over the possibilities for genuine democracy, Michels eventually settled for Fascism,* which was both authoritarian and based on broad appeal. He died in Rome on May 3, 1936.

RSC

MILIZIA VOLONTARIA PER LA SICUREZZA NAZIONALE. See **VOLUNTARY MILITIA FOR NATIONAL SECURITY**

MILLO DI CASALGIATE, ENRICO. Italian admiral and military hero of the Dardanelles, he was born on February 12, 1865, at Chiavari, and died on June 14, 1930, at Rome. Millo became a captain in 1901, and in 1912, during the Italian-Turkish War, led the daring and controversial reconnaissance, naval rescue, and return in the Straits of the Dardanelles, which won him a military medal of valor and the admiration of all Europe. He served during World War I* and was governor of Dalmatia,* 1918–20.

WR

MINGHETTI, MARCO. Born in Bologna on November 8, 1818, Minghetti came from a well-to-do bourgeois family. In his youth he spent several years in Paris and travelled extensively in other countries, taking a particular interest in science and agriculture. He joined the intellectual movement for unification after attending the Congress of Italian Scientists in Pisa in 1839.

In 1846–47 he participated in the movement to liberalize the political and judicial system in the Papal States.* He was a deputy in the Roman Assembly during the revolutions of 1848* and a prominent advocate for moderate liberalism.

He met Cavour* in 1852 and wrote a treatise on central Italy at his behest. He spent the late 1850s in Turin, where he lent his support to Cavour's anti-Austrian policy. In 1859 he played a crucial role in preparing the ground for the annexation of the central Italian regions to the kingdom of Victor Emmanuel II.*

Elected to the first Italian parliament, Minghetti served as minister of the interior and of finance before becoming prime minister (March 24, 1863–September 28, 1864). During his tenure as prime minister he negotiated the September Convention* (1864) by which France removed her troops from Rome, and he transferred the capital from Turin to Florence.

In 1869 he returned to political activity as minister of agriculture and later on as minister plenipotentiary to Vienna. In July 1873 he served again as prime minister, but he also retained the finance portfolio in order to pursue his long-standing aim of a balanced budget. Within days of achieving that goal in 1876, however, he was ousted by the electoral success of the *Sinistra storica** (see Sinistra, La*).

An advocate of decentralized government, Minghetti tried in vain to get his parliamentary colleagues to establish regional governments with real powers. He wrote on economic issues, freedom of worship, and the role of political parties in government. He died in Rome on December 10, 1886.

CML

MINTO, GILBERT ELIOT, EARL OF. The second earl of Minto (November 16, 1782–July 31, 1859) was educated at Edinburgh for a diplomatic career and served briefly as British ambassador to Berlin in the 1830s. Thereafter he became a familiar figure in Whig cabinets. The best known episode of his career occurred in 1847–48 when Palmerston sent him to Italy to persuade its rulers of the need for liberal reform to insure against revolution. Yet, as he travelled southward through the peninsula he encountered the wave of revolution sweeping northward from Palermo, and soon he too was caught up in cries of independence for Italy. Palmerston's diplomacy was stood on its head, thereby ruling out further British encouragement for Italian aspirations for another decade. Minto retired from political life in 1852.

JWB

MINUTOLO, ANTONIO CAPECE. See **CANOSA, ANTONIO CAPECE, PRINCE OF**

MIRABELLO, CARLO. Admiral and reformer of the navy, Carlo Mirabello was born on November 17, 1847, at Tortona (Alessandria) and joined the navy in 1865, in time to participate in the fleet's Adriatic campaign during the Third War of Independence (see War of 1866*). He subsequently became an expert in hydrography and made significant contributions to that branch of the service, particularly to the scientific knowledge pertaining to the Italian coast and to regions around the Red Sea.

In collaboration with Admiral Giovanni Bettolo, Mirabello promoted the build-up of the Italian fleet at the beginning of this century, notably as the result of the parliamentary inquiry on the navy, concluded in 1903. Mirabello had already made a name for himself as commander of the Italian squadron in China, a position to which he was named in 1902 in the aftermath of Italy's embarrassing failure to win a concession at San Mun in 1899.

Giovanni Giolitti* named Mirabello senator and minister of the navy in 1903; he held the latter position in all successive governments until December 1909. During that time, Mirabello not only introduced many reforms in the navy, but also increased its size, promoting the construction of dreadnoughts. This policy made Italian naval superiority a critical factor in the Tripolitan war, at which time, thanks to Mirabello's work, it was the world's fourth largest fleet. Mirabello died in Milan on March 24, 1910.

BFB

MIRACOLO ECONOMICO. See **ECONOMIC MIRACLE**

MIRAFIORI, COUNTESS OF. See **RATTAZZI, URBANO**

MISLEY, ENRICO. This Modenese lawyer, liberal conspirator, and entrepreneur was born in 1801. Completing his education at Pavia in 1822, Misley joined a liberal Modenese plot to force constitutional government upon Duke Francis IV while supporting the duke's interest in the Sardinian throne. Between 1826 and 1830 he remained in touch with Francis, who knew of his contacts with Italian exiles abroad. Committed to the unity of central Italy, Misley served as Ciro Menotti's* agent in approaching Italian exiles in London and Paris. In France he contacted moderates who supported constitutional monarchy. He also sought ties with Lafayette and other French liberals. Antonio Panizzi* in London thought Misley was deluded by his faith in the July Monarchy liberals and his belief in a self-sustaining central Italian revolution. Misley was in Paris in February 1831, when the Modenese revolution erupted (see Revolutions of 1831*), and thus escaped arrest. He launched various business ventures in Spain between 1835 and 1848 and furnished support to the Regent Maria Christina in her war against the Carlists. His English contacts aided Cavour* in negotiating a loan from the London Hambro Bank in 1851. Attracted to the economic expansion in Catalonia, Misley spent the 1850s in Barcelona, where he died in 1863.

MSM

MITO DEL MEZZOGIORNO. See **FORTUNATO, GIUSTINO**

MIXED BANKS. See **BANCA COMMERCIALE ITALIANA** and **CREDITO ITALIANO**

MODERNISM IN ITALY. This term is broadly applied to philosophical, historical, theological, and sociopolitical currents of thought in late nineteenth- and early twentieth-century Catholicism. Modernism was officially condemned on September 8, 1907, in Pius X's* encyclical, *Pascendi*. This movement attemped to reconcile the Church and her teachings to the modern world by employing philosophical speculation, scientific investigation, historical criticism, and biblical exegesis to the Catholic experience.

In Italy Modernism captured the imagination of many young liberal Catholics and Christian Democrats, thus focusing on sociopolitical concerns. In the realm of politics, Don Romolo Murri,* a liberal of the Opera dei Congressi,* founded the Lega Democratica Nazionale, urging Catholic participation in politics and reform of the Church. In the fields of theology and philosophy Don Salvatore Minocchi and Ernesto Buonaiuti led the Modernist surge. The independence of Murri's followers from the Church authorities, especially in politics, alarmed Pius X, and he issued a series of admonishments (*Pieni d'animo*, 1906, and *Lamentabli*, 1907) to "wayward" Italian priests before his condemnation of Modernism and its political and social effects in 1907.

For further reference see: G. Martini, *Cattolicismo e storicismo* (Naples: Edizioni Scientifiche Italiane, 1951).

RJW

MONARCHIST PARTY. See **NATIONAL MONARCHIST PARTY**

MONCALIERI, PROCLAMATION OF. In the elections of July 1849, following the Piedmontese defeat at the battle of Novara,* the Chamber that emerged had a strong contingent from the Left (see Sinistra, La*) and Center-Left which showed itself hostile to the crown and little disposed to accept Austrian terms. The peace treaty agreed upon in Milan on August 6, 1849, after difficult negotiations, was a moderate one, but there were those in the Chamber who objected because no guarantee had been provided for Lombards and Venetians who had fled to Piedmont. In November the Chamber decided to postpone further action on the treaty until the government assured the safety of Lombard and Venetian emigrants of Piedmontese citizenship.

The prime minister, Massimo D'Azeglio,* considered delay in the approval of the peace dangerous. Therefore, he dissolved the Chamber on November 20, 1849, and urged Victor Emmanuel II* to issue a personal admonition to his subjects. That same day the King issued a proclamation from the royal chateau of Moncalieri in which he criticized the conduct of the dissolved Chamber and urged the voters in the nation to elect sensible candidates in the forthcoming election. Although the proclamation of November 20 was an extraordinary—and, indeed, extraconstitutional—measure that evoked some criticism, others saw it as a necessary step to preserve the peace and the constitutional system in Piedmont. The elections of December 1849 resulted in a victory for the Ministry, and on January 9, 1850, the new Chamber quickly approved the treaty with Austria by a vote of 112 to 17, with 7 abstentions. Shortly thereafter the Senate approved it 50 to 5.

FJC

MONTAGNANA, RITA. Born in Turin on January 6, 1895, this Italian Communist Party (PCI)* leader and feminist activist was the wife of Palmiro Togliatti* from 1924 to 1947. She was an early Socialist and labor activist and was present at the founding of the PCI in 1921. A party delegate to the Third International, Montagnana performed a variety of anti-Fascist activities. In Spain in 1937–39, she worked as a translator for Radio Moscow. Returning to Italy in 1944, she was in charge of the party's women's commission, and was one of the founders of the Unione Donne Italiane.* After the war she sat in the Constituent Assembly of 1946.* Elected senator, she served as a member of the party's Central Committee from 1945 to 1956.

MJS

MONTECITORIO, PALACE OF. A Roman palace, presently the home of the Chamber of Deputies* of the Italian Parliament, it was constructed by Carlo Fontana, under the papacy, according to a design by Bernini. Until 1870 it was the Palace of Justice, except during the Napoleonic period, when it was the site of the Prefecture. The palace takes its name from the Roman "Colonna citatoria" in Campo Marzo—the site of the magistrates' meetings. As the meeting place of the Chamber of Deputies it has been the scene of many heated debates, especially during the nation's emerging years.

WR

MONTENOVOSO, PRINCE OF. See **D'ANNUNZIO, GABRIELE**

MONTESSORI, MARIA. This educator and originator of the method of education called the Montessori system was born in Chiaravalle near Ancona on August 31, 1870. Her father was a military man of noble background and her mother, Renilde Stoppani, was a niece of Antonio Stoppani, the philosopher-priest. When she was about twelve, the family moved to Rome. Interested first in mathematics and engineering, she later turned to biology and medicine. In 1894 she received a medical degree from the University of Rome, the first woman to do so. Following her graduation, she lectured on anthropology at the University of Rome and served as an assistant physician at the psychiatric clinic where she came into contact with retarded children.

It was her interest in retardation that led her to study the works of Jean Itard and Edouard Seguin, which paved the way for providing therapy for such children. She was invited to lecture in Rome on the education of the feebleminded, and her course led to the creation of the orthophrenic school, which she directed for two years, 1899–1901. While lecturing on pedagogy at the University of Rome (1901–7), she came to the conclusion that the methods she had evolved for the retarded might be employed in the education of normal children. To test her ideas, she opened the Casa dei Bambini (Children's House) in the San Lorenzo district of Rome (1906). From her experience in this and other schools, she evolved the Montessori method, which gained worldwide popularity.

Building upon her conclusion that every child has the spontaneous urge to learn, she sought to free the child from the rigid discipline that then characterized formal education. In her schools she instructed the teachers (directresses) to provide the children with materials that would arouse their interests. As word spread of the success of her approach, she was sought as a lecturer in Europe and abroad. She introduced her methods to Spain in 1917, assuming direction of the Montessori Institute in Barcelona, and in 1919 established one in London. Returning to Italy in 1922, she was appointed inspector of schools, but left the country in 1934 during the Fascist period, when she was accused of pacifism. She eventually made the Netherlands her permanent home and died there on May 8, 1952.

For further reference see: E. M. Standing, *Maria Montessori: Her Life and Work* (New York: Mentor-Omega Books, 1962).

RCo

MONTINI, GIOVANNI BATTISTA. See **PAUL VI**

MORAVIA, ALBERTO. Alberto Moravia is the pseudonym of Alberto Pincherle, the novelist, essayist, and critic, and the Italian writer best known outside Italy since World War II.* Born in Rome on November 28, 1907, of Jewish-Catholic parents, Moravia first gained critical attention for his novel *Gli indifferenti* (The Time of Indifference; 1929), published at his own expense. After the German occupation of Rome, following Mussolini's* fall in 1943, Moravia was forced into hiding. In the postwar period he quickly became an international celebrity. He published *La romana* (The Women of Rome; 1947), *Racconti romani* (Roman Tales; 1954), *La ciociara* (Two Women; 1957), *La noia* (The Empty Canvas; 1960), and *L'attenzione* (The Lie; 1965). His approach to fiction, critics have said, is "more akin to that of the American realist" than to that of the traditional Italian *verismo* (the realism of Giovanni Verga* and Luigi Capuana). At the end of World War II Moravia was drawn briefly to the Roman Catholic Church; but when some of his books were placed on the *Index*, he reverted to his earlier skepticism. Moravia continues to write and has lately published several travel journals.

AP

MORELLI, SALVATORE. A leading advocate of universal suffrage and women's rights in the first Italian parliament, Morelli was born to a middle-class family near Brindisi in 1830. He studied law in Naples but never practiced because he became involved in the revolutions of 1848* on the democratic side. Arrested and tried in the early 1850s, he spent several years in the island prison of Ventotene and then under house arrest in Lecce. Freed by the victory of Giuseppe Garibaldi's* troops, he became active in Neapolitan politics. Morelli made his mark on the city council of Naples for his advocacy of mass education. In 1867 he ran for Parliament from the district of Sessa Aurunca. As a deputy, he joined Mauro Macchi,* Giuseppe Ricciardi,* and others in the fight for women's legal and political equality. His book, *La donna e la scienza o la soluzione dell'umano problema* [Woman and science or the solution to the human problem] (Naples, 1862) became a classic among advocates of women's rights.

In the 1870s Morelli joined with Garibaldi, Giuseppe Ferrari,* and other democrats in a campaign for franchise reform of which his newspaper, *Il Suffragio Universale*, was the standard-bearer. Morelli died in Rome in 1880.

CML

MORO, ALDO. This prominent postwar Christian Democratic politician, prime minister, and party general secretary was born in Puglia on September 23, 1916. His parents were both educators, his father being an inspector for the Ministry of Public Instruction and his mother, Fida, an elementary school teacher. One of five children, Moro attended school in Taranto, where he continually placed at the top of the class. An obese and studious boy, he was often teased by his classmates.

Raised in a strongly Catholic atmosphere, he was active in Church-sponsored youth groups both in the Gioventù Cattolica Italiana at the liceo and in the Federazione Universitaria Cattolica Italiana (FUCI)* at the university. Moro began his study of law at the University of Bari, where he was president of the local Catholic student chapter. In 1939 he transferred to Rome, becoming the national president of the FUCI. As president of this university organization, Moro followed Pope Pius XII's* line on behalf of peace in Europe and neutrality for Italy. In 1942 he resigned his position after being drafted for military service.

In 1945 Moro, then a professor of law at the University of Bari, was elected to the Constituent Assembly* on the Christian Democratic list and began a distinguished political career. He was subsequently elected to the Chamber of Deputies* in 1948 and was appointed by Alcide De Gasperi* to serve as undersecretary to the foreign minister, a post he retained until 1950. In 1954 Moro accepted his first cabinet post, minister of justice, under Antonio Segni,* and subsequently served as minister of public instruction in the government of Andone Zoli* before becoming secretary of the Christian Democrats in 1959. Moro initiated talks with the Socialists which resulted in the parliamentary coalition of the Centro-Sinistra (see Christian Democratic Party*) and eventually led to the formation of his first government in 1963. He served as prime minister until June 1968.

After a series of electoral gains by the Italian Communist Party (PCI)* in the early 1970s, Moro began to urge Christian Democrats toward the ''Compromesso Storico,'' an agreement in which the PCI would refrain from voting against the Christian Democrats in return for an informal voice in governmental policy.

In 1978 Moro became the most sensational victim of the Red Brigades,* a left-wing terrorist organization. He was kidnapped outside his home and after a fruitless fifty-four-day search by massive security forces, his body was found in May in the trunk of a car in the center of Rome.

For further reference see: Corrado Pizzinelli, *Moro* (Milan: Longanesi, 1969).

RJW

MOSCA, GAETANO. Political scientist and jurisprudent, Mosca's renown rests on his elaboration of the theory of an elite ruling class. He was born on April

1, 1858, in Palermo, and died on November 9, 1941, in Rome. Lecturer in constitutional law at the universities of Palermo (1885–88) and Rome (1888–96), professor at Turin (1896–1923) and Rome (1923–33), holding at the latter the chair of history of political institutions and doctrines, Mosca's first major work (*Sulla teorica dei governi e sul governo parlamentare* [On the theory of governments and parliamentary government], 1884) was a severe critique of parliamentary government, containing the basic ideas developed in his *Elementi di scienza politica* (The Ruling Class; 1896), expounding the thesis that all governments, no matter what their form, consist of an elite of birth, money, talent, or traditional functions. Patently undemocratic but misunderstood as illiberal, Mosca's theories were grounded in comparative historical studies of political institutions, in which he saw as undeniable the fact that the majority never rules, but is ruled by an elite, the best of which is an open one that renews itself by co-optation and whose rule rests on a tacit consensus or "representation" of the ruled. Hence the questionable logic of attempts to convert Mosca's ideas into a justification of the Fascist regime, toward which Mosca was at first benevolently neutral, until December 1925, when in a Senate speech he criticized Fascist legislation as subverting the very parliamentary regime he had so severely castigated but whose accomplishments in Italy between 1848 and 1914 he now lauded as impressive. Mosca himself participated in parliamentary life: he served as deputy from 1909 to 1919 and as senator from 1919, and was also undersecretary for colonies under Antonio Salandra* (March 1914–June 1916).

For further reference see: Mario Delle Piane, *Gaetano Mosca: Classe politica e liberalismo* (Naples: Edizioni Scientifiche Italiane, 1952); James H. Meisel, *The Myth of the Ruling Class: Gaetano Mosca and the "Elite"* (Ann Arbor: University of Michigan Press, 1958).

SS

MOVIMENTO SOCIALE ITALIANO. See MSI

MSI. This political party of postwar Italy was formally established in 1946. Known as the *Movimento Sociale Italiano* (Italian Social Movement), the party is recognized for its distinct neo-Fascist posture and ideology. It mourns and extols the triumphant achievements of Fascism* and the divine leadership of its leader, Benito Mussolini.* Its philosophy is centered on the Fascist corporative state, on antiregionalism, and on law and order. It is intensely nationalist, and it openly advocates a Center-Right political coalition. In the sphere of foreign policy, it is tenaciously anti-Communist and therefore pro-Western, though harboring some resentments against the Anglo-Saxon democracies.

Electorally, the MSI's best performance occurred in the elections of 1953, when it captured twenty-nine seats in the Italian Chamber of Deputies.* Its worst performance was registered in the elections of 1968, with twenty-four seats in the Chamber. In the 1972 elections MSI and the Monarchists presented a joint list, capturing fifty-six seats. This figure went down to thirty-five seats in the elections of 1976 and to thirty seats in those of 1979.

The political secretary of the party is the fiery Giorgio Almirante, and its organ is *Il Secolo d'Italia*.

PVB

MUNICH AGREEMENT. This agreement resulted from the conference held in Munich by the leaders of Germany, Italy, Great Britain, and France on September 29–30, 1938, to resolve the German-Czechoslovak crisis over the Sudetenland. British Prime Minister Chamberlain and French Premier Daladier had been ready to meet most of Hitler's demands regarding that territory, but they had also insisted on a diplomatic settlement to the crisis. Mussolini* favored a conference because it would give prestige to him as the "broker." The Munich Agreement provided for almost immediate occupation of some zones by Germany but also stipulated that an international commission would decide in which other districts plebiscites would be held. Czechoslovakia, at Hitler's insistence, was to solve the problem of its Polish and Hungarian minorities. After it had done so, Germany and Italy were to follow Great Britain and France in guaranteeing the new frontiers. The International Commission held no plebiscites, and not one of the signatories of the treaty offered the truncated Czechoslovakia a guarantee. Hitler, in effect, tore up the Munich Agreement in March 1939.

JKZ

MURAT, JOACHIM. This Napoleonic general and King of Naples was an innkeeper's son, born at La Bastide, France, on March 25, 1767. Murat attached himself to Napoleon I* early in the French Revolution. He served in the Italian and Egyptian campaigns, married Caroline Bonaparte (1800), and commanded the cavalry at the battle of Marengo* and in many other battles. He was proclaimed King of Naples on August 1, 1808, and despite close French supervision was able to introduce numerous reforms into Naples. Murat abandoned the Emperor in 1813 in order to retain his throne, but during the Hundred Days he launched an ill-timed attack on the Austrians which led to the Neapolitans' defeat at Tolentino (May 3, 1815). After escaping to Corsica, Murat made a last desperate attempt to regain power, but was captured by Bourbon troops and executed at Pizzo on October 13, 1815.

WDG

MURATORI, LODOVICO ANTONIO. Italian scholar, historiographer, and antiquarian, Muratori was born at Vignola (near Modena) on October 21, 1672. He studied at Modena under the Benedictine Benedetto Bacchini, becoming a disciple of the critical-historical methods of Mabillon and the Benedictines of St. Maur. In the same year that he was ordained a priest (1694), Muratori was appointed one of the curators of the Ambrosian Library in Milan. He soon published the *Anecdota* in two volumes (1697–98), which incorporated selected historical texts from manuscripts discovered in the library.

In 1700 he was invited by the duke of Modena to be archivist and librarian for the duchy. During his long sojourn there he published numerous works. The most important was the *Rerum italicarum scriptores* (1723–51), twenty-eight volumes of documentary sources which brought to public attention the social history of the medieval Italian communes.

This great collection was accompanied by a series of seventy-five historical studies on those same communes: *Antiquitates italicae medii aevi* [Italian medieval antiquities] (1738–43), in which Muratori showed an acute awareness of the links between culture and morals, customs and institutions. Quite properly considered the "father of Italian history," Muratori died in Modena on January 23, 1750.

FFA

MURRI, ROMOLO. Murri was born in Monte S. Pietrangeli (the Marches) on August 27, 1870, and died in Rome on March 12, 1944. After studying in local seminaries, he attended the Collegio Capranica in Rome and was ordained in 1893. During the same year he took courses at the University of Rome, where he came under the influence of Antonio Labriola,* the first Italian Marxist philosopher. Although his Thomistic philosophy was far removed from Marxism, Murri was impressed with Labriola's views on history and on the development of the proletariat. Deeply conscious of socioeconomic injustices, Murri, together with others of similar persuasion, founded an association of Catholic university students in 1894. Its aim was to do battle against the bourgeois state and to bring about a renovation of society based on democracy and Christianity. The journalistic mouthpiece for the Murri adherents was *Cultura Sociale*. Calling themselves Christian Democrats, Murri and his followers published (1899) a program calling for the democratization of Italian political life, the formation of corporations along occupational lines, a reform of the tax structure, social legislation, protection for small landowners and rural workers, and general and gradual disarmament. These demands were later incorporated into the platform of the Italian Popular Party* (1919). In the meantime, however, Murri quarreled with Pope Pius X* over the issue of Modernism* and was excommunicated. His disenchantment with the formal Church led him to reexamine the relationship between the individual and the Church and to conclude that an individual's first obligation was to his own conscience.

In 1943 Murri was reconciled with the Church. He is considered the spiritual ancestor of the left wings of the postwar Christian Democratic Party.*

EC

MUSSOLINI, ARNALDO. This director of *Il Popolo d'Italia* and younger brother of Benito Mussolini* was born on January 11, 1885, at Dovia di Predappio and named for Arnaldo of Brescia. From 1903 to 1905 he was a worker in Switzerland, and on returning to Italy became administrator in an agricultural school in Cesena. He served in World War I,* and on November 1, 1922, became director of *Il Popolo d'Italia*, beginning his political and journalistic career. A man of some conscience and religion, he influenced his brother in relations with the Catholic Church, especially with regard to the reconciliation of 1929 (see Lateran Accords*). He died in Milan on December 21, 1931.

WR

MUSSOLINI, BENITO. Benito Mussolini, founder and leader ("Il Duce") of Italian Fascism,* was premier (1922–43), ruling as dictator after 1925. He was born in Predappio on July 29, 1883, the son of an anticlerical, Socialist black-smith. Largely self-educated, he shared his father's views, adding to them ideas picked up from reading Louis Auguste Blanqui, Friedrich W. Nietzsche, and Georges Sorel. An itinerant schoolteacher and journalist, Mussolini spent a few years in Switzerland and the Austrian Trentino before marrying (1910) Rachele Guidi, a peasant from his home town. She bore him five children: Edda, Vittorio, Bruno, Romano, and Anna Maria. Edda's husband, Count Galeazzo Ciano,* became the Duce's foreign minister in 1936.

A revolutionary Socialist with syndicalist leanings, Mussolini was jailed for his opposition to the Libyan War (see Ouchy, Treaty of*) in 1911–12. Thereafter, he became editor of the Italian Socialist Party (PSI)* newspaper in Milan, *Avanti!**
At first he denounced World War I* but soon reversed himself and called for Italy's entry on the side of the Triple Entente.* Expelled from the Socialist Party for this, he launched his own newspaper in Milan, *Il Popolo d'Italia* (November 1914), later to become the organ of his Fascist movement. He served in the army until wounded in 1917.

In Milan on March 23, 1919, Mussolini and a few other veterans founded the revolutionary, nationalistic Fasci di Combattimento ("Fighting Leagues"). At first the Fascist movement did poorly, but after the threat of a Socialist revolution collapsed (1920) it developed into a powerful radicalism of the Right, gaining the support of many landowners in the lower Po Valley, industrialists, and army officers. Fascist Blackshirt squads carried on local civil war against Socialists, Communists, Catholics, and Liberals. Mussolini survived challenges from Dino Grandi* and other rivals.

Opportunistically renouncing his republicanism and threatening a Fascist March on Rome,* Mussolini secured a mandate from Victor Emmanuel III* to form a coalition government (October 28, 1922). In 1924 his government almost fell during the Aventine Secession* in parliament following the assassination of the Socialist Giacomo Matteotti (see Matteotti Crisis*). Counterattacking, the Duce imposed a single-party, totalitarian regime in 1925–26. In ensuing years he devised the institutions of the corporate state and negotiated the Lateran Accords* with the Vatican (February 11, 1929), the latter being his most enduring legacy.

In the mid-1930s the strutting dictator began an aggressive foreign policy, conquering Ethiopia,* helping General Franco in the Spanish Civil War,* and taking Albania.* The Rome-Berlin Axis* (1936) was expanded into a military Pact of Steel* (May 1939). In spite of this, Mussolini did not join Hitler in World War II* until France was falling in June 1940. During the next two years he also declared war on Greece, Yugoslavia, the Soviet Union, and the United States. A series of military defeats plus a nonconfidence vote by the Fascist Grand Council set the stage for Victor Emmanuel III to overthrow him on July 25, 1943. Soon after, the Fascist state disintegrated.

On September 12, the Germans rescued the sickly ex-Duce and made him head of a puppet northern Italian Social Republic (see Salò, Republic of*). In April 1945 he started to surrender to the Italian Armed Resistance* in Milan but decided instead to flee with his mistress, Clara Petacci. Captured by Italian partisans at Lake Como, they were shot on April 28 at Giulino di Mezzegra, and their bodies were strung up in a Milan piazza. Later, Mussolini was buried at Predappio. His widow died on October 31, 1979, and is buried near him.

A skillful journalist and demagogue, Mussolini was popular with most Italians until the late 1930s. He lost their support when he dragged his country into a war that it was unprepared to fight.

For further reference see: Ivone Kirkpatrick, *Mussolini* (New York: Hawthorn, 1964); Denis Mack Smith, *Mussolini* (New York: Knopf, 1982); Renzo De Felice, *Mussolini* (Turin: Einaudi, 1965–81).

CFD

MVSN. See **VOLUNTARY MILITIA FOR NATIONAL SECURITY**

N

NAPOLEON I. Napoleon I, Emperor of the French, was of Italian ancestry. Born Napoleon Buonaparte in 1769 in Corsica (ceded by Genoa to France only the year before), he spoke and was taught Italian until he went off to school in France at age nine. During his early triumphs in Italy (1796–97; 1800) he used his background and linguistic skill to ingratiate himself with Italians. Later, he gave the Italian states similar governments and laws, and reduced their number.

Napoleon never consciously fostered pan-Italian nationalism or promoted unification, despite his statements at St. Helena. His system of roads and waterways gave him the lie. It was not designed to tie the Italian states together, but to connect them, separately, to France. His one great gesture toward unity was to give Italy a common language of administration—Tuscan—via the dictionary of the Florentine Accademia della Crusca.

Napoleonic Italy comprised three parts: the Kingdom of Italy in the North (the former Cisalpine Republic,* enlarged by Venetia and the eastern Papal States*); the Kingdom of Naples in the South; and the areas annexed to France (Genoa, Parma, Tuscany, and papal territories including Rome). Napoleon's sister Elisa was grand duchess of Tuscany (technically part of France) and princess of Lucca* and Piombino (not annexed). Rome and environs comprised two departments under General Sextius Alexandre François Miollis. Italy and Naples were constitutional monarchies; Napoleon was King of Italy, which was ruled (1805–14) by his viceroy, Eugène de Beauharnais (Josephine's son). Joseph, Napoleon's elder brother, was the first King of Naples (1806–8), succeeded by Marshal Joachim Murat* and his wife, Caroline Bonaparte (1808–15), who prolonged the life of their kingdom by defecting to the Allies in 1814.

The law of all the states was the Code Napoléon. All had French-style administrations and court systems. Everywhere, feudalism was abolished, careers opened to talent, rights and duties of citizenship extended to all males (including Jews), the power of the Church reduced, public welfare promoted, public works erected, school systems enlarged and centralized, and scholarship and creativity encouraged. Everything was best implemented in the Kingdom of Italy, which had progressive Italian leaders such as Franceso Melzi d'Eril,* Giuseppe Prina, Giovanni Scopoli, and Giovanni Paradisi, and the support (though it was not slavish) of the poet Vicenzo Monti, the sculptor Antonio Canova, and the scientist Alessandro Volta. Elsewhere, especially in Rome, many changes were nominal. Even in Rome, however, the French left marks of Napoleonic imagination and energy. Much of the Colosseum was restored, as was the Arch of Titus; the Temple of Vespasian and the Column of Trajan, long buried, were unearthed.

It is not surprising that Italian historians see Napoleon as a major force in the emergence of modern Italy. It was Murat, however (as King Gioacchino Napoleone of Naples), who first fought for Italian unification. In 1815, when Napoleon returned from Elba, Murat turned against the Allies, marched his army against the Austrians in the North, and proclaimed the independence of all Italy—under himself. He had been convinced by intellectuals and members of secret societies (notably Antonio Maghella and Giuseppe Zurlo) that the people would rise up and support him. They did not. He lost his throne and, within the year, his life. Nevertheless, his exploits are celebrated, along with the more telling contributions of the Emperor of the French.

For further reference see: C. Zaghi, *Napoleone e l'Italia* (Naples: Cymba, 1966); A. Fugier, *Napoléon et Italie* (Paris: J. B. Janin, 1947); G. Natali, *L'Italia durante il regime Napoleonico* (Bologna: R. Pàtron, 1955); *L'Italie jacobine et napoléonienne*, special issue of *Annales Historique de la Révolution Française* (Paris, 1977); J. Rambaud, *Naples sous Joseph Bonaparte* (Paris: Plon-Nourrit, 1911); A. Valente, *Gioacchino Murat et l'Italia meridionale* (Turin: Einaudi, 1976); M. Andrieux, *Les Français à Rome* (Paris: Fayard, 1968); A. Varni, *Bologna Napoleonica* (Bologna: M. Boni, 1973); O. Connelly, *Napoleon's Satellite Kingdoms* (New York: Free Press, 1965).

OC

NAPOLEON III. Napoleon III was French Emperor from 1852 to 1870 and a key figure in assisting Cavour* in breaking Austrian hegemony in Italy. He was born on April 21, 1808, in Paris, and died on January 9, 1873, in Chislehurst, England. Louis Napoleon, nephew of Napoleon I,* served as president of the Second Republic (1848–52) before overthrowing it to create the Second Empire. As president, Louis restored Pius IX* to power in the Papal States,* from which he had been chased during the revolutions of 1848,* and left a garrison in Rome to protect him. Though politically expedient because pleasing to French Catholics, this policy entangled Napoleon in contradictions when, as Emperor, he championed Italian nationalism, which was a threat to the Pope's temporal power.

Genuinely sympathetic to Italian nationalism and convinced that it would inevitably triumph, and ambitious to extend French power, Napoleon first permitted Cavour to voice the grievances of Italian liberals at the Congress of Paris* (1856) and then plotted with him at Plombières (1858) (see Plombières Agreement*) to provoke Austria to war and to wrest Lombardy* and Venetia from her. Napoleon planned an Italian Confederation of four states under the nominal presidency of the Pope, which would be led by Victor Emmanuel II,* whose kingdom would expand to include Lombardy, Venetia, Parma, Modena, and the Legations.* In 1859 Franco-Sardinian forces drove Austria from Lombardy, but Napoleon, threatened by Prussia and alarmed by revolutions in central Italy, concluded an armistice at Villafranca.* Lombardy went to Sardinia, but Austria kept Venetia. After permitting Victor Emmanuel to annex most of central Italy through plebiscites in 1860, Napoleon received Nice and Savoy as compensation. Shortly thereafter he watched Giuseppe Garibaldi's* expedition with helpless fascination. When Cavour proposed that Victor Emmanuel push south through papal territory to regain control of the situation, Napoleon secretly consented, but he persisted in preserving papal sovereignty over Rome.

For further reference see: J.P.T. Bury, *Napoleon III and the Second Empire* (London: English Universities Press, 1964); J. M. Thompson, *Louis Napoleon and the Second Empire* (New York: Noonday Press, 1955); "Il Secondo Impero e L'Italia," in Franco Valsecchi, *L'Italia del Risorgimento e l'Europa delle nazionalità* (Milan: A. Giuffrè Editore, 1978).

RCu

NAPOLEON III ET L'ITALIE. This brochure, published in Paris on February 4, 1859, called for a restructuring of the political order in Italy to satisfy Italian nationalism. Written by Arthur de La Guéronnière with the assistance of Eugene Rendu, it was revised in many parts by Napoleon III,* who had commissioned it. The brochure argued against Austrian hegemony in Italy and in favor of a confederation with Rome as its capital and the Pope as its titular head. Recognized immediately as the Emperor's handiwork, this brochure contributed to the tension preceding the war of 1859.*

RCu

NATHAN, ERNESTO. This radical/Masonic (see Freemasonry*) mayor of Rome (1909–13) was born in London on October 5, 1845, of parents who were strong supporters of Giuseppe Mazzini* and Giuseppe Garibaldi.* Nathan settled permanently in Rome in 1871, and his house became a center where leading Italian political and cultural figures met. A Mason since 1887, he was grand master between 1896 and 1904 and then from 1917 to 1919. He was responsible for the national seat, the Palazzo Giustiniani, in 1901. Nathan mobilized the lodges to work for the creation of a laic state in Italy. His mayorality was noted for economy, efficiency, and improvement in municipal services. It was also marked by bitter exchanges with Catholics, nationalists, and segments of the conservative liberals over his anticlericalism, which they charged was an attack on Christianity itself. Nathan died in Rome on April 9, 1921.

RSC

NATIONAL CONSERVATIVE ASSOCIATION. See JACINI, STEFANO

NATIONAL FUEL TRUST. See **ENI**

NATIONALIST ASSOCIATION. See **ITALIAN NATIONALIST ASSOCIATION**

NATIONAL MONARCHIST PARTY. This post-World War II Italian political party supports restoration of the monarchy in Italy. It was founded by Alfredo Covelli and Achille Lauro. The party was formed after the June 1946 referendum establishing the Republic and had the support of the conservative nobility and certain popular classes, especially in those zones of the South which were the backbone of the Monarchist electorate. In the 1953 election it gained forty seats, and in 1958 supported the government of Andone Zoli.*

WR

NATIONAL SOCIETY. See **SOCIETÀ NAZIONALE ITALIANA**

NATIONAL UNION OF LIBERAL AND DEMOCRATIC FORCES. See **AMENDOLA, GIOVANNI**

NATO. See **NORTH ATLANTIC TREATY ORGANIZATION, ITALY AND**

NAZIONE, LA. See **NEWSPAPERS**

NENNI, PIETRO. Pietro Nenni, a Socialist leader, was born in Faenza on February 9, 1891, and died in Rome on January 1, 1980. He made his political debut in the Republican Party* before World War I.* He supported Italian entry into the war in 1915 and collaborated briefly on Mussolini's* *Popolo d'Italia.* After the war Nenni broke decisively with Mussolini and with the Republicans. He joined the Italian Socialist Party (PSI)* in 1921, and in 1923 was both editor of *Avanti!** and leader of those Socialists who rejected fusion with the Italian Communist Party (PCI)* and entry into the Communist International. With the onset of complete dictatorship after 1925, Nenni became a strong proponent of reunification between the reformist Unitary Socialist Party and the revolutionary Italian Socialist Party and led the reunited party after 1930. Nenni, who had been an opponent of close cooperation with the Communists, reversed himself after 1934 when confronted with the growing Fascist danger. From 1934 to 1939 he led the party into the "Unity of Action" pact with the Italian Communist Party. In 1936 and 1937 he helped organize the Italian volunteers for the Republican government in the Spanish Civil War.* The Nazi-Soviet Pact of August 1939 brought about a revolt against his leadership of the Socialist Party. Nenni was ousted as secretary but eventually resumed the leadership after 1943. He represented the Socialists on the National Liberation Council and served as vice-president of the Council of Ministers and as minister for the Constituent Assembly of 1946* in the government of Alcide De Gasperi.*

The Socialist Party under Nenni continued to support unity of action with the Communists and faced another split in January 1947 with the formation of the Socialist Party of the Italian Workers (later Italian Socialist Democratic Party). That same year saw Nenni's Socialists and the Communists ousted from the government. Only after the Soviet invasion of Hungary in 1956 did Nenni break his alliance with the Italian Communist Party. He then led the Socialist Party into an alliance with the Christian Democratic Party* after 1962 and into a brief fusion with the reformist Social Democratic Party between 1966 and 1968.

For further reference see: Pietro Nenni, *La battaglia socialista contro il fascismo* (Milan: Mursia, 1977); idem, *Intervista sul socialismo italiano*, ed. G. Tamburrano (Bari: Laterza, 1977).

AJD

NEO-GUELF MOVEMENT. An Italian form of liberal Catholicism at mid-nineteenth century, neo-Guelfism attempted to reconcile the preservation of the temporal power with a popular movement for Italy's independence and unification. The term was coined by detractors of liberal Catholicism, especially Gabriele Pepe and Giuseppe Ferrari,* but Catholic intellectuals accepted it and used it with pride. The foremost spokesman for the movement was the Piedmontese theologian Vincenzo Gioberti.* In contrast to the influential French theorist Joseph de Maistre, Gioberti wanted a synthesis of democratic nationalism and Catholicism which would appeal to the Italian masses. The goal of the neo-Guelf movement was to establish a political order in Italy in which the Pope could be at once the spiritual leader of the universal Church and the temporal leader of all Italians. As a strategy to achieve this goal, neo-Guelf leaders proposed the founding of an Italian federation over which the Pope would preside. Their aspirations came close to being realized in 1846–47 when Pope Pius IX* was elected and introduced liberal reforms in the Papal States.* Gioberti's movement could count on the support of prominent liberals like Cesare Balbo* and of intellectuals like Carlo Troya* and Alessandro Manzoni.* But even so, it never built a solid national network, nor did it have much success among the Italian masses. Hence, the revolutions of 1848* dealt it a blow from which it never recovered.

The outbreak of revolution in France emboldened the critics of neo-Guelfism. They began to think that a democratic republic was possible in Italy as in France. Later, the revolutionary war against Austria in northern Italy forced Pius IX to clarify his position vis-à-vis the national movement. Although sympathetic to it, he refused to take sides in a struggle between two Catholic countries. His refusal to send papal troops to aid the Lombard revolutionaries in April 1848 marked the end of neo-Guelfism as a viable political movement. True to its origins, it survived as an intellectual movement of Italian liberal Catholics.

CML

NERI, POMPEO. This functionary and political economist was employed in the Hapsburg administration of Tuscany and Milan under Maria Theresa, Francis

I, and Peter Leopold of Hapsburg-Lorraine.* Born in Florence in 1706, his early education was at a seminary in Siena. From there he passed to the University of Pisa, where he received a degree in law in 1726. He followed his father's footsteps into the ducal bureaucracy at Florence in 1735, and with the extinction of the Medici in 1737 was made secretary to the Council of Regency for Hapsburg-Lorraine. Pompeo Neri became one of the chief technicians and architects of the Hapsburg reforms in Tuscany, where he was author of administrative projects in the 1740s, and at Milan, where he was made president of the commission to complete a new Catasto (tax list) in 1748. He returned to Florence in 1758, and after 1765 was one of the most trusted advisers of Peter Leopold. He was involved particularly with legislation introducing free trade in grain in 1767 and with the new regulation of communal and municipal government. He was author of a number of treatises on administrative matters that reveal the practical concerns of the Italian Enlightenment,* particularly his *Discorso sopra lo stato artico e moderno della nobiltà toscana* [Discourse on the ancient and modern condition of the Tuscan nobility] (1748), *Relazione dello stato in cui si trova l'opera del censimento di Milano* [Report on the state of the census taking in Milan] (1750), *Osservazioni sopra il prezzo legale delle monete* [Observations on the legal value of money] (1751), and *Discorso sopra la materia frumentario* [Discourse on wheat products] (1766). He died in 1776.

For further reference see: Franco Venturi, *Illuministi italiani* (Naples: Ricciardi, 1958), 3: 945–50.

RBL

NEUTRALITY, IN WORLD WAR I. Italy's declaration of neutrality in the European conflict on August 3, 1914, at first met with near-unanimous approval in the country, materially and morally unprepared for war. But during the ten months preceding Italy's intervention on the side of the Triple Entente* in May 1915, the country divided between neutralists who sought to escape the horrors of war and perhaps extract territorial compensation from Austria as the price of Italy's continued neutrality, and assorted interventionists who favored war either because they did not believe that Austria would ever make such compensations or because of ideological hostility toward Austria and Germany, Italy's allies for more than three decades. The country's division did not end in May 1915, compromising the war effort and contributing to the postwar disarray.

SS

NEWSPAPERS. Following Italy's unification under a liberal regime, journalism experienced a prolific and lively existence until stifled by the Fascist dictatorship. Milan's *Corriere della Sera,** founded in 1876 as an independent journal favored by moderate liberals, achieved primacy under the innovative direction of Luigi Albertini* after 1900. A staff of specialized editors, resident and roving correspondents, and contributors recruited from Italy's cultural and political elite made possible wide national and international coverage of news and commentary. The Milanese *Secolo*, founded in 1866 by Edoardo Sonzogno, for a time had the largest circulation in Italy. An organ of radical democracy, it was rich in political coverage. Also in Milan was *La Perseveranza* (1860–1920), the voice of Lombard conservatism, with Ruggiero Bonghi* as its editor for a number of years. *L'Osservatore Cattolico* (1864–1907) was long directed by Don Davide Albertario,* a militant supporter of the papacy; he was succeeded by Filippo Meda* in 1902. In November 1914 Milan saw the birth of Mussolini's* *Popolo d'Italia*, destined to become the chief organ of Fascism.* Rome rivaled Milan for journalistic primacy. *La Tribuna* was founded in 1883 as an organ of the Left (see Sinistra, La*). After 1910, under Olindo Malagodi,* it became especially influential in parliamentary coverage. *Il Giornale d'Italia*,* founded by Sidney Sonnino* in 1901, quickly acquired national prominence under Alberto Bergamini*; and *Il Messaggero*, founded in 1878 in small format and liberal-democrat in politics, at first acquired a large circulation by its emphasis on local news, which later became wider and more varied. *Avanti!*,* founded in Rome in 1896 and transferred to Milan in 1911, was the principal organ of Italian socialism. Among its editors were such luminaries as Leonida Bissolati,* Claudio Treves,* Enrico Ferri,* and, in 1912, Benito Mussolini. The current *Osservatore Romano* was founded in 1861 and soon became the authoritative voice of the Vatican. *L'Idea Nazionale*,* which was founded in 1911 and became daily in 1914, was the expression of the Nationalist Party, its editors and contributors including many of Fascism's future ideologues. In Turin the principal newspaper was *La Stampa*,* begun as the *Gazzetta Piemontese* in 1867 and renamed in 1895. After Alfredo Frassati assumed its direction in 1900, he made it a rival of the *Corriere della Sera* in the distinction of its national and international coverage, as well as Giovanni Giolitti's* ever-loyal supporter. Florence's major newspaper for a long time was *La Nazione*; it was founded in 1859 by Tuscan moderates and distinguished by the collaboration of major political and literary figures, as was Bologna's *Il Resto del Carlino*, founded in 1885 as a liberal organ. Genoa's chief newspaper was *Il Secolo XIX*, founded in 1886, rivaled by *Il Lavoro*, established in 1903 as the voice of Genoese labor and reformist socialism. Venice's *Gazzetta di Venezia*, which dated from 1799, became a daily in 1866, changing its liberal orientation to conservatism when it absorbed the *Giornale di Venezia* in 1906. *Il Mattino* of Naples, founded in 1891 by Edoardo Scarfoglio,* soon became the newspaper of widest circulation in the South. Two newspapers contested for primacy in Sicily: the liberal *Giornale di Sicilia* of Palermo, founded in 1860, and Catania's democratic *Corriere di Sicilia* (1879–1930). The fate of Italy's press under Fascism is indicated, in brief, by the acquisition by Fascist interests in 1926 of the *Corriere della Sera*, *La Stampa*, and *La Tribuna*, which merged with *L'Idea Nazionale* in 1926, and by the suppression of *Avanti!*, also in 1926.

For further reference see: Valerio Castronovo, *La stampa italiana dall'unità al fascismo* (Bari: Laterza, 1970); Alfredo Signoretti, *La stampa in camicia nera, 1932–1943* (Rome: G. Volpe, 1968).

SS

NICOTERA, GIOVANNI. Minister of the interior (1876–77, 1891–92), Nicotera's evolution from democratic republicanism to partisan authoritarianism effectively barred his way to higher reaches of power. He was born on September 9, 1828, in Sambiase (Catanzaro), and died on June 13, 1894, in Vico Equense (Naples). A Mazzinian and a conspirator against Bourbon rule, he was wounded in the defense of Rome in 1849 and again in the Sapri expedition of 1857. He was freed from life imprisonment with the liberation of Sicily in 1860. Nicotera followed Giuseppe Garibaldi* in his ventures in 1862, 1866, and 1867. He served as a deputy to parliament from 1861 until his death. As one of the leaders of the Left (see Sinistra, La*) he became minister of the interior when Agostino Depretis* came to power in March 1876, but was forced to resign in December 1877 because of arbitrary use of his office. He broke with Depretis, and in 1883 joined four other Depretis opponents to form the Pentarchy* of the Left. Becoming increasingly conservative, Nicotera served under Antonio Di Rudinì* as minister of the interior (February 1891–May 1892) in the first government of the Right (see Destra, La*) since 1876 and practiced a severe policy against radical democratic agitation.

SS

NIGRA, COSTANTINO. Diplomat and philologist, he was instrumental in Piedmont's diplomatic relations with France in the years immediately preceding Italian unification. Born in Aosta on June 11, 1820, after studies at Turin, where he earned a law degree in 1849, he entered the Piedmontese foreign office. In 1856 he accompanied Cavour* to the Congress of Paris* and impressed Napoleon III.* Thereafter he became chief diplomatic emissary between Paris and Turin. He was at Plombières (see Plombières Agreement*), later negotiating the details of the Franco-Piedmontese alliance and those of the cession of Nice and Savoy to France. He remained in Paris until 1876, first as minister plenipotentiary and then as ambassador. Thereafter he served at St. Petersburg, London, and Vienna. In 1899 he represented Italy at the Hague Peace Conference. Nigra was the editor of several works on Italian folklore and popular poetry. He retired in 1904 and died in Rapallo on January 6, 1907.

FFA

NITTI, FRANCESCO SAVERIO. This political economist and statesman was born in Melfi in the Basilicata on July 19, 1868, and began his career by championing the cause of the South. He was professor of public finance at the University of Naples, and entered parliament in 1904 as the representative of Muro Lucano. In 1911, while a member of the Radical Party,* he accepted the portfolio of agriculture in the fourth ministry of Giovanni Giolitti* (March 1911–March 1914).

During the war he led an economic and financial mission to the United States (the summer of 1917) and served as minister of the treasury in Vittorio Orlando's* cabinet (October 1917–January 1919). He resigned on the eve of the peace conference because of his disagreement with the foreign minister, Sidney Sonnino,* on the terms to be attained in the peace. He was later to attack the treaties in a trilogy of books that denied that Germany was solely responsible for the war, and noted that the treaty terms would not assure the peace of the Continent.

From June 1919 to June 1920 Nitti served as prime minister and had to deal with the postwar crisis in Italy. He was responsible for implementing the system of proportional representation and sought to solve the Fiume* crisis by agreement with Yugoslavia. An opponent of Fascism,* he was forced to flee Italy in 1924 and was captured by the Germans in France in 1943. Released at the war's end, he returned to Italian political life and became a prominent member of the National Democratic Union Party. In 1948 he was named to the Senate.* He died in Rome on February 20, 1953.

For further reference see: Frank J. Coppa, "Francesco Saverio Nitti: Early Critic of the Treaty of Versailles," *Risorgimento* 2, no. 2 (1980): 211–19; Vincenzo Nitti, *L'opera di Nitti* (Turin: Piero Gobetti Editore, 1924).

FJC

NOCE, TERESA. This Communist Party activist, feminist, author, and journalist was born in Turin on July 29, 1900. Noce joined the Young Socialists in 1919 and in 1921 was part of the new Italian Communist Party (PCI).* Active clandestinely for the party in the twenties and thirties, she organized anti-Fascist women and served as a journalist in the Spanish Civil War.* She suffered frequent arrest and imprisonment between 1939 and 1945. After 1945 she was part of the party's Central Committee, was elected as deputy, and sponsored a variety of legislation relating to women's issues. Author of *Ma domani fa giorno* [Tomorrow the sun will rise] (1952), *Gioventù senza sole* [Youth without sunshine] (1978), and *Rivoluzionaria professionale* [A professional revolutionary] (1977), she died in 1980.

MJS

NOI DONNE. This women's journal was first published in Paris (1937–39) by the Unione Donne Italiane* (UDI) to mobilize women for peace and against Fascism.* It was published clandestinely during the Armed Resistance* by numerous GDD units (see Gruppi di Difese...*) in the northern provinces. The first legal issue appeared in Naples in August 1944. The journal was transferred to Rome in September 1944, and it became the fortnightly publication of UDI in October. Currently published as a weekly, it covers a wide range of women's concerns, ranging from abortion to sports.

MJS

NON ABBIAMO BISOGNO. This encyclical letter was issued by Pope Pius XI* on June 29, 1931, during the controversy between the Italian Catholic Action* and the Fascist regime. In this letter the Pope protested against the violence and invectives launched by government officials against Catholic youth organizations and accused the government of attempting to monopolize the young for the Fascist Party (see Fascism*). He described the regime as one "based on ideology which clearly resolves itself into a true and real pagan worship of the state, which is no less in contrast with the natural rights of the family than it is in contradiction to the supernatural rights of the Church.'' The Fascist concept of the state was therefore incompatible with Catholic doctrine. The Pope specifically stated that he was not condemning the party as a whole but only those elements of its program and those activities of the government that were in opposition to Catholic doctrine and practice.

The encyclical letter was the personal work of Pius XI, who also took the precautionary measure of sending the text abroad, where it would be published simultaneously with the original Italian text.

Mussolini* affected scorn for the doctrinal position assumed by the pontiff. After two additional months of bitter controversy, a compromise was reached. The existence of Catholic Action was preserved, but its activities were strictly confined to the religious and recreational spheres.

                                                                                                                        EC

NON EXPEDIT. The papal position after 1871 that it was ''not expedient'' for Italian Catholics to participate in the political life of a state that had despoiled the Church of its temporal power, the *non expedit* was confirmed by Pius IX* in 1874 and converted into an absolute prohibition in 1877. It did not apply to administrative elections, in which Catholics participated with increasing numbers from the 1880s onward. Repeatedly confirmed by Leo XIII,* it was relaxed prior to the general elections of 1904 by Pius X,* who was fearful that continued Catholic abstentionism would facilitate a success by the parties of the Extreme Left (see Sinistra, La*). With the encyclical *Fermo proposito* (1905), Pius X reconfirmed the prohibition in principle but left it to the prudence of local bishops to decide when it should be suspended. In 1913 the *non expedit* was practically annulled by an agreement (the Gentiloni Pact*) lifting the prohibition in 330 of the 508 electoral constituencies. After the formation of the Italian Popular Party* in 1919, Benedict XV* formally abrogated the prohibition.

                                                                                                                        SS

NORTH ATLANTIC TREATY ORGANIZATION, ITALY AND THE. This military alliance was formed in April 1949 because of profound concern on the part of Western Europe, the United States, and Canada over communism in the years immediately following World War II.* NATO comprises Belgium, Canada, Denmark, France, the Federal Republic of Germany, Greece, Iceland, Italy, Luxembourg, the Netherlands, Norway, Portugal, Spain, Turkey, the United Kingdom, and the United States.

The admission of Italy to NATO was disputed and, as a result, delayed. The opposition was both foreign and internal. Britain initially opposed Italian participation in the military alliance. Internally, Prime Minister Alcide De Gasperi* and his foreign minister, Carlo Sforza,* believed that neutrality was most appropriate for Italy. Eventually these two statesmen became convinced that Italian participation was in the best interests of the country.

Hence, De Gasperi and Sforza decided to push for Italy's admission. But it was not easy for the Italian parliament to approve entry into NATO. The treaty was opposed by the Communists, and by other parties on the Left. The Socialists declared their neutrality. De Gasperi also had problems with the left wing of his party, whose members were skeptical about Italy's participation in the security pact. To persuade members of his own party, De Gasperi discreetly asked the Holy See to exert influence on the Christian Democratic skeptics. Eventually, the Italian parliament ratified the treaty.

Even after parliamentary approval, Italian participation in NATO never worked well, for it was characterized first by a challenge and later by passive participation. The challenge was initiated by Giovanni Gronchi,* the third president of the Italian Republic. In 1956 he argued that NATO was no longer tailored for the realities of the times. He coined the term "neo-Atlanticism," contending that the situational factors of 1956 were intrinsically different from those of 1949. Hence, a new "vista" was necessary in Italian foreign policy. This new vista ultimately signified a neutralist position for Italy. The matter exploded in 1958, when Aldo Moro* and Amintore Fanfani* launched "the opening to the Left" (*l'apertura a sinistra*), which, in foreign policy, called for a de-emphasis of the military aspects of NATO. The elevation of John XXIII* to the Petrine chair in 1958 was of considerable impact in making the alliance with the Socialists possible.

With the *apertura a sinistra*, NATO assumed a secondary position. Even so, Italian participation in the security pact has seldom been more than nominal. Italy's appropriations for NATO have been consistently low, especially when compared with those of the other members. Furthermore, whatever appropriations were made by the Italian government were spent on nonmilitary matters.

For further reference see: Domenico Bartoli, *Da Vittorio Emanuele a Gronchi* (Milan: Longanesi, 1961); Guglielmo Negri, *La direzione ed il controllo democratico della politica estera in Italia* (Milan: Giuffrè, 1967).

PVB

NOVARA, BATTLE OF. A battle in the war for Italian independence, it was fought on March 23, 1849, between the Sardinian and Austrian forces. The Sardinians were completely defeated, bringing about the abdication of King Charles Albert of Sardinia (see Charles Albert of Savoy*) in favor of his son, Victor Emmanuel II,* who became King of Italy in 1861.

WR

NUOVO AVANTI! The Socialist newspaper *Nuovo Avanti!* was published in Paris during the mid-1930s, when a group of Italian Socialists led by Pietro Nenni,* Giuseppe Saragat,* and Angelo Tasca* decided that a new collaborative relationship with the Italian Communist Party (PCI)* was needed in order to promote the general cause of anti-Fascist unity of action. The newspaper, which was named ''Nuovo'' to distinguish it from the Socialist Party's main organ, *Avanti!*,* articulated the new direction in Italian anti-Fascist politics that was expressed in the unity of action pact signed on August 17, 1934, by the Italian Socialist Party (PSI)* and the Communist Party.

                                                                                        FR

O

OBERDAN (OBERDANK), GUGLIELMO. An Italian irredentist martyr (see Irredentism*), he was born in Trieste* on February 1, 1858. Oberdan took refuge in Rome in July 1878 to escape Austrian military service. He became convinced that a dramatic incident was needed to highlight the fate of the Italians abandoned to Austrian rule. The scheduled visit of Emperor Francis Joseph* to Trieste for late September 1882 provided the opportunity. Armed with bombs, Oberdan left Rome on September 14, with the Austrian Donato Ragosa. The Austrian secret police were informed of the assassination plot by two of Oberdan's irredentist acquaintances, who probably were spies. Oberdan was seized at Ronchi on September 16, while Ragosa eluded Austrian security. After his trial Oberdan was sentenced to death by hanging. He was executed on December 20, 1882, with "Long Live Italy! Long Live Free Trieste!..." on his lips.

RSC

OJETTI, UGO. This journalist, writer, art historian, and critic was born in Rome on July 15, 1871. His studies of Italian art and artists from the Renaissance on won him much fame. Ojetti's numerous novels, collections of essays, plays, and autobiographical accounts demonstrated his versatility. He founded and directed *Dedalo* (1920–33), a review dedicated to the figurative arts; *Pegaso* (1929–33), a literary periodical; and *Pan* (1933–40), a review of art, music, and letters. Best known as a journalist, he was dispatched on many special assignments (including some to the United States) by the *Corriere della Sera*,* on whose staff he served from 1898. During his lifetime he published more than fifty volumes. Ojetti died in Florence on January 1, 1947.

RSC

OLIVETTI, ANGELO OLIVIERO. This corporativist theorist and Fascist publicist was born in Ravenna on June 21, 1874, and died in Spoleto on November 17, 1931. A revolutionary syndicalist by 1905, Olivetti was especially influential as editor of *Pagine Libere* (1906–11, 1920–22). He supported the

Libyan War (see Ouchy, Treaty of*) and promptly advocated Italian intervention in World War I,* becoming a leader in the revolutionary interventionist Fascio Rivoluzionario d'Azione Internazionalista.

Olivetti was central in the revision that led from revolutionary syndicalism* to corporativism,* but he was skeptical about Fascism* at first and became an active Fascist only during the Matteotti Crisis* of 1924, when there seemed a chance of forcing Fascism onto a corporativist order. He served on the Commission of Eighteen established to design new institutions, but he became quite critical of the bureaucratic and party interference that damaged corporativism in practice.

DDR

ONB. See **BALILLA**

ON THE HOPE OF ITALY. See *SPERANZE D'ITALIA, DELLE*

OPENING TO THE LEFT. See **CHRISTIAN DEMOCRATIC PARTY** and **NORTH ATLANTIC TREATY ORGANIZATION, ITALY AND THE**

OPERA DEI CONGRESSI. A Catholic social and political movement of the late nineteenth and early twentieth centuries, the Opera dei Congressi was founded in 1874 as an organization of Catholic laymen devoted to serving the interests of the papacy. Eschewing labels of conservative, liberal, or moderate, the members of the Opera saw themselves simply as Catholics adhering to the Syllabus of Errors* and intent on defeating the anticlerical Italian state that had dispossessed the Pope. A rigidly hierarchical organization that demanded strict obedience to Church leaders, the Opera established committees in each diocese, nurtured the growth of a Catholic press, and actively supported the foundation of Catholic schools. Aside from these endeavors and the usual religious activities, the members of the Opera were encouraged to stand for office in local elections that were exempted from the strictures of the *non expedit.**

During much of the century, the Opera was controlled by the "intransigenti," those Catholics who simply refused to accept the legitimacy of the Italian state and who shunned any conciliation whatsoever. This lack of participation in national politics led the Opera to develop a network of social programs, including the establishment of rural credit banks (Don Luigi Cerutti), associations for the protection of emigrants (Bishop Scalabrini), cooperatives, and peasant unions. The Opera set up a section on "Christian Economy" and began to organize the urban poor, sponsoring over 600 societies in the cities by 1897.

The growing influence in the Opera of the Christian Democrats (those Catholics under Don Romolo Murri* and Don Luigi Sturzo* who asserted some independence in politics from the papacy and who relied on Catholic social organizations for popular political support) alarmed the more conservative Opera leaders. At the 1903 congress, the Christian Democrats (see Christian Democratic

Party*) gained effective control of the leadership of the Opera with the election of Giovanni Grosoli. Two weeks later, Pius X,* fearful of Modernist trends among the "democristiani," dissolved the central organization of the Opera dei Congressi.

For further reference see: G. De Rosa, *Storia politica dell'Azione Cattolica in Italia*, 2 vols. (Bari: Laterza, 1953–54).

RJW

OPERA NAZIONALE BALILLA. See BALILLA

OPERA NAZIONALE DOPOLAVORO. See DOPOLAVORO

OPERA VIGILANZA REPRESSIONE ANTIFASCISMO. See OVRA

ORANO, PAOLO. This Fascist journalist and academic, born in Rome on June 15, 1875, began his career in 1903 as a writer for the Socialist newspaper *Avanti!*,* and was codirector of the syndicalist *Pagine Libere* in 1907–8 and director of *La Lupa* of Florence in 1910–11. Orano moved to a "national syndicalist" position when he supported Italian intervention in World War I.* He joined the Fascist Party (see Fascism*) after 1919 and served the regime as deputy to parliament in 1921 and 1924 and as editor of the Rome edition of the *Popolo d'Italia* in 1924 and 1925. Subsequently, Orano became professor of journalism and rector of the University of Perugia. He was a leader of the anti-Semitic campaign of 1938 and was made a senator in 1939. In 1943 he rallied to the Italian Social Republic (see Salò, Republic of*). He died in a concentration camp in Padula in 1945.

AJD

***ORDINE NUOVO, L'.* See GRAMSCI, ANTONIO**

ORIANI, ALFREDO. Oriani was a writer who criticized both the aesthetics and the politics of post-*Risorgimento* Italy in his novels, plays, and historical essays. Born in Faenza on August 22, 1852, he developed a disgust for cultural positivism and parliamentary politics as a law student at the University of Rome. Abandoning law, he retired to his villa, "Il Cardello," in the Romagna,* where he led a reclusive existence as a writer until his death on October 18, 1909.

As a novelist, Oriani received little critical or popular recognition during his lifetime. His novels expressed the tortured anguish and violent revolt typical of deracinated intellectuals at the turn of the century. *La disfatta* [The defeat] (1896), *Vortice* [The whirlpool] (1899), and *Olocausto* [The holocaust] (1902) are considered the best examples of his fiction.

Oriani claimed to have been influenced by Hegel in his historical writing, which was characterized by inattention to sources and a mystical idealism concerning Italy's destiny. In works such as *Fino a Dogali* [Until Dogali] (1889) and *La lotta politica in Italia* [The political struggle in Italy] (1892), he lamented how the petty, sterile, and corrupt machinations of parliamentarianism had supplanted the grand vision of Italy's future painted by the heroes of the *Risorgimento*.* He predicted, however, that the dialectic of renewal would continue and that Italy would fulfill its mission in a future marked by revolution and war. This mission included the annexation of Trent and Trieste* and a revival of African empire. Because of his advocacy of nationalism, imperialism, and war in the name of idealism, both the Nationalists and the Fascists exalted Oriani posthumously as a precursor of their respective parties.

MSG

ORLANDO, VITTORIO EMANUELE. As prime minister (1917–19), Orlando led Italy through the military disaster of Caporetto* and to victory, only to fail at the Paris Peace Conference.* He was born on May 19, 1860, in Palermo, and he died on December 1, 1952, in Rome. Orlando was an internationally renowned jurist; the author of numerous works on public law and administration; and professor of constitutional law at the universities of Modena (1885) and Messina (1886), of administrative law at Palermo (1889), and of public and constitutional law at Rome (1901–31). In parliament (1897–1925) he sat among the Liberal Left. Orlando held cabinet posts under Giovanni Giolitti* (Education, 1903–5; Justice, 1907–9); Antonio Salandra* (Justice, 1914–16); and Paolo Boselli* (Interior, 1916–17). In the last post he attemped to reconcile the neutralist Giolittians, Socialists, and Catholics to the war effort, succeeding to the premiership in the midst of the Caporetto catastrophe (October 29, 1917). During the last year of the war he was faced by divisions within the government over full implementation of the Pact of London* in contrast with Yugoslav claims to territories promised to Italy under the pact. The crisis culminated at the Paris Peace Conference, where Orlando and Foreign Minister Sidney Sonnino* clashed with President Woodrow Wilson (April 1919), especially over Fiume.* Shaken by general discontent with the dubious fruits of victory, Orlando resigned in June 1919. After failing twice in 1922 to form a national coalition government to end the postwar parliamentary paralysis, Orlando gave his support to Mussolini* in November 1922, and was included in the governmental list of candidates in the April 1924 elections. Disillusioned in his hopes that Fascism* could be transformed into a constitutional movement, he openly broke with it in January 1925 and resigned from the Chamber in August. In 1931 he resigned his university chair to avoid taking the oath of loyalty to the regime; and although he supported the Ethiopian War (1935), he opposed participation in World War II,* and was among the King's advisers in the coup that ousted Mussolini on July 25, 1943. Orlando resumed his university post in 1944, when he became president of the Chamber of Deputies, and in June 1946 was elected to the Constituent Assembly.* In 1948 he was appointed senator for life under the Republic.

For further reference see: Vittorio Emanuele Orlando, *Memorie, 1915–1919,* ed. Rodolfo Mosca (Milan: Rizzoli, 1960); Giulio Cianferotti, *Il pensiero di V. E. Orlando e la giuspubblicistica italiana fra ottocento e novecento* (Milan: Dott. A. Giuffrè Editore, 1980).

SS

ORSINI, FELICE. After an early Jesuit education, this Romagnol republican and revolutionary (1819–58) studied law and philosophy at Bologna. The fanatically anticlerical son of a *carbonaro*, he participated in many uprisings in the Romagna* between 1831 and 1848. Orsini's call for prison reforms resulted from his own experience in papal prisons in 1844, when both he and his father were arrested. Perceiving republicanism as historically rooted in Italy, Orsini served as a volunteer in the Venetian Republic in 1848 and became a representative in the Mazzinian Constituent Assembly in Rome in February 1849. As French troops entered Rome, Orsini went into exile in southern France and wrote his memoirs of the Roman Republic. His role in the abortive Mazzinian risings of 1852–54 led to imprisonment after his arrest in Transylvania in December 1854. Later estranged from Giuseppe Mazzini,* Orsini joined other radicals in Paris who blamed Napoleon III* for failing to help Italy and plotted the assassination attempt of January 14, 1858. Defended by Jules Favre, Orsini wrote to Napoleon III from jail to plead Italy's cause, and his letter was read at the trial and published in the *Moniteur*. He was guillotined on March 13, 1858, but his abortive plot led indirectly to the Plombières meeting that year (see Plombières Agreement*) between the Emperor and Cavour.*

For further reference see: Alessandro Luzio, *Felice Orsini* (Milan: L. F. Cogliati, 1914); F. Orsini, *Lettere*, ed. A. M. Ghisalberti (Rome: Vittoriano, 1936); *Memorie politiche,* ed. Leopoldo Marchetti (Milan: Rizzoli, 1962); Michael St. John Packe, *Orsini: The Story of a Conspirator* (Boston: Little, Brown, 1957).

MSM

ORTES, GIAMMARIA. A Venetian cleric and economist (1713–90) whose major work, *Dell'economia nazionale* [On the national economy], was published in 1774, Ortes was an original but somewhat paradoxical critic of the mercantilistic monetary theory of value. He was neither a Physiocrat, in the sense of considering land the basic source of wealth, nor a proponent of labor value, although he advocated the division of labor and free trade. He held wealth to be fixed in quantity and dependent on population size, which made him in some aspects of his theories a precursor of Malthus, whom he also resembled in his defense of institutions promoting inequalities of landed wealth, including the *fedecommessi* (deeds of trust), and in his pessimistic view of the prospects for achieving material progress. In the last year of his life he published *Riflessioni* *sulla popolazione delle nazioni per rapporto all' economia nazionale* [Reflections on the impact of national populations on the national economy].

RBL

OSSERVATORE CATTOLICO, L'. See **NEWSPAPERS**

OSSERVATORE ROMANO, L'. A Vatican newspaper, the current *Osservatore Romano* was founded as a daily in 1861, although it had predecessors in 1849 and 1851. Begun as an independent "moral-political newspaper," after 1870 it became the authoritative but unofficial organ of the Holy See, publishing the Italian texts of papal speeches and pronouncements as well as other official Church announcements. Its editors are appointed by the Secretariat of State, and the *Osservatore*'s editorials and major articles are presumed to reflect the Vatican's views. During the Fascist dictatorship and the German occupation, *L'Osservatore Romano* was frequently the source of information not found in any other Italian publication.

SS

OTTOLENGHI, GIUSEPPE. See **JEWS IN ITALY**

OUCHY, TREATY OF. It terminated the Italo-Turkish War over Libya,* with preliminary and definitive provisions signed, respectively, October 15 and 18, 1912, at Ouchy (a suburb of Lausanne), Switzerland. Its text was published on November 26. Italy was acknowledged to be in occupation of Libya (Tripolitania and Cyrenaica) and it pledged to pay to the Turkish treasury an unspecified sum equal to Libya's share of Turkey's national debt. Amnesty was declared for Turkish inhabitants of Libya and for Italian residents of the Dodecanese Islands* seized by Italy during the war. Italy was to withdraw from the islands once Turkish evacuation of Libya was complete. The sultan was to attend to Ottoman civil and judicial interests in Libya, and to maintain his religious authority.

RSC

OVRA. This special and secret police, more an arm of the Fascist Party than of the Italian state, was created at the end of 1926 following four attempts to take Mussolini's* life in 1925–26. The first attempt was made by Tito Zaniboni,* a former Socialist deputy, who planned to shoot the Duce as he spoke from the balcony of the Palazzo Chigi. In the second, Violet Gibson, a deranged Irishwoman, shot Mussolini as he emerged from the city hall in Rome. In the third attempt, the anarchist Gino Lucetti attempted to throw a bomb under a car in which Mussolini was passing. Finally, Anteo Zamboni sought to shoot Mussolini when he appeared in Bologna. In 1926 Arturo Bocchini was appointed chief of police and developed this inspectorate or police force charged with the responsibility of suppressing every manifestation against Fascism* and its leaders. Precisely what the letters OVRA stood for is still uncertain. Some claim that they stood for Opera Vigilanza Repressione Antifascismo, while others have opted for Opera Volontaria Repressione Antifascista. Denis Mack Smith has maintained that the term was meaningless and was invented by Mussolini to intimidate opponents.

FJC

P

PACCIARDI, RANDOLFO. One of Italy's most prominent anti-Fascists and a major figure in the Republican Party* (PRI), Pacciardi was born in Grosetto on January 1, 1899. Forced to flee Mussolini's* Italy, he took up residence first in Switzerland and then in France, organizing Italian resistance to Fascism.* He seized the opportunity of the Spanish Civil War* to combat Mussolini and became commander of the famous Garibaldi Brigade.

After World War II* Pacciardi helped to establish the Republican Party and brought such figures as Ugo La Malfa,* Luigi Salvatorelli,* and Ferruccio Parri* into its ranks. In 1963, objecting to La Malfa's domination of party affairs ("comparable to that of [Palmiro] Togliatti[*] in the Communist Party," he said), Pacciardi left the PRI and attempted to establish a political movement called the Nuova Repubblica, which sought a strong presidential republic. In 1980, after years outside the Party, the man who in 1946 coined the slogan "Better in prison with the Communists than in a government with the Christian Democrats" returned to Republican politics.

RJW

PACELLI, EUGENIO. See PIUS XII

PACELLI, FRANCESCO. See LATERAN ACCORDS

PACT OF ROME (1890). A programmatic statement of Italian radical democracy formulated at a congress in May 1890, the Pact of Rome was authorized by Felice Cavallotti* and supported by independent republican Giovanni Bovio* and Socialist Andrea Costa.* It called for the revision of the constitution to reduce the powers of the executive, parliamentary initiative, pay for members of parliament, administrative decentralization, a volunteer militia, withdrawal from the Triple Alliance,* expropriation of untilled lands, an eight-hour work day, freedom of labor to organize, social insurance laws, a single and progressive tax on incomes, reform of the judicial system, and tuition-free education at all levels. The pact's program long remained the guiding beacon of Italian non-Socialist democracy.

SS

PACT OF ROME (1918). This agreement was reached in April 1918 under Italian sponsorship at a congress of oppressed nationalities committed to the destruction of the Austro-Hungarian Empire. The pact's assertion of the right of the peoples represented to realize or complete their national unity and independence did not accord with Foreign Minister Sidney Sonnino's* insistence on the full implementation of the Pact of London* (April 1915), the terms of which contrasted sharply with Yugoslav aspirations in the Adriatic. The Pact of 1918, supported by Prime Minister Vittorio Orlando,* was another sign of his differences with Sonnino, which played havoc with Italy's position at the Paris Peace Conference* in 1919. It is not to be confused with the program of identical name propounded by Extreme Left (see Sinistra, La*) elements in Italy in 1890.

SS

PACT OF STEEL. This military alliance between the regimes of Fascist Italy and Nazi Germany, signed on May 22, 1939, required each signatory government to support the other if it became involved in a war. Mussolini,* angered over Hitler's sudden annexation of Austria in March 1938 and still tied down himself in the Spanish Civil War,* had evaded alliance talks with the Nazi government for over a year. His sudden decision to conclude such a pact with Hitler reflected his belief in Germany's inevitable ascendancy in Europe and a desire to win major territorial gains for Fascist Italy. Mussolini surmised wrongly that Hitler would not actually unleash a war before 1943.

When Hitler started World War II* in September 1939, Mussolini chose "nonbelligerency" for Italy on the ground that Italy was not militarily or economically prepared. He changed his mind and plunged into the fighting on June 10, 1940, when Germany seemed on the edge of total victory in France. Italy's participation in the war exposed its unreadiness, Hitler's unwillingness to consult his ally in making decisions, and the lack of harmony in the objectives of Germany and Italy. Mussolini's fall from power on July 25, 1943, led to the dissolution in September of the alliance, which had never been popular in Italy.

For further reference see: F. W. Deakin, *The Brutal Friendship* (New York: Harper and Row, 1962); Elizabeth Wiskemann, *The Rome-Berlin Axis* (London: Collins, 1966); Mario Toscano, *Le origine diplomatiche del patto d'acciaio* (Florence: G. C. Sansoni, 1956).

JKZ

PAGANO, FRANCESCO MARIA. A leading eighteenth-century Neapolitan jurist and writer and a disciple of Giambattista Vico* and Antonio Genovesi,* he was born in Brienza (Lucania) on December 18, 1748. After earning a law degree, he was appointed professor of ethics and criminal jurisprudence at the University of Naples in 1770. In 1787 he published the acclaimed *Considerazioni sul processo criminale* [Considerations on the criminal process]. Influenced by events in France, he early joined the liberal movement in Naples, and when in 1794 some Neapolitan Jacobins* were arrested, he defended them. Although a justice of the Admiralty Tribunal (1794), he was soon denounced (1795) for his liberal activities, stripped of his teaching post, and imprisoned (1796). Released in 1798, he fled to Rome and Milan, but returned to Naples when the Parthenopean Republic* was proclaimed in January 1799. Pagano was actively involved in the provisional government and its defense. After the Bourbons' return in June, he was arrested and hung on October 29, 1799.

FFA

PAGINE LIBERE. See **ORANO, PAOLO**

PALLAVICINO TRIVULZIO, GIORGIO. A distinguished member of the liberal patriciate of Lombardy,* Pallavicino was born in Milan on April 29, 1796. In his youth he joined the secret society of the Federati* and took part in the abortive Piedmontese revolution of 1821 (see Revolutions of 1820–21*). He was one of three Lombard leaders who negotiated with King Charles Albert of Savoy* in the hope that he would introduce liberal reforms in his kingdom. He returned to Milan in December 1821 but was soon arrested. His confession to the Hapsburg police led to the arrest of Federico Confalonieri* and other liberals. Like them, Pallavicino served time in the Spielberg fortress, but he was pardoned in 1835 and did not join them in forced emigration to the United States.

In the spring of 1848 he had a chance to regain the respect of his former political friends by joining the anti-Austrian rebellion. He became one of the most prominent members of the Lombard Provisional Government, which favored constitutional monarchy and union with Piedmont-Sardinia. After the failure of the revolution he settled in Turin, where he remained very active politically. In 1857, with the Venetian Daniele Manin,* Pallavicino founded the Società Nazionale Italiana,* which tried to unify all segments of the Italian nationalist movement under a program of independence, territorial unity, and constitutional government. In 1859 Pallavicino played a major role in the annexation movements of North-Central Italy, and in 1860 he represented the King in Naples. Having served in the Sardinian legislature in the 1850s, he was made a senator at the time of unification. He died at Genestrelle, near Casteggio, on August 4, 1878, leaving interesting memoirs that were edited for publication by his wife and daughter.

CML

PAN. See **OJETTI, UGO**

PANIZZI, ANTONIO. Librarian and patriot, he was born in Brascello near Modena on September 16, 1797. He attended the University of Parma and received a degree in law but did not have much time to practice his profession because his association with the Carboneria* led to his exile in 1821. He left for Switzerland and in 1822 found his way to England, where he was well received by Piedmontese and Lombard exiles, especially Ugo Foscolo.* To support himself Panizzi wrote articles and taught Italian; in 1828 he became professor of Italian language and literature at the University College, London. In 1831 he was named assistant librarian of the British Museum and in 1856 assumed the post of chief librarian, which he held until 1867. While at the British Museum his ninety-one rules became the basis of the museum's catalogue, which he reorganized; he also restructured the main reading room. Never forgetting his homeland, Panizzi maintained a correspondence with Cavour,* Massimo D'Azeglio,* Giuseppe Mazzini,* and Giuseppe Garibaldi,* among others. His essays and pleas on behalf of Italy played a part in winning over English public opinion to the cause of Italian independence and unity. Knighted in 1869, he died in London on April 8, 1879.

FJC

PANTALEONI, DIOMEDE. This well-known physician and political figure was born in Macerata on March 21, 1810. He received his degree in medicine at the University of Rome and practiced his profession prior to his involvement in political matters. Elected to the Chamber conceded by Pius IX* in 1848, he assumed a moderate position and opposed the extreme measures of the radical Left (see Sinistra, La*). Following the Pope's flight from Rome he suggested that a deputation be sent to Gaeta* to urge him to return to the capital. Consequently, he opposed the calling of the constituent assembly which voted for the termination of the papacy's temporal power. Despite his opposition to the creation of the Roman Republic, he remained in the capital during its brief existence.

Pantaleoni remained in Rome following the papal restoration but made frequent and long trips to Piedmont, France, Germany, and England, forming friendships with some of the leading figures in these countries. He sought to persuade Pius IX to return to a constitutional course and favored the reformism of Marco Minghetti* and Giuseppe Pasolini.* Like them, he too eventually adhered to the politics of Cavour,* who incorporated parts of the Papal States* into the Kingdom of Italy.* In 1861 Cavour entrusted Father Carlo Passaglia* and Pantaleoni with the task of securing papal approval for the annexation by having Pius renounce the temporal power. This diplomatic mission ended in failure, and Pantaleoni was asked to leave Rome.

Pantaleoni found his way to Paris, continued to correspond with his friends and associates in the moderate constitutional party in Italy, and still favored a diplomatic solution to the Roman Question.* This was the position he assumed when he entered the Italian Senate at the end of 1883. In 1884 he published a volume on the Roman Question entitled *L'idea italiana nella soppressione del potere temporale dei papi* [The Italian idea in the suppression of the temporal power of the popes]. He died in Rome on May 3, 1885.

For further reference see: Massimo D'Azeglio and Diomede Pantaleoni, *Carteggio inedito* (Turin, 1888).

FJC

PANTALEONI, MAFFEO. This well-known economist and political figure, the son of Diomede Pantaleoni* and an English mother, was born in Frascati on July 2, 1857. He studied the classics in Germany and took his degree in law at the University of Rome (1881). At twenty-five he became professor of economics at the University of Camerino and subsequently taught at the schools of commerce in Venice, Bari, and the University of Naples. In 1902 he succeeded Angelo Messedaglia* in the chair of economics at the University of Rome.

In 1882 his work on the shifting of taxation, *La teoria della traslazione dei tributi* [Theory of the transfer of taxes], appeared; it remains a classic treatment of the subject. A few years later his chief work in economic theory, *Principi di economia pura* [Principles of pure economy] (1889), which analyzed the theory of marginal utility, was published in Florence. In his other works he estimated the national wealth of Italy and elaborated the theory and technique of index numbers.

Pantaleoni, like his lifelong friend Vilfredo Pareto,* disagreed with many of the policies of the liberal, parliamentary regime, commencing with his criticism of its colonial policy in Africa. In 1901 he entered the Chamber of Deputies as a Radical, but after a few years left the party as well as the Chamber. A bitter opponent of socialism, during the Giolittian decade (1903–14) Pantaleoni found himself in harmony with the Nationalists. He was among the first to favor intervention in World War I* and fought the pacifists.

During and after the war Pantaleoni was increasingly involved in political journalism, writing articles for a series of newspapers and reviews. These were collected and published in five volumes. For a time he served as Gabriele D'Annunzio's* director of finance in Fiume* but soon parted company with the first Duce. He supported Mussolini* and the Fascist regime, and in 1923 represented the Italian government on the League of Nations Committee of Control for Austria. That same year he was appointed to serve in the Italian Senate. He died of a heart attack on October 29, 1924, while addressing the International Savings Congress held in Milan.

For further reference see: Edwin Seligman, "Pareto and Pantaleoni: Personal Reminiscences of Two Italian Economists," *Political Science Quarterly* 45 (1930): 340–46; P. Sraffa and A. Loria, "Maffeo Pantaleoni," *Economic Journal* 34 (1924): 648–54.

FJC

PANUNZIO, SERGIO. Sergio Panunzio, an influential Fascist theorist from the revolutionary syndicalist current and a major proponent of corporativism,* was born in Molfetta on July 20, 1886, and died in Rome on October 8, 1944. Panunzio enjoyed a successful academic career, winning a chair in political science at the University of Rome in 1927. He served the regime in a variety of posts, most notably as director of the first specifically Fascist institution of higher education, the Facoltà Fascista di Scienze Politiche at the University of Perugia. He was most important as a publicist, playing a central role in the debates surrounding each step toward a corporativist system.

As a syndicalist, beginning in 1903, Panunzio was especially concerned with the socializing attributes of socioeconomic organization. When it became clear, by 1910, that revolutionary syndicalism* could make little headway in the Italian labor movement, Panunzio spearheaded the revision that led many syndicalists through interventionism to Fascist corporativism. His mature conception was totalitarian, populist, and decentralizing. As a way of involving ordinary people more constantly and directly in public life, he proposed to organize society by economic sector and to diffuse legislative capacity into the resulting corporative groupings. Panunzio's conception differed considerably from the elitist and coercive versions of Fascist corporativism espoused by Alfredo Rocco* and Carlo Costamagna.

Panunzio was a persistent critic of the defects of Fascist corporativism in practice, but he continued until the fall of the regime to portray Fascism* in grandiose terms, as the solution to a universal crisis of modern liberalism. Thus, he ended up a mythmaker, giving Mussolini's* dictatorship a veneer of revolutionary legitimacy.

DDR

PAOLI, PASQUALE. Corsican patriot (1725–1807) Paoli's sojourn in Naples (1739–54) with his exiled father, Giacinto, exposed him to the Neapolitan Enlightenment,* especially through the influence of Antonio Genovesi.* He returned to Corsica and emerged as a leader of the continuing Corsican struggle against control by Genoa. Combining elements of enlightened despotism with grass-roots communal government, Paoli established at Corte a general council of elected representatives of heads of Corsican families. He enlisted the support of Corsican clergy while pursuing an anticurial policy, organized a modern army while a state prison helped to contain brigandage,* and established a new university. His antifeudal measures sought a more modern agrarian system and revived Mediterranean commerce. Protesting the cession to France of the island in 1768, he went to England, where Whigs hailed him as a liberal hero. An elected member of the Constituent Assembly in Paris in 1790, he served as military commander of Corsica but broke with the Convention (the new constituent assembly entrusted with the revision of the superseded monarchical Constitution) in 1793 and negotiated with the British to send a fleet to occupy Corsica. Rather than securing Corsican independence, Paoli's efforts made the island a diplomatic pawn. Yet he remained a symbol of the modern liberator, and James Boswell proclaimed him worthy of a place in the *Lives* of Plutarch.

MSM

PAOLUCCI, RAFFAELE. Raffaele Paolucci was born in 1892. A professor of surgery and a politician, he joined the Italian Nationalist Association* after heroic service in World War I.* Elected to parliament in 1921, he helped organize the Nationalist paramilitary Blue Shirt squads. After the merger between the Nationalist Association and the Fascist Party in March 1923, Paolucci became a member of the conservative and monarchist wing of Fascism.* In late 1924, during the crisis over the murder of Giacomo Matteotti (see Matteotti Crisis*), he attempted to organize a revolt of conservative deputies against Mussolini.* After 1945 Paolucci became a senator for the National Monarchist Party.*

AJD

PAPAL GUARANTEES, LAW OF. This law, enacted in Italy on May 13, 1871, unilaterally attempted to regulate relations between the Kingdom of Italy* and the Holy See after the seizure of Rome and its incorporation into the new state in 1870.

Composed of two sections, it defined the prerogatives of the Pope and of the Holy See, on the one hand, and specified the relationship between Church and state in Italy, on the other. By implication it sought to resolve the issue of papal temporal power raised by Italy's absorption of the Papal States* into the Kingdom.

The Pope was accorded royal status, and his person was declared to be sacred and inviolable. He was guaranteed full freedom to exercise all his prerogatives as head of the Church, with full rights of communication with Catholics world-wide. His right to full sovereignty in diplomacy was conceded. The law also guaranteed extraterritoriality for the Vatican and other apostolic palaces, villas, museums, and libraries.

Furthermore, the Italian government accorded the papacy an annual grant of 3.225 million lire; this sum was regularly deposited for the Holy See but was never recognized or drawn upon by the popes. For its part, the Italian government forbade any restrictions on meetings of the clergy in territory under its rule and also renounced any requirement of loyalty to the King of Italy on the part of bishops as well as any right of control over acts of clerical authorities unless they violated Italian law.

The Law of Guarantees was never recognized by the popes, who continued to regard themselves as prisoners in the Vatican and the victims of a usurping power which had denied papal temporal power. Relations with Italy were ulti-mately regularized by the Lateran Accords* of February 11, 1929, negotiated and ratified by Mussolini's* government and the Vatican under Pius XI.*

BFB

PAPAL STATES. The Papal States comprised the territory in central Italy ruled by the popes. They first took definite form in the middle of the eighth century, when the territory that the popes had ruled *de facto* since the fall of the Roman Empire was formally confirmed to them by the Frankish kings who dominated Italy. The immediate purpose of this temporal power was to provide the papacy with the revenue to carry out its spiritual mission; the long-term purpose was to provide the papacy with the political independence considered necessary for its spiritual freedom of action. Militarily weak, the states depended upon the papacy's spiritual prestige for protection; but this proved inadequate when, in 1797, the armies of revolutionary France invaded and eventually annexed the territory. The temporal power was restored by the Congress of Vienna* in 1815; but by this time the experience of the progressive and secular French administration had stimulated dissatisfaction with the antiquated ecclesiastical regime. The secretary of state, Ercole Consalvi,* attempted to satisfy this discontent with a reform program, but he was driven from power by the reactionaries in 1823. The reactionary policy that was followed after his fall provoked the 1831 revolution (see Revolutions of 1831*), which was suppressed only by Austrian intervention. The urgent need for reform was now evident; but nothing was done, and discontent continued to grow. By 1846, when Pius IX* came to power, it was too late for his program of moderate reform to satisfy public opinion. In November 1846 he had to flee a radical uprising, and was restored only by French intervention. Thereafter the Papal States were clearly dependent on foreign protection, and when in 1870 the French garrison was withdrawn, the Italian army occupied Rome. With the formal annexation of Rome to Italy on October 6, 1870, the Papal States came to an end.

For further reference see: Mario Varavale and Alberto Caracciolo, *Lo stato pontificio* (Turin: UTET, 1978).

                                                                           AJR

PAPE ET LE CONGRÈS, LE. This was a brochure that appeared in Paris on December 22, 1859. While authored by Arthur de La Gueronnière, it was immediately attributed to Napoleon III,* who had in fact inspired it. It invited the Pope to consider the benefits of relinquishing all of his territories, with the exception of the Patrimony of St. Peter. The smaller his territory, the author contended, the greater would be his spiritual authority. France would not help restore the rebellious Legations* to papal control, nor would it permit Austria to do so. The brochure aroused a passionate controversy and aborted the congress that France had called to deal with the Italian Question.

                                                                           RCu

PAPINI, GIOVANNI. This critic, novelist, poet, and journalist was a central figure—with Giuseppe Prezzolini*—in the Modernist-pragmatist literary movement that brought Italy into the mainstream of European culture before World War I.* Born in Florence on January 9, 1881, and for the most part privately educated, Papini was a precocious writer. With the young Prezzolini, he co-founded the activist literary-philosophical journal *Leonardo* (1903–5), contributed anti-Socialist, pro-nationalist articles to *Il Regno** (1903–5), and wrote for Prezzolini's *La Voce** (1908–16). In 1913, with Ardegno Soffici* and others, he founded *Lacerba*, for a time the major literary organ of Italian Futurism.* But Papini was too restless to be an adherent of any new movement for long. His shifts from pragmatism to Futurism, from agnosticism to Catholicism, and from critical severity to enthusiastic encouragement of new writers, mirror in a highly personal manner the main currents and countercurrents of Italian cultural life in his time.

The writings that early made his reputation include the precocious *Crepuscolo dei filosofi* [Twilight of the philosophers] (1906); *Il pilota cieco* [The blind pilot] (1907); the autobiographical novel *Un uomo finito* [The failure] (1912); and *Stroncature* [Savage reviews] (1916). His controversial "conversion" to Christianity expressed itself in *Storia di Cristo* [Life of Christ] (1921); *Sant'Agostino* [St. Augustine] (1929); and *Dante Vivo* [The living Dante] (1933). Papini nearly lost his eyesight in 1935. In 1939 he published his fervent *Italia mia* [My Italy]; but during World War II* he sank into a mood of profound pessimism. By 1952 a severe paralysis began to set in. Nevertheless, he continued his literary activity until his death in Florence on July 7, 1956.

AP

PARETO, VILFREDO. This Italian economist, sociologist, and political theorist was born in Paris on July 15, 1848, the son of an exiled Mazzinian engineer, Raffaele Pareto, and his French wife, Marie Meténier. Little is known about the family's exile, which ended in 1858. Vilfredo completed his education at the Polytechnic Institute in Turin and in 1870, following his graduation, went to Rome to serve as a managerial engineer with the Roman Railway Company. He transferred to Florence in 1874 to assume the directorship of the Valdarno Iron Works. There he commenced his crusade against protectionism and the policies of the various Italian ministries.

Pareto was drawn to the study of economics by the works of Maffeo Pantaleoni* and Leon Walras. In 1893, with the retirement of Walras, he assumed the chair in political economy at the University of Lausanne. Following the death of his uncle Domenico in 1898, Pareto inherited a considerable fortune, which enabled him to withdraw to a villa at Céligny in Switzerland and write. His first important publication was the two-volume *Cours d'économie politique* [The course of political economy] (1896–97), which sought to present economics within the framework of the natural sciences. The *Manuale di economia politica* [Manual of political economy] (1903–5), his most important work in economics, brought forward a general theory of economic equilibrium more refined than that of Walras.

Convinced that economics alone could not provide an adequate explanation for concrete social events, he turned to sociology, becoming one of its leading theorists. Pareto's sociological theory centers upon the concept of logical and nonlogical actions: the first linking means to an end, and the second lacking such a linkage. He stressed in his *Trattato di sociologia generale* [The mind and society: A treatise on general sociology] (1916), his major sociological work, that men were motivated by sentiments (residues) and provided rational explanations for their nonlogical conduct (derivations). He also maintained that while governments claimed to be founded on reason, they all relied on force, and even where universal suffrage prevailed, an oligarchy governed, disguising its actions by invoking the will of the people. His theory of elites assumed the domination of the less able by the more competent, as well as the domination of the state by the political elite.

Critical of representative government in general, Pareto led the campaign against the Italian parliamentary regime in the two decades before World War I.* His polemic against the liberal state influenced both the Nationalists and the Fascists. Mussolini,* who hailed Pareto as one of his teachers and as a precursor of Fascism,* nominated him to the Senate in March 1923. Opposed to all ideologies and suspicious of all parties, Pareto approved of some of the early political actions of Fascism but had reservations about its economic policies. He died in Switzerland on August 19, 1923, before Fascism had become a regime and before the onset of the ''totalitarian state.''

For further reference see: Giovanni Busino, *Gli studi su Vilfredo Pareto oggi* (Rome: Bulzoni Editore, 1974); Franz Borkenau, *Pareto* (London: Chapman and Hall, 1936); G. H. Bousquet, *Vilfredo Pareto, sa vie et son oeuvre* (Paris: Payot, 1928); Franco Ferraroti, ed., *Per conoscere Pareto* (Rome: Arnaldo Mondadori Editore, 1973).

FJC

PARINI, GIUSEPPE. The leading poet of eighteenth-century Italy, Parini was born in Bosio (near Milan) on May 22, 1729. He was educated at Milan and took holy orders in 1754. In 1752 he published *Alcune poesie di Ripano Eupilino*, which assured his early entrance into intellectual circles. The publication of the blank verse poem *Il mattino* in 1763 established his popularity and influence and marked a distinct and positive departure from the prevailing Italian literary mode in its robust realism and subtle irony. The Austrian plenipotentiary, Count Carlo Firmian,* took an interest in Parini and appointed him editor of the *Milan Gazzette* in 1768, and, in the following year, to a specially created chair of literature at the Palatine School in Milan.

His major work, *Il giorno*, encompasses, in four parts, the already mentioned *Mattino*, *Mezzogiorno* (1765), *Vespro* (1780), and *Notte* (1801), in which with unerring wit and skillful irony he instructs a young nobleman how to spend his day. He died on August 15, 1799, in Milan.

FFA

PARIS, CONGRESS OF. Convened at the conclusion of the Crimean War* in February 1856, the congress sought to find a viable solution to the ''Eastern Question.'' Russia's expansion toward the Mediterranean was checked by denying her control over the mouth of the Danube; imposing further naval restrictions on her in the Black Sea; and eliminating her protectorate over Moldavia, Wallachia, and Serbia, as well as her claim to interfere in Turkish affairs on behalf of Christian minorities. The Ottoman Empire, in turn, was included in the Concert of Europe, and its independence and territorial integrity guaranteed. In reality, the Congress of Paris portended other changes by affording Moldavia and Wallachia the opportunity to unite as an independent Rumania a few years later, and by allowing Cavour* to raise the question of Italian aspirations before an international forum. Committed to preserve an existing balance of power, the congress unwittingly ushered in a new age of nationalism.

JWB

PARIS PEACE CONFERENCE, ITALY AT THE. Italy's position at the Paris Peace Conference (1919) was compromised by the fact that the United States was not a signatory to the Pact of London* of April 1915, and therefore not bound by its provisions, as were England and France. While President Woodrow Wilson was agreeable to the cession of the Trentino,* the Cisalpine Tyrol (with over 200,000 German-speaking inhabitants), Trieste,* and most of Istria* (with a large Yugoslav population), he demurred regarding Fiume,* which, although half Italian, had not been assigned to Italy by the Pact of London and was claimed by Yugoslavia. Wilson also supported Yugoslav demands for the province of Dalmatia,* granted to Italy by the pact but preponderantly Yugoslav in population. Italy could therefore either stand on the letter of the Pact of London, and renounce all claims to Fiume (which was Foreign Minister Sidney Sonnino's* position), or, as Prime Minister Vittorio Orlando* preferred, bargain for all of Istria and Fiume and renounce Dalmatia. But at first the Italian delegation claimed Fiume in addition to all that was promised Italy in the Pact of London. When, on April 13, 1919, President Wilson appealed to the Italian people over the heads of the Italian delegation, Orlando and Sonnino withdrew from the conference in protest, returning to an enthusiastic welcome in Italy. The enthusiasm did not last; and when the conference proceeded with the peace treaties in Italy's absence, Orlando and Sonnino returned to Paris early in May. The subsequent failure to reach any compromise with Wilson and the Yugoslavs was one factor in the overturning of Orlando's government by an adverse vote in parliament on June 19, 1919. Although the Treaty of Saint-Germain with Austria (September 10, 1919) accorded Italy most of what it had been promised in the Pact of London, the sensation of defeat at the peace tables persisted long thereafter, occasioning Gabriele D'Annunzio's* seizure of Fiume (September 12) and a bitter nationalist resentment that was to feed the nascent Fascist movement.

For further reference see: René Albrecht-Carrié, *Italy at the Paris Peace Conference* (New York: Columbia University Press, 1938); Silvio Crespi, *Diario,*

1917–1919: Alla difesa d'Italia in guerra e a Versailles, 2nd ed. (Milan: Mondadori, 1938).

SS

PARLIAMENT, STRUCTURE OF, BEFORE 1922. Under the Piedmontese constitution of 1848 (the *Statuto**), adopted by the Kingdom of Italy* in 1861, parliament consisted of two houses: a Senate of lifetime royal appointees with no limit of number, and a Chamber of Deputies whose members were elected for a term of five years among eligible male citizens over age thirty, without remuneration until after 1912. Elected by male suffrage enlarged in 1882 and made nearly universal by 1912 (1.9 percent of the population eligible to vote in 443 single-member constituencies in 1861; 6.9 percent in 135 multiple-member constituencies in 1882, returned to 508 single-member colleges in 1892; 23.2 percent in 1913; and 27.3 percent with proportional representation in 1919), the Chamber of Deputies increased its ascendancy over the Senate under Cavour* and his successors, making of the Senate a largely honorific body by the end of the century. Although the executive power and the appointment and dismissal of ministers were royal prerogatives (Articles 5, 65, 67), parliamentary practice increasingly made the government a creature of the two houses, especially the deputies, whose vote of no confidence, although not binding on the King, customarily required the government's resignation. Legislative power was shared by king and parliament (Article 3); but tradition and the *Statuto*'s requirement that all tax and budgetary bills be presented first to the lower house (Article 10) gave legislative primacy to the Chamber of Deputies. Similarly, foreign policy was within the royal domain; however, Article 5's specification that all treaties entailing financial obligations or territorial changes be approved by parliament restricted royal initiative but did not extinguish it; witness Humbert I's* role in entering the Triple Alliance* (1882) and Victor Emmanuel III's* efforts to bring Italy into World War I* in May 1915. Finally, it was a parliament paralyzed by irreconcilable factionalism that made possible Victor Emmanuel's freedom to appoint Mussolini* prime minister in October 1922, soon after which both parliament and crown were reduced to subject status.

For further reference see: Gaetano Arangio-Ruiz, *Storia costituzionale del regno d'Italia, 1848–1898* (Florence: G. Civelli, 1898); Alberto Caracciolo, *Il parlamento nella formazione del regno d'Italia* (Milan: A. Giuffrè, 1960); Giampiero Carocci, ed., *Il parlamento nella storia d'Italia* (Bari: Laterza, 1964).

SS

PARRI, FERRUCCIO. Ferruccio Parri, born in 1890 in Piedmont, came from a family of democratic, Mazzinian convictions. A young officer in World War I,* he fought at the front and served later in the High Command. His anti-Fascist activities began in 1921 and were stimulated by the Matteotti Crisis* of 1924. After the installation of the dictatorship in 1925 he helped leading Socialists escape from Italy. Arrested in 1927, he spent the next five years in and out of

Fascist prisons. He was amnestied in 1932 and worked for a decade in economic research, while associated in Milan with the Justice and Liberty movement.* In 1942 he was again arrested and held for six months.

In early 1943 Parri participated in the founding of the Action Party.* After Italy's surrender to the Allies in September of that year, he became a principal organizer of the partisan Armed Resistance* in northern Italy behind the German lines. He was an Action Party member of the Committee of National Liberation of Upper Italy (CLNAI*) and the *de facto* head of the Volunteers of Liberty Corps, the military command of the anti-Fascist partisan units fighting behind the Nazi lines.

After the war ended in Europe in June 1945, Parri became the prime minister of Italy. These were difficult times, and his cabinet fell after five months in office. The Action Party dissolved in 1946, and he joined the Republican Party.* He served as a senator, first in the Republican Party, and in 1958 was elected as an independent senator on the Socialist list. In 1963 Parri was appointed a life senator. Parri died on December 8, 1981, at the age of ninety-one.

NK

PARTHENOPEAN REPUBLIC. The Parthenopean Republic was the state established in southern Italy by revolutionary France and its Neapolitan sympathizers after General Championnet fought his way into Naples on January 23, 1799. Ancient Naples was known as Parthenope, hence the name chosen for the new republic which, for five months, replaced the Kingdom of Naples, whose Bourbon ruler, Ferdinand I,* had fled to Sicily. A provisional government planned the abolition of feudal practices and other reforms but was frustrated by its own inexperience, French interference and exactions, and popular opposition to a novel regime propped up by foreign troops. It also had to contend with a counterrevolutionary movement led by Cardinal Fabrizio Ruffo* and the Second Coalition, and backed by Admiral Nelson's fleet.

Military reverses in northern Italy in the spring of 1799 forced the French to withdraw from the South. Unassisted, the Republic crumbled before Ruffo's forces, which were motivated by a thirst for booty, hatred of the foreigner, devotion to the monarchy, and religious faith. Upon his return to Naples Ferdinand wreaked vengeance upon all who had cooperated with the Parthenopean state, thereby alienating many Neapolitan intellectuals.

RCu

PARTITO COMMUNISTA ITALIANO (PCI). See **ITALIAN COMMUNIST PARTY**

PARTITO D'AZIONE. See **ACTION PARTY**

PARTITO LIBERALE ITALIANO. See **ITALIAN LIBERAL PARTY**

PARTITO NAZIONALE FASCISTA. See **FASCISM**

PARTITO NAZIONALE MONARCHICO. See **NATIONAL MONARCH-IST PARTY**

PARTITO POPOLARE ITALIANO. See **ITALIAN POPULAR PARTY**

PARTITO REPUBBLICANO ITALIANO. See **ITALIAN REPUBLICAN PARTY**

PARTITO SOCIALISTA DEMOCRATICO ITALIANO. See **SARAGAT, GIUSEPPE**

PARTITO SOCIALISTA ITALIANO (PSI). See **ITALIAN SOCIALIST PARTY**

PASCOLI, GIOVANNI. The poet who in 1905 succeeded Giosuè Carducci* in the chair of Italian literature at Bologna, Pascoli was born at San Mauro di Romagna on December 31, 1855. By 1876 Pascoli had lost six of his closest relatives, including his father, by assassination. *Myricae*, a collection of poems, is Pascoli's masterpiece. The focus in the first half is on the doings and concerns of the peasants. The theme of the second half is death. The work is a reflection of his personal tragedy and of the human condition in contrast to the naive optimism of the rationalist school. Pascoli died in Bologna on April 6, 1912.

RSC

PASOLINI, GIUSEPPE. This *Risorgimento** political figure and statesman was born in Ravenna on February 8, 1815. With his close friend Marco Minghetti* he was one of the principal exponents of the moderate liberal national party in the Papal States.* In 1845 he became friendly with Cardinal Mastai, bishop of Imola and the future Pius IX.* Reportedly, it was at the Pasolini Villa at Monterico near Imola that Mastai was exposed to liberal sentiments and read such works as Cesare Balbo's* *On the Hope of Italy* (see *Speranze d'Italia, Delle**) and Vincenzo Gioberti's* *On the Moral and Civil Primacy of the Italians*. Following Mastai's accession to the papacy, Pasolini was among the first laymen to serve as a papal minister, being appointed minister of commerce, agriculture, and industry in February 1848.

Pasolini was among those who urged Pius IX to grant his subjects the constitution that was promulgated in March 1848. However, following the Pope's allocution of April, in which he announced that he could not declare war upon Austria, Pasolini and the other lay ministers resigned in protest. Serving as vice-president of the Council of Rome during the Roman Republic, Pasolini left for Florence following its collapse. During Pius IX's visit to his northern provinces in 1857, Pasolini met with him and urged a return to moderate reformism, but to no avail.

From 1857 to 1859 Pasolini served as mayor of Ravenna and in 1859 played a major part in preparing for the union of the provinces of central Italy with Piedmont. He was appointed to the Senate in 1860, and Cavour* also named him governor of Milan, where he remained until 1862, when he was named prefect of Turin. Shortly thereafter he served as foreign minister in Luigi Farini's* government (1862–63), and thereafter was entrusted with political missions to England and France (1863–64). Following the war of 1866* he was appointed the King's commissioner to Venice, where he remained until 1867. Thereafter he retired from political life until 1876, when he assumed the presidency of the Senate. He died in Ravenna on December 4, 1876.

FJC

PASOLINI, PIER PAOLO. One of the leading figures of his generation, Pasolini was a poet, polemicist, novelist, and filmmaker. Born in Bologna on March 5, 1922, he attained a degree in letters, and it was his contact with the "Borgate"—the settlements of the unemployed outside Rome—that inspired his first novel, *Ragazzi di vita* [The boys] (1955), as well as the film which he wrote and directed, *Accatone* (1961). His poetry included "Le cenere di Gramsci" and an anthology in Friulian dialect, *Canzoniere italiane*. Pasolini's later films were *Mamma Rosa* (1962), *The Gospel According to St. Matthew*—a controversial life of Christ (1964)—and *Il Decamerone* (1971). He was brutally murdered in Rome on November 1, 1975.

WR

PASSAGLIA, CARLO. This theologian, born in Lucca* on May 9, 1812, entered the Society of Jesus in 1827 and by 1845 became professor of dogmatic theology at the Gregorian University in Rome. Constrained to go abroad during the revolutions of 1848,* he returned to Restoration Rome in 1849, resuming his chair and writing theological tracts. In 1850 he played an important part in preparing the definition of the Immaculate Conception, on which he produced three copious volumes. Subsequently, he found himself increasingly in conflict with the superiors of the Jesuits and left the order at the end of 1858. Protected by the Pope, he was awarded a chair at the Sapienza and was one of the theologians entrusted with the task of studying the question of the temporal power. He concluded that Pius IX* could renounce the temporal power to safeguard the interests of the Church.

At the suggestion of Diomede Pantaleoni,* Cavour's* agent in Rome, Passaglia sought to negotiate with cardinals Giacomo Antonelli* and Vincenzo Santucci for a solution to the Roman Question.* This attempt proved abortive, and Passaglia was constrained to leave Rome. He fled to Turin, where he was granted the chair of moral philosophy at the university there. Passaglia, who was laicized, still sought some conciliation between church and state, and this was reflected in his works and the journals he directed. These attempts earned him the criticism of the Church, to which he was only reconciled on his deathbed, when he retracted. He died in Turin on March 12, 1887, without seeing the conciliation he so desired.

FJC

PASSANANTE, GIOVANNI. See HUMBERT I

PASTORE, GIULIO. Minister in numerous postwar Christian Democratic cabinets, Pastore was born in Genoa on August 17, 1902. An activist in Catholic workers' movements prior to the Fascist consolidation of power, he was forced to resign his position as editor of *Il Cittadino*, a working-class daily. With the fall of Mussolini,* Pastore resumed his role in democratic politics and was elected to the first postwar Chamber of Deputies.* He held a number of cabinet-level positions, including minister for the development of the Mezzogiorno, and was reelected to the Chamber for the last time in 1968. On October 4, 1969, Pastore died after heart surgery.

RJW

PATTO GENTILONI. See GENTILONI PACT

PAUL VI. Pope from 1963 to 1978, Giovanni Battista Montini was born on September 26, 1897, of devout parents in Concesio, a small village outside of Brescia, and was raised in an atmosphere of political activism. His father, Giorgio, was an adviser to Pope Benedict XV,* a prominent politician serving in the Chamber of Deputies as a member of Don Luigi Sturzo's* Italian Popular Party* and the editor of the Catholic daily *Il Cittadina di Brescia*. Plagued by poor health, Giovanni Battista was nonetheless an exceptional student. He entered the seminary of the Brescia diocese in 1916 and was ordained in May 1920. Because of his brilliant academic record, the young priest was sent to Rome to study at the famous school for Vatican diplomats, La Pontificia Accademia Ecclesiastica. After his graduation, Don Montini was sent to the papal embassy in Warsaw, but returned to Italy after only six months abroad. After studying in Paris briefly, he established himself in Rome, serving in the Vatican Secretariat of State and as the Assistente Ecclesiastico to the Catholic University students of the Federazione Universitaria Cattolica Italiana (FUCI)* (1925–33). During the Mussolini* years, Montini distinguished himself as a quiet but persistent anti-Fascist, continuing his work among Catholic students and his research and teaching at the Pontificio Instituto.

In 1937 Pope Pius XI* appointed Montini Vatican undersecretary of state to Eugenio Cardinal Pacelli, the future Pius XII.* During World War II* Monsignor Montini worked quietly on behalf of the Jews in Slovakia and Hungary and on behalf of the persecuted Serbs in Croatia. In 1954 Pius XII raised him to the post of archbishop of Milan, where he gained a reputation as the "worker's bishop.'' Four years later Pius' successor, John XXIII,* bestowed upon Montini the red hat of a cardinal.

On June 21, 1963, when John XXIII died in the midst of Vatican II,* Cardinal Montini became the 260th successor of St. Peter, taking the name of Paul.

As pontiff, Montini continued Vatican II, bringing it to a successful conclusion in 1965. A reserved, ascetic, and intellectual man, Paul presided over the Roman Catholic Church in a period of radical change and was often criticized for his stand on birth control (encyclical *Humanae vitae*) and his attempts to limit more radical doctrinal interpretations of Vatican II. Always a progressive champion of the poor and of the Third World, Montini died on August 6, 1978, at Castel Gondolfo.* In his later years he was shaken by the political violence in Italy of the seventies, culminating in the assassination of his friend, former Italian prime minister Aldo Moro.*

For further reference see: W. E. Barret, *Shepherd of Mankind* (Garden City, N.Y.: Doubleday, 1964); Antonio Fappani and Franco Molinari, eds., *Giovanni Battista Montini giovane. Documenti inediti e testimonianze* (Turin: Marietti, 1979).

                                                                                                    RJW

PAVESE, CESARE. Italian poet, novelist, diarist, critic, and translator, Pavese was born near Turin in Santo Stefano Belbo on September 9, 1908. He introduced the works of Joyce and Faulkner to the Italian audience, and his *Moby-Dick* is one of the great classic translations. Pavese was a political prisoner under the Fascists, but later worked as an editor for Einaudi, and received the Strega Prize for literature. His major novels are *Paesi tuoi* [The harvesters] (1941), *Il compagno* [The comrade] (1947), *La casa in collina* [The house on the hill] (1949), and finally *La luna e i falo* [The moon and the bonfires] (1950). His main themes are loneliness and the inability to surmount it. Pavese committed suicide in a Turin hotel on August 27, 1950.

                                                                                                    WR

PCI. See **ITALIAN COMMUNIST PARTY**

PECCI, GIOACCHINO. See **LEO XIII**

PEGASO. See **OJETTI, UGO**

PELLA, GIUSEPPE. Prime minister of Italy in 1953 and the chief architect of the "economic miracle,"* Giuseppe Pella was born to a family of poor sharecroppers on April 18, 1902, in Valdengo (Piedmont). He took a doctorate in political economy at the University of Turin and in the 1930s represented Italian textile interests at various international conferences.

In 1946 Pella was elected as a Christian Democrat to the Constituent Assembly* that drew up the Italian Constitution. In the same year he began his collaboration with Alcide De Gasperi,* entering the latter's government as undersecretary of finance. Pella subsequently served as minister of finance and as budget minister, becoming identified with a sound money policy, until 1953, when he formed his own government of technocrats. During his brief five-month tenure as prime minister, Pella weathered a crisis with Yugoslavia over Trieste* but could not unite the various factions of the Christian Democratic Party* the way De Gasperi had done. In later governments Pella served as foreign minister, minister of the budget, and minister of finance. Even during the economic difficulties of the 1970s, an aging Pella preached cautious optimism and faith, arguing that "a great deal of the possibility of [economic] salvation is in ourselves." He died in Rome on May 31, 1981, at the age of seventy-nine.

RJW

PELLICO, SILVIO. Italian revolutionary, author, and Christian moralist, Pellico was born in Saluzzo (Cuneo) on June 25, 1789. His earliest interests were in poetry and the theater, where romantic tragedies such as his renowned *Francesca da Rimini* (1815) linked his name with those of men like Vittorio Alfieri* and Ugo Foscolo.*

Attracted to revolutionary activities, Pellico wrote for the patriotic journal *Il Conciliatore*,* suppressed by the Austrians in 1819, and joined the Carbonari (see Carboneria*) in 1820. He was arrested by the Austrian police, sentenced to death for treason, and ultimately condemned to years of imprisonment. Pellico's decade-long experience in Austrian prisons ranging from Milan to the Spielberg in present-day Czechoslovakia provided the material for the Christian meditations published in *Le mie prigioni* [My life as a political prisoner] (1832) after his release. His later life was spent in Turin, where he died on January 31, 1854. Both nationalists, indicting Austrian cruelty, and clericals, citing his renunciation of violence, claimed Pellico as their own.

For further reference see: B. Allasson, *La vita di Silvio Pellico* (Milan: Mondadori, 1933); I. Rinieri, *Della vita e delle opere di Silvio Pellico* (Turin: R. Streglio, 1898–1901).

JCR

PELLOUX, LUIGI. Prime minister (1898–1900), Pelloux is always associated with the constitutional crisis that occurred at the end of the century. He was born on March 1, 1839, in La Roche (Savoy), and died on October 26, 1924, in Bordighera. A career soldier, he participated in the wars of 1859* and 1866,* and in September 1870 commanded the artillery that breached the gates of Rome. Elected to the Chamber in 1880, where he sat at the Left (see Sinistra, La*), he was made general by 1885 and senator in 1896. Pelloux was minister of war under Antonio Rudinì (February 1891–May 1892), Giovanni Giolitti* (May 1892–November 1893), and again Rudinì (July 1896–December 1897). At the time of the grave May 1898 disturbances, he acted with restraint as corps commander in the Bari area. Successor to Rudinì as prime minister in June 1898,

Pelloux attempted to calm the country with amnesties and reforms; but in 1899 he introduced a number of bills restricting the exercise of public liberties, thereby arousing the Extreme Left and eventually losing the support of the Liberal Left led by Giuseppe Zanardelli* and Giolitti. Faced by parliamentary obstructionism, Pelloux implemented the restrictive bills by decree (July 20, 1899). When the Roman Court of Cassation ruled the decree procedurally invalid (February 1900) and parliamentary obstructionism resumed, Pelloux called for elections (June 1900). Failing to receive the popular mandate he expected, he resigned at the end of the month, ending the crisis.

SS

PENTARCHY. This parliamentary alliance of five leaders of the Historic Left (see Sinistra, La*)—Benedetto Cairoli,* Francesco Crispi,* Giovanni Nicotera,* Alfredo Baccarini, and Giuseppe Zanardelli*—broke with Agostino Depretis* over the issue of transformism.* In May 1883 dissatisfaction with Depretis' increasingly conservative policies and close cooperation with the Right (see Destra, La*) led to a cabinet crisis during which Baccarini and Zanardelli resigned. An alliance of the ''pure'' Left was subsequently inaugurated in Naples on November 25, 1883. The new group's sympathies were anticlerical, pro-irredentist, and favorable to the grievances of the South and the lower classes. Crispi's acceptance of a position in Depretis' government in April 1887, however, signalled the Pentarchy's demise.

RJ

PEPE, GUGLIELMO. Neapolitan general and liberal Italian patriot, he was born at Squillace in Calabria on February 13, 1783. Pepe served in the army of the Parthenopean Republic* (1799) and fought with Napoleon I* against the Austrians at the battle of Marengo* (1800). Later he joined the army of the Kingdom of Naples under Joseph Bonaparte, continued in service under Joseph's successor, Joachim Murat,* for whom he commanded a brigade in Spain (1811–13), and distinguished himself during Murat's unsuccessful campaign to maintain his throne (1815).

In 1818 the restored Bourbon king entrusted Pepe with command of a division. When revolution erupted in 1820 (see Revolutions of 1820–21*) he had sufficient prestige within the Neapolitan army and among both Muratists and Carbonari (see Carboneria*) to assert leadership. He pressed the King to grant the Spanish constitution of 1812 and assumed command of the military. Defeated by the Austrians at Rieti (1821), Pepe was unable to save the liberal regime and went into exile. He returned to Naples after the revolutions of 1848.* Given command of a force sent to fight the Austrians in the North, he rejected Ferdinand II's* subsequent order recalling him and led some 2,000 men to Venice to assist Daniele Manin.* After the city fell (1849) he fled to Paris. He died in Turin on August 8, 1855.

RCu

PERSANO, COUNT CARLO DI. See **WAR OF 1866** and **LISSA**

PERSEVERANZA, LA. See **NEWSPAPERS**

PERTINI, ALESSANDRO. This political leader, journalist, and president of Italy was born in Stella on September 25, 1896. After serving in World War I,* he joined the Italian Socialist Party (PSI)* and soon took a strong position against Fascism.* Condemned for an anti-Fascist work in 1926, he was imprisoned for ten months for supporting the expatriation of Filippo Turati.* Emigrating to France, Pertini lived there as a worker and was twice arrested for political activity. In 1927 he returned clandestinely to Italy, but was recognized and sentenced to eleven years in prison. In 1943 he was freed, and with Giuseppe Saragat* and Pietro Nenni* helped reorganize the Socialist Party. He fought in Rome as a partisan and was condemned to death by the Nazi SS. Escaping to Milan, he became secretary of the PSI for occupied Italy and in 1944 took part in the liberation of Florence. From 1945 to 1946, and also in 1950, he was director of *Avanti!,* * and in 1948 became senator and president of the Socialist senators' group. Since 1953 a member of the governing committee of the party and director of *Il Lavoro Nuovo* (1947), in June 1968 he became president of the Chamber of Deputies* and in July 1978 president of the Republic.*

WR

PERUZZI, UBALDINO. A distinguished Tuscan liberal of the *Risorgimento* * and the scion of an ancient Florentine banking family, Peruzzi was born in Florence on April 2, 1822. He participated in the revolutions of 1848* on the moderate side but withdrew from political activity in the 1850s. After the flight of the grand duke from Tuscany in 1859, Peruzzi became head of the Tuscan provisional government and was instrumental in the annexation of Tuscany to the Kingdom of Northern Italy. He served as a deputy from 1860 to 1890 and as senator from 1890 until his death at Antella, near Florence, on September 9, 1891. After the transfer of the Italian capital from Turin to Florence, Peruzzi was also very active in local affairs and served several terms as mayor of Florence in the 1860s and 1870s.

CML

PETER LEOPOLD OF HAPSBURG-LORRAINE. The third son of Maria Theresa and the Emperor Francis I, Peter Leopold (1747–92) succeeded to his father's personal domain as grand duke of Tuscany in 1765 while his elder brother became Emperor as Joseph II. He was educated at Vienna in the era of reforms following the War of the Austrian Succession, and later proved to be an astute and capable ruler. In Florence he received collaboration and support from functionaries in the native bureaucracy appointed by the regents for his father, including Pompeo Neri,* Giulio Rucellai, Angelo Tavanti, and Francesco Maria Gianni.* The ensuing reform movement gave the duchy a European reputation for enlightened government. In 1767 Tuscany became one of the first European states to introduce freedom in the grain trade. To encourage manufacturing, the guilds of Florence and other cities were suppressed. In the 1770s the attention of the reformers turned to local government and to the administrative dominance of Florence, which dated from the time of the Renaissance Republic. There followed a significant restructuring of local communal institutions. In the 1780s further measures, affecting the relationship between church and state, encountered local resistance. With the new criminal code of 1786, Tuscany became the first state to abolish capital punishment. There were limits, however, to the success of the reform movement. Plans for a cadastral survey, for a new land tax, and for a Tuscan constitution and consultative assembly were abandoned. But Tuscany emerged as one of the most successfully restructured of the eighteenth-century Italian states. Following the death of his brother at Vienna in 1790, Leopold succeeded to the imperial title as Leopold II. As Emperor he was confronted with the political and diplomatic problems accompanying the outbreak of the French Revolution. On his death in 1792 he was succeeded at Vienna by his eldest son, Francis II,* while the Grand Duchy of Tuscany reverted to his second son, Ferdinand III.*

For further reference see: Adam Wandruska, *Pietro Leopolde: Un grande riformatore* (Florence: Valecchi, 1968).

RBL

PHYSIOCRACY. This school of economic thought was most typical of the Enlightenment* in France in the 1750s and 1770s, but it also attracted adherents in Italy. The center of the school in Paris was François Quesnay (1694–1774), whose *Tableau économique* was published in 1758. In contrast with the customary wisdom of his day, which emphasized the importance of specie in precious metals, Quesnay held that all wealth was derived from nature through agriculture. Farmers (the *classe productive*) were the only true producers of wealth. The seeming wealth produced by those engaged in nonagricultural pursuits, including the bourgeoisie (the *classes steriles*), was no more than the value of the raw materials utilized. Proper operation of the natural laws of economics should provide equitable distribution of net profits from the agricultural sector throughout the economy, through free operation of the market, returning a sufficient advance to the primary sector to assure economic growth. Quesnay's ideas were further developed by others, such as the Marquis de Mirabeau, Mercier de la Rivière, and Dupont de Nemours. Important doctrines of Physiocracy were the circular flow of wealth, laissez-faire, and the concept of a single tax on the net product of agriculture. The definition of wealth, and the distinction between productive and sterile classes, fell under criticism with the revival of interest in labor value by Adam Smith in the 1770s, and Physiocracy lost credibility as an integral system. In Italy, Physiocratic doctrine evoked much interest among contemporary economists, although with some differences. Although applauding the attention given to agriculture and to free trade in grain, the Italians were hesitant to accept blanket de-emphasis of manufacturing, and generally viewed the "economic laws" of Physiocracy with suspicion. They favored a more historical and empirical approach. The Neapolitan representative in Paris, Abate Ferdinando Galiani, in his *Dialogues sur le commerce des blés* [Dialogues on the grain trade] (1770), criticized doctrinal application of free export of grain. In Tuscany a split developed between Physiocratic (Pompeo Neri* and Angelo Tavanti) and anti-Physiocratic (Francesco Maria Gianni*) advisers of Duke Peter Leopold* on the issues of a single tax on agriculture and the degree of tariff support for manufactured goods. At Milan, Cesare Beccaria,* although a strong promoter of agricultural improvement and free trade, based his economic theory on utilitarian principles more similar to those of Adam Smith than to those of Quesnay.

For further reference see: George Weulersse, *Le mouvement physiocratique en France de 1756 à 1770*, 2 vols. (Paris: F. Alcan, 1910); Franco Venturi, *Italy and the Enlightenment* (New York: New York University Press, 1972).

RBL

PICCOLE ITALIANE. See **BALILLA**

PICCOLO CORRIERE D'ITALIA, IL. See **LA FARINA, GIUSEPPE**

PINCHERLE, ALBERTO. See **MORAVIA, ALBERTO**

PIOMBINO. The Società Alti Forni e Fonderia di Piombino was established in 1897 and began production in 1899 with a relatively small and technologically old-fashioned charcoal blast furnace and a foundry for iron tubing. Two years later, the blast furnace was shut down and pig iron production was suspended. This marked the end of the old establishment and the beginning of the modern one.

By 1905 Piombino was producing its own coke and using it to produce pig iron. By 1919 it had doubled its coking and blast furnace capacity, had added three Siemens-Martin furnaces and a rolling mill, and had become one of the largest and most technologically advanced steelmaking plants in Italy.

Piombino, along with a number of other iron and steel firms, gave the Società

Ilva* authority to manage its plants in 1911. At the end of World War I,* the firms merged to become a single corporation—Ilva, Alti Forni e Acciaierie d'Italia.

JSC

PIRANDELLO, LUIGI. Major playwright, novelist, and short-story writer of twentieth-century Italy, Pirandello became a dominant figure in European drama with the staging of his *Sei personaggi in cerca d'autore* [Six characters in search of an author] in 1921. He received the Nobel Prize in literature in 1934. Born in Agrigento, Sicily, on June 28, 1867, Pirandello studied at the universities of Palermo, Rome, and Bonn (Germany) before settling in Rome, where he began publishing poems, translations, short stories, and novels. In 1894 he married Antonietta Portulano, who bore him three children but later went mad. He started teaching, and abruptly found acclaim with the novel *Il fu Mattia Pascal* [The late Mattia Pascal] in 1904. In all, he wrote six other novels and some 250 short stories, most of them included in *Novelle per un anno* [A year's worth of short stories] (1920). He was past fifty when he turned seriously to playwriting. His first stage success was the Sicilian comedy *Liolà*, which echoes Machiavelli's *Mandragola*. The major plays fall into three overlapping categories, the first exploring the nature of theater, the second the complexities of personality, and the third the categorical imperatives of human community, religious faith, and high art. Besides *Six Characters*, his best plays include *Così è (se vi pare)* (It is so [if you think so]; 1917); *Enrico IV* (Henry IV; 1922); *Ciascuno a suo modo* (Each in his own way; 1924); *La nuova colonia* (The new colony; 1928); *Lazzaro* (Lazarus; 1929); *Questa sera si recita a soggetto* (Tonight we improvise; 1930); *Come tu mi vuoi* (As you desire me; 1930); *I giganti della montagna* (The mountain giants; incomplete, 1936). Pirandello travelled much in his later years as head of his own theatrical company, honored nationally and internationally. He died in Rome on December 10, 1936.

For further reference see: Anne Paolucci, *Pirandello's Theater* (Carbondale: Southern Illinois University Press, 1974); Gaspare Giudice, *Pirandello: A Biography* (London: Oxford University Press, 1975).

AP

PIRELLI, ALBERTO. An industrialist and public figure, he was born in Milan on April 28, 1882. As the younger son of Giovan Battista Pirelli, who in the late 1870s had founded the family firm in rubber and cable production, he shared the management of the enterprise with his brother Piero (1881–1956). During and after World War I* Alberto held important government posts and served as Italy's economic representative at the Versailles Conference. After the March on Rome* he became a fervent admirer of Mussolini.* His confidence in Mussolini eventually extended to the entire Fascist corporative state, which he praised for recognizing the importance of private enterprise. Pirelli died in 1971 in Casciago (Varese).

For further reference see: his two-volume work, *Economia e guerra* (Milan: Istituto per gli studi di politica internazionale, 1940), and his political recollections in *Dopoguerra 1919–1932. Note ed esperienze* (Milan: Instituto per gli studi di politica internazionale, 1961).

                                                                                                    RS

PISACANE, CARLO. The scion of an upper-class Neapolitan family with a tradition of military and government service to the Bourbons, Pisacane was born in Naples in 1818. He attended the prestigious Nunziatella military academy and began a promising career as an army officer. However, in 1847 his career came to a sudden end when he became involved in a love affair with a married woman, Enrichetta Di Lorenzo Lazzari. With her he fled abroad, where he gradually drifted into exile circles and became politicized. In the spring of 1848 he returned to Italy to defend the Milanese revolutionary government against the Austrians and later the Roman Republic against the French. Once again in exile, in 1851 he published a controversial account of the Lombard campaign, *Guerra combattuta in Italia negli anni 1848–1849* [War fought in Italy in the years 1848–1849]. Although sympathetic to Mazzinian nationalism before the revolution, in the 1850s Pisacane was influenced by Carlo Bianco's theory of guerrilla warfare and by French Socialist thought. In his *Saggi storici-politici-militari sull'Italia* [Historical, political and military essays on Italy], published posthumously in 1858–59, he argued that the Italian Revolution had to be a social revolution first and foremost and that it could be initiated by inciting the impoverished peasant masses of the South to rebellion. With Giuseppe Mazzini's* knowledge (but not his consent), in 1857 Pisacane planned a military expedition to his native Kingdom of Naples for the purpose of starting a peasant rebellion and overthrowing the hated Bourbon government. His goals were stated in a *Testamento politico* [Political testament], published after his death. The expedition ended in tragic failure, and Pisacane himself was killed on the plain of Sapri on June 2, 1857.

                                                                                                    CML

PIUS VI. Pope from 1775 to 1799, he was born Giovanni Angelo Braschi in Cesena on March 22, 1717. He entered the priesthood in 1738. Rising steadily in the Curia, he became a cardinal in 1773 and was elected pope at the conclave of 1775. His first fifteen years were marked by a losing battle with the Austrian Emperor and various German and Italian princes who aimed at reducing papal authority within their states. A still more serious conflict arose from the French Revolution. The Pope's condemnation of the Civil Constitution of the Clergy led to a break with the French government in 1791. Relations deteriorated steadily as the revolution became more radical and more anticlerical, until in 1797 Napoleon I Bonaparte (see Napoleon I) invaded the Papal States* and forced Pius VI to yield a large part of his territory. In 1798 the French seized Rome itself, replaced the papal government with a Roman Republic,* and carried the aged Pope off into captivity in France. He died at Valence, in Dauphiny, on August 29, 1799.

AJR

PIUS VII. Pope from 1800 to 1823, he was born Barnaba Chiaramonti at Cesena on August 14, 1742. He joined the Benedictine order in 1758. Having won a reputation as a theologian, he became a cardinal and bishop of Imola in 1785. During the French invasion of 1797, he created a sensation by declaring, in a homily that became famous, that the democratic form of government was not incompatible with Christianity, and, indeed, sprang from it. Partly because of the reputation for open-mindedness toward the modern world which this won him, he was elected pope at the conclave of 1800. His greatest problems were created by relations with Napoleon I.* At first, all went well: he signed the Concordat of 1801, which allowed the revival of the Church in France and became a model for the reorganization of church-state relations in the post-revolutionary era. In 1804, he crowned Napoleon Emperor. Relations then began to deteriorate when Napoleon sought to extend his control over the Church and to compel the papacy to take part in his conflict with England. Angered by Pius' opposition, he occupied the Papal States* in 1808, and in 1809 had the Pope imprisoned in France. The fall of Napoleon allowed Pius to return to Rome in 1814. His last years were devoted to repairing the damage done by the revolutionary era to the Church, and to attempting the reform of the Papal States. He died in Rome on August 20, 1823.

AJR

PIUS VIII. Pope from 1829 to 1830, he was born Francesco Saverio Castiglioni at Cingoli on November 20, 1761. He first became prominent as an expert in canon law. In 1800 he was named bishop of Montalto; here, his refusal to bow to Napoleonic encroachments upon the freedom of the Church led the Emperor to have him imprisoned at Milan in 1810. In 1816 he was named a cardinal and appointed archbishop of Cesena. Enjoying general respect among the cardinals, he was nearly elected pope in 1823, and was elected in 1829 as Pope Pius VIII. The brevity of his pontificate prevented him from realizing his plans for the reform of the Papal States* and the propagation of Catholicism outside Europe; perhaps his most important move was to recognize the July Monarchy created by the 1830 revolution in France, thus saving the Church from a dangerous association with the legitimist cause. He died in Rome on November 30, 1830, after a reign of only twenty months.

AJR

PIUS IX. Giovanni Maria Mastai Ferretti, born in Senigallia on May 13, 1792, was elected pope on June 16, 1846, and wore the tiara until his death in the Vatican on February 7, 1878. The longest reigning pope, he played a part in

European affairs, influenced the course of the *Risorgimento*,* and more than anyone else shaped the character of the Catholic Church and the papacy prior to Vatican II.*

Afflicted with epilepsy in his youth, he received holy orders in April 1819 and was assigned to the Roman orphanage of Tata Giovanni, where he remained until 1823. From 1823 to 1825 he accompanied the apostolic delegate to Chile and Peru and upon his return to Rome served as the director of the San Michele hospice until 1827. From 1827 to 1832 he was archbishop of Spoleto, afterward becoming bishop of Imola. While in Imola he was made a cardinal, in 1840; he was elected pope six years later.

During the first two years of his pontificate, Pio Nono's moderate reformism contrasted sharply with the conservative course of his predecessor, Gregory XVI,* and contributed to his liberal image. Meanwhile, patriots in the peninsula, influenced by Vincenzo Gioberti's* *Del primato morale e civile degli Italiani* [On the moral and civil primacy of the Italians], and by the new Pope's selection of Cardinal Gizzi as his secretary of state, expected Pius to provide the leadership for Italian unification. His failure to do so contributed to the revolutionary upheaval of 1848 in Rome (see Revolutions of 1848*), his flight from the capital to Gaeta* in the Kingdom of the Two Sicilies,* and the establishment of the Roman Republic in 1849. The Republic did not survive the year, toppled by the intervention of the Catholic powers—France, Austria, Spain, and Naples.

Following his restoration and return to Rome in 1850, Pius, who had earlier been hailed as the figure destined to reconcile liberty and religion, was condemned as the high priest of illiberalism. The loss of the greater part of his state to the Piedmontese, who proclaimed the Kingdom of Italy* in 1861, convinced Pius that a war was being waged upon the papacy and religion. He responded with the encyclical *Quanta cura*, to which was appended the Syllabus of Errors* (1864), which catalogued the principal errors of the times and included a condemnation of the separation of church and state, liberalism, nationalism, and democracy.

Pius, who supervised the affairs of the Church, left the execution of diplomatic matters and affairs of state in the hands of his secretary of state, Cardinal Giacomo Antonelli.* He reestablished the hierarchy in England (1850) and the Netherlands (1853), and favored the restoration of neoscholasticism. His devotion to Mary led to the proclamation of the Immaculate Conception on December 8, 1854. On April 12, 1855, he escaped injury when the floor of one of the rooms in the convent of Sant'Agnese collapsed, plunging him and more than a hundred seminarians to the story below. Some considered it miraculous that all escaped unharmed, while others considered the event symbolic of the fall of the papacy.

Determined to protect the prerogatives of the bishop of Rome and the dogmatic unity of Catholicism against liberal currents, Pius favored centralization in the Church, which became one of the hallmarks of his pontificate. Thus, the ecclesiastical particularism remaining in some nations was eliminated, and the autonomy of the bishops of the Eastern Churches, united with Rome, was reduced.

This increase in Roman and papal influence culminated with the declaration of papal infallibility (July 18, 1870), proclaimed during the course of Vatican Council I* (1869–70), convoked by Pius. Shortly thereafter, on September 20, 1870, the Italians entered Rome and made it their capital, eliminating what remained of the Papal States and ending the temporal power. Pio Nono's refusal to accept the loss of his state provoked the Roman Question,* which troubled relations between Italy and the Vatican for half a century, while his refusal to reach an accommodation with Otto von Bismarck* and the Liberals in Germany led to the *Kulturkampf*, Bismarck's conflict with the Catholic Church.

Pius found it difficult, if not impossible, to negotiate with those he considered responsible for the plight of the Church and the undermining of Christian values. This contributed to his self-imposed imprisonment in the Vatican and his sustained intransigence. Although liberals in Europe and patriots in Italy condemned his actions, the Catholic masses in Europe and America were moved by his goodness, simplicity, and courage in the face of adversity. Soon after his death there was talk of his beatification, and his cause was formally opened in 1955.

For further reference see: Alberto Serafini, *Pio IX. Giovanni Maria Mastai Ferretti dalla giovinezza alla morte nei suoi scritti e discorsi editi e inediti. I: Le vie della Divina Provvidenza, 1792–1846* (Città del Vaticano: Tipografia Poliglotta Vaticana, 1958); Frank J. Coppa, *Pope Pius IX: Crusader in a Secular Age* (Boston: Twayne Publishers, 1979); E.E.Y. Hales, *Pio Nono: A Study in European Politics and Religion in the Nineteenth Century* (Garden City, N.Y.: Doubleday, 1954); Giacomo Martina, *Pio IX (1849–1850)* (Rome: Università Gregoriana Editrice, 1974); also see the journal *Pio IX. Studi e Ricerche sulla Vita della Chiesa dal Settecento ad Oggi.*

FJC

PIUS X. The only pope to be canonized since 1712, Pius X initiated the codification of the Code of Canon Law (1904), effected liturgical and organizational reforms, relaxed the prohibition against Catholic participation in Italian national politics, and dealt severely with Modernism* within the Church. Born Giuseppe Melchiorre Sarto on June 2, 1835, in Riese (Treviso), he died on August 20, 1914, in Rome. Of humble origins and manner, to which he always remained true, he was ordained in 1858 and served as curate and pastor until appointed chancellor of the Treviso diocese in 1875. Bishop of Mantua in 1884 and cardinal patriarch of Venice by 1893, his cares were preeminently pastoral. Elected pontiff on August 4, 1903, the "nonpolitical" Pius X was soon faced by a crisis with the French government culminating in its unilateral repeal (1905) of the Concordat of 1801. His decision to permit some Catholic participation in the Italian elections of 1904 to check the growth of the anticlerical parties, and his further relaxation of the *non expedit** in 1909 and 1913, showed him to be more tolerant toward the Italian liberal state. But he was inflexibly opposed to the scriptural liberalism of Alfred Loisy and George Tyrrell and the Christian social democracy of Romolo Murri.* Holding Catholic dogma to be immutable, Pius twice condemned the Modernist theses in 1907; two years later he founded the Pontifical Biblical Institute to guide Catholic scriptural studies. His edicts and encyclicals on religious instruction, public prayer, sacred music, holy communion, and the Immaculate Conception attest to his traditional piety, which, with his charity and concern for the poor, formed the basis for his canonization in 1954.

For further reference see: Ernesto Vercesi, *Tre papi: Leone XIII, Pio X, e Benedetto XV* (Milan: Edizioni Athena, 1929); Dino Secco Suardo, *Da Leone XIII a Pio X* (Rome: Cinque Lune, 1967).

SS

PIUS XI. The Roman pontiff for much of the Fascist period, Ambrogio Domiano Achille Ratti was born to a working-class family on May 31, 1857, in the Lombardian hill town of Desia, the fourth child of Francesco and Teresa Ratti. In 1877 Achille Ratti entered the diocesan seminary and on December 20, 1879, was ordained a priest. After receiving a doctorate in canon law from the Gregoriana and degrees in theology and philosophy, Ratti embarked on a thirty-one-year career as a librarian that culminated in his appointment as director of the Vatican Library in 1913. During these years Ratti authored many scholarly articles, indulged his passion for mountain climbing, and stayed in close touch with his Milanese friends, among them relatives of the future Pope Paul VI.*

Ratti's placid life among his incunabula was interrupted in 1919 when Benedict XV* appointed him apostolic visitor, and later, nuncio to Poland, raising him simultaneously to the rank of archbishop. The nuncio's stay in Poland was brief, but Ratti was shaken by the near victory of the Bolsheviks in the 1921 Russo-Polish War, which only strengthened his anti-Communist sentiments. Recalled to Rome shortly thereafter, he was given the red hat of a cardinal and in June 1921 was appointed to the see of Milan.

In 1922 Achille Cardinal Ratti was chosen pope, taking the name Pius XI. A willful man, Papa Ratti, although he welcomed Mussolini's* initiatives toward Catholicism, often clashed with the Duce concerning Church rights in Fascist society. Known as the "pope of Catholic Action,"* he championed this lay organization, but withdrew his support from the Catholic Partito Popolare (see Italian Popular Party*). Confident of the efficacy of concordats, Pius presided over the 1929 *Conciliazione* in Italy (see Lateran Accords*) and negotiated concordats with many nations, including Nazi Germany. He openly clashed with Mussolini by claiming extensive educational rights in the encyclical *Divini illius magistri** (1929) and by condemning the anti-Catholic excesses of the regime in *Non abbiamo bisogno** (1931). In 1938 the Pope, exasperated with Nazism, issued his stinging repudiation of Hitlerism in *Mit Brennender Sorge*. Upon his death on February 10, 1939, at the age of eighty-two, Mussolini is reputed to have sighed, "At last that stubborn old man is dead."

For further reference see: Carlo Confalonieri, *Pio XI visto da vicino* (Turin: Editrice S.A.I.E., 1957); Zsolt Aradi, *Pius XI: The Pope and the Man* (Garden City, N.Y.: Hannover House, 1958).

RJW

PIUS XII. The 258th Roman pontiff, who reigned from 1939 to 1958, Eugenio Pacelli was born on March 2, 1876, within the Aurelian walls, in the shadow of the Vatican. He was the third child born to Filippo and Virginia Pacelli, members of the Papal or "black nobility." Young Pacelli studied at the Gregoriana as a seminarian and was ordained on Easter Sunday, 1899. Two years later, Don Pacelli entered the Vatican Secretariat of State, beginning a long tenure of service in the diplomatic corps. After holding a series of positions in the Curia, Pacelli was appointed nuncio to Munich and three weeks later was consecrated titular archbishop of Sardes. In 1920 he became the first apostolic nuncio to the new German Republic and remained in that country until 1929, when he was summoned to Rome by Pius XI* and given the red hat of a cardinal.

In the Rome of his birth once again, Pacelli's career flourished. In 1930 he was made secretary of state, replacing the aged Cardinal Pietro Gasparri,* and in 1935 he was appointed camerlengo, holding both prestigious posts simultaneously. Upon the death of Pius XI in 1939, Cardinal Pacelli was elected pope on March 2, 1939. He took the name Pius XII.

Pacelli's papacy endured for nineteen years and was marked by controversy. He worked tirelessly to keep Europe from plunging into World War II,* and failing this, to keep Italy neutral. Although technically correct and impartial in his relations with Axis* and Allies alike, Pius XII's policies were colored by his ardent anti-Communism, which led him to welcome the Axis campaign against the Soviet Union. Although the Pope directed the Church in Europe, and especially in Rome, to discreetly assist the Jews, and although he established the Vatican Information Service to distribute aid to, and information about, thousands of refugees, Papa Pacelli was widely criticized at the war's end for his public silence concerning Nazi crimes.

On the whole, Pius XII's papacy was marked by conservative doctrinal trends, but he did spur nascent stirrings for reform with the encyclicals *Mystici corporis* (1943), *Mediator Dei*, (1947), and *Divino affante* (1943). However, in 1950 he attempted to restrain the theological speculation that *Divino affante* encouraged with the encyclical *Humani generis*.

On October 11, 1958, Pius XII died at the age of eighty-two in the papal residence in Castel Gondolfo.* His death marked the end of an era for a Church poised on the edge of major reform.

For further reference see: Saul Friedlander, *Pius XII and the Third Reich* (London, 1965); Oscar Halecki, *Eugenio Pacelli: Pope of Peace* (New York:

Farrar, Straus and Young, 1951); J. Derek Holmes, *The Papacy in the Modern World 1914–1978* (New York: Crossroad Publishing Co., 1981).

RJW

PLACET. A term for the approval given by a secular ruler to ecclesiastical acts or enactments, required for them to have binding force within his territory, it applied to acts emulating from ecclesiastical authorities within his territory, as distinct from the exequatur,* which was required for papal acts.

The placet, or Regium Placet ("the royal consent"), first appeared in Europe around 1400. Its first appearance in Italy was in Sicily in the fifteenth century. After unification, it was retained in force by a law of 1863, but was eventually abolished by the Concordat of 1929 (see Lateran Accords*). Never fully accepted by the Church, it was long a major source of conflict in church-state relations.

AJR

PLI. See ITALIAN LIBERAL PARTY

PLOMBIÈRES AGREEMENT. Named after a spa in the Vosges region, the agreement resulted from a secret colloquy on July 20, 1858, between Camillo Benso di Cavour* and Napoleon III.* The French Emperor committed France to the support of Piedmont-Sardinia in a war against Austria, provided it could be justified to French and European public opinion as a defensive war.

Formalized by treaty on December 10, 1858, the agreement stipulated that in the event of a victory a federation of four states would be created under the presidency of the Pope: (1) a Kingdom of Upper Italy (Piedmont, Lombardy-Venetia, Parma, Modena, and the Papal Legations*); (2) a Kingdom of Central Italy (Tuscany, Umbria, the Marches); (3) Rome and the remainder of the Papal States*; and (4) the Kingdom of Naples. In exchange for her support, France was to receive the city of Nice and the Duchy of Savoy, and the young Princess Clotilde, daughter of Victor Emmanuel II,* was to marry Napoleon III's cousin, Prince Jerome Bonaparte.

The Plombières Agreement marked the success of the anti-Austrian policy initiated by Cavour in 1856. This policy was designed to free northern Italy of Austrian influence through an alliance between the King of Sardinia and the moderate elements of the Italian nationalist movement on the one hand, and, on the other, through a change in the European balance of power. Cavour's initiative coincided with Napoleon III's desire to regain for France some of the prestige lost in the unpopular Crimean War* and thereby to strengthen his regime.

After Plombières Cavour focused his efforts on creating tension on the Austro-Sardinian border and provoking the Austrian government into military action.

The result of his efforts, aided by a domestic political crisis in Austria, was the Lombard campaign of 1859 (see War of 1859*).

CML

PNF. See **FASCISM**

PNM. See **NATIONAL MONARCHIST PARTY**

PODRECCA, GUIDO. A brilliant satirist for *Avanti!*,* Podrecca was very active in early congresses of the Italian Socialist Party (PSI),* generally following the reformist line. As the years passed Podrecca became more conservative. In 1911 and 1912, for example, he openly supported the Libyan War (see Ouchy, Treaty of*) and published a book justifying the government's action, giving reasons that resembled nationalist arguments. In 1912 the delegates at the Congress of Reggio Emilia expelled him, and he joined the new Reformist Socialist Party founded by Leonida Bissolati.* He advocated Italian intervention in World War I* after 1914 and became an early supporter of Fascism* in the postwar period, participating in the meeting that initiated the movement at the Piazza San Sepolcro in Milan in 1919.

SD

POINCARÉ, RAYMOND, ITALIAN POLICIES OF. This French statesman and ardent nationalist (1860–1934) served as premier (1912–13, 1922–24, 1926–29) and as president (1913–20). Neither Italophile nor Italophobe, Raymond Poincaré considered French interests in relations with Italy. In 1912 he responded forcefully to the Italian interception of three French ships. In 1915 he helped draw Italy into World War I,* but regretted Allied concessions. Nevertheless, during the Paris Peace Conference* he urged the maintenance of good relations with both Italy and the United States, and in April-May 1919 bitterly criticized Premier Georges Clemenceau's* rejection of the former. In 1923 his concessions gained Mussolini's* support of the Ruhr occupation. Throughout the 1920s he conciliated Mussolini's Italy, but at the lowest possible French cost.

JB

POLITECNICO, IL. See **CATTANEO, CARLO**

POLITICA, LA. The most influential political review of the Fascist years, *La Politica* was founded in Rome in December 1918 by the nationalist ideologues (and later Fascists) Francesco Coppola* and Alfredo Rocco.* Following the latter's death in 1935, Coppola carried on alone. At the beginning the review featured an occasional article by Benedetto Croce* and Guido De Ruggiero.* It was consistently against the League of Nations, arbitration, disarmament, and the pursuit of peace as deliberate instruments of the Western democracies determined to safeguard their empires while preventing new countries like Italy from gaining their rightful "place in the sun." This review terminated publication in 1943.

RSC

POPOLO D'ITALIA, IL. See **MUSSOLINI, ARNALDO; MUSSOLINI, BENITO;** and **NEWSPAPERS**

POPULAR PARTY. See **ITALIAN POPULAR PARTY**

PRESIDENT OF THE REPUBLIC. The formal head of state, a position created by the Constitution of 1948,* the president is elected for a seven-year term by an electoral college composed of both houses of parliament and three representatives from each region, except Valle d'Aosta, which has only one. The president appoints the prime minister (who must receive parliamentary approval), five lifetime senators, and five judges of the Constitutional Court.* Although the president has a substantial number of formal powers, most of his acts must be approved by a cabinet member. Presidents of the republic have included Enrico De Nicola,* who served as provisional president (1946–48), Luigi Einàudi* (1948–55), Giovanni Gronchi* (1955–62), Antonio Segni* (1962–64), Giuseppe Saragat* (1964–71), Giovanni Leone* (1971–78), and Alessandro Pertini* (1978–).

EER

PREZZOLINI, GIUSEPPE. Giuseppe Prezzolini, writer, organizer, and disseminator of Italian culture, was born in Perugia on January 27, 1882, the son of a prefect. A man of inexhaustible curiosity and energy, Prezzolini was in the forefront of the idealistic reaction against positivism, socialism, scientism, and statism. Brilliant but lacking profound convictions, Prezzolini remained a cynic, unable to harness his talents and vigor to a single cause. From 1908 until 1914, he directed *La Voce** and made of it an agency of cultural nationalism and absolute historicism. In 1911 he established the *Libreria* of *La Voce*, which published many volumes, including translated works of foreign authors, and compiled and printed anthologies in several fields of learning. Prezzolini was an early advocate of intervention in World War I* and served in an official, noncombatant role. His early admiration for Mussolini* survived the murder of Giacomo Matteotti in 1924 (see Matteotti Crisis*), but was to be undermined by the Italian conquest of Ethiopia* in 1935–36 and the adoption of a foreign policy that was hostile to Great Britain and France. Prezzolini took pride in insisting that he had actually discovered the future Duce by having given him a national forum in *La Voce* in the pre-1914 years. The *Voce* publishing house brought out the first biographical study of Mussolini, that by Torquato Nanni (1915). By contrast, however, Prezzolini was never an enthusiastic supporter of the regime. Its violent methods and the church-state *Conciliazione* of 1929 (see

Lateran Accords*) aroused his concern, as did Italy's role in the development of the Rome-Berlin Axis.* Perhaps significantly, Prezzolini chose to be in the United States between 1930 and 1950 as professor of Italian literature at Columbia University and director of its Casa Italiana. Many people, anti-Fascists in particular, charged that the Casa had become an outpost of Fascist propaganda. This was never satisfactorily proved. While at Columbia, Prezzolini was responsible for the *Repertorio bibliografico di storia e della critica della letteratura italiana (1902–42)* [Alphabetical bibliography of the history and criticism of Italian literature], published in four volumes between 1937 and 1948. He returned to Italy after the war, but soon moved to Lucerne, Switzerland. He wrote for the Italian weekly *Il Borghese* and the dailies *Il Tempo* and *La Nazione*. His literary productivity consisted of fifty-seven books and seventy anthologies. He contributed articles to 136 periodicals or reviews in many countries. His most self-revealing works are *L'Italiano inutile* [The useless Italian] (1954); *Storia di un'amicizia* [History of a friendship] (2 vols., 1966–68); his correspondence with Giovanni Papini* in the years 1900–1956; *Diario, 1900–1944* (2 vols., 1978); and *Prezzolini: Un secolo di attività* [Prezzolini: A century of activity]. He died in Lugano, Switzerland, on July 14, 1982.

RSC

PRI. See **ITALIAN REPUBLICAN PARTY**

PRINETTI, GIULIO. Prinetti was a political figure who played a part in the Franco-Italian rapprochement at the turn of the century. Born in Milan on November 8, 1851, he received a degree in engineering from the Polytechnic Institute of Milan and in 1882 entered the Chamber of Deputies. In the Chamber he sat among the deputies of the Extreme Right and in 1887 was entrusted with the portfolio of public works in the second ministry of Antonio Di Rudinì.* He resigned from the cabinet when the prime minister moved closer to the liberal Giuseppe Zanardelli.* In keeping with his conservative tendencies, he joined Sidney Sonnino* and Luigi Pelloux* in combatting the obstructionism of the Extreme Left in 1899–1900.

Subsequently, Prinetti moderated his ultraconservative sentiments and entered the Zanardelli-Giolitti* cabinet (1901–3). As foreign minister he signed an agreement with France (see Prinetti-Barrère Agreements*) that not only confirmed the Visconti-Venosta-Barrère agreement of 1900 defining spheres of influence in North Africa, but also provided for reciprocal neutrality should either of the states be attacked by a third party or constrained to assume the offensive as a result of a direct provocation. Thus, while he renewed the Triple Alliance* with Austria and Germany, he emasculated it by means of his accord with France. Early in 1903 Prinetti was stricken by paralysis and forced to withdraw from the cabinet. He died in Rome on June 9, 1908.

FJC

PRINETTI-BARRÈRE AGREEMENTS. These secret 1902 Franco-Italian accords edged Italy toward neutrality between France and Germany. A series of agreements from 1896 to 1902 resolved a fifteen-year period of Franco-Italian tension. In 1896 the status of Italians in Tunisia was more clearly established. Two years later a commercial accord concluded a tariff war. In 1900 Ambassador Camille Barrère,* French foreign minister Théophile Delcassé,* and Italian foreign minister Emilio Visconti-Venosta* exchanged recognition of Italian interests in Libya* and French interests in Morocco. In 1902 Barrère and Italian foreign minister Giulio Prinetti* recognized Italian and French spheres of influence in Libya and Morocco respectively; Italian leaders also agreed to remain neutral if Germany initiated a war with France.

For further reference see: G. Déthan, "La rapprochement franco-italien après la chute de Crispi jusqu'aux accords Barrère-Visconti-Venosta sur le Maroc et la Tripolitaine (1896–1900)," *Revue d'Histoire Diplomatique*, 70 (October-December 1956): 323–39; P. Milza, "La politique étrangère française et l'Italie (1896–1902)," *Rassegna Storica Toscana* 13, no. 1 (January-June 1967): 47–80.

JB

PROMESSI SPOSI, I. See **MANZONI, ALESSANDRO**

PROPAGANDA DUE. This Masonic lodge (see Freemasonry*), led by Licio Gelli, grand master, created a scandal which in May 1981 led to the collapse of the government of Arnaldo Forlani, which was replaced by that of the Republican Giovanni Spadolini, the first postwar premier who was not a member of the Christian Democratic Party.* The activities of the lodge, which contained a membership from the military, parliament, and criminals, were brought to public attention when the police, searching for accomplices of Michele Sindona, uncovered a membership list that implicated some of the most important figures in Italy, including three members of the cabinet. Criticized as a "state within a state" and accused of bribing its friends and blackmailing its enemies, Propaganda Due was seen to plot the destruction of the constitutional state by altering the political system in a rightward direction.

FJC

PSDI. See **ITALIAN SOCIALIST PARTY (PSI)** and **SARAGAT, GIUSEPPE**

PSI. See **ITALIAN SOCIALIST PARTY (PSI)**

PSIUP. See **ITALIAN SOCIALIST PARTY (PSI)**

PUCCINI, GIACOMO. The major composer of Italian opera in the twentieth century, Puccini was born on December 22, 1858, in Lucca.* He was from a family of composers famous for church music in Lucca for several centuries. He studied at the Milan Conservatory. On May 31, 1884, his first opera, *Le Villi*, was staged in Milan with much success. His other works (with year of first performance) are *Edgar* (1889); *Manon Lescaut* (1893); *La Bohème* (1896); *Tosca* (1900); *Madama Butterfly* (1904); *La fanciulla del west* (1910); *La rondine* (1917); *Il trittico: Il tabarro, Suor Angelica, Gianni Schicchi* (1918); and *Turandot* (1926). While his middle period—especially *La Bohème, Tosca,* and *Madama Butterfly*—is still the most popular with the public, his later works have become increasingly known and appreciated through performance. Puccini died in Brussels while undergoing treatment for cancer of the throat on November 29, 1924. He is buried at Torre del Lago at the villa he lived in most of his life. The house is now a Puccini museum and archive.

JLD

Q

QUADERNI DI GIUSTIZIA E LIBERTÀ. See **JUSTICE AND LIBERTY MOVEMENT**

QUADRAGESIMO ANNO. Pope Pius XI's* social encyclical was issued on May 15, 1931, the fortieth anniversary of *Rerum novarum.* Quadragesimo anno* discussed social and political justice in the corporative state, rejected the legitimacy of class distinctions, and emphasized the organization of society along vocational lines for the common good. These "corporations" would be "composed of representatives of the unions of workingmen and employers of the same trade or profession" who would work toward peaceful collaboration. Both strikes and lockouts were forbidden in the corporative order and the "public authority" would settle outstanding differences.

The encyclical, although criticizing capitalism and Marxism, did not endorse Mussolini's* regime. Rather, it criticized Fascism,* labeling the New Order as "excessively bureaucratic and political."

RJW

QUADRILATERAL. The Quadrilateral was a strategic zone in northern Italy. Austrian military domination of the North Italian plain derived from control of the area enclosed by the Mincio and the Adige, the former guarded by Mantua and Peschiera, the latter by Verona and Legnago. These fortresses covered the approaches to the key Alpine passes linking Italy with southern Austria; they thus formed a "Quadrilateral" within which Austrian forces could regroup and receive reinforcements. This zone played a major part in Napoleon I's* Italian campaigns, and it was the refuge to which Count Radetzky* withdrew in 1848, as well as the stronghold from which he launched his subsequent reconquest of northern Italy. The fortresses remained in Austrian hands through the war of 1866,* after which they were ceded to the Kingdom of Italy.*

WDG

QUADRIPARTITO. See **ITALIAN REPUBLICAN PARTY**

"QUESTIONI URGENTI." This was the second of two articles in which Sidney Sonnino* put forth his political beliefs and programs on the issues he thought most important for Italy in the wake of national problems during the 1890s, which culminated in the assassination of King Humbert I* in 1900. As with "Quid agendum?,"* the first article, this essay appeared in *Nuova Antologia* (September 16, 1901, vol. 189: 316–45). "Questioni urgenti" carried yet further Sonnino's departure from the antiparliamentarian positions marking his career between 1896 and 1900.

Noting changes he expected to appear in the new century that he felt would make great demands on governments, Sonnino appealed to enlightened conservatives (in his language, "the constitutional parties") to unite and organize for progressive goals. More than before, he warned against threats arising from an increase in socialism and clericalism and challenges they presented to the liberal monarchy.

For Sonnino, "Questioni urgenti" was a manifesto addressed to the old ruling groups who had united Italy and who must now work to achieve reforms he deemed essential if Italy were to confront demands from various social forces coming to the fore in the twentieth century. Fundamental to his program were sweeping tax reforms and initiatives that would foster a cooperative alliance of capital and labor. The proposals in this essay epitomize the conservative reform program characteristic of Sonnino's parliamentary initiatives in the years when he was spokesman for the opposition to Giovanni Giolitti* during the period preceding World War I.* More reminiscent of that of an English Tory, the *noblesse oblige* that permeated Sonnino's thinking is evident concerning school legislation, liberalized agrarian contracts, strikes, municipalized public services, and protective legislation for emigrants.

BFB

"QUID AGENDUM?" An article by Sidney Sonnino* written in the aftermath of Humbert I's* assassination, it was published in the *Nuova Antologia* of September 16, 1900. In it, Sonnino called for national political unity behind the new King for the purpose of realizing a reform program that would free Italy from the ills that had afflicted her during the 1890s and that had led to the discontent culminating in Humbert's murder. As in "Torniamo allo Statuto,"* the author blamed Italy's particular mode of parliamentarianism for the country's plight. However, on this occasion Sonnino appealed for a truce between all parties and parliamentary groups to achieve a unitary effort for the national good.

The proposed agenda for national renewal espoused by Sonnino called for a two-pronged set of reforms in the sociopolitical area, on the one hand, and for economic and financial innovation, on the other. The comprehensiveness of Sonnino's ideas is demonstrated by the range of topics included: civil justice, the civil service, elementary schools, collaboration of labor and capital in industrial production, revised farm contracts, municipalization of public services, protective legislation for emigrants, commercial treaties, railroad concessions, the merchant marine, and local tax reform. The program became the foundation of the political platform Sonnino developed in the following years and which he later incorporated in the plan of government for his first Prime Ministry in 1906. Sonnino further refined his thoughts in "Questioni urgenti,"* published one year later.

For further reference see: "Quid agendum?" found in Sidney Sonnino, *Scritti e discorsi extraparlamentari, 1870–1920*, ed. Benjamin F. Brown (Bari: Laterza, 1972), 1: 679–708.

BFB

R

RACCOGNIGI, AGREEMENT OF. This pact between Russia and Italy, dated October 24, 1909, provided that each would try to maintain the status quo in the Balkans, but, more important, that Italy recognized Russia's interest in the Straits while the Tsarist regime acknowledged Italy's claim to Tripoli. In October 1908 Great Britain and France, Russia's associates in the Triple Entente,* had refused their approval of a Russian plan to send Tsarist warships through the Straits even though Austria-Hungary had agreed to such a proposal in return for Russian consent to the Austro-Hungarian annexation of Bosnia-Herzegovina. Italy's allies, Germany and Austria-Hungary, had been similarly cool to her Tripolitan ambitions.

JKZ

RADETZKY, VON RADETZ JOSEPH WENZEL, COUNT. Austrian military commander and governor of northern Italy, he was born at Vienna on February 10, 1766. Radetzky fought in all the major campaigns against Napoleon I* and was chief of staff under Prince Schwartzenberg (1813–15); he attained the rank of field marshal in 1836. As commander of the forces in Italy, he directed the retreat from Milan in March 1848 and the concentration in a defensive position within the Quadrilateral.* In July he overwhelmed Charles Albert of Savoy* at the battle of Custozza,* drove him from Lombardy,* and reoccupied Milan. After completing his defeat of the Piedmontese at the battle of Novara* (May 23, 1849), Radetzky pressed the siege of Venice; the city capitulated on August 24, 1849. After serving as governor-general of Lombardy-Venetia (see Lombardy-Venetian Kingdom*) through his ninety-first year (1849–57), he died in Vienna on April 15, 1858.

WDG

RADICAL PARTY. With unification achieved under a liberal monarchy after 1861, Italy's democratic elements, largely republican, were faced by a dilemma: accept the monarchy and try to democratize it, or remain in permanent and extraparliamentary opposition. Under the leadership of Agostino Bertani,* a group of radical democrats gradually abandoned their prejudicial republicanism and entered parliament, where, alongside intransigent republicans and a nucleus of Socialists, they formed the Extreme Left, in distinction from the Liberal Left, which had risen to power in 1876. Strong primarily in the Po Valley among lower middle and professional classes, radical democracy espoused universal manhood suffrage, administrative decentralization, a variety of socioeconomic reforms, irredentism,* anticlericalism, friendship toward republican France, and hostility toward the Triple Alliance.* With the ascendancy of Felice Cavallotti,* the Radicals organized their cadres and increasingly differentiated themselves from the Socialists, their competitors for mass support, as well as from intransigent Republicans. The three groups nevertheless collaborated in their opposition to Francesco Crispi* and Luigi Pelloux* in the 1890s; but after 1900, the Radical Party, most numerous of the three in parliament, and pursuing a policy of acting as a bridge between liberalism and socialism, moved in the direction of consistent collaboration with the government, supporting Giuseppe Zanardelli* and Giovanni Giolitti* (1901–3, 1903–5), and participating in ministries led by Sidney Sonnino* (1906), Luigi Luzzatti* (1910–11), and Giolitti (1911–14). Divided over the Libyan War (1911–12) (see Ouchy, Treaty of*), opposed to Giolitti's transactions with the Catholics in the elections of 1913, and fearful of losing ground to the rising Italian Socialist Party (PSI)*, early in 1914 left-wing Radicals forced the resignation of the three Radical ministers from the government, prompting Giolitti to resign. During the national debate in 1914–15 on participation in World War I,* most Radicals favored intervention on the side of the Triple Entente,* especially France, with which the party had close ties. With the political realignment following the end of the war, the Radical Party disintegrated in the wake of the electoral successes of the Socialist Party and the Catholic Popular Party (see Italian Popular Party*), with which it could not compete for mass popular support. Its current revived form faces similar problems.

For further reference see: Raffaele Colapietra, *Felice Cavallotti e la democrazia radicale in Italia* (Brescia: Morcelliana, 1966); Alessandro Galante Garrone, *I radicali in Italia, 1849–1925* (Milan: Garzanti, 1973); Giovanni Spadolini, *I radicali dell'Ottocento: Da Garibaldi a Cavallotti*, 3rd ed. (Florence: F. Le Monnier, 1972).

SS

RAMPOLLA DEL TINDARO, MARIANO. This cardinal and secretary of state was born in Polizzi, Sicily, on August 17, 1843. He studied in Rome and in 1866 was ordained. He subsequently served the Secretariat of State in the Congregation for Extraordinary Ecclesiastical Affairs and in 1874 was named a canon of St. Maria Maggiore. In 1875 he went to Spain as counselor in the Nunciature, becoming chargé d'affaires in 1876. In 1877 he was recalled to Rome and made secretary of the Congregation for the Propagation of the Faith and then secretary of the Congregation for Extraordinary Ecclesiastical Affairs.

Consecrated titular archbishop of Heraclea in 1882, that same year he was made nuncio to Spain, where he advised the clergy not to favor the Carlist cause. Named cardinal in 1887, some months later he became secretary of state under Leo XIII* and held that post till Leo's death in 1903. As secretary of state he assumed an intransigent position on the Roman Question,* opposed renewal of the Triple Alliance,* moved closer to Republican France, and sought cordial relations with Russia. He bitterly opposed the policies of Francesco Crispi.*

During the conclave of 1903, when it appeared that Rampolla might be the next pope, Cardinal Puzyna of Austria-Hungary imposed his government's veto. This right was respected, but Pius X,* Leo's successor, hastened to eliminate this privilege. Rampolla served Pius as secretary of the Holy Office and president of the Pontifical Biblical Commission until his death in Rome on December 16, 1913.

FJC

RANZA, ANTONIO. See **JACOBINS**

RAPALLO TREATY OF 1920. This Italo-Yugoslav pact, signed on November 12, 1920, by the two foreign ministers, Carlo Sforza* and Ante Trumbic, represented a compromise effort to solve the Italian-Yugoslav boundary and the Fiume* problem. The Paris Peace Conference* had upheld Yugoslavia's claim to this Adriatic port city on the grounds that it was more Yugoslav than Italian and that Italy already possessed the larger port of Trieste.* The Rapallo Treaty provided that Fiume would become a Free State while Zara and some Adriatic islands would be given to Italy, and Italy would renounce claims to Dalmatia.* Mussolini's* Fascist government in Italy was unhappy with the Rapallo Treaty. On January 27, 1924, Mussolini's government succeeded in signing a new Treaty of Rome with Yugoslavia which gave the city of Fiume to Italy but granted to Yugoslavia economic rights in its harbor as well as the nearby Port Baros.

JKZ

RASSEGNA SETTIMANALE, LA. This influential journal of politics, literature, arts, and sciences was founded in Florence in January 1878 by Sidney Sonnino,* Leopoldo Franchetti,* Enea Cavalieri, and Francesco Guicciardini, and was closely modeled on the British weekly *The Saturday Review*. Its articles reflected varying political viewpoints but with a special concern for the promotion of moderate reforms, particularly emphasizing the social responsibility of the ruling classes in economic and administrative programs in southern Italy. Although the weekly never achieved a large circulation, its contributors included such distinguished authors as Giustino Fortunato,* Giosuè Carducci,* Cesare Lombroso, Marco Minghetti,* Matilde Serao,* Giovanni Verga,* and Pasquale Villari.*

In late 1878, Sonnino and Franchetti moved the journal to Rome and continued its publication in weekly form until January 27, 1882, when it became a daily newspaper entitled *La Rassegna*. The paper continued the program of its weekly predecessor but became more politically identified with the Center group in parliament, where most of its founders had won seats. Under the editorship of Michele Torraca, *La Rassegna* distinguished itself for its attacks on the "emptiness" of the old political parties and for its focus on contemporary social and economic questions. It also warmly supported Italian colonial expansion in Africa and the transformism* of Agostino Depretis,* issues that often drew it into polemics with other leading Roman dailies.

On November 1, 1886, *La Rassegna* ceased publication due to irreconcilable differences between Torraca and the paper's owners, principally Sidney Sonnino.

BFB

RATTAZZI, URBANO. Rattazzi was born in Alessandria on June 29, 1808, and died in Frosinone on June 5, 1873. After practicing law in Casale, he ran for parliament in 1848 and distinguished himself as the author of legislation uniting Lombardy* to Piedmont-Sardinia. He held several cabinet posts in the governments of Count Gabrio Casati and Vincenzo Gioberti* and made a reputation as a spokesman for the constitutional Left (see Sinistra, La*). He broke with Gioberti over the issue of Piedmontese intervention against the democratic governments of Tuscany and Rome.

After Charles Albert's* defeat at the battle of Novara,* Rattazzi became the leader of a Center-Left opposition party which joined Cavour's* Center-Right forces to form the so-called *connubio** in 1852. When Cavour became prime minister for the first time, in 1852, Rattazzi and his followers were rewarded with cabinet posts. The Rattazzi-Cavour alliance lasted until 1858, but not without disagreements over regulation of religious orders and over the activities of Mazzinian dissidents. A major dispute between these leading figures of Piedmontese politics arose also over King Victor Emmanuel II's* plans to marry his mistress, the Countess of Mirafiori. Rattazzi took the side of the King, whose closest friend and confidante he remained for years.

In the summer of 1859, as president of the Sardinian Chamber of Deputies, he spoke against the Villafranca* armistice and against the cession of Nice and Savoy to France. Head of the moderate opposition to the governments of Cavour and Bettino Ricasoli,* Rattazzi became prime minister in 1862 and then again in 1867. In both instances he was forced to resign by a coalition of radical and conservative deputies united in their condemnation of his equivocal dealings with Giuseppe Garibaldi* and his revolution-minded followers. Rattazzi's inaction while Garibaldi organized his forces for a march on Rome reflected the King's desire to achieve by revolutionary means what could not be achieved by diplomacy. But Rattazzi paid a heavy political price for his loyalty to Victor Emmanuel II. His second resignation, following the battle of Mentana,* dealt a severe blow to the "constitutional opposition," bringing the Italian parliament one step closer to transformism.*

For further reference see: Adolfo Omodeo, "Per l'interpretazione della politica di U.R.,'' in *Difesa del Risorgimento* (Turin: Einaudi, 1951), pp. 573–90. See also several essays in Gianni Di Stefano, ed., *1862: La prima crisi dello stato unitario* (Trapani: Corrao, 1966). For Rattazzi's personal life see the gossipy memoirs of Madame Rattazzi (Maria Letizia Bonaparte-Wyse), *Rattazzi et son temps* (Paris: Dentu, 1881–83).

CML

RATTI, ACHILLE. See **PIUS XI**

RED BRIGADES. The Red Brigade movement evolved out of the Metropolitan Collective of Milan, an organization founded on September 8, 1969, by dissident student and worker groups, led by Renato Curcio (representing the students), and by Corrado Simioni and Franco Troiano (representing the workers). This leftist extraparliamentary band rejected the compromise policies of the Italian Communist Party (PCI)* and the Italian Socialist Party (PSI)*; in the early 1970s it began to wage an underground terrorist campaign against the state, including bombings, kidnappings, and armed attacks on government officials and policemen. It was by far the most active of all Italian terrorist groups during the 1970s, taking credit for fifty-five deaths and sixty-eight ''kneecappings.'' The Red Brigade kidnapping and murder of Prime Minister Aldo Moro* in 1978 was the terrorist event of the decade.

It is not possible to say definitively what the Red Brigades represent in history. The movement's connection with other terrorist groups, both domestic and foreign, is a matter of debate among experts, as is the question of how much support, if any, the Red Brigades receive from the KGB. Then, too, the relationship between Antonio Negri, the extraparliamentary Left's major thinker, and the Red Brigades is still a matter for the courts to decide. According to their own pronouncements, the Red Brigades want to create a Communist state through revolution, and their immediate objectives are to discredit the PCI and to undermine the Italian parliamentary state through terror.

RD

RED SHIRTS. See **GARIBALDI, GIUSEPPE**

RED WEEK. The week of June 6–13, 1914, was so called because of police-civilian clashes over popular demonstrations and the general strike, climaxed by the proclamation of republics in Ravenna and Forlì. Renewed anarchist activity, splits in Socialist, syndicalist, and republican ranks over Libya,* uncertainties following universal manhood suffrage, doubts concerning Giovanni Giolitti's* dealings with Catholics, and unemployment due to cutbacks in local public work projects all contributed to the radicalization of Italian society. The charge of police brutality was raised as six worker demonstrators were killed at Rocco Gorga on January 16, 1914. Although many anarchists, Socialists, syndicalists, and republicans cooperated during Red Week, there was no central or unified command. Antimilitarism was the common denominator, with the anarchist Errico Malatesta* and the Socialist Mussolini* opting for revolution. In restoring order, 16 civilians were killed and 600 were injured, while security forces, excepting the military, suffered 2 killed and 408 slightly injured.

RSC

REGIONAL GOVERNMENTS UNDER THE REPUBLIC. These are the semiautonomous governments of the twenty geographical regions that have been created since 1948 (see Regions in the Republic*). Each region has an authorizing statute that functions as a constitution; a popularly elected unicameral Regional Council; an Executive Committee (*Giunta*); and a president. The *Giunta* and the president are elected by the council from its membership and must retain the confidence of the council. Regional governments have authority to legislate in a large number of fields of local and regional concern and to exercise financial autonomy. Actions of regional governments must conform to national policy and the constitution of the Republic.

EER

REGIONS IN THE REPUBLIC. These twenty geographical areas have been created since 1948 with semiautonomous governments (see Regional governments under the Republic*). Two types of regions were authorized by the constitution: five special regions, which had unique cultural, linguistic, or socioeconomic characteristics; and fifteen (originally fourteen) ordinary regions. The special regions are Valle d'Aosta, Trentino-Alto Adige,* Sicily, and Sardinia, which were established by 1949, and Friuli-Venezia Giulia, which was established in 1963. After much delay, governments for the ordinary regions were established in 1970. The ordinary regions are Piedmont, Lombardy,* Veneto, Liguria, Emilia-Romagna, Umbria, the Marches, Tuscany, Abruzzi, Molise, Latium, Campania, Apulia, Basilicata, and Calabria.

EER

REGNO, IL. Enrico Corradini's* Florentine pioneer weekly political review, *Il Regno*, which appeared on November 29, 1903, resulted from the cultural-intellectual ferment that gripped Florentine youth. *Leonardo** (1902) stressed philosophy, the *Regno* politics, and *Hermes** (1904) art and literature. Corradini was the director of the *Regno*, with Giovanni Papini* as editor and Giuseppe Prezzolini,* Emilio Bodrero, G. A. Borgese, Mario Calderoni, Aldemiro Campodinico, Maffio Maffii, Pier L. Occhini, and Vilfredo Pareto* as major contributors. The review represented Corradini's first practical undertaking following his conversion to nationalism in 1896.

As the name indicates, the *Regno*'s emphasis was on national problems, including Italy's poor international competitive position, irredentism,* emigration,* the feeble ruling class, and the absence of patriotic solidarity, among others. Scholars credit the *Regno* for having initially raised many issues of critical national importance. Some believe that the problems enunciated and the solutions proposed formed the root ideas of nationalism, and eventually sought fulfillment via Fascism.* Bodrero, Maffii, Occhini, and a number of enthusiastic self-styled subscribers, "the friends of the *Regno*," followed Corradini into the Italian Nationalist Association* of 1910. Financial difficulties, lack of groundswell enthusiasm, and the disaffection of Papini, Prezzolini, and Borgese forced Corradini to relinquish control to Aldemiro Campodonico and the National Young Liberals on March 31, 1905. The *Regno* collapsed December 25, 1906.

For further reference see: Monique de Taeye-Henen, *Le nationalisme d'Enrico Corradini et les origines du fascisme dans la revue florentine "Il Regno" 1903–1906* (Paris: Didier, 1973).

RSC

REPUBBLICA SOCIALE ITALIANA. See SALÒ, REPUBLIC OF

REPUBLICAN PARTY, POSTUNIFICATION. Forever loyal to Mazzinian traditions, Italy's Republican Party seemed destined to extinction with the creation of the liberal monarchy in 1861; but it finally triumphed with the erection of the Republic in 1946, and declined following the fulfillment of its principal aim. After a period of conspiratorial agitation against the monarchy in the 1860s and 1870s, a growing number of Republicans (Giovanni Bovio,* Agostino Bertani,* Felice Cavallotti,* Napoleone Colajanni,* Salvatore Barzilai*) abandoned the boycott of parliament and entered the Chamber, espousing a democratic program mixed with the vague voluntary socialism at times propounded by Giuseppe Mazzini* and Giuseppe Garibaldi.* The chief article of republican faith nevertheless remained the calling of a constituent assembly to allow Italians the freedom to choose between monarchy and republic. Weakened in the 1880s by defections toward radicalism and socialism, the Republicans, strongest in central Italy, organized a formal party in 1895, participated in the Extreme Left's parliamentary obstructionism against the government of Luigi Pelloux* (1899–1900), and reached their apex of parliamentary representation in 1900 with twenty-nine seats. With the advent of the Giolittian era and increasing democratization of Italian institutions, republicanism's appeal declined, and the party's parliamentary representation fell to seventeen in 1913. It almost disappeared in 1919 (four seats), rising slightly, to six in 1921 and to seven in 1924. Always refusing to participate in "His Majesty's Government," the Republicans opposed foreign policy favoring the Triple Alliance* and colonial ventures, although on the question of the Libyan War (1911–12) (see Ouchy, Treaty of*) they experienced a serious schism. Ardent irredentists, most Republicans favored intervention in World War I* on the side of the Triple Entente,* moved by the desire to acquire Trent and Trieste* and by ideological preference for republican France. With the establishment of a dictatorship by the former Republican Mussolini,* the party ceased to exist, to be reborn in the second postwar period (see Italian Republican Party*). Although among the smaller parties, it has participated in many postwar coalition governments, and in June 1981 the Republican Giovanni Spadolini became prime minister.

For further reference see: Fernando Manzotti, *Partiti e gruppi politici dal Risorgimento al fascismo* (Florence: F. Le Monnier, 1973); Carlo Morando, *I partiti politici nella storia d'Italia* (Florence: F. Le Monnier, 1968); Mario Vinciguerra, *I partiti italiani dal 1848 al 1955*, 3rd ed. (Rome: Centro Editoriale dell'Osservatore, 1956).

SS

RERUM NOVARUM. The first modern social encyclical on the "conditions of the working man," *Rerum novarum* was promulgated on March 15, 1891, by Pope Leo XIII.* Welcomed with much enthusiasm in Catholic circles and labeled the "Magna Carta of Labor," the encyclical condemned laissez-faire capitalism and scientific socialism while suggesting the formation of organizations of employers and employees as the best way to promote social justice. Rejecting class divisions and conflict, Leo admitted the right to strike as a last resort and proclaimed the worker's right to protection against economic and social injustice. In the event that the laborer could not assert his own rights, he wrote, it became incumbent upon the state to intervene on his behalf.

In Italy many Catholic groups, including those of the Opera dei Congressi,* were spurred to social action by *Rerum novarum*, and the advances of the Catholic Christian Economy organization among the urban poor were legitimized by the social teachings of this encyclical.

RJW

RESISTANCE, ARMED. The Armed Resistance was the anti-Fascist, anti-German struggle in northern Italy following Pietro Badoglio's* announcement of the armistice with the Allies (September 8, 1943). Fighters were grouped in two wings: (1) autonomous units, recruited from disbanded elements of the Italian army and supportive of the royal government in the South; and (2) a stronger, politically reforming wing identified with the Committees of National Liberation (see CLN*). Communist "Garibaldi" partisans accounted for 40 percent of the resisters; Action Party* "Giellisti," 25 percent; Socialists, Christian Democrats, and Liberals, 35 percent. The latter two parties often worked with the autonomous units. In January 1944 the Committee of National Liberation for Upper Italy (CLNAI*) was formed in Milan to serve as a five-party clandestine government. In June it set up a military command over the CVL* (Corpo Volontari della Libertà), as the resisters were known. The Allies maintained liaison with the Resistance and sent in supplies. Growing tension with the Allies was reduced by the Caserta agreements of December 7 whereby the Allies promised substantial aid if the Resistance obeyed all orders, including the surrender of arms at war's end. At the same time, the Italian government in Rome recognized the CLNAI as its "delegate."

Milan's liberation (April 25, 1945) marked the culmination of the Armed

Resistance. Some 250,000 Italians took part in the struggle at various times. Total casualties exceeded those of the Allied forces in Italy. Although Ferruccio Parri,* northern leader of the Action Party, became premier in June 1945, the political influence of the Armed Resistance rapidly subsided.

For further reference see: Charles F. Delzell, *Mussolini's Enemies*, rev. ed. (New York: Howard Fertig, 1974); idem, "The Italian Anti-Fascist Resistance in Retrospect: Three Decades of Historiography," *Journal of Modern History* 47 (March 1975): 66–96.

CFD

RESTO DEL CARLINO, IL. See **NEWSPAPERS**

REVEL, OTTAVIO. See **THAON DI REVEL, OTTAVIO**

REVOLUTIONS OF 1820–21. The first liberal revolutions in Italy, they were marked by the primacy of political and constitutional issues over social ones and were the first significant threat to the international order established at the Congress of Vienna.* The revolutions began in the Kingdom of the Two Sicilies,* where army officers led uprisings to protest the restoration of absolute monarchy and other traditional institutions of the Bourbon dynasty. The rebellious officers had close ties with the leaders of the Spanish revolutionary movement that had begun in 1820 among troops stationed in the port of Cadiz who were destined to fight in the South American colonies.

The Neapolitan rebels wanted King Ferdinand I* to grant a constitution; the Sicilians clamored for the Constitution of 1812, which the King had abrogated. Under pressure from his own army and from prominent elements in the civilian population, the King granted a constitution. But soon after he sought the help of the conservative powers of Europe to restore the absolute monarchy. In 1821, in fact, the liberal movement in the Two Sicilies was crushed by Austrian military intervention.

Milan and Turin were the other focal points of liberal *moti* in 1820–21. In the Lombard capital the movement for liberalization of the Austrian regime was led by prominent intellectuals, professional men, and landowners. The unveiling of a large conspiracy led to numerous arrests. Among those sentenced to house arrest was the philosopher Gian Domenico Romagnosi.* Others were sentenced to harsh prison sentences in the Spielberg fortress or to exile overseas. Federico Confalonieri* and Silvio Pellico,* author of the famous memoir *Le mie prigioni* [My imprisonment], were among those who suffered this fate.

In Turin, opponents of the very conservative policies of King Victor Emmanual I* pinned their hopes not on the heir apparent, Charles Felix,* but on the young Charles Albert of Savoy*-Carignano, who had been raised by liberal parents. The conspirators, among them Charles Albert's close friend Santorre di Santarosa,* were elated at the abdication of Victor Emmanuel I. In the absence of Charles Felix from Turin, Charles Albert became regent. But at the last minute he refused to lead a coup against the legitimate heir to the crown of Savoy. His apparent betrayal of the liberal cause earned him the lasting enmity of Piedmont's liberal elite.

Everywhere the revolutions of 1820–21 ended in failure. But from the experience of failure Italian intellectuals, including Giuseppe Mazzini,* who witnessed the exodus of defeated liberals from his native Genoa, learned an important lesson. Small elite groups, no matter how determined, could not hope to overthrow the old regime. Only a broadly based revolutionary movement could accomplish that goal.

CML

REVOLUTIONS OF 1831. In February 1831 revolutions broke out spontaneously in the duchies of Parma and Modena and in the Papal States* due to disaffection generated by the economic depression of the 1820s and discontent with the restoration governments of the post-1815 period.

In the Duchy of Parma a provisional government headed by Count Filippo Linati, who had served in various Napoleonic governments, momentarily replaced the Duchess Marie Louise. In Modena, following the abortive plot of Ciro Menotti,* a dictatorship under the liberal Biagio Nardi established a provisional government after Duke Francis IV fled to neighboring Mantua. Both provisional governments were short-lived and accomplished limited reform, mainly with regard to greater freedom of the press, although Nardi, a landowner, also attempted some tax reform. By March both Marie Louise and Francis IV returned to power with Austrian help.

Revolutionary leadership in the Papal States was assumed by Bologna, where the legate, before fleeing on February 5, designated a provisional government headed by a lawyer, Giovanni Vicini. The new regime declared the end of the Pope's temporal rule and moved to establish, with other rebellious parts of the Papal States, a provisional government of the United Italian Provinces. Devotion to the nonintervention principle prevented unity between this government and that of the duchies, while Bologna's narrow municipalism, concerned with communal liberties, impeded cooperation. Various communes, from Ferrara to Rimini and from Urbino to Perugia, produced, through provisional governments, a common wave of anticlericalism and measures of emancipation from the economic burdens and institutional controls of clerical rule. Liberal members of the commercial, agrarian, and professional middle class often led these revolutions, but police reports also reveal artisan participation and limited peasant involvement. Capitulation to Austrian troops at Ancona in March ended the revolts and restored papal control, although petitions from various communes, demanding economic and administrative reform, continued after 1831. On an international level, in May the memorandum of 1831,* signed by Austria, Prussia, Russia, England, and France, was directed to Gregory XVI* on the question of reform.

MSM

REVOLUTIONS OF 1848. A turning point in the emergence of a modern Italian state, the revolutions of 1848 began with a revolt in Palermo (January

12, 1848) against the conservative Bourbon regime. The revolution then spread to the mainland. In March, after news of similar events in Paris and Vienna, it became nationwide. The main issues, already aired during the abortive revolutions of 1820–21* and 1831,* were the introduction of constitutional government along the French or British models and Italy's independence from foreign powers, especially Austria. In contrast to their predecessors, however, the revolutionaries of 1848 also aimed at the attainment of Italian national unity. The groundwork for such unity was laid in the decade preceding the revolution by the followers of Giuseppe Mazzini* and by prominent liberal intellectuals such as Massimo D'Azeglio* and Vincenzo Gioberti.*

Following the Palermo revolt, Sicilian and Neapolitan liberals, though frequently at odds among themselves, pressured King Ferdinand II* to grant a constitution (February 11, 1848). Within a month his example was followed by the Grand Duke of Tuscany, Charles Albert of Savoy,* and Pope Pius IX.* Although imposed on the Italian rulers by popular agitation, these constitutions (statuti) reflected the political aspirations of moderate liberals determined to leave political rights and power in the hands of male, educated property owners.

So long as the Italian rulers respected the constitutions they had granted and so long as one of them, Charles Albert of Savoy, waged war against Austria in northern Italy, the revolutions remained under moderate liberal leadership. This was true even in Milan, where the urban lower classes took part in the anti-Austrian insurrection of March 18–22, 1848 (the Five Days of Milan). And it was also true in Venice, where a republican government was proclaimed. But in July-August 1848 democratic leaders began to challenge the moderate liberal governments. After Charles Albert's defeat at the hands of the Austrian army (August 6, 1848) a democratic government under the lawyer Francesco Domenico Guerrazzi came to power in Tuscany, and democratic elements challenged the moderate liberals in the Papal States.* Toward the end of 1848 the revolutions took a radical turn. This trend culminated with the proclamation of the Roman Republic on February 9, 1849. The new government, headed by Giuseppe Mazzini, his disciple Aurelio Saffi, and the old Jacobin Carlo Armellini, proclaimed the demise of the temporal power, drafted a democratic constitution, and claimed to represent the whole of Italy.

The failure of the revolutions began in the Italian state which had given them birth, the Kingdom of the Two Sicilies.* Already on May 15, 1848, King Ferdinand II had staged a nearly successful coup against the fledgling parliamentary system. Thereafter, with the support of conservative groups and the army, he kept up the pressure. The revolutionary movement became hopelessly divided between moderate liberals, who clung to their ideal of constitutional monarchy even in the face of the King's hostility, and democrats, who proposed to involve the peasantry in the revolution by the promise of land reform. Similar divisions weakened the democratic governments of Guerrazzi in Tuscany and Daniele Manin* in Venice.

In the early part of 1849, supporters of the revolutions—their hopes for unity dashed by the defeat of Charles Albert's army—flocked to Mazzini's Roman Republic, which came close to having an all-Italian government. But Mazzini's experiment in democratic republicanism began when the counterrevolutionary tide was already sweeping through Europe.

In June 1849 the army of Napoleon III,* turned defender of monarchical legitimacy, overcame the republican army led by Giuseppe Garibaldi* and Carlo Pisacane.* After months of siege, Venice surrendered to the Austrian army in August. The revolutions thus ended in failure, and were followed by a second Restoration. But the experience of a national movement, common to revolutionary leaders in every state, was never forgotten. It became the basis for both the renewed Mazzinian militancy of the early 1850s and the moderate liberal networks that coalesced in the Italian National Society (see Società Nazionale Italiana*) in 1857.

For further reference see: volume 3 of Giorgio Candeloro's *Storio dell'Italia moderna*, 8 vols. (Milan: Feltrinelli, 1959–74); Franco Della Peruta, *I democratici e la rivoluzione italiana* (Milan: Feltrinelli, 1958); Raymond Grew, *A Sterner Plan for Italian Unity* (Princeton: Princeton University Press, 1963); Paul Ginsborg, *Daniele Manin e la rivoluzione veneziana del 1848–1849* (Milan: Feltrinelli, 1978); Clara M. Lovett, *The Democratic Movement in Italy, 1830–1876* (Cambridge, Mass.: Harvard University Press, 1982).

CML

RICASOLI, BETTINO. Born in Florence on March 9, 1809, Ricasoli was the scion of an ancient and distinguished patrician family. A member of the Accademia dei Georgofili since his youth, he devoted much time to the improvement of the family estate at Brolio in Tuscany. In the 1840s he joined Vincenzo Salvagnoli, Raffaele Lambruschini, and other aristocrats in advocating constitutional reform of the grand ducal government as well as economic and cultural cooperation among the Italian governments of the time.

He participated in the revolutions of 1848,* but his clashes with the democratic faction led by F. D. Guerrazzi eventually led him to call for the return of the Grand Duke. During the Second Restoration, Ricasoli withdrew again to his estate and became involved in a reclamation project in the Maremma.

After the ousting of the Grand Duke in 1859, Ricasoli returned to Florence. He served in the provisional government and engineered the annexation of his native region to the Kingdom of Sardinia under Victor Emmanuel II.*

In June 1861 he succeeded Cavour* as prime minister because he enjoyed the support of a majority in the Chamber. But he could not gain the trust of the King, who preferred his rival, the Piedmontese Urbano Rattazzi.* Forced to resign in March 1862, Ricasoli did not return to office until June 1866, when Italy faced war with Austria and a disastrous financial crisis.

Ricasoli had a deep interest in religious reform and in reconciliation between church and state. In 1867 he attempted to negotiate an agreement but ran afoul of the strong anticlerical currents in the Chamber. After his second resignation over this issue, he ceased to play an active role in national politics, though he remained active in Tuscan affairs. He died at his ancestral home of Brolio on October 23, 1880.

CML

RICCI, RENATO. See **BALILLA**

RICCIARDI, GIUSEPPE. A major figure of the democratic movement in the Kingdom of the Two Sicilies,* Ricciardi was born in Naples in 1808 and died there in 1882. He was the son of a Neapolitan noblewoman and of the magistrate Francesco Ricciardi, who had received the title of Count of Camaldoli from King Joseph Bonaparte. Thus, Ricciardi was brought up during the Restoration in a family that was politically out of favor. Although his formal education was sketchy at best, Ricciardi showed a precocious talent for political journalism, which brought him to the attention of the police in the early 1830s. He escaped harassment or possible arrest by undertaking the traditional grand tour abroad. In 1848, however, he was one of the leading figures in the anti-Bourbon revolution (see Revolutions of 1848*). Concerned with the social question, he wished to attract the peasantry to the cause of Italian unity; but episodes of violence and land seizure pushed him toward a more conservative position. After the unification he became one of the leading parliamentary spokesmen for social reform, suffrage reform, and women's rights. He was also one of the first and most enthusiastic sponsors of divorce legislation.

CML

RICHECOURT, EMMANUEL FRANCOIS JOSEPH IGNACE DE NAY, COMTE DE. Noble and functionary of the ducal administration of Lorraine at Nancy, Richecourt (1694–1759) was transferred to Florence on the succession of Francis of Lorraine as Grand Duke of Tuscany in 1737. There he became the chief figure in the Council of Regency that governed for Francis, then Emperor in Vienna. He was responsible for the first period of the Hapsburg reforms in Tuscany, including the first measures regarding the Church, the regulation of *fedecomessi* (deeds of trust), and feudal jurisdictions. He was replaced by Marshal Botta-Adorno in 1757.

RBL

RIFORMA GENTILE. See **GENTILE REFORM**

RIGHETTI, IGINO. President of the Federazione Universitaria Cattolica Italiana (FUCI)* from 1925 to 1934 and founder of the Catholic Movimento Laureati, Igino Righetti was born in 1904 near the town of Rimini. Raised in a Catholic atmosphere, Righetti studied in Bologna and at the University of Rome, where he received his degree in law. As a student, he was active in the Partito Popolare (see Italian Popular Party*) and in 1925 was appointed president of the FUCI, the organization of Catholic university students. In this capacity, Righetti worked closely with Giovanni Battista Montini, the future Pope Paul VI,* leading the students on a decidedly anti-Fascist course. In 1934 he founded the Movimento Laureati, an organization of Catholic university graduates, many of whom were destined for important positions in the postwar Christian Democratic Party.* He died of nephritis in 1938 at the age of thirty-four.

RJW

RIGHT. See **DESTRA, LA**

RIGOLA, RINALDO. See **CGL**

RISORGIMENTO. This nineteenth-century movement led to the unification of Italy and the proclamation of national independence. The Italian word for resurgence or resurrection was also the name chosen by Cavour* for his newspaper, founded in December 1847. The term indicates something that once existed, came to an end, and then was revived. Because no Italian state embracing the entire peninsula had ever existed before the proclamation of the Kingdom of Italy* in 1861, it is clear that the term does not refer solely to a territorial settlement; rather, the *Risorgimento* was a movement of ideas before it became a political solution. In many ways the *Risorgimento* was a spiritual process that called for the transformation of Italian life and the affirmation of national autonomy. Initially the word had a predominantly literary or cultural significance, only later assuming a political-territorial meaning as well.

Politically, the groundwork for the *Risorgimento* was paved by the French Revolution, which had led to a reorganization of the peninsula as well as to the introduction of liberal and national ideas. At the Congress of Vienna* (1815), Italian national interests were ignored as Austria secured Lombardy* and Venetia, and members of the Hapsburg family were placed on the thrones of Tuscany, Parma, and Modena. The Restoration prompted opposition and the formation of a number of secret societies opposing the settlement, most notably the Carbonari (see Carboneria*). Revolutions erupted in the Kingdom of the Two Sicilies* (1820), Sardinia (1821), Modena, and the Legations* of the Papal States* (1831), all of which were suppressed with Austrian assistance (see Revolutions of 1820–21*; Revolutions of 1831*).

In 1831 Giuseppe Mazzini* founded his Giovine Italia,* or Young Italy, which in turn inspired another wave of revolutions, no more successful than those of the Carbonari, culminating in the revolutionary upheaval of 1848. Vincenzo Gioberti's* suggestion that the papacy assume leadership of the national movement, advocated in his *Del primato morale e civile degli Italiani* [On the moral and civil primacy of the Italians], was also discredited by the conduct of Pope Pius IX* during the revolutions of 1848.*

Following the Second Restoration of 1849, the Kingdom of Sardinia, under the leadership of Count Cavour, assumed direction of the national movement.

Cavour's diplomacy, in conjunction with the daring expedition of Giuseppe Garibaldi* to Sicily and the organization of the Italian National Society (see Società Nazionale Italiana*), led to the creation of the Kingdom of Italy in 1861. Unification was not yet complete, however; in 1866 Italy acquired Venice, and on September 20, 1870, finally occupied Rome. It was only after World War I* and the Treaty of Saint-Germain that Italy acquired the so-called Italia Irredenta (Istria* and the Trentino*) and the South Tyrol.

For further reference see: S. J. Woolf, *The Italian Risorgimento* (New York: Barnes and Noble, 1969); Luigi Salvatorelli, *The Risorgimento: Thought and Action* (New York: Harper and Row, 1970); Alessandro Galante Garrone, "Risorgimento e antirisorgimento negli scritti di Luigi Salvatorelli," *Rivista Storica Italiano* 78 (September 1968): 513–43; Raymond Grew, *A Sterner Plan for Italian Unity: The International Society in the Risorgimento* (Princeton: Princeton University Press, 1963); Emiliana P. Noether, *Seeds of Italian Nationalism, 1700–1815* (New York: Columbia University Press, 1951).

FJC

ROBILANT, CARLO FELICE, COUNT DI. Foreign minister between October 1885 and April 1887, Robilant's reformulation of Italy's position in the Triple Alliance* from suppliant to equal partner made him one of the most capable diplomats since Cavour.* He was born August 8, 1826, in Turin, and died on October 17, 1888, in London, where he was serving as ambassador. After a distinguished military career in three wars (1848–49, 1860, and 1866*), Robilant served as Italian envoy to Austria-Hungary between 1871 and 1885. Opposed to Italy's hasty entry into the Triple Alliance with Austria and Germany in 1882, as foreign minister he exploited the discomfiture of Italy's allies during the Balkan crises of 1885–87 when, as a condition for the renewal of the alliance in February 1887, he secured for Italy a role of parity with Austria in future dispositions of the Balkans. He also promoted Italy's position with the Anglo-Italian-Austrian Mediterranean Agreements* (February–March 1887).

SS

ROCCO, ALFREDO. Alfredo Rocco, Fascist theorist, minister of justice, and a major architect of the Fascist state, was born in Naples on September 9, 1875, and died in Rome on August 28, 1935. Rocco had already embarked on a successful academic career in law when he emerged as the most forceful spokesman of the Italian Nationalist Association* in 1914. But he developed his mature political conception only after the war, responding to the trade-union challenge of the *biennio rosso* and to the difficulties that Italy faced in international economic competition. Since the liberal state seemed too weak to respond to either challenge, he proposed to transform the Italian state, using socioeconomic groupings to enable a revitalized political elite to control the threatening mass society and to galvanize the nation's energies for production, international economic competition, and imperialist war. But while Rocco felt that the Italian state must move toward totalitarianism, extending its sovereignty and mobilizing people more fully, he remained a juridical rationalist; his conception required codified law and had no place for charisma, intuition, or terror.

In Rome in December 1918 Rocco and Francesco Coppola* began publishing *La Politica,** a major Nationalist, and later Fascist, review. Rocco became minister of justice in January 1925, as Mussolini* was beginning to develop a specifically Fascist order, and quickly achieved considerable power, since he impressed Mussolini with his energy and technical competence. Over the next several years he drafted a series of laws that transformed the Italian state, expanding its sovereignty and enhancing the power of the executive. His syndical law of April 3, 1926, established juridical recognition of trade unions and their collective contracts, outlawed strikes and lockouts, and instituted a labor magistracy to deal with labor conflicts.

Rocco left office as part of the shake-up of the Fascist hierarchy in July 1932. He was made a senator in 1934 and served as rector of the University of Rome until his death in 1935.

For further reference see: Alfredo Rocco, *Scritti e discorsi politici,* 3 vols. (Milan: A. Giuffrè, 1938); Paolo Ungari, *Alfredo Rocco e l'ideologia giuridica del fascismo* (Brescia: Morcelliana, 1963).

DDR

RODANO, MARIA LUISA CINCIARI. A prominent figure in Italian left-wing politics and the contemporary women's movement, she was born in Rome on January 21, 1921. Rodano was an active anti-Fascist and part of the Armed Resistance* in Rome (1943–44). She was also one of the founders and organizers of the Catholic Left, which joined the Italian Communist Party (PCI)* in 1946. A member of the initiating committee for the Unione Donne Italiane* in 1944, she later served as its president. Rodano served for several terms as both deputy and senator.

MJS

ROMAGNA. This province in east-central Italy, centered in Ravenna, is so named because it was among the last Italian territories held by the Eastern Roman Empire. The Romagna came under papal control in the late Middle Ages. Papal administration became unpopular after French rule during the Napoleonic era had given the inhabitants a taste of efficient secular government. Restored to the papacy in 1814, the Romagna became a center of plots and revolutions against the temporal power. In 1859 a revolution overthrew papal rule, and the province became part of the Italian state in 1860.

AJR

ROMAGNOSI, GIAN DOMINICO. Influential philosopher, jurist, and writer, Romagnosi was born in Salsomaggiore on December 11, 1761. After earlier studies at Piacenza, he earned a law degree at Parma (1786). In 1791 he published his well-known work, *Genesi del diretto penale* [Origins of penal law], in which he argued that the right to punish belongs to society. In the same year, he assumed a civil judgeship at Trent, and from 1793 to 1802 practiced law there. During this time, he published *Cosa é equalita?* (1792) and *Cosa é libertà?* (1793).

In 1802 he became professor of public law at Parma and published his most famous work, *Introduzione allo studio del diretto pubblico universale* [Introduction to universal public law] (1805). In 1807 he was nominated adviser to the minister of justice of the Kingdom of Italy and assumed the chair of civil law at Pavia. He then founded and became director of the Special School of Politics and Law in Milan in 1808. From 1812 to 1814 he edited the *Giornale di Giursprudenza Universale*.

After the Restoration, dismissed from all positions, he was allowed to run a private law school. In 1821 he was arrested and accused of treason but was soon released. Forbidden to teach, he was also kept from accepting a position at the Ionian University of Corfu. Romagnosi spent the remainder of his days dependent upon the good will of friends and writing for a variety of journals. He died in Milan on June 18, 1833.

Although influenced by Enlightenment* thought, Romagnosi was basically Vichian in his belief that the nature of man can only be determined in a social-historical context. Romagnosi saw man as a collective being who progresses through time via laws which he sought to define in light of the ongoing dialectic between tradition and opportunity.

For further reference see: Alessandro Levi, *Romagnosi* (Rome, 1936); Enrico Sestan, ed., *Opere di G. D. Romagnosi, C. Cattaneo and G. Ferrari* (Milan: R. Ricciardi, 1957).

FFA

ROMAN QUESTION. Under this heading are included a number of problems regarding relations between church and state in Italy from the decade of unification to the Lateran Accords* of 1929. Between 1859 and 1861, the "Question" revolved around papal protests and international complications over Italian seizure of most of the Church's temporal domains in the process of unifying the peninsula. From 1861 to 1870, the issue became the acquisition of Rome as Italy's capital either by negotiation, as attempted by Cavour,* Bettino Ricasoli,* and Marco Minghetti,* or by force, as tried by Giuseppe Garibaldi* in 1862 and 1867. Either approach involved difficulties with other Catholic countries, especially imperial France, self-appointed protector of the remains of the Papal States,* with a temporary compromise reached in the September Convention* (1864), undone by Garibaldi's incursion into the Roman provinces and consequent French military intervention (battle of Mentana,* 1867). With France involved in war against Prussia in 1870, the Lanza-Sella government felt free to occupy Rome (September 1870), ending papal temporal power, after which Pius IX* secluded himself in the Vatican palaces as a "prisoner," rejecting the privileges and assurances accorded the Church in the Law of Papal Guarantees* (May 1871). Italian relations with France during the early years of the Third Republic continued to be difficult owing to French Catholic sympathy for the Pope, whose persistant refusal to recognize the Kingdom of Italy* was expressed by such prohibitions as the *non expedit** (1874), occasioning in reaction a growth of Italian anticlericalism, especially among the Left (see Sinistra, La*) and the Extreme Left. Continued papal hopes that Rome might be reacquired through international pressure was one factor in Italy's joining the Triple Alliance* (1882), securing thereby *de facto* ratification by Austria and Germany of Italy's rightful possession of Rome. But the Alliance, aimed in part against France, led the latter repeatedly to raise the Roman Question as a way of pressuring Italy to loosen its ties with Germany. With the gradual rapprochement between Italy and France after the late 1890s, and following the worsening of French-Vatican relations after 1900, Pius X,* although never renouncing the papacy's traditional claims to Rome, nevertheless moved in the direction of a less hostile attitude toward the Italian state, gradually relaxing the *non expedit* from 1904 to 1913. By 1919 negotiations were in progress toward a reconciliation, culminating in the Lateran Agreements of February 1929, whereby, in return for Italian recognition of a sovereign Vatican City state and monetary compensations, the papacy recognized the Italian Kingdom with Rome as its capital, substantively resolving the Roman Question.

For further reference see: S. William Halperin, *The Separation of Church and State in Italian Thought from Cavour to Mussolini* (Chicago: University of Chicago Press, 1937); Arturo C. Jemolo, *Church and State in Italy, 1850–1950*, trans. by David Moore (Oxford: Blackwell, 1960).

SS

ROMAN REPUBLIC OF 1798–99, THE. This was one of the French-inspired sister republics that emerged after Napoleon I's* first Italian campaign of 1796. A few months after the Treaty of Campoformio, a diplomatic incident (the murder of General Duphot) occasioned the French occupation of Rome by General Berthier, which occurred in February 1798. Roman patriots proclaimed the Republic on the Forum and planted a liberty tree on the Campidoglio, while political exiles returned. Pius VI* left the city for exile in Tuscany before his ultimate transfer to France, where he died. The constitution of the Roman Republic was modeled on the French constitution of 1795, although names were changed to provide for consuls, tribunes, and a senate. Legislation abolished fiefs and *fedecomessi* (deeds of trust) and limited clerical incomes, and a political life developed through the *Monitore di Roma*, political clubs, and leaders such as Vincenzo Russo.* Further developments depended on the French occupation. Formation of the Roman Republic was one of the contributing causes for the outbreak of the War of the Second Coalition,* and it did not survive the French defeats of the summer of 1799. Papal rule was restored for Pius VII* in 1800, and Rome was not occupied again by the French until 1808.

For further reference see: V. E. Giuntella, "La giacobina repubblica romana (1798–99)," in *Archivio dello Società Romana di Storia Patria* (Rome, 1950).

RBL

RONCALLI, GIUSEPPE. See **JOHN XXIII**

ROSMINI-SERBATI, ANTONIO. This idealist philosopher, theologian, and statesman was born in Rovereto (South Tyrol), on March 25, 1787. Rosmini became a priest in 1821 against the wishes of his aristocratic parents. In 1828 he founded the still active institute of the priests of charity known as the Rosminians. His philosophical and theological writings, meanwhile, were earning him the respect and discipleship of many important religious and literary figures, most notably Alessandro Manzoni.* Politically, Rosmini championed a Dante-like vision of a universal state with the Pope as supreme moral and spiritual arbiter but with state power directly exercised by politically constituted governments. In 1848 he petitioned the Pope not to call foreign armies into Italy, and his two major works of that year, *Delle cinque piaghe della santa chiesa* [The five wounds of the Church] and *La costituzione secondo la giustizia sociale* [A constitution based on social justice], were immediately placed on the *Index*. His major philosophical writings include *Nuovo saggio sulle origine delle idee* [New essay on the origin of ideas] (1830) and *Trattato della coscienza morale* [Treatise on moral conscience] (1840). He began a systematic exposition of his thought with *Introduzione alla filosofia* [Introduction to philosophy] (1850). But it has been left to later scholars to gather and systematize his many writings. Especially in the works that later greatly influenced Giovanni Gentile* and Benedetto Croce,* Rosmini drew conclusions about God, the Trinity, creation, and Christology that were condemned as unorthodox by popes Pius IX* and Leo XIII.* It has been argued, however, that those conclusions are not essential to Rosmini's basic perspective. He retired in relative silence to Stresa in the 1850s, and died there on July 1, 1855.

For further reference see: C.R.H. Leetham, *Rosmini, Priest, Philosopher, and Patriot* (Baltimore: Helicon Press, 1958).

HP

ROSSELLI, CARLO. Carlo Rosselli was born in Rome on November 16, 1899. After serving in the Italian army during World War I,* he attended the University of Florence, where he studied history and economics under the tutelage of Gaetano Salvemini.* He played a crucial role in 1924–25 in forming the first underground anti-Fascist movement in Italy, was coeditor with Pietro Nenni* of *Quarto Stato* in 1926, and in the next three years was at the center of anti-Fascist opposition until his deportation to the island of Lipari. During his nineteen-month confinement there he wrote his major theoretical work, *Liberal Socialism*.

Escaping to France in 1929, Rosselli founded the Justice and Liberty movement* in Paris. For the next eight years, he was a leading figure in the non-Communist anti-Fascist Left, and was active in promoting a wide variety of initiatives aimed at subverting the Fascist and Nazi regimes. In August 1936 he led a group of Loyalist volunteers into battle in Catalonia shortly after the outbreak of the Spanish Civil War.* On June 9, 1937, while recuperating from phlebitis in Normandy, he was assassinated, along with his brother Nello (1900–1937), at Bagnoles-de-l'Orne by members of a French right-wing terrorist group, the *cagoulards*, who carried out the murder as paid agents of the Italian Fascist government.

For further reference see: Nicola Tranfaglia, *Carlo Rosselli dall'interventismo a Giustizia e Libertà* (Bari: Laterza, 1968); various authors, *Giustizia e Libertà nella lotta antifascista e nella storia d'Italia—Attualità dei fratelli Rosselli a quaranta anni dal loro sacrificio* (Florence: La Nuova Italia, 1978).

FR

ROSSI, ERNESTO. This economist and political activist was born in Caserta on August 25, 1897, and died in Rome on February 9, 1967. He was a disciple of Luigi Einàudi* and of Antonio De Vita De Marco.* A chance encounter with Gaetano Salvemini,* then teaching in Florence, marked the direction Rossi maintained as a man of thought and action until his death in 1967. In 1925 Rossi was a member of the group that helped Salvemini to publish and distribute *Non Mollare*, the first anti-Fascist clandestine publication in Italy. Together with Riccardo Bauer and others he was instrumental in organizing the Justice and Liberty movement* in Italy, which was founded by Carlo Rosselli* and other exiles in the fall of 1929. Arrested in October 1930 and sentenced to twenty years' imprisonment, he regained his freedom after the overthrow of the Fascist dictatorship in July 1943. A radical in the European connotation of the term, he saw better chances for social justice in the workers' struggle within a market economy than in collectivism. In the immediate post-world war period he campaigned strenuously for European federalism. A regular contributor to *Il Mondo* and other progressive publications, he also wrote *I padroni del vapore* [The owners of the steamship], *Abolire la miseria* [Abolish poverty], *Il malgoverno* [Misgovernment], *Una spia del regime* [A spy of the regime], *Il manganello e l'aspersorio* [The club and the aspergillum], and other books, and edited a selection of essays by Luigi Einàudi.

MS

ROSSI, PELLEGRINO LUIGI EDOARDO. This statesman, Italian jurist, and peer of France was born in Carrara on July 13, 1787. He became professor of law at the University of Bologna (1812), but his career was interrupted by political events and the support he provided Joachim Murat.* Following Murat's fall, Rossi fled to Switzerland (1815) and then moved to France. While abroad he remained vitally interested in his homeland but became increasingly skeptical of radical and revolutionary solutions and championed a moderate reformism. He acquired French citizenship, became professor of political economy at the

Collège de France, and in 1839 was made a peer. His expertise in juridical and economic matters, familiarity with developments in the Italian peninsula, and friendship with Guizot all contributed to his being named ambassador of France to Rome in 1845. He held this position until the fall of the July Monarchy early in 1848.

After that event Rossi chose to remain in Rome. During the tumultuous days after the Pope's allocution of April 1848, in which he refused to declare war upon Austria, Pius IX* looked to Rossi for support. In September 1848 the Pope appointed him minister of the interior and effective head of the government. Rossi was disliked both by the democrats and by the intolerant clericals, and his determination to preserve the temporal power and negotiate the formation of an Italian League earned him the enmity of the political clubs. On November 15, 1848, he was assassinated by Dante Costantini as he attempted to enter the Palace of the Chancery for the opening of parliament. This precipitated a revolution in Rome, the flight of Pius IX to Gaeta,* and the establishment of the Roman Republic in 1849.

FJC

ROSSINI, GIOACCHINO ANTONIO. This Italian composer's masterpiece, *Il barbiere di Siviglia* (1816), is famous worldwide. Born in Pesaro on February 29, 1792, he studied music in Bologna. He produced his first opera, *La cambiale di matrimonio*, at age eighteen, but his first real success was *Tancredi* (1813). Between 1815 and 1823 Rossini composed twenty operas. His production of *Guglielmo Tell* in 1829 brought his opera-writing career to a close. Departing from convention, Rossini's *Guglielmo Tell* marks a transitional stage in the history of opera. He produced little in the years from 1832 until his death at Passy, outside Paris, on November 13, 1868.

FJC

RUDINÌ, ANTONIO STARABBA, MARQUIS DI. First prime minister of the Right* (see Destra, La*) (1891–92) after fifteen years of governments by the Left (see Sinistra, La*), Rudinì's efforts at reconciliation with the Left and Extreme Left foundered in 1898, ending his second ministry and his political career. He was born on April 16, 1839, in Palermo, and died on August 7, 1908, in Rome. He conspired against Bourbon rule in 1860 before Giuseppe Garibaldi's* expedition. In 1864 Rudinì was appointed mayor of Palermo, where he showed much courage in helping crush a clerical-Bourbonist rising in September 1866, after which he became prefect, occupying the same post in Naples in 1868. The next year he briefly became minister of the interior under Luigi Menabrea* although not a member of parliament, to which he was soon elected and where he sat uninterruptedly until his death. With Minghetti's death in 1886, Rudinì became leader of the Right, clashing with his fellow Sicilian, Francesco Crispi,* whom he succeeded as prime minister in February 1891, forming a government predominantly of the Right but with Giovanni Nicotera* of the Left at the Interior Ministry. Rudinì attempted to reduce expenditures, even in the military; opposed the colonial expansionism practiced by Crispi; and, while renewing Italy's membership in the Triple Alliance* in 1891, sought to improve relations with France. The general failure of his policies and the heterogeneous composition of his government led to his resignation in May 1892. He returned to office after the fall of Crispi's last government following the colonial defeat at Adowa* in March 1896; limited Italy's colonial presence to Eritrea*; recognized France's protectorate over Tunisia (September 1896); attempted reductions in military expenditures; and sought to improve Sicily's economic conditions by endeavoring to end the tariff war with France. When the Left and Extreme Left abandoned him because of his Draconian repression of the disturbances of May 1898, while the Right condemned him for his earlier permissive policies, which allegedly made repression necessary, Rudinì resigned in June 1898.

For further reference see: Bolton King and Thomas Okey, *Italy Today* (London: Nisbet and Co., 1909).

SS

RUFFO, FABRIZIO. Born at Castello di San Lucidio, Calabria, on June 3, 1744, he entered holy orders and rose rapidly in the papal service, becoming a cardinal. After the French conquest of Italy in 1798, he fled to Sicily with the King of Naples. Early in 1799 he returned to Calabria, where he aroused a holy war of the devout peasantry against the French and their liberal Italian supporters. His "Army of the Holy Faith" (the Sanfedisti*) quickly reconquered Naples. Ruffo promised pardon to the defeated liberals; however, the King ignored his promise and carried out a bloody persecution. Disillusioned, the cardinal retired from politics. He died in Naples on August 12, 1827.

AJR

RUMOR, MARIANO. Prime minister of Italy from 1968 to 1970, he was born on June 6, 1915, in Vicenza. A graduate of the University of Padova, he participated in the Armed Resistance* and was elected on the Christian Democratic list from Verona to the Constituent Assembly of 1946.*

In 1948 Rumor was elected to the Chamber of Deputies* and in 1951 became undersecretary for agriculture. He served as minister of agriculture under Antonio Segni,* Fernando Tambroni,* and Amintore Fanfani,* and as minister of the interior under Giovanni Leone.* In December 1968, in the midst of labor and student unrest, Rumor, then political secretary of the Christian Democrats, formed a Center-Left government composed of Socialists, Republicans, and the Christian Democratic Party.* Eighteen months later Rumor's government fell. In 1977 this former prime minister was exonerated from any connection with the Lockheed scandals by a committee of the Chamber of Deputies.

RJW

RUSSO, VINCENZO. A doctrinaire rationalist and revolutionary, he was deeply influenced by the thought of the French Enlightenment.* Born in Palma on June

16, 1770, he was educated in the Seminary of Nola and completed his legal studies at Naples. A member of several radical Neapolitan clubs, he was condemned for his activities by the repressive Bourbon regime and fled, in 1797, to Milan and Switzerland. On the heels of the French armies, he returned to Rome in 1798, where he took part in political events and wrote *Pensieri politici* [Political thoughts], a work which, while attempting to sustain the idea of a democratic republic, shows the author to be a utopian dreamer. With the fall of the Bourbons in 1799, he returned to Naples, where he was active in the affairs of the short-lived Parthenopean Republic.* Taken prisoner in the Bourbon reaction, he was hung on November 17, 1799.

FFA

S

SACRO EGOISMO. A phrase meaning "sacred egoism," it was used by Premier Antonio Salandra* upon taking over the Foreign Ministry following the death of Antonino San Giuliano* on October 16, 1914. He exhorted the Foreign Ministry staff to exclude all sentiments and considerations "except that of an exclusive and unlimited devotion to our country, a sacred egoism for Italy." Since this was during the period of neutralilty,* Salandra meant that Italy had a sacred duty to consider its own interests foremost—an appeal for unity while his government formulated a policy. Critics and supporters alike, however, seized upon *sacro egoismo* as symbolizing Italy's aims in the intervention crisis that followed, resulting in participation in World War I* on the side of the Triple Entente.*

PJD

SALANDRA, ANTONIO. Premier of Italy (1914–16) at the start of World War I,* Antonio Salandra was born in Troia, Foggia province of Apulia, on August 13, 1853. He studied philosophy and law under the mentorship of Francesco De Sanctis* at the University of Naples, obtaining a law degree in 1872. He soon established a reputation with a series of juridical and economic studies. In 1879 De Sanctis, then minister of public instruction, sponsored Salandra for a chair in administrative law at the University of Rome. While at Rome Salandra met Silvio Spaventa* and also formed a close friendship with Sidney Sonnino,* collaborating with the latter on *La Rassegna Settimanale.** This helped establish in him a political philosophy of the Historical Right (see Destra, La*), emphasizing the authority of the state and the rule of law.

Salandra began his political life in 1886 when he entered the Chamber of Deputies, sitting on the Center-Right. He identified with "the party of constitutional opposition" against parliamentary opportunism and Giovanni Giolitti.* He served as undersecretary in the first ministry of Antonio Di Rudinì* (1891–92) and in the last ministry of Francesco Crispi* (1893–96). His political career progressed as he was named minister of agriculture in the second government of Luigi Pelloux* (1899–1900), minister of finance in the first Sonnino cabinet (1906), and minister of the treasury in Sonnino's second cabinet (1909–10).

During the Libyan War (see Ouchy, Treaty of*) and successive Balkan conflicts, Salandra directed his attention to international problems and convinced himself that Italy's most pressing problem was its lack of military preparedness.

On March 21, 1914, following Giolitti's resignation, Salandra became premier as a self-styled liberal-conservative, along with Sonnino the recognized parliamentary leader of the opposition.

World War I intervened, placing Salandra on center stage in a world historical drama. He initially declared neutrality* for Italy. But after the death of Foreign Minister Antonino San Giuliano* in October 1914, he became deeply embroiled in controversy with the use of the term *sacro egoismo** to define Italy's war aims. After naming Sonnino foreign minister in November, he moved progressively to favor Italy's entry into the conflict on the Allies' side. He signed the Pact of London* in April 1915 and denounced the Triple Alliance* on May 3, 1915.

In the midst of a continuing governmental crisis, Salandra undertook a bold stroke and tendered his resignation to the King on May 13. The resignation was refused, and on May 23 Salandra led Italy into World War I by declaring war on Austria. After the retreat in the Trentino* and a series of domestic errors, Salandra resigned in June 1916.

He was a delegate to the Paris Peace Conference* in 1919 and represented Italy at the League of Nations in 1923. He openly supported Fascism* and had sought an accord with Mussolini* to form a government with the Fascists. Later he called for a return to constitutional government, but retired from public life in 1925. In 1928 he was named senator. Salandra left two volumes of memoirs: *La neutralità italiana, 1914. Ricordi e pensieri* and *L'intervento, 1915*. He died in Rome on December 9, 1931.

For further reference see: Giovambattista Gifuni, *Salandra inedito* (Milan: Pan, 1973); Brunello Vigezzi, *L'Italia dalla neutralità all'intervento* (Milan-Naples: Ricciardi, 1967).

                                                                                          PJD

SALÒ, REPUBLIC OF. The Italian Social Republic, Mussolini's* Fascist regime in northern Italy (1943–45), established its headquarters at Salò on Lake Garda. Since many older Fascist hierarchs had broken with Mussolini, it was administered largely by the fanatical and racialist wing of the Fascist Party (see Fascism*). Mussolini, deprived of his erstwhile monarchical and conservative allies, tried to revert to his republican and populist origins. His Salò regime, however, won no mass support and was rightly perceived as a puppet of Nazi Germany. Without German troops to protect it, the Salò Republic crumbled before the combined assault of Allied armies and Italian partisans in April 1945.

                                                                                          ACas

SALVADORI, GIULIO. One of the principal collaborators on Angelo Sommaruga's* *Cronaca Bizantina*,* Salvadori was born near Arezzo on September

14, 1862, and died in Milan in 1928. He abandoned aestheticism and Carduccianism in the mid-1880s, returning with passionate zeal to his childhood Catholic faith. For nearly a half century thereafter he was one of the major figures in the revival of Italian Catholicism, as a lyceum and university teacher, as an organizer of Catholic educational groups (Operai della Parola, 1887), as a poet (*Canzoniere civile*, 1889), and as the editor of a famous Catholic journal (*L'ora Presente*, 1894–97) that attempted to popularize the ideas contained in the papal encyclical *Rerum novarum** (1891).

Salvadori was deeply influenced by the latitudinarian religious ideas of Paul Desjardins (1859–1940), until the latter unrestrainedly took up the cause of Modernism.* Although he then became increasingly conservative, he opposed Fascism* from his faculty position at the Catholic University of the Sacred Heart in Milan. Toward the end of his life Salvadori interpreted the modern world of bolshevism, Fascism, and liberalism as a gigantic illness, the only antidotes for which were the wisdom and love of the Holy Father. He is a candidate for beatification in the Catholic Church.

RD

SALVATORELLI, LUIGI. Luigi Salvatorelli, who was born on March 11, 1886, in Marsciano, Perugia, and died in Rome on November 3, 1974, was a historian and a journalist. His research on early Christianity won him a chair at the University of Naples. In 1921 he left his academic career to become an editor of Turin's *La Stampa.** A democratic liberal, he was a staunch anti-Fascist. His book *Nazionalfascismo* (1923) interpreted Fascism* as a reactionary phenomenon that reflected the confused hopes of petty bourgeois groups fearful of losing status in a rapidly changing society. Compelled to leave *La Stampa* in 1925, he resumed his studies of medieval and modern history, among which are *Sommario della storia d'Italia dai tempi preistorici ai nostri giorni* [A concise history of Italy] (1939) and *Risorgimento: Pensiero e azione del Risorgimento* [*Risorgimento* thought and action] (1970). A founder of the Action Party* (1942), he later joined the Democratic-Republican Concentration and directed the Rome weekly *La Nuova Europa* (1944–46). In 1956 he and Giovanni Mira published *Storia d'Italia nel periodo fascista* [History of Italy in the Fascist period]. From 1949 until 1974 he wrote for *La Stampa*.

CFD

SALVEMINI, GAETANO. An extremely influential historian, social critic, and *meridionalista*, Salvemini was born in Molfetta (Bari) in 1873. He was also an active member of the Italian Socialist Party (PSI)* and criticized the reformist leadership for its neglect of the South. On the pages of *Critica Sociale** and in the party congresses Salvemini argued that the South was the crucial political obstacle to reforms because Giovanni Giolitti's* shady practices in this region guaranteed him a majority in the Chamber of Deputies. The northern Socialists ignored these activities, Salvemini charged, because Giolitti treated their constituents well. Salvemini described government interference in southern elections and Giolitti's cooperation with the underworld in the classic *Il ministro della mala vita*. As a political remedy for the South he advocated universal suffrage, a measure he believed would counteract government intervention, increase Socialist representation, and make reforms possible. Salvemini insisted that the party give universal suffrage top priority, something which Filippo Turati* opposed because he feared such a measure would increase the Catholic vote. Anna Kuliscioff* and Claudio Treves* supported Salvemini, leading to a dispute within the leading Socialist group. The most serious effects, however, occurred when the reformists of the right, especially Leonida Bissolati* and Ivanoe Bonomi* seized upon universal suffrage as a pretext to support Giolitti, a move that Salvemini angrily opposed. In 1911 Salvemini left the party over the Southern Question* and founded his own newspaper, *L'Unità*.*

Salvemini was among the earliest and most prestigious opponents of Fascism,* going into exile in 1925. In 1934 he began teaching at Harvard University. He spoke and wrote against Fascism and during his time in the United States inspired the group of anti-Fascists located in the Boston area which published the review *Controcorrente*. In 1949 he appeared to reevaluate his position on Giolitti in a famous introductory essay to a book written by A. William Salomone. Although he made it clear that Giolitti could be interpreted in a better light only by comparing him to Mussolini,* Salvemini set off a major historiographical debate on Giolitti's role, especially with regard to the development of Italian democracy.

In addition to his political role and his importance as a critic of modern Italy, Salvemini is noted for his extensive writings on the history of medieval Italy. After World War II* he returned to Italy; he died in Sorrento on September 6, 1957.

For further reference see: Massimo L. Salvadori, *Gaetano Salvemini* (Turin: Einaudi, 1963); A. William Salomone, *Italy in the Giolittian Era* (Philadelphia: University of Pennsylvania Press, 1960).

SD

SANFEDISTI. The name was first applied to the armed bands of peasants organized by Cardinal Fabrizio Ruffo* into the "Army of the Holy Faith," which in 1799 overthrew the French satellite republic in Naples. The Sanfedisti represented the spontaneous resistance of the southern peasants, deeply Catholic and devoted to their traditional rulers, to a regime that offended their deepest convictions. After 1815 the term was applied to the reactionary secret societies organized to oppose those of the liberals; it was also applied, more generally, to those who supported "throne and altar" against revolution.

AJR

SAN GIULIANO, ANTONINO PATERNÒ CASTELLO, MARQUIS DI. Foreign minister (December 1905–February 1906; March 1910–October 1914), San Giuliano was an assertive defender of Italian interests in the Mediterranean,

North Africa, and the Balkans. He was born on December 10, 1852, in Catania, and died on October 16, 1914, in Rome. He served as mayor of Catania at twenty-six, as deputy at thirty, and as an active parliamentarian under Agostino Depretis.* San Giuliano remained close to Giovanni Giolitti,* whom he first served as undersecretary for agriculture (May 1892–November 1893). He was an opponent of Antonio Di Rudinì's* policy of colonial retrenchment after 1896. San Giuliano was minister of posts and telegraphs under Luigi Pelloux* (May 1899–June 1900) and foreign minister under Alessandro Fortis* at the time of the Algeciras Conference* (January 1906). Although loyal to the Triple Alliance,* he favored the French position in the Moroccan question. He was ambassador to London between 1906 and 1909, and in 1910 began his long tenure at the Foreign Ministry in the successive governments of Luigi Luzzatti,* Giolitti, and Antonio Salandra.* He promoted the Italian venture in Libya* (1911–12), obstructed Serbian and Austrian expansion in Albania,* and refused to sanction Austria's plans for a preventive war against Serbia in 1913. With the outbreak of war in 1914, although seriously ill, he steadfastly resisted pressures from both the Central Powers and the Triple Entente,* charting the course of a vigilant and negotiated Italian neutrality.*

SS

SAN MUN AFFAIR. See **CANEVARO, FELICE NAPOLEONE**

SANTAROSA, SANTORRE ANNIBALE DE ROSSI DI POMAROLO, COUNT DI. This patriot and revolutionary figure was born in Savigliano on October 18, 1783. He served as syndic of Savigliano in 1808 and then as subprefect of La Spezia under the French. Head of a division in the Ministry of War (1816) under the restored government, he longed for the creation of an Italian state under a constitutional monarchy. Counting upon the support of Charles Albert of Savoy,* Santarosa was the moving spirit behind the revolutions of 1820–21* in Piedmont, which ended with Austrian intervention and the withdrawal of the constitution. Forced into exile, he went to Paris and, after his arrest there, found his way to England. At the end of 1824 he left for Greece and was killed while fighting as a simple soldier on the island of Sfacteria on May 8, 1825.

FJC

SAPRI EXPEDITION. See **PISACANE, CARLO**

SARACCO, GIUSEPPE. Prime minister (June 1900–February 1901) and dean of the Italian parliament, his major achievement was the pacification of parliament and the country after the crisis of obstructionism and the assassination of King Humbert I* in 1900. He was born on October 9, 1821, in Bistagno (Alessandria), and died on January 19, 1907, in Acqui. A member of parliament from December 1849 to 1865 when, failing reelection, he was appointed senator, at first he sat at the Right (see Destra, La*) as a Cavourian (see Cavour*), then moved toward the Center-Left, and eventually became less partisan. Secretary-general for public works in Urbano Rattazzi's* cabinet (March–December 1862) and secretary-general of finance in Alfonso La Marmora's* first cabinet (October 1864–December 1865), Saracco was public works minister under Agostino Depretis* (April–July 1887) and twice under Francesco Crispi* (August 1887–March 1889; December 1893–March 1896). In other periods he was vice-president of the Senate (March 1878–February 1880; June 1886–April 1887) and president (November 1898–June 1900; February 1901–October 1904).

SS

SARAGAT, GIUSEPPE. This Socialist leader, born September 19, 1898, joined the reformist Unitary Socialist Party in 1922. In exile after 1926, he was a member of the Directorate of that party and one of the architects of the reunification of the reformist and maximalist wings of Italian socialism in 1930. Considered an early opponent of ''unity of action'' with the Italian Communist Party (PCI)* in 1934, Saragat gradually shifted ground under the impact of Nazism. He helped found the domestic underground of the Italian Socialist Party (PSI)* during the 1930s and collaborated on the *Nuovo Avanti!** and *Politica Socialista*. In 1939 he joined with most other Socialists in breaking with the Communist Party after the Hitler-Stalin Pact of August, but Saragat again shifted in 1943 when he signed the alliance between the Italian Socialist, Communist, and Action parties (see Action Party*).

After 1945 Saragat emerged as the leader of the anti-Communist right wing of the Italian Socialist Party. In 1947, at the Palazzo Barberini congress of the Socialist Party, he led the dissidents who formed what became the Italian Social Democratic Party.

Saragat served as a member of numerous postwar Italian governments and was elected president of the Republic* from 1964 to 1971. He is currently a senator for life and president of the Social Democratic Party.

AJD

SARTO, GIUSEPPE MELCHIORRE. See **PIUS X**

SBARBARO, PIETRO. Famous in the 1880s as the ''mad professor,'' Sbarbaro (1838–93) authored books and edited newspapers with a pronounced monarchist point of view. He blamed the woes of the nation on the parliamentary system, and in his notoriously salacious newspaper, *Le Forche Caudine* (financed by Angelo Sommaruga*), Prime Minister Agostino Depretis* was denounced as ''the new Circe.'' The House of Savoy looked with disdain on the eccentric professor's blustering activities, and the Depretis government shut down *Le Forche Caudine* in 1885, destroying the Casa Sommaruga in the process.

Sbarbaro went to prison for a time but was released when the voters of Pavia elected him to parliament in December 1885. A lasting political career failed to materialize, and after a brief exile in Switzerland he returned to Italy and served a five-year prison sentence. Free for the last two years of his life, through illness and poverty Sbarbaro continued to edit newspapers until the end.

RD

SCAPIGLIATURA. The *scapigliatura* literary movement of the 1860s and 1870s, centered in Milan, also flourished in Turin and Genoa, and eventually spread south to include Naples. Celebrating *la vie bohème*, it rejected middle-class morality. The major figures in the movement were Giuseppe Rovani (1818–74), Cletto Arrighi (1830–1906), Emilio Praga (1839–75), Iginio Ugo Tarchetti (1841–69), Arrigo Boito (1842–1918), Giovanni Camerana (1845–1905), and Carlo Dossi (1849–1910). Some of the *scapigliati* painted; others wrote music; however, the movement was essentially a literary phenomenon. These writers translated mid-nineteenth-century French literature, principally the books of Baudelaire, Gérard de Nerval, Alfred de Musset, Théophile Gautier, Rimbaud, and, through them, Poe into Italian.

RD

SCARFOGLIO, EDOARDO. Edoardo Scarfoglio was born in Paganico (L'Aquila) in 1860 and died in Naples in 1917. A failed poet and an unfulfilled novelist who turned to literary criticism, Scarfoglio became one of the so-called *bizantini maggiori* on Angelo Sommaruga's* *Cronaca Bizantina** from 1881 to 1884. His best critical pieces of this period were collected in *Il libro di Don Chisciotte*, an anthology modeled on Giosuè Carducci's* *Confessioni e battaglie* (1883–84). The Abruzzese aesthete and anti-Socialist advocate of imperialism then switched to political journalism, and with his wife, Matilde Serao,* he founded the extremely conservative *Corriere di Napoli* in 1888. Disputes with the paper's financial backer, the Neapolitan millionaire Matteo Schilizzi, caused Scarfoglio and Serao to leave the *Corriere*, and in 1892 they founded *Il Mattino*. This paper rapidly became an institution in Italian journalism, and Scarfoglio, under the pseudonym "Tartarin," used it to advance Francesco Crispi's* expansionist policies in Africa and his anti-Socialist policies at home.

The Italian disaster at Adowa* and the subsequent political turmoil in Italy, culminating in the May Days of 1898, temporarily gave him a more sober outlook on the country's future, however. Scarfoglio then turned uneasily to Giovanni Giolitti* as the last and best hope for all Italians who feared the onslaught of socialism; thus, for the next ten years *Il Mattino* was the voice of Giolittianism in southern Italy. That alliance ended with Giolitti's overtly democratic fourth ministry and with his failure to win a great empire in the Libyan War (see Ouchy, Treaty of*).

Scarfoglio was disappointed again, this time by Antonio Salandra.* Convinced that German might was invincible, he waged a vigorous editorial campaign in 1914–15 against intervention on the side of the Triple Entente.* Scarfoglio could only see defeat and revolution issuing from the war. This view isolated him from the main currents of Italian politics after 1915, and by the time of his death, just a few weeks before Caporetto* and the Russian Revolution, *Il Mattino* had lost its position as the leading interpreter of the ideas and sentiments of the southern bourgeoisie.

RD

SCELBA, MARIO. An active collaborator of Don Luigi Sturzo* and a prominent member of the Christian Democratic Party,* Scelba was born in Catania on September 5, 1901. As a young man, he joined Catholic student organizations—the Federazione Universitaria Cattolica Italiana (FUCI)* and the Laureati—received his law degree from the University of Rome, and was a member of the Partito Populare Italiano (PPI) (see Italian Popular Party*). When the party was dissolved in 1926, Scelba remained in contact with its leaders, Sturzo and Alcide De Gasperi,* and wrote anti-Fascist articles in *La Punta* and *Conquiste Sociali* under a pseudonym.

Scelba was one of the chief organizers of the Christian Democrats, and accepted a cabinet post in the 1945 government of Ferruccio Parri.* Later, under De Gasperi, he served in various ministerial positions. A member of the Chamber of Deputies* from 1948 to 1968, Scelba became prime minister in February 1954, his government lasting until July 1955. In 1968 he was elected to the Senate* and was subsequently very active in the European Parliament, becoming its president from 1969 to 1971.

RJW

SCHUSCHNIGG, KURT VON. Kurt von Schuschnigg, an Austrian political leader, was born at Riva Sul Garda in 1897 and died in Austria in 1977. He was Austrian Christian Socialist chancellor from July 1934 to March 1938. He continued the clericocorporativist regime of his predecessor, Engelbert Dollfuss,* who was assassinated in July 1934. Until about 1936 he enjoyed support from Mussolini.* At Berchtesgaden in February 1938, Hitler demanded of Schuschnigg concessions undermining Austrian independence. Schuschnigg returned to Austria and called for a plebiscite on the issue of independence. Hitler used this as a pretext for annexing Austria in March and imprisoning Schuschnigg. Mussolini did not object and in return received Hitler's pledge of perpetual friendship. Imprisoned between 1938 and 1945, Schuschnigg later taught in the United States. He retired to the Tyrol, where he died.

JAL

SCIALOJA, ANTONIO. A liberal political leader and economist, Scialoja was born at San Giovanni a Teduccio (Naples) on August 1, 1817, to a family of pasta manufacturers. He studied political economy and by the 1840s was well established in an academic career that took him as far as the University of Turin. Having joined the liberal faction in the revolutions of 1848,* Scialoja became minister of agriculture and commerce. He broke with the advocates of constitutional monarchy after the attempted royal coup of May 15, 1848. Arrested in 1849 and sentenced in 1852, he was allowed to emigrate to Turin, where he taught economics and published treatises on finance and taxation. In 1860 Scialoja joined Giuseppe Garibaldi's* provisional government in Naples as minister of finance. He served in the Chamber from 1860 to 1865 and in the Senate from 1865 until his death. As minister of finance during the war of 1866* he issued the controversial decree on the inconvertibility of the lira into gold. Scialoja served as minister of education from 1870 to 1872, but after his resignation from that post he abandoned active involvement in politics and resumed his scholarly pursuits. He ended his career as a financial adviser to the Egyptian government and died on the island of Procida on October 13, 1877.

CML

SCLOPIS DI SALERANO, PAOLO FEDERICO. Jurist and statesman, he was born in Turin on January 10, 1798. Liberal in his outlook, he opposed the violent overthrow of the established order and favored gradual reforms instead. Thus, though he entered the circle of liberals surrounding Cesare Balbo,* he did not take part in the revolutions of 1820–21.* With the accession of Charles Albert of Savoy* to the Piedmontese throne in 1831, Sclopis was a member of the commission appointed to reform the country's laws and in particular to devise a new civil code. Later he took part in the elaboration of the constitution granted by Charles Albert (see *Statuto**). With the onset of the constitutional regime he entered the Balbo government as minister of justice and favored the conclusion of a new concordat with the Holy See. When this proved impossible, he questioned the unilateral alteration of church-state relations demanded by the Left (see Sinistra, La*) and supported by Count Cavour.* He entered the Senate in 1849 and presided over it from 1863 to 1864. In that house he often spoke on church-state issues, opposing the suppression of the religious orders and the introduction of civil matrimony. Opposed to the September Convention* of 1864, from that year onward he increasingly removed himself from political life. In 1864 he was elected president of the Royal Academy of Turin, a position he held until his death. In 1871 he presided over the international commission to settle the Alabama controversy between the United States and Great Britain. He died in Turin on March 8, 1878.

FJC

SECOLO, IL. See **NEWSPAPERS**

SECOND VATICAN COUNCIL. See **VATICAN II**

SECOND WAR OF ITALIAN INDEPENDENCE. See **WAR OF 1859**

SECOND WORLD WAR. See **WORLD WAR II, ITALY IN**

SEGNI, ANTONIO. Twice prime minister and once president (1962–64) of the postwar Italian Republic, Antonio Segni was born on February 2, 1891, to a wealthy family of Sardinian landowners. He received his doctorate in law from the University of Rome in 1913 and embarked upon a career in academia as a professor and in politics as a member of Don Luigi Sturzo's* Partito Popolare (see Italian Popular Party*). His political activity was interrupted by the Fascist suppression of the Popolari, but his academic career flourished, culminating in his appointment in 1943 as rector of the University of Sassari.

In 1944 Segni entered the first Christian Democratic government in Italian history as undersecretary for agriculture and forestry, rising to minister under Alcide De Gasperi.* Responsible for sweeping agricultural reforms and extensive land distribution, Segni became the target of right-wing attacks in the early fifties. He also served as minister of public instruction under De Gasperi before being called to form his own government in 1955. It lasted until 1957. Prime minister again from 1959 to 1960, Segni became president in 1962 but was forced to resign in 1964, when he suffered a near-fatal stroke. He died on December 1, 1972.

RJW

SELLA, QUINTINO. Thrice finance minister, famous for his quest for a balanced budget, Sella was the chief architect of early united Italy's financial policies; a vigorous if unpopular leader of the post-Cavourian Right (see Destra, La*); and an internationally distinguished man of science. He was born on July 7, 1827, in Sella di Mosso (Novara), and died on March 14, 1884, in Biella. After a career as an engineer, mineralogist, mathematician, and university professor (Turin), he entered politics in 1860 and remained in the Chamber until his death. Finance minister under Urbano Rattazzi* (March–December 1862) and again under Alfonso La Marmora* (September 1864–December 1865), whose fall he occasioned by proposing drastic tax increases to meet calamitous budgetary deficits, Sella's longest tenure as finance minister came under Giovanni Lanza* (December 1869–July 1873). In fact the strongest man in the government, he approached a balanced budget at the cost of "ferocious taxation" and "economics to the bone"; virtually vetoed the King's preference to side with France against Prussia in the war of 1870; insisted on the occupation of Rome (September 1870); and supported the Law of Papal Guarantees* (May 1871). But Sella's unpopularity, to which he was notoriously indifferent, weighed heavily on the Right, a part of which defected, leading to the fall of the Lanza-Sella government in July 1873. He never returned to ministerial office.

SS

SENATE OF THE REPUBLIC. The Senate is the upper or second house of the Italian parliament. Since 1963 the Senate has 315 elected members who are chosen for a five-year term. In addition, each president of the Republic* may appoint five lifetime senators, and former presidents are lifetime senators. Senate seats are generally apportioned to the regions on a population basis, and senators are elected by voters who are at least twenty-five years of age. A modified proportional representation system is used, which results in a Senate that is politically similar to the Chamber of Deputies.* The Senate exercises powers equal to those of the Chamber of Deputies, but the lower house is the more prestigious body.

EER

SEPTEMBER CONVENTION. This agreement was signed between the government of Marco Minghetti* and the French Empire on September 15, 1864, to regulate the Roman Question.* Napoleon III* agreed to withdraw French troops from Rome within two years in return for a pledge from the Italian government to respect and protect what remained of the temporal power of the papacy from outside incursions. As a sign that the Italians had abandoned Rome, they promised to move their capital from Turin to another city within six months. Eventually they decided to move the capital to Florence. In the convention the Italians withdrew their opposition to the formation of a papal army of volunteers drawn worldwide, so long as such a force remained defensive and did not threaten Italian territory. Finally, the Minghetti government agreed to pay part of the debt of the papal territory that had been previously incorporated into the Italian Kingdom.

From the first the convention aroused controversy. It angered Italian patriots such as Giuseppe Garibaldi,* who refused to renounce Rome; it sparked riots in Turin that precipitated the fall of Minghetti; and, finally, it upset Pius IX,* who responded at the end of 1864 with his encyclical *Quanta cura*, to which was appended the Syllabus of Errors* condemning liberalism and nationalism, among other things.

FJC

SERAO, MATILDE. Born of a Greek mother and a Neapolitan patriot in exile, Matilde Serao (1856–1927) was perhaps Italy's best-known woman writer during her lifetime. She was extremely prolific, and many of her works were regularly translated into English and other languages. Her best writing described the social conditions of Naples in books such as *Il paese di Cuccagna* [The land of Cockayne], *Il ventre di Napoli* [The belly of Naples], and *Leggende napoletane* [Neapolitan legends].

Serao also occupies an important place in the history of Italian journalism, being one of Italy's first newspaperwomen. She went to Rome in 1882, where the success of her early stories gave her entrée into the hectic milieu of late nineteenth-century Italian journalism. She contributed to the most stylish periodicals of the time, including *Capitan Fracassa* and the *Cronaca Bizantina*,* meeting such people as Gabriele D'Annunzio* and the mercurial journalist Edoardo Scarfoglio,* whom she married in 1884 and with whom she was to have a stormy and unhappy relationship. With Scarfoglio she founded and coedited a number of newspapers, the most important of which was the Neapolitan *Il Mattino*. In 1904 she split from Scarfoglio and founded *Il Giorno*, which she ran for many years.

Despite their tendency to be too long, Serao's works give an extraordinary picture of social conditions in the Italy of the period à la Flaubert. Her best love novels, such as *Fantasia* [Fantasy] and *Cuore infermo* [The sick heart], make important statements on the repressed condition of women, even though they are less powerful than her portrayals of the plight of poor women in works such as *Suor Giovanna della Croce* [Sister Giovanna of the cross], *Telegrafi dello stato* [State telegraphs], and *La ballerina* [The ballet dancer]. Serao also described well the political corruption of Rome during the late nineteenth century and ended her career with an antiwar novel, *Mors tua* [Your death], which reportedly provoked Mussolini* into vetoing her for the Nobel Prize. Finally, Serao should be remembered for her writings on etiquette and for her travel book on the Holy Land, *Nel paese di Gesù* [In the country of Jesus].

SD

SETTEMBRINI, LUIGI. A politician, teacher, and man of letters who was active in the Neapolitan *Risorgimento*,* Settembrini was born in Naples on April 17, 1813. He attacked the Bourbon government in a celebrated pamphlet, *Protesta del popolo delle Due Sicilie* [Protest from the people of the Kingdom of the Two Sicilies], published in 1847. As cofounder in 1848 of a secret society, Unità Italiana, he was arrested and imprisoned during the repressive aftermath of the revolutions of 1848*. He escaped while being deported and returned to accept the chair of Italian literature at the University of Naples in 1861. His most noted works include the *Lezioni di letteratura italiana* [Lessons from Italian literature] (1866–72) and his *Ricordanze* [Recollections] (1879–80). After being nominated to the Senate in 1873, he died in Naples on November 4, 1876.

MSG

SETTIMO, RUGGIERO. A Sicilian politician who played an active role in the revolutions of 1820–21* and 1848,* he was born in Palermo on May 19, 1778. Settimo served as minister of the navy (1812–13) and minister of war (1813–14) after the granting of the constitution of 1812. Subsequently identified with liberalism and the cause of Sicilian autonomy, he was a member of the "Committee of Safety" in 1820 and became president of the provisional government in Palermo in 1848. Escaping to Malta in 1849, he died there on May 2, 1863, after being nominated to the Italian Senate.

MSG

SEVEN WEEKS WAR. See WAR OF 1866

SFORZA, CARLO. A prominent diplomat and politician who served both the parliamentary governments of the pre-Fascist period and the early governments of the Republic, Carlo Sforza was born of a noble family in Montignoso on September 25, 1873. Educated at home and groomed by his father, Count Giovanni Sforza, for a career in the diplomatic corps, Carlo began his service abroad in 1911 as a minister plenipotentiary to China and subsequently was transferred to Serbia. Italian High Commissioner in Turkey at the end of World War I,* Sforza returned to Rome in 1919, serving first as undersecretary for foreign affairs in the government of Francesco Nitti* and then as minister under Giovanni Giolitti* (1919–21).

Sforza was the Italian ambassador in Paris when the March on Rome* brought Mussolini* to power in 1922. Rather than serve the Fascists, he resigned his post and went into exile, living in France, Belgium, England, and the United States. During this period he authored many books and articles on European diplomacy and politics. With the fall of Fascism,* Sforza returned to Italy, becoming a minister in the coalition government (April–June 1944) and later playing an important role in international affairs in the governments of Ivanoe Bonomi* and Alcide De Gasperi.* A strong supporter of a close alliance with the United States and hostility toward the USSR, Sforza remained a prominent figure in Italian politics until his death in Rome on September 4, 1952.

RJW

SICCARDI LAWS. These reform measures were introduced under the Massimo D'Azeglio* government for the purpose of adapting the relationship of church and state in Piedmont to the requirements of the newly instituted constitution. Siccardi, a jurist long involved in ecclesiastical affairs and keeper of the seals, introduced the bills in parliament on February 25, 1850, after failure to obtain Roman approval for alteration of the 1841 Concordat.

The laws provided for the abolition of ecclesiastical tribunals and clerical immunities; prohibitions of donations of property to religious bodies without prior governmental approval; and abandonment of penalties for the nonobservance of religious feasts. Passed by parliament with the approbation of the Left (see Sinistra, La*), though not without serious debate in the Senate, they were signed by the King on April 9, 1850. D'Azeglio thought they demonstrated the vigor of the constitution; many Catholics viewed them as a unilateral abrogation of a treaty and a declaration of war upon the Church.

JCR

SIDOLI, GIUDITTA BELLERIO. A dedicated revolutionist, Sidoli was one of the most prominent women activists in Giuseppe Mazzini's* inner circle. She was born in Milan in 1804. The sister of Carlo Bellerio, a student leader in the 1821 riots in Pavia, at the age of sixteen she married Giovanni Sidoli of Reggio Emilia, who was convicted in 1822 of conspiracy against the Duke of Parma. He fled into exile, losing his substantial property, and was soon followed by Giuditta and their four young children. But Giovanni Sidoli died in 1829, and his widow then returned to Reggio Emilia. The abortive revolution of 1831* put

Giuditta Sidoli in jeopardy again, and she fled to Marseilles with her fellow Emilian, Giuseppe Lamberti. Through Lamberti, Mazzini's right hand in France, she became active in the Young Italy (Giovine Italia*) network and met Mazzini, with whom she fell in love. Although very fond of her, however, he refused then, as always, to make a commitment to marriage and family. For two decades Sidoli devoted her energies to the revolutionary cause, moving constantly in and out of Italy to escape surveillance, while her children remained with relatives in Reggio Emilia. She returned there in 1852 but was arrested when revolutionary literature and other items were found in her home. Her oldest daughter, Elvira, then persuaded her to settle in Turin, where she died on March 28, 1871.

CML

SIGHELE, SCIPIO. A prominent irredentist spokesman and a resident of Nago, in the Trentino,* Sighele was born in Brescia on June 24, 1868. He held university positions in Italy in sociology and criminology. Such studies as *La coppia criminale* [The criminal couple] (1893) and *La donna nuova* [The new woman] (1898) were widely translated. Difficulties of Italians under Austrian rule spurred Sighele to join with the imperialist and conservative Enrico Corradini* in the formation of the Italian Nationalist Association* of 1910. He favored ethnic-cultural defense for Austria's Italian subjects until international circumstances sanctioned liberation. On April 21, 1912, Sighele resigned from the association over its antidemocratic posture. Intensifying irredentist activity provoked his expulsion from Nago on June 2, 1912. Sighele died on October 21, 1913, and was interred at Nago on November 16.

RSC

SILONE, IGNAZIO. Ignazio Silone was the pseudonym of Secondo Tranquilli, who was born in Pescina dei Marsi (L'Aquila) on May 1, 1900, and died in Geneva on August 22, 1978. A writer and politician, he helped lead the Socialist youth federation into the new Italian Communist Party (PCI)* in 1921. After a decade of holding important posts within the Communist movement, Silone was ousted from the Central Committee and expelled from the party in 1930 over his opposition to Stalinist practices. Silone remained an exile from Fascism* in Switzerland, where he wrote the novels *Fontamara* (1934) and *Pane e vino* [Bread and wine] (1936). During World War II* he helped reorganize the political bureau of the Italian Socialist Party (PSI)* in Switzerland. His active political career briefly resumed when he was elected as a Socialist deputy to the Constituent Assembly of 1946,* but in 1947 he left the party along with those Socialists who rejected an alliance with the Communists. After 1948 Silone became an exponent of "humanist socialism." He was editor of *Tempo Presente* and president of the Italian Association for Cultural Freedom. His other writings include *La scuola dei dittatori* [School for dictators] (1938) and *Uscita di sicurezza* [Emergency exit] (1965).

AJD

SINISTRA, LA. Originally a term used to designate democratic and republican elements in the Piedmontese parliament of 1848, from the 1850s onward, and especially after unification, the Sinistra (the Left) came to mean that wing of Italian liberalism which accepted constitutional monarchy but did not wholly renounce those democratic origins that distinguished it from the Liberal Right (see Destra, La*). The radically democratic and republican elements formerly associated with the Left thereafter became known as the Extreme Left (Estrema). When the Liberal Left came to power in 1876, it enacted part of its program of electoral, fiscal, and educational reforms; but the moderate character of these reforms made possible increased collaboration with the Liberal Right (transformism*), and alienated the two ''Lefts'' from each other even more, until the crisis of the late 1890s, when they joined in opposition to the government of Luigi Pelloux.* This collaboration, in which the newly formed Italian Socialist Party (PSI)* participated, marked the origins of the fitful alliance between Liberal and Extreme Left characteristic of the Giolittian era, during which the Radicals, having accepted the permanence of constitutional monarachy, came closer to the Liberal Left, while the Republicans and Socialists, opposed to monarchy on principle, comprised the anticonstitutional part of the Extreme Left. The long rule by the Liberal Left was interrupted in 1914 by the accession of Antonio Salandra's* government of the Right, and came to a definitive end with the postwar political realignment.

SS

SISMONDI, JEAN CHARLES LEONARD, SIMONDE DE. Economist, literary critic, and historian (1773–1842), he was born at Geneva, where he received his early education. Genevan politics obliged him to flee to England in 1793 and then to Tuscany, where he wrote an early work on agronomy: his *Tableau de l'agriculture toscane* (1801). Suspected of Jacobinism (see Jacobins*) during the reaction of 1799, he returned to his native land. His mature ideas developed through the contradictory currents of the Napoleonic period. His economic works, *De la richesse commerciale* (1803) and *Nouveaux principes d'économie politique* (1819), developed ideas of Adam Smith and Jean Baptiste Say. In criticizing Say's law of markets he developed an underconsumption theory of economic crises. His literary works were encouraged by Mme. de Staël, whose circle he frequented at Geneva. As a result he wrote his *Histoire des républiques italiennes du moyen age* (1807–8), an important work for the revival of interest in medieval Italy, and particularly in the liberties of the Italian city-states. His *De la litterature du midi de l'Europe* (1813) particularly reflects the influence of de Staël, whose interest in climate as a determinant of national character, however, he abandoned in favor of a more historical and political view, which he developed further in his lengthy *Histoire des Français* (1821–42). Sismondi also maintained a large literary correspondence with leading contemporaries.

For further reference see: J. R. de Salis, *Sismondi, 1773–1842* (Paris: H. Champion, 1932).

                                                                                                        RBL

SOCIALIST PARTY. See **ITALIAN SOCIALIST PARTY**

SOCIAL QUESTION. This generic term refers to a number of socioeconomic problems evident in Italy during the latter part of the nineteenth century and the early years of the twentieth. The term came into currency soon after unification in reference to the depressed conditions of the peasantry throughout Italy, but especially in the South (see Southern Question*), so that for a time "southern" and "social" questions were almost synonymous. The inquiries initiated by Agostino Bertani* (1872), the studies by Leopoldo Franchetti* and Sidney Sonnino* on conditions in the southern provinces (1875, 1877), and the massive parliamentary report on the state of Italy's agriculture and peasantry (Stefano Jacini,* 1881–85) were major factors in focusing national attention on the lot of the peasantry. By the end of the century, the question became enlarged owing to the problems attendant on increased industrialization, and on the agitation of the question by militant socialism, as well as by the Church in the encyclical *Rerum novarum** (1891). With regard to industrial workers, the issues consisted of the conditions and remuneration of work and the related problems of labor organization and the right to strike. For the peasantry, the problems were the lot of day and seasonal laborers, labor contracts, sharecropping agreements, and land tax assessments. The burden of indirect taxes weighed on both industrial workers and poor peasantry, as did inadequate educational opportunities and emigration.* Early legislative responses to the question produced a nominally compulsory elementary education law (1877), complete abolition of the grist tax (see Macinato*) (1884), inadequately funded old age pension programs (1895, 1898), a modest child labor law (1886), minimal industrial accident insurance (1883, 1898), and a law to guide and protect emigrants (1901). Greater progress in attenuating the sharpness of the social question, made dramatically evident by the disturbances of the Fasci Siciliani* (1893–94) and the events of May 1898, occurred during the Giollittian era (1901–14), when, in addition to various programs for the economic recovery of the South, a series of reforms was enacted, including a more liberal attitude toward the organization of labor and the right to strike; new laws on child and female labor (1902); laws extending the age of, and enforcing the provisions for, compulsory elementary education (1904, 1906, 1910); laws on a weekly day of rest (1907); maternity benefits for working women (1907); compulsory accident insurance for workers in Sicilian sulphur mines (1908); reduction of excise taxes (1907–8); and a state monopoly of life insurance, the yield from which was assigned to the national fund for invalidity and old age pensions (1912). These reforms hardly ended the social question, but they did indicate an increased willingness to address it. The Fascist regime introduced a comprehensive but not always effective body of social legislation, much enlarged during the post-Fascist period.

For further reference see: Pasquale Villari, *Scritti sulla questione sociale in Italia* (Florence: Sansoni, 1902); Angiolo Cabrini, *La legislazione sociale, 1859–1913* (Rome: Bontempelli, 1913); Giustino Fortunato, *Il Mezzogiorno e lo stato italiano*, 2 vols., 2nd ed. (Florence: Vallecchi, 1926).

SS

SOCIETÀ ALTI FORNI E FONDERIA DI PIOMBINO. See **PIOMBINO**

SOCIETÀ BANCARIA ITALIANA. The Società Bancaria Italiana (SBI) was officially established in October 1904 when the Società Bancaria Milanese (founded in 1898) absorbed the assets of the bankrupt Banco di Sconto e di Sete and changed its name. The bank expanded quickly over the next two years (its assets jumped in value from 36 million lire to 182 million lire) and became, by its own reckoning, the third largest ordinary credit "mixed" bank in the country and the most "Italian" of them all.

The SBI, following the example of larger rivals like the Banca Commerciale Italiana* and the Credito Italiano,* was committed to financing industry, especially the creation and growth of new corporate enterprises. By 1905 it had already participated in the establishment of eighteen different companies, including firms in textiles, automobiles, sugar refining, construction, engineering, and electric power production. The expansion was perhaps too rapid; by 1907 the bank was in serious financial difficulty and was saved from collapse by the intervention of the Banca d'Italia.* The bank's directors indicated in their annual report of 1908 that they intended to pursue a more prudent and cautious investment policy in the future.

In 1914 the SBI was merged with the Società Italiana di Credito Provinciale to form the Banca Italiana di Sconto. This new institution was the creation of Ansaldo,* the giant steelmaking and engineering firm, and by the end of World War I* was nearly the equal of the Banca Commerciale Italiana.

JSC

SOCIETÀ BANCARIA MILANESE. See **SOCIETÀ BANCARIA ITALIANA**

SOCIETÀ NAZIONALE ITALIANA. Founded in July 1857 by Daniele Manin,* leader of the Venetian Revolution of 1848 (see Revolutions of 1848*), and Giorgio Pallavicino Trivulzio,* a prominent liberal patrician from Lombardy,* the SNI was a major protagonist of the struggle for Italian independence and unity.

Except for the Mazzinian networks, the SNI was the most successful, cohesive, and widespread political organization of the *Risorgimento** era. Its members, especially in north-central Italy, were instrumental in preparing the ground for the military campaigns and annexationist demonstrations of 1859–60. Although their means were subversive and revolutionary, the leaders of the SNI were committed to a constitution such as the Sardinian *Statuto** of 1848, which left broad powers in the hands of the monarch, and to a legislature elected by mature men of means.

Despite the SNI's very moderate political ideology, prominent democratic activists such as the Lombard Agostino Bertani* joined it in 1858–59 when they realized its potential for success within the context of Cavour's* foreign policy. However, the leadership of the society remained in the hands of those moderate liberals who were to head Italy's government from the unification until 1876.

CML

SOCIETÀ OPERAIE. Among the earliest forms of working-class organizations in Italy, the Società were founded in northern Italy in the 1850s. After the unification they spread to other parts of the country as well. The leadership came almost entirely from Mazzinian cadres who believed in Italian national unity and in the need to integrate the lower classes in the political revolution. Rank-and-file members came from salaried workers, especially in urban areas, but also from artisans.

Mazzinian militants such as Maurizio Quadrio, Aurelio Saffi, and Bartolomeo Francesco Savi, as well as independent democratic activists such as Mauro Macchi,* expected the Società to provide the foundation of a democratic state that would eventually replace the one created by the liberals. Members of the Società took an oath of allegiance similar to that of Young Italy (see Giovine Italia*) and pledged to help one another in need. Cooperative banks, evening schools, and kindergartens were often created to provide services otherwise lacking in working-class communities. In the 1880s the Società lost members and leaders to the emerging Italian Socialist Party (PSI),* but they continued to exist as symbols of a native, non-Marxist tradition of secular and democratic politics.

CML

SOFFICI, ARDEGNO. Ardegno Soffici was born in Rignano sull'Arno on April 7, 1879. He was an artist and writer who moved from impressionism, to Futurism,* to neoclassicism. He collaborated before 1914 on the reviews *La Voce** and *Lacerba*, became an ardent supporter of Italian entry into World War I* in 1915, and documented the war on the Italian front in *Kobilek* and *Ritirata dei Friuli*. Soffici was an early member of the Fascist Party (see Fascism*) and influenced Fascist art along rural and neoclassical lines. He died in 1964 at Forte dei Marmi (Lucca).

AJD

SOFFITTA, LA. See **LERDA, GIOVANNI**

SOLARO DELLA MARGARITA, CLEMENTE, COUNT. This political figure and Piedmontese diplomat was born in Cuneo on November 21, 1792. During the French occupation of Piedmont, he developed a deep religious sentiment and an attachment to the Savoy dynasty, coupled with a profound distrust of liberalism. He received his degree in law in Turin in 1812 and after the Restoration (1816) served as secretary to the legation in Naples. An ardent supporter of the Carlists, he was named minister plenipotentiary to Madrid in 1826 and remained there until 1834. In 1835 Charles Albert of Savoy* entrusted him with the Ministry of Foreign Affairs, and in this office Solaro pursued a conservative and legitimist course. In 1839 he managed to reestablish the nunciature in Turin, which had been suspended since 1753. The count left office at the end of 1847 and from 1854 to 1860 sat in the Chamber of Deputies, where he attacked the ecclesiastical and foreign policies of Cavour.* He died in Turin on November 12, 1869.

FJC

SOLFERINO, BATTLE OF. A decisive battle in the struggle for Italian independence, it was fought on June 24, 1859, between the Austrian troops under the command of Emperor Francis Joseph,* and the French and Sardinian forces under Emperor Napoleon III* and Victor Emmanuel II.* It ended with the overwhelming defeat of the Austrians, whose losses numbered 22,000, compared to 17,000 for the Allies. The results of this battle led to the meeting of the two emperors at Villafranca.*

WR

SOMALIA. A republic in northeast Africa bordering Ethiopia* and Kenya, it was formerly the British Somaliland Protectorate (1885–1960) and the colony of Italian Somaliland (Somalia Italiana). Through the efforts of Vincenzo Filonardi,* an Italian chartered company rented the coastal ports of Somalia from the Sultan of Zanzibar (1893–96). In 1905 a successor company went bankrupt, and amidst charges of scandal and slavery the Italian government formally proclaimed a colony. In its mostly nomadic semi-desert colony, Italy promoted the development of banana plantations at great expense and little profit. In 1935–36 Somalia was a staging ground for the Italian invasion of Ethiopia. Occupied by the British early in World War II,* subsequently the colony became a UN Trust Territory under Italian administration and gained its full independence in 1960. It merged with the British protectorate of Somaliland, leaving more than 1 million ethnic Somalis and a persistent irredentist problem in the Ogaden province of Ethiopia and the northern frontier district of Kenya.

RLH

SOMMARUGA, ANGELO. As Rome's most eminent publisher and literary impresario from 1881 to 1885, Sommaruga (1857–1941) brought forth more than 130 books, and his newspaper-journal holdings included five titles. His principal publication and the one which has given its name to this five-year period in Italian cultural history was the *Cronaca Bizantina*,* an aesthetic journal featuring the prose and poetry of Giosuè Carducci* and Gabriele D'Annunzio.* Sommaruga's downfall occurred when he financed the yellow journalism of Pietro Sbarbaro* in *Le Forche Caudine*, a scurrilous newspaper that assailed the powerful ministry of Agostino Depretis.* When the government counterattacked by shutting down the newspaper, Sommaruga's entire establishment was destroyed in the operation.

The young publisher went to trial in 1885, was imprisoned briefly, and then was allowed to leave the country. His subsequent publishing endeavors in South America ended in bankruptcy, after which he spent many years as an antique furniture dealer, operating between Paris and Buenos Aires. Near the end of his life Sommaruga began to write various memoir articles and an autobiography; these remain valuable sources of information and also contain vivid portraits of early Humbertian cultural life.

RD

SONNINO, SIDNEY COSTANTINO. This politician is famed for his two one-hundred-day governments and for his leadership of the parliamentary opposition during the Giolittian era. Sonnino was born in Pisa on March 11, 1847, the second son of Isacco Sonnino, a wealthy Jewish banker from Livorno, and his wife, Georgina Menhennet Terry, an English lady reared in Portugal and Egypt. Baptized into his mother's Anglican faith, Sonnino was taken back to the family home in Alexandria, Egypt, where he remained until political events forced his father to terminate his long career there in 1850 and return permanently to Italy. When Sidney and his older brother, George, were old enough to enter *ginnasio*, the family moved from Livorno to an imposing palace in Florence just as the Grand Duchy of Tuscany was absorbed into the Kingdom of Italy. After completing preparatory schooling, Sonnino entered the University of Pisa, from which he was graduated in 1865 with a law degree. Following a brief apprenticeship in a Florentine law firm, he entered the diplomatic corps in 1867 and served successively in Madrid, Vienna, Berlin, and finally Paris, where he witnessed the events of the Commune, the most influential experience in his life.

Frustrated by the formalities of diplomatic life, Sonnino returned to Florence in 1871 and began the literary and political activity his personal fortune permitted and which engaged him until his death. Beginning with pamphlets and articles on universal suffrage, proportional representation, agrarian economics, and a variety of social issues, Sonnino went on to coauthor, with Leopoldo Franchetti,* the famed *Inchiesta in Sicilia* (see Sonnino and Franchetti, *Inchiesta in Sicilia**) and to found *La Rassegna Settimanale*.*

Sonnino first entered political life in 1877 as mayor of the Tuscan commune of Montespertoli, site of one of the family's several estates and that which he inherited on his father's death in 1878. Sonnino remained active in local politics there until World War I,* a period during which he was simultaneously a member of the provincial council of Tuscany. In 1880 he was elected to the Chamber of Deputies from San Casciano in Val di Pesa, the district encompassing Monte-spertoli, an office to which he was reelected ten times and held until 1919.

From his entry into parliament, Sonnino sat in the Center with a group initially composed of young men distinguished by their moderate views and enlightened social goals. As deputy, Sonnino spoke less frequently than many of his colleagues but earned a reputation for personal integrity, independent views, consummate skill in economic and social issues, and occasional acerbic exchanges, particularly with deputies of the Left (see Sinistra, La*). With the passage of the years, Sonnino grew more conservative, although he always considered himself a reformer. His speeches and political writings often reflected his profound admiration of English constitutional government. His interpretation of English political models often caused him, however, to be erroneously considered a spokesman for a German chancellorship form of government. Respected though he was, Sonnino never attracted a personal political following of any size, and his only constant ally through his long political career was Antonio Salandra.*

For a few months in 1889, Sonnino was undersecretary of the treasury in Francesco Crispi's* first government. When Crispi returned as prime minister in 1893 Sonnino served as minister of the treasury and of finance. In addition to authoring the bill that created the Banca d'Italia* in 1892, Sonnino, as minister under Crispi, is credited with balancing the budget and saving Italy's finances in the wake of the banking scandals earlier in the 1890s.

Always the advocate of Italian colonial expansion, Sonnino was profoundly disturbed by Italy's defeat at Adowa* in 1896. That disaster, coupled with social crises such as the Fasci Siciliani* and the Milan riots of 1898, pushed Sonnino into a period of political authoritarianism and reaction. This phase was highlighted by his famed article "Torniamo allo Statuto"* in 1897, and finally by his role as leader of the majority under Luigi Pelloux.* In that capacity he led the fight to change the Chamber's rules so as to gag the democratically oriented "obstructionists."

King Humbert I's* assassination in 1900 so deeply affected Sonnino that he underwent a return to his earlier moderate conservatism, as his contemporary articles "Questioni urgenti"* and "Quid agendum?"* demonstrate. He also founded in 1901 the Rome daily, *Il Giornale d'Italia*,* as a vehicle for his concern with the Mezzogiorno and his desire to promote socioeconomic reforms, albeit with a spirit of benevolent paternalism. In 1906 Sonnino was called to form a government and did so with the first inclusion in a cabinet of representatives of the Extreme Left as well as with external support from the Socialists. The program Sonnino enunciated bore some similarity to that of the minimalist Socialists and was utilized in large measure by Giovanni Giolitti* for his long ministry from 1906 to 1909. When Sonnino's government fell after only one hundred days, he was so disillusioned that he virtually withdrew from politics for the following year. However, Austria's annexation of Bosnia-Herzegovina in 1908 roused his long commitment to Italian irredentism* and brought him back to parliamentary activism. He was called again to form a government in December 1909, but its spiritless character suggested that the arrangement was little more than an interim device to prepare the way for a return of the Giolittian group to government. When his second cabinet fell after only one hundred days, Sonnino identified himself with the cause of Italian colonial expansion in Libya* and the institution of universal male suffrage. His backing of these two programs somewhat reconciled him with Giolitti, whom he had opposed for two decades.

Taken by surprise at the outbreak of war in 1914, Sonnino first favored maintaining Italy's commitment to the Triple Alliance,* but he soon moved to favor neutrality* and intervention on the side of the Triple Entente.* When Salandra named him foreign minister in November 1914, Sonnino became the principal architect of the Treaty of London,* which brought Italy into the war in 1915 alongside England, France, and Russia. As the only minister remaining in office with all the wartime governments, Sonnino went to the Paris Peace Conference* determined to assure Italian territorial compensation, particularly in the Adriatic. Failing in this goal, partially due to the application of Woodrow Wilson's principles of self-determination, Sonnino left office when the government of Vittorio Orlando* resigned and did not run for his old seat at the elections later in 1919. Although he was named senator in 1920, Sonnino withdrew as a disillusioned man and spent considerable time at Il Romito, his seaside castle near Livorno, where he was buried after his death in Rome on November 24, 1922.

Sonnino, who remained a bachelor throughout his life, was the only Protestant ever to be prime minister of Italy. Beyond his political and journalistic activities, he dedicated himself to scholarly pursuits, particularly the study of Dante. He founded the Casa di Dante in Rome, which he wanted to be a monument to his career.

There is no biography of Sonnino in English and only a few brief pieces on him in Italian, the best of which is Camillo Montalcini's introduction (pp. xi–lxxii) in the first volume of Sidney Sonnino, *Discorsi parlamentari*, 3 vols. (Rome: Tipografia dello Stato, 1925). See also Sidney Sonnino, *Opera omnia*, ed. Benjamin F. Brown and Pietro Pastorelli, 8 vols. (Bari: Laterza, 1972–81).

BFB

SONNINO AND FRANCHETTI, *INCHIESTA IN SICILIA*. This classic 1877 work by Sidney Sonnino* and Leopoldo Franchetti* first called public attention to the socioeconomic problems of the Italian Mezzogiorno and launched serious scientific study of the Southern Question,* particularly in Sicily. The Sonnino-Franchetti initiative had its origins in the official parliamentary inquiry authorized in 1875 after general recognition that the exceptional measures applied in Sicily had not succeeded in reestablishing order in the island. The parliamentary group was directed to go to Sicily to investigate conditions there and report its findings and proposals.

Believing that an official group would not gain the Sicilians' confidence and ascertain their true feelings or be able to perceive the nature of the island's problems, Sonnino and Franchetti, together with Enea Cavalieri, undertook to conduct their own parallel and private study of the area. The three men toured Sicily on horseback from January to May 1876, interviewing people from all walks of life and recording their impressions of social, economic, political, and administrative conditions. On returning home to Florence, Sonnino and Franchetti published their findings in two volumes entitled *Inchiesta in Sicilia*. Sonnino's volume was subtitled *I contadini* [The peasants] and Franchetti's was called *Le condizioni politiche e amministrative della Sicilia* [Political and administrative conditions in Sicily]. Cavalieri's manuscript, which survived until 1925, was never published.

Upon their appearance in early 1877, the two volumes roused enormous interest throughout Italy but notably hostile criticism and bitter resentment from the landowning classes in Sicily. Nevertheless, the work achieved almost immediately favorable comment for its accuracy despite the bleak picture portrayed. Several of the proposals made by the authors, such as support for peasant land ownership and various plans for combatting the Mafia,* were regarded as quite daring for the time. Still, the Sonnino-Franchetti inquiry from the time of its publication completely overshadowed the Bonfadini report, as the official parliamentary study was known.

Although the recommendations of Sonnino and Franchetti were largely ignored, the study laid permanently to rest the myth of Sicily as the garden of the Mediterranean. Enduring interest in the *Inchiesta* is shown by its translation into German (Dresden: Carl Tittmann, 1906) and two subsequent Italian editions (Florence: Barbera, 1925; and Florence: Vallecchi, 1974). The first edition was published in Florence by Barbera in 1877.

BFB

SOUTHERN QUESTION. A major historical issue of national politics, it addresses the problem of integrating the economically disadvantaged regions of the South into the national state. The term originally referred to the former territories of the Kingdom of the Two Sicilies,* but since 1945 it designates other underdeveloped areas as well, including Sardinia, the minor islands, and specific provinces in Central Italy. Public awareness of the Southern Question developed slowly in the decades following national unification. The rapid liberation and annexation of the South in 1860–61 allowed no opportunity for assessing its resources and needs. Ignorance of southern poverty, the desire to centralize the public administration, and ill-founded optimism that progressive, honest, and efficient leadership would quickly solve the problems of the South set the stage for the outbreak of brigandage.* Furthermore, there was broad resentment of government policies on taxation, compulsory military conscription, and economic protectionism. Soil exhaustion, pervasive deforestation, illiteracy rates that in some areas hovered around 90 percent, and an inefficient agriculture based on latifundian estates and absentee ownership were major and largely unacknowledged causes of the Southern Question.

In the 1860s government officials concentrated on suppressing brigandage and restoring law and order by military means. Private sociological investigations conducted in the early 1870s by Leopoldo Franchetti* and Sidney Sonnino* and the parliamentary *Inchiesta agraria* of 1877–85 documented the problems of the South and pointed to the need for comprehensive remedial measures. At the turn of the century champions of the South known as *meridionalisti*, including effective publicists like Giustino Fortunato,* Gaetano Salvemini,* and Pasquale Villari,* launched a vigorous and partly successful campaign to dramatize the seriousness of the Southern Question. Their documented claims that government policies since the 1860s had actually increased the gap between North and South by promoting the economic development of the former at the expense of the latter helped convince parliament to pass special legislation between 1900 and 1914 to reduce taxes, combat malaria, provide public works, and encourage the industrialization of the Naples area. These programs were continued and even stepped up in the period between the two world wars in spite of the Fascist regime's reluctance to officially recognize the persistence of the Southern Question. The most systematic efforts to solve the Southern Question belong to the period since 1945. The Cassa per il Mezzogiorno,* the Industrial Reconstruction Institute (IRI),* and other government agencies have implemented land reforms, industrial development, public projects, and social security programs of immediate and long-term benefit for the South. Most important, migration in the context of European Economic Community agreements has provided an outlet for surplus labor. The Southern Question remains nevertheless a pressing issue in national politics due to the persisting problem of uneven regional development.

For further reference see: Rosario Villari, ed., *Il Sud nella storia d'Italia* (Bari: Laterza, 1961).

                                                                                        RS

SPADOLINI, GIOVANNI. See **CHRISTIAN DEMOCRATIC PARTY; ITALIAN REPUBLICAN PARTY;** and **PROPAGANDA DUE**

SPANISH CIVIL WAR, ITALIAN PARTICIPATION IN. Despite flamboyant rhetoric and the bombardment of Corfu, Mussolini* did not deviate from traditional Italian foreign policy during the first decade of his rule. Yet he did evince a desire to enhance Italy's position in the Mediterranean, including the Balearic Islands. To that end he sought to make the most of the visit to Rome in November 1923 of the Spanish king, Alfonso XIII, and General Miguel Primo de Rivera, who had assumed dictatorial powers in September. The establishment of the Second Spanish Republic in 1931 promised to prove an impediment to Mussolini's ambitions in the Western Mediterranean. In 1934 he pledged aid to Spanish monarchists conspiring to overthrow the Republic.

The Spanish Civil War was the result of class antagonisms and conflicting social philosophies within Spain itself. Outside influences played little part in bringing about the conflagration. But outside forces were decisive in determining which camp, Loyalist or rebel, would prevail.

Italian military support of the insurgent generals began within a few days of their uprising on July 17, 1936. While it was German crews and transport planes that enabled most of the Army of Africa to cross from Spanish Morocco to Andalusia—the first airlift—Italian aircraft were in action against Republican warships in the Strait of Gibraltar.

The military strength represented by the trained, well-equipped Moroccan soldiery—in itself of crucial importance amid the collapse of authority—was significantly augmented in the months to come by the weapons and fighting men sent Franco by Mussolini and Hitler. The Italian military contribution included hundreds of aircraft, both bombers and fighters, thousands of artillery pieces, tanks, and trucks, and the services of nearly 100,000 men, including infantry, earning the CTV (Corpo Truppe Volontarie) the place of honor in Franco's victory parade. This was supported by a diplomatic and propaganda effort that further vitiated the Nonintervention Agreement to which Italy officially adhered. (Some 4,000 anti-Fascist Italians fought in the International Brigades, the Garibaldi Battalion distinguishing itself in the defeat of Mussolini's army at Guadalajara.)

Italian intervention in the Spanish conflict was prompted mainly by strategic and ideological considerations, buttressed by Mussolini's personal quest for glory and, after the defeat at Guadalajara, by the need to avenge the loss and safeguard the prestige of the Fascist regime. Although the Italians and Germans intervened independently of each other, they were brought together by their common struggle in Spain. There their friendship and alliance were forged.

For further reference see: Gabriel Jackson, *The Spanish Republic and the Civil War, 1931–1939* (Princeton: Princeton University Press, 1965); Dante A. Puzzo, *Spain and the Great Powers, 1936–1941* (New York: Columbia University Press, 1962); John F. Coverdale, *Mussolini and Franco: Italian Intervention in the Spanish Civil War* (Princeton: Princeton University Press, 1974).

DAP

SPAUR, KARL VON. Karl von Spaur, Bavarian minister in Rome, 1832–48, was born on March 3, 1794, in Wetzler, Bavaria, to an aristocratic family with a long tradition of government service. Entering the Bavarian diplomatic service, he held various posts in Vienna, Berlin, and Frankfurt before his appointment in 1832 as minister to the Holy See. A conservative who believed firmly in the union of church and state against revolution, he worked to promote closer relations between Bavaria and the Vatican, winning the trust of the papacy by his role in settling various religious disputes. His most notable exploit took place when he helped Pope Pius IX* to escape from Rome after the radical uprising of November 1848 (see Revolutions of 1848*). He died on October 26, 1854, while en route to Florence.

AJR

SPAVENTA, BERTRANDO. Philosopher and historian of philosophy, by linking Hegel's thought with earlier Italian philosophy (Giordano Bruno, Tommaso Campanella) he laid the foundation for the twentieth-century neo-Hegelianism of Benedetto Croce* and Giovanni Gentile.* Born in Bomba (Chieti) on June 26, 1817, Spaventa became a priest in 1840 to please his family; but by the 1850s he was in Turin, writing anti-Catholic tracts on academic freedom. He taught briefly in Turin and Bologna before settling at the University of Naples in 1861, where he remained until his death on February 20, 1883. For his writings on the principles and history of philosophy, and on Hegel, Bruno, Campanella, Kant, and Vincenzo Gioberti,* see especially *Scritti filosofici* (1900) and *Da Socrate a Hegel* (1905), edited by Gentile.

HP

SPAVENTA, SILVIO. This patriot and political figure was born in Bomba (Chieti) on May 10, 1822. He settled in Naples, where he and his brother Bertrando opened a school that stressed philosophy. In March 1848 he established the journal *Il Nazionale*, which sought a federal solution to the Italian question, and in April 1848 was elected to the Neapolitan Chamber of Deputies.

Disillusioned with the constitutionalism of the Bourbon government, in conjunction with Luigi Settembrini,* Filippo Agresti, and Cesare Braico, he founded Unità Italiana, a secret society that sought unification. Arrested during the reaction of 1849, Spaventa was subjected to a long trial that aroused the conscience of Europe because of the corruption of the judges and the bribing of witnesses. He was condemned to death, but his sentence was commuted to imprisonment and then exile.

He returned to Italy in 1859 and supported the policies of Cavour.* Finding his way to Naples on the eve of Giuseppe Garibaldi's* arrival, he served as minister of police during Luigi Carlo Farini's* tenure there. Subsequently he was nominated undersecretary of the interior in the Farini-Minghetti ministry and had to assume much of the responsibility for the suppression of the disorders in Turin following the announcement of the September Convention.* In 1873 he was named minister of public works in the last cabinet of the Destra* presided over by Marco Minghetti.*

Spaventa championed a strong state above political parties and favored nationalization of the country's railroads. His proposal for state control was opposed by the Tuscan deputies, who withdrew their support from the government, precipitating the fall of the Destra in 1876. In 1889 he was nominated to the Senate. He died in Rome on June 21, 1893.

For further reference see: Silvio Spaventa, *Discorsi parlamentari* (Rome: Tipografia della Camera dei deputati, 1913); G. Farolfi, *Il concetto di stato in Silvio Spaventa* (Bologna, 1946).

FJC

SPEDIZIONE DEI MILLE. See **GARIBALDI, GIUSEPPE**

SPERANZE D'ITALIA, DELLE. This book by Cesare Balbo* was published in 1844 and dedicated to Vincenzo Gioberti.* Analyzing the various hopes of ridding northern Italy of Austrian control, Balbo found a league of Italian princes unlikely, and a national agitation similar to Ireland's impossible (since Italy had no Daniel O'Connell), while foreign help was fraught with the dangers of foreign occupation. According to Balbo, the only hope for the independence of Lombardy* and Venetia resided in the possibility of a war leading to a dissolution of the Turkish Empire into which Austria would be drawn. Details concerning a future confederation were unresolved by Balbo, though he disliked republics and preferred a strong prince like Charles Albert of Savoy* who would ultimately establish a deliberative government. Unlike Gioberti's *Primato*, published the year before, Balbo's work did not place much stock in the prospect of papal leadership and saw Italy's hope in Piedmont's establishment of a strong Italian kingdom north of the Po. The book was an immediate success and found its place in the literature of the moderate liberals.

MSM

SPINI, GIORGIO. This historian of modern Italy was born in Florence on September 23, 1916, and is a graduate of the University of Florence, where he subsequently taught. Spini's range of scholarship is vast. His two major works are *Storia dell'età moderna* [History of the modern age] (3 vols., 1962) and *Autobiografia della giovane America. La storiografia americana dai padri pellegrini all'indipendenza* [Autobiography of young America: American historiography from the pilgrim fathers to independence] (1968).

RSC

SPIRITO, UGO. Ugo Spirito, philosopher and university professor, was born in Arezzo on September 9, 1896, and died in Rome in 1979. He was a student of the idealist philosopher Giovanni Gentile.* Spirito was attracted to the philosophy of law and to economic theory, emerging as one of the leading corporative theorists in Italy. Along with Arnaldo Volpicelli, he edited the journal *Nuovi Studi di Diritto Economia e Politica*. In 1932, at the corporative congress of Ferrara, Spirito developed the theory of the corporation as owner of the means of production. He believed that only in this way could the dichotomy between the individual and society be overcome. Spirito thus carried corporative theory (see Corporativism*) to a collectivist extreme that was rejected by most Fascists as a form of communism.

AJD

STAMPA, LA. A newspaper founded in 1867 as the *Gazzetta Piemontese* and renamed in 1895, *La Stampa* of Turin has long rivaled Milan's *Corriere della Sera** for primacy in Italian journalism, both in the quality of its coverage and in circulation. Refashioned from provincial to national scope by Luigi Roux, and especially by Alfredo Frassati after 1900, *La Stampa* has counted distinguished journalists, men of letters, scholars, and political figures among its editors and contributors. Anti-Fascist and always loyal to Giovanni Giolitti* and his progressive liberalism, Frassati sold his interests in *La Stampa* in 1926, when it fell into Fascist hands. In the post-Fascist period it resumed its Left-Center orientation and its former journalistic excellence.

For further reference see: Valerio Castronovo, *"La Stampa" di Torino e la politica interna italiana, 1867–1903* (Modena: Società Tipografica Editrice Modenese, 1962); idem, *La Stampa italiana dall'unità al fascismo* (Bari: Laterza, 1970).

SS

STARACE, ACHILLE. Achille Starace was secretary of the National Fascist Party from 1931 to 1939. Born in Gallipoli (Lecce) in 1889, he served as a combat infantry officer in World War I,* and was awarded many decorations for valor. One of the first adherents to Fascism,* he organized and led Fascist action squads in the Trentino.* Of the many posts he held, the most important and sensitive was that of national secretary of the party. Under his leadership membership rose from 1 million in October 1932 to 2.6 million by December 1939. Starace, however, failed to invigorate the ranks, as many of the old guard refused to step aside. His attempt to use the party as an instrument of national unity and fascistization was widely resented. Starace's efforts and those of his predecessor, Roberto Farinacci,* to give Fascism a unique set of gestures, called *costume e mistica fascista*, and the pushing of the cult of the Duce were his most controversial actions. As war neared, Starace called for tightening of discipline, compulsory attendance at patriotic rallies, public processions, more spirited ideological lectures, formalized greetings, and enforced deference to rank and ritual, all of which had apish, arbitrary, and totalitarian overtones. To silence mounting criticism, Mussolini* felt compelled in December 1939 to replace him with the more congenial Edoardo Muti. Despised by the anti-Fascists, Starace was shot by partisans in Milan on April 28, 1945, and late that evening his body (along with those of Mussolini, Farinacci, and Clara Petacci) was suspended head downward at Piazzale Loreto in Milan.

RSC

STATUTO. The Sardinian Constitution of 1848, which became the Constitution of the Kingdom of Italy* in 1861, the *Statuto* was written by the ministers of

King Charles Albert of Savoy* in response to popular demonstrations in Genoa and Turin. Reluctantly, Charles Albert agreed to proclaim it on February 8, 1848. His half-hearted acceptance of a new role as a constitutional monarch violated a pledge he had given his predecessor, Charles Felix,* in exchange for forgiveness of his liberal past. The *Statuto* sanctioned a sharing of power between the monarch and a parliament chosen by a highly restricted electorate. Ministers, however, remained responsible to the monarch, who maintained control over foreign and military policy. The *Statuto* proclaimed Roman Catholicism to be the state religion but safeguarded the rights of religious minorities.

CML

STERBINI, PIETRO. This writer and political figure was born in Frosinone (in the Papal States*) in 1795. He studied medicine at the University of Rome, where he received his degree. Politics and literature were his other passions, and this was reflected in his tragedy *La vestale*, which was presented in 1827 but quickly prohibited by the police. During the revolutions of 1831* in central Italy, Sterbini attempted to provoke a revolution in Rome but failed. He was forced into exile and eventually found his way to Marseilles (1835), where he practiced medicine and became active in Giuseppe Mazzini's* Young Italy (Giovine Italia*) (1840). Following the election of Pius IX* in June 1846, and the granting of amnesty to political offenders in July, Sterbini returned to Rome.

During the period of Pio Nono's reformism, Sterbini pressed for broader changes through his journal, *Il Contemporaneo*, and through the Popular Club of Rome, over which he presided. Elected a member of the Chamber in May 1848, for a time he pursued the policies of Terenzio Mamiani Della Rovere,* but after Mamiani's dismissal became increasingly radical. He was particularly upset with the Pope's refusal to join the other Italian states in waging war upon Austria.

Sterbini opposed the selection of Pellegrino Rossi* as minister and was allegedly implicated in the November 15, 1848, assassination of Rossi. He was one of the figures responsible for imposing a radical government upon the reluctant Pope and served in it as minister of public works and commerce. Following the flight of Pius to Gaeta,* Sterbini was elected a member of the constituent assembly and voted for the abolition of the temporal power and the creation of the Republic. During the rule of the triumvirate, he did not play an active part in affairs because of his differences with Mazzini. Following the French invasion and the Restoration, Sterbini left for France. He returned to Italy following the proclamation of the Kingdom of Italy* (1861), and died in Naples on October 1, 1863.

For further reference see: Luigi Carlo Farini, *Lo stato romano dall'anno 1815 al 1850*, 3rd ed. (Florence: Felice Le Monnier, 1853).

FJC

STRASSOLDO, GIULIO. A Hapsburg bureaucrat during the Restoration era, Strassoldo was born in Gorizia on September 4, 1773, of a noble Friulian family, and rose rapidly in the Imperial administration. As governor of Lombardy* after 1818, his use of the police and censorship powers won him the hatred of liberals. He was not, however, a reactionary, but favored moderate reforms in the tradition of enlightened despotism, and he disapproved of the procedures used in prosecuting the Lombard conspirators during 1821–23. He died in Milan on May 9, 1830.

AJR

STRESA FRONT. This alignment of Great Britain, France, and Italy against Germany was agreed to by the three prime ministers in a meeting at Stresa on April 11, 1935. Their collaboration reflected Anglo-French concern over Germany's illegal rearmament policy, and Mussolini's* concerns over Hitler's threat to Austria's independence. In the Stresa pact the three governments condemned the violation of treaties which could endanger the peace of Europe and reaffirmed their belief in the necessity of preserving the independence and integrity of Austria. The Stresa Front collapsed in the winter of 1935–36, in the wake of the Anglo-German Naval Agreement and Britain's persuasion of the League of Nations to impose economic sanctions on Italy for its assault on Ethiopia.*

JKZ

STURZO, LUIGI. Born in Caltagirone, Sicily, on November 26, 1871, Sturzo came from a deeply religious family of the Sicilian rural aristocracy. From 1883 to 1891 he studied at the seminaries of Acireale, Noto, and Caltagirone. During these years he aspired to the priesthood, seeing himself in the role of preacher and professor of philosophy. The publication of *Rerum novarum** in 1891 profoundly influenced his thought, making him aware of concrete social problems. After his ordination in 1894 he went to Rome, where, amid studies at the Thomistic Academy and the Gregorian University, he became involved in the social apostolate. Together with Romolo Murri* he became active in the Opera dei Congressi.* In 1898 he received his degree from the Gregorian University and returned to Caltagirone to continue the work of organizing the Catholic masses, especially the rural workers.

In 1905 Sturzo was elected provincial councillor. It was in this capacity that he announced his political program on December 29, 1905. He proposed a national party of Catholics that would be independent of the Church and would not bear the word "Catholic" in its title, although its guiding principles would be based on Christianity. The party would end the hegemony of the ruling liberal classes. The call for such an organization turned out to be premature; the papal ban on Catholic participation in national politics, though modified in 1905, militated against the formation of a party of Catholics. Not until 1918, when Pope Benedict XV* completely rescinded the *non expedit*,* was it possible for the Italian Popular Party* to come into being (January 18, 1919).

The new party reflected the views not only of Don Sturzo but also of the Christian Democrats, who had once followed the lead of Romolo Murri. The platform of the party called for proportional representation, decentralization, women's suffrage, an elective senate (to represent nationwide academic, administrative, and trade-union organizations), extension of land ownership, social legislation, liberty for the Church, and disarmament. Sturzo was the party's political secretary, but his dual role as priest and political leader was an embarrassment to Pope Pius XI,* who hoped to reach an accord with Mussolini.* In July 1923 Sturzo resigned as political secretary, motivated also by veiled threats of Fascist reprisals against the Church if he continued in his post. He remained active in the party until October 1924, when, acceding to the wishes of Cardinal Pietro Gasparri,* papal secretary of state, he went into exile. With London as his headquarters, Sturzo made trips to Paris, wrote sociological and historical books, contributed articles to Catholic journals, assisted refugees from Italian Fascism,* and kept abreast of international developments.

After the signing of the Lateran Accords* (1929), Sturzo proposed the formation of an Italian Popular Party in exile, which would take over when Mussolini fell from power. But Sturzo's project failed for several reasons: his closest associates were dead by 1933; money was lacking; and information about internal developments in Italy was scanty. Ill health made it almost impossible for him to adjust to the rigors of wartime London, and in 1940 he left England and went to the United States, where he lived in New York and Florida.

With the liberation of Rome in June 1944, Sturzo prepared to return to his native country. His early return was blocked, however, by Alcide De Gasperi,* the head of the Christian Democratic Party,* who feared that Sturzo, long famous for his republican views, would polarize Italian Catholics over the institutional question. Pope Pius XII,* through the apostolic delegate Amleto Cicognani, also urged his delay in returning to Italy. In September 1946, after the institutional referendum had taken place, Sturzo, now seventy-five, returned to the country he had left twenty-two years earlier. He was disappointed in the Italy and the Rome that he found; above all, he was disappointed in the Christian Democratic Party. He thought the new party inclined toward socialism and disapproved of all the measures undertaken on behalf of Southern Italy, with the sole exception of the Cassa per il Mezzogiorno.* He found himself frequently at odds with De Gasperi. In the spring of 1952, at the express invitation of the Pope, he sought to bring about a coalition of all the parties of the Right and Center in the forthcoming administrative elections in Rome in order to prevent a Communist victory. Although his role turned out to be minimal, Sturzo was subsequently maligned for having become involved in the maneuver. In the same year as the so-called Sturzo Operation, President Luigi Einàudi* appointed him senator for life. In the Senate* Sturzo declined to join the group made up of Christian Democratic senators, choosing instead a mixed group in order to preserve his freedom of action. During these years he resided at a convent of the Canossian Sisters, leaving the convent only to attend Senate meetings. When he died in Rome on August 8, 1959, he was first buried in a crypt of the Church of San

Lorenzo Fuore le Mure, and later (July 1962) in a mausoleum erected in the Church of SS. Salvatore in his native Caltagirone.

For further reference see: Gabriele De Rosa, *Sturzo* (Turin: UTET, 1977); Francesco Piva and Francesco Malgeri, *Vita di Luigi Sturzo* (Rome: 5 Lune, 1976).

EC

SYLLABUS OF ERRORS. This document was the most controversial doctrinal statement of the popes in modern times because of its blanket condemnation of contemporary political movements and thought systems. Pope Pius IX* issued the encyclical *Quanta cura* on December 8, 1864, with an appended list—or "syllabus"—of eighty "errors" of the times that had already been condemned in other acts, decrees, or allocutions. The encyclical reminded Catholics of the care taken by the popes in watching over the Church and its integrity. Noting the specific threats he perceived to religion in the nineteenth century, particularly from secularism, Pius branded "erroneous" ideas such as pantheism, naturalism, rationalism, indifferentism, socialism, communism, clandestine societies, Bible societies, clerico-liberalism, and others. Special attention was devoted to the errors relating more directly to the Church and its rights in civil society, with special emphasis on the indissolubility of marriage.

In view of the increasing hostility to papal temporal power, notably in the movement for Italian unification, any attack on papal sovereignty was singularly condemned. The liberalism of the 1860s was said to be especially erroneous for its promotion of religious freedom. The eightieth and final "error" became instantly the most criticized and publicized: "It is an error to believe that the Roman Pontiff can or should reconcile himself to progress, liberalism, and contemporary civilization."

The effect of the Syllabus was instant and widespread. Liberal Catholics could not accept it, and traditional or conservative Catholics viewed it as a declaration of war on the contemporary heresies they had been fighting. But the extremity of expression in the Syllabus was such as to make its opponents appear reasonable and thus served to negate its desired purpose. Although never withdrawn, the Syllabus was slowly and tacitly ignored by Pius IX's successors. Nevertheless, its legacy created an image of a Church in opposition to many modern innovations.

BFB

SYNDICALISM. Initially a Socialist current emphasizing the role of the trade union, as opposed to a political party, in creating socialism, Italian syndicalism became a major source of Fascist corporativism* and provided Fascism* with such ideologues and functionaries as Sergio Panunzio,* Michele Bianchi,* and Edmondo Rossoni. The syndicalist current began to develop within the Italian Socialist Party (PSI)* around 1902, spearheaded by Arturo Labriola* and Enrico Leone as a revolutionary, anticollaborationist alternative to reformism. The Italian syndicalists borrowed only selectively from Georges Sorel, with his emphasis on myth and violence, and they did not share the anarchist faith in spontaneous popular insurrection. They focused instead on the process of psychological development through trade-union activity that, they argued, was gradually engendering superior forms of social life among the organized industrial workers.

Syndicalism appeared to have a promising future in the labor movement by 1905, but it encountered defeat thereafter, largely because its major tactic—the militant strike—seemed counterproductive to most workers. During the prewar period, revolutionary syndicalism remained influential only in a few organizations, especially in Parma, Ferrara, Piacenza, and Milan, under such leaders as Alceste De Ambris* and Filippo Corridoni.* This failure in practice led the syndicalists to begin reassessing their conception around 1910. Almost all of them supported Italian intervention in World War I* and came to argue that socialism had to be a national proposition. But more significant was their conclusion that the target of revolution ought to be parliamentary liberalism, not capitalism, and that occupational groupings could provide the basis for a new politics. After World War I, their neosyndicalist blueprint appealed to disaffected young veterans seeking an alternative to both liberalism and orthodox socialism.

Longtime syndicalists were involved with the Fascist trade-union movement from its inception in 1921, but the syndicalist contribution to Fascism was not limited to the defense of working-class interests. Rather, the syndicalists offered a conception of the overall purpose of the Fascist revolution, suggesting a way of overcoming parliamentary liberalism and ordinary politics through a corporativist system based on occupational groupings.

For further reference see: Alceo Riosa, *Il sindacalismo rivoluzionario in Italia* (Bari: De Donato, 1976); David D. Roberts, *The Syndicalist Tradition and Italian Fascism* (Chapel Hill: University of North Carolina Press, 1979).

DDR

T

TAMBRONI ARMAROLI, FERNANDO. This Christian Democratic political figure, born in Ascoli Piceno in 1901, served as minister of the interior in a number of postwar cabinets and presided over the controversial government of 1960, which accepted the support of the Neo-Fascist Party. A notable who had close ties with the president of the Republic,* Giovanni Gronchi,* in April 1960 he formed a transition government that had the support of the MSI* and thus opposed Aldo Moro's* mandate that the Christian Democrats reject the parliamentary support of the Extreme Right and look to the Left. Since his government was deemed temporary, it was reluctantly accepted by the left wing of the party.

Italians of the Left and Center were upset when it became obvious that Tambroni sought to consolidate his power and prolong the life of his government by favoring lower prices on sugar, meat, and gasoline, and by appealing to conservatives through his championing of law and order. In May and June, when there were popular demonstrations in Ravenna and Bologna against the installation of American missiles and strikes in Reggio-Emilia provoked by wage issues, the police acted energetically on the direct orders of the prime minister. Agitation increased in the peninsula, but this did not deter the Tambroni government from authorizing the MSI to hold its national congress in Genoa the first week in July 1960. This decision provoked further demonstrations.

Tambroni, who was accused of turning the Christian Democrats and the country toward the Right, created a new solidarity among the anti-Fascist parties, with the Communists, who had become increasingly isolated, playing the key role in the opposition to Tambroni's new course. There were skirmishes with the police in Genoa; the violence soon spread to other cities of the peninsula and became particularly bitter in the capital, where dozens were injured. Indeed, the explosive situation penetrated the Italian parliament, where there were clashes between the Extreme Right and the Extreme Left in both the Chamber of Deputies* and the Senate.*

Cesare Merzagora, president of the Senate, called for a "truce" that would permit an objective examination of the situation, but feelings were too aroused to heed the suggestion. Charges and countercharges were hurled by the Left and Right. Although it could not be shown that Tambroni had deliberately provoked the disorders in order to restrict liberties and ally the Christian Democratic Party* with the parties of the Right, his flirtation with the MSI, whatever his motives, and the reaction it provoked in the country, alarmed the moderate and Left factions in the party, which disavowed his experiment. Tambroni was therefore forced to resign on July 18, 1960. He died three years later.

FJC

TANLONGO, BERNARDO. See **BANCA ROMANA, SCANDAL OF THE**

TANUCCI, BERNARDO. This Tuscan statesman and lawyer was very influential in the state affairs of Naples for over forty years. He was born in Stia on January 20, 1698. As teacher of jurisprudence at Pisa, his writings attracted the attention of Carlo Bourbon, duke of Parma. He accompanied Carlo to Naples when the latter became king in 1734. He became minister of justice in 1752 and minister of foreign affairs and the royal household in 1754. When in 1759 Carlo became King of Spain, Tanucci headed the regency council in Naples and was later chief minister under Ferdinand IV.

After the birth of Carlo III, a power struggle ensued between Tanucci and the ambitious and meddlesome Queen Maria Carolina. Dismissed in October 1776, he died in Naples on April 29, 1783. Applying Enlightenment* ideas, Tanucci reduced Church power, softened the penal law, reformed the government, and strengthened the position of the Bourbon throne.

FFA

TARTARIN. See **SCARFOGLIO, EDOARDO**

TASCA, ANGELO. Angelo Tasca, Socialist leader and historian, was born on November 19, 1892, in Moretta (Cuneo) and died in Paris on March 3, 1960. A founder and leader of the Italian Communist Party (PCI)* from 1921 to 1929, he was expelled from the party by Stalin in 1929 for rightist deviations (Bukharinism). He became a French citizen in 1936 and a member of both the French and Italian Socialist parties (see Italian Socialist Party, PSI*). Tasca wrote extensively on foreign policy during the 1930s for the Socialist press and led the faction of Italian socialism which was most opposed to cooperation with the Italian Communist Party during the Popular Front era (1934–39). In 1940, after the fall of France, Tasca collaborated with Vichy, while simultaneously working for the Belgian and British Resistance. His most famous work is *Rise of Italian Fascism* (1938), republished in Italian in 1950.

AJD

TAVIANI, PAOLO EMILIO. An important Christian Democratic politician and minister of the post-World War II period, Paolo Emilio Taviani was born in Genoa on November 6, 1912. He received his law degree from the University of Genoa, fought in the Italian Armed Resistance,* and was elected to the Chamber of Deputies* on the Christian Democratic list in 1945. He rose rapidly in the hierarchy of the party, becoming its national secretary in 1949 and serving in various ministerial posts including Defense, Finance and Treasury, Southern Affairs, and Interior. Taviani took a hard line against the Red Brigades,* setting a policy excluding negotiation for the freedom of political prisoners. This stand, opposed by Amintore Fanfani* and Giovanni Leone,* was articulated by Taviani during the celebrated *Caso Sossi* (on April 18, 1974 the Red Brigades kidnapped the Genoese judge Mario Sossi), but was not strongly criticized until after the assassination of Aldo Moro,* which called into question the wisdom of the hard line taken by the Christian Democratic Party.*

RJW

TENCA, CARLO. One of the most influential writers and journalists of the *Risorgimento** period, Tenca devoted his creative life to the Italian national cause. He was born on October 19, 1816, in Milan. After being educated there, he collaborated on the periodicals *Italia Musicale, Corriere delle Dame*, and *Rivista Europea*, becoming literary editor of the latter in 1845. After the revolutions of 1848* he edited *Ventidue Marzo*, the official organ of the provisional government, and after that, the *Italia del Popolo*. When the Austrians returned, he left for Florence to direct the *Costituente Italiana*. At the end of 1849 he returned to Milan and founded the influential weekly *Crepuscolo*, in which he sought to inspire Italians with a sense of their own destiny. During its life, Tenca managed to deal skillfully with the censors so that *Crepuscolo* was published without interruption from January 6, 1850, to March 5, 1859, when the Austrians withdrew. Tenca served in the Italian Chamber of Deputies (1859–65), was involved in Milanese civic affairs, and died in Milan impoverished, after a long illness, on September 4, 1883.

FFA

TERNI. The Società Altiforni, Acciaierie e Fonderie di Terni was founded on March 10, 1884, by a group composed of the state, some banks, and a few industrialists. The intention of the founders was to build in Italy a modern steel mill that would, among other things, meet the needs of the Italian military, especially the navy, for armor plating, guns, and ammunition. The choice of Terni in Umbria as the location for the new enterprise was dictated primarily by strategic and personal considerations rather than by economic ones.

The early years of the company were difficult. Thus, in 1887, one year after it opened for business, Terni was saved from imminent disaster by its principal creditors—the government, the Banca Nazionale del Regno, and the Banca Generale—when they agreed to increase their loans to the firm. A few years later Terni was in trouble again, this time because of the banking crisis in Italy. In this instance, an arrangement was worked out with the newly created Banca d'Italia* for the slow retirement of Terni's debt, which the bank had assumed from the firm's major creditors.

From the mid-1890s, the firm, along with the economy, began to prosper. By 1903 Terni was producing 62 percent of Italy's steel output and 80 percent of domestically produced iron rails. It had also managed to overcome technical difficulties and was able to produce armor plating for ships at least equal in quality to that produced by Krupp.

After 1904 Terni entered into a trust-building phase. It established links with shipbuilding firms and with the Società Elba, and it helped found the Società Ilva.* It also became associated with the Banca Commerciale Italiana.* By 1910 a kind of loose holding company under the general control of the Banca Commerciale Italiana had come into existence, with Terni at its center, which combined iron and steel plants, shipyards, and armaments production.

Although Terni benefited from war demand, its growth did not match that experienced by Ansaldo.* Thus, while the decline in military demand after the war created adjustment problems for Terni, they were not as severe as those faced by some of its competitors. Terni had also begun to diversify during the war, into electronic power production and electrochemicals, and it was in these areas that expansion was especially rapid during the 1920s. In 1933 control of Terni was assumed by the Industrial Reconstruction Institute (IRI).*

JSC

TERRACINI, UMBERTO. Umberto Terracini, a Communist leader, was born in Genoa on July 27, 1895. He was founder of the review *Ordine Nuovo* (in 1919). In 1921 he helped found the Italian Communist Party (PCI).* Arrested in 1926, Terracini was condemned to twenty-three years in prison and was not liberated until September 1943. A critic of Stalin while in prison, Terracini was expelled from the Communist Party in 1943 but was readmitted in 1944. He served in the Armed Resistance* from 1943 to 1945, was elected a deputy to the Constituent Assembly of 1946,* and became its president in 1947. Terracini has been a senator of the Republic since 1948.

AJD

TERUZZI, ATTILIO. This Fascist politician was born in Milan on May 5, 1882, and died in Procida on April 26, 1950. He was one of the vice-secretaries of the National Fascist Party (see Fascism*) (1921–23); was actively involved in the planning for the March on Rome* in October 1922; participated in the fusion negotiations between the Italian Nationalist Association* and the Fascist Party in March 1923; and was undersecretary at the Interior Ministry in 1925 and 1926. Subsequently, Teruzzi was governor of Cyrenaica (see Libya*) from

1926 to 1929 and served as a high official in the Fascist militia until his appointment as minister of Italian Africa in 1937.

AJD

TERZA PAGINA, LA. The cultural page of Italian daily newspapers, unique for its combination of articles on a wide variety of subjects in literature, philosophy, criticism, politics, and the arts, the "third page" evolved as a traditional feature of Italian journalism in the first decade of the twentieth century with the purpose of expanding newpaper coverage beyond the more traditional areas of political, governmental, and international events. *Il Giornale d'Italia** of Rome initiated the feature less than a month after the paper's founding. To counter charges that his daily was colorless and dull, Alberto Bergamini,* the paper's editor, expanded the issue of December 2, 1901, to six pages to accommodate four long articles on the current dramatic production of Gabriele D'Annunzio's* *Francesca da Rimini*.

The publication of articles of cultural interest did not become an immediate and consistent feature of any single page, but when six-page editions appeared, the third page more and more frequently carried items of literary, musical, and artistic interest. Gradually original works of fiction, commentary, criticism, and other features were published by the *Giornale d'Italia*, some on a regular basis.

In 1903, when *La Tribuna* enlarged its edition to six pages, it too began carrying a similar third page. This daily was the first to name a staff primarily responsible for such cultural features. Other major dailies soon followed these examples, most significantly *Corriere della Sera** of Milan in 1905.

As the feature evolved, each paper's third page tended to publish articles reflecting, to an extent, its own political orientation. Many new authors and schools of thought received their first public exposure on the third page, and the first publication of works of various famous writers first appeared in this format. The third page tradition has thus essentially combined the functions ascribed to monthly journals or commercial publishing houses in other countries.

BFB

THAON DI REVEL, OTTAVIO. The career of this political figure, born in Turin on June 26, 1803, began in the Piedmontese financial administration. A conscientious Catholic and trusted minister of Charles Albert of Savoy* from 1844 to 1848, he was elected to the Chamber of Deputies in December 1848 and remained in that house until he was made a senator in 1861. A moderate constitutionalist, he was one of the signers of the *Statuto*,* but urged the government to pursue a cautious policy that would respect the rights of the Church. Therefore, he fought the financial and ecclesiastical policies of Count Cavour,* opposing the Siccardi Laws,* the Civil Matrimony Bill, the Law of Convents, and all attempts to move the nation's capital to Rome.

Revel regretted Cavour's decision of 1852 to break with the Right (see Destra, La*) and ally with Urbano Rattazzi* and the Center-Left. It was he who dubbed the alliance between Cavour and Rattazzi the *connubio*,* or marriage. Following the proclamation of the Kingdom of Italy,* Revel opposed the September Convention* of 1864 with France, which provided for the transfer of the Italian capital from Turin to Florence. He died in Turin on February 10, 1868.

FJC

THIRD WAR FOR NATIONAL LIBERATION. See **WAR OF 1866**

THOUSAND, THE. See **GARIBALDI, GIUSEPPE**

TITTONI, TOMMASO. Four times foreign minister between 1903 and 1919, until 1909 Tittoni struggled to mitigate the differences between Italy and its Austrian and German allies. He was born on November 16, 1855, in Rome, and died on February 7, 1931, in Manziana (Bracciano). Tittoni was conciliatory toward Catholics while active in Roman municipal and provincial politics. He served as liberal conservative deputy to parliament (1886–97), prefect of Perugia (1898–1900) and of Naples (1900–3), and senator (December 1902). Tittoni was also foreign minister under Giovanni Giolitti* (November 1903–March 1905) and Alessandro Fortis* (March–December 1905). Briefly ambassador to London (1906), he became foreign minister again under Giolitti (May 1906–December 1909). While ambassador to Paris (1910–16) he favored Italy's intervention on the side of the Triple Entente* in 1915. As foreign minister under Francesco Nitti* (June–November 1919), he strove in vain to resolve the Fiume* question, over which he resigned. As president of the senate (December 1919–January 1929), he did not oppose the Fascist regime.

SS

TOGLIATTI, PALMIRO. Of Piedmontese origin, Togliatti was born in Genoa on March 26, 1893, and attended high school in Sardinia. His father was a modest state employee and strongly religious—hence the younger Togliatti's first name, for Palm Sunday, on which he was born. In 1911 he received a scholarship to the University of Turin. Though he probably joined the Italian Socialist Party (PSI)* in 1914, Togliatti was more influenced by figures like Gaetano Salvemini,* Georges Sorel, and Benedetto Croce.* During World War I* he served in the army health corps.

In 1917 he became a reporter for the Socialist press, but his real political education began when he joined Antonio Gramsci,* Angelo Tasca,* and Umberto Terracini* in founding the Turinese weekly *L'Ordine Nuovo*. There he was especially known for his biting column on cultural subjects. In 1921 he and the *Ordine Nuovo* group joined Amadeo Bordiga* and others in founding the Italian Communist Party (PCI).* The following year he became a member of the Central Committee and wrote frequently for the party press. After attending the Fifth Congress of the Communist International (CI), he returned to Italy and joined Gramsci and the CI in the struggle to wrest party control from Bordiga. Their victory was completed with the Congress of Lyons (January 1926). Togliatti, under the direction of Gramsci, wrote the "Lyons Theses."

After the arrest of Gramsci in November 1926, Togliatti became the leader of the PCI. Until the dissolution of the CI in 1943, Togliatti was also a major figure in that organization. In the CI Togliatti at first favored a nondogmatic line. By 1929, however, the increasingly hard line of the CI forced Togliatti to adjust the line of the PCI to that of the International. For many years thereafter, Togliatti was regarded as a Stalinist, though he disagreed with many of Stalin's ideas and actions.

In 1934, while in France, Togliatti directly experienced the new Popular Front against Fascism* which the French Communists, Socialists, and Left Radicals had formed. Similarly, he and his party arrived at a pact of unity with the Italian Socialists. This new line of broad unity against Fascism, much more congenial to Togliatti, is embodied in his remarkable *Lectures on Fascism* given at the Leninist School in Moscow. Later in 1935, Togliatti gave a major speech at the Seventh Congress of the CI in which he stressed the unity of the fight against Fascism, the struggle for peace, and the defense of the USSR.

In the summer of 1937, Togliatti was sent to Spain as the representative of the CI to the Spanish Communist Party. Through the experience of the Spanish Civil War,* Togliatti developed the conception of a "democracy of a new type," an idea that became the basis for the politics of the PCI. Spain (and later Italy) could undergo a "bourgeois-democratic" revolution, but one led by the working class on the basis of radical social and economic changes. Among the last defenders of the Spanish Republic, Togliatti arrived in Algeria on March 24, 1939. After a brief return to the Soviet Union, he was back in France in early August. Shortly after the signing of the Nazi-Soviet Pact, he was arrested by the French police. Apparently unrecognized, Togliatti spent six dangerous months in prison and was finally back in the USSR in May 1940. From June 27, 1941, to May 11, 1943, he delivered (as one "Mario Correnti") more than one hundred radio broadcasts to Fascist Italy. When appropriate he informed his audience of military developments and continually urged armed resistance to the regime.

On March 27, 1944, Togliatti was finally able to return to Italy. In a famous speech at Naples, he ended the sectarian tendencies of some members of his party by giving sole priority to national unity of all popular forces in the defeat of Fascism. Even the question of the monarchy would be left to the postwar period. The ensuing armed struggle against Fascism made the PCI, for the first time, a great national party (1,770,896 members at the end of 1945). At the Fifth Congress of the PCI (December 1945–January 1946), Togliatti called for a democracy of a "new type" in Italy. It would be a multiparty progressive democracy dedicated to the elimination of the roots of Fascism. At the Constitutional Assembly of 1946,* Togliatti even urged inclusion of the Lateran Accords* in the new constitution.

This phase of national unity was ended with Alcide De Gasperi's* elimination of both the PCI and the PSI from the government in the spring of 1947 and by the defeat of the Left in the April 1948 elections. Togliatti himself was nearly killed by a crazed neo-Fascist; only his insistence on calm prevented a bloody insurrection. The Cold War years from 1947 to 1955 were difficult and unproductive for Togliatti. In its enforced isolation, the PCI reverted to dogmatism.

Paradoxically, the year 1956—that of the Twentieth Congress of the Communist Party of the USSR and of Hungary—began one of the most fruitful periods of Togliatti's life. In an interview with *Nuovi Argomenti*, he (alone among Communist leaders) used Khrushchev's devastating "secret" speech as the basis for demanding a historical study of Stalinist degenerations and for an "Italian road to socialism." At its Eighth Congress (December 1956), the PCI adopted Togliatti's program of (1) peaceful coexistence; (2) polycentrism; (3) the refusal to accept any leading party or state in world communism; and (4) the unity of the struggle for democracy and socialism.

In August 1964, Togliatti made a last trip to the USSR, where he hoped to discuss recent developments. While vacationing at Yalta, he wrote his so-called Promemoria. It provided both a summary of the situation in the world Communist movement and important considerations on a strategy for the future; for Communists in the West, he urged the building of ever broader alliances through the struggle for peace and democracy; for Communists in the Socialist countries, he insisted on the need for greater democracy, frankness, and self-criticism. Struck by a cerebral hemorrhage, he died at Yalta on August 21, 1964. His leadership helped to transform the PCI from a small band of dedicated outlaws into the largest Communist Party in the West and a major element in Italian politics.

For further reference see: Palmiro Togliatti, *Lectures on Fascism* (New York: International Publishers, 1976); idem, *Opere*, ed. Ernesto Ragionieri (Rome: Editori Riuniti, 1967–76); Donald Sassoon, *The Strategy of the Italian Communist Party* (New York: St. Martin's Press, 1981).

JMC

TONIOLO, GIUSEPPE. A pioneer in Italian Social Catholicism, he was born in Treviso on March 7, 1845, and died in Pisa on October 7, 1918. From 1863 to 1867 he studied at the University of Padua. In 1878 he joined the faculty at the University of Pisa as a professor of political economy; he remained at Pisa until the end of his life. In 1878 he married Maria Schiratti, by whom he had seven children. After the dissolution of the Opera dei Congressi* (congress movement) he became the head of the Unione Popolare of Italian Catholics. He staunchly supported the papacy, and in the controversy between the supporters and detractors of Romolo Murri* in the Christian Democratic movement, he was vehemently anti-Murri.

Toniolo was an apostle rather than a leader of Italian Christian Democracy.* With his basic premise the primacy of Christian ethics in the socioeconomic sphere, he saw Christian civilization as an instrument for the elevation of the lower classes. While defending the concept of private property, he insisted that surplus wealth be used for the needs of the poor, especially the landless. He also believed in the coparticipation of industrial workers in the profits of a company and advocated legislation to control money operations, including the stock exchange. He supported unions, and while his preference was for horizontal unions that included both capital and labor, he encouraged workers to form their own organizations when their employers refused to join them. Toniolo was opposed, however, to an alliance with the Socialists. Instead, he favored a national parliament that included the representation of economic groups (corporativism*).

Regarding democracy, he distinguished between its accidental and essential elements. According to Toniolo, the essence of democracy was liberty, and it could exist in any form of government. The monarchy of St. Louis IX of France in the Middle Ages was, in Toniolo's view, more democratic that the republic of Oliver Cromwell in seventeenth-century England. He thus considered the class antagonisms of his own day to be abnormal, a product of secularism and technology. He had a great admiration for the medieval commune, the order and ethical dimension of which he exaggerated. Toniolo maintained that the age of capitalism would be followed by the age of the worker, and in the Catholic world this would be accomplished through a union between the working classes and the Pope.

For further reference see: Giuseppe Toniolo, *Democrazia cristiana, concetti e indirizzi*, 2 vols. (Città del Vaticano: Edizione del Comitato Opera Omnia di G. Toniolo, 1949).

EC

"TORNIAMO ALLO STATUTO." The most famous piece of political literature of the antiparliamentarian school of thought in the era of the liberal monarchy, it was published in the *Nuova Antologia* of January 1, 1897. Signed only "A Deputy," the article was soon correctly attributed to Sidney Sonnino,* who never publicly acknowledged its authorship.

Written in anticipation of the semicentennial of the promulgation of the *Statuto** by Charles Albert of Savoy,* the article reflects contemporary disillusionment with national political development relative to the idealism implicit in some *Risorgimento** concepts of what the liberal monarchical state ought to become.

Sonnino's thesis was that the Italian parliament had gradually usurped constitutional powers reserved to the throne by the *Statuto*. The result, he argued, was crass political maneuvering amongst parties and the consequent fostering of two forces, clericalism and socialism, which threatened the fabric of Italian society. According to Sonnino's interpretation, this dual menace could be averted and national well-being recouped by returning to the crown those executive powers presumably granted to it by the *Statuto*.

This proposal roused impassioned debate in the critical times in which it appeared. The concept was interpreted as a call for royal absolutism with a Bismarckian type of chancellorship as was current in imperial Germany, thus denying the practice of ministerial responsibility as it had developed in Italy. For the expression of these views, Sonnino was branded the archconservative of Italian politics, particularly when this article was later coupled with the authoritarian positions he took in the Chamber as leader of the majority during the second government of Luigi Pelloux* in 1899–1900.

The seeds of "Torniamo allo Statuto" first appeared in another unsigned Sonnino article, "Il parlamentarismo e la monarchia," published in *La Rassegna Settimanale** of January 18, 1880. Sonnino's persistant refusal to debate the ideas of the 1897 article obscured his apparent goals until long after his death. The posthumous appearance of Sonnino's diary shows his inspiration for "Torniamo allo Statuto" to have derived from his perception of British parliamentary and monarchical practices.

For an annotated text of "Torniamo allo Statuto," see: Sidney Sonnino, *Scritti e discorsi extraparlamentari, 1870–1920*, ed. Benjamin F. Brown (Bari: Laterza, 1972), 575–97.

BFB

TOSCANINI, ARTURO. This conductor dominated Italian musical life in both opera and symphonic music for the first half of the twentieth century. He also became internationally known, especially in America, where he was conductor of the famous NBC Symphony. Toscanini was born in Parma on March 25, 1867. He studied at the Parma Conservatory and became a member of an opera orchestra, as cellist, in Rio de Janeiro at the age of nineteen. He conducted various Italian opera orchestras and by 1898 he was conducting at La Scala. From 1928 to 1936 he conducted the New York Philharmonic and later conducted the best orchestras in Europe and America. Although briefly attracted to Fascism* at its birth, he soon turned against it and became strongly opposed to the Mussolini* and Hitler regimes. He left Bayreuth, where he had conducted at the Wagner festival, because of Hitler, and he later left the Salzburg festival for the same reason. Toscanini died on January 16, 1957, in New York City, and is buried in Milan.

JLD

TRANQUILLI, SECONDO. See **SILONE, IGNAZIO**

TRANSFORMISM. A practice of political compromises and transactions between nominally opposing parties, a transformism of sorts (the *connubio**) originated as early as the 1850s with the collaboration of Cavour* of the Right (see Destra, La*) and Urbano Rattazzi* of the Left (see Sinistra, La*); but it is Agostino Depretis* who made transformism into a system of government during the 1880s. The permanence of the practice derived from the fact that, after unification, such issues as taxation, electoral reform, administrative decentralization, and foreign policy divided not only Right from Left but also both Liberal formations, each of which was a conglomerate of ideological, regional, and personal diversities. Given the need of a stable parliamentary majority in order to govern effectively, Depretis of the Left and Marco Minghetti* of the Right collaborated to this end in the 1880s. The practice reached its height with the advent of the Giolittian era (1901–14), making it possible for Giovanni Giolitti* to dominate the political scene for more than a decade. Its critics alleged that transformism and its consequent compromises corrupted parliamentary life and obstructed the formation of the classic two-party system. Its supporters viewed it as a form of consensus politics designed to avoid destructive confrontations, especially with the growth of the parties of the Extreme Left, whose "domestication" into collaborationist formations within the liberal parliamentary system constituted Giolitti's principal political aim.

SS

TRECCANI, GIOVANNI. See **GENTILE, GIOVANNI**

TRENTIN, SILVIO. Silvio Trentin was born on November 11, 1885, in San Bonà di Piave (Venice). After serving as a reconnaissance specialist in World War I* he resumed his career as a professor of public law. In 1925 he resigned his professorship in Venice in protest against Fascist laws requiring state employees to conform with the aims of the regime. In February 1926 he emigrated with his family to Auch, and late to Toulouse, where from 1934 to 1943 he was among the most militant leaders of the Justice and Liberty movement.* From 1928 to 1934 he published several works on the Fascist legal system, and in 1935 his reflections on the crisis of liberalism and the need for a thoroughgoing Socialist transformation of bourgeois institutions were articulated in the book *La crise du droit et de l'état* [The crisis of law and the state].

In 1942 Trentin founded a Resistance movement in Toulouse, *Libérer et Fédérer*. In 1943 he was active in forging anti-Fascist unity with representatives of the Italian Socialist Party (PSI)* and the Italian Communist Party (PCI).* In early September 1943 he returned to Italy, where he helped organize the Armed Resistance* in the region of Venetia. In November he was arrested in Padua. While in prison he became ill and was released under police surveillance. He died in Treviso of a heart ailment on March 12, 1944.

For further reference see: Silvio Trentin, *Scritti inediti—testimonianze e studi*, ed. Paolo Gobetti (Parma: Guanda, 1972); Frank Rosengarten, *Silvio Trentin dall'interventismo alla Resistenza* (Milan: Feltrinelli, 1980).

FR

TRENTINO; ALTO ADIGE. This frontier region between Italy and Austria, the southern portion (Trentino) having Trent as its major city, was long a center of Italian irredentism* before World War I.* The northern portion (Alto Adige: Südtirol) became a source of Austro-Italian tensions when acquired by Italy in 1919 and retained in 1947. Preponderantly Italian in language, the Trentino was incorporated by Austria into the county of Tyrol after the Napoleonic Wars.

Repeatedly sought by Italy during the wars for independence (see Revolutions of 1848*; Wars of 1859,* 1866*), acquisition of the Trentino, whose strategic position commands the Lombard and Venetian plains, was one of the goals of Italy's intervention in World War I. The Treaty of Saint-Germain (1919) awarded Italy the Trentino, and also the Alto Adige (South Tyrol) up to the Brenner Pass. The Alto Adige had a German-speaking population of more than 200,000, which Mussolini* sought to Italianize and which Germany annexed during the course of World War II.* By the terms of the Treaty of Paris (February 1947), Italy retained both the Trentino and Alto Adige, the two erected into an autonomous region in 1948 with special linguistic and cultural guarantees for the German-speaking population. Nevertheless, there have been sporadic incidents of violence by extremist elements in the Alto Adige area.

SS

TRESCA, CARLO. The most dynamic of the radical intellectuals and labor agitators who defended the interests of Italian immigrants in the United States from the 1890s to World War II* was born in Sulmona on March 9, 1879. Editor of *Il Germe* (The seed) at age twenty-two, Tresca conducted a press campaign against the political notables of his home town of Sulmona in the Abruzzi that resulted in criminal proceedings for libel. Condemned to imprisonment, he fled the country in June 1904, immigrating to the United States.

Through the intervention of Socialist immigrants from the Abruzzi, Tresca was invited to Philadelphia to become director of *Il Proletario*, the official organ of the Italian Socialist Federation of North America. After twenty months he left *Il Proletario* to publish his own newspaper, *La Plebe*. Tresca transferred his base of operations to Pittsburgh, where he hoped to lead the Italian coal miners and mill workers of Western Pennsylvania in militant action. When heavy fines and jail sentences failed to discourage *La Plebe*'s crusade, Tresca found himself the target of a hired assassin.

By 1912 Tresca's reputation for skillful agitation had become well established in labor circles, and in the wake of the great textile workers' strike of that same year, the Industrial Workers of the World (IWW) invited him to lead Italian demonstrators in the campaign to liberate the imprisoned strike leaders Arturo Gionvannitti and Joe Ettor. During the next four years, Tresca assisted the IWW (the "Wobblies") in several of the most ferocious industrial struggles of the era. The strike of iron miners on the Mesabi Range in Minnesota in 1916 nearly resulted in Tresca's being lynched and then convicted on a trumped-up murder charge. A deal to liberate him was negotiated between local authorities and some Wobbly leaders. This deal, however, alienated IWW chieftain William D. ("Big Bill") Haywood and ended Tresca's association with the syndicalist labor union.

In the midst of the Justice Department's campaign to wipe out radicalism, Tresca became involved in one of America's most famous political trials—the Sacco-Vanzetti case. His strategy generated nationwide publicity and financial support for "the good shoemaker and the poor fishpedlar." However, by the time the Sacco-Vanzetti case reached its tragic climax, Tresca had long since become preoccupied with another struggle—the fight against Fascism.* Long before the March on Rome,* Tresca had judged Fascism to be the "White Guard" of capitalism, and in the pages of *Il Martello* he excoriated Mussolini* as the archtraitor of the working class. Mussolini sought to silence his transatlantic opponents and Tresca was one of his targets. In 1923 the Italian ambassador demanded that the American government suppress *Il Martello*. Federal authorities hastened to comply and prosecuted Tresca on bogus charges of sending obscene matter (in reality, a two-line advertisement for a book on birth control) through the mails. Sentenced to a year and a day, Tresca spent four months in a federal penitentiary in 1925 before public protest forced President Coolidge to commute his sentence to time served. The Fascists then resorted to violence. During a rally in Harlem's "Little Italy" in 1926, a bomb was hurled at him and other anti-Fascist leaders.

By the 1930s Tresca had become an implacable foe of the Communists, as well as the Fascists. Originally one of the few anarchists willing to collaborate with Communists in the fight against Fascism, Tresca ceased to consider them worthy allies when he observed Stalinism in action. Above all, it was the Communists' ruthless suppression of the anarchist revolution in Catalonia and Aragon during the Spanish Civil War* that convinced him of the need to resist them as determinedly as the Fascists.

After Pearl Harbor, Tresca obstructed both Communists and former Fascists in their efforts to infiltrate the Italian-American Victory Council and the Mazzini Society,* the latter being the leading organization of Italian anti-Fascists in the United States. On the night of January 11, 1943, an assassin fired a bullet into Tresca's brain. His killers were never brought to justice.

For further reference see: Nunzio Pernicone, "Carlo Tresca," *La Parola del Popolo* (November-December 1979).

NP

TREVES, CLAUDIO. He was the most prominent reformist leader after Filippo Turati* and a close friend and collaborator of both Turati and Anna Kuliscioff.* Born in Turin on March 24, 1869, he moved to Milan in 1898 in order to be closer to his two friends. He was elected to the Chamber of Deputies in 1906 and served until 1926. Treves was the editor of *Il Tempo*, the most important reformist daily. *Il Tempo* ceased publication in 1909, after which Treves became editor of *Avanti!*,* replacing Leonida Bissolati.* In 1911 he was instrumental in accomplishing the delicate operation of transferring *Avanti!* from Rome to Milan after it ran into financial trouble. Under his editorship the party newspaper opposed the Libyan War (see Ouchy, Treaty of*) and followed Turati's line. After the Reggio-Emilia Congress in 1912, Treves was replaced as editor by Benito Mussolini,* who drastically altered the newspaper's policy. Before World War I* Treves temporarily took the helm of *Critica Sociale*ute during Turati's illness.

Treves opposed Italian entrance into the war. Nationalists blamed him for the Caporetto* defeat because of his famous antiwar statement, "This winter, no longer in the trenches." In 1926, after the Fascist victory, Treves went into exile in Paris, where he became one of the most prestigious opponents of the Fasicst regime, working in the Concentrazione Antifascista* and running *La Libertà*. He died in Paris on June 11, 1933.

For further reference see: Gaetano Arfe, *Storia del socialismo italiano, 1892–1926* (Turin: Einaudi, 1965).

SD

TRIBUNA, LA. See **MALAGODI, OLINDO** and **NEWSPAPERS**

TRIENNIO. See **JACOBINS**

TRIESTE. Acquisition of Trieste was one of the major goals of Italian irredentism* before World War I.* But as Trieste was its chief outlet to the seas, the Austro-Hungarian Empire resisted all Italian claims, even the minimum request for an Italian-language university in the city. The desire for Trieste and the whole Istrian peninsula was one of the reasons for Italy's entrance into war against its former Austrian ally in 1915; Italy acquired the area in 1919. Occupied by German troops in September 1943, and by Anglo-American and Yugoslav forces in 1945, Trieste became the source of international controversy, resolved temporarily in 1947 by the creation of a Free Territory, and permanently in 1954, with the city of Trieste and a coastal strip (Zone A) assigned to Italy, and the rest of the territory (Zone B) to Yugoslavia.

SS

TRIPARTITE PACT. Signed on September 27, 1940, the alliance was originally between Germany, Italy, and Japan and recognized the "new world order" that was to be established, with Germany and Italy dominating the West, and Japan dominant in Asia. In addition to recognition of these blocs, the Tripartite Pact called for mutual assistance in the event another nation entered the war. Although not specifically mentioned, it was intended to keep the United States out of the war. A month after the signing of the Tripartite Pact, Mussolini's* forces attacked Greece, but there was no coordinated strategy with the German forces.

Matsuoka Yōsuke, the Japanese foreign minister, and the Army Supreme Headquarters believed the Tripartite Alliance would help to bring an end to the war in China; it was a major element in their foreign policy. That policy was, in part, a result of the U.S. abrogation of the Treaty of Commerce in 1940. To secure needed resources, the Japanese army decided on a move into Southeast Asia, and the success of that venture depended upon the alliance with the European powers, Italy and Germany, and a neutrality pact with Russia. Matsuoka Yōsuke believed the alliance would strengthen Japan's negotiations with the

United States. As with the earlier Anti-Comintern Pact,* more countries signed the Tripartite pact during the course of the war.

BDQ

TRIPLE ALLIANCE. This political and military partnership between Germany, Austria-Hungary, and Italy, an expansion of the alliance of 1879 between the two Germanic powers, came into existence on May 20, 1882. Germany and Austria-Hungary chiefly valued the new pact for its provisions of military support or benevolent neutrality in the event that a member was attacked by France or Russia. Italy's allies refused to guarantee its possession of Rome, although they discouraged the papacy's efforts to regain all or part of that city. Italy's primary interest in the Triple Alliance lay, however, in its desire to win back its North African ambitions, which had been blocked by France. The revised treaties of 1887 and 1891 did provide statements of German support for Italy's claim to Tripoli, but both Germany and Austria-Hungary urged restraint upon their ally in this regard because they did not want to upset France or the Ottoman Empire, the suzerain of the Tripolitan territory.

Frustration with its allies on the Tripolitan issue led Italy into pacts with France (1900) and Russia (1909) in which those states recognized its claims to Tripoli. But its neutrality pact with France (1902) and its good relations with Great Britain and Russia also indicated that its leaders increasingly respected the strength of the Triple Entente* powers. Awareness of that strength and the refusal of its allies to pledge Italy territorial compensations if they won the war, a violation of their treaty, were apparently the main reasons for Italy's decision to remain neutral when World War I* broke out in August 1914.

For further reference see: Luigi Albertini, *The Origins of the War of 1914*, 3 vols., trans. and ed. Isabella M. Massey (1952–57; reprint Westport, Conn.: Greenwood Press, 1980); Federico Chabod, *Storia della politica estera italiana dal 1870 al 1896* (Bari: G. Laterza, 1951.)

JKZ

TRIPLE ENTENTE. This diplomatic combination came into existence when Great Britain concluded sphere-of-influence agreements with France in April 1904 and with Russia, France's ally, in August 1907. Earlier these states had been major rivals for empire. Germany had refused to aid an overextended British government because it would not join the Triple Alliance,* while France had already realized that it could make no further advances in North Africa if faced with hostile British naval power. The heart of their agreement was a French offer of a free hand to Great Britain in Egypt in return for a similar concession to France in Morocco. Both Conservative and Liberal British leaders viewed the massive German protest against France's demands on Morocco in 1905 as a disguised attack on the new Anglo-French friendship, and they favored closer ties with both France and Russia. Even though the Tsarist regime had been shaken by a lost war with Japan and a domestic revolution in 1905, it proved to be a difficult associate. The major part of the Anglo-Russian agreement assigned control over the Persian Gulf to Great Britain and over a northern sphere of Persia to Russia. The Russian government encroached heavily on the freedom of the Persian monarchy and pursued an agressive course in the troubled Balkans, policies that distressed its British friends. Nevertheless, the Triple Entente held up in the great crisis of 1914 because the British cabinet felt deeper concern about Germany's conduct and intentions than it did about Russia's.

For further reference see: George Monger, *The End of Isolation: British Foreign Policy, 1900–1907* (1963; reprint Westport, Conn.: Greenwood Press, 1976); Luigi Albertini, *The Origins of the War of 1914*, 3 vols., trans. and ed. Isabella M. Massey (1952–57; reprint Westport, Conn.: Greenwood Press, 1980).

JKZ

TRIPOLITANIA. See LIBYA

TROPPAU, CONGRESS OF. See METTERNICH-WINNEBURG, CLEMENT VON

TROYA, CARLO. A historian who participated in the Neapolitan revolutions of 1820–21* and 1848,* he was born in Naples on June 7, 1784. Troya favored the neo-Guelf school (see Neo-Guelf movement*) of *Risorgimento* thought. He served as intendent of the Basilicata in 1821 and as president of the Neapolitan cabinet in 1848. Founder of the Società Storica in Naples in 1844, he published a series of historical works culminating in his four-volume *Storia d'Italia nel Medioevo* [History of Italy in the Middle Ages] (1839–55). He died in Naples on July 28, 1858.

MSG

TURATI, AUGUSTO. Augusto Turati, secretary of the Fascist Party (see Fascism*) from March 1926 to October 1930, was born in Parma on August 25, 1888, and died in Rome in August 1955. He saw front-line service during World War I,* winning several decorations, then was active as a radical democrat before joining the Fascist movement in Brescia in 1921. Sympathetic to neo-syndicalism, he helped organize the Fascist labor movement in Brescia province and led the much-publicized strike of the Fascist metalworkers' union in 1925.

Compared to Roberto Farinacci,* his predecessor as party secretary, Turati was tactically moderate and was not disposed to challenge Mussolini.* However, he viewed the party as a revolutionary instrument, and he sought to foster a partnership between the party and the Fascist economic organizations as the basis for a new corporativist order. Nevertheless, his rivalries with Fascist union chief Edmondo Rossoni and corporations minister Giuseppe Bottai* limited his effectiveness. Turati helped to promote Rossoni's ouster in 1928, but ultimately such infighting contributed to his own demise as party secretary in 1930.

DDR

TURATI, FILIPPO. Born in Canzo (Como) on November 25, 1857, Turati was the founder and most important historical leader of the Italian Socialist Party (PSI).* He studied at the University of Bologna and later participated in the *Scapigliatura*,* a movement of artists, writers, and bohemians centered in Milan in the 1870s. In 1883 he published his most important sociological work, "Il delitto e la questione sociale," in which he argued that crime was caused by poor social conditions. He then turned to politics, becoming associated with the Partito Operaio Italiano (POI).

In 1885 Turati met his life companion, Anna Kuliscioff,* a Russian woman who was already an experienced agitator and who was to have great influence on him. In 1889 he was among the principal founders of the Lega Socialista Milanese, a forerunner of the Socialist Party. The Lega's program reflected Turati's brand of Marxism, which had become supreme. In 1891 he took over a review founded by his friend Arcangelo Ghisleri and transformed it into a forum for the dissemination of his ideas—*Critica Sociale*.* Through *Critica Sociale*, a more popular newspaper entitled *Lotta di Classe*, prodigious activity among the workers, and organizational talent, Turati established the Italian Socialist Party in 1892 against overwhelming odds.

Turati believed in a gradual, nonviolent road to socialism. Reforms were necessary to achieve socialism; liberty and democracy were necessary to achieve reforms. This line of thinking led Turati to advocate alliances with democratic elements of the bourgeoisie in order to prevent reaction, to which he believed Italian society was particularly prone. Since the need to fight repression was preeminent for Turati, he independently instituted a policy of alliances in Milan against Francesco Crispi* in 1894 and sought party sanction for his policy. After the riots of 1898 the party successfully followed his ideas in defeating government reaction, despite Turati's imprisonment.

After his release, Turati made cooperation a normal feature of Socialist conduct designed to prevent reaction and achieve reforms. The result was widespread opposition among Socialists, which Turati overcame long enough to deliver Socialist votes to the liberal Zanardelli*-Giolitti* cabinet, which depended on those votes to stay in power. This support brought spectacular benefits to the workers in 1901 and 1902, allowing Turati to keep control of the party. Changing political and economic conditions, however, favored the left wing.

In 1903 and 1904 Turati's position weakened, a major factor inducing him to turn down an offer of a cabinet position. In 1905 the reformists recovered and, aided also by their premier role in organized labor, recaptured control of the party until the outbreak of the Libyan War (see Ouchy, Treaty of*).

After 1912 Turati opposed Benito Mussolini's* extremist positions, but had not been able to dislodge him from the leadership when World War I* began.

Turati was a leading neutralist during World War I. During the postwar crisis Turati opposed the maximalists, who advocated a Communist revolution on the Soviet model, stating that their policies would bring disaster. His desire to maintain Socialist unity prompted Turati to avoid a political solution to the Fascist threat until it was too late. When he participated in talks aimed at setting up an anti-Fascist coalition his party expelled him. Turati founded the Partito Socialista Unitario (Unitary Socialist Party), with Giacomo Matteotti, his "spiritual son," as secretary. Matteotti was murdered by Fascist thugs in 1924 (see Matteotti Crisis*), provoking the protest known as the Aventine Secession,* in which Turati played a large role.

The Aventine Secession failed to prevent Mussolini from securing absolute power. In 1926 Turati fled Italy in a daring escape. He was helped by Carlo Rosselli,* Ferruccio Parri,* and Alessandro Pertini,* among others. In Paris Turati became the spiritual head of the anti-Fascist resistance. He helped found the Concentrazione Antifascista* to coordinate the activities of the disparate exile groups and gained international exposure for them. He also advocated the re-unification of the two Socialist parties, which took place in 1930. In 1931 he achieved his last goal, agreement between the Justice and Liberty movement* and the Concentrazione. Turati died in Paris on March 29, 1932.

For further reference see: Spencer DiScala, *Dilemmas of Italian Socialism: The Politics of Filippo Turati* (Amherst: University of Massachusetts Press, 1980); Filippo Turati and Anna Kuliscioff, *Carteggio*, 6 vols. (Milan: Feltrinelli, 1949–78).

SD

TURIELLO, PASQUALE. This political author is frequently called the first conscious and systematic Italian imperialist. Born on January 3, 1836, in Naples, he lived all his life in that city, dying there on January 13, 1902. Turiello fought during the *Risorgimento*,* in September 1860 joining a band of Neapolitans that advanced on Benevento, deposing the local papal authorities; in 1866 and 1867 he marched with Giuseppe Garibaldi.* Turiello abandoned law practice in 1862 for teaching and journalism, working as a correspondent for the Milanese *Perseveranza* and as an editor for the Neapolitan *Patria*. Politically, Turiello became a leading voice of the Neapolitan Right, serving as adviser to Antonio Di Rudinì* before they broke in 1896.

The 1882 publication of *Governo e governati in Italia* made Turiello famous. Noting the deterioration since 1860 of the southern peasantry's lot and the wide gap throughout Italy between government and people, Turiello rejected liberalism and "parliamentarianism." The author proposed instead greatly strengthening the power of the executive; replacing parliament with a system of representation by economic class; instituting paramilitary education; and pursuing vigorous colonial policies. In later works Turiello accentuated his antiparliamentary and pro-imperialist themes (see, for example, the second edition of *Governo e governati*, 1889–90; *Politica contemporanea*, 1894; and *Il secolo XIX*, 1902).

For further reference see: Massimo L. Salvadori, *Il mito del buon governo* (Turin: Einaudi, 1963); Giuseppe Imbucci, *Ideologia e questione sociale in Pasquale Turiello* (Rome: Istituto Luigi Sturzo, 1971).

RJ

TWO SICILIES, KINGDOM OF THE. One of the sovereign states in Italy prior to its unification, the Kingdom of the Two Sicilies consisted of the southern part of the Italian peninsula and the island of Sicily. Welded into a single realm, known as the Kingdom of Sicily, by the Normans in the twelfth century, the two regions remained united under Norman, Hohenstaufen, and Angevin rulers until 1282. An Aragonese invasion of the island in that year limited Angevin rule to the mainland, and, by dividing the realm, resulted in two monarchs styling themselves kings of Sicily, although the mainland came to be conventionally called the Kingdom of Naples. When Alfonso of Aragon seized Naples from the Angevins in 1442 he reunited the mainland and island and adopted the title King of the Two Sicilies. After Naples and Sicily came under Spanish rule in 1503 they were separately administered by viceroys until the War of the Spanish Succession (1702–13) transferred the Neapolitan kingdom to Austria, and that of Sicily, briefly, to Savoy.

The War of Polish Succession (1733–38) ended with the Spanish Bourbon Don Carlos controlling both kingdoms, independent of Spain. His son Ferdinand's reign (1759–1825) witnessed invasions by French revolutionary and Napoleonic armies which drove Ferdinand to Sicily and brought to the mainland first the Parthenopean Republic* (1799) and then a decade (1806–15) of reforming rule under Joseph Bonaparte and Joachim Murat.* After his restoration in 1815, Ferdinand, titling himself Ferdinand I,* created the Kingdom of the Two Sicilies by fusing Sicily to Naples in a unitary state. Punctuated by the revolutions of 1820–21* and 1848,* the rule of his successors—Francis I* (1825–30), Ferdinand II* (1830–59), and Francis II* (1859–60)—was characterized by conservative policies antithetical to the national movement. Giuseppe Garibaldi's* expedition in 1860 overturned Bourbon rule and led to the incorporation of the entire South into the new Kingdom of Italy.*

For further reference see: Harold Acton, *The Bourbons of Naples* (London: Methuen and Co., 1956); idem, *The Last Bourbons of Naples* (London: Methuen and Co., 1961); Benedetto Croce, *History of the Kingdom of Naples* (Chicago: University of Chicago Press, 1970); Denis Mack Smith, *A History of Sicily*, 2 vols. (New York: The Viking Press, 1968); Giuseppe Galasso, *Il Mezzogiorno nella storia d'Italia* (Florence: Felice Le Monnier, 1977).

RCu

U

UCCIALLI, TREATY OF. This treaty of commerce and friendship was signed by Menelik II* in 1889 two months after he became Emperor of Ethiopia,* and by Italy's representative, Count Pietro Antonelli. The treaty's immediate advantage to Menelik was the provision of modern arms to the new emperor and the protection of Ethiopians abroad (particularly in Jerusalem) by the Italian consular corps. By extension, Menelik acceded to the Italian occupation of the Red Sea coastlands, which in the following year became the colony of Eritrea.* The Italian government also understood the treaty to place Italy in a special relationship to Ethiopia, widely perceived in Europe to be an Italian protectorate over Ethiopia. By 1891 Menelik unilaterally abrogated the treaty, and after several years of diplomatic and frontier skirmishes the two countries went to war. After initial successes on the battlefield, the Italians met with military disaster at Adowa* on March 1, 1896. By the terms of the peace treaty, Italy renounced all claims to a protectorate over Ethiopia under the terms of the Treaty of Uccialli.

RLH

UDI. See **UNIONE DONNE ITALIANE**

UMANITÀ NOVA, L'. See **MALATESTA, ERRICO**

UMBERTO I AND UMBERTO II. See **HUMBERT I** and **HUMBERT II**

UNGARETTI, GIUSEPPE. This lyric poet, with Eugenio Montale, made Italy "the poetic center of continental Europe." Born in Egypt on February 10, 1888, of Tuscan parents, Ungaretti was educated there and in Paris (1912–15). His World War I* poems, *Il porto sepolto* [The sunken port] (1916) and, in French, *La guerre* [War] (1919), launched his literary career and earned him the favor of Mussolini.* *Allegria di naufragi* [The joy of shipwrecks] has been the title of several editions of collected poems. His complete works make up the two volumes of *Vita di un uomo* [Life of a man], separately titled *Tutte le poesie* [Complete poems] (1969) and *Saggi ed interventi* [Essays and addresses] (post-humous, 1974). Ungaretti taught in Brazil (1937–42) but was back in Italy for the end of the war. He was thereafter widely honored in Italy and abroad, and died in Milan on June 1, 1970.

AP

UNIONE DONNE ITALIANE. This women's mass organization had its roots in the anti-Fascist women's front in Paris in the 1930s and in the GDD (see Gruppi di Difese. . . *) of the Armed Resistance.* The UDI was officially founded in Rome (September 1944) at the instigation of Communist and Socialist women who hoped to maintain and expand women's political activism. Averaging 400,000 members since 1945, the UDI has been linked to parties of the Left, although since the 1960s it has attempted to establish greater autonomy, pressuring both parties and the government to deal with women's issues. Headquartered in Rome, it publishes the weekly *Noi Donne*.

MJS

UNIONE ELETTORALE. A Catholic political action group designed to organize local electoral intervention, the Unione Elettorale was established in 1905 by Pope Pius X.* As part of the general reorganization of the Opera dei Congressi* set forth in the encyclical *Il fermo proposito*, the Unione served as an umbrella group for Catholics in politics; and in elections in which the *non expedit** did not apply, it directed Catholic votes to individual candidates. The Unione often asked candidates to submit to questioning in order to determine their suitability for Catholic support.

Giovanni Giolitti* and other ''non-Catholic'' politicians were generally willing to make concessions to the Unione in return for Catholic support. The 1913 general election, in which the *non expedit* was lifted in two-thirds of the contests so as to allow Catholics to oppose Socialists and anticlericals, was a good example of the influence of the Unione Elettorale. The importance of the organization diminished with the foundation of the Partito Popolare (see Italian Popular Party*) in 1919 and the total involvement of Catholics in Italian politics.

RJW

L'UNITÀ. A weekly newspaper founded in 1911 by Gaetano Salvemini* after his exit from the Italian Socialist Party (PSI),* *L'Unità* expressed Salvemini's hostility to parties as organizations dominated by economic interests and by politicians who, despite their rhetoric, wound up exercising an essentially conservative function. Salvemini believed that these parties, and especially the Socialist Party, needed the spur of independent groups which, free from organized party discipline, were better able to present fresh ideas for discussion.

L'Unità was notable for agitating certain themes that Salvemini had brought up during his last years as a Socialist. For example, the newspaper emphasized reforms for the South, putting into effect Salvemini's idea that Italian democrats should concentrate on this issue rather than scattering their resources on less crucial problems. It also attacked protectionism, the economic organizations within the Socialist Party that supported it, and reformism, its political expression. Despite these attacks, however, the newspaper remained attentive to developments within the Socialist Party, looking for signs of change and finding collaborators such as Ugo Guido Mondolfo. *L'Unità* had enormous appeal to the younger generation of Socialists. Angelo Tasca* and Amadeo Bordiga,* who would head opposing factions in the Italian Communist Party (PCI),* wrote for *L'Unità*, and years later the Communist Party's more famous daily newspaper adopted the same title. *L'Unità* ceased publication at the end of 1920.

SD

UNITÀ ITALIANA. See **SETTEMBRINI, LUIGI**

UNITY OF ACTION PACT. See **NENNI, PIETRO**

UOMO QUALUNQUE. See **COMMON MAN'S MOVEMENT**

UTRECHT, TREATY OF. A treaty ending the War of the Spanish Succession, it was signed by the major European powers on April 11, 1713. It divided the Spanish dependencies, with the following specifically Italian provisions: (1) Austria was to receive Milan, Naples, and Sardinia; (2) Savoy was to receive Sicily as a kingdom, as well as advantageous boundary revisions in northern Italy. In 1720 Austria exchanged Sardinia for Sicily, thus making the House of Savoy kings of Sardinia.

WDG

V

VALERIO, COLONEL. See **AUDISIO, WALTER**

VALERIO, LORENZO. A political figure of the Left (see Sinistra, La*), he was born in Turin on November 24, 1810. Valerio was director of a silk manufacturing enterprise and was known for his liberal ideas and his desire to free the economy. In 1844 he was among the founders of the Agrarian Association, which favored free trade. Following the reforms of October 1847 in Piedmont, he founded the journal *La Concordia* and was elected to the Chamber of Deputies. In that house he bitterly criticized those responsible for the defeat at the hands of Austria. Initially a supporter of Vincenzo Gioberti,* he turned against him when the latter proposed intervening against the democratic government established in Tuscany. Valerio founded *Il Diritto*, a mouthpiece of the Left that opposed the policies of Cavour.* However, he did support the war of 1859* against Austria and in 1862 was nominated to the Senate. In 1865 he was named prefect to Messina, where he died on August 26, 1865.

FJC

VATICAN CITY. See **LATERAN ACCORDS**

VATICAN COUNCIL I. The twentieth ecumenical council of the Roman Catholic Church, it was held at St. Peter's Basilica in Rome from December 8, 1869, to July 18, 1870. The Council was convened by Pope Pius IX* to offset the growing spirit of Modernism* and liberalism in the Church and in society. At the same time, Pius was locked in a bitter struggle to preserve the temporal power of the Church from the expanding designs of the *Risorgimento.**

Approximately 700 bishops, accompanied by teams of theologians, attended the opening session of the Council on December 8, 1869. Protestant and Orthodox leaders were invited but did not attend. While Rome did not encourage the participation of heads of state, the Austrian emperor and several Italian princes allied with the Papal States* were present at the opening ceremonies. Civil governments were generally apprehensive about the Council, fearing it would confirm Pius' Syllabus of Errors* (1864).

The Council preparations were carried out primarily through the work of six theological deputations, dealing with the issues of doctrine, discipline, religious orders, missions, politico-religious affairs, and ceremonies. Once the Council began, these deputations came under the direction of official conciliar committees headed by cardinals and bishops. These committees were, in turn, coordinated by a central committee, which determined the order of deliberations at the general assemblies of the Council. In addition to these general assemblies or congregations (eighty-six in all), there were four public sessions whose role was to formally ratify decisions of the general congregations. Ultimately, the Council produced two major documents: *Dei filius*, on matters of faith and reason, solemnly promulgated at the third public session (April 24, 1870), and *Pastor aeternus*, on the authority of the Pope, dogmatically proclaimed at the fourth and final public session (July 18, 1870). The final vote on *Pastor aeternus*, which included the contested definition of the doctrine of papal infallibility, was 533 in favor and only 2 opposed, but most of the minority opposition had already left the Council. While all the minority bishops ultimately submitted to the Council decrees, many complained bitterly of the rigid control that the Pope had exercised over the Council and of alleged high-handed tactics employed by the "infallibilist party" and the officials of the Roman Curia. Small groups of Swiss, German, and Austrian Catholics rejected the doctrine of papal infallibility, sparking the "Old Catholic" schism from the Church.

The day after the definition of papal infallibility the Franco-Prussian War erupted. Once the French troops had left Rome as a result of the war, the Italians invaded the Pontifical State and annexed it after a plebiscite (October 6, 1870). Pius IX suspended the Council *sine die* on October 20, 1870. Despite this historic loss of the temporal power, the papacy emerged from Vatican I with more authority and vigor than before.

For further reference see: Don Cuthbert Butler, *The Vatican Council: 1869– 1870*, ed. Christopher Butler (Westminster: The Newman Press, 1962); Henri Rondet, *Vatican I* (Paris: P. Lethielleux, Editeur, 1962); Frank J. Coppa, *Pope Pius IX: Crusader in a Secular Age* (Boston: Twayne Publishers, 1979).

RB

VATICAN II. An ecumenical council called by Pope John XXIII* and continued by his successor, Paul VI,* Vatican II (1959–65) marked the beginning of a new era for the Roman Catholic Church. The constitutions, decrees, and declarations of the Council reformed both the structure and the liturgy of the Church in a manner unseen since the Council of Trent. Due especially to the impetus of Pope Paul, the moderates and the liberals among the Church Fathers managed to exert the greatest influence. Cardinals Augustine Bea, Julius Döpfner, and Giacomo Lecaro distinguished themselves as progressives, while among the most influential conservatives were cardinals Alfredo Ottaviani, Ernesto Ruffini, and Michael Browne.

The Council's pronouncements dealt with almost every aspect of Catholic life, including reforms of the liturgy and the sacraments, the role of the Church in the Third World, and Christian education. The clergy was called to renewal and the role of the laity in Church affairs was emphasized. The ecumenical spirit of the Council was demonstrated in the invitations extended to some ninety-three non-Catholic observers and in the Decree on Ecumenism.

The Council was ended in 1965, with Paul VI setting up a number of permanent commissions to see to the implementation of the decisions of Vatican II.

For further reference see: Walter M. Abbot, ed., *Documents of Vatican II* (New York: Guild Press, 1966).

RJW

VENEZIA GIULIA. A region situated in the northeastern section of Italy and officially known as Friuli-Venezia Giulia, it consists of approximately 7,845 square kilometers, with a population of 1,232,520 inhabitants. Trieste,* with a population of 272,423, is the capital of the region. Following World War II,* Trieste became *l'enfant terrible* for the United Nations and for the Allied Powers, causing great tension between Italy and Yugoslavia. Initially declared a Free Territory, in 1954 Trieste was returned to Italy, while a good part of the Venezia Giulia was ceded to Yugoslavia.

PVB

VERDI, GIUSEPPE. The major composer of Italian opera in the nineteenth century, Verdi was born at Le Roncole, a village near Busseto in the Duchy of Parma, on October 10, 1813. He studied music in Milan with several private tutors, having been rejected by the Milan Conservatory. His first opera, *Oberto, Conte di San Bonifacio*, was performed at La Scala in 1839 and was a modest success. His first major success was *Nabucco* (1842), which established him as a major opera composer in Italy. His other major operas (with date of first performance) are: *I Lombardi* (1843), *Macbeth* (1847), *Rigoletto* (1851), *Il trovatore* (1853), *La traviata* (1853), *I Vespri siciliani* (1855), *Simon Boccanegra* (1857), *Un ballo in maschera* (1859), *La forza del destino* (1862), *Don Carlo* (1867), *Aïda* (1871), *Otello* (1887), and *Falstaff* (1893). While his earliest works tend to be dramatically exciting but musically predictable, his later works are subtle in their uses of both voice and orchestra for maximum dramatic effect. Verdi died of a stroke in Milan on January 27, 1901.

JLD

VERGA, GIOVANNI. Verga was one of Italy's greatest novelists, celebrated abroad by writers such as D. H. Lawrence. Born in Catania, Sicily, on August 31, 1840, he was active in the mid-century political uprisings. After 1865 he lived mostly in Florence and Milan, but returned to Catania in 1884. By then he had written his popular *Storia di una capinera* [Story of a blackcap] (1871) about the anguish of a young nun revealed through letters; many short stories (some translated by D. H. Lawrence), including *Cavalleria rusticana* (later dramatized for Eleanora Duse and made into an opera by Mascagni); several aristocratic-bohemian novels; and the first of his two great novels in the naturalist-realist or *verismo* style, *I malavoglia* [The house by the medlar tree] (1881). *I malavoglia* was to have been the first of a series of novels, generally titled *I vinti* [The vanquished], covering the whole spectrum of Italian social classes. Actually, Verga completed only one other volume for the series, *Mastro-don Gesualdo* (1889), and part of a third. A fervent patriot and a critic of Socialist panaceas, the great Sicilian novelist lapsed into silence after 1906, and died in Catania on January 27, 1922.

AP

VERRI, ALESSANDRO. This Milanese writer of the Enlightenment* and younger brother to Pietro Verri* was born in 1741 into a patrician family of Milan, where he received his early education. He collaborated with his brother and with others of the Accademia dei Pugni at Milan in the publication of the journal *Il Caffè** in 1764–66. In later life he lived at Rome, where he maintained an important correspondence with his brother and developed his literary talents. He was author of a *Storia d'Italia* that was not published in his lifetime, of translations of Shakespeare, of novels, and particularly of a work entitled *Le notti romane* (1792) that was modeled in part on Edward Young's *Night Thoughts* and was an important early expression of Italian romanticism. He died in 1816.

RBL

VERRI, PIETRO. Milanese economist and writer of the Enlightenment,* he was born in 1728 to a patrician family habilitated for offices in the city and active in its politics. His father Gabriele was an official of the Hapsburg administration. Educated at Milan, Rome, and finally at the Jesuit Collegio dei Nobili at Pavia, he travelled to Vienna, served in the Imperial army during the Seven Years War, and in 1764 began a career as Hapsburg functionary in Milan that continued nearly until his death. He was employed chiefly in the financial administration, where he attained the rank of councillor of state in 1783. Inspired by the French Encyclopedists, he published works on moral philosophy (*Meditazioni sulla felicità*, 1767; *Osservazioni sulla tortura*, 1777) and treatises on the public economy of Milan, including *Riflessioni sulle leggi vincolanti* (1769), on the grain trade. His major work was his *Storia di Milano*, of which the first volume was published in 1783. With his younger brother Alessandro* he became the center of a group of intellectuals, including Cesare Baccaria,* Paolo Frisi,* and G. Panini, in a society called the Accademia dei Pugni, which served briefly as the central focus of the Lombard reformers and published a journal in 1764–66 entitled *Il Caffè*,* in which his articles appeared. In later life, he became dissatisfied with the Hapsburg administrative policy under Joseph II, and on the

French occupation of 1796, supported the patriots of the Cisalpine Republic.*
He died in 1797.

For further reference see: E. Greppi, A. Giulini, and L. F. Cogliati, *Carteggio
di Pietro e di Alessandro Verri dal 1766 al 1797* (Milan, 1910–42); Nino Valeri,
Pietro Verri (Milan, 1937); Emiliana P. Noether, *Seeds of Italian Nationalism,
1700–1815* (New York: Columbia University Press, 1957).

RBL

VICO, GIAMBATTISTA. The author of the *Scienza nuova* [The new science]
and the most prominent intellectual figure of eighteenth-century Italy, Vico was
born in Naples on June 23, 1668, and was educated there. After serving as a
tutor, he assumed the professorship of rhetoric at the University of Naples in
1697. Originally interested in jurisprudence, he wrote a number of important
works on law. However, after failing to gain the chair of jurisprudence at Naples
in 1723, he turned to history and philosophy.

In 1725 he published his great work, *Principi d'una scienza nuova* [Principles
of a new science]. In 1735 Charles III, in a much belated gesture, appointed
him royal historiographer, a post he held, together with his university position,
until his death on January 20, 1774.

In the *Scienza nuova* Vico fashioned a highly original synthesis, combining
Enlightenment* ideas about natural law and Renaissance literary theory with
Plato's notion of the relation between sense data and ideas, Tacitus' insight into
the historical process, the inductive method of Bacon, the materialism of Hobbes,
and the idealism of Descartes. What resulted was a new approach to, and concept
of, the sociohistorical process.

Against the prevailing Enlightenment belief that a science of human nature
can result from a study of physical nature, Vico maintained that one understands
only what one has made. Thus, only God, not man, can fully understand nature.
Man can, however, know himself through an inductive investigation of what he
has made: history, rationality, and culture. Thus, the laws of history as well as
a science of the mind can be discovered through an inquiry into the dialectic
between consciousness and nature, taking place over time and resulting in a
specific historical dynamic.

For further reference see: *The Autobiography of Giambattista Vico*, trans. Max
Fisch and Thomas Bergin (Ithaca: Cornell University Press, 1944); Benedetto
Croce, *The Philosophy of Giambattista Vico*, trans. R. G. Collingwood (London:
Howard Latimer, 1913).

FFA

VICTOR EMMANUEL I. King of Piedmont-Sardinia from 1802 to 1821, he
was born on July 24, 1759, in Turin. Victor Emmanuel was brought up in the
Catholic and conservative atmosphere of the Sardinian court. Of mediocre ability,
but strong and self-assured, he received little real education. With French control
of Piedmont, he fled with the court to Sardinia in 1798. Exasperated by what
he perceived as the fatalism of his brother, Charles Emmanuel III, he eagerly

assumed the throne when the former abdicated in June 1802. Soon disillusioned, he remained in Sardinia, a bitter exile, until 1814. Restored to power, at the Vienna Congress he obtained Genoa, but was deeply frustrated by Austrian control of Lombardy.* When a revolt burst forth in Turin in 1821, the rebels demanded democratic reform and action against Austria. Opposed by conscience to a constitution and intelligent enough not to engage in a futile struggle, he abdicated on March 13, 1821, in favor of his brother, Charles Felix.* He died at Moncalieri on January 10, 1824.

FFA

VICTOR EMMANUEL II. The last King of Sardinia and the first King of Italy, Victor Emmanuel was born in Turin on March 14, 1820, the son of Charles Albert of Savoy*-Carignano, and of Maria Teresa of Tuscany. He spent part of his childhood at the Tuscan court and enjoyed a carefree youth in Piedmont. In 1842 he married Maria Adelaide, daughter of the Austrian viceroy in Lombardy-Venetia (see Lombardo-Venetian Kingdom*), the Archduke Rainier of Hapsburg.

Victor Emmanuel disapproved of his father's concessions to the liberals in 1848, but he fought bravely to keep Austrian troops out of northern Italy. He also opposed the resumption of war against the Austrians in 1849, yet he proved ready to lead the country upon his father's abdication and was able to negotiate favorable surrender terms with Field Marshal Joseph Radetzky.*

In the 1850s, despite his distrust of constitutional government and his repression of a democratic uprising in Genoa, he upheld the *Statuto* * granted by his father. However, he preferred to surround himself with ministers who were clearly loyal to him. He was also made very uneasy by the anticlerical policies of Cavour* and other liberal ministers that culminated in the passage of the Siccardi Laws* in 1852.

Victor Emmanuel became reconciled with Cavour when the latter's foreign policy began to bear fruit with the Sardinian presence in the Crimean War* and at the Congress of Paris* of 1856. King and minister thereafter cooperated closely in the sequence of steps that led from the Plombières Agreement* with France in 1858 to the war with Austria and the territorial annexations of 1859 (see War of 1859*). That collaboration, however, nearly broke down at the time of the conquest of the South, when Cavour feared Giuseppe Garibaldi's* influence over the King.

On March 18, 1861, Victor Emmanuel was proclaimed King of Italy; but he insisted on maintaining his dynastic last name, in order to signify the historical continuity of the House of Savoy. Cavour was able to persuade a majority of the Chamber of Deputies to go along. After Cavour's death, however, Victor Emmanuel resumed a more active role, especially in matters of diplomacy and war. Like Giuseppe Mazzini* and Garibaldi, with whom he kept in touch through Italian and foreign emissaries, Victor Emmanuel pinned his hopes for Italian ascendancy in Europe upon the disintegration of the Hapsburg Empire. Thus, he supported revolutionary movements, especially in the Balkans.

The occupation of Rome by the Italian army on September 20, 1870, marked the end of Victor Emmanuel's active involvement in politics. However, in 1873 he travelled to Vienna and Berlin for a diplomatic rapprochement that foreshadowed the Triple Alliance.* In 1876 he witnessed the advent of the *Sinistra storica* (see Sinistra, La*) to power and the stabilization of a parliamentary system of government that was quite compatible with the interests of the monarchy. He died in Rome on January 9, 1878.

For further reference see: Vittorio Bersezio, *Il regno di Vittorio Emanuele II. Trent'anni di vita italiana*, 8 vols. (Turin: Roux, 1878–95); Denis Mack Smith, *Victor Emmanuel, Cavour and the Risorgimento* (New York: Oxford University Press, 1971).

CML

VICTOR EMMANUEL III. Italy's longest-reigning monarch (1900–1946), Victor Emmanuel III contributed to the rise and fall of Fascism.* He was born on November 11, 1869, in Naples, son of Humbert I,* then prince of Piedmont, and Margherita of Savoy; he died in Alexandria, Egypt, on December 28, 1947. Given a spartan upbringing under the tutelage of Colonel Egidio Osio, he received a number of military commands, rising to the rank of army corps commander in 1897. In 1896 he married Princess Elena of Montenegro.* Uncommonly short in stature, weak in the legs, and reserved in manner, when he formally ascended the throne (August 11, 1900) after his father's death by assassination, he affirmed his faith in the liberal monarchy. Subsequently he gave his support to the Zanardelli*-Giolitti* ministry of the Left (see Sinistra, La*) (1901–3) and promoted reconciliation with France, weakening Italy's ties to the Triple Alliance.* During the ritual visits to Europe's major capitals (1902–3), he pointedly did not go to Vienna. For more than a decade he supported the democratizing policies of Giolitti, but broke with him on Italy's intervention in World War I* in May 1915, supporting Prime Minister Antonio Salandra,* who favored war against Austria, whereas Giolitti insisted on continued neutrality.* During the postwar crisis, the King played a passive role until October 1922, when, fearing a civil war and receiving conflicting advice, he refused to invoke martial law to cope with the Fascist March on Rome,* thus assuring Mussolini's* accession. Again, during the Matteotti Crisis* of late 1924, he refused to move against Mussolini, thus confirming the dictator's permanence in power. Victor Emmanuel's attitude on the Ethiopian War is in dispute; he nevertheless accepted the crown of Emperor of Ethiopia* in May 1936. In April 1939 he became King of Albania,* after Mussolini ordered the occupation of that country. Clearly opposed to entrance into World War II* on the side of Germany, he acquiesced to it in June 1940; but toward the end of 1942 he sought a way out, achieved by an armistice with the Allies on September 3, 1943, after Mussolini was ousted by a royal coup on July 25, 1943. Despite some Allied support, Victor Emmanuel's permanence as king was opposed by most Italian anti-Fascist parties. Consequently, in June 1944 he delegated his royal powers to his son, who later became Humbert II.*

Hoping to save the dynasty, on the eve of a referendum on retention of the monarchy he abdicated in favor of Humbert (May 9, 1946) and went into exile. But in the referendum of June 2, a majority of Italians opted for a republic.

For further reference see: Silvio Bertoldi, *Vittorio Emanuele III* (Turin: UTET, 1970); Domenico Bartoli, *La fine della monarchia* (Milan: Mondadori, 1966); Silvio Scaroni, *Con Vittorio Emanuele III* (Milan: Mondadori, 1954).

SS

VIDONI PACT. The Vidoni Pact was an agreement of October 2, 1925, between Confindustria,* representing industrial employers, and the General Confederation of Fascist Syndicates, representing workers. The two organizations agreed to recognize one another as exclusive representatives for management and labor and to exclude all nonaffiliated organizations from collective bargaining in industry. The agreement also provided for the abolition of workers' factory councils (*commissioni interne di fabbrica*), many of which were still controlled by Socialists and Communists, through which labor representatives sought to monitor and influence managerial decisions. Signed at Fascist headquarters in the Vidoni Palace in Rome, the agreement was sanctioned by the authority of party secretary Roberto Farinacci.* While this pact strengthened the Fascist labor unions led by Edmondo Rossoni, which had been unable to liquidate their Socialist and Communist rivals in open competition, it also forced Fascist organizers to desist in their battle to gain control of factory councils. The provisions of the Vidoni Pact anticipated those of the Labor Law of April 3, 1926, which extended the principle of collective bargaining by officially recognized associations to all sectors of the economy, and went on to outlaw strikes and lockouts and to establish special labor courts for compulsory arbitration of unresolved labor disputes. Industry accepted the agreement with some reluctance for fear that it might lose freedom of action, but Confindustria used it nevertheless to strengthen its representational role in industry. Following the agreement, Confindustria aligned itself fully with the Fascist regime and was granted a permanent seat on the Grand Council.

For further reference see: Ferdinando Cordova, *Le origini dei sindacati fascisti, 1918–1926* (Rome-Bari: Laterza, 1974).

RS

VIENNA, CONGRESS OF. This peace congress followed the Napoleonic Wars, 1814–15. After the downfall of Napoleon I,* the statesmen of Europe met at Vienna in September 1814 to arrange a peace settlement. Their principal goal was a stable international order that would ensure the peace of Europe; they hoped to attain this goal by establishing a balance of power, by redistributing territory so as to satisfy the ambitions of the powers, and by creating a ring of strong states around France to restrain her from future aggression. The settlement of Italy was largely in Metternich's* hands, because the other powers had agreed that the peninsula was in Austria's sphere of influence. Viewing Italian nationalism as dangerous, Metternich made no concession to it: Italy remained divided into small states, all more or less under Austrian control. Lombardy* and Venetia formed part of the Austrian Empire, while Tuscany, Modena, and Parma were ruled by members of the Hapsburg family. Since the restoration of the Papal States* was largely due to Austrian support, the papacy, in gratitude, tended to follow Vienna's line of policy. In Naples, Metternich had at first been inclined to support Joachim Murat,* the French general whom Napoleon had placed on the throne. Eventually, alarm at Murat's relations with the Italian nationalists and pressure from the Bourbon monarchies of France and Spain led Metternich to replace Murat with the former Bourbon king, Ferdinand I,* who in return bound his kingdom closely to Austria by a treaty of alliance. Only Piedmont remained relatively free of Austrian domination; it was strengthened by the acquisition of the former republic of Genoa so that it might bar the northwest of Italy against French attack.

In general, the Congress was successful in its primary aim, establishing a stable international order: the century of peace that Europe enjoyed between 1815 and 1914 was its legacy. The dark side of the Congress was its rejection of the rising forces of liberalism and nationalism; ignored at Vienna, those forces henceforth turned against the 1815 settlement, leading to a half-century of revolution. This was particularly true of Italy. Indignant at the continued division and foreign domination of the peninsula, Italian patriots began the long, drawn out struggle of the *Risorgimento*,* which in the end established a united Italy on the ruins of the Vienna settlement.

For further reference see: Charles Webster, *The Congress of Vienna* (London: H. M. Printing Office, 1919); Emil Lengyel, *The Congress of Vienna, 1814–1815* (New York: Watts, 1974).

AJR

VIGANÓ, RENATA. This literary figure whose writings popularized the experiences of women of the Armed Resistance* was born in Bologna in 1900 and died there in 1976. Trained as a nurse, she worked in that capacity with the partisan brigades, 1943–45. Her prize-winning novel *Agnese va a morire* [Agnese goes to her death] (1947) and subsequent writings such as *Donne della Resistenza* [Women of the resistance] (1955) illustrate the role women played in the Resistance.

MJS

VILLAFRANCA, ARMISTICE AND PEACE PRELIMINARIES OF. The armistice and peace preliminaries of Villafranca followed the battle of Solferino* and brought to an end the fighting in the Second War for Independence (see War of 1859*). On July 6, 1859, with the Austrians still in control of the Quadrilateral* of fortresses, Napoleon III* offered Francis Joseph* an armistice, which the Austrian Emperor accepted. It was Francis Joseph who chose Villafranca as the place where the belligerents could meet to discuss the terms. On July 11, Napoleon III rode to Villafranca and together with Francis Joseph fixed the terms that would prevail in the peace. The two decided to favor the formation of an Italian Confederation under the presidency of the Pope; that Austria would cede Lombardy* to France, except for the fortresses of Mantua and Peschiera; that France in turn would transfer this territory to Piedmont; that the Veneto would remain under Austrian control but would form part of the Italian Confederation; that the Grand Duke of Tuscany and the Duke of Modena would be returned to their respective thrones and each would proclaim a general amnesty; and finally to ask the Pope to introduce reforms in his government.

Neither Cavour* nor Victor Emmanuel II* was invited to Villafranca, and the Piedmontese prime minister urged his King to refuse the terms in a stormy encounter at the King's camp at Monzambano on July 10. Unable to continue the war without the French, Victor Emmanuel felt that he had no choice but to accept the agreement but did so only insofar as it affected him. This was an important proviso, for he assumed no obligation to adhere to the formation of the Confederation and the restoration of the rulers of the duchies. Nonetheless, Cavour resigned the evening of July 11, enraged that Napoleon had not kept the Plombières Agreement* to liberate Italy from the Alps to the Adriatic. The terms of Villafranca were finalized in the Treaty of Zurich* (November 1859) but the dukes were never restored and the Italian Confederation never materialized.

FJC

VILLARI, PASQUALE. Italy's outstanding historian of the nineteenth century was born in Naples on October 3, 1826. Villari was active in the revolutions of 1848* and was sent into exile. Pursuing an academic career, he taught at Pisa (1859–65) and at Florence (1865–1913). His *Storia di Girolamo Savonarola e dei suoi tempi* [The life and times of Girolamo Savonarola] (1859–61) and *Niccolò Machiavelli e i suoi tempi* [Niccolo Machiavelli and his times] (1877–82) are masterpieces of modern historiography which have gained him a European reputation. Villari sat in united Italy's parliament for a decade, was appointed senator (1884), and served as minister of education (1891). He remained active in his concern for the political union of the Italian people until his death in Florence on December 17, 1917.

HP

VILLIERS, GEORGE WILLIAM FREDERICK. See **CLARENDON, GEORGE WILLIAM FREDERICK VILLIERS, EARL OF**

VINCIGUERRA, MARIO. Mario Vinciguerra was born in Naples in 1887. In the late 1920s he tried to carry on the kind of anti-Fascism* begun by Giovanni Amendola.* In 1930 he coedited, with Renzo Rendi, an underground bulletin called *L'Alleanza Nazionale* [The national alliance for freedom], in which he said that it was up to the liberal "men of order" to provoke the crisis of Fascism* and also "to save Italy from the opposite threat of Communism." In December 1930 he was sentenced to fifteen years in prison; he served six years of his sentence and was then amnestied. After World War II* he published several important works on the history of Italian political parties.

FR

VISCONTI, LUCHINO. The producer-director who was a founder of the school of Italian filmmaking known as neorealism was born in Milan on November 2, 1906. His first major work was *Ossessione* (1942), followed by *La terra trema* (1946). His career culminated in the films *Rocco and His Brothers* (1962), *The Leopard* (1963), *The Damned* (1969), and *Death in Venice* (1970). In live theater he introduced the works of Jean-Paul Sartre, Arthur Miller, and Tennessee Williams to the Italian audience. Visconti died on March 17, 1976, in Rome.

WR

VISCONTI-VENOSTA, EMILIO. Foreign minister for approximately twelve years between 1863 and 1901, Visconti-Venosta consistently sought to prevent Italy from becoming a client state of either France or Germany in the rivalry between those two powers. He was born on January 22, 1829, in Milan, and died on November 28, 1914, in Rome. A participant in the Milanese revolt against Austria (March 1848) and a Garibaldian volunteer in the war of 1848, he broke with Giuseppe Mazzini* during the 1850s and became an adherent of Cavour.* Visconti-Venosta was a deputy to parliament from 1860 to 1866; when appointed senator, he always sat at the Right (see Destra, La*). He was secretary-general for foreign affairs (1862–63) and first became foreign minister under Marco Minghetti* (March 1863–September 1864), negotiating the September Convention* with France. He served as foreign minister under Bettino Ricasoli* (June 1866–April 1867) and under Giovanni Lanza* (December 1869–July 1873). He supported neutrality in the Franco-Prussian War (1870), helped fashion the Law of Papal Guarantees* (1871), worked to attenuate Italy's strained relations with the new French republic, and under Minghetti (July 1873–March 1876) sought to improve Italy's relations with Austria while avoiding involvement in an anti-French German alliance. With the fall of the Right in 1876, Visconti-Venosta's career experienced a twenty-year eclipse, which ended in July 1896, when he became foreign minister under Antonio Di Rudinì* (until June 1898), then under Luigi Pelloux* (May 1899–June 1900), and finally under Giuseppe Saracco* (June 1900–February 1901). During these five years he labored to reduce Italy's dependency on the Triple Alliance* by improving relations with France—which had deteriorated under Francesco Crispi* because of a tariff war and the Tunisian question—and prepared the way for the Franco-Italian entente of 1902 regarding respective interests in Morocco and Tripoli. In 1906 he was Italian representative at the Algeciras Conference,* where he sided with France in its dispute with Germany over Morocco.

For further reference see: Samuel William Halperin, *Diplomat under Stress: Visconti-Venosta and the Crisis of 1870* (Chicago: University of Chicago Press,

1963); Federico Chabod, *Storia della politica estera italiana dal 1870 al 1896* vol. 1, *Le premesse* (Bari: Laterza, 1951).

SS

VISCONTI-VENOSTA, GIOVANNI. Giovanni Visconti-Venosta was a man of letters who was politically active as a youth in the *Risorgimento** in Lombardy.* Born in Milan on September 4, 1831, he participated with his more famous brother, Emilio,* in propaganda and demonstrations against Austria, which culminated in his exile to Piedmont in 1859. After unification, he held several public offices but increasingly devoted his energies to literature. His writings include short stories, caricatures, parodies, and a memoir of the Lombard *Risorgimento* entitled *Ricordi di gioventù* [Memoirs of youth] (1904). He died on October 1, 1906, in Milan.

MSG

VISCONTI-VENOSTA–BARRÈRE AGREEMENT OF 1900. See **PRINETTI, GIULIO**

VITTORIALE DEGLI ITALIANI. See **D'ANNUNZIO, GABRIELE**

VITTORINI, ELIO. This novelist was born in Syracuse on July 27, 1908, and died in Milan on February 12, 1966. Author of *Piccola borghesia* [Petty bourgeoisie] (1931), *Garofano rosso* [The red carnation] (1933), and *Conversazione in Sicilia* [Conversation in Sicily] (1941), he passed from dissident Fascism* to overt opposition to the Fascist regime. He joined the Armed Resistance* and the Italian Communist Party (PCI)* during World War II.* Vittorini edited the Milanese edition of the Communist daily *L'Unità* in 1945 and the influential literary and political journal *Il Politecnico* in 1945 and 1946. He left the Communist Party in 1946 after a dispute with Palmiro Togliatti* over the relationship of literature to politics. His important postwar works are *Uomini e no* [Men and non-men] (1945) and *Le donne di Messina* [Women of Messina] (1949).

For further reference see: Elio Vittorini, *Diario in pubblico* (Milan: Bompiani, 1957).

AJD

VITTORIO VENETO, BATTLE OF. This battle, which lasted from October 24 to November 3, 1918, was fought at the end of World War I.* General Armando Diaz* had planned a two-pronged attack against Austria-Hungary: from the mid-Piave sector to the foothills around Vittorio-Veneto, with a subsidiary attack against Monte Grappa. The Italians met fierce resistance at first, but on October 29 the tide turned, and Vittorio Veneto, which gave its name to the Italian victory, was entered on the thirtieth. The next day resistance collapsed on Monte Grappa and the Austrian High Command ordered the evacuation of Venetia. On November 3 Udine and Trent were occupied while the navy landed troops at Trieste.* A military delegation of the moribund empire signed an armistice at Villa Giusti the same day. In this battle the Italians suffered some 39,000 casualties, while the Austrians had some 30,000 killed and wounded and another 427,000 taken prisoner.

FJC

VOCE, LA. Giuseppe Prezzolini's* Florentine weekly review of culture, initiated in December 1908 after the *Leonardo** and *Regno** experiences, *La Voce* represented the intellectual's commitment to moral rearmament and patriotic education on the many questions of Italian life and European developments. This weekly's main contributors were Benedetto Croce,* Giovanni Gentile,* Guido De Ruggiero,* Giovanni Papini,* Luigi Ambrosini, Giovanni Amendola,* Luigi Einàudi,* Giuseppe Lombardo Radice, and Benito Mussolini.* Cultural nationalism was *La Voce*'s objective. In its pages an attempt was made to overcome the provincialism and excessive theorizing characteristic of Italian culture and to find a satisfactory substitute for positivist thought, as well as an alternative to Giovanni Giolitti's* liberalism. Gaetano Salvemini's* withdrawal in 1911 dramatized the Vocist's turn to an antidemocratic sentiment. In 1914 Prezzolini attempted to have the *Voce* support a reconstructed and dynamic idealism. Failure led him to surrender its direction, in May 1916, to Giuseppe De Robertis. As a reaction to its many initiatives, the periodical, now bimestrial, became exclusively a review of art and literature, proposing a culture pure and extraneous from the distracting concerns of the day. The *Voce* lasted until December 1916.

For further reference see: Emilio Gentile, *"La Voce" e l'età giolittiana* (Milan: Pan, 1972).

RSC

VOLPE, GIOACCHINO. This historian of modern Italy was born in Paganica (Aquila) on February 16, 1876. Volpe was director of the Institute of Contemporary Italian History at the University of Rome, where he also taught medieval studies, his first interest. An infantry officer in World War I,* he embraced Fascism* and served as a Fascist deputy, 1924–29. His *Storia del movimento fascista* [History of the Fascist Movement] (1939) was a partisan undertaking. His greatest work, *L'Italia moderna* [Modern Italy] (3 vols., 1943–52), was more objective. Volpe broke with Fascism during World War II* over Mussolini's* Italian Social Republic (see Salò, Republic of*). Spared undue humiliation over his Fascist past, Volpe continued to be a productive and acclaimed teacher and scholar until his death at Sant'Arcangelo (Forlì) on October 1, 1971.

RSC

VOLPI, GIUSEPPE. This industrialist and Fascist minister was born on November 19, 1877, in Venice and died in Rome on November 16, 1947. In 1905 he founded the Società Adriatica di Elettricità and became a leader in the movement for Italian political and economic penetration in the Balkans and the Ot-

toman Empire. Volpi favored Italian intervention in World War I* and was
president of both the Committee of Industrial Mobilization during the war, and
of the Association of Italian Joint Stock Companies in 1919. He also served as
governor of Tripolitania (Libya*) (1921–25). Volpi was made count of Misurata
in 1925, served as finance minister from 1925 to 1928, and was president of the
Italian Confederation of Industry from 1934 to 1943 (see Confindustria*).

AJD

**VOLUNTARY MILITIA FOR NATIONAL SECURITY (MILIZIA VO-
LONTARIA PER LA SICUREZZA NATIONALE).** This militia (MVSN)
was created to give the Fascist squads a military organization and to provide for
their legitimization. It was stipulated in the Fascist Grand Council Declaration
of July 25, 1923, that its membership would not exceed 500,000 and would be
drawn from the party. However, with the impact of the Ethiopian War it grew
rapidly to 763,000 in 1938. Its specific task was to preserve the Fascist order
and thwart any attempt or gesture of sedition against the Fascist government.
As it evolved it was divided into two main groups: the general militia, forming
over 95 percent of the total; and special branches that included the rest. The
former, unpaid, volunteered their service to the regime and were used to combat
counterrevolutionary activity and to provide premilitary instruction to those between eighteen and twenty; they prepared themselves for mobilization in defense
of the regime. For their efforts, they were provided with various services, including free medical care. Those in the special militia were attached to specific
government services and departments, such as railways, posts and telegraphs,
and ports, and functioned as Fascist inspectors. The first commander of the
militia was Emilio De Bono,* one of the coordinators of the March on Rome.*

For further reference see: Alberto Aquarone, ''La milizia volontario nello stato
fascista,'' *La Cultura* 2 (May and June 1964); Adrian Lyttelton, *The Seizure of
Power* (London: Weidenfeld and Nicolson, 1973).

FJC

**VOLUNTARY ORGANIZATION FOR THE REPRESSION OF ANTI-
FASCISM.** See **OVRA**

W

WAR OF 1859. Sometimes called the Second War for Italian Independence, the war of 1859 was fought by the armies of Piedmont-Sardinia and France, with the assistance of Italian volunteers, against Austria. The war resulted in the liberation of Lombardy* from Austrian troops and was followed by the creation of a Kingdom of North Italy under King Victor Emmanuel II.*

The stage for this war was set by the anti-Austrian propaganda of the Società Nazionale Italiana* and by Cavour's* diplomacy. In June 1858, Cavour secured French support for his anti-Austrian policy (see Plombières Agreement*). At the same time, extensive reforms of the Sardinian army were being completed, and volunteers from all parts of Italy received training and weapons in Piedmont.

In the early part of 1859, however, Cavour's plans were almost thwarted by British attempts at mediation of the growing rift between Piedmont-Sardinia and Austria. In February 1859, Napoleon III* himself began to retreat from his Plombières position and sought to avoid war by calling for an international conference. Cavour and his political allies feared that their carefully laid plans had come to nought.

In April, however, Emperor Francis Joseph* and his minister, Count Buol, faced with mounting domestic problems, tried to hasten a resolution of the crisis by confrontation. On April 19, Austria delivered an ultimatum to the Sardinian government to demobilize its army and to stop recruiting and training volunteers. The ultimatum was rejected on April 23, and Austrian troops began to cross the Ticino River on April 29.

In the first two weeks of the war Sardinian troops bore the brunt of the Austrian offensive. By early June, however, French troops had reached the Po Valley and Giuseppe Garibaldi's* Cacciatori delle Alpi were securing control of several mountain passes in northern Lombardy. The decisive military encounters took place on June 24, at the battle of Solferino* between French and Austrian troops and at San Martino between Sardinian and Austrian troops. Although tactically superior, the French, who had suffered heavy losses, decided not to pursue the enemy into Venetia. The Austrians, therefore, were able to regroup around their military strongholds at Mantua and Peschiera.

To the chagrin of Cavour and his political allies throughout Italy, on July 5, 1859, Napoleon III opened negotiations with Francis Joseph. The negotiations were concluded on July 11, 1859, with the signing of the Villafranca armistice.* Lombardy was annexed by the Kingdom of Sardinia but Venetia remained under Austrian rule until 1866.

For further reference see: chapters 15–16 in Piero Pieri, *Storia militare del Risorgimento* (Turin: Einaudi, 1962); Adolfo Omodeo, "Da Plombières a Villafranca," in *Difesa del Risorgimento* (Turin: Einaudi, 1955), pp. 280–95.

CML

WAR OF 1866. Sometimes called the Third War for Italian Independence, the war of 1866 resulted in the liberation of Venetia from Austrian rule. This had been an important objective of Italian foreign policy since the unification, but one that the Italian government had been unable to attain without benefit of a powerful alliance against Austria.

The opportunity for such an alliance presented itself in July 1865 with the unfolding of a confrontation between Austria and Prussia that began over the issue of Schleswig-Holstein and culminated in war a year later. In February-March 1866, Otto von Bismarck* began to build a coalition that would support Prussia in a future military confrontation with Austria. The government of General Alfonso de La Marmora* was quick to seize on Prussian overtures. An alliance was signed on April 8, 1866, albeit on terms disadvantageous to Italy. She pledged military support if Prussia attacked Austria within three months. But she received no pledges of Prussian help in the event of an Austrian attack. Nonetheless, the alliance did offer the best prospect for the acquisition of Venetia.

Upon the outbreak of hostilities between Prussia and Austria, on June 16, 1866, Baron Bettino Ricasoli* became head of the government, replacing La Marmora, who took charge of the military campaign under the King's direction. Inadequate coordination with the Prussian allies, a seriously flawed logistical system, and tensions among the generals combined to stall the Italian military effort as early as June 24, 1866. At the battle of Custozza (1866)* Italian troops were defeated by a smaller Austrian force. Thereafter, Italian hopes of victory focused on the navy's new, foreign-built battleships, which were superior to the Austrian ones in both tonnage and equipment. But the difficulty of training crews to different specifications and the ineptness of Piedmontese Admiral Carlo Persano led to further disappointments.

Under pressure to redress the military balance through a victory at sea, on July 20, 1866, Persano ordered an attack on the Austrian base at Lissa,* off the Dalmatian coast. But the Austrian warships under the command of Admiral Wilhelm von Tegethoff arrived to protect the base. Although neither side could claim victory in the ensuing battle, Lissa became synonymous with Italian humiliation because it marked the failure of Persano's strategy and the loss of several new ships.

In the meantime, however, the decisive Prussian victories in central Europe prompted Napoleon III* to offer his services as the mediator who could bring the war to an end, and thereby preserve the European balance of power. As part of the mediation, Napoleon III arranged for the indirect transfer of Venetia and the Mantua area from Austrian to Italian sovereignty as specified in his earlier agreement with Austria. The transfer was sanctioned by a popular plebiscite on October 21, 1866.

CML

WARS OF THE FIRST AND SECOND COALITIONS, ITALY IN THE.

On the outbreak of the wars of the French Revolution in April 1792 the Italian states were at peace, and, except for the French occupation of Savoy and Nice in November 1792, remained undisturbed until the first Italian campaign of Napoleon Bonaparte (see Napoleon I*) in 1796. In 1792, however, Italian authorities had sought out suspected native sympathizers of the Jacobins,* and there had been serious repressions at Naples and elsewhere in 1793. After the execution of Louis XVI, Naples, Sardinia, and Tuscany joined the major powers in the First Coalition—Austria, Prussia, England, and Spain. With the establishment of the Directory in 1795, Italian exiles in Paris, among them Filippo Buonarroti,* sought to secure the liberation of Italy. The Directory, however, did not intend to revolutionize Italy, and Bonaparte's invasion of May 1796 was part of the general strategy against Austria. The Republic of Alba in Piedmont (1796) was rapidly suppressed, and the activity of Italian patriots was only gradually recognized as the military campaign in Lombardy* reached its conclusion. Subsequently, Bonaparte permitted formation of the Cispadane Republic at Modena—which was incorporated into the Cisalpine Republic* centered at Milan in June 1797—and also the establishment of the Ligurian Republic* in the old territory of Genoa. Through the Treaty of Campo Formio* with Austria (October 1797), which ended the War of the First Coalition, the French continued to hold Lombardy and Genoa, while Venice, which had also been occupied by the French, was ceded to Austria.

French occupation of the Papal States* and the creation of the Roman Republic* in February 1798, as well as the occupation of Naples and the creation of the Parthenopean Republic* in January 1799, preceded the War of the Second Coalition. The French occupied Rome after the murder of General Duphot in December 1797, and developments during the following summer led to resumption of war. The French fleet was destroyed by Admiral Nelson at Aboukir off the coast of Egypt in August 1798, blocking Bonaparte in Egypt. The Second Coalition, in which the major powers were Austria, England, Russia, and Naples, was formed at this point. Ferdinand IV of Naples attempted to invade the Roman Republic in December, but was defeated by the French and fled to Sicily. The French also occupied Tuscany. However, in the summer of 1799 the armies of the Second Coalition won sweeping victories in Italy and in northern Europe. Naples was occupied by a peasant army of Sanfedisti* led by Cardinal Fabrizio Ruffo.* The crisis led to the coup d'état of 18–19 Brumaire (November 9–10, 1799) and Bonaparte's seizure of power in France. The War of the Second Coalition concluded with Napoleon's Second Italian Campaign, his defeat of the Austrians at the battle of Marengo* (June 1800), and the treaties of Lunéville with Austria (February 1801) and Amiens with England (March 1802). In Italy, Lunéville recognized the restored Cisalpine and Ligurian republics.

For further reference see: Giorgio Candeloro, *Storia dell'Italia moderna*, vol. 1, *Le origini del Risorgimento, 1700–1815* (Milan: Feltrinelli, 1956); R. R. Palmer, *The Age of Democratic Revolution*, vol. 2 (Princeton: Princeton University Press, 1964).

RBL

WORLD WAR I, ITALY IN. After ten months of bitter and anguishing controversy, dividing parliament and country between neutralists and interventionists, Italy entered World War I on May 24, 1915 (against Austria but not Germany) by what some have considered a coup d'état by king and government against the Giolittian majority in parliament and the Socialist and Catholic masses in the country. Convinced that Italy's participation was necessary to complete its territorial unification and achieve strategic security in the Alps and the Adriatic, the Salandra*-Sonnino* government committed Italy to the Triple Entente* in the Pact (Treaty) of London* of April 26, 1915. As reward for its intervention, Italy was promised the Trentino,* the Cisalpine Tyrol, Istria* with Trieste,* most of Dalmatia,* a number of Adriatic islands, and a share in the postwar colonial spoils. The government's expectation that Italy's intervention would lead to an early Entente victory proved to be illusory. The prolongation of the war beyond 1915, the five fruitless and costly battles of the Isonzo* (May 1915–March 1916), a major reversal in the Trentino in May–July 1916, and sharp differences between the government and the supreme commander, General Luigi Cadorna,* led to Salandra's resignation in June 1916. There followed Paolo Boselli's* National Union government, which finally declared war on Germany (August 28, 1916), but failed to rally many neutralists, especially the Socialists, to the war effort. Economic difficulties, autocratic conduct of military operations by General Cadorna, and the foreign policy of Sonnino,* who would not modify the terms of the Pact of London, all worked to exacerbate the divisions within the government and the country. The disaster of Caporetto* (October–November 1917) eliminated Cadorna from the military scene; he was replaced by General Armando Diaz,* who restored the army's morale and integrity, resisted repeated Austro-German offensives on the Piave (November 1917–June 1918), and eventually achieved a major victory at the battle of Vittorio Veneto* (October–November 1918). Sonnino's differences with Prime Minister Vittorio Orlando* (October 1917–June 1919) and with the democratic interventionists over the problem of how to deal with Yugoslav claims to territories promised to Italy in the Pact of London served to divide the country further at the moment of final victory, bought at the cost of nearly three and a half years of war and 600,000 dead. These difficulties contributed to Italy's difficulties at the Paris Peace Conference* and to the consequent disillusionment over the fruits of victory.

For further reference see: Brunello Vigezzi, *L'Italia di fronte alla prima guerra mondiale*, vol. 1, *L'Italia neutrale* (Milan: Riccardo Ricciardi, 1966); Ferdinando Martini, *Diario, 1914–1918*, ed. Gabriele De Rosa (Milan: Mondadori, 1966); Luigi Cadorna *La guerra alla fronte italiana*, 2 vols. (Milan: Treves, 1923).

SS

WORLD WAR II, ITALY IN. In World War II Italy moved from "nonbelligerency," 1939–40, to belligerency alongside Nazi Germany, 1940–43, to defeat and occupation, 1943–45. Italy's unpreparedness for war persuaded Mussolini* in September 1939 to ignore his commitment to Hitler, embodied in both the Rome-Berlin Axis* and the Pact of Steel.* But the Fascist Duce chafed at the parallel drawn with Liberal Italy's neutrality* in 1914, and by March 1940 he was resolved on intervention at the earliest opportunity. Persuasion and threat by the United States, Britain, and the Vatican were to no avail. The Nazis spring blitzkrieg threatened to terminate hostilities before Italy could join in, and on June 10, 1940, twelve days before the French surrender, Mussolini dragged his country into World War II.

The venture roused little enthusiasm among Italians. Faintheartedness at the grass roots combined with incompetence at the top of the Fascist hierarchy to produce a woeful record. Since the attack on France brought meager profit, Mussolini in October 1940 launched his "parallel war" by invading Greece. Military disasters, however, immediately necessitated a saving intervention by German forces. Similarly, the Germans were constrained to take over direction of the Mediterranean and North African campaigns. Further humiliations included the destruction of half the Italian fleet at anchor in Taranto harbor and the loss of the East African empire. Nonetheless, Mussolini would not disengage his nation from the war and continued its subservience to Germany. In the wake of the Nazi attack on the USSR he contributed an Italian contingent to the Russian front, and on December 11, 1941, joined Hitler in declaring war on the United States. In sum, Italy and her resources were made to serve the German war effort, which accounted partly for the privations visited on Italy's civil population in 1942–43. These, in turn, provoked the first overt manifestations of proletarian unrest under the Fascist dictatorship.

The catalyst for change, however, was the expulsion of Axis troops from North Africa, followed by the Anglo-American conquest of Sicily in July 1943. On July 25 the Fascist Grand Council passed a motion of no confidence in the Duce's handling of the war, and King Victor Emmanuel III,* seizing this cue, dismissed and imprisoned Mussolini. The new royal government under Marshal Pietro Badoglio,* although anxious to leave the war, delayed accepting Allied unconditional terms until September 3, when an armistice was signed at Cassibile.

The Germans, in turn, occupied the Italian peninsula as far south as Salerno, where the Allies landed on September 8.

For the final twenty months of the war, then, Italy was divided between two occupying forces. In the North Mussolini, rescued by Nazi commandos, was installed as head of the so-called Republic of Salò,* a German puppet regime. More representative of Italian sentiment was the broad-based, though leftist-led, anti-Nazi Armed Resistance.* Partisans proved capable of mounting formidable military operations in the German rear, and in April 1945 caught and executed Mussolini. The Allies advanced from the South slowly and painfully; Rome was liberated in June 1944 and was spared devastation by being designated an open city, but not until spring 1945 did Allied forces reach the Po Valley. The royal regime, having declared war on Germany in October 1943, achieved the informal status of Allied cobelligerent. This was to prove invaluable to Italy in the post-1945 peace negotiations.

For further reference see: Knox MacGregor, *Mussolini Unleashed, 1939–1941: Politics and Stategy in Fascist Italy's Last War* (New York: Cambridge University Press, 1982); F. W. Deakin, *The Brutal Friendship: Hitler, Mussolini and the Fall of Fascism* (London: Weidenfeld and Nicolson, 1962); David W. Ellwood, *L'alleato nemico: La politica d'occupazione anglo-americana in Italia, 1943–1946* (Milan: Feltrinelli, 1977).

ACas

WORLD WAR II, TREATY WITH ITALY ENDING. This series of protocols formally and officially ended the state of war between the Big Four—France, Great Britain, the United States, and the Soviet Union—and Italy. The treaty was signed on February 10, 1947, after the final draft had been approved by the twenty-one nations that participated at the Paris conference, July 30–October 15, 1946. The Italian Constituent Assembly* ratified the text on February 10, 1947.

Negotiations for the drafting of the text lasted more than a year. They proved to be arduous because of persistent differences among the Big Four. These differences involved territorial questions vis-à-vis Italy's borders with Yugoslavia, Austria, and France; Italian colonies; disposition of her fleet; limitations on future Italian rearmament; and reparations payable to the victorious powers for damages caused by the Italian military forces. The pivotal provisions of the treaty can be summarily condensed as follows:

Territorial Clauses. The central question involved Italy's borders with Yugoslavia. The epicenter of this disputed area was the city of Trieste,* for which Italy had always nourished a strong sentiment, an economic interest, and a sense of ''manifest destiny'' born of historical precedent. Thus the fierce determination of the Italian government not to yield the city. Ultimately, Trieste remained under Anglo-American jurisdiction as a Free Territory until October 1954, when an agreement was reached allowing Italy to retain the entire city, while most of the Venezia Giulia* was ceded to Yugoslavia. Other important territorial losses were the African colonies, the Dodecanese Islands,* several islands along the Adriatic coast, and four small frontier areas to France. The South Tyrol—another sensitive region for Italy—has remained under Italian jurisdiction.

Reparations. They were stipulated as follows: $100 million to the Soviet Union; $125 million to Yugoslavia; $105 million to Greece; $25 million to Ethiopia*; and $5 million to Albania.* France, Great Britain, and the United States renounced their claims to Italian property in their respective territories. As a quid pro quo, they received nominal indemnities from Italy.

Military Forces. The treaty sanctioned precise limits: 185,000 men for the Italian army, 65,000 *Carabinieri*, 25,000 men and 350 planes for the air force, 25,000 men for the navy, in addition to two warships, four cruisers, four destroyers, twenty torpedo boats, and an insignificant number of smaller vessels.

For further reference see: United States Department of State, "Draft Peace Treaty with Italy," *Selected Documents, Paris Peace Conference 1946* (Washington, D.C.: U.S. Government Printing Office, 1946), pp. 75–162.

PVB

Y

YOUNG ITALY. See **GIOVINE ITALY**

Z

ZACCAGNINI, BENIGNO. See CHRISTIAN DEMOCRATIC PARTY

ZAMBONI, ANTEO. See OVRA

ZANARDELLI, GIUSEPPE. Prime minister from 1901 to 1903, Zanardelli's reputation rests primarily on his incorruptibility and selfless devotion to liberal principles. He was born on October 29, 1826, in Brescia, and died on December 26, 1903, in Maderno. Zanardelli was a participant in the insurrection and resistance of Brescia against Austria in 1848–49 and again in 1859. Deputy to parliament from 1860 until his death, Zanardelli always sat with the Liberal Left (see Sinistra, La*). In the 1860s he frequently criticized the Right (see Destra, La*) for its suppression of Garibaldian and Mazzinian groups. As minister of public works under Agostino Depretis* (March 1876–November 1877), Zanardelli voiced the Left's opposition to state assumption of the railways as excessively increasing the functions of government and fostering a ''public-employeemania.'' He served as minister of the interior in the government of Benedetto Cairoli* (March–December 1878). Severely criticized for his permissive policy on public liberties after an attempted assassination of King Humbert I* in November 1878, Zanardelli persisted in his theory of punishment after the fact, as against restrictive preventive measures. As minister of justice under Depretis (May 1881–May 1883), he promoted the electoral reforms of 1882, favoring enlarged but not universal suffrage. Opposed to Depretis' transformismo,* in May 1883 Zanardelli joined four other opponents of Depretis to form the Pentarchy.* Reconciled with Depretis, he became minister of justice again (April–July 1887), continued in this office under Francesco Crispi* (August 1887–February 1891), and authored the monumental unified penal code of 1890, abolishing the death penalty. President of the Chamber of Deputies from November 1892 to February 1894, in December 1893 he declined to form a new government rather than suffer an Austrian veto to the appointment of Trentino-born General Oreste Baratieri as foreign minister. During 1894–95 he strenuously opposed Crispi's increasingly repressive manner of government. Again president of the Chamber between April and December 1897, Zanardelli became justice minister under Antonio Di Rudinì* (December 1897–May 1898), but opposed the latter's severe repression of the May 1898 disturbances. Reelected president of the Chamber in November 1898, he resigned in May 1899 in protest against Luigi Pelloux's proposed restrictive laws on public liberties. In April 1900 he joined, with Giovanni Giolitti,* the Extreme Left's parliamentary obstructionism against the Pelloux laws and helped bring Pelloux down in June 1900. Chosen prime minister in February 1901, Zanardelli, with Giolitti as minister of the interior, began a reorientation of domestic politics and hastened the ongoing rapprochement with France. The Zanardelli-Giolitti combination rallied the Extreme Left (whose votes twice saved the government from defeat, in 1901 and 1902), promoted the growth of labor organizations, and in general initiated the process of political and social democratization characteristic of the coming Giolittian era.

For further reference see: Carlo Vallauri, *La politica liberale di Giuseppe Zanardelli, dal 1876 al 1878* (Milan: A. Giuffrè, 1967); A William Salomone, *Italy in the Giolittian Era: Italian Democracy in the Making, 1900–1914*, 2nd ed. (Philadelphia: University of Pennsylvania Press, 1960).

SS

ZANIBONI, TITO. Tito Zaniboni, a militant Socialist, was born in Monzambano (Mantua) on February 1, 1883, and died in Rome on December 27, 1960. He was arrested on November 4, 1925, after being accused of plotting to shoot Mussolini.* A member of the Unitary Socialist Party who had previously been elected to parliament, Zaniboni's plot served as a pretext for further crackdowns against the Socialists. Condemned to thirty years in prison, Zaniboni was released after the fall of Fascism.* In 1944 he was given responsibility for purging former Fascist officials. He later took charge of settling persons who had been displaced by the war.

SD

ZELANTI. During the eighteenth and nineteenth centuries, the *Zelanti* formed the strongest party within the Roman Curia. It was noted for its ultramontanism and hostility to any interference by the secular authorities in the affairs of the Church. After the French Revolution, the *Zelanti* became bitterly hostile to liberalism and, in particular, to any attempt at reform in the Papal States.*

AJR

ZOGU, AHMED. See **ALBANIA**

ZOLI, ANDONE. The eighteenth premier in post-World War II Italy, Zoli was born on December 16, 1887, in Forlì. The son of a landowner, he was graduated from the faculty of law of the University of Bologna. As a member of the Partito

Popolare (see Italian Popular Party*), Zoli was an ardent anti-Fascist before his party's suppression in 1926, and from 1943 to the war's end, he was active in the Tuscan section of the Armed Resistance.*

In 1948 he was elected senator on the list of the Christian Democrats, subsequently holding a number of ministerial portfolios before becoming prime minister in 1957. Zoli's government was formed by the first noncoalition cabinet in Italian postwar history, and was noted for its fiscal rigor and disdain for the neo-Fascists. He resigned the premiership in 1958 and died in February 1960.

RJW

ZURICH, TREATY OF. The peace concluded by Austria, France, and Sardinia on November 10, 1859, gave definite form to the private agreement reached by Napoleon III* and Francis Joseph* during their meeting at Villafranca* on July 11, 1859. Vehemently regretted by Cavour,* it was reluctantly accepted as inevitable by Victor Emmanuel II.* The set of treaties making up the complete peace provided for the cession by Austria of Lombardy* to Sardinia through France. Suggestions were also incorporated into the treaties concerning a confederation of Italian states headed by the Pope, and the maintenance of the status quo in the center of the peninsula.

JCR

APPENDICES

Appendix **A**

Chronology of Important Events

1700–1721	Pontificate of Pope Clement XI
1702–13	War of the Spanish Succession
1713	Treaty of Utrecht ends War of the Spanish Succession; Spanish possessions in Italy ceded to Austria, Duchy of Savoy becomes a kingdom
1721–24	Pontificate of Pope Innocent XIII
1724–30	Pontificate of Pope Benedict XIII
1725	Publication of Giambattista Vico's *Scienza nuova*
1729	Outbreak of revolt in Corsica against Genoa
1730	Death of Victor Amedeus II, duke of Savoy, and, after 1713, king
1730–40	Pontificate of Pope Clement XII
1730–73	Reign of Charles Emmanuel III, king of Sardinia
1731	Antonio Farnese, duke of Parma-Piacenza, dies without heirs; conflict over control of duchy follows
1733–38	War of Polish Succession; Italian campaigns lead to territorial readjustments in Italy
1735	Charles of Bourbon, eldest son of Philip V of Spain and his second wife, Elisabetta Farnese, recognized as ruler of independent kingdom of Naples and Sicily
1737	Gian Gastone Medici dies without heirs; Francis, duke of Lorraine, becomes grand duke of Tuscany
1740–58	Pontificate of Pope Benedict XIV
1740–48	War of the Austrian Succession
1748	Philip of Bourbon, second son of Philip V of Spain and his second wife, Elisabetta Farnese, recognized as ruler of Parma-Piacenza
1751	Publication of Ferdinando Galiani's *Della moneta*
1754	Antonio Genovesi begins lecturing on ''commerce and mechanics'' at University of Naples
1755	Pasquale Paoli emerges as leader of Corsican revolt against Genoa

1758–69	Pontificate of Pope Clement XIII
1759–1825	Reign of Ferdinand IV, king of Naples and Sicily
1764–66	*Il Caffè* published in Milan
1764	Publication of Cesare Beccaria's *Dei delitti e delle pene*
1765–90	Reign of Leopold I, grand duke of Tuscany, considered the most enlightened ruler in Italy
1768	Corsica ceded to France by Genoa
1769–74	Pontificate of Pope Clement XIV
1770	Publication of Ferdinando Galiani's *Dialogues sur le commerce des blés* in Paris by Diderot
1773	Suppression of Jesuit order by Pope Clement XIV
1773–95	Reign of Victor Amedeus III, king of Sardinia
1775–99	Pontificate of Pope Pius VI
1789	Beginning of French Revolution
1796–1802	Reign of Charles Emmanuel IV, king of Sardinia
1796	Napoleon's first Italian campaign begins
1796–99	French-inspired republics established in Italy
1797	Peace of Campo Formio between France and Austria; Napoleon gives Venice to Austria, ending the independence of the Venetian republic
1800	Battle of Marengo: Napoleon again defeats Austria
1800–1823	Pontificate of Pope Pius VII
1801	Peace of Lunéville between France and Austria; Italy passes under French hegemony
1801	Cisalpine Republic established in northern Italy
1802–21	Reign of Victor Emmanuel I, king of Sardinia
1802	Cisalpine Republic renamed Republic of Italy
1804	Republic of Italy becomes Kingdom of Italy
1806	Kingdom of Naples passes under French control; King Ferdinand IV withdraws to Sicily under British protection
1812	Ferdinand IV grants Sicily a constitution at the urging of Lord Bentinck, English adviser
1814	Napoleon abdicates as emperor of France; collapse of the Napoleonic Kingdom of Italy
1815	Congress of Vienna restores European dynastic and territorial order; Lombardy and Venetia become provinces in Hapsburg empire; Austrian hegemony over Italy prevails
1820–21	Liberal conspiracies and revolutions in Naples, Turin, Milan, and the Papal States
1830–31	Liberal revolutions in Turin, Modena, and the Papal States
1831–34	First attempts at insurrection by Mazzini's organization, Young Italy
1843–45	Major unrest in the Papal Legations

1846	Giovanni Maria Mastai-Ferretti is elected pope and takes the name Pius IX
1846–47	Apparent triumph of the neo-Guelf movement
1847	Pius IX creates a Consulta di Stato, Council of Ministers, and Civic Guard
1848–49	Revolutions in all Italian states
1850–52	Major political trials in Lombardy, Venetia, the Papal States, and the South
1853–54	Abortive Mazzinian insurrections in Milan, the Lunigiana, and Genoa
1855	Sardinian intervention in the Crimean War against Russia
1856	Sardinian participation in the Paris Peace Conference
1856	Founding of the Italian National Society
1857	Failure of Pisacane's revolutionary expedition to the South
1857	Cavour comes to an understanding with the Italian National Society
1858	Orsini attempts to assassinate Napoleon III
1858	Secret talks at Plombières between Cavour and Napoleon III
1859	Outbreak of war against Austria; with French help Piedmont annexes Lombardy and the Duchies
1859	Villafranca armistice
1860	Pius IX issues a bull of excommunication that collectively condemns all those who conspired to deprive the Pope of his possessions
1860	Expedition of the Thousand; annexation of the Kingdom of the Two Sicilies, the Marches, and Umbria
March 1861	Proclamation of Victor Emmanuel II of Savoy as King of Italy
June 6, 1861	Death of Cavour
August 29, 1862	Garibaldi halted at Aspromonte on his way to liberate Rome
September 1864	Approval of September Convention with France
June 1865	Capital transferred from Turin to Florence
June–October 1866	War against Austria; acquisition of Venetia
September 1866	Insurrection in Palermo, Sicily
November 3, 1867	Garibaldi defeated at Mentana in his second attempt to liberate Rome
July 1868	Enactment of grist tax
September 20, 1870	Seizure of Rome by Italian troops
May 13, 1871	Law of Papal Guarantes
June 1871	Capital moved from Florence to Rome
March 10, 1872	Death of Mazzini
1874	Confirmation of the *non expedit*

March 1876	Fall of the Right; accession of Depretis and the Left; the "parliamentary revolution"
July 1877	Coppino compulsory elementary education law
January 9, 1878	Death of Victor Emmanuel II; accession of Humbert I
February 7, 1878	Death of Pius IX; February 20: election of Leo XIII
June–July 1878	Congress of Berlin
May 1881	France assumes protectorate over Tunisia
January–May 1882	Electoral reform laws; extension of suffrage
May 1882	Italy joins Germany and Austria-Hungary in the Triple Alliance
June 2, 1882	Death of Garibaldi
1883	Confirmation of transformism; formation of the Pentarchy
1884	Complete repeal of the grist tax
1885	Publication of the Jacini parliamentary inquiry on agriculture and agricultural classes
January 1887	Destruction of an Italian column at Dogali, East Africa
February 1887	Renewal of the Triple Alliance
July 1887	Death of Depretis and accession of Crispi
1888	Beginning of tariff war with France
May 1889	Treaty of Uccialli between Italy and Menelik II of Ethiopia
January 1890	Promulgation of unified penal code (Zanardelli code); formation of Italian colony of Eritrea
May 1890	Pact of Rome of democratic parties
May 1891	Renewal of Triple Alliance; the encyclical *Rerum novarum*
August 1892	Formation of Italian Workingmen's Socialist Party, Genoa Congress
December 1892	Beginning of Banca Romana scandal
August 1893	Massacre of Italian emigrant workers at Aigues-Mortes, France
December 1893	Disturbances of the Fasci Siciliani
January 1894	Repression of the Fasci Siciliani by Crispi
March 1, 1896	Italian defeat at Adowa, Ethiopia
March 5, 1896	Fall of the last Crispi ministry
January 1897	Sonnino's article "Torniamo allo Statuto"
May 1898	Rudinì repression of popular disturbances ("Fatti di Maggio")
June 1899	Beginning of parliamentary obstructionism against Pelloux's "extraordinary laws"
July 1899	Government by decree
March 1900	Resumption of parliamentary obstructionism
June 1900	General elections; resignation of Pelloux

June 29, 1900	Assassination of Humbert I; accession of Victor Emmanuel III
February 1901	Formation of the Zanardelli-Giolitti ministry and the beginning of the Giolittian era
June 1902	Prinetti-Barrère Agreement and the beginning of the Franco-Italian Entente; renewal of the Triple Alliance
July 20, 1903	Death of Leo XIII
August 4, 1903	Election of Pius X
September 1904	General strike throughout Italy
November 1904	General elections; partial suspension of the *non expedit*
February 1906	First Sonnino "Ministry of a Hundred Days"; Radicals and Republicans enter a government
May 1906	Beginning of Giolitti's long ministry (third)
September 1907	Papal encyclical against Modernism (*Pascendi dominici gregis*)
December 28, 1908	Earthquake in Sicily and Calabria; destruction of Messina and Reggio
October 1909	Racconigi Agreement between Italy and Russia
December 1910	Formation of Italian Nationalist Association
June 1911	Enactment of Credaro education reform law
September 29, 1911	Italian declaration of war on Turkey and the beginning of the Libyan (Tripolitanian) War
June 1912	Enactment of near-universal manhood suffrage law
July 1912	Socialist Party Congress of Reggio Emilia and the emergence of Mussolini
October 1912	Peace Treaty of Ouchy-Lausanne ending the Libyan War
December 1912	Last renewal of the Triple Alliance
October–November 1913	General elections; Gentiloni Pact
March 1914	Fall of Giolitti's fourth ministry and accession of Salandra
June 1914	"Red Week" and general strike
August 3, 1914	Italy declares its neutrality in the European War
August 20, 1914	Death of Pius X
September 3, 1914	Election of Benedict VX
November 25, 1914	Mussolini expelled from Socialist Party
April 26, 1915	Signature of Pact (Treaty) of London committing Italy to war on the side of the Entente
May 24, 1915	Italy declares war on Austria-Hungary
June 1916	Fall of Salandra and formation of the Boselli National Union Government
August 28, 1916	Italy declares war on Germany
October 24, 1917	Beginning of the battle of Caporetto and the retreat to the Piave River
April 1918	Pact of Rome of the oppressed nationalities
June 1918	Battle of the Piave

October–November 1918	Battle of Vittorio Veneto
January 1919	Formation of the Italian Popular (Catholic) Party
March 23, 1919	"Birth" of the Fascist movement
April 1919	Confrontation between President Wilson and the Italian delegation at the Paris Peace Conference over Fiume
September 1919	D'Annunzio seizes Fiume
September 1920	Occupation of the factories in northern Italy
November 1920	Treaty of Rapallo with Yugoslavia
December 1920	Ousting of D'Annunzio from Fiume
January 1921	Formation of the Italian Communist Party
May 1921	General elections; election of Mussolini and thirty-four followers to parliament
June 1921	Fall of the last Giolitti ministry
January 22, 1922	Death of Benedict XV
February 6, 1922	Election of Pius XI
October 28–30, 1922	March on Rome
October 31, 1922	Mussolini forms his first government
November 20, 1922	Mussolini attends opening of Lausanne Conference
January 14, 1923	Decree establishes Fascist Militia (MVSN)
April 1923	Left-wing Popular Party members withdraw from Mussolini's cabinet
July 15, 1923	Decree establishes fairly rigid control of press
August 29, 1923	Italy seizes Corfu; evacuates it on September 27
December 21, 1923	Palazzo Chigi Pact between Confindustria and Fascist labor syndicates
January 27, 1924	Italian-Yugoslav treaty; Fiume annexed by Italy
April 6, 1924	Parliamentary elections under Acerbo law; Fascist victory
May 30, 1924	Giacomo Matteotti's speech challenging the election
June 10, 1924	Fascists assassinate Matteotti in Rome
June 27, 1924	Aventine Secession from parliament begins
January 3, 1925	Mussolini's coup d'état; beginning of dictatorship
January 12, 1925	Alfredo Rocco becomes minister of justice (1925–32)
February 12, 1925	Roberto Farinacci becomes secretary of PNF (1925–26)
April 21, 1925	Giovanni Gentile's "Manifesto of the Fascist Intellectuals"
May 1, 1925	Benedetto Croce's "Countermanifesto"; law creating Dopolavoro (Leisure Time) organization
October 2, 1925	Palazzo Vidoni Pact between Confindustria and Confederation of Fascist Corporations
October 5–16, 1925	Mussolini represents Italy at Locarno Conference
December 10, 1925	Law creating National Organization for Maternity and Child Welfare
December 24, 1925	Decree makes Mussolini "Capo del Governo"

March 30, 1926	Augusto Turati becomes secretary of PNF (until 1930)
April 3, 1926	Rocco Labor Law and antistrike law; law creates Balilla Youth Organization
April 21, 1926	Fascist Labor Charter (*Carta del Lavoro*)
November 6, 1926	"Exceptional decrees" on public safety; dictatorship is complete
February 1, 1927	Fascist Special Tribunal for the Defense of the State begins its proceedings
May 17, 1928	New Fascist electoral law
December 9, 1928	Decree establishes Fascist Grand Council
February 11, 1929	Lateran Pacts signed between Italy and Vatican
September 12, 1929	Dino Grandi is appointed minister of foreign affairs
October 8, 1930	Giovanni Giuriati becomes secretary of PNF (1930–31)
October 1930	Mussolini begins talks about "Fascism for export"
May 15, 1931	Pope Pius XI's encyclical, *Quadragesimo anno*, on the corporative state
June 29, 1931	Pope Pius XI's encyclical, *Non abbiamo bisogno*
November 1, 1931	Fascists impose loyalty oath upon professors
December 7, 1931	Achille Starace becomes secretary of PNF (1931–39)
July 20, 1932	Mussolini takes back from Dino Grandi the portfolio of minister of foreign affairs (1932–36)
October 28, 1932	Tenth anniversary of March on Rome; Mussolini publishes "Doctrine of Fascism"
November 12, 1932	New statute of the PNF
Spring 1933	Mussolini proposes Four-Power Pact with Britain, France, and Germany
July 22, 1933	Mussolini takes portfolio of minister of war
November 6, 1933	Mussolini takes portfolios of ministers of navy and air
February 5, 1934	Law on Formation and Functions of the Corporations
March 18, 1934	Rome Protocols signed (Italy, Austria, Hungary); Mussolini proclaims Fascism a "universal phenomenon"
April 11–14, 1934	Stresa Conference of Italy, France, and Britain
June 14, 1934	Mussolini and Hitler meet in Venice
July 25, 1934	Attempted Nazi Putsch in Austria; murder of Chancellor Engelbert Dollfuss
December 6, 1934	Wal Wal clash between Italian and Ethiopian forces
January 7, 1935	Franco-Italian (Laval-Mussolini) agreement concerning Libyan border
October 2, 1935	Italy invades Ethiopia
October 11–19, 1935	League of Nations imposes economic sanctions against Italy, effective November 18

November–December 1935	Hoare-Laval plan for settling Ethiopian crisis at Ethiopia's expense
May 9, 1936	Mussolini proclaims victory over Ethiopia
June 11, 1936	Count Galeazzo Ciano is named foreign minister (1936–43)
July 18, 1936	Spanish Civil War begins (1936–39)
October 25–27, 1936	German-Italian pact concerning Austria; beginning of Rome-Berlin Axis
January 2, 1937	Anglo-Italian "Gentlemen's Agreement" regarding Mediterranean interests
September 28, 1937	Mussolini visits Hitler in Berlin
October 27, 1937	Law creates GIL (Italian Youth of the Lictors)
November 6, 1937	Italy joins Germany and Japan in Anti-Comintern Pact
December 11, 1937	Italy withdraws from League of Nations
March 11, 1938	Mussolini gives approval to Hitler's annexation of Austria
March 30, 1938	Mussolini takes title, "Maresciallo d'Italia"
April 16, 1938	Anglo-Italian Pact regarding Ethiopia and Spain
May 3–9, 1938	Hitler visits Rome and Florence
July 14, 1938	Fascist Manifesto of the Racist Scientists
September 29, 1938	Munich Conference of Hitler, Mussolini, Chamberlain, and Daladier on Czechoslovakia-Germany crisis
November 17, 1938	Decree law on Defense of the Italian Race
November 30, 1938	Anti-French demonstrations in Italian Chamber
January 19, 1939	Law creates Chamber of Fasces and Corporations
February 10, 1939	Pope Pius XI dies
February 15, 1939	Fascist School Charter announced
March 2, 1939	Election of Cardinal Eugenio Pacelli to be Pius XII
April 7, 1939	Italy invades Albania
May 22, 1939	Italy and Germany sign Pact of Steel political and military alliance
September 1, 1939	Hitler invades Poland, starting World War II; Italy remains "nonbelligerent"
September 1, 1939	Ettore Muti appointed PNF secretary
March 18, 1940	Mussolini confers with Hitler at Brenner; promises to enter the war
June 10, 1940	Italy declares war on France and Great Britain
June 22, 1940	Armistice signed between France, Germany, and Italy
September 27, 1940	Germany, Italy, and Japan sign Tripartite Pact in Berlin; aimed at United States
October 28, 1940	Italy invades Greece
November 11, 1940	British naval and air power knocks out three Italian capital ships at Taranto naval base
March 28–29, 1941	British naval victory over Italians, Cape Matapan

Spring 1941	Britain liberates Italian East Africa, reinstates Haile Selassie to throne in Ethiopia
April 6, 1941	Germany invades Yugoslavia and Greece
April 10, 1941	Germany and Italy divide up Yugoslavia; proclamation of "independent" Croatia, under Italian domination
June 16–21, 1941	United States closes Italian and German consulates; Italy and Germany close U.S. consulates
June 22, 1941	Italy joins Germany in invasion of Soviet Union
December 11, 1941	Italy and Germany declare war on United States
July 1, 1942	German General Erwin Rommel's offensive from Tobruk is halted at El Alamein, seventy miles west of Alexandria
October 23–November 10, 1942	British African offensive drives Axis forces from El Alamein back into Libya
November 8, 1942	Allied forces land in French North Africa
February 5, 1943	Mussolini "changes the guard" in his cabinet; names Count Ciano to be ambassador to the Holy See; Mussolini takes over Foreign Ministry portfolio
March 1943	Wave of industrial strikes in Turin and Milan
May 8–12, 1943	End of conflict in North Africa
July 10, 1943	Allied invasion of Sicily
July 19, 1943	Mussolini confers with Hitler at Feltre in Venetia
July 24–25, 1943	Fascist Grand Council, led by dissidents (Ciano, Grandi, Bottai) votes nonconfidence in Mussolini; Victor Emmanuel III dismisses Mussolini and names Marshal Pietro Badoglio the new head of the government; Mussolini is arrested
September 3, 1943	Allied invasion of southern Italy (Calabria)
September 8, 1943	Allied invasion at Salerno; announcement of Italian armistice signed September 3; beginning of Armed Resistance in German-occupied northern Italy
September 9, 1943	King Victor Emmanuel III and Marshal Badoglio flee to southern Italy
September 10, 1943	German troops occupy Rome
September 15, 1943	Germans rescue Mussolini; soon he establishes puppet "Social Republic" in the North at Salò
September 29, 1943	Badoglio signs "long armistice" at Malta
October 30, 1943	Allied Tripartite Declaration of Moscow regarding Italy
November 1943	New Republican Fascist Party holds Congress at Verona in North
January 8–10, 1944	Verona trial of Fascist "traitors"; Ciano executed
January 22, 1944	Allies land at Anzio
April 12, 1944	Victor Emmanuel III announces plans to name Crown Prince Humbert to be Lieutenant General of the Realm, effective upon liberation of Rome

June 4, 1944	Rome captured by Allies; Prince Humbert takes over
July 27, 1944	The Carlo Sforza "purge law" enacted to punish Fascist crimes
September 10, 1944	Second Quebec Conference between Churchill and Roosevelt; liberalization of economic policy in Italy
December 16, 1944	Mussolini's last public address, in Milan
April 25, 1945	Liberation of Milan; CLNAI assumes temporary power; Mussolini flees Milan
April 28, 1945	Mussolini and mistress, Claretta Petacci, captured by partisans; are executed at Giulino di Mezzegra near Lake Como
May 2, 1945	German armies in Italy surrender to Allies
June 1946	Proclamation of Italian Republic
1947	Italian peace treaty is signed
January 1948	Implementation of the constitution adopted in 1947
April 1948	First parliamentary elections under the new constitution; the Christian Democrats are victorious
May 11, 1948	Luigi Einàudi elected president
April 1949	Italy's entry into NATO
April 1951	Italy's entry into the European Coal and Steel Community
1954	Death of Alcide De Gasperi
April 29, 1955	Giovanni Gronchi elected president
February 1962	First Center-Left government under Amintore Fanfani
May 6, 1962	Antonio Segni elected president
December 28, 1964	Giuseppe Saragat elected president
1966	Floods in North and Central Italy destroy many art treasures
December 29, 1971	Giovanni Leone elected president
November 1974	Premier Aldo Moro forms Christian-Democratic/Republican government
1977	Italy and Yugoslavia ratify agreement ending World War II border dispute
1977	Pragmatic Accord, supported by Christian Democrats, Communists, Socialists, Social Democrats, and Republicans
May 1978	Red Brigades kidnap and kill Aldo Moro
June 1978	President Leone resigns in face of corruption charges
July 9, 1978	Alessandro Pertini elected president
October 1980	Arnaldo Forlani forms new four-party coalition government
June 1981	Appointment of first premier, Giovanni Spadolini (Republican), not a Christian Democrat
August 1983	Bettino Craxi first Socialist prime minister of Italy
June 11, 1984	Death of Enrico Berlinguer, leader of the PCI

Appendix B

Chronology of Ministries of Piedmont and Italy

March 16–July 27, 1848	Balbo: Cesare Balbo
July 27–August 15, 1848	Casati: Gabrio Casati
August 15–October 11, 1848	Alfieri: Cesare Alfieri Di Sostegno
December 16, 1848–February 21, 1849	Gioberti: Vincenzo Gioberti
February 23–March 27, 1849	later, Chiodo: Agostino Chiodo
March 27–May 7, 1849	De Launay: Gabriele De Launay
May 7, 1849–May 21, 1852	D'Azeglio: Massimo D'Azeglio
May 21–November 4, 1852	D'Azeglio: Massimo D'Azeglio
November 4, 1852–May 1, 1855	Cavour: Camillo Benso Cavour
May 4, 1855–July 19, 1859	Cavour: Camillo Benso Cavour
July 19, 1859–January 21, 1860	La Marmora: Alfonso La Marmora
January 21, 1860–March 23, 1861	Cavour: Camillo Benso Cavour
March 23–June 12, 1861	Cavour: Camillo Benso Cavour
June 12, 1861–March 3, 1862	Ricasoli: Bettino Ricasoli
March 3–December 8, 1862	Rattazzi: Urbano Rattazzi
December 8, 1862–March 24, 1863	Farini: Luigi Carlo Farini
September 28, 1864	later, Minghetti: Marco Minghetti
September 28, 1864–December 31, 1865	La Marmora: Alfonso La Marmora
December 31, 1865–June 20, 1866	La Marmora: Alfonso La Marmora
June 20, 1866–April 10, 1867	Ricasoli: Bettino Ricasoli
April 10–October 27, 1867	Rattazzi: Urbano Rattazzi
October 27, 1867–January 5, 1868	Menabrea: Luigi Federcio Menabrea
January 5, 1868–May 13, 1869	Menabrea: Luigi Federico Menabrea
May 13–December 14, 1869	Menabrea: Luigi Federico Menabrea
December 14, 1869–July 9, 1873	Lanza: Giovanni Lanza
July 10, 1873–March 25, 1876	Minghetti: Marco Minghetti

March 25, 1876–December 25, 1877	Depretis: Agostino Depretis
December 26, 1877–March 23, 1878	Depretis: Agostino Depretis
March 24–December 19, 1878	Cairoli: Benedetto Cairoli
December 19, 1878–July 2, 1879	Depretis: Agostino Depretis
July 14–November 25, 1879	Cairoli: Benedetto Cairoli
November 25, 1879–May 29, 1881	Cairoli: Benedetto Cairoli
May 29, 1881–May 25, 1883	Depretis: Agostino Depretis
May 25, 1883–March 30, 1884	Depretis: Agostino Depretis
March 30, 1884–June 29, 1885	Depretis: Agostino Depretis
June 29, 1885–April 4, 1887	Depretis: Agostino Depretis
April 4, 1887–July 29, 1887	Depretis: Agostino Depretis
March 9, 1889	later, Crispi: Francesco Crispi
March 9, 1889–February 6, 1891	Crispi: Francesco Crispi
February 6, 1891–May 15, 1892	Di Rudinì: Antonio Di Rudinì
May 15, 1892–December 15, 1893	Giolitti: Giovanni Giolitti
December 15, 1893–March 10, 1896	Crispi: Francesco Crispi
March 10–July 11, 1896	Di Rudinì: Antonio Di Rudinì
July 11, 1896–December 14, 1897	Di Rudinì: Antonio Di Rudinì
December 14, 1897–June 1, 1898	Di Rudinì: Antonio Di Rudinì
June 1–June 29, 1898	Di Rudinì: Antonio Di Rudinì
June 29, 1898–May 14, 1899	Pelloux: Luigi Pelloux
May 14, 1899–June 24, 1900	Pelloux: Luigi Pelloux
June 24, 1900–February 15, 1901	Saracco: Guiseppe Saracco
February 15, 1901–November 3, 1903	Zanardelli: Giuseppe Zanardelli
November 3, 1903–March 12, 1905	Giolitti: Giovanni Giolitti
March 28–December 24, 1905	Fortis: Alessandro Fortis
December 24, 1905–February 8, 1906	Fortis: Alessandro Fortis
February 8–May 29, 1906	Sonnino: Sidney Sonnino
May 29, 1906–December 11, 1909	Giolitti: Giovanni Giolitti
December 11, 1909–March 31, 1910	Sonnino: Sidney Sonnino
March 31, 1910–March 29, 1911	Luzzatti: Luigi Luzzatti

March 30, 1911–March 21, 1914	Giolitti: Giovanni Giolitti
March 21–November 5, 1914	Salandra: Antonio Salandra
November 5, 1914–June 18, 1916	Salandra: Antonio Salandra
June 18, 1916–October 30, 1917	Boselli: Paolo Boselli
October 30, 1917–June 23, 1919	Orlando: Vittorio Emanuele Orlando
June 23, 1919–May 21, 1920	Nitti: Francesco Saverio Nitti
May 21–June 15, 1920	Nitti: Francesco Saverio Nitti
June 15, 1920–July 4, 1921	Giolitti: Giovanni Giolitti
July 4, 1921–February 26, 1922	Bonomi: Ivanoe Bonomi
February 26–August 1, 1922	Facta: Luigi Facta
August 1–October 31, 1922	Facta: Luigi Facta
October 31, 1922–July 25, 1943	Mussolini: Benito Mussolini
July 27, 1943–April 22, 1944	Badoglio: Pietro Badoglio
April 22–June 18, 1944	Badoglio: Pietro Badoglio
June 18–December 12, 1944	Bonomi: Ivanoe Bonomi
December 12, 1944–June 21, 1945	Bonomi: Ivanoe Bonomi
June 21–December 10, 1945	Parri: Ferruccio Parri
December 10, 1945–July 13, 1946	De Gasperi: Alcide De Gasperi
July 13, 1946–February 2, 1947	De Gasperi: Alcide De Gasperi
February 2, 1947–May 31, 1947	De Gasperi: Alcide De Gasperi
May 31, 1947–May 23, 1948	De Gasperi: Alcide De Gasperi
May 23, 1948–January 27, 1950	De Gasperi: Alcide De Gasperi
January 27, 1950–July 26, 1951	De Gasperi: Alcide De Gasperi
July 26, 1951–July 16, 1953	De Gasperi: Alcide De Gasperi
July 16–August 17, 1953	De Gasperi: Alcide De Gasperi
August 17, 1953–January 18, 1954	Pella: Giuseppe Pella
January 18–February 10, 1954	Fanfani: Amintore Fanfani
February 10, 1954–July 6, 1955	Scelba: Mario Scelba
July 6, 1955–May 19, 1957	Segni: Antonio Segni
May 19, 1957–July 1, 1958	Zoli: Adone Zoli
July 1, 1958–February 15, 1959	Fanfani: Amintore Fanfani
February 15, 1959–March 25, 1960	Segni: Antonio Segni
March 25–July 26, 1960	Tambroni: Fernando Tambroni
July 26, 1960–February 21, 1962	Fanfani: Amintore Fanfani
February 21, 1962–June 21, 1963	Fanfani: Amintore Fanfani

June 1963–December 1963	Leone: Giovanni Leone
December 4, 1963–June 24, 1964	Moro: Aldo Moro
July 23, 1964–January 21, 1966	Moro: Aldo Moro
February 23, 1966–June 24, 1968	Moro: Aldo Moro
June 24, 1968	Leone: Giovanni Leone
December 13, 1968	Rumor: Mariano Rumor
August 6, 1969	Rumor: Mariano Rumor
March 1970	Rumor: Mariano Rumor
August 6, 1970	Colombo: Emilio Colombo
February 17, 1972–February 26, 1972	Andreotti: Giulio Andreotti
June 26, 1972–June 12, 1973	Andreotti: Giulio Andreotti
March 15, 1974	Rumor: Mariano Rumor
November 23, 1974	Moro: Aldo Moro
February 12, 1976	Moro: Aldo Moro
June 1976	Andreotti: Giulio Andreotti
March 13, 1978	Andreotti: Giulio Andreotti
February 1, 1979	Andreotti: Giulio Andreotti
August 1979–September 1980	Cossiga: Francesco Cossiga
October 1980–May 1981	Forlani: Arnaldo Forlani
June 1981	Spadolini: Giovanni Spadolini
November 1982	Fanfani: Amintore Fanfani
August 1983	Craxi: Bettino Craxi

Appendix C

Presidents of the Italian Republic

Enrico de Nicola, elected liberal provisional president by the Constituent Assembly, June 28, 1946

Luigi Einàudi, elected May 11, 1948

Giovanni Gronchi, elected April 29, 1955

Antonio Segni, elected May 6, 1962

Giuseppe Saragat, elected December 28, 1964

Giovanni Leone, elected December 29, 1971

Alessandro Pertini, elected July 9, 1978

Appendix **D**

Kings of Piedmont and Italy

Emmanuel Philibert	1553–80
Charles Emmanuel I	1580–1630
Victor Amadeus I	1630–37
Charles Emmanuel II	1637–75
Victor Amadeus II	1675–1730
Charles Emmanuel III	1730–73
Victor Amadeus III	1773–96
Charles Emmanuel IV	1796–1802
Victor Emmanuel I	1802–21
Charles Felix	1821–31
Charles Albert	1831–49
Victor Emmanuel II	1849–78 (king of Italy after 1861)
Humbert I	1878–1900
Victor Emmanuel III	1900–1946
Humbert II	1946

Appendix E

Popes (Eighteenth Century to Present)

1700–1721	Clement XI (Giovanni Francesco Albani)
1721–24	Innocent XIII (Michelangelo dei Conti)
1724–30	Benedict XIII (Pietro Francesco Orsini)
1730–40	Clement XII (Lorenzo Corsini)
1740–58	Benedict XIV (Prospero Lambertini)
1758–69	Clement XIII (Carlo Rezzonico)
1769–74	Clement XIV (Giovanni Vincenzo Antonio Ganganelli)
1775–99	Pius VI (Giovanni Angelo Braschi)
1800–1823	Pius VII (Barnaba Chiaramonti)
1823–29	Leo XII (Annibale della Genga)
1829–30	Pius VIII (Francesco Saverio Castiglioni)
1831–46	Gregory XVI (Bartolomeo Alberto-Mauro-Cappellari)
1846–78	Pius IX (Giovanni M. Mastai Ferretti)
1878–1903	Leo XIII (Gioacchino Pecci)
1903–14	St. Pius X (Giuseppe Melchiorre Sarto)
1914–22	Benedict XV (Giacomo Della Chiesa)
1922–39	Pius XI (Achille Ratti)
1939–58	Pius XII (Eugenio Pacelli)
1958–63	John XXIII (Angelo Giuseppe Roncalli)
1963–1978	Paul VI (Giovanni Battista Montini)
1978 (thirty-four days)	John Paul I (Albino Luciani)
1978-	John Paul II (Karol Wojtyla)

Index

Note: Page numbers in *italic* indicate main entries.

About the Editor

FRANK J. COPPA currently serves as Professor and Chairman of the Department of History at St. John's University in Jamaica, New York. In addition to editing and co-editing six other volumes, he has written *Planning, Protectionism and Politics in Liberal Italy; Camillo di Cavour; Pope Pius IX: Crusader in a Secular Age*; and articles appearing in *Catholic Historical Review, Journal of Modern History, Journal of Economic History,* and *Journal of Italian History* among others.